FOUR
SOFTWARE
TOOLS

with WordPerfect, VP-Planner, and dBASE III Plus

WADSWORTH SERIES IN COMPUTER INFORMATION SYSTEMS

FOUR

SOFTWARE

TOOLS

with WordPerfect, VP-Planner, and dBASE III Plus

DOS for IBM PC and MS DOS

Word Processing Using WordPerfect

Spreadsheets Using VP-Planner

Data Base Management Using dBASE III Plus

Tim Duffy
Professor of Accounting in Data Processing
Illinois State University

Wadsworth Publishing Company
Belmont, California
A Division of Wadsworth, Inc.

Computer Science Editor: Frank Ruggirello
Editorial Associate: Reita Kinsman
Managing Designers: Julia Scannell and James Chadwick
Print Buyer: Karen Hunt
Designer: Vargas/Williams/Design
Cover: Vargas/Williams/Design
Compositor: Thompson Type

Printed in the United States of America
1 2 3 4 5 6 7 8 9 10—92 91 90 89 88   14

Library of Congress Cataloging-in-Publication Data

Duffy, Tim.
  Four software tools: with WordPerfect, VP-Planner, and dBASE III
  Plus.

  p.   cm. — (Wadsworth series in computer information systems)
  Includes index.
  ISBN 0-534-08820-1
  1. PC DOS (Computer operating system)   2. MS-DOS (Computer
operating system)   3. WordPerfect (Computer program)   4. Stephenson,
Jim. VP-Planner (Computer program)   5. dBASE III PLUS (Computer
program)   I. Title.   II. Series.
QA76.76.063D845   1988
005.36—dc19   87-12510
                                                CIP

_____ To Michael

CONTENTS IN BRIEF

CONTENTS

Contents

Contents

Contents

xx   Contents

PREFACE

Institutions of higher education are increasingly under pressure to develop and implement courses in their curricula that deal with the microcomputer. Accredited colleges of business are under pressure from AACSB to integrate the microcomputer into just about every aspect of their curriculum. Colleges of education are being pressured to prepare teachers to teach high school and elementary classes dealing with the microcomputer. Community colleges are being pressured to develop courses that prepare students to use the microcomputer effectively in a business environment.

The three applications of word processing, data base management, and spreadsheets immediately suggest themselves as the primary applications in developing a curriculum to teach students how to apply the computer as a tool to solve school-related, private, or business-related problems. In addition to understanding how these three application packages work, a user must have a working knowledge of the disk operating system provided by a manufacturer.

A major problem in developing and teaching microcomputer applications classes is finding an appropriate text. There are few texts currently on the market that deal with DOS, word processing, spreadsheets, and data base management. In the past, if all of these software packages were to be covered, either students had to buy four books at substantial expense, or teachers had to prepare and supply an inordinate number of handouts on the use of the software packages. This text solves this problem by presenting all four elements in one book.

Objective of Textbook

The objective of this text is to teach students to solve realistic problems using the most readily available "off the shelf" general applications software. It is not necessary to go into detail about each package, since the primary goal of most applications courses is to get students to the point where they feel comfortable using the computer to solve problems. Therefore, a general introduction and familiarization with the more commonly used aspects of each general applications package is the most desirable approach.

The general applications software packages covered in this textbook are WordPerfect 4.2 (word processing), VP-Planner (spreadsheets), and dBASE III Plus (data base management). An introduction to microcomputers as well as extensive coverage of the IBM Personal Computer Disk Operating System (PC-DOS) are included.

After completing this textbook, students will have the skills/tools necessary to solve numerous problems using WordPerfect 4.2, VP-Planner, and dBASE III Plus.

Applications Software

Three packages have emerged as de facto standards in each of the general applications software areas discussed above. WordPerfect 4.2, developed by the WordPerfect Corporation, is now the best-selling word processing package for business use. dBASE III Plus, developed by Ashton-Tate, is typically used as the data base management standard.

Lotus 1-2-3 is, without doubt, the standard against which all other spreadsheet packages are measured. Many packages have not only imitated

1-2-3, but substantially improved on this approach to spreadsheet development. VP-Planner, distributed by Paperback Software, is one of the spreadsheet packages that, according to numerous reviewers, offers an excellent alternative to 1-2-3. Not only does VP-Planner totally emulate 1-2-3, but it improves on the original product in many small ways; the most important of which is the ability to access and manipulate any dBASE II, dBASE III, or dBASE III Plus data base file.

One of the real problems that faces educators today is how to acquire inexpensive, well-written software that truly represents programs that students will be expected to use in the business world. Each of the above companies has entered into an agreement with Wadsworth Publishing Company to solve this problem of acquiring quality software by making available through Wadsworth educational versions of each of these software packages for use in the classroom. Information about how you can receive the applications software can be obtained by contacting your local Wadsworth representative or by writing or calling Elizabeth Scott, Sales Services Manager, or Frank Ruggirello at Wadsworth Publishing Company, Ten Davis Drive, Belmont, California 94002, telephone: 415-595-2350. The software is available for IBM Personal Computers and IBM compatible computers (MS-DOS).

Note that Appendix A contains specific instructions to students about characteristics of the software that might differ from the full-blown packages. For example, the dBASE III Plus limits file size to 31 records.

Hardware Rationale

The introduction of the IBM Personal Computer revolutionized the world of third-party applications software for microcomputers. The IBM PC was capable of addressing much more memory—and was therefore capable of running programs that could more properly address many larger problems—than were any previous computer systems. This is especially true in the area of spreadsheets: many existing packages were rewritten to take advantage of the additional memory available on the IBM. The IBM so revolutionized the microcomputer world that it has emerged as the standard by which other computers are judged.

Hardware Requirements

An IBM PC or IBM compatible computer, with two disk drives and 256K of RAM memory, is required. You will also need a color monitor or monochrome graphics board to properly display the VP-Planner graphics on the screen. The printer (with graphics capabilities, if it is to be used to print VP-Planner graphs) is also required for printing documents, reports, graphs, or worksheets.

Structure of Text

This textbook works best in a "hands-on" environment; that is, the step-by-step exercises in the text make most sense when an individual is sitting at a computer, or has easy access to one, so that an immediate response to some action can be generated. (A symbol like the one in the left margin highlights all hands-on material.)

Each of the above packages in covered is some detail, but the text assumes that each software package has already been configured for use. If a package has not been configured to a specific machine, please refer to the documentation for that package.

The software packages can be covered in any order. You are encouraged to cover at least the first two chapters, however, before going on to one of the specific packages.

Sample Files and Learning Aids

A number of sample diskette files—which include sample worksheets, text files, and data base files—have been provided for use with text lessons and exercises. At the end of each chapter, exercises are offered to provide quick feedback to students on their progress. In addition to the written exercises, hands-on computer exercises are included in most chapters to provide students with feedback through various challenging applications of material covered in each chapter.

At the end of the text, appendixes present command summaries of WordPerfect 4.2 and dBASE III Plus as well as a graphic depiction of the various menus used in VP-Planner. An extensive glossary of computer terms used in the text appears at the back of the book, as do keyboard templates for each of the four software tools.

Teaching Aids

An Instructor's Manual is provided free to each adopter of the text. The Instructor's Manual contains a lecture outline as well as transparency masters for each chapter. A disk containing all of the finished worksheets at the end of each spreadsheet chapter is also included. As an extra bonus, this disk also contains a VP-Planner GRADBOOK template that adoptors can use for tracking their grades. The GRADBOOK template is completely macro driven and makes the tedious process of tracking grades much easier.

The computerized text generator Micro-Pac is also available to each adopter of *Four Software Tools*. Micro-Pac makes the process of generating a test easy. It includes true/false, multiple choice, fill-in, and short-answer test questions. Contact your Wadsworth representative for a copy, or call Helga Newman at 415-595-2350.

Optional Casebook

An optional casebook for *Four Software Tools* is also available from Wadsworth Publishing Company. The casebook presents advanced topics for selected software and is designed to give students valuable problem-solving experience via realistic case applications that emphasize hands-on use of the microcomputer through task-oriented exercises. The casebook includes:

28 challenging cases that go into far greater depth than the usual introductory textbook applications

A broad range of material from finance, budgeting, agriculture, accounting, and many other areas selected for their professional value

Background material/discussion for each of the advanced cases

ACKNOWLEDGMENTS

When I first started writing the original textbook, *Four Software Tools*, I did not realize what a tremendous effort such an endeavor entailed. I soon learned that a multitude of people are needed to make a textbook a success. These individuals include family, friends, colleagues, and many people in the publishing business. I am deeply indebted to my wife, Wendy, who initially encouraged me to start on the first version of this text. Without her encouragement the original text may never have been finished.

I also owe tremendous thanks to my department chair, Dr. James A. Hallam. Jim Hallam has also always been an encouraging influence. His greatest strength has always been his willingness to support his faculty in their efforts to improve their classroom teaching ability through training, travel, or use of additional technology. His encouraging words over the past thirteen years have been greatly appreciated.

Julia Bradley of Mount San Antonio College, David Van Over of the University of Houston, Robert Schuerman of Cal Poly San Luis Obispo, and John Turcher of Robert Morris College reviewed the manuscript for this edition and made many thoughtful suggestions. Thanks, too, to the reviewers of the original manuscript: Professors Margaret "Kit" Ellis, Seattle Central Community College; Mike Goul, Arizona State University; Richard Hatch, San Diego State University; Stephen Johnson, Linn-Benton Community College; and Judith Scheeraen, Westmoreland County Community College.

The efforts of the individuals at Wadsworth Publishing Company must definitely also be acknowledged, because they are responsible for turning a dog-eared manuscript into professional, final copy. Frank Ruggirello, senior computer science editor, is without equal in the the publishing business. Frank is always a joy to talk to or to visit. His judicious use of Giants game tickets, great restaurants, excellent brown sauce, and peaceful rides along the ocean will always be remembered with fondness. Reita ("Ollie") Kinsman, editorial associate, was always able to solve just about any problem that arose. Hal Humphrey, production editor, did a great job shepherding the project through to completion.

A many times overlooked ingredient in the success of a textbook is the sales staff of a publishing company. Without their marketing efforts, any text, no matter how good, would fail. There is no doubt in my mind that the Wadsworth corporation has one of the finest, most professional sales staffs in the country. Individuals like Ragu Raghaven (Wadsworth's most successful sales rep), Serina Beauparlant (former editorial assistant), and Harriet McQuarie (ISU's marketing rep), along with the efforts of many others in marketing textbooks, will always be greatly appreciated. Many of these people will always be considered friends.

Finally, I would like to dedicate this text to our newborn son, Michael. Michael's bright-eyed smiles are all that's needed to work his way into Mommy's and Daddy's hearts. Michael feels that he is especially entitled to this dedication, since he delayed his birth one week so that Daddy could finish the manuscript for this textbook by the arranged deadline.

TOOL ONE

INTRODUCTION TO MICROCOMPUTERS AND DOS

Chapter 1

Microcomputer Hardware

After completing this chapter, you should be able to:

List and describe the five parts of a microcomputer system

List and describe the four component hardware parts of a microcomputer

Define and discuss a number of technical terms related to microcomputers

List and describe the different types of monitors

List and describe the different types of printers

Describe different storage media available for microcomputers

Discuss how to handle diskettes properly

Figure 1.1
A microcomputer system is composed of five not-so-equal parts. The most important of these is people. They determine the success or failure of the remaining four: hardware, software, documentation/procedures, and data/information.

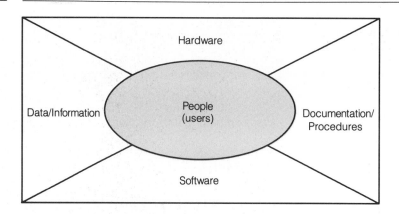

A typical **microcomputer system** used at home or in a business is composed of five parts: (1) people (users), (2) hardware, (3) software, (4) documentation/procedures, and (5) data/information (see Figure 1.1). The people part of the system is almost self-explanatory. Individuals typically have some problem or application that they try to solve or implement with the help of the computer. Satisfying the needs of these people is critical to the success of the system. If users are not satisfied with the way their problems are solved, the system will be deemed a failure. It is very important, therefore, that the proper hardware, software, and documentation and/or procedures be selected for problem solving.

The hardware component of the microcomputer system, consisting of the computer equipment, can be seen and touched. The software component, in contrast, is intangible and consists of the set of instructions to the hardware that is used to solve a problem or perform some type of process. The documentation/procedures component contains the instructions on how to run a particular piece of software or how to perform a particular process, such as changing the paper on the printer. The data/information component contains the facts, figures, or text data that are used by the computer to solve a problem.

The physical, touchable part of a computer system, the hardware component, has four parts: (1) input, (2) processing, (3) output, and (4) storage (see Figure 1.2). As is the case with component stereo systems, different manufacturers put these components together in different ways. Some manufacturers put all the components into one "box" or container; others separate each part, placing each in its own box. But no matter how a computer is manufactured, it has all four basic components.

Most hardware components include a number of chips for storage or control purposes. A **chip** is an electronic entity that contains the circuitry needed to perform some task or function. There are usually a number of chips in any microcomputer and several in any hardware device; they are composed of one or more semiconductors (extremely small electronic components) on a wafer of a ceramic-like substance called *silicon*.

Input

The standard **input** device for a computer is the keyboard. Most keyboards attached to computers contain the standard **QWERTY** keys—the key arrangement found on most typewriters. In addition to these standard keys, computers typically have a number of other keys that perform a variety of tasks.

If you look at the IBM PC keyboard (see Figure 1.3), you will see that it has three parts: the function keys (in the left-hand part of the keyboard), the

Figure 1.2
A typical IBM PC hardware configuration. (Courtesy of IBM)

alphanumeric keys (in the middle), and the numeric key pad (in the right-hand area). Let's examine the role of some important keys.

Function keys (usually labeled F1, F2, and so on) are special-function keys that allow you to answer questions, issue instructions, or select items from a menu of options. Each individual piece of software determines how and for what function each of these keys is used; the process each key performs differs from one piece of software to another.

Escape key is ordinarily used to issue a command designed to get a user out of trouble. It can be used to cancel or interrupt a previous command.

Control key is used to send a command to the computer or to a piece of software. The control key is held down while one or more other keys are depressed at the same time. Instructions often use the caret symbol (^) to indicate that the Control key should be depressed. For example, ^PrtSc indicates that the Control key and the PrtSc key should both be depressed at the same time.

Shift key functions like the shift key on a typewriter. It allows you to enter an upper-case character when you are in lower-case mode. When you are in upper-case mode (Caps Lock on), it allows you to enter a lower-case character.

Caps Lock key is somewhat like the Shift Lock key on a typewriter, with a few differences. It is used when all capital letters are to be entered; however, it does not bring into operation the special characters above the numeric keys in the alphanumeric key area or the upper line of any other nonalphabetic key. For this to happen, the Shift key must be held down while the appropriate other key is depressed.

Enter key, the large rectangular key above the PrtSc key, is used to tell the computer to accept a command. It must be depressed for the computer to be able to respond. This means usually that the Enter key must be pressed after any command.

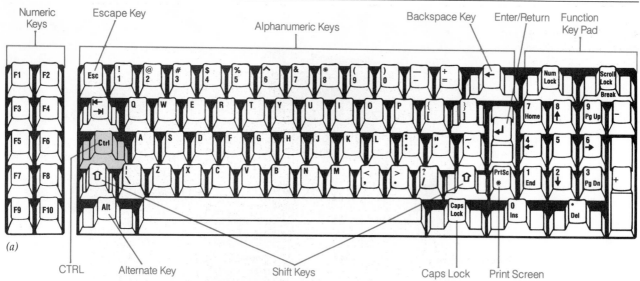

Numeric Keys | Escape Key | Alphanumeric Keys | Backspace Key | Enter/Return | Function Key Pad

CTRL | Alternate Key | Shift Keys | Caps Lock | Print Screen

(a)

Figure 1.3
(a) An IBM PC has three parts: function keys, alphanumeric keys, and numeric key pad; (b) a Koala touch-pad is an additional accessory used with graphics. (Courtesy of IBM)

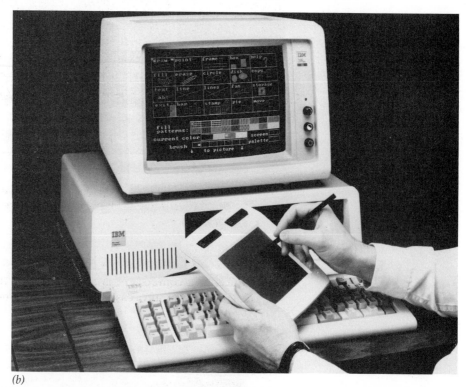

(b)

Alt key is somewhat like the Control key. Some pieces of software require that the Alt key and some other key be held down together for some action or process to occur.

PrtSc key, when held down with the Shift key, allows you to transfer to the printer almost anything that appears on the monitor of your machine; some graphics may not be so easily transferred.

Besides the keyboard, a number of other input devices can be attached to a computer. The mouse is a hand-held device that signals the computer to move the cursor on the display screen and can issue a "yes/no" command to the computer. (The *cursor* is the blinking dash that appears on your screen that

Figure 1.4
Some of the parts included on a typical IBM PC microcomputer system board. (Courtesy of IBM)

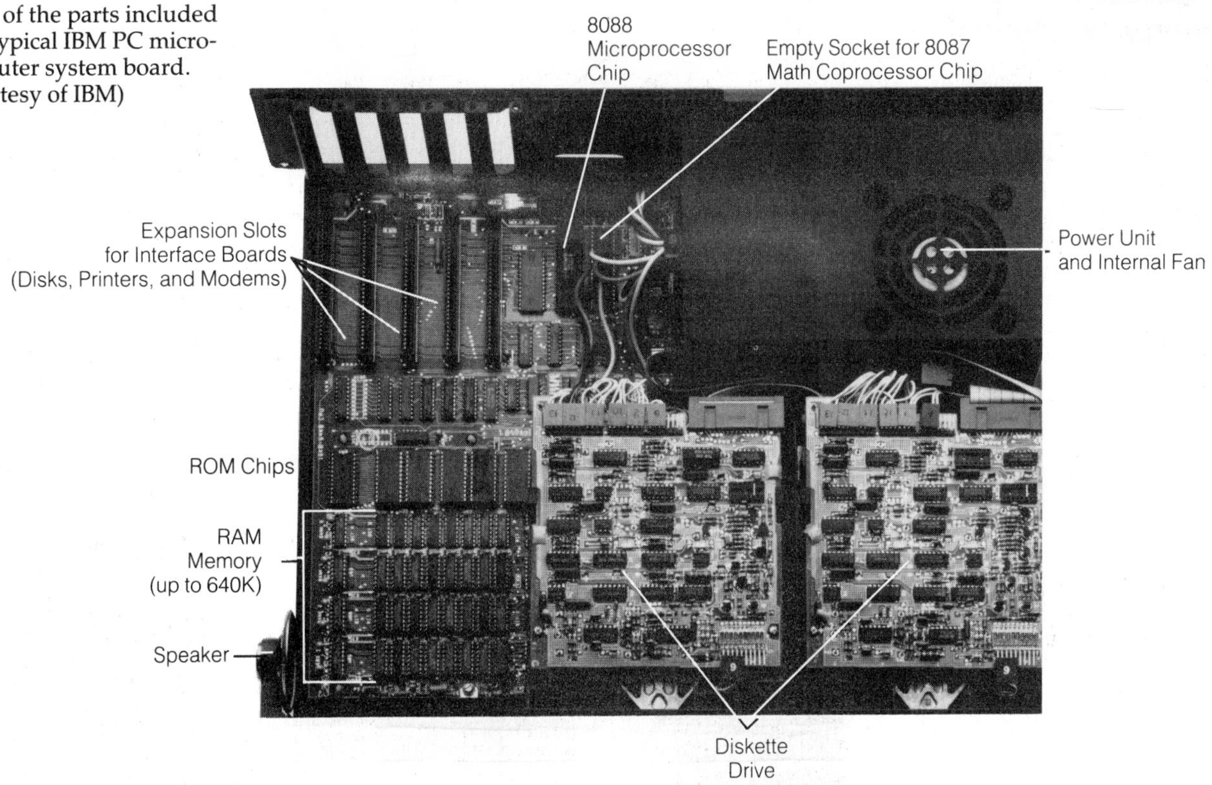

8088 Microprocessor Chip

Empty Socket for 8087 Math Coprocessor Chip

Expansion Slots for Interface Boards (Disks, Printers, and Modems)

Power Unit and Internal Fan

ROM Chips

RAM Memory (up to 640K)

Speaker

Diskette Drive

shows where the next character you enter will appear.) Other devices include touch pads, touch screens, light pens, voice recognition units, and bar code recognition units.

Processing

The processing component is composed of a number of different parts (see Figure 1.4): (1) microprocessor, (2) primary memory, (3) buses and boards, and (4) interfaces.

Microprocessors

The heart of a computer system is the **microprocessor**, or processing component, typically called the Central Processing Unit or **CPU**. The CPU is responsible for controlling data flow and executing program instructions upon the data. This component does all of the system's adding, subtracting, multiplying, and dividing, and its comparing of numbers and characters.

Different computer manufacturers use different microprocessors, but before these differences can be addressed, a brief explanation of some basic computer terms is in order.

A computer performs all its operations in a language called *binary notation*. In this language, every character (letter, numeral, or symbol) entered on the keyboard is instantly translated into a combination of 1's and 0's, called a *base two* (or *binary*) *equivalent*. Figure 1.5 displays some examples of decimal numbers and their binary equivalents.

Decimal	Binary
0	0
1	1
2	10
3	11
4	100
5	101
6	110
7	111
8	1000
9	1001
10	1010

The system's *binary code* determines how any specific character is represented in binary digits. Most microcomputers use the American Standard Code for Information Interchange, or **ASCII**, to represent data (see Figure 1.6). Notice that upper- and lower-case letters have different binary codes (as well as different hex and decimal codes, which we discuss later). For this reason, you must be specific about the characters you enter in a computer: a capital "A" does not mean the same thing to a computer as a lower-case "a."

A **bit** (short for *binary digit*) is the smallest unit of computer storage; each bit can represent a 1 or a 0. A computer uses groupings of bits to store data, and by combining bits in different ways, it can store enormous amounts of information.

The next smallest unit of computer storage, called a **byte**, is simply a grouping of eight bits. Individual bytes store binary codes that represent specific numeric digits or characters; one byte can hold any of 256 different values, depending on how the 1's and 0's are ordered. To store the letters *CPU* in memory, a computer would need three bytes—one for each character.

Finally, a **K** of storage represents 1,024 bytes. Most people think of a K as being equal to approximately 1,000 bytes, making it easier to perform mental calculations when determining the amount of storage involved. For example, a 256K system is popularly thought of as containing slightly more than 256,000 bytes, although it actually contains exactly 262,144 (1,024 × 256) bytes.

Familiarity with these terms is essential to understanding the various families of microprocessor chips: 8-bit, 16-bit, and 32-bit. The 8-bit microprocessors use 8 bits (one byte) at a time, 16-bit microprocessors usually use 16 bits (two bytes) at a time (see Figure 1.7), and 32-bit microprocessors usually use 32 bits (four bytes) at a time.

Computers differ significantly in the speed at which they work and in the amount of storage they possess. Speed is affected by three major factors. First, the larger the number of bits handled at one time, the faster the CPU should be; thus, a 16-bit computer is usually faster than an 8-bit computer. Second, the rating of the **system clock** indicates how fast operations can be performed in the computer. System clocks are rated in millions of cycles per second, or MHz (megahertz); most operate at between 4 and 16 MHz. A computer with a 4-MHz clock can be expected to perform at about one-half the speed of a computer with an 8-MHz clock. Third, a **coprocessor** can affect the computer's speed. Often used exclusively for mathematical manipulation, the coprocessor is usually placed in the microcomputer to take the burden of manipulating numbers off the CPU, allowing it to perform other tasks. To

Figure 1.6

ASCII code for single numeric digits and for upper- and lower-case letters of the alphabet.

Binary	Hex	Decimal	Symbol	Binary	Hex	Decimal	Symbol
0110000	30	48	0	1010110	56	86	V
0110001	31	49	1	1010111	57	87	W
0110010	32	50	2	1011000	58	88	X
0110011	33	51	3	1011001	59	89	Y
0110100	34	52	4	1011010	5A	90	Z
0110101	35	53	5	1100001	61	97	a
0110110	36	54	6	1100010	62	98	b
0110111	37	55	7	1100011	63	99	c
0111000	38	56	8	1100100	64	100	d
0111001	39	57	9	1100101	65	101	e
1000001	41	65	A	1100110	66	102	f
1000010	42	66	B	1100111	67	103	g
1000011	43	67	C	1101000	68	104	h
1000010	44	68	D	1101001	69	105	i
1000101	45	69	E	1101010	6A	106	j
1000110	46	70	F	1101011	6B	107	k
1000111	47	71	G	1101100	6C	108	l
1001000	48	72	H	1101101	6D	109	m
1001001	49	73	I	1101110	6E	110	n
1001010	4A	74	J	1101111	6F	111	o
1001011	4B	75	K	1110000	70	112	p
1001100	4C	76	L	1110001	71	113	q
1001101	4D	77	M	1110010	72	114	r
1001110	4E	78	N	1110011	73	115	s
1001111	4F	79	O	1110100	74	116	t
1010000	50	80	P	1110101	75	117	u
1010001	51	81	Q	1110110	76	118	v
1010010	52	82	R	1110111	77	119	w
1010011	53	83	S	1111000	78	120	x
1010100	54	84	T	1111001	79	121	y
1010101	55	85	U	1111010	7A	122	z

make use of this chip, however, the computer software must specify that the coprocessor be used for the mathematical work; otherwise, the slower CPU will be used.

The amount of storage permitted by different types of CPUs varies considerably. An 8-bit microprocessor permits a maximum addressable (that is, usable) storage of 64K or 65,536 bytes, a 16-bit microprocessor permits a maximum addressable storage of 1,000K or 1 million bytes, and a 32-bit microprocessor permits a maximum addressable storage of 16,000K or 16 million bytes. Some 8-bit computers get around their storage limitation by using **banked memory**. For example, although the Apple IIe is capable of handling 128K, it cannot address all 128K at one time; instead, it has two banks of 64K each and can address only one of these at any given moment. To use all 128K it must switch from one of the 64K banks to the other.

Which CPU should you purchase? For a typical user, the speed of the CPU and the amount of addressable storage are not very important. The determining factor should be the software. Choose the software best capable of solving your problem, and then purchase a computer capable of running that software.

(a)

(b)

(c)

(d)

Figure 1.7

Typical 16-bit computers. (a) Senior Partner courtesy of Panasonic Industrial Co.; (b) Kaypro 286i computer courtesy of Ron Powers, Kaypro Photo Department; (c) Hewlett-Packard Touchscreen computer courtesy of Hewlett-Packard; (d) NEC APC III courtesy of NEC Information Systems, Inc.

Primary Memory

Every computer contains internal storage space—**primary memory**—which can be used by the computer for a number of different functions: to contain data, either "raw" (date read from a file) or "refined" (data that have been manipulated); to contain program instructions for manipulating the data; and to contain the operating system for the computer. The amount of memory a computer has determines how long and, therefore, how complex a program can be. In a computer with limited memory, a complex program may have to be broken down into a number of subprograms to fit. The amount of memory also determines how much data can be stored in the computer, placing limits, for example, on the maximum size of a document. (Any storage outside the computer, such as on magnetic disks, is called **secondary storage**.)

RAM Memory. A computer uses two types of memory: RAM and ROM. **RAM**, which stands for Random Access Memory, is the memory accessible to the computer user. The user can put information into RAM memory, change information already stored there, or erase stored information. In addition, RAM memory holds data and program instructions vital to the computer's functioning; and the total amount of RAM determines which programs can be run and how much data can be processed. VP-Planner, for example, is a program capable of using every byte of available RAM memory; the so-called user-friendly programs also take up a lot of RAM memory. Generally, the more user-friendly a program is, the more RAM it needs.

RAM memory usually consists of **volatile memory**—memory that does not hold data after the computer's electrical current is turned off. What happens if you have typed a letter on the computer but turn the computer off before you remember to store it? The letter is irretrievably lost. Some recent computers use a nonvolatile memory called "bubble memory," but this feature is expensive.

ROM Memory. **ROM**, which stands for Read Only Memory, is used to hold permanent programs and information needed by the computer. Information contained in a ROM chip can be read, but it cannot be changed by the user; it is permanently "burned into" the chip.

Basic start-up program instructions are often found in ROM memory. The BASIC program language may be held in ROM (IBM PC); likewise, a number of utility programs or software packages may be held in ROM memory. An example of a ROM program is the Lotus 1-2-3 package "on a chip" held in the HP portable computer. Nonetheless, for the typical user, ROM memory becomes important only when the computer has a number of ROM-resident programs.

Buses and Boards

The computer system's processing unit, together with any memory connected to it, constitutes the computer proper; any piece of hardware connected to the computer is referred to as a **peripheral**. Examples of peripherals include the video display, disk drives, printers, keyboard, and modem.

A computer passes information to a peripheral and receives information from it through an entity called a **bus**. Buses vary greatly from computer to computer, but there are two basic types of bus systems: open bus systems and closed bus systems. On its main system board (sometimes called a mother board), an **open bus system** contains expansion slots that allow users to expand the system as they see fit. The IBM XT, for example, has eight expansion slots. Depending on your computer, you can use these slots to add such peripherals as a printer, a modem, a plotter, a second printer, and even a fancy, esoteric device like an environment controller to control living conditions in your house. All you have to do is plug an interface board (see Figure 1.8) into an empty slot on the main system board and then attach the peripheral to it. The IBM PC and its compatibles, along with the Apple II computer, are examples of open bus computers.

A computer with a **closed bus system** comes with plugs, called established ports, that accept device cables from the peripherals. Expanding such a

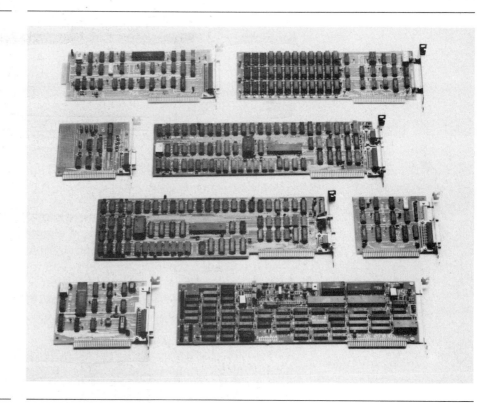

computer system is not a problem until all the ports are filled or until you wish
to add a device or controller that cannot be accommodated by the ports of your
computer—an environmental control device, for example.

Interfaces

The bus system allows the computer to communicate within itself and with
the peripherals. But communication between the computer and a peripheral
cannot occur without an interface. An **interface** (adapter) is a board containing
circuitry that connects a peripheral to the bus system (on an open bus system).
(On a closed bus system, the interface is built into the computer.)

Interfaces are either parallel or serial. A **parallel interface** transmits all
the bits contained in a byte of storage simultaneously. At least eight wires, one
for each bit, are needed to carry the information; most parallel devices, however, have many more wires, for performing a number of data-checking and
message-carrying functions. The standard method of parallel data transmission is called **centronics**.

A **serial interface** transmits the bits contained in a byte one at a time. Only
two wires are needed: one to send bits and the other to receive them. Other
lines handle the data-checking and message-carrying functions. No real standards for serial transmission have been established in the computer industry,
and as a result, a serial interface is more difficult to work with than a parallel
one. Parallel transmission is faster, but serial transmission allows information
to be transmitted farther (parallel devices usually restrict cable length to under
15 feet). Disks and printers usually use parallel transmission; printers, terminals, and (especially) modems usually use serial transmission.

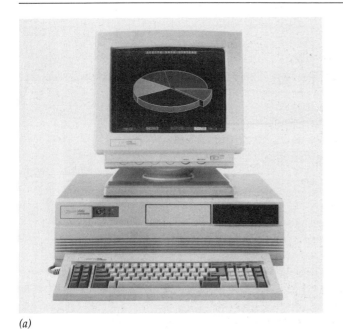

(a)

(b)

Figure 1.9
Three IBM PC-AT compatible computers: (a) Zenith Data Systems A-248, (b) PC's Limited 286, and (c) Compaq Deskpro. (Courtesy of Zenith Data Systems, PC's Limited, and Compaq Computer Corporation)

(c)

IBM Compatibility

There is no doubt that IBM established an industry standard when it introduced its PC in 1981. For a significant period of time, IBM was one of the few companies that provided a powerful MS-DOS computer. Over the years, however, this situation has changed dramatically. Dozens of firms are now producing high-quality machines at prices less than IBM charges and with additional features, such as faster clock speeds, that many consumers find desirable. After IBM introduced its PC-AT model, a microcomputer with an 80286 32-bit microprocessor and a 16-bit data bus, it took competitors only a short time to introduce clones (see Figure 1.9). Many of these machines work two or three times faster than the original AT.

(a)

(b)

(c)

The true 32-bit microprocessor market evolved even before IBM was able to introduce a microcomputer centered around the 80386 microprocessor chip (see Figure 1.10). The 80386 microprocessor chip allows multiple users and multiple applications to run at one time.

Portability

Consumers have long been demanding a truly portable computer—one that can be easily transported in a briefcase or placed under an airplane seat. But they have been especially critical of portable computers that reached the market without the capabilities that they found in their desk-top computers. Above all, users demanded screens that were easy to use.

(b)

(a)

Figure 1.11
Two full-featured portable microcomputers: (a) Zenith Data Systems S-181 portable with an 8088c microprocessor chip and (b) Compaq Portable III with an 80286 microprocessor chip. (Courtesy of Zenith Data Systems and Compaq Computer Corporation)

The manufacturers that have entered this market (see Figure 1.11) fall into two groups. The first group provides a machine that is battery powered and has a highly readable Liquid Crystal Display (LCD) (usually using double-twist technology), one or more disk drives (usually 3.5-inch drives), and a truly low weight (usually under 12 pounds).

The second group of vendors markets machines that are bulkier but have much more power. For example, their machines might have a hard disk capable of storing twenty million or more characters, a diskette drive, an extremely readable (gas plasma) screen, and a faster, more powerful microprocessor chip (80286); but they usually must be powered by regular 110-volt service.

Output

Monitors

The primary **output** device used with microcomputer equipment is the **monitor**, which gives the user instant video feedback. Attachable monitors of many different types exist (see Figure 1.12); other monitors may be built into the main computer box itself. The screens may present displays in black and white, green and white, yellow and brown, or any other two colors.

Video displays can be divided into seven groups:

1. **Televisions** must be attached to a device called a radio-frequency (rf) modulator if they are to work effectively. Although televisions make adequate display screens for games, the resolution (or clarity) of their display is not good for applications such as word processing or

(a)

(b)

(c)

(d)

Figure 1.12
Output display devices that
can be attached to a micro-
computer. (a) Color Monitor
courtesy of IBM; (b) and (c)
Princeton Graphic monitors
courtesy of Princeton
Graphic Systems, an Intelli-
gen Systems Company; (d)
Kaypro portable courtesy
Ron Powers, Kaypro Photo
Department; (e) Hewlett-
Packard portable courtesy of
Hewlett-Packard.

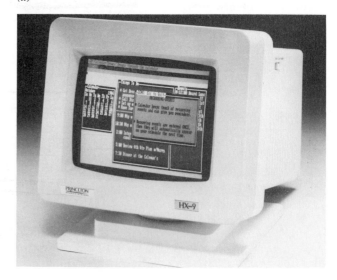

spreadsheets. Working with such a device can quickly produce eye fatigue.

2. **One-color display monitors**—for example, black-and-white monitors—operate with one active color. The image displayed on these devices is better than that on a television, but it can still cause eye fatigue after long periods of time. Most one-color display monitors use a 5 × 7 dot matrix. Each dot (or **pixel**) turns on or off depending on the character to be displayed.

3. **Monochrome monitors** are similar to one-color monitors except that they have many more pixels per character, which results in a much crisper display.

4. **Color monitors** are excellent for presenting graphics, displaying graphs of data, and playing games. They are not good for working with text data found in spreadsheets and word-processing, however, because the images frequently "tear" (split) on the screen, and the pixels frequently appear multicolored.

5. **Flat screen/LCD monitors** have recently been developed for lap computers. They contain a liquid-crystal screen or some other type of display that does not need a large tube. LCD displays have black characters on a white/gray background; they are found on many watches and calculators, are usually lightweight, and sometimes suffer from poor readability.

6. **Enhanced Graphics Adapter (EGA) monitors** present the clearest, most vivid graphics of any current monitor. They use 640 × 350 dot resolution to present crisper, more colorful images. Most are capable of showing sixty-four or more different colors with extremely high resolution (see Figure 1.13).

7. **Multipurpose monitors** are comparatively recent arrivals in the marketplace. They are able to handle regular monochrome graphics, color, and EGA signals, thereby providing a user with three monitors in one case (see Figure 1.14).

Figure 1.13
Princeton Graphic Systems SR-12P EGA graphics monitor. (Courtesy of Princeton Graphic Systems. Copyright 1986. Used by permission.)

Figure 1.14
Sony multi-sync CPD-1302
monitor capable of handling
both color and EGA graphics.
(Courtesy of Sony Corporation of America)

One way to perform very different applications (including graphics) on
a computer is to hook two monitors to the computer. The monochrome monitor can be used for text-related applications, and the color monitor can be used
when graphics are needed.

Printers

Video displays are ideal for displaying output that does not need to be pre-
served. When the information must be retained, however, a **printer** is used to
generate an image of the output on paper.

Printers are available in a number of different types. **Dot matrix printers**,
the most common type hooked to microcomputers, use dots to form the characters (see Figure 1.15). A single print head, usually containing either seven or
nine print needles (some of the more recent printers have as many as twenty-
four), moves across the paper, impacting the print needles to form each character. The number of print needles in the head determines the quality of the
letters formed: the more needles, the crisper the letter. The speed of these
printers varies from 80 characters per second (cps) to about 450 cps.

Thermal printers produce a print style that looks similar to dot matrix,
but the characters are formed by burning dots into the paper. Most thermal
printers work only on special types of paper. Output speed is about 80 cps.

Letter-quality printers, whose output appears to have come from a typewriter, are also called **daisy wheel printers**. They have one of two types of
print mechanism: a daisy wheel (so called because the characters on the print
wheel resemble the petals of a daisy) or a print thimble (see Figure 1.16). These
devices print at speeds of 10 to 60 cps.

Ink-jet printers shoot little jets of ink onto the paper in patterns that form
characters. These printers can produce output on a par with that of a cheap

Figure 1.15
Two dot matrix printers. (IBM Personal Computer Graphics Printer courtesy of IBM; NEC Pinwriter P2 courtesy of NEC Information Systems, Inc.)

Figure 1.16
Typical thimble print heads. (Courtesy of NEC Information Systems, Inc.)

dot matrix printer, or they can match letter-quality printers (see Figure 1.17). Output speed exceeds 200 cps. Instead of ribbons, these printers use disposable ink cartridges (see Figure 1.18).

Laser printers use xerographic technology to form characters on paper by means of electronic charges, forming the characters with a toner and bonding the toner to the paper with heat (see Figure 1.19). This same process is used extensively in modern copiers. Laser printers print about eight to ten pages per minute; the technology has only recently been applied to microcomputer printers.

Figure 1.17
The graphics capability of an
ink-jet printer. (Courtesy of
Hewlett-Packard)

Figure 1.18
The disposable ink cartridge
used in the Hewlett-Packard
ThinkJet printer. (Courtesy of
Hewlett-Packard)

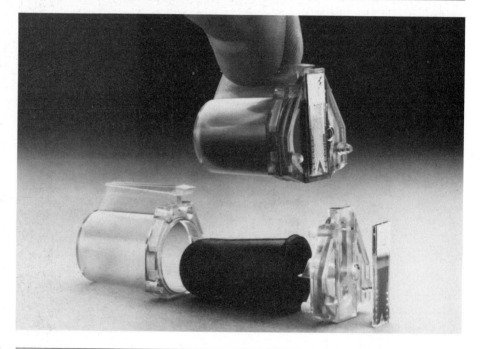

Plotters

The **plotter**, an output device that is growing in popularity (see Figure 1.20), draws pictures using computer technology. At least one pen moves on the plotter, and the paper may also move. Most of today's plotters allow users to produce multicolored drawings by directing the plotter to stop for a change of pens.

Figure 1.19
A Hewlett-Packard LaserJet printer. (Courtesy of Hewlett-Packard)

Figure 1.20
A number of Colorwriter plotters manufactured by Gould Electronics. (Courtesy of Gould Electronics)

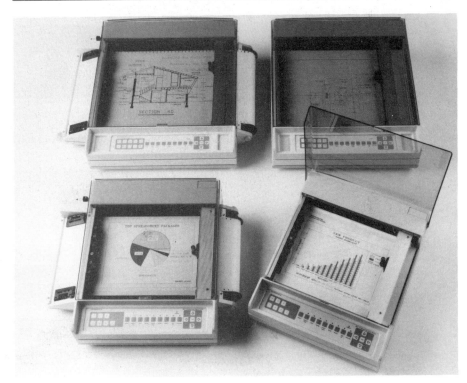

Secondary Storage

Floppy Disks (Diskettes)

As mentioned, RAM memory is volatile: When the power goes off, anything in RAM is lost. The most common **nonvolatile storage** medium used by microcomputers is variously called the **floppy disk**, the disk, and the **diskette**. It is simply a circle cut from a sheet of Mylar plastic (see Figure 1.21) that has a ferrous oxide coating capable of holding magnetic spots. Diskettes come in

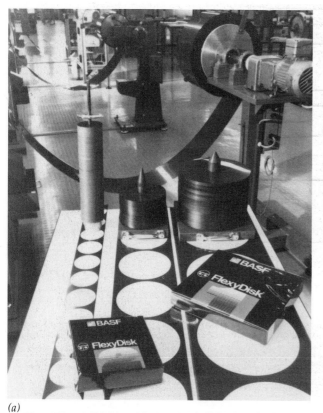

(a)

(b)

Figure 1.21
(a) Manufacturing line where disks are cut from Mylar plastic and (b) machine producing the
Mylar. (Courtesy (a) BASF Systems Corporation and (b) Polaroid)

different sizes (identified by diameter), but the most common size for microcomputers is 5.25 inches.

Before a new disk can be used, it must be prepared so that the computer
can recognize it and record data on it. The process of preparing a disk for use,
called **formatting** because it is performed by the FORMAT command, will be
discussed later.

Disks provide storage for data, documents, and programs that need to
be kept for an extended period of time. Without disks, a computer's only
storage medium is RAM memory, and the contents of RAM memory are
destroyed when the power to the CPU is turned off.

Diskettes are usually contained in protective paper envelopes (see Figure
1.22). Outside their envelopes, they look much alike (see Figure 1.23): spongy,
5.25-inch diskettes with flimsy black plastic covers. The term *floppy disk* alludes
to the flimsiness of the protective cover and to the flexibility it gives. Need-
less to say, a user must exercise caution when handling this flimsy storage
medium.

Several features are common to all diskettes. All have some type of
printed label that indicates the name of the manufacturer and identifies the
top side of the diskette. A diskette is always placed in a disk drive with its
label up, and the end with the label goes in the drive last. (The *disk drive*
contains a mechanism for reading information from or writing information to
the disk.)

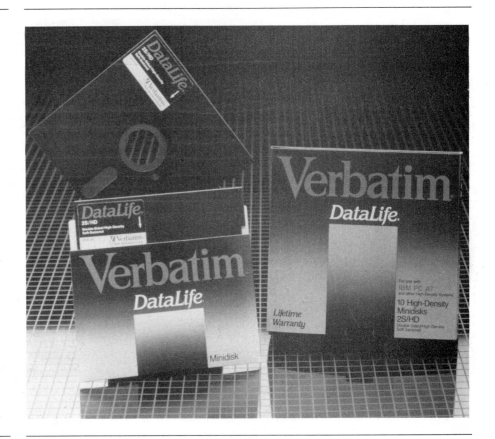

igure 1.22
Typical 5.25-inch diskettes.
(Courtesy of Verbatim
Corporation)

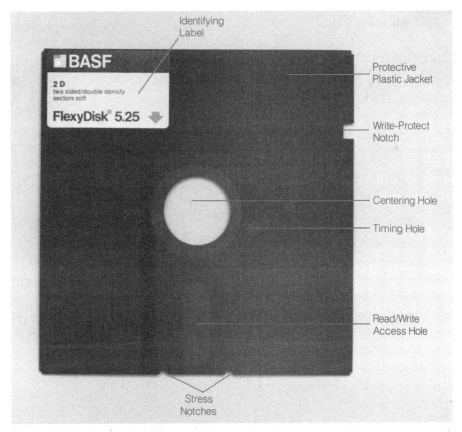

Figure 1.23
Various features of a typical
5.25-inch diskette. (Courtesy
of BASF Systems
Corporation)

Two round holes are visible at the center of the disk. The larger one, called the **centering hole**, is clamped by the disk drive, which then rotates the disk inside its protective cover. On a good-quality disk, the centering hole is surrounded by a plastic ring that reinforces the disk in case it does not automatically center inside the protective cover and gets pinched by the disk drive. The smaller hole to the right of the centering hole is the **timing hole**, which indicates the beginning of a track or sector, telling the disk drive where to start reading or writing. (If there is only one hole on the diskette, the diskette is *soft-sectored*; if there is more than one hole, the diskette is *hard-sectored*.)

Below the centering hole is an oval hole called the **read/write access hole**. Data are read from or recorded onto the disk by the read/write heads which are positioned over this opening. Data are written onto the disk in concentric circles (see Figure 1.24) called **tracks**. More than one file can be contained by a track because the track is subdivided into units of storage called **sectors**, each of which is capable of holding 512 bytes of data. There are nine sectors per track, forty tracks per side, and two sides per disk. The total storage space on a disk is therefore 368,640 bytes ($512 \times 9 \times 40 \times 2$). Another common measurement of storage space for computers is based on the unit K, which is equal to 1,024 bytes (characters). When 368,640 is divided by 1,024 the result is 360; a diskette thus has 360K of storage.

On a computer designed to handle **soft-sectored disks**, the tracks are divided into sectors during the formatting process; **hard-sectored disks** already have their tracks divided into sectors. IBM computers and IBM compatibles use soft-sectored disks, as do most other computers. You cannot use hard-sectored disks in computers whose disk drives are designed for soft-sectored disks, nor can you use soft-sectored disks in computers whose disk drives are designed for hard-sectored disks.

Figure 1.24
A 5.25-inch disk with tracks and sectors.

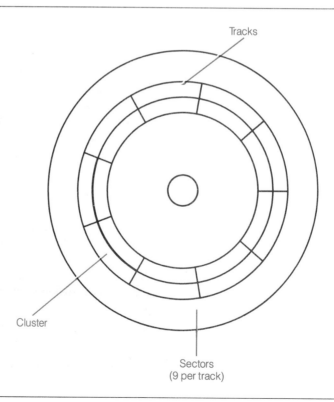

Below the read/write access hole are two small semicircular holes called stress notches. They enable the diskette to bend without creasing the protective jacket.

Along the upper right-hand edge of the diskette is a rectangular notch known as the **write-protect notch**. If you cover this notch, data on the diskette can be read, but writing and erasing cannot occur. Many diskettes accompanying software packages and holding original programs don't have a write-protect notch, thus permanently protecting the information on the diskette from alteration or erasure. The diskette scratches easily. Manufacturers try to protect it by gluing a piece of feltlike cloth to the inside of the flimsy protective cover, to trap small foreign particles that gather on the diskette as it whirls around inside the jacket. The cloth is also lubricated with a substance such as silicone to decrease drag and promote longer disk life by reducing abrasion caused by rubbing against the material. Treating diskettes with care and common sense dramatically increases their useful lives.

Diskette Do's and Don't's

1. Copy (back up) everything! Never trust a single diskette with important data or files.

2. Don't write on the diskette envelope with a ball-point pen. No matter how lightly you try to write, the concentrated pressure created by the pen will more than likely damage the thin Mylar disk. It is best to write the label prior to affixing it to the diskette; failing that, use a felt-tip pen—and be careful.

3. When you are through using the diskette, place it inside its protective envelope. This will help keep dust, dirt, pop, coffee, and so on from getting inside the protective cover.

4. Store diskettes vertically, like records. Don't lay them flat or at an angle, or they will bend and warp.

5. Don't touch the diskette surface with fingers, tissue, or solvents. Both surfaces contain data. If you put an unprotected diskette on a dusty table, you can easily contaminate the data surface.

6. Place a label on every diskette. This will help you avoid not being able to locate a disk because it was formatted by someone who thought labels weren't important.

7. Don't bend or crease diskettes. If you plan to mail one, take special care to pack it carefully with one of the plastic protective mailing devices.

8. Be especially careful when inserting a diskette into the disk drive. It's very easy to catch something on a piece of internal machinery and crease the fragile diskette. If this should happen, back up the diskette at once! Don't take any chances with your disk files!

9. Close the disk drive door gently; don't let it snap shut. It's important that the diskette center itself as the door closes. Snapping the door can catch the diskette off-center and pinch the fragile plastic, causing permanent damage.

10. Keep diskettes away from magnetic fields which are generated by magnets, some color monitors, and the older telephones.

11. Don't expose diskettes to temperature extremes, such as in direct sunlight, on tops of radiators, in trunks of cars, or next to cold windowsills.

12. Use plenty of common sense in dealing with fragile diskettes. Careless handling can and will wipe out hours of work in an instant.

Hard Disks

In the last few years, hard-disk systems have become increasingly popular. They offer greater storage capacity and provide faster data retrieval. Two basic types of hard disk are available: one that has a removable cartridge and one that has a fixed disk commonly known as a Winchester disk (see Figure 1.25c). The Winchester, which was first developed by IBM for use on mainframe computers, is the more popular of the two among microcomputer users.

A **hard disk** contains one or more rigid platters for recording data. Like floppy disks, these rigid platters have a metal oxide coating for holding the magnetic charges that represent characters. The platters rotate on a spindle at about 3,600 rpm.

(a)

(b)

(c)

Figure 1.25
(a) ST4192N—Seagate full-height 5¼-inch high performance hard disk drive with embedded controller, SCSI interface, and 160 meg of formatted capacity. The drive has an average access time of 17 msec.
(b) ST157R—Seagate 3½-inch hard disk drive with ST412/RLL interface and 49 megabytes of formatted capacity. The drive features an average access time of less than 30 msec and only 9 watts power.
(c) Typical half-height Winchester hard disk with tape back-up system. (Courtesy of (a,b) Seagate Technology and (c) Alloy Computer Products)

A Winchester hard disk is held inside a sealed unit that contains the recording platters and the read/write heads; in contrast, a hard disk with a removable **cartridge** uses a removable platter. The removable cartridge consists of a rigid platter that is capable of rotating within a plastic case, which, in a slot on the disk drive, is spun by the disk drive to the proper speed. Some hard disk units use both the removable cartridge and a Winchester drive. On both types of hard disks, the read/write heads "float" over the recording surface at a distance of about fourteen-millionths of an inch to read or record data. A stepping motor positions the arm with the read/write heads at the appropriate track to get to the required data (see Figure 1.25b).

The diameter of the platters varies from 3 to 5.25 inches, and the amount of data that can be stored on a disk also varies greatly. Rather than being measured in K (thousands), storage on a hard disk is measured in **megabytes (meg)**—millions of bytes of storage.

Some precautions must be taken when using hard disks. Because the read/write heads are so close to the recording surface, contaminants such as a hair or piece of dust on the platters cause the read/write head to jump up and then crash into the recording surface. The sealed environment of the Winchester almost eliminates the problem of contamination and head crashes, but these can occur with removable cartridges.

Another problem facing users of hard-disk technology is how to back up the data contained on the disk. Hard disks with removable cartridges are easy to back up because data on the fixed disk can simply be copied onto a removable cartridge. Winchester disks, however, are more difficult to back up. Most computer manufacturers enable data on a Winchester to be copied onto a floppy disk, but if a floppy disk can store a maximum of 360K, approximately twenty-eight of these disks will be required to back up a 10-meg hard disk. This can be very time-consuming. Some hard-disk manufacturers are making the back-up process easier, however, by making available cartridge tape units that have a ¼-inch tape cartridge for holding the back-up data (see Figure 1.26). These tapes can store from 10 to 40 meg of data, cutting the back-up process from three hours to as little as ten minutes.

Figure 1.26
A 24-megabyte external hard disk with magnetic tape backup. (Courtesy of Tallgrass Technologies Corporation © 1985)

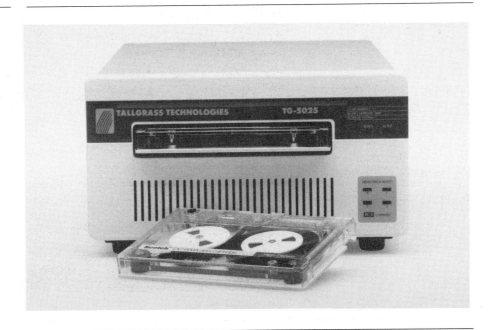

Chapter Review

A microcomputer system is composed of five separate parts: (1) people (users), (2) hardware, (3) software, (4) documentation/procedures, and (5) data/information. The human element is the most important part because a person using a microcomputer usually has some type of important problem to solve.

The hardware component consists of the equipment (boxes) that constitutes the microcomputer. The four component hardware parts consist of (1) input, (2) processing, (3) output, and (4) storage. The heart of the hardware configuration is the microprocessor chip.

A number of different types of monitors and printers can be attached to a microcomputer system and used as output devices. The major nonvolatile storage device is the diskette, a fragile storage medium that must be treated with care.

The two basic types of computer memory are RAM and ROM. Data and program instructions are stored inside the computer in RAM. The smallest piece of RAM, the byte, is capable of holding one character of storage. Pieces of data are stored in RAM using a binary system of 0's and 1's, in a code called ASCII. ROM is used primarily by the computer.

Key Terms and Concepts

ASCII
banked memory
bit
bus
byte
cartridge
centering hole
centronics
chip
closed bus system
color monitor
coprocessor
CPU
daisy wheel printer
diskette
dot matrix printer
EGA monitors
floppy disk
formatting
function keys
hard disk
hard-sectored disks
ink-jet printer
input
interface
K
laser printers
LCD monitors
megabyte (meg)

microcomputer system
microprocessor
monitor
monochrome monitor
multipurpose monitors
nonvolatile storage
open bus system
output
parallel interface
peripheral
pixel
plotter
primary memory
printer
QWERTY
RAM
read/write access hole
ROM
secondary storage
sectors
serial interface
soft-sectored disks
system clock
thermal printer
timing hole
tracks
volatile memory
write-protect notch

Chapter Quiz

Multiple Choice

1. Which of the following items is part of the microcomputer?
   a. RAM (Random Access Memory)
   b. Interface *adaptor & bus*
   c. ROM (Read Only Memory)
   d. Bus *peripheral*
   e. All of the above are part of a microcomputer

2. Which of the following is not an output device?
   a. Printer
   b. Plotter
   c. Monitor
   d. Keyboard
   e. All of the above are output devices

3. Which of the following statements is correct?
   a. RAM is the nonvolatile memory.
   b. ROM is the memory used to hold data and instructions.
   c. The bus is used to move data and instructions from one part of the computer to another.
   d. The laser printer uses new technology to make it an input device.

4. Which of the following terms do(es) not apply to a diskette?
   a. Sector
   b. Track
   c. Soft-sectored
   d. Byte
   e. All of the above terms apply to a diskette

5. Which of the statements below is false?
   a. About eight "families" or types of microprocessor are currently on the market.
   b. A 32-bit processor will probably be slower than an 8-bit processor.
   c. RAM restrictions will not usually restrict the type of software you are allowed to run on your computer.
   d. b and c.
   e. All of the above are false.

True/False

6. A letter-quality printer is typically faster than a dot matrix printer.

7. A diskette is an example of nonvolatile storage.

8. As a general rule of thumb, the more bits a microprocessor chip can handle at one time, the more memory it can address and the faster it operates.

9. Hard disks are typically faster and more reliable than diskettes.

10. Monochrome display monitors are easier to read than one-color monitors because they use more pixels.

Answers

1. e 2. d 3. c 4. e 5. e 6. f 7. t 8. t 9. t 10. t

Exercises

1. Define or describe each of the following:
   a. microprocessor   h. centronics
   b. bit   i. pixel
   c. byte   j. track
   d. ASCII   k. sector
   e. RAM   l. K
   f. ROM   m. meg
   g. bus

2. List some typical input devices for a microcomputer.
   a.

   b.

   c.

   d.

3. The standard code used for storing information in microcomputers is the _____ code.

4. Differences among 8-, 16-, and 32-bit microprocessing computer chips limit the amount of addressable _____ memory.

5. Memory that is only capable of 64K functioning at one time but that has a total storage capacity of 128K is called _____ memory.

6. The type of monitor that displays characters with the pixels (dots) close together is the _____ display.

7. _____ memory is available to the user, but _____ _____ memory is used only by the machine.

8. The unit of storage required to hold a numeric digit or character is called a(n) _____ .

9. A _____ interface transmits a bit at a time, while a _____ transmits at least eight bits at once.

10. The terms diskette and _____ disk are synonymous.

11. A K of memory is equal to about _____ bytes, and a meg of memory equals about _____ bytes of storage.

12. List some advantages and disadvantages using hard disk storage devices.
    Advantages:
    a.

    b.

    Disadvantages:
    a.

    b.

13. Why is the human element so important in a microcomputer system? Do you know of any examples of individuals not satisfied with their microcomputers because they were inappropriate to the users' particular problem?

14. A printer that prints characters using dot patterns is called a _____ _____ printer.

15. A _____ chip greatly speeds up processing that involves mathematical manipulation.

Chapter

2

Microcomputer

Software

After completing this chapter, you should be able to:

List and describe the three classifications of software

List and describe the five classifications of application software

Describe the role of integrated application software

Describe the function of the IBM Disk Operating System (DOS)

List and describe the various parts of DOS

List and describe the rules for file names

Describe how to prepare a disk(ette) for use

Describe how to start (boot) the computer system

Describe how DOS uses the prepared disk

Describe how DOS uses characters called ''wild cards''

Describe how DOS uses various keys to give commands

Chapter 1 covered the hardware component—the seeable, touchable portion—of a microcomputer system. This chapter covers the **software** component—the set of individual instructions issued to the computer to enable it to manipulate or process the data.

The three general categories of software (see Figure 2.1) are (1) operating systems, (2) programming languages, and (3) application programs. An **operating system** is a collection of programs and utilities designed to make it easy for the user to create and manage files, run programs, and operate the system devices attached to the computer. Without its operating system, a computer is just a collection of useless hardware. Various computer operating systems are on the market, including CP/M, PC DOS, MS DOS, and CP/M 86. The IBM PC DOS operating system will be discussed in detail later in this chapter.

Programming Languages

Programming languages enable the user to write a set of instructions to solve a particular problem. The most common programming language on microcomputers today is **BASIC**; others include FORTRAN, **COBOL**, and PASCAL. BASIC, in particular, has many versions, so a BASIC program written on one computer often must be changed before it can be run on another computer. Most people interested in microcomputers find it reassuring that they need not know how to program in order to use a computer effectively.

A high-level, humanly intelligible programming language cannot be used on a computer without a language processor. **Language processors** are software packages that translate instructions prepared in a specific programming language, such as BASIC or COBOL, into the binary machine language of the computer. The translation is done by either a compiler or an interpreter.

A **compiler** is a piece of software that translates a complete program into machine language, while simultaneously checking for any errors that have been made by the programmer. It accepts a **source code** (the set of program instructions written in a high-level language) and generates the **object code** (the translated binary instructions that are executable by the computer). The object program, which is the program that performs all actual processing, becomes operative if there are no errors in the source program.

An **interpreter**, instead of translating the program all at once, translates one instruction at a time during the execution of the program. BASIC is one programming language that makes use of an interpreter to translate high-level instructions individually into machine language (as long as no errors are

Figure 2.1
Types of software.

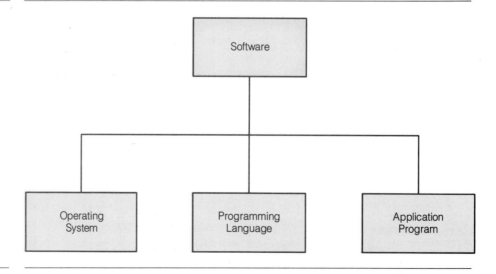

present). This process occurs every time the computer executes a BASIC instruction.

The major difference between a compiler and an interpreter is speed. A compiler translates a program only once and thereafter executes the object code, but an interpreter must translate a program instruction every time that instruction is executed. Compiler programs generally execute three to five times faster than interpreter programs.

Application Programs

Application programs are precoded sets of generalized instructions for the computer; each program is written to accomplish a certain goal. A general ledger package, a mailing list program, and PacMan are all examples of application programs. To use an application program, you do not have to know anything about programming because its writer has already taken care of the programming needed to solve the type of problem it addresses.

Application software can be divided into five core applications of interest to most users (see Figure 2.2): (1) electronic spreadsheets, (2) word processing, (3) communications, (4) data base management, and (5) graphics.

Electronic Spreadsheets

Electronic spreadsheet programs allow users to manipulate various data that can be expressed in rows and columns. A *cell* (the intersecting point of a row and a column) can contain text, numbers, or formulas, which set up the interrelationship of a cell with other cells. Whenever you change the contents of

Figure 2.2
Types of application software.

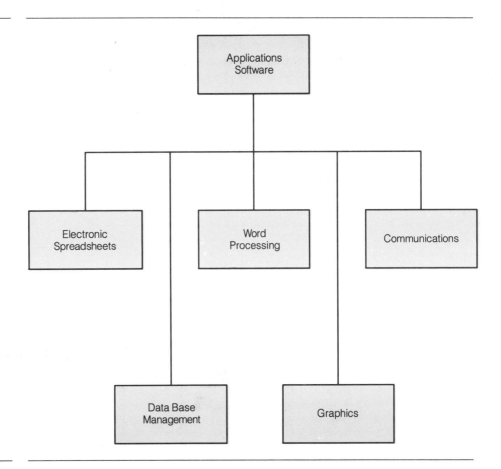

one cell, the spreadsheet automatically recalculates everything. **VisiCalc**, designed by Dan Flystra and Dan Bricklin while they were graduate students at the Harvard Business School, was the first spreadsheet introduced for microcomputers; it was originally designed to run on the Apple II computer. The introduction of VisiCalc led businesspeople to view the microcomputer as a potentially useful business tool rather than as a plaything.

Many different spreadsheet packages have since been produced for microcomputers that incorporate tremendous improvements in power and capability over the original VisiCalc. The spreadsheet you will be studying later is the **VP-Planner** spreadsheet program. Just as VisiCalc was responsible for businesses purchasing Apple microcomputers, Lotus 1-2-3 and spreadsheet packages like VP-Planner have been responsible for businesses purchasing IBM PC microcomputers.

Sophisticated spreadsheet packages can do much more than manipulate rows and columns of numbers; they have advanced features such as "if-then-else" logic (which allows you to check the value contained in a worksheet cell and take actions based on that value), tests for "less than or greater than," and the ability to determine the minimum, maximum, or average value in a range of numbers. Some spreadsheets also allow the importing or exchanging of information with other application programs. This feature enables users to perform additional calculations with data already possessed or to print out reports.

The following are only a few of the business and personal applications that spreadsheet programs can be used to accomplish:

> product planning
>
> production forecasting
>
> marketing
>
> materials and labor requirements
>
> merger and acquisition of real estate
>
> cash flow analysis
>
> checkbook registers
>
> personal balance sheet

The usefulness of an electronic spreadsheet alone has justified many microcomputer purchases by individuals and businesses. Once you become familiar with the usage and capability of the electronic spreadsheet, it will become an indispensible productivity tool.

Word Processing

How often, in drafting a memo, letter, report, or term paper, have you filled a wastebasket with "reject" paper? How often have you crossed out or erased lines and phrases? How often have you tried to squeeze additional comments between lines or on the side of the page? How often would you have given anything to be able to move a paragraph or section easily from one place to another?

Word processing simplifies the task of creating, editing, redrafting, and printing a document and improves personal productivity and efficiency by (for example) allowing you to duplicate a letter without retyping the whole thing or to recall the document six months later without having to leaf through a ton of paper to find it. The major benefit of this automated process is the ease with which it allows you to generate an almost perfect document. Word processing will not necessarily reduce the time it takes you to produce an original report from scratch; in fact, it may take you longer. But perfection is now within the grasp of the individual preparing a report because changes can now be made that would have taken too much time to do manually.

Not only can word processing reduce turnaround time, increase efficiency, improve recall of documents, and allow the duplication of originals and the standardization of forms, but software enhancements to word processing packages have been designed that will also check spelling and, at the instruction of the user, automatically correct misspelled words. The word processing package you will be examining later is **WordPerfect**. It is one of the most commonly used word processing packages on the market.

Communications

Communications application packages allow you to obtain and transmit information over telephone lines. Many businesses use terminals to communicate with computers at other locations; many microcomputers are also capable of communicating with other computers. But whereas a terminal is merely a communications device that allows a user to receive or transmit information to a computer, a microcomputer can perform the terminal's function and can process information as a stand-alone computer system.

A microcomputer gains the ability to communicate over telephone lines by means of a device called a **modem**—an abbreviation for *modulator-demodulator*. A modem translates the computer's binary signals (0's and 1's) into audible sounds that can be communicated over a telephone line; the process is then reversed at the other end of the line.

A modem can be either internal (placed inside the machine in an expansion slot; see Figure 2.3) or external (connected to a serial interface on the computer; see Figure 2.4), and it may come with a variety of features. For example, it may have an auto-answer capability that allows the computer to answer the phone, or it may have an **auto-dial** capability that allows the

Figure 2.3
The modem here is entirely contained on this board, which fits into a vacant expansion slot inside the computer. (Courtesy of Prometheus Products of Fremont, California)

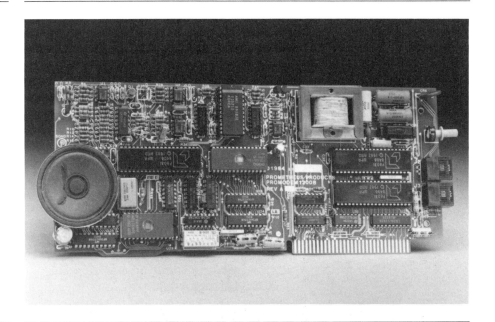

computer (via the modem) to dial a desired number automatically. Features such as these increase the modem's cost.

Both internal and external modems translate data at a speed measured as a **baud** rate. Many modems transmit thirty characters per second, or roughly 300 baud; other modems can transmit at 1,200 and 2,400 baud.

The increased communications capabilities of microcomputers made possible by the modem have created a new industry that provides information to computer owners. Through the Dow Jones News/Retrieval, for example, you can get information about stocks or sell and purchase stock. The Source allows you to book an airline reservation, rent a car, place a hotel reservation, or purchase consumer goods.

A number of microcomputers can be connected to form a **local area network (LAN)** (see Figure 2.5) that links computer equipment in an office or building so that users can share data, hard disks, or printers. Modems are not needed to attach a computer to the network.

Data Base Management

Data base management programs permit you to organize and keep records and files in whatever manner you want and to update, manipulate, and use this information in virtually unlimited ways. For example, assume that you are the personnel director of a firm that employs 1,000 employees. Your firm has placed information about each of the 1,000 employees in a data base file. Let's say the firm gets a request from the government for information on how many of its employees are over fifty-five years of age. Without computer assistance, you would be forced to go through each individual's file folder to see if that person was over fifty-five. With a computer, however, if information about the birth date of each employee is already on file, you just interrogate the data file with a statement like LIST FOR YEAR < 1931, which causes the system to list those individuals who were born before 1931.

A data base management software package allows users to access information from the file quickly, saving vast amounts of time. The data base management package that you will be examining later is **dBASE III Plus. dBASE II**, a predecessor of dBASE III Plus, was the first relational data base created for microcomputers.

Graphics

Once you have produced a final product, its effectiveness depends on the manner in which it is presented. It is extremely important that your audience not be burdened with reading 10 or 100 pages of text data that could be summarized in one graphic display. The ability to convert raw data into **graphic displays** (see Figure 2.6) can be accomplished through a number of useful software programs such as Chart-Master and VP-Planner. Plotters and color printers are available to produce hard copy of a graph; devices are also available to take a graph from the screen and produce a slide. The graphics feature of VP-Planner will be covered later in this text.

Integration

As you can see, the five core applications described thus far can be very beneficial to a microcomputer user. They are at their most powerful when they enable the user to combine information generated by one software package with that generated by another.

Figure 2.4
An external modem that hooks up to a serial port (expansion card) contained on the computer. (Courtesy of Prometheus Products of Fremont, California)

Figure 2.5
The expansion cards, cables, and software necessary for connecting microcomputers together in a local area network. (Courtesy of Novell, Inc., Orem, Utah)

Some packages provide two or more of these core applications in one software package. VP-Planner and Lotus 1-2-3 are two such **integrated packages**. Both contain a powerful spreadsheet with low-level data base management and medium-level graphics. Since Lotus 1-2-3's introduction in 1983 and the advent of VP-Planner, several packages (including Framework, Symphony, and Intuit) that combine all five core applications have appeared.

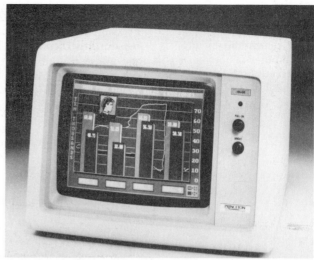

Figure 2.6

Effective use of graphics to present information. (Courtesy of Princeton Graphic System, an Intelligen Systems Company, and Polaroid Corporation)

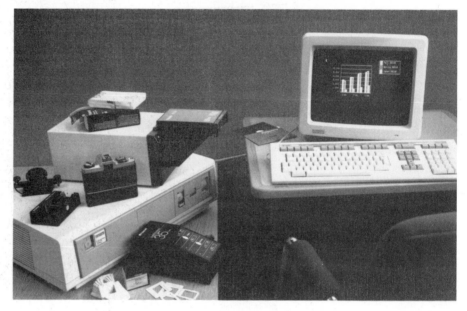

The five core application areas represent general software application packages that can be used to solve a variety of different problems and are not limited in their use. In addition to these, many specific, special-use application software programs exist which are designed to solve only one type of problem. These include the following:

Grading programs for teachers

General ledger

Accounts receivable and payable

Payroll

Inventory control

Mailing lists

Computer games

Educational programs

Personal accounting

Practical software programs have also been written for personal use. Financial programs are available that allow an individual to track checks written, credit charges made, and the tax-deductibility of various expenses, as well as generate monthly income and balance statements. Sophisticated stock portfolio programs are available that enable you to access the Dow Jones data base, get information, and buy or sell stock from your home.

Educational software is in plentiful supply. Besides the variety of special-purpose application programs, which address everything from learning the alphabet to preparing for the SAT exam, a special computer programming language called LOGO is available to help young children learn programming and improve their problem-solving skills. The range of educational software and the areas it covers are very broad and include many examples of excellent programming.

Business software is also abundant in the marketplace. Software has been written to solve just about any business problem, from general ledger to payroll; many programs written by reputable software firms have withstood the scrutiny of public accounting firms. Numerous vertically marketed software packages address specific industries, such as real estate or the health professions.

These are only a few of the many available software packages designed to solve very specific types of problems. The wide assortment of application packages allows a user to take advantage of the programming efforts of other individuals, without needing to know how to program.

Productivity Software

A new classification of software has emerged over the past few years that allows an individual to be more efficient by providing programs to perform repetitive tasks quickly. These flexible software packages can be used by a wide spectrum of people. Two examples of such packages are desktop organizers and outliners.

Desktop Organizers. Desktop organizers are primarily RAM-resident software packages that can include such capabilities as calculators, notepads, automatic dialers, and appointment calendars. The term **RAM-resident** means that once the program is loaded into memory, it stays there until either the machine is turned off or you tell it to erase itself. The advantage of using a RAM-resident piece of software is that you do not have to insert a disk in a drive to load a program. You simply issue a command to activate the program residing in RAM.

One such desktop organizer, Sidekick, is a RAM-resident program developed by Borland International. This package was the first of this software genre to be marketed and has been tremendously successful. It contains all of the functional parts mentioned above and displays each part in a separate window on the screen (see Figures 2.7 and 2.8).

One of the features that many people in business use is the calculator. Sidekick allows you to use your favorite spreadsheet package to enter formulas and, without leaving your spreadsheet package, to invoke Sidekick's calculator to check your work.

Outliners. **Outliner** software assists you in outlining ideas, goals, or tasks. Some outline processors contain a built-in word processor that allows you to imbed major blocks of text within your outline. Outlining packages contain three basic types of lines: title, headline, and subhead. The title is actually a headline: both contain only one line of text. The title provides you with information about the goal of the outline, and a headline gives you some idea of the information that is to follow. The indented lines of information below each headline are the subheads. These subheads can in turn be followed by lower levels of subheads.

One popular outline processor is Think Tank. Using Think Tank outlines allows you to look at details of a step by expanding a subhead to show the "smaller" items that follow (see Figure 2.9) or to show the "big picture" by hiding subheads and only showing headlines (see Figure 2.10). Outline processors can be used for preparing a paper, planning a house, developing a

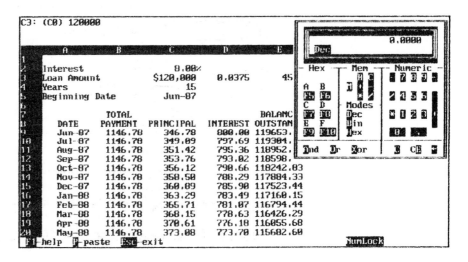

Figure 2.7
Calculator window of Sidekick, which can be invoked from within another software package such as Lotus 1-2-3.

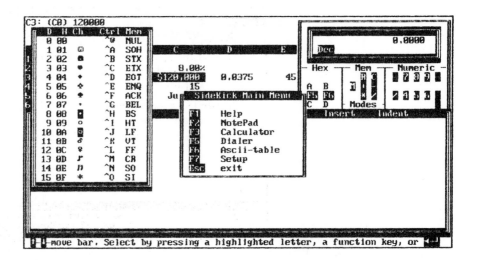

Figure 2.8
Various Sidekick windows active over a Lotus 1-2-3 worksheet.

sales strategy, or any other process that requires a logical step-by-step planning process.

IBM PC DOS

This section introduces the IBM Personal Computer Disk Operating System (DOS) and provides introductory information about various DOS commands required in day-to-day use of the IBM PC. For more information, refer to the Disk Operating System reference manual, written by Microsoft.

Knowledge of the Disk Operating System is critical because this software establishes the environment in which users operate the computer and in

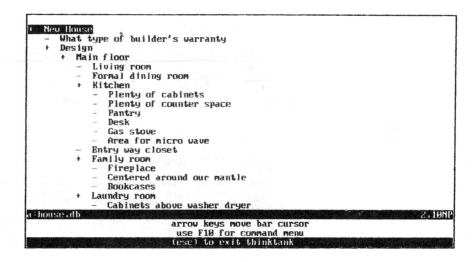

Figure 2.9
Expanded Think Tank outline with title, headings, and subheadings.

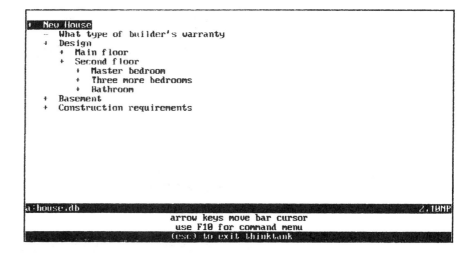

Figure 2.10
Collapsed Think Tank outline.

which computer programs are run. The operating system sets many practical limits on a computer's usefulness.

The IBM Personal Computer **Disk Operating System (DOS)** is a collection of programs designed to make it easy for users to create and manage files, run programs, and use the system devices attached to the computer. If no operating systems for microcomputers existed, every user would need a degree in computer science to use one effectively.

When IBM decided to manufacture its PC, it contracted with the software firm **Microsoft** to develop the new computer's operating system. Microsoft markets virtually the same operating system, under the name MS DOS, to many of the "clone" manufacturers of IBM-compatible computers. The two operating systems, for all intents and purposes, are identical.

Parts of DOS

The DOS is divided logically into three parts: (1) the I/O handler, (2) the Command Processor, and (3) utility programs (see Figure 2.11). The I/O handler is composed of the "hidden" files called IBMBIO.COM and IBMDOS.COM. The I/O handler manages each character that is typed, displayed, printed, received, or sent through any communication adapter. It contains all the routines for managing data to be stored on the disk, whether the data consist of a program, a document, accounts receivable information, or something else. The Command Processor, which is found in the file called COMMAND.COM, has a number of built-in functions (also called subprograms) that handle most DOS tasks, including copying files, running programs, and looking at a disk's "table of contents" to determine which files are currently stored there. The utility programs are used for "housekeeping" tasks that don't readily fit in the Command Processor. Each utility program is contained on a disk as a separate file, collectively referred to as external files. Utilities handle such tasks as formatting diskettes, comparing files and/or diskettes, and reporting the available free space on a diskette.

Each disk that contains DOS contains the four core pieces of DOS:

1. The **boot record** contains the program responsible for loading the rest of DOS into the PC. The boot record is contained on every disk that has been formatted, regardless of whether it contains DOS.

Figure 2.11
Component parts of DOS.

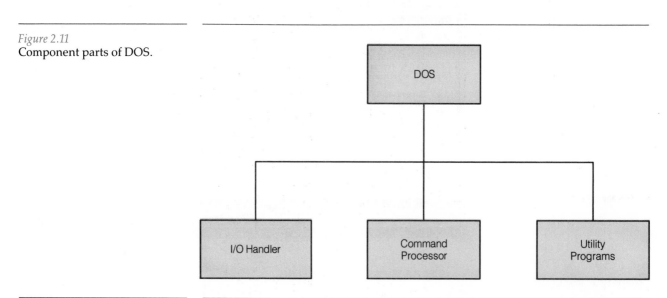

2. The **IBMBIO.COM program** acts as the I/O handler program, handling all inputs and outputs to and from the computer.

3. The **IBMDOS.COM program** acts as the file manager and contains a series of file-related functions that can be used by DOS on files residing on a diskette.

4. The **COMMAND.COM program** accepts DOS commands and runs the appropriate programs.

Only the COMMAND.COM program appears in the directory of a diskette. The others are "hidden" program files that reside on the diskette but do not appear in the directory.

When DOS is placed on a disk, it needs a lot of storage space to contain all of the above parts. In fact, DOS requires about 40K of storage space on a 360K disk, leaving about 320K of storage available on a DOS disk for programs and data. DOS does not have to be placed on data disks, but it should be placed on any disks that have programs to be run.

File Names

A **file** is a collection of related information that can take the form of data or of instructions for manipulating those data. In other words, files can be either data files or program files. Users keep track of the files on a diskette by name. Each file name must be unique; if you try to record a file using a name that already exists on the diskette, the first file will be destroyed and replaced with the contents of the second file.

Within space and special character limitations, you can name your file anything you wish. Diskette **file names** can be one to eight characters in length and can be followed by a one- to three-character **file-name extension**, set off by a period. A student data file for grades, for example, might be called STUDGRAD.TXT. The components of this name are labeled in Figure 2.12.

The characters that can be used for file names are

A–Z	!	}
0–9	'	_
$	(	^
&	)	~
#	-	`
@	{	

Any other characters are invalid. An invalid character is assumed to be a delimiter, which truncates the file name. Imbedded spaces are not allowed.

File names should reflect the data held in the files. If you are taking an English 101 course and wish to create a file to hold the first term paper for this class, a good file name would be ENGTP1—an abbreviation for English Term

---

Figure 2.12
Components of a file name.

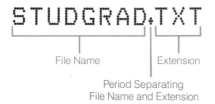

Paper 1. When used, the optional file-name extension should immediately follow the file name. The same character set allowed for file names can be used for file-name extensions. All other characters are invalid. You must include the extension when you refer to a file that has a file-name extension; otherwise, DOS will be unable to locate the file. (The exceptions to this rule are when the extension is BAT, EXE, or COM.) DOS instructions to a computer are contained in .BAT files. A typical .BAT file is the AUTOEXEC.BAT file, which contains instructions for the computer when it is first started. Compiled program files like .EXE and .COM files perform specific tasks. DOS utility files contain either a .EXE or a .COM extension.

Generally, special characters should not be used in file names since some software packages do not allow them, and difficulties may arise if you try to use such a file with a number of different packages. In addition, Microsoft may use some of these as commands to DOS in a future version of DOS. For example, the %, <, >, and \ characters were allowable in DOS 1.0 and DOS 1.1, but they are no longer valid beginning with DOS 2.0.

You may store as many as 112 files on a diskette, and the diskette itself will hold up to 360K of storage. A single diskette file, therefore, can be up to 360K in size as long as it is the only file on the entire diskette. A hard disk, however, does not have this limitation, and DOS allows a file to be up to a billion bytes in size.

Directory

The names of any files stored on a diskette are kept in a system area known as the **directory**, which contains the file name and file extension as well as information about the size of the files and the dates and times when they were created or last updated. The directory of a disk can be listed by using the **DIR** command. For example, a disk directory might yield the following list:

```
A>dir
Volume in drive A has no label
Directory of A:\

COMMAND  COM      17792      10-20-83      12:00p
PROCEDUR          17408      11-23-84      12:03a
INTRNOUT           3968      11-23-84      12:02a
AIS               32256       1-01-80      12:52a
INTRNOUT BAK       3968      11-22-84       1:01p
AISOUTL            2816      10-24-84      12:09a
ARTICLE           14592      11-01-84      12:02a
INTAUDI           11136      11-15-84       3:26p
INTERN   BAK      12032      12-04-84       5:36p
INTCOVER BAK        768      12-11-84      12:06a
INTCOVER            768      12-11-84      12:02a
INTERN            12032      12-05-84      12:02a
ISECON   BAK      15488       1-01-80      12:03a
ISECON            15488       1-01-80      12:09a
         File(s) 173056 bytes free
```

Notice that the above directory listing contains one or more blanks, or spaces, between the file name and the file extension. This is simply how DOS displays directory information. If you wish to access or to execute a file, you must place the period between the file name and the extension.

Next to the directory is a system area known as the **file allocation table (FAT)**. Its job is to keep track of which sectors belong to which files and to keep track of all available space on the diskette so that new files can be created and stored in unused areas of the diskette. Each diskette has one directory and two copies of the file allocation table. If the system has a problem reading the first copy of the file allocation table, it reads the second.

Preparing a Disk

It is important to understand how DOS keeps track of files because these system areas are required on all diskettes that DOS is expected to recognize (not just on the DOS diskette itself but also on other diskettes). The only way to mark this information on a diskette is to use the **FORMAT** utility program that resides on the DOS diskette. Consequently, every diskette must be formatted before it can be used by DOS. FORMAT does not have to be used every time you wish to put information on a diskette—only the first time, before a diskette is used.

FORMAT writes on every sector of a diskette, finds and write-protects any tracks having bad sectors, sets up the directory, sets up the file allocation table, and puts the boot record program at the beginning of the diskette. It can also create a copy of DOS on a new diskette, if that option is specified in the original command. In this manner, a diskette can be set up that contains DOS and still has plenty of space for data.

Either of the following two commands would format a diskette. The first, which both formats the diskette and places DOS on the diskette, should be used any time a piece of application software is to reside on a disk. The second command simply formats the diskette, without placing DOS on it; it should be used on a disk that is only to hold data to be processed by a program.

```
FORMAT B:/S
FORMAT B:
```

The Boot Process

The task of starting a computer has long been known as the **boot process**, a term derived from the old expression "pulling oneself up by the bootstraps." There are two basic ways to initiate the boot process. The first, known as a **cold start**, involves starting the computer when the power is off. The second, a **system reset** or **warm start**, involves pressing the CTRL + ALT + DEL keys simultaneously.

When you do a system reset or turn on the computer, the CPU executes a small program contained in ROM, called the bootstrap loader, which starts disk drive A and reads into RAM the boot record containing the bootstrap program on disk. The bootstrap program now starts to execute. It checks the directory of the disk to make certain that the IBMBIO.COM and the IBMDOS.COM programs reside in consecutive entries on the disk, and it loads first the IBMBIO.COM program and then the IBMDOS.COM program into RAM.

The IBMBIO.COM program now starts to execute. This part of DOS checks to see what equipment is attached to the computer and prepares each piece for use. This **initialization** process causes a printer hooked up to the computer to move its write head and click. After IBMBIO.COM has finished, the IBMDOS.COM program starts to execute, performing initialization work that allows data to be passed to and stored on disk. When IBMDOS.COM is finished, the COMMAND.COM file is brought in from the disk and placed in RAM, completing the boot process.

One last task is performed automatically by DOS when the boot process has finished: DOS automatically checks for an **AUTOEXEC.BAT** file on the boot disk. If it finds the file, it starts executing the DOS commands found in it. If there is no AUTOEXEC.BAT file on the disk, a prompt is displayed on the screen requesting the date. This may be entered with either dashes (the mm-dd-yy format) or slashes (the mm/dd/yy format) as the delimiters. If a date is not entered and the RETURN key is pressed, the system will default to 1-01-80, and any files saved during this session will have the default date as the creation or change date. After the date has been entered, the operator is prompted for the time, which may be entered with either colons (the hh:mm:ss format) or periods (the hh.mm.ss format) as the delimiters. The entry 10:42:23 indicates that the time is 10:42 and 23 seconds.

After the date and time have been entered, three lines are displayed at the top of the screen:

```
The IBM Personal Computer DOS
Version 3.10 (C)Copyright IBM Corp 1981, 1982, 1983
A>
```

A> is the DOS prompt from the command processor. Whenever A> is displayed (as it is above), the command processor is ready to accept commands, and the system is waiting for a command to be entered. The date and time entered are recorded in the directory for any files that are created or changed during this session.

Versions of DOS

Since the introduction of the IBM PC and the development of its operation system by Microsoft, there have been a number of versions of DOS for the PC and compatibles. These include 1.1, 2.0, 2.1, 3.0, 3.1, and 3.2. The digit to the left of the decimal point indicates the version of the operating system, whereas the digit to the right of the decimal point indicates the release of the operating system. The 1.0, 2.0, and 3.0 versions represent the first releases of their respective versions.

Version 1.X was the original operating system for the IBM PC computer and compatibles. This operating system truly represents the infancy of the PC. Many of the commands that now appear in operating systems did not even exist in this version. Also, many commands that were in this first version have been significantly altered to perform other tasks in addition those originally expected of them. This first version of DOS also supports only floppy disk drives.

Version 2.X was a major upgrade of version 1.X and was the operating system that was developed specifically for the IBM XT microcomputer. This version of DOS was the first Microsoft version to support the hard-disk drives and allows you to create directories and subdirectories for storing programs and files in separate, independent areas on a disk. It also allows you to configure the way that DOS is to use memory for input/disk buffers operations as well as allowing you to reassign the use of various disk drives.

Version 3.0 was another upgrade of DOS that appeared about the same time as the IBM AT microcomputer. Although it does not take advantage of the full power of the 80286 microprocessor chip and was not designed specifically for the AT, it still represents an advance in the power of this operating system. The operating system provides a number of advanced features, some of which are (1) creating its own RAM disk, (2) supporting networking (version 3.2), (3) supporting 3.5-inch disk drives (version 3.2), and (4) letting you use a different drive specifier to refer to another drive or path.

As DOS was evolved from version to version since the introduction of the PC, the tasks that it has been expected to perform have become increasingly complex. This increased responsibility has gradually resulted in the increased size of DOS on disk and a corresponding increase in the amount of required memory. The table that follows depicts the growth of DOS.

DOS Version	Disk Space (bytes)	Memory (bytes)
1.1	13,663	12,400
2.0	39,660	24,576
2.1	40,320	26,576
3.0	58,926	37,024
3.1	62,122	37,040
3.2	68,668	43,712

Starting DOS

If the computer power is off (cold start):

1. Insert the DOS diskette or the program disk with DOS (label side up and thumb on label) in disk drive A (the left-hand disk drive).
2. Close the drive door.
3. If a printer or other peripherals are attached, turn their power switches to the ON position.
4. Turn the system unit power switch (located on the right-hand side, toward the rear of the machine) to the ON position.

If the computer power is already on (system reset or warm start):

1. Insert the DOS diskette or the program disk with DOS (label side up and thumb on label) in disk drive A.
2. Close the drive door.
3. Depress and hold down both the CTRL and ALT keys; then depress the DEL key. Release the three keys.

Either of these procedures automatically loads DOS into memory. Starting the computer and loading DOS takes from 3 to 45 seconds, depending upon how much memory is in the PC.

The actions performed by the computer when you powered it up differ in one respect from the actions it performs when you do a system restart. When the computer is first turned on, it automatically performs a memory check to ensure that all of the RAM locations are capable of storing and retrieving data correctly; it does not perform this task during a system reset. The memory check consumes most of the computer's start-up time, and the more memory on a machine, the longer the test takes.

Default Drive

The "A" in A> (the DOS prompt) designates the **default drive**, thereby telling DOS which of the diskettes to search to get a file or execute a program. DOS searches only the diskette located in the default drive to find file names you enter, unless and until you specify another drive. The default, therefore, can be viewed as the current drive.

DOS always starts a computer with diskettes with the default drive set to A. Additional drives attached to the computer are specified by consecutive letters of the alphabet: B for the second disk drive, C for the third, and so on. It does not matter whether the user types upper- or lower-case letters, because DOS always translates them to upper case.

The default drive can be changed by entering the designation letter of the desired drive, followed by a colon. To change to disk drive B, for example, you would change the prompt as follows:

```
A>_           [original drive]

A>B:_         [new drive designation]

B>_           [new prompt]
```

B is now the default (current) drive, and henceforth DOS will search only the diskette located in disk drive B to find file names you enter, unless and until another drive is specified.

How DOS Uses the 5.25-inch Disk

Most disk drives record forty-eight tracks per inch (tpi) on diskette; only a ⅚-inch strip of disk actually holds tracks. With 48-tpi drives, then, only forty usable tracks are actually created. These tracks are labeled 0 through 39.

Tracks are divided into sectors, usually eight or nine per track. The IBM, unless told to do something else, will automatically divide a track into nine sectors, creating 720 total sectors on a diskette (40 tracks × 9 sectors × 2 sides). Of these 720 sectors, 12 are reserved by the system to be used as follows:

4 sectors are used by the FAT (2 copies, with 2 sectors per copy).

7 sectors are used to hold the directory.

1 sector is used to hold the boot program in the boot record.

DOS's use of these sectors, therefore, leaves 708 sectors (with a total user storage of 362,496 bytes) available on a diskette formatted without the operating system.

Space within a track is allocated in increments called **clusters** (see Figure 2.13). A cluster on a single-sided diskette consists of one sector; a cluster on a double-sided diskette consists of two adjacent sectors. Once a cluster is allocated to a file, it must be entirely filled before another cluster will be allocated to the file by the system.

Another important disk concept is the **cylinder** (see Figure 2.13). On a floppy disk there are forty tracks on each side of the diskette, each track on the top side lying directly above the corresponding track on the bottom side. All like-numbered tracks on all recording surfaces constitute a cylinder. In the case of the floppy disk, then, two tracks make up each cylinder. DOS refers to the bottom of the disk as side 0 and the top as side 1. On a double-sided diskette, DOS starts storing data on the outermost track (referred to as track 0) of side 0, filling sectors 0 through 8. It then goes to side 1 to use track 0, sectors 0 through 8; then back to side 0 to use track 1, sectors 0 through 8; and so on.

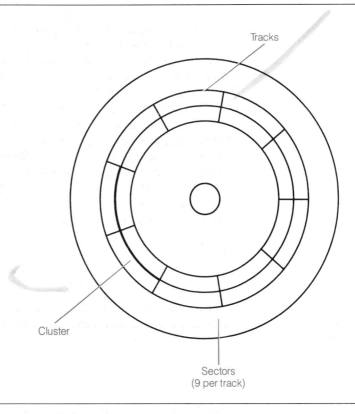

Figure 2.13
Cylinders and clusters on
a disk.

Tracks

Cluster

Sectors
(9 per track)

This process continues until the entire diskette is full. (If the diskette is single-sided, of course, DOS does not switch sides.)

The cylinder concept allows the disk drive to access information much faster than would otherwise be possible. The read/write heads need only be activated electronically from one side to another until the cylinder of storage is filled, at which point the read/write head can position itself mechanically to the next cylinder. Mechanical delay is always more time-consuming then electronic delay.

Global File-name Characters (Wild Cards)

Global file-name characters, also known as wild cards, enable users to execute commands against files whose names have one or more characteristics in common. The two wild cards used in DOS are ? and *.

The ? Character. A ? in a file name or extension indicates that any character can occupy that position. For example, a computer will respond to the command

```
DIR REPORT?.*
```

by listing all directory entries on the default drive having file names of seven characters and beginning with REPORT; the entries listed may have any character in the seventh position and (because an * was marked after the period) may have any (or no) extension. Files that would be listed by the above DIR command include

```
REPORT1
REPORTA
REPORTB  ENG
REPORT4  BUS
```

The * Character.   An * in a file name or extension indicates that any character can occupy that position and any remaining positions in the file name or extension. For example, a computer will respond to the command

```
DIR W*.*
```

by listing all directory entries on the default drive having file names beginning with W and having any (or no) extension. The file names in this example may be from one to eight characters in length, and the extensions may be one to three characters in length. (The second * in the above command tells DOS to list any files that start with a W and *also* have a file extension.) Files that would be listed by the above DIR command include

```
WS        COM
WSOVLY1   OVR
WINSTALL  COM
WORK01
```

Control Keys

Control keys are used whenever commands or input lines are entered. When two keys are required to convey a command, for example CTRL-BREAK, the first key must be depressed and held down while the second key is depressed. Control keys include the following:

ENTER—makes a line or command available to the computer

CTRL-BREAK—stops a program that is executing

CTRL-S—stops output to the screen temporarily so that it can be examined (restart the output by again depressing CTRL-S)

SHIFT-PRTSC—sends anything except graphics displayed on the monitor to the printer

CTRL-PRTSC (or CTRL-P)—toggles the printer echo either on or off

ESC—cancels the current line (many programs also use this key to stop processing or get out of some difficulty)

Back Arrow—moves the cursor back one position

Function Keys—used by various packages to cut down on the number of keystrokes required to enter a command

NUM LOCK—activates either the numeric key pad or the arrow keys and other special function keys

DOS Editing Keys

DOS editing keys allow you to make changes to the last DOS command that you entered, a feature that can save many keystrokes.

DEL—skip one character in the current line

ESC—cancel the current line without changing the data in the instruction buffer

F1—copy and display one character from the instruction buffer to the cursor position in the current line

F2—copy all characters from the instruction buffer up to a specified character and place them in the current line

F3—copy all remaining characters from the instruction buffer up to the current line

F4—skip all characters in the instruction buffer up to a specified character

F5—place the current line in the instruction buffer for more editing

INS—insert characters at the current cursor location using this toggle

The F3 key is probably the most important of the keys listed above. DOS uses an instruction **buffer** (a temporary holding area) to hold the last instruction you gave it; that instruction can be summarily reissued by depressing the F3 key.

Chapter Review

The three basic types of software for microcomputers are (1) operating systems, (2) programming languages, and (3) application programs. You do not have to know how to program to make effective use of today's microcomputers.

If you do decide to program, you will probably use a high-level language such as BASIC or PASCAL. The instructions of these programming languages must be converted into a machine-readable format before they can be executed by the computer. The translation process is performed by either a compiler or an interpreter.

Application programs are prewritten programs that are used to solve specific user problems. The five basic problem areas addressed by applications software are (1) electronic spreadsheets, (2) word processing, (3) data base management, (4) communications, and (5) graphics. A number of these general applications can be combined in one piece of software by a process known as integration. Integration allows you to pass data/information quickly from one application to another and to manipulate or process it without having to leave one application and start another.

The disk operating system (DOS), a critical piece of software that is loaded into the machine at start-up time, allows you to perform once-laborious tasks (formatting a disk, copying files, or listing the directory of a disk) with ease.

Information stored on a disk is contained in files. Each file must have a unique file name. File names follow rather rigid naming conventions.

DOS uses disk drives in executing commands. It also uses information contained on special areas of the disk or in files. Global (wild card) characters can be used to access some of this information, if it is file-related.

Key Terms and Concepts

A> (DOS prompt) 48
application program 35
auto-dial 38
AUTOEXEC.BAT 48

BASIC 34
baud 38
boot process 47
boot record 44

buffer
cluster 50
COBOL *pg* 34
cold start 47
COMMAND.COM 44 45
communications 37
compiler 34
control keys 52
cylinder 50
data base management 38
dBASE II 38
dBASE III 38
default drive 50
DIR 46
directory 46
disk operating system (DOS) 44
DOS editing keys 52
electronic spreadsheet 35
file allocation table (FAT) 41
file name 45
file-name extension 45
files 45
FORMAT 47
global file-name characters
　(wild cards) 51

graphic display 38
IBMBIO.COM 44-45
IBMDOS.COM 43 45
initialization
integrated packages 29
interpreter 34
language processor 34
local area network (LAN) 38
Microsoft 44
modem 37
object code 34
operating system 34
outliner 41
programming language 34
RAM-resident 41
software 4
source code 34
system reset 47
VisiCalc
VP-Planner
warm start (system reset) 47
word processing 36
WordPerfect 37
? 51 *wild cards in DOS*
*

Chapter Quiz

Multiple Choice

1. Which of the following is not an example of application software?
   a. WordPerfect
   b. VisiCalc
   c. BASIC
   d. VP-Planner
   e. dBASE III Plus
   f. All of the above are examples of applications software

2. Which of the following is not a benefit of word processing?
   a. Easy to make changes
   b. Allows user to move parts of a document to new locations
   c. Increases efficiency
   d. May check your spelling
   e. All of the above are benefits of word processing

3. Which of the statements below is(are) false?
   a. A modem can only be an input device
   b. The term *baud* refers to how fast data are transmitted
   c. Two modems, one at each end, are needed for computers to communicate using telephone lines
   d. Auto-dial features are not typically found on modems
   e. a and d are false

4. Which of the statements below is false?
   a. A file name can have up to eight characters
   b. A file name must have an extension
   c. A period must appear between a file name and its extension
   d. The file-name extension can have one to three characters
   e. All of the above statements are true

5. DOS is NOT made up of which of the following parts?
   a. boot record
   b. IBMBIO.COM
   c. IBMDOS.COM
   d. COMMAND.COM
   e. It is composed of all of the above parts

True/False

6. You do not have to format a disk before you use it for the first time.

7. The difference between a cold boot and a system reset is that the RAM memory is not checked during the system reset.

8. Only the diskette on the default drive is checked during a search for files unless the computer is otherwise instructed.

9. DOS keeps track of where files are stored by using the file allocation table (FAT).

10. Global characters (wild cards) are normally not much help in formulating useful DOS commands.

Answers

1. c 2. e 3. e 4. b 5. e 6. f 7. t 8. t 9. t 10. f

Exercises

1. Define or describe each of the following:
   a. software
   b. compiler
   c. interpreter
   d. application program
   e. electronic worksheets
   f. word processing
   g. modem
   h. baud
   i. data base management
   j. integration
   k. DOS
   l. cold boot
   m. system reset (warm boot)
   n. default drive

2. A(n) _compiler_ translates a program all at once, whereas a(n) _interpreter_ translates a program a statement at a time.

3. The _source code_ code of a program is written by a programmer.

4. List the five core software applications.
   a. _Word processing_
   b. _Communications_
   c. _Data Base management_

d. *Graphics*

e. *Electronic spreadsheets*

5. The device that translates digital signals into audible noises that can be transmitted across telephone lines is called a(n) *modem* .

6. *Integration* allows you to pass data quickly from one application to another.

7. The _____ interfaces between the user and the hardware.

8. The company named _____ wrote the DOS for the IBM PC.

9. List and describe the four parts of IBM PC DOS.
   a.

   b.

   c.

   d.

10. List and describe the parts of a file name. Place an * to the left of the required part(s).
    a.

    b.

11. List the pieces of information given by the directory command for each file.
    a.

    b.

    c.

    d.

    e.

12. The *Boot (Format)* command is used to prepare a disk for use.

13. A *Cold* boot requires that the power to the machine be off beforehand.

14. The disk that is automatically searched is the _____ _____ disk.

15. Of the 720 sectors created on the disk, only 702 are available to the user. The remaining sectors are taken up by _____, _____, and _____ .

16. Like-numbered tracks from both recording surfaces are called _____ _____ .

17. The wild card character _____ is used to identify a variable in only one position.

18. If a file was originally created with a file extension, that extension must be used any time that the file is referenced in the future. The exceptions to this rule are when the extension is
    a.

    b.

    c.

19. Up to _____ files can be stored on a single diskette.

20. Two adjacent sectors that are used for storing data in a file are called a(n) _____ .

Computer Exercises

1. Enter the following commands using your DOS system disk. Describe what happens.
   a. `DIR *.COM`
   b. `DIR ?I*.COM`
   c. `DIR ?I*.*`
   d. `DIR *.*`

2. What happens when you press the F3 key?

3. When are you required to use a period (.) with a file name?

4. List the three keys that are used for a system reset (warm boot), and then perform one.
   a.

   b.

   c.

5. What two pieces of information does DOS automatically prompt you for when the boot process is finished (provided there is no AUTOEXEC.BAT file present)?
   a.

   b.

6. What is the DOS prompt that automatically appears on the screen after the boot process is finished for a diskette-based system?

Chapter 3

Commonly Used IBM PC DOS Commands

After completing this chapter, you should be able to:

Distinguish between internal and external DOS commands

Describe the processes of redirection and piping

Discuss the format notation of DOS commands

Discuss information common to all DOS commands

Discuss each diskette-oriented DOS command in detail

This chapter contains information about DOS commands that are commonly used in a diskette-based microcomputer environment. If you want more information about a particular command, you should refer to the 2.0 or 2.1 Disk Operating System reference manual, written by Microsoft.

The two types of DOS commands are internal and external. **Internal commands** are executed immediately because they are built into the command processor COMMAND.COM. **External commands** reside on diskettes as separate, external files (also referred to as utilities) and must be read from the appropriate diskette before they can be executed. This means that the diskette containing a command file must already be in a drive, or DOS will be unable to execute it.

Format Notation

Format notation refers to the rules that must be followed when entering commands for DOS. These rules are sometimes referred to as *syntax*. The following rules indicate how DOS commands are to be entered.

Rules Common to All DOS Commands

1. Any words shown in capital letters must be entered exactly as shown. They can, however, be entered as any combination of upper- and lower-case letters because DOS automatically changes all letters to upper case.

2. Supply any items shown in lower-case letters.

3. Items in square brackets ([ ]) are optional.

4. Ellipsis points (. . .) indicate that the item they accompany can be repeated as many times as desired.

5. All punctuation (except square brackets)—commas, equal signs, question marks, colons, slashes, and so on—must be included where shown.

Commands are usually followed by one or more **parameters**—information of any kind that is entered in addition to the command name. For example, the name of the file to be copied and the destination drive for the copy are parameters for the COPY command.

A **delimiter** is a character that shows where one part of a command ends and another part begins. Common delimiters are the space, comma, semicolon, equal sign, and tab key, although generally only the space (usually represented in instruction manuals as the character b) is used. A period is not a delimiter. Commands and parameters must always be separated by delimiters.

Examples:

```
ERASE FILE01
RENAME OLDFILE NEWFILE
```

No part of a file name can be separated by a delimiter.

Examples:

```
B:REPORT.DOC        [correct]
A: REPORT DOC       [incorrect twice]
```

You can end commands while they are running by pressing CTRL + BREAK. It may take a while for the command to affect the computer. The CTRL + C command works in the same fashion.

Operationally, drives can act in either of two roles: A source drive is one that data are transferred from, and a target drive is one that data are transferred to. Depending on the particular operation involved, a drive may function as either the source drive or the target drive.

NOTE TO NETWORK USERS Some adopters of this textbook may be using a networked device. Such individuals cannot use the following commands. If you do try to use such a command, DOS responds with the following message:

```
Cannot <command> to a network device
```

The <command> entry is the name of the command that you entered at the keyboard. The commands covered in the text that do not work over a network on a shared or attached device are

```
CHKDSK
DISKCOPY
FORMAT
LABEL
SYS
```

Information About Specific DOS Commands

Information about each DOS command described on the following pages is divided into five areas: (1) the command itself is named; (2) the purpose (function) of the command is presented; (3) the syntactical format of the command is detailed, with any optional parameters; (4) the nature of the command is given, identifying whether it is part of DOS (internal) or is a utility (external); and (5) any remarks or explanations about the command are given.

ASSIGN (Drive) Command

Function: This command allows you to tell DOS to direct read/write request for one disk drive into read/write request for another drive.

Format: ASSIGN [x[=]y[,,,]]

Type: External

Remarks & Examples: The [x] parameter tells DOS which drive is to be reassigned, and the [y] parameter tells DOS which drive you want to receive the read/write requests.

Once the command is issued, DOS converts x internally so that any request for that drive is automatically directed toward device y. Both drives (x and y) must be physically present on your machine.

To reset all drives to their previous settings, simply enter the command ASSIGN.

The ASSIGN command is especially useful when you have, for instance, installed a hard drive on your system and are still running software that was written for a two-diskette drive system. For example, you may have a budget system that was written using BASIC. Such a system might expect the program disk to reside in drive A and the data disk to reside in drive B. The ASSIGN command allows you to place both the program and data files on device C (the hard drive) by using the following command:

```
C>ASSIGN A=C B=C
```

Once the above command is issued, DOS now looks for any files on drive C. This means that if you issue a DIR B: command, you actually receive a directory listing of physical drive C. Once you have finished with your budgeting system, you can reset the drives to their original values by issuing another ASSIGN at the DOS prompt.

```
C>ASSIGN
```

ATTRIB (Attribute) Command (DOS 3.x)

Function: This command allows you to change the read-only attribute of a file. This determines whether a file can only be read or can be both read and written.

Format: `ATTRIB[+R|-R][d:][path]filename[.ext]`

Type: External

Remarks
&

Examples: The +R parameter is used to set a file to read-only status, and the -R parameter is used to remove the read-only status of a file. The `[d:][path]filename[.ext]` portion is used to specify the file you want to mark as read-only or to check its status. Global file names are permissible.
The following example sets the attribute of the file named STUDGRAD.TXT to read-only.

```
A>ATTRIB +R STUDGRAD.TXT
```

Once the command above is issued, you can verify that the read-only attribute has been changed by entering this command:

```
A>ATTRIB STUDGRAD.TXT
```

The ATTRIB command now displays the following message on your screen:

```
R     A:\STUDGRAD.TXT
```

The R at the beginning of the line indicates that the file has a read-only status. You can, in other words, obtain information from this file, but you can not execute a write that will record information to this file.

The following command removes the read-only status from the STUDGRAD.TXT file.

```
A>ATTRIB -R STUDGRAD.TXT
```

If you now issue another ATTRIB command to check the new status of the STUDGRAD.TXT file, the following information is displayed to your screen.

Command

```
A>ATTRIB STUDGRAD.TXT
```

Result

```
A:\STUDGRAD.TXT
```

The STUDGRAD.TXT file no longer has a read-only status. This means that you can now read as well as write to that file.

The following command resets all files on drive B that have a .DOC file extension to read-only status:

```
A>ATTRIB +R B:*.DOC
```

CHKDSK (Check Disk) Command

Function: This command allows you to analyze the directory and the file allocation table (FAT) disk and produces diskette and memory status reports. CHKDSK can also repair errors in the directories or FAT.

Format: `CHKDSK [d:][filename][/F][/V]`

Type: External

Remarks
&
Examples: CHKDSK temporarily makes the drive specified in d: the default drive. If CHKDSK ends prematurely (because, for example, you replied A to a diskette error message), the default drive changes to the drive that CHKDSK was checking.

CHKDSK will not automatically correct errors found in the directory or FAT unless you specify the /F parameter. If the /F parameter is not specified, CHKDSK functions but does not actually make corrections, allowing you to analyze the possible consequences of making a correction. It is generally inadvisable to make corrections unless there is a major problem; if the error is in the directory or FAT itself, a large part of the data on the disk can be lost.

If the /V parameter is specified, a series of messages (one for each file) identifying the status of each file will be displayed.

CHKDSK FILENAME tells if the file specified (in this case, FILENAME) has been stored in contiguous sectors on disk. When a disk has recently been formatted, the 512 individual byte sectors used to store files will store input files contiguously. After some files have been erased and other files added, however, DOS will still attempt to store any new files or additions to existing files in the first vacant sector. Occasionally, a large file will end up being stored in a number of nonadjacent sectors as a result. Such a file, referred to as a **fragmented file**, will slow DOS's reading speed because the read/write heads will have to be moved physically to a number of different locations on disk.

If the number of noncontiguous locations reported by CHKDSK is large, re-forming the file by using the COPY command may improve performance.

CHKDSK does not prompt you to insert a diskette in the specified drive; it automatically assumes that the diskettes are in the appropriate drives and begins to execute shortly after the ENTER key has been pressed.

The status report displayed by CHKDSK contains the following pieces of information:

1. Disk Report—

   Total disk space

   Number of bytes used for hidden or system files

   Number of bytes used for user files

   Bytes used by tracks containing bad sectors

   Bytes available for use

2. RAM Report—

   Bytes of total memory (RAM)

   Bytes of available (unused) memory

After the diskette has been checked, error messages (if any) are displayed, and a status report like the following appears:

```
362496 bytes total disk space
 22528 bytes in 2 hidden files
135168 bytes in 1 user files
 (4608 bytes in bad sectors)
204800 bytes available on disk
262144 bytes total memory
249744 bytes free
```

Notice that two hidden files were reported in the above status report. These are the DOS system files IBMBIO.COM and IBMDOS.COM, which are hidden from normal directory searches.

You should run CHKDSK occasionally for each diskette to ensure the integrity of the file structures.

Examples of some uses of CHKDSK follow.

1. Run the CHKDSK program which resides on drive A against the disk in drive B.

   ```
   A>CHKDSK B:
   ```

2. Tell CHKDSK to correct any errors in the above example automatically.

```
A>CHKDSK B:/F
```

3. Find out if the file REPORT has much fragmentation.

```
A>CHKDSK REPORT
```

4. Find out if any of the files on the disk in drive A: are fragmented.

```
A>CHKDSK *.*
```

5. With B as the default drive, execute CHKDSK from drive A against the diskette in drive B.

```
B>A:CHKDSK
```

CLS (Clear Screen) Command

Function: This command clears the monitor screen.

Format: CLS

Type: Internal

Remarks
&
Examples: This command clears the monitor screen upon execution, leaving only the DOS prompt in the upper left-hand corner of the screen. CLS does not affect memory or disk storage.

COPY Command

Function: This command allows you to copy one file or a number of files with the same name characteristics to another diskette. It also allows you to copy one or more files and create a new file with a different name on the same disk. In the latter case, a different name must be given to the new copy.

Format: COPY [/A/B]filespec[/A][/B]
                     [d:][filename[.ext]][/A][/B]
             or
             COPY [/A/B]filespec[/A][/B]
                     [d:][filename[.ext]][/A][/B][/V]

Type: Internal

Remarks
&
Examples: The parameter filespec is the source file. The parameter [d:][filename[.ext]] is the target file.
             Only the commonly used aspects of the COPY command are discussed here. For more coverage, refer to the DOS manual.
             In the following example, the file REPORT will be copied onto the diskette contained in drive B. Because no name for

the new file is specified, it will have the same name as the original file. For the same reason, the source drive and the target drive must be different; otherwise, an error message will be displayed.

```
A>COPY REPORT B:
```

In the following example, the file FILE01 will be copied from the diskette in disk drive B onto the diskette in default drive A, with no change in the file name.

```
A>COPY B:FILE01
```

In the following example, all of the files from the diskette in the default drive will be copied onto the diskette in drive B. The file names will remain unchanged, and each will be displayed as its file is copied. This method is very useful if the files on the default drive diskette (drive A) are fragmented.

```
A>COPY *.*B:
```

In the following example, file FILE01 will be copied, and the copy will be renamed FILE01.BAC. Because a drive is not specified, the default drive will be used. Both files now reside on the same disk.

```
A>COPY FILE01 FILE01.BAC
```

In the following example, file FILE01 will be copied, and the copy on the disk in drive B will be renamed FILE01.BAC. But because a target drive is specified, two copies of the file will be made: One will reside on the disk in drive A and have the name FILE01; the other will reside on the disk in drive B and have the name FILE01.BAC.

```
A>COPY FILE01 B:FILE01.BAC
```

In the following example, file FILE01.ABC will be copied from the diskette in drive A onto the diskette in drive B, and the copy will be named FILE01.XXX.

```
A>COPY FILE01.ABC B:*.XXX
```

DATE Command

Function:	This command allows you to change the date that has been stored by DOS (today's date). Ultimately, the date is placed in the directory entry for any files that are created or altered and resaved during this session.
Format:	DATE [mm-dd-yy]
Type:	Internal

Remarks
&
Examples: If a valid date is entered with the DATE command, the new date is accepted by DOS. Otherwise, the DATE command produces the following prompt:

```
Current date is day mm-dd-yy
Enter new date:_
```

The system displays the day of the week in the day location. Don't worry that you have never told it the day of the week: DOS has a formula for calculating this piece of information.

To leave the date unchanged, press ENTER.

The valid delimiters within the date are hyphens (-) and slashes (/). This means that the dates 4-23-85 and 4/23/85 are both correct. DOS also allows you to mix these delimiters, so the date 4/23-85 also works.

Any date is acceptable as today's date as long as the digits are in the correct ranges for each field. This means, for example, that you can't enter 16 for a month (12 is the maximum) or 35 for a day (31 is the maximum). DOS also does not allow you to enter a date prior to 1-1-80.

If a mistake is made, the error message INVALID DATE is displayed.

DIR (Directory) Command

Function: This command allows you to obtain lists of all files contained in the directory or of specified files or families of files. A line is displayed for each file and includes the file name, extension (if any), file size, and date and time of creation (or updating).

Format: DIR [d:][filename[.ext]][/P][/W]

Type: Internal

Remarks
&
Examples: The /P parameter causes the display to pause after twenty-three lines have been displayed. The message Strike a key when ready... is then displayed.

The /W parameter produces a five-column-wide display of the directory. Only the file name and extension for each file are displayed.

The wildcard characters ? and * can also be used with the file-name and extension parameters.

In the following example, all directory entries on the default drive will be listed.

```
DIR
```

In the following example, all directory entries on the diskette in drive B will be listed.

```
DIR B:
```

A typical directory listing might look like this:

```
A>DIR
Volume in drive A has no label
Directory of A:\

COMMAND    COM    17792    10-20-83    12:00P
WSOVLY1    OVR    41216     6-21-84     3:30P
WSMSGS     OVR    29056     4-12-83
WINSTALL   OVR    38528     3-02-83
WS         INS    43776     3-02-83
WSU        COM    21376     1-01-80    12:04a
WINSTALL   COM     1152     3-02-83
WST        COM    21376     6-21-84     3:29P
INSTALL    EXE    36352     3-28-84     8:00a
AUTOEXEC   BAT       11     1-01-80    12:01a
MM         INS     2816     3-28-84     8:01a
WSD        COM    21376     6-21-84     3:30P
WS         COM    21376     6-21-84     3:28P
MAILMRGE   OVR    13568     3-28-84     8:03a
SYSTEM1            128      1-01-80    12:00a
PISANI            640       1-30-85    12:07a
CHKDSK     COM     6400    10-20-83    12:00P
LETTER            128       1-01-80     4:21a
PRINT             128       1-01-80    12:03a
DIR1                0       1-01-80    12:52a
      20 File(s) 11264 bytes free
```

The file name, extension, size of the file, creation date, and time of creation are given for each file on the diskette. At the end of the directory listing is given the amount of available storage on the disk.

In the following example, all directory entries on the diskette in the default drive that start with a W will be listed.

```
A>DIR W*.*
```

The listing elicited by the above instruction might look like this:

```
A>DIR W*.*
Volume in drive A has no label
Directory of A:\

WSOVLY1    OVR    41216     6-21-84     3:30P
WSMSGS     OVR    29056     4-12-83
WINSTALL   OVR    38528     3-02-83
WS         INS    43776     3-02-83
WSU        COM    21376     1-01-80    12:04a
WINSTALL   COM     1152     3-02-83
WST        COM    21376     6-21-84     3:29P
WSD        COM    21376     6-21-84     3:30P
WS         COM    21376     6-21-84     3:28P
       9 File(s) 11264 bytes free
```

Only files that begin with a W are included in this directory listing.

In the following example, all directory entries on the diskette in the default drive that have an extension of .COM will be listed.

```
A>DIR *.COM
```

The listing elicited by the above instruction might look like this:

```
Volume in drive A has no label
Directory of A:/

COMMAND     COM    17792    10-20-83    12:00P
WSU         COM    21376     1-01-80    12:04P
WINSTALL    COM     1152     3-02-83
WST         COM    21376     6-21-84     3:29P
WSD         COM    21376     6-21-84     3:30P
WS          COM    21376     6-21-84     3:28P
CHKDSK      COM     6400    10-20-83    12:00P
MORE        COM      384    10-20-83    12:00P
         8 File(s) 8192 bytes free
```

The DIR /P command causes a directory listing to be displayed to the screen one page at a time. After the twenty-third line, the following message is displayed at the bottom of the screen:

```
Strike a key when ready ..._
```

The DIR /W command is used to get a display of only the file names and extensions of the diskette files. The names are displayed in five columns, and the amount of available storage is also given.

```
                Volume in drive A has no label
                Directory of A:/

COMMAND  COM   WSOVLY1  OVR   WSMSGS  OVR   WINSTALL  OVR   WS
WSU      COM   WINSTALL COM   WST     COM   INSTALL   EXE   AUTOEXEC BAT
MM       INS   WSD      COM   WS      COM   MAILMRGE  OVR   SYSTEM1
PISANI         CHKDSK   COM   LETTER        PRINT           DIR1
            20 File(s) 11264 bytes free
```

DISKCOPY (Copy Diskette) Command

Function: This command allows you to copy the contents of the diskette that is in the specified source drive onto the diskette that is in the specified target drive—exactly as the information appears on the source disk.

Format: DISKCOPY [d:][d:][/1]

Type: External

Remarks
&
Examples: The first parameter specified is the **source drive**, and the
           second is the **target drive**. The /1 parameter causes
           DISKCOPY to copy only side 0 (the first side) of the
           diskette, regardless of whether the disk is single- or double-
           sided. The same drives (or different ones) can be specified as
           source and target. If the drives are the same, a single-drive
           copy operation is performed. At appropriate times, a
           prompt to insert the diskette is displayed; when this has
           been done, DISKCOPY prompts the user to press any key in
           order to continue.
               The following command will cause DOS to load in the
           DISKCOPY file from the default disk drive.

```
A>DISKCOPY A: B:
```

           The contents of a disk to be placed in drive A are to be
           copied to a disk to be placed in drive B. The following
           message is displayed:

```
Insert source disk in drive A:
Insert target disk in drive B:
Strike any key when ready:
```

           The DISKCOPY program will then check to see if the disk
           in drive B is formatted. If it isn't, DISKCOPY will format it.
           It will then perform the copy process and after copying will
           display the following prompt:

```
Copy another (Y/N)?_
```

           If Y is depressed, the next copy will be done on the
           originally specified drives, and DISKCOPY will again
           prompt the user to insert the source and target disks. If N is
           depressed, the command ends.
               The following command is different from the one above
           in that it expects the source disk to be in drive B and the
           target disk to be in drive A:

```
DISKCOPY B: A:
```

           Because preexisting files on the target disk will be
           destroyed when the copy process begins, it is important that
           you understand how the command will work and that you
           develop consistency when using DOS copy commands. This
           will result in fewer instances of accidental data destruction.
               If both parameters are omitted, a single-drive copy
           operation is performed, using the default drive. On a single-
           drive system, all prompts are for drive A, regardless of any
           drive specifiers that have been entered.
               Diskettes subjected to a lot of file creation and deletion
           activity become fragmented, because diskette space is
           allocated to files on the basis of where the first available

opening is. Since a diskette with fragmented files can degrade performance by requiring excessive head movement and rotational delays in finding, reading, or writing a file, the CHKDSK *.* command should be used on busy disks from time to time to identify the extent of fragmentation. If a lot of fragmentation exists, use the COPY command to eliminate it.

The following command, for example, can be used to copy all the files (in unfragmented order) from the diskette in drive A to the diskette in drive B:

```
COPY A:*.*   B:
```

WARNING It is safest to use preformatted disks when using DISK-COPY. You should also make certain that there are no bad sectors on the target disk. Since the copy generated is a mirror image, good data can end up being placed in a bad sector during a DISKCOPY operation.

ERASE Command

Function: This command is used to delete a specific file or group of files from the diskette in the designated drive. (If no drive is specified, the default drive is used.)

Format: ERASE filespec
or
DEL filespec

Type: Internal

Remarks
&
Examples: The shortened form **DEL** can be used in place of ERASE.

The global characters ? and * can be used in the file name and in the extension. *Global characters should be used with caution*, however, because several files can easily be erased with a single command. If proper care is not taken in using this command, a user may inadvertently delete all of the files on a diskette.

To erase all files on a diskette, enter

```
ERASE [d:]*.*
```

The system files IBMBIO.COM and IBMDOS.COM cannot be erased because they are hidden files and are not accessible to you.

If *.* is used to erase all the files on a diskette, DOS issues the following message to verify that all files are to be erased:

```
Are you sure (Y/N)?
```

You then enter Y and depress ENTER to erase or enter N and depress ENTER to cancel the command.

In the following example, the file FILE01.PRG will be erased from the diskette in drive A:

```
A>ERASE FILE01.PRG
```

FORMAT Command

Function: This command is used to initialize the diskette in the designated or default drive so that it conforms to a recording format that DOS can use. FORMAT analyzes the entire diskette for defective sectors, initializes the directory, sets up space for the file allocation table, and records the boot program in the boot record.

Format: FORMAT [d:][/S][/1][/8][/V][/B]

Type: External

Remarks
&

Examples: All new diskettes must be formatted. An unformatted disk is unrecognizable to DOS.

If the /S parameter is specified in the FORMAT command, the operating system files IBMBIO.COM, IBMDOS.COM, and COMMAND.COM are copied from the default diskette onto the newly formatted disk. Using the /S parameter creates a system disk, with all the operating system files necessary to boot the system. The external utility programs, however, must be copied from a DOS master disk.

If you specify the /1 parameter, the target diskette is formatted for single-sided use.

The /8 parameter tells FORMAT to prepare the disk with eight sectors per track, instead of the default number of nine per track. You should let DOS use the default number so that you gain the additional 40K of disk space.

The /V parameter, which prompts the user for a volume label, cannot be used with the /8 parameter. You will be prompted for the volume name and can enter up to eleven characters. Thereafter, the volume name will appear when the DIR and CHKDSK commands are executed, further identifying the disk for you.

The /B parameter creates a disk with eight sectors per track and leaves room for IBMBIO.COM and IBMDOS.COM to be placed on the disk at a later time with the SYS command. Because it does not record these files onto the disk, any version of the IBM operating system can be placed there.

Formatting destroys any previously existing data on the diskette. Do *not* format a disk that contains data you will need later, or it will be lost forever.

During the formatting process, discovery of any defective sectors in a track results in the whole track's being marked RESERVED. This prevents any sectors in the **reserved track** from being allocated to a data file.

The DOS system files are marked as hidden files. FORMAT produces a status report that indicates (on separate lines) the following information:

total disk space

space marked as defective

space currently allocated to files

amount of space available for future files

The following command causes the diskette in drive B to be formatted and the operating system files to be copied:

```
A>FORMAT B:/S
```

The system begins by issuing the following message:

```
Insert new diskette for drive B:
and strike any key when ready
```

After you insert the appropriate diskette and strike any key, the system issues the following message while diskette formatting is taking place:

```
Formatting...
```

Once the formatting is complete, the system issues this message:

```
Formatting...Format complete
System transferred

362496 bytes total disk space
 40960 bytes used by system
 (4608 bytes in bad sectors)
316928 bytes available on disk

Format another (Y/N)?_
```

Enter Y to format another diskette; enter N to end the FORMAT program.

The FORMAT B:/S command causes DOS to be placed on a nine-sectored track disk, creating what is known as a **system disk**. This is desirable when the disk is to contain programs for use, and it permits the system to be booted from the disk.

If the disk is to be used only to store data (a so-called **slave disk**), the FORMAT B: command should be selected. This command performs all the tasks mentioned above except placing the files IBMBIO.COM, IBMDOS.COM, and COMMAND.COM on the disk. The system cannot be booted from such a disk; if booting is attempted, DOS will display the message:

```
Non-System disk or disk error
Replace and strike any key when ready
```

LABEL (Volume Label) Command (DOS 3.x)

Function: This command allows you to create, change, or delete a volume label on a disk.

Format: `LABEL [d:][volume label]`

Type: External

Remarks
&
Examples: The second `[d:]` parameter is used to tell DOS the drive of the disk you want to label. If no drive identifier is used, the default drive is assumed.

The `[volume label]` parameter is used to specify the new label for the disk to be named. This label can contain up to eleven characters. If no label is specified, DOS gives you the following prompt (the xxx's represent the current volume name):

```
Volume in drive x is xxxxxxxxxx

Volume label (11 characters, ENTER for
none)?
```

The label placed on the disk is the same type of label that can be placed on a disk when the /V parameter is used on the FORMAT command. To declare a new label, simply enter the desired characters and press ENTER. If the disk has an existing label, it is replaced when you press ENTER.

To delete an existing volume label, do not enter any characters, but simply press ENTER. You will then receive this prompt:

```
Delete current volume label (Y/N)?
```

Press Y and then press ENTER. The volume label on the disk is now deleted.

MORE (Filter) Command

Function: This filter command causes one screenful (twenty-three lines) of information from the specified file to be displayed. The command then pauses and displays the message `--More--`; any keystroke causes the next screenful of text to be displayed.

Format: `MORE`

Type: External

Remarks
&
Examples: The following statement will display a screenful of data from the file FILE03.PRG:

```
MORE <FILE03.PRG
```

MORE then displays the prompt `--More--` at the bottom of the display. Press any key, and MORE continues this process, twenty-three lines at a time, until the end of file is reached. The system prompt is then displayed on the screen.

The following command will produce a display of the diskette directory, sorted by file name order, twenty-three lines at a time:

```
DIR¦SORT¦MORE
```

This command will produce a screenful of information like that below:

```
              24 File(s) 7168 bytes free
Directory of A:\
Volume in drive A has no label
    %PIPE1     $$$         0    1-01-80    1:35a
    %PIPE2     $$$         0    1-01-80    1:35a
    AUTOEXEC   BAT        11    1-01-80   12:01a
    CHKDSK     COM      6400   10-20-83   12:00P
    COMMAND    COM     17792   10-20-83   12:00P
    DIR1                   0    1-01-80    1:32a
    INSTALL    EXE     36352    3-28-84    8:00a
    LETTER             128      1-01-80    4:21a
    MAILMRGE   OVR     13568    3-28-84    8:03a
    MM         INS      2816    3-28-84    8:01a
    MORE       COM       384   10-20-83   12:00P
    PISANI             640      1-30-85   12:07a
    PRINT              128      1-01-80   12:03a
    SORT       EXE      1408   10-20-83   12:00P
    SYSTEM1            128      1-01-80   12:00a
    WINSTALL   COM      1152    3-02-83
    WINSTALL   OVR     38528    3-02-83
    WS         COM     21376    6-21-84    3:28P
    WS         INS     43776    3-02-83
    WSD        COM     21376    6-21-84    3:30P
    WSMSGS     OVR     29056    4-12-83
    WSOVLY1    OVR     41216    6-21-84    3:30P
    WST        COM     21376    6-21-84    3:29P
    WSU        COM     21376    1-01-80   12:04a
```

Notice the temporary %PIPEx.$$$ files at the beginning of the directory listing; if you enter a regular DIR command, you will see that these files have disappeared. Notice, too, that no information is given about the amount of available storage on the disk.

The MORE command is similar to the TYPE command, except that the user does not have to pause and restart the display manually. MORE does this automatically.

PRINT Command

Function: This command causes the system to perform background printing of a list (queue) of on-disk files on the printer, while the computer is performing other tasks such as executing a program.

Format: `PRINT [[d:][filename[.ext]][/T][/C][/P]...]`

Type: External

Remarks
      &

Examples: When PRINT has control of the printer, do not try to print out a document from some other program such as WordStar. If you do, the WordStar document will appear in the middle of the document that was already printing at the time.

Background printing—printing on a disk-based file—is accomplished when the CPU is idle and waiting for data or for an operation to finish.

The /T parameter cancels the printing for any files in the queue. The current file stops printing, the paper advances to the top of the next page, and the printer bell is sounded. For example, the following command empties the print queue:

```
PRINT /T
```

The /P parameter adds a file to the print queue. For example, the following command places the files LETTER.DOC, RESUME.DOC, and NAMES.TXT in the print queue:

```
PRINT LETTER.DOC /P RESUME.DOC NAMES.TXT
```

The /C parameter cancels a specific file or files in the print queue. For example, the following command removes any file that has PROG as a file name (no matter what the extension is):

```
PRINT PROG.*/C
```

And the following command removes the three files PROGO1, PROGO2, and PROGO3 contained on drive A from the print queue:

```
PRINT A:PROGO?/C A:PROGO2 A:PROGO3
```

If just the PRINT command is given, PRINT displays the file names currently in the queue.

When you invoke PRINT for the first time, DOS responds with the prompt:

```
Name of list device [PRN]:
```

Unless you want to change the output device, just depress the ENTER key. This is the only time that DOS will prompt for the device. If the device must be changed after PRINT has been used, a system restart (CTRL + ALT + DEL) will be necessary.

Files are printed in the order in which they are placed in the queue.

For PRINT to operate, of course, the file must reside on disk.

RENAME (or REN) Command

Function: This command allows you to change the name of an existing file specified in the first parameter to the new name and extension specified in the second parameter.

Format: `REN[AME] filespec filename [.ext]`

Type: Internal

Remarks
&

Examples: The abbreviated form **REN** can be used for the RENAME command. The global characters ? and * can also be used with this command.

In the following example, file FILE03 on drive B will be renamed NEWFILE:

`RENAME B:FILE03 NEWFILE`

In the following example, file FILE03 on drive B will be renamed FILE03.XY:

`REN B:FILE03 *.XY`

SORT (Filter) Command

Function: This filter command reads, sorts, and then writes data onto the appropriate device.

Format: `SORT [/R] [/+n]`

Type: External

Remarks
&

Examples: The /R parameter causes the sort to be done in reverse order. If this parameter is not specified, the information will be sorted in ascending order. It is important to notice that the standard ASCII collating sequence determines the order of the sort.

The /+n parameter indicates the column at which the sort is to start. If no parameter is specified, the sort automatically begins at the first column.

The maximum size a sortable file can be is 63K.

Unless redirection is used, the information sorted is displayed on the screen. Different sorts can be accomplished as follows:

`DIR |SORT/+10` [displays the directory sorted by extension]

`DIR |SORT/+14` [displays the directory sorted by file size]

`DIR |SORT/+24` [displays the directory sorted by date]

`DIR |SORT/+24|MORE` [displays the directory sorted by date, one screen at a time]

The following command causes the directory to be displayed on the screen, sorted by file name:

```
DIR :SORT
```

In the typical display below, notice the temporary %PIPEx.$$$ files used by the sort filter.

```
          24 Files(s) 13312 bytes free
Directory of A:/
Volume in drive A has no label
    %PIPE1    $$$       0    1-01-80    2:08a
    %PIPE2    $$$       0    1-01-80    2:08a
    AUTOEXEC  BAT      11    1-01-80   12:01a
    CHKDSK    COM    6400   10-20-83   12:00P
    COMMAND   COM   17792   10-20-83   12:00P
    DIR1            1066    1-01-80    1:36a
    INSTALL   EXE   36352    3-28-84    8:00a
    LETTER           128    1-01-80    4:21a
    MAILMRGE  OVR   13568    3-28-84    8:03a
    MM        INS    2816    3-28-84    8:01a
    MORE      COM     384   10-20-83   12:00P
    PISANI           640    1-30-85   12:07a
    PRINT            128    1-01-80   12:03a
    SORT      EXE    1408   10-20-83   12:00P
    SYSTEM1          128    1-01-80   12:00a
    WINSTALL  COM    1152    3-02-83
    WINSTALL  OVR   38528    3-02-83
    WS        COM   21376    6-21-84    3:28P
    WS        INS   43776    3-02-83
    WSD       COM   21376    6-21-84    3:30P
    WSMSGS    OVR   29056    4-12-83
    WSOVLY1   OVR   41216    6-21-84    3:30P
    WST       COM   21376    6-21-84    3:29P
    WSU       COM   21376    1-01-80   12:04a
```

The following directory command places the disk directory in alphabetical order by file extension:

```
DIR :SORT/+10
```

Notice that the available bytes of storage line is imbedded within the directory output on the typical display below. This happens because the sort filter sorts everything that it receives from the DIR command without distinguishing between a file line and a text line.

```
    LETTER           128    1-01-80    4:21a
    SYSTEM1          128    1-01-80   12:00a
    PRINT            128    1-01-80   12:03a
    PISANI           640    1-30-85   12:07a
    DIR1            1049    1-01-80    2:08a
          24 File(s) 5120 bytes free
```

```
%PIPE1     $$$        0    1-01-80    2:08a
%PIPE2     $$$        0    1-01-80    2:08a
AUTOEXEC   BAT       11    1-01-80   12:01a
MORE       COM      384   10-20-83   12:00P
WINSTALL   COM     1152    3-02-83
CHKDSK     COM     6400   10-20-83   12:00P
COMMAND    COM    17792   10-20-83   12:00P
WSU        COM    21376    1-01-80   12:04a
WS         COM    21376    6-21-84    3:28P
WST        COM    21376    6-21-84    3:29P
WSD        COM    21376    6-21-84    3:30P
SORT       EXE     1408   10-20-83   12:00P
INSTALL    EXE    36352    3-28-84    8:00a
MM         INS     2816    3-28-84    8:01a
WS         INS    43776    3-02-83
MAILMRGE   OVR    13568    3-28-84    8:03a
WSMSGS     OVR    29056    4-12-83
WINSTALL   OVR    38528    3-02-83
WSOVLY1    OVR    41216    6-21-84    3:30P

Volume in drive A has no label
Directory of A:\
```

Redirection can also be used with the SORT command; in this operation, an input and/or output file can be specified.

SORT /+6<NAMES.TXT>SORTED.NAM [starts sorting input file NAMES.TXT, beginning at the sixth column, and places the sorted information in file SORTED.NAM]

SORT <GRADES.TXT [sorts file GRADES.TXT, beginning at the first column, and displays the data on the screen]

SYS (System) Command

Function: This command is used to place a copy of DOS on the disk in the specified drive.

Format: SYS d:

Type: External

Remarks
  &

Examples: For you to use this command properly, one of the following conditions must exist:

1. The directory must be empty.
2. The diskette must have been formatted with the /S parameter.
3. The diskette must have been formatted with the /B parameter.

This will ensure that space exists at the beginning of the diskette for the IBMBIO.COM and IBMDOS.COM files. DOS requires that these two files reside in the first two directory entries.

The SYS command allows the user to transfer a copy of DOS to an application program diskette that is designed to hold DOS but (because of copyright restrictions) does not. On such a diskette, room has been reserved for the DOS files, and the first two entries in the directory have been left blank for the IBMBIO.COM and IBMDOS.COM files. The SYS command will transfer these files to the new disk and place them in their allocated positions.

TIME Command

Function: Permits a user to change or enter a new time for the system. This date will then become part of any directory entry of a new file.

Format: `TIME [hh:mm:ss.xx]`

Type: Internal

Remarks
&

Examples: Upon receiving a valid time entry from the user, DOS stores that information until the system is shut down or until a new time is entered. In the latter case, the system displays the following prompt:

```
Current time is hh:mm:ss.xx
Enter new time:_
```

In this prompt, hh is for hours, mm is for minutes, ss is for seconds, and xx is for hundredths of a second.

To leave the time as currently set, press ENTER.

A 24-hour clock pattern is used. This means that 1:00 P.M. is entered as 13:00. Most people are concerned only with hours and minutes; the seconds and hundredths do not have to be used.

If partial time information (for example, just hours) is entered, the remaining fields are shown as zeros.

The valid delimiters for time fields are colons (:)—separating hours, minutes, and seconds—and the period (.)—separating seconds and hundredths of a second.

If an invalid time or invalid delimiter is entered, the `Invalid time` message will be displayed.

In the following example, when the ENTER key is depressed, the time recorded by the system will be changed to 18:25:00.00

```
A>TIME
Current time is 00:25:16.65
Enter new time:18:25_
```

TYPE Command

Function: This command causes the contents of the requested file to be displayed on the screen.

Format: `TYPE filespec`

Type: Internal

Remarks
&

Examples: Depress CTRL-PRTSC if you want the contents of a file to be
printed as they are being displayed. Depress CTRL + S to
cause the output to pause, and then press any other key to
continue scrolling.

     Text files appear in a legible format; other files, however,
such as object program files, may contain nonalphabetic or
nonnumeric characters that render them unreadable.

     In the following example, file FILE03.PRG on the diskette
in drive B will be displayed on the screen:

```
TYPE B:file03.prg
```

VER (Version) Command

Function: This command causes the version number of the DOS
currently in RAM memory to be displayed on the screen.

Format: VER

Type: Internal

Remarks
&

Examples: The DOS version is displayed in X.XX format, as in the
example below:

```
A>VER
IBM PERSONAL COMPUTER DOS Version 2.10
```

VOL (Volume) Command

Function: This command causes the disk volume I.D. of the specified
drive to be displayed on the screen.

Format: VOL [d:]

Type: Internal

Remarks
&

Examples: For a diskette's volume name to be displayed, the diskette
must have been formatted using the /V parameter. If no
drive is specified, the volume I.D. of the diskette in the
default drive is given.

     Following is an example of a VOL command executed for
a diskette with a volume I.D.:

```
A>VOL
Volume in drive A is TIMDISK
```

Following is an example of a VOL command executed for a
diskette with no volume I.D.:

```
A>VOL B:
Volume in drive B has no label
```

Redirection

Redirection

The **standard input device** on the IBM PC is the keyboard, and the **standard output device** is the display screen. The **redirection** feature, which was introduced with DOS 2.0, allows the IBM PC to accept input from a device other than the keyboard and to send output to a device other than the display screen.

Before DOS 2.0 appeared, the IBM PC had only a crude method of redirecting output: via the CTRL-PRTSC key sequence or via the CTRL-P sequence. These key sequences turn the printer on and echo any output displayed on the screen to the printer. This older method is commonly used with the DIR command to make a permanent copy of the directory of a disk that contains many files. This listing can then be referred to whenever the user wants to remember the name of a specific file.

With the newer redirection feature, either a device name or a file name can be used in the redirection command. For example, the command DIR>PRN will direct the PC to place the output on the printer without displaying anything on the screen, effectively redirecting the output from the screen to the printer.

This redirection feature can also be used with a variety of manipulations that involve the SORT command.

Example:

```
A>SORT <NAMES >SNAMES   [takes the input from the file called
NAMES, sorts it, and sends the output of the sort to the file called
SNAMES]
```

Piping

Piping is a method of sharing generated input and output among different programs by creating and using temporary, intermediate files. The output from one program thus becomes the input to another program.

These files, which appear briefly with names like %PIPE1.$$$, affect such things as the amount of available storage for a short time. After the command has been executed, the storage area used by these files is released for reuse.

The concept of piping is important to filter command programs. A **filter program** performs some type of data manipulation on a file, such as sorting the file or breaking it down into displayable chunks. Two common filter commands are MORE and SORT.

Example:

```
A>DIR:SORT   [generates a screen-listing of the directory, sorted in
order by file name]
```

In response to the above command, DOS quickly performs a number of tasks. First, the DIR command is executed, and output from the DIR command is sent to the temporary file $PIPE1.$$$. Next, the SORT filter command is executed, using as input the %PIPE1.$$$ file, and SORT arranges the directory information on the screen. The $PIPE1.$$$ file is then deleted, and the disk storage it occupied is released.

Examples:

```
A>DIR:SORT>NEWDIR   [generates a sorted listing of the directory in
file-name order and puts the output in the file called NEWDIR]
```

`A>DIR!MORE` [generates a screen-listing of the diskette directory, one screen at a time]

Piping can be invoked only at the DOS command level.
Three characters are involved in this process of redirection:

< establishes a source of input other than the keyboard

> establishes a target of output other than the monitor

>> establishes a target of output other than the monitor and also adds any new material to the end of an existing file (a process known as appending)

These symbols can be used at the DOS prompt level; they must be placed before the appropriate file name.

The > character will erase any preexisting information in the receiving file. If this is not desired, use the >> designation for the receiving file, and the new information will be added to the old file rather than replacing it.

Examples:

`A>DIR >DIRDISK1` [directs the output received from the directory command to a newly created (or newly erased) file called DIRDISK1]

`A>NEWFILE <OLDFILE` [makes the source of NEWFILE input the file called OLDFILE, rather than the keyboard]

`A>DIR >>DIRDISK1` [directs the output received from the directory command to the file called DIRDISK1, appending the new data to the existing contents of DIRDISK1]

DOS Command Summary

ASSIGN	Changes a drive assignment so that another drive name can be used
ATTRIB	Changes read-only status of a file
CHKDSK	Checks the status of a disk and prepares the status report
CLS	Clears the display monitor
COPY	Copies one or more files
DATE	Changes the system date
DEL	Deletes one or more files
DIR	Lists the files in the directory
DISKCOPY	Copies a complete diskette
ERASE	Deletes one or more files
FORMAT	Prepares a disk for use
LABEL	Changes the volume name of a disk
MORE	Displays a screenful (twenty-three lines) of data on the monitor
PRINT	Queues and prints disk-based data files
RENAME	Renames disk files
SORT	Sorts data files
SYS	Places DOS on a disk

TIME	Changes the system time
TYPE	Displays file contents on the monitor screen
VER	Displays the DOS version number
VOL	Displays the volume I.D. of a diskette

DOS Commands by Function and Type

Time: DATE, TIME
File: COPY, DEL, DIR, ERASE, PRINT, RENAME, TYPE
Disk: CHKDSK, DISKCOPY, FORMAT, VOL
Filters: MORE, SORT
System: CLS, SYS, VER

Internal Commands	External Commands (Utilities)
CLS	ASSIGN
COPY	ATTRIB
DATE	CHKDSK
DEL	DISKCOPY
DIR	FORMAT
ERASE	LABEL
RENAME	MORE
TIME	PRINT
TYPE	SORT
VER	SYS
VOL	

Chapter Review

The two basic types of DOS commands are internal and external. Internal commands are part of the DOS file COMMAND.COM. To execute one of these, you need only enter the command from the keyboard. External commands reside on disk(ette) as separate, external files. For one of these to be executed, the disk it is on must reside in the default drive or in a drive that you specify with a drive identifier.

The standard input and output devices, respectively, are the keyboard and the monitor. Input can be specified for redirection via the < character; output can be redirected via the > character. Input and/or output can be directed to a file or to another device by using redirection.

Piping, which is directly linked to redirection, involves creating temporary files to share input and/or output. Temporary files created by piping commands appear as %file.$$$ in a directory. When they are no longer needed by the system, they are automatically deleted. The filter commands SORT and MORE make use of piping.

Each DOS command has characteristics in common with other DOS commands; DOS also makes use of a common format notation. Diskette-oriented commands all have unique features that can only be expressed adequately when discussed in detail.

Key Terms and Concepts

ASSIGN command
ATTRIB command
CHKDSK command

CLS (clear screen) command
COPY command
DATE command

DEL (delete) command
delimiter
DIR (directory) command
DISKCOPY (copy diskette)
  command
ERASE command
external command
filter programs
FORMAT command
format notation
fragmented file
internal command
LABEL command
MORE (filter) command
parameter
piping
PRINT command
redirection

REN
RENAME command
reserved track
slave disk
SORT (filter) command
source drive
standard input device
standard output device
SYS (system) command
system disk
target drive
TIME command
TYPE command
VER (version) command
VOL (volume) command
$<$
$>$
$>>$

Chapter Quiz

Multiple Choice

1. Which of the statements below is false with respect to copying files using IBM PC DOS?
   a. DISKCOPY is the command used to reform fragmented files.
   b. COPY can create a copy of a file on the same disk, but a different name must then be used.
   c. COPY can be used to create a back-up file on another disk.
   d. DISKCOPY creates an exact copy of a disk's contents. It does this sector by sector and track by track.

2. The FORMAT command does all but which of the following tasks?
   a. Divides each track into eight or nine sectors
   b. Marks any track having a bad sector(s) as reserved
   c. Builds the directory
   d. Builds the file allocation table
   e. Performs all the above tasks

3. Which of the following statements is false with respect to redirection and piping?
   a. It is never possible to see the %file.$$$ files.
   b. Output can be redirected to the printer by using the PRINT parameter.
   c. When output is directed to a file, it always destroys the file's previous contents.
   d. Both b and c are false.
   e. All of the above are false.

4. Which of the commands below cannot use the * or ? wild cards?
   a. ERASE
   b. COPY
   c. CHKDSK
   d. DISKCOPY
   e. DIR
   f. All of these commands can use wild cards.

5. Which of these commands will cause the contents of the file FILE1 on a disk in drive A: to be copied to a disk in drive B:?
   a. A>COPY FILE1 A:
   b. B>COPY A:FILE1
   c. A>COPY FILE1 A:FILE1.BAK
   d. Both a and b
   e. All of the above will accomplish the task.

True/False

6. If you do not give a drive specifier in a command, DOS assumes that the command you have just entered is to be executed against the default drive.

7. An external command must reside on the default disk unless a drive specifier is given.

8. The COMMAND.COM file contains the external DOS commands.

9. The ERASE and DEL commands can be used interchangeably.

10. The computer can be booted from a slave disk.

Answers

1. a 2. e 3. d 4. d 5. b 6. t 7. t 8. f 9. t 10. f

Exercises

1. Define or describe each of the following:
   a. internal command   e. COPY versus DISKCOPY
   b. external command   f. filter
   c. redirection   g. system versus slave diskette
   d. piping

2. List three internal DOS commands.
   a.

   b.

   c.

3. List three external DOS commands.
   a.

   b.

   c.

4. Give the following FORMAT commands:
   a. Format the disk in drive A, placing the operating system on it.
   b. Format the disk in drive A without placing the operating system on it.
   c. Format the disk in drive B, placing the operating system on it.
   d. Format the disk in drive B without placing the operating system on it.

5. Without changing the default drive, give the following COPY commands:
   a. Copy file FILE1 from the default disk A and create file FILE1.BAK on drive A.
   b. Copy file FILE1 from the default disk A onto the diskette in drive B.
   c. Copy file FILE1 from disk B and copy it onto the diskette in default drive A, using the same name.
   d. Copy file FILE1 from disk B and copy it onto the diskette in default drive A, using the name FILE1.BAK.

6. The default drive is A. Enter the command that would erase file FILE1 from the diskette in drive B, without changing the default drive.

7. The DOS command that is used to reform fragmented files is the _____ _____ command.

8. The DOS command that is used to examine the directory and print a table of contents is the _____ command.

9. Two commands that can be used to delete unwanted files are
   a.

   b.

10. The command used to create a "carbon" copy of the disk in drive A onto the disk in drive B is _____ .

11. The SORT and MORE commands are called _____ _____ commands.

12. Two commands that can be used to tell you the amount of available space on a disk are
    a.

    b.

13. The DOS command that is used to install the various DOS system files on a disk is the _____ command.

14. The format notation [ ] means that these parameters are _____ _____ when using this command.

15. A temporary file created by piping has the file extension of _____ _____ .

16. The copy command that will also copy all the files of one disk onto another disk is the COPY _____ .

17. What happens when you enter the command ERASE *.*? What prompt do you receive? What happens if you continue?

18. What is the difference between the MORE and the TYPE commands?

Computer Exercises

1. Enter the following DIR commands:
   a. Display the directory, one page at a time.
   b. Display the directory using the wide parameter option.
   c. Using the SORT filter, list the files in alphabetical order by the extension.
   d. Using the SORT filter, list the files in order by file size.
   e. Using the SORT and MORE filters, display the contents of the directory, one screen at a time. Sort the directory by file name.

2. Clear the screen, using the CLS command.

3. Check the version of your DOS, using the VER command.

4. Use the VOL command to see if there is a volume name on your disk.

5. Change the date and time of the system. Use the DATE and TIME commands to verify that the change was properly made.

6. What is the date on the SEMPCINT.DOC file? What command do you have to use to get the date?

7. Run CHKDSK on your diskette. Fill in the following blanks:
   _____ bytes total disk space
   _____ bytes in _____ hidden files
   _____ bytes in _____ user files
   _____ bytes in bad sectors
   _____ bytes available on disk
   _____ bytes total memory
   _____ bytes free

8. Make a back-up copy of the SEMPCINT.DOC file on your disk, using the COPY command. What did you name it? _____

9. Run CHKDSK again, and fill in the blanks:
   _____ bytes total disk space
   _____ bytes in _____ hidden files
   _____ bytes in _____ user files
   _____ bytes in bad sectors
   _____ bytes available on disk
   _____ bytes total memory
   _____ bytes free

10. Make a back-up copy of the SEMPCINT.DOC file on your disk, using the COPY command.
    a. Copy it onto another file on your disk.
    b. Copy it onto another disk.

11. Erase the SEMPCINT.DOC file.

12. List (TYPE or MORE) the contents of the back-up file of SEMPCINT.DOC on your screen. Give the instruction that you used: _____.

13. Use the MORE command to list out the SEMPCINT.DOC file.

14. Use the redirection command to place the information from the DIR command into a disk file called DIR1.

15. Use the MORE command to look at the DIR1 file.

16. Recreate the SEMPCINT.DOC file from your back-up copy.

17. Use the MORE command to list the BOOKEXER file.

18. Use the SORT command (and give the command you used) to list the directory in the following ways:
    Alphabetically by file name _____
    Alphabetically by file extension _____

Chapter

4

Advanced

DOS Concepts

After completing this chapter, you should be able to:

Tell what a batch file does

Discuss the types of batch files

Discuss how to create batch files

Discuss how to create batch files with replaceable parameters

Discuss the concept of directories

Discuss common directory commands

Discuss the concept of active directory

Discuss how to use the CONFIG.SYS file to configure your system

Discuss how to set up a RAM disk using the VDISK.SYS file inside the CONFIG.SYS file

Batch Files:
The DOS Automator

The Disk Operating System (DOS) gives you tremendous power on your computer. DOS allows you to perform tasks on files such as copying, deleting, renaming, listing them as they occur in the directory, and listing them in sorted order. DOS also allows you to customize the operating environment to meet your specific needs. Customization involves placing any number of DOS commands in a file and then executing the commands contained in that file. The file that contains these DOS commands is known as a **batch file**.

A batch file then feeds its DOS commands to DOS. Once DOS receives a command from a batch file, it executes it and tries to access any other commands in that file. A batch file can have any file name but is required to have a .BAT file extension. The .BAT file extension indicates to DOS that the file contains system commands rather than text, machine language, or any other data.

What are the advantages of using a batch file? Batch files can save you large amounts of time. You can tell DOS to execute all DOS commands in the file by typing the batch file's name. Since the commands are already correctly entered into the file, you don't have to worry about making mistakes in any of the DOS commands or file names.

Why is the term *batch* used in referring to a batch file? The term goes back to the early days of data processing when batches of machine-readable documents or system commands were submitted to a computer. The computer's operating system would process a batch of operating system instructions at one time, while a computer program would process a batch of machine-readable documents at one time. With early computers, information could not be entered interactively as it was needed. Instead, information was recorded on punched cards, magnetic disks, or magnetic tapes and then entered into the machine. There was very little interaction between the operator and the machine or between a user and the computer.

Batch files on today's microcomputers contain frequently executed sequences of DOS commands. Such sequences include booting the machine, entering date and time, and then starting a program; copy commands for backup for critical files; and using batch jobs to make it easier for beginners to use the microcomputer.

How Batch Files Work

There are two types of batch files. The first executes automatically upon booting the system (AUTOEXEC.BAT); the second can be executed only by entering its name from the keyboard. When you are executing the second type of batch file, you do not have to include the .BAT file extension.

When DOS executes the commands in a batch file, it follows the same steps that it uses in executing any DOS command. It checks to see if the command is contained in the COMMAND.COM file (internal command). If the command is not an internal command, it checks to see if the command is contained on the default disk (unless a drive identifier was used). It assumes that such a command contains either a .COM or .EXE file extension. If DOS is unable to find a .COM or .EXE file, it checks to see if there is a file on the indicated disk with an appropriate .BAT file extension. When DOS encounters any one of these circumstances, it starts to execute that command/batch file.

The user does not have to wait for all of the commands in a batch file to be executed before stopping the process. You can stop a batch file at any time by entering a Ctrl + Break command or a Ctrl + C command. Either of these commands bring the following message:

```
Terminate batch job (Y/N)?_
```

If you press the N key, the batch file continues processing. If you press the Y key, DOS returns you to the default disk with the standard DOS prompt (i.e., A> or B>).

An AUTOEXEC.BAT batch file executes during the boot process immediately after DOS has been loaded into RAM memory. Note that you can have only one AUTOEXEC.BAT file on a disk at any one time. If there happens to be more than one, DOS executes the first AUTOEXEC.BAT file that it finds in the directory. Here is a sample AUTOEXEC.BAT batch file:

REM Start-up procedure

Date

WP

Notice that the batch file contains only three commands. **REM** displays the message start-up procedure on the screen. The Date command prompts the user for the date. After the date has been entered, the WP command starts the WordPerfect word processing program. Thus this batch file allows an individual, without much knowledge of a computer, to use a WordPerfect disk that contains DOS and this batch file and, without having to learn any DOS commands, do their word processing. Remember, it does not matter to DOS whether a command is in upper-case letters, lower-case letters, or a combination of the two.

Rules for Creating Simple Batch Files

The following rules are imposed by DOS when you name and create a batch file:

You can create batch files by using either the DOS COPY command to copy commands to a batch file or by using a wordprocessor in nondocument or programming mode.

Please note that when you use the COPY option, DOS erases all the data in a file and starts fresh. You cannot modify an existing batch file with the COPY command.

The file name of a batch file must be entered according to standard DOS procedures; that is, it can have one to eight allowable characters.

The file extension *must* be .BAT.

The file name cannot be the same as a DOS internal command or as any file with a .COM or .EXE file extension, because DOS cannot differentiate between such commands and may execute the internal command instead of the .BAT command. If another file residing on the disk has the batch file name but a different file extension, DOS executes the file that it finds first in the directory.

Creating Batch Files

Batch files can be created in a number of ways, two of which are covered here: using the COPY CON: facility of DOS or using the nondocument mode of a word processor. The **COPY CON:** procedure uses the DOS copy feature to copy all commands entered at the keyboard to the batch file. The COPY CON: convention is most appropriate when you are creating a small batch file. If you have to make changes to a large batch file, a word processor is better because you don't want to destroy your existing text and start from the beginning. The following steps would be required to create the AUTOEXEC.BAT file:

1. A>COPY CON:AUTOEXEC.BAT

2. REM Start-up procedure

3. DATE

4. TIME

5. ^Z

Let's examine each of these steps. The COPY CON: portion of step 1 tells DOS that a file is to be created from entries generated at the keyboard. The AUTOEXEC.BAT tells DOS the name of the file to be created.

Steps 2–4 contain the commands that are to be placed in the file. DOS knows you are finished with a line when you press the ENTER key.

Step 5 contains a ^Z entry. The ^Z indicates the end of the file to DOS. DOS now knows to record all commands in the file to disk. The ^Z is achieved not by entering the characters ^Z but by pressing the F6 function key. When you press the F6 key, DOS stores the file to disk under the name used in the COPY CON: command (AUTOEXEC.BAT).

A frequent problem in using the COPY CON: facility is error correction. Once you press ENTER, you cannot make changes in a line. If you make mistakes, continue entering the various DOS commands and make any changes using the nondocument mode of a word processor.

This batch file could be entered using the nondocument or programming mode of a word processing language. Remember, nondocument mode does not embed any special ASCII control sequences in a file. After the AUTO-EXEC.BAT file has been opened, the above commands can be entered exactly as they appear.

There is no difference in how the two files execute. The only difference is in how they are created. Most people, once they are familiar with a word processor, prefer to create batch files with their nondocument mode, because errors are much easier to correct.

Executing a Batch File

The following rules apply when you are ready to tell DOS to execute a batch file:

DOS assumes that the batch file resides on the default drive unless you indicate otherwise by using a drive identifier (for example, C:SAMPLE.BAT).

To start a batch file, simply enter the file name. You do not have to enter the .BAT file extension.

Once the batch file is located by DOS, the operating system begins executing commands residing in the batch file one at a time. When one command has been executed, DOS automatically loads the next command and tries to execute it.

If DOS loads an instruction and is unable to interpret it, a `Syntax error` message is displayed.

Once a batch file has begun execution, you can stop it by entering a CTRL + Break or Ctrl + C DOS interrupt command. Once one of the above commands is entered, DOS displays the following message:

```
Terminate batch job (Y/N)?_
```

If you answer N, the batch file continues to execute, and the next command is read and executed. If you answer Y, the stream of commands coming from the batch file is interrupted, and you are returned to DOS (a system prompt is displayed to the screen).

If you have removed the disk, DOS will prompt you to reinsert the disk containing the batch file. If you simply want to stop the execution, enter another interrupt command (Ctrl + Break or Ctrl + C); otherwise, reinsert the original disk and press any key to continue.

Substituting Data in Batch File Execution

Most DOS commands require one or more pieces of data (parameters) that tell the operating system exactly how to execute a command and on which files it should be executed. The Rename command, for example, requires two parameters: The first parameter indicates which file is to be renamed, and the second supplies the new name.

DOS provides you with the ability to substitute parameters for DOS commands that reside in a batch file. This is accomplished by indicating to DOS when and where replaceable parameters are to be used. **Replaceable parameters** are pieces of information in a DOS command that might change from one uses to the next. A replaceable parameter is represented by a percent sign (%) followed by a single digit (i.e., %1). This convention allows you to designate ten pieces of information that can be supplied by commands residing in a batch file (%0 through %9).

One application of a replaceable parameter enables you to print a text file quickly and easily without starting up a word processing software package. This is accomplished by a batch file with the single DOS statement:

```
COPY %1 PRN
```

This batch file takes any output and redirects it to the printer. You could name this batch file PRINTIT.BAT. The PRINTIT.BAT name allows DOS to differentiate this file name from the DOS PRINT command. Now, when you want to print a file—for example, MEMO—enter the command

```
PRINTIT MEMO
```

When DOS receives this command, it locates the batch file PRINTIT and passes the parameter MEMO to the COPY command. It then takes the contents of the file MEMO and sends it to the printer.

Sample Batch Files

Many of today's IBM or IBM compatible computers have expanded memory cards that allow you to add up to 640K of regular RAM to your microcomputer. This extra RAM allows you to turn part of your RAM into an electronic disk that can be used to store program files and pass them, with tremendous speed, to the CPU. If you use programs such as WordStar that require a lot of disk I/O, a RAM disk can give you much faster processing.

The following batch file allows you to create a RAM disk as you boot the system. This particular example makes use of a utility provided by the Quadram Corporation on their multifunction card. Of course, this batch file has to be named AUTOEXEC.BAT and would be stored on the disk containing all of the WordStar program files.

```
QM2 QD=10, QC=0, QS=0, BATCH
COPY *.*C:
C:
WS
a:
```

Let's examine these statements. The first calls the Quadram utility QM2 and tells it, among other things, to create a RAM disk. This becomes **device** C: (this first statement can be replaced by the VDISK statement in the CONFIG.SYS file, discussed later in this chapter). The next statement takes all of the files that appear on the disk in drive A and copies them, one at a time, to the RAM disk. The next statement makes the RAM disk (default C>) the default drive. The fourth statement starts WordStar. The last statement changes the default drive to A when you exit WordStar.

The next example of a batch file contains the statements necessary for starting VP-Planner so that graphs can be displayed on the monitor using a Hercules or Hercules compatible graphics card; these statements are as follows:

```
DATE
HGC FULL
VP
```

The first command prompts you for the date and then resets the computer's system date from the data that you enter at the keyboard. The HGC FULL command executes the HGC-COM file and places the Hercules graphics card in graphics mode so that it can display worksheet-generated graphs. The last command starts VP-Planner.

Introduction to Disk Directories

Before we look at directories, let's review how DOS prepares a regular double-sided disk via the FORMAT command. When DOS is finished formatting a disk, it prepares the **directory** and places it in seven sectors. This directory can hold up to 112 files. DOS, in essence, limits the number of files that you can place on your disk. DOS also limits the number of files that a directory can hold on other types of disks. Here is a list of the type of disk and its maximum number of files:

Disk Type	Maximum Files
Single sided	64
Double sided	112
High density (AT)	224
Hard disk	512

Although DOS appears to limit the number of files that can be stored on a disk, it is not really the case. Can you imagine that a high-density disk with 1.2 meg of storage or a hard disk with 10 to 20 meg, or more, is able to store only a limited number of files? You can circumvent this apparent limitation on any disk by using subdirectories. Directories can be used on diskettes, but they are most frequently used on hard disks and high-density diskettes.

The main directory is referred to as the **root directory**, and any additional directories are **subdirectories**. Subdirectories allow you to store more information (files) on a disk and to organize your disk more effectively. This means that you can place your word processing programs and files in a subdirectory for word processing or your data base management programs and data base files in a data base subdirectory. Such an organization is shown in Figure 4.1.

Each of the subdirectories depicted here can be divided into other subdirectories. The data base directory might be subdivided into two subdirectories, one to be used for holding business-related data files and the other for personal data files.

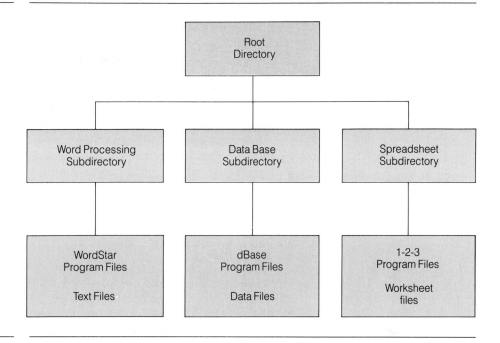

Directories and Directory Commands

A subdirectory is like a root directory except that it is itself a file and contains DOS housekeeping entries in a regular directory, but it does not have the size limitation of the root directory. A subdirectory can expand indefinitely (or until there is no more disk space).

Since a subdirectory is a file, it must be named. However, it cannot be built like other files. Rather, the commands used are the following:

Command	*Purpose*
Make directory (**MKDIR**) [**MD**]	Build a file to contain the new directory entries.
Change directory (**CHDIR**) [**CD**]	Move to another directory and make that the active directory.
Remove directory (**RMDIR**) [**RD**]	Delete the file containing the directory.
Tree	Display all directories on the disk.

The first three directory commands are internal commands. They can be executed either by their complete DOS name (in parentheses) or their abbreviated name [in brackets]. The Tree (found only in PC DOS) is an external command and resides as a separate file on disk. The syntax of these commands is discussed in greater detail at the end of the chapter.

Before you make a subdirectory, you should plan how you want to store data on your disk. You may decide to store programs and information by application type such as depicted in Figure 4.1, or you may plan to store programs and information by project. A third possibility is to combine these two techniques, storing information by project within an application.

The Make Directory (MD) Command. Once you have an idea of how you want to store your information, you can build the subdirectories that will hold the information. This is accomplished via the MKDIR (MD) command.

If you want to work along with an example, format a system disk and copy these files to it:

CHKDSK.COM

FORMAT.COM

DISKCOPY.COM

MORE.COM

SYS.COM

TREE.COM

SORT.EXE

ANSI.SYS

A directory listing of the files on the disk would now appear as follows:

```
Volume in drive A is TIM DUFFY
Directory of A:\

COMMAND      COM      17792      10-20-83      12:00P
CHKDSK       COM       6400      10-20-83      12:00P
FORMAT       COM       6912      10-20-83      12:00P
DISKCOPY     COM       2576      10-20-83      12:00P
MORE         COM        384      10-20-83      12:00P
SYS          COM       1680      10-20-83      12:00P
TREE         COM       1513      10-20-83      12:00P
SORT         EXE       1408      10-20-83      12:00P
ANSI         SYS       1664      10-20-83      12:00P
        9 File(s)  294912 bytes free
```

You are now ready to build three subdirectories for storing information: for word processing (WP), spreadsheets (SS), and data base management (DB). Each is created by using the MD commands:

```
A>MD WP
A>MD DB
A>MD SS
```

After each command is entered, drive A starts up to record information from that subdirectory file's. You can now issue a DIR command, and the following information will be displayed on your screen:

```
Volume in drive A is TIM DUFFY
Directory of A:\

COMMAND      COM      17792      10-20-83      12:00P
CHKDSK       COM       6400      10-20-83      12:00P
FORMAT       COM       6912      10-20-83      12:00P
DISKCOPY     COM       2576      10-20-83      12:00P
MORE         COM        384      10-20-83      12:00P
SYS          COM       1680      10-20-83      12:00P
TREE         COM       1513      10-20-83      12:00P
SORT         EXE       1408      10-20-83      12:00P
ANSI         SYS       1664      10-20-83      12:00P
WP                  <DIR>                 3-29-86      12:05a
DB                  <DIR>                 3-29-86      12:05a
SS                  <DIR>                 3-29-86      12:05a
       12 File(s)  291840 bytes free
```

Notice that this listing shows that DOS is treating the directories as files. The original listing had nine files, but after you created the subdirectories, it has twelve files. You can differentiate a subdirectory from a file by the < DIR > message (abbreviation for directory) which is displayed in place of the extension and file size data. Notice that the date on which the subdirectory was created (the system date stored in the machine at startup time) is also listed.

Also notice that the bytes free entry has changed since the three subdirectories were created. Each subdirectory takes a minimum of 1K, or 1024, characters of storage.

The Change Directory (CD) Command. Once your subdirectories have been created, you can reach a subdirectory via the CD (change directory) command. To move from the root directory to the data base (DB) subdirectory, you enter the CD DB command. To make sure that you have moved to the right subdirectory, you can issue the DIR command to see where you are. The following output will be displayed on your monitor.

```
Volume in drive A is TIM DUFFY
Directory of A:\DB

.          <DIR>      3-29-86       12:08a
..         <DIR>      3-29-86       12:08a
      2 File(s) 291840 bytes free
```

The output of this DIR command is just a bit different from the output of the root directory. Notice that the second line of this directory listing contains A:\DB. This denotes the sudirectory that is considered by DOS to be active. You can always tell when you are at the root directory because the output of the DIR command will give the default drive followed only by a backslash, for example, A:\.

You can also use the CD command to find out where you are in a subdirectory tree since the CD causes DOS to respond with the current active directory:

```
CD          (command)
A:\DB       (response)
```

If you were at the root directory, the same command would produce a different response:

```
CD
A:\
```

You can also use the CD command to leave the subdirectory and return to the directory above in the hierarchy by entering CD .. or CD\, but if you use the first option, be sure to put a space between the CD and the two periods. Entering one of these commands moves you from the current subdirectory to the directory immediately above it. In this case, if you are at the DB subdirectory, you are taken to the root directory.

The Active (Current) Directory

The active (current) directory concept is especially important in a hard disk or high density disk environment. After you have moved to a subdirectory in your hard disk, you can switch the default drive to one of your diskette drives, and DOS will remember which is the active subdirectory. If you copy files from the diskette to the hard disk drive that contains the active (current) subdirectory, they will be placed in that subdirectory.

For example, suppose that your current active subdirectory is on drive B. Also suppose that you have changed your default drive from B to A but want to copy a file called MEMO.TXT back to your active subdirectory on drive B. All that is required is to enter the following command:

```
A>COPY MEMO.TXT B:
```

Since DOS remembers which is the active subdirectory, it automatically copies the file to that subdirectory.

When you are copying information from one directory to another, remember that both the directory and the file name must be used. For example, if you want to copy the FORMAT.COM file from the root directory to the DB directory, you enter the following DOS command:

```
A>COPY FORMAT.COM \DB
```

This command translates as: Take the file called FORMAT.COM and copy it to the DB subdirectory; use the existing name. Now, if you want to refer to the FORMAT.COM file as it exists in the DB subdirectory while you are in the root directory, enter \DB\FORMAT.COM. When you refer to files in directories other than the active directory, you must use their full names. The subdirectory is part of that name.

While remaining at the root directory, you can copy the FORMAT.COM file from the DB subdirectory to the WP subdirectory by using the following command:

```
A>COPY \DB\FORMAT.COM \WP
```

Again, you must specify all of the sending information, which in this case is the name of the subdirectory and the name of the file, and all of the receiving information, which (unless you are going to change the name of the file) is only the receiving directory. The complete name for a file, including the complete subdirectory name, is referred to as the **path**.

The Tree Command. You may someday use a microcomputer system that is not familiar to you, in which case you may not know what subdirectories are on a disk or which files are in which subdirectory. Then the PC DOS TREE command will be extremely helpful. The TREE command is an external file that must reside on one of the disks. In this example, it is in the root directory. The TREE command generates the following output:

```
DIRECTORY PATH LISTING FOR VOLUME TIM DUFFY

Path: \SS
Sub-directories: None

Path: \WP
Sub-directories: None

Path: \DB
Sub-directories: None
```

This information might not be enough for you. The TREE command also has a /F parameter that lists any files found in a directory in addition to the directory name. The TREE /F command generates the following display:

```
DIRECTORY PATH LISTING FOR VOLUME TIM DUFFY

Path: \SS
Sub-directories: None

Files:            None

Path: \WP
Sub-directories: None

Files:            FORMAT .COM

Path: \DB
Sub-directories: None

Files:            FORMAT .COM
```

The Remove Directory (RD) Command. Assume that the DB subdirectory is no longer needed. Since you do not want to waste the disk space taken up by this directory and its files, you want to erase it. However, the ERASE command cannot be used to remove a directory. You must use the RMDIR (RD) command. First, all files must be deleted from the directory with the ERASE *.* command. If you forget to remove any file from the subdirectory, DOS will display the error message:

```
Invalid path, not a directory
or directory not empty
```

If you receive this error message, simply go to that directory and erase the rest of the files from it; then issue the RD command to remove the subdirectory.

PATH: Executing Commands without Changing Directories

Assume that you have a computer system with a hard disk (device C) and two diskette drives (devices A and B). While you are working on drive A, you want to execute the DOS command CHKDSK. This command, however, resides in the subdirectory DOSFILES that you created to hold the external DOS files. (This saves room on the root directory and also provides storage that is easy for you to remember.) The problem is that you must switch to the DOSFILES subdirectory, issue the DOS command CHKDSK, and then switch back to your current drive or directory and resume work. This process takes several change drive (CD) commands, which you would like to avoid.

The PATH command provides the capability to automatically search specified drives or directories if the desired file cannot be found in the active disk or directory. It can be used for any file with a .EXE, .COM, or .BAT file extension.

Path Command.

Function: The PATH command searches specified drives and directories for commands or batch files that are not found on the current drive or directory.

Format: PATH [[d:]path[[;[d:]path...]]
             or
             PATH;

Type: Internal

Remarks
    &

Examples: The PATH command allows you to specify a list of drives
           and subdirectory names separated by semicolons. When
           you now enter a command that is not found in the current
           active disk or subdirectory, DOS searches the named drives
           and subdirectories in the sequence you entered them; the
           current drive or subdirectory is left unchanged.

Entering PATH with no parameters displays the current path. Entering
PATH; (with only a semicolon) resets the search path to the current drive and
subdirectory, which is the DOS default.

A path can be any valid series of subdirectories separated by a backslash.
Each separate path must be separated by semicolons, and the search by DOS
for the program or batch file will be in the order of the drives and subdirectories specified in the PATH command. If the file cannot be found in the current
directory and the designated paths, a Bad command or filename message will appear. If you give a bad drive name or subdirectory, DOS will skip
that parameter without displaying an error message.

If, in the example above, you want to tell DOS to automatically go to the
DOSFILES subdirectory if it is unable to find a specified program or batch file
in the active drive or subdirectory, you should give the following PATH
command:

```
PATH c:\dosfiles
```

Now, when a command is entered, DOS first searches the active disk
and subdirectory; if it is unable to locate the desired program file, it searches
the DOSFILES subdirectory to see if it is located there. If it finds the appropriate file, the command is executed; and if it is unable to locate the file, the
message Bad command or file name appears on the monitor.

You may want DOS to search two subdirectories for command files. For
example, you might want DOS to examine the DOSFILES subdirectory
and the UTILITY subdirectory as well. This is accomplished via the following
command:

```
PATH c:\dosfiles;c:\utility
```

Now when a command is entered, DOS first searches the active disk or
subdirectory. If it is unable to locate the desired program file, it searches the
DOSFILES subdirectory to see if the file is located there; if it is not, it searches
the UTILITY subdirectory. If it finds the file, the command is executed; if it is
unable to locate the file, the message Bad command or file name appears on the monitor.

DOS Directory Commands

CHDIR (or CD) Command.

Function: Changes the current DOS directory or displays the current
           directory of the default drive.

Format: CD [d:][path]
           or
           CHDIR [d:][path]

Type: Internal

Remarks
&

Examples: The abbreviated form CD can be used for the CHDIR
command.
    Use the [d:] parameter to specify the drive on which
the subdirectory that you want to change resides or on
which you want to display the current directory.
    The CD\ command moves you from the current
subdirectory to the root directory. The CD . . command
moves you from the current directory to the next higher
directory.

MKDIR (or MD) Command.

Function: Creates a subdirectory on a specified drive named by the
characters following the command.

Format: MD [d:][path]
            or
            MKDIR [d:][path]

Type: Internal

Remarks
&

Examples: The abbreviated form MD can be used for the MKDIR
command.
    Use the [d:] parameter to specify the drive on which
you wish to create the subdirectory. If no drive is specified,
the default drive is assumed.
    DOS specifies no limit to the number of directories that
you can create. The only limitation is the amount of storage
available on your default device. Neither is there a limit to
how many times a file name can appear on a disk as long as
each occurrence is in a different subdirectory.

RMDIR (or RD) Command.

Function: Removes the subdirectory of the name composed of the
characters following the command.

Format: RD [d:][path]
            or
            RMDIR [d:][path]

Type: Internal

Remarks
&

Examples: The abbreviated form RD can be used for the RMDIR
command. All files must be erased from the subdirectory
before it can be removed. If files remain in the subdirectory
and the RD command is executed, the following error
message will be displayed on the monitor:

```
Invalid path, not a directory
or directory not empty
```

You cannot remove root directories from a disk.

Tree Command.

Function: Displays all of the directories on a disk and, using an optional parameter, lists the files of the root directory and of each subdirectory.

Format: TREE [d:][/F]

Type: External

Remarks
&
Examples: Use the [d:] and [path] optional parameters that appear before the TREE command to tell DOS in what drive and what subdirectory this external file resides. Use the optional [d:] following the TREE command to tell DOS against which drive to execute the command. Use the optional [/F] parameter to tell DOS to list each file contained in each subdirectory.

Configuring Your System

DOS, beginning with version 2.0, enables you to use commands that customize or configure your computer system. Any time that you start DOS via a boot operation, DOS searches the root directory of the active drive for a file named **CONFIG.SYS**. If the CONFIG.SYS file is found, DOS reads that file and uses the commands in it to customize its environment. If CONFIG.SYS is not found, DOS uses default values.

The CONFIG.SYS file can be created in a number of ways: You can use the COPY command to create it, you can use the EDLIN editor, or you can use your word processing package. This file can contain various commands, but only the commands commonly used to configure your system are covered here: Assign, Break, Buffers, Country, Device, and Files.

Assign. The Assign statement (covered in Chapter 3) can be used in a CONFIG.SYS file to reassign device names. You must have the ASSIGN.COM file on your boot disk.

Break. The Break option can be either on or off and allows you to instruct DOS to check for a control break (CTRL + Break) when a program requests DOS to perform any tasks. The default for DOS is off. If you want DOS to search for Ctrl + Break whenever it is requested, use the command BREAK = ON. This is especially useful if you wish to break out of a program compile (such an operation produces few or no standard device operations).

Format: BREAK = [ON¦OFF]

Buffers. The Buffers option permits you to determine the number of disk buffers that DOS is to allocate in memory when it starts (the default is two for a PC and three for an AT). A buffer is part of RAM that is used by the computer to hold information that has been read, is to be written to disk, or is to be printed.

Format: BUFFERS = x

The x represents a number between 1 and 99 and is the number of disk buffers that DOS allocates in RAM when it starts. Each of these buffers requires 512 bytes of RAM. Since DOS automatically starts with two buffers, only 1024 bytes are used for buffers. This 1K of buffer storage may not be enough for such simple operations as looking at the directory of a diskette or a subdirectory of a hard disk, especially if there are many small files. A small number of buffers means that a lot of shifting of data has to occur in this reserved area. Therefore, a directory listing takes much less time when more buffers are allocated in RAM.

Data base applications also require more buffer space. A small number of buffers (for example, the default value 2) means that the response of the data base in retrieving data from disk is going to be slow. Any data base program that makes use of relative addressing (a topic to be covered later in the text) requires a larger number of buffers to increase performance.

How many buffers should you set aside? This is determined by the size of your computer and the types of processing applications that you want to perform. Since each buffer takes up 512 bytes, you probably don't want to specify 50 of them when you have a machine with only 128K of storage. Too many buffers can have a negative effect on the performance of your machine. When you increase the number of buffers too much, DOS spends too much time searching the buffers for data. For most applications about twenty buffers are sufficient.

Country (DOS 3.1). The Country command is used to display the format for the date, time, currency symbol, and the decimal separator for various countries.

Format: `COUNTRY = xxx`

The xxx is a three digit international country code for the telephone system. The default value is 001 (United States). The following countries and their respective codes are supported by DOS 3.1:

United States	001
Netherlands	031
Belgium	032
France	033
Spain	034
Italy	039
Switzerland	041
United Kingdom	044
Denmark	045
Sweden	046
Norway	047
Germany	049
Australia	061
Finland	358
Israel	972

Device. The Device command allows you to specify the name of a file containing a device driver. A number of standard drivers are automatically loaded into memory by DOS. For instance, the standard input, standard output, standard printer, diskette, and fixed disk device drivers are automatically loaded by DOS during the boot process. The Device command allows you to load special drivers that come with DOS (ANSI.SYS or VDISK.SYS) that come with DOS on the DOS Master Disk.

The ANSI.SYS driver file located on disk provides a standard interface for programs, regardless of which manufacturer made them. This driver allows you to program applications that do not have to access the ROM BIOS (which is different in most machines and causes most of the compatibility problems of software) but instead send special instructions using this driver.

Format: `DEVICE = ANSI.SYS`

The **VDISK.SYS** driver file located on the DOS master disk enables you to set a RAM disk using part of your computer's memory. This RAM disk simulates all of the properties of a diskette in a disk drive. RAM disks have a number of advantages: Since their speed is limited only by the speed of RAM, they are fast; more than one RAM disk can be installed; if you have an AT computer with extended memory (more than 1 meg), you can use that memory for one or more RAM disks; you can specify the amount of RAM memory for each disk.

RAM disks also have a few disadvantages. Each one increases the size of DOS by 720 bytes. Most importantly, however, if power is lost or you forget to transfer files to a physical disk, all of the contents of the RAM disk are lost and cannot be recovered.

Format: `DEVICE = vdisk.sys[bbb][sss][ddd][/E[:m]]`

The `[bbb]` parameter is the size of the RAM disk in K and is specified as a decimal number. The default size is 64K. The allowable range is between 1 and the amount of memory actually installed in your machine. It would usually be between 128 and 320K.

The `[sss]` parameter is the sector size in bytes. The sizes that you can use are 128, 256, and 512 (the default value is 128).

The `[ddd]` parameter is the number of files that are allowed in the directory of the RAM disk (64 is the default). This value, if entered, can be between 2 and 512.

The /E parameter tells DOS to place the RAM disk in extended memory, and the m parameter tells DOS how many sectors of data are to be transferred at one time (the default is 8). This value, if entered, can be between 1 and 8.

The following sample VDISK command installs a 320K RAM disk with 512 byte sectors and 128 directory entries. The VDISK.SYS file is found on the default drive.

`DEVICE = VDISK.SYS 326 512 128`

When you start your computer using DOS 3.1, VDISK displays the following message when it executes:

`VDISK Version 2.0 virtual disk x`

This message means that DOS has encountered the DEVICE = VDISK.SYS command in the CONFIG.SYS file and is trying to execute it to install the RAM disk with the drive letter x.

Files. This command allows you to specify the maximum number of files that can be open at any one time (the default value assigned by DOS is 8).

Format: `FILES = x`

The x can be any number between 8 and 255. The default value is 8, which means that no more than eight files can be open at any one time. What does this mean to you? Any file access, whether it is a read, write, or close, is performed by telling DOS which file such a task is to be performed against.

When a file is opened, DOS reserves a fixed amount of memory called a *control block* to handle I/O for this file. The size of this area depends on the value specified in the FILES = command. A number commonly used for this option is 15. This is especially valid when you are using a program, such as dBASE III, that allows you to have several data files open at any one time.

Creating the CONFIG.SYS File. One of the easiest ways to create a CON-FIG.SYS file is to use the COPY command of DOS. This is accomplished by issuing the COPY CON:CONFIG.SYS command. This command places you in the line-by-line editor of DOS, and you can enter any commands that you want. Be sure, however, that the command is correct before you press the ENTER key, since you cannot go back and correct any errors. When you have finished entering the desired commands, depress the F6 key (a ^Z appears) to indicate to DOS that you have finished.

The following lines represent the commands necessary to create a CON-FIG.SYS file that will set the number of buffers to 20 and the number of files to 15, and that will create a 256k RAM disk with 256 byte sectors and a directory containing 64 entries.

```
COPY CON:CONFIG.SYS
BUFFERS = 20
FILES = 15
DEVICE = VDISK.SYS 256 256 64^Z
```

Chapter Review

Three advanced topics are covered in this chapter: batch file commands, directory commands, and commands used for configuring the system.

Batch files allow you to save DOS commands to a file with a .BAT file extension and then execute those commands by entering the name of the batch file. The commands in the batch file are executed one at a time by DOS as though you were entering them from the keyboard.

There are two types of batch files: the first type is an AUTOEXEC.BAT, and the second type is a file with a .BAT file extension. The major difference between the two types of files is that an AUTOEXEC.BAT file is automatically executed by DOS when the boot process has finished and a regular batch file must be invoked by the name of the file.

Directories and subdirectories are used to divide disk storage space into functional units. This allows you to place all word processing files in one directory, all spreadsheet files in another directory, and all data management files in still another directory. Directories are most appropriate on a hard disk but can be used as easily on diskettes. The major advantage of directories, besides allowing you to group similar files, is that the file number limitations that DOS places on the root directory can be avoided by building a subdirectory.

A number of directory commands are available in DOS. The MKDIR (MD) command allows you to build a directory. The CHDIR (CD) allows you to move in a downward or upward direction from one directory to another. Once all files have been erased from a directory, the RMDIR (RD) command can be used to delete a directory.

The CONFIG.SYS file can be used to configure your system. The CON-FIG.SYS file can contain instructions to DOS on how many files to have open at one time. It can also contain information to DOS about how many disk buffers for receiving disk I/O to have active at any one time. The CON-FIG.SYS file can also contain the VDISK command used to construct a RAM disk. The instructions contained in the CONFIG.SYS file are used by DOS during the boot process to configure the system.

Key Terms and Concepts

batch file	MKDIR (MD)
Break	Path
Buffers	RMDIR (RD)
CHDIR (CD)	REM
CONFIG.SYS	replaceable parameters
COPY CON:	root directory
Country	subdirectory
Device	Tree
directory	VDISK.SYS

Chapter Quiz

Multiple Choice

1. Which of the following statements about batch files is true?
   a. Batch files are automatically executed by DOS.
   b. Batch files contain special instructions in binary for DOS.
   c. DOS automatically searches the root directory of the system disk from which the boot process occurred for an AUTOEXEC.BAT file.
   d. A batch file can only be named AUTOEXEC.BAT.
   e. None of the above statements is true.

2. A batch file cannot contain
   a. Frequently executed DOS commands.
   b. Commands needed upon booting the computer.
   c. Commands that are used to configure the system by setting up disk I/O buffers.
   d. Commands used to start a software package.
   e. All of the above commands can be in a batch file.

3. A root directory is
   a. The first directory created to hold a subdirectory's files.
   b. The first directory that you make on disk.
   c. A directory that has subdirectories beneath it.
   d. The directory that is automatically created by DOS when it initializes a disk.
   e. None of the above statements is true.

4. Which of the following directory commands is used to display your location in a subdirectory?
   a. MD
   b. CD
   c. RD
   d. TREE
   e. None of the above

5. Which command is used to create a RAM disk using the CONFIG.SYS file?
   a. RAMDISK
   b. VDISK
   c. BUFFERS
   d. RAMBUFFR
   e. None of the above

True/False

6. The CONFIG.SYS file is located and the commands in it are executed any time that you start a new program.

7. Batch commands are executed one at a time by DOS.

8. The root directory of a disk is always limited by the number of files that can be stored in it.

9. Most of the DOS commands that deal with disk directories are internal commands.

10. Once the standard drivers have been loaded by DOS, DOS searches the boot disk to see if a CONFIG.SYS file resides on it and finishes the start-up process.

Answers

1. c 2. c 3. d 4. b 5. b 6. f 7. t 8. t 9. t 10. t

Exercises

1. Define or describe each of the following:
   Root directory
   Batch file
   VDISK.SYS

2. The _____ batch file is automatically executed once the boot process has finished.

3. The _____ command is used to build a batch file without invoking a word processor.

4. A batch file can be interrupted by entering the _____ series of keystrokes.

5. The _____ key is depressed once you have finished entering the batch file from DOS.

6. The character that is used to indicate replaceable parameters is _____ .

7. The directory created automatically on any disk device during the format process is called the _____ directory.

8. A double-sided 5.25-inch disk can store a maximum of _____ files without using directories.

9. Directories are created using the _____ DOS command.

10. Directories are erased by using the _____ DOS command.

11. Before a directory can be removed, all files must be removed using the DOS _____ command.

12. The directory command that is part of PC DOS but not MS DOS is the _____ command.

13. A directory is actually viewed by DOS as a _____ of data.

14. When you issue a DIR command, a directory has a _____ entry in place of the file extension and file size entries.

15. The _____ command is used to find out where you are in a series of directories and subdirectories.

16. The file named _____ contains instructions that tell DOS how to configure the system.

17. The _____ command tells DOS how much memory to use for disk I/O operations.

18. The _____ command tells DOS how many files can be open at any one time.

19. The _____ file allows you to build a RAM disk in memory.

20. The file that contains the standard method of accessing devices without going through the ROM BIOS is the _____ file.

Computer Exercises

The following exercises are necessary to create files that are needed later in the text. Any time that you see the ^Z entry you are to depress the F6 function key.

1. If you have a Hercules monochrome graphics board or a Hercules compatible board and want to see graphics when running VP-Planner, create a batch file called RUNVP.BAT using the following steps:

```
COPY CON:RUNVP.BAT
DATE
HGC FULL
VP^Z
```

Before you can invoke the RUNVP.BAT file, you must have copied the HGC.COM file to your VP-Planner disk.

2. On the system disk that you use to boot your computer, place the following CONFIG.SYS file. This diskette with the CONFIG.SYS file should then be used to boot your computer any time that you want to use dBASE III Plus.

```
COPY CON:CONFIG.SYS
FILES = 15
BUFFERS = 20^Z
```

TOOL TWO

WORD PROCESSING WITH WORDPERFECT

Chapter
5

Introduction to
WordPerfect

Chapter Objectives

After completing this chapter, you should be able to:

Understand basic concepts of word processing

Define and discuss common word processing terminology

Discuss the steps involved in using word processing packages

Discuss the various parts of the WordPerfect package

Discuss the parts of the status line of the entry screen

Discuss a number of cursor movement commands

Discuss a number of elementary WordPerfect commands necessary for the novice

Most people must be able to express their thoughts or needs by the written word, at least occasionally. It is usually desirable to clarify what has been committed to paper by refining, rephrasing, and restating. **Word processing** can be defined as the manipulation of text data including creating a document, editing and changing it, storing and retrieving it, and printing it.

Word processing has usually been accomplished using handwritten or typewritten pages, but with either method the process of revising text is difficult and time-consuming. When using a typewriter, for example, you have to retype the entire page even if you want to make only one change. Or if time constraints disallow retyping, you must "cut and paste," using scissors, correction tape, correction fluid, and maybe glue, and then copy the patched document on a copy machine before anything approaching a professional-looking document can be achieved.

Word processing software makes changing a document much easier by automating the process of entering, editing, revising, storing, and printing. One of the most important aspects of computerized word processing (see Figure 5.1) is that you do not have to plan the original document carefully. Rather, you can compose the document while sitting at the keyboard; a rough outline is all that you need at the outset. Composing at the keyboard may require some practice on your part, but you will soon get used to composing documents as you enter them. You may also find that you don't forget to make points that somehow slip your mind when you are handwriting text. You can then print out or review the document and make changes. Thus word processing greatly increases productivity.

Word processing began in the early 1900s with the introduction of the mechanical typewriter. The qwerty keyboard of this device was designed to prevent keys from jamming rather than to increase the speed of data entry by the user. The system was recognized as a vast improvement over handwriting; nonetheless, during the period from 1930 to 1950, various methods of automating the process of producing repetitive documents were attempted.

In the early 1960s IBM introduced the **mag typewriter**, which used a magnetic tape cartridge for sequential access to stored documents. This was hailed as a dramatic advance because it allowed a user not only to store, retrieve, and then type a document but also to make immediate insertions, deletions, and corrections on the original without having to retype the entire document.

Line editors, the original word processors, are software development aids that allow a programmer to make changes in a line of program code. The program must be stored on some type of disk device, and only one line at a time can be changed and formatted in the program because line editors cannot deal with anything larger than one line.

During the late 1960s and early 1970s, many large computer manufacturers decided to enter the word processing market by marketing add-on software packages that could be attached to existing mainframes or by introducing stand-alone word processing machines. Many mainframe word processing packages were too complicated to learn to use without special training, so businesses that originally purchased add-on packages have since shifted to dedicated word processing technology.

Stand-alone word processors are computers whose sole task is word processing. They are fast, easy to use, and extremely flexible in their ability to produce printed output. The screen usually shows exactly what will appear on the printed page. Most mainframe word processing packages required the user to embed strange control codes in the text to perform specific functions—such as centering a line of text, indenting a paragraph, underlining a block of

Figure 5.1
Typical hardware configuration used for word processing (Courtesy of NEC Information Systems, Inc.)

text, or setting margins or tabs—and to see the document as it would appear in print, the user had to print it.

Until the early 1980s, the stand-alone word processor appeared to be the answer to most users' needs. Its major drawback was its high cost: A stand-alone word processing device typically cost $15,000 to $20,000, including computer, monitor, disk drives, printer, and software. Only large organizations could assume such an expense for such a tool. In addition, the units were so large that a significant part of a room had to be reserved for each one. Today's models are less bulky than their predecessors, but they still have limited processing versatility.

During the late 1970s, word processing packages were introduced for microcomputers. The first was developed by Bob Barnaby and Seymour Rubinstein for one of the first microcomputers, the IMSAI. Word processing packages for microcomputers are commonly a composite of mainframe and stand-alone word processing programs with some new additions. Examples include Electric Pencil, WordStar, Samna III, Word, WordPerfect, and Scripsit.

At first, word processing on microcomputers suffered many of the same limitations as mainframe software and so did not threaten the stand-alone word processing market. It was not easy to use, and it was less powerful than the software on the dedicated systems. In recent years, however, microcomputer word processing software has succeeded in closely matching the features provided by manufacturers such as CPT and Wang. Because of the versatility of the software, the user can choose from a wide array of computers and printers to optimize the match of software and hardware to the application.

The lower costs of microcomputer word processing have had an impact on large and small organizations alike. Large businesses have been able to expand the word processing function beyond the "pool" concept, placing personal equipment in the hands of individuals. Small businesses have found that they can afford word processing. And now individuals are finding that they too can afford this powerful tool.

One major difference among microcomputer-based word processing packages is how they handle document size. Some packages limit the size of the document to the amount of available RAM, making ten to sixteen pages the effective maximum. In contrast, what can be referred to as **virtual-file allocation** word processing packages contain only about six to twelve pages of a document in RAM at one time, saving the remainder on disk.

A later trend in microcomputer word processing software was the addition of writing aid programs such as spelling and grammar checkers and thesauruses. Some word processing software comes with these options built in, whereas others make them installable at additional cost. Add-on programs compatible with many word processing packages are also available from third-party vendors.

A still later add-on feature has been desk-top publishing. **Desk-top publishing** gives the user typeset quality such as you see in newspapers and textbooks. It also allows you to combine text with pictures.

One problem that continues to plague vendors of word processing software for microcomputers is that the keyboards on most microcomputers are not arranged very well for the typist. A number of companies now offer a variety of replacement keyboards (see Figure 5.2).

Ever since line editors became available to computer programmers for making on-line changes to programs, people have used the computer for editing functions such as moving, copying, inserting, and deleting text. Changes over the past few years, however, have signaled a development beyond using the computer for mere editing and printing.

Overview of WordPerfect

WordPerfect is judged by many software reviewers to be one of the best word processing packages on the market. It provides you with great flexibility. The WordPerfect software package is composed of the word processor, a merge program, Speller, Thesaurus, and other advanced features.

Word Processing

The word processing portion of WordPerfect provides most of the power needed by a typical person. It allows you to type your text (document) into a file on disk and then later to store the document. You can also make manual corrections of spelling or grammar in the document, rearrange blocks of text or make other changes required by the process known as **revision**, and print your document.

What appears on the screen in WordPerfect is more or less what will appear on the printed page: If you tell WordPerfect to indent a paragraph, the paragraph is indented on the screen; if you want the output to be double-spaced, it is double-spaced on the screen. This feature applies to most commands, except some print commands.

WordPerfect also has the virtual-file feature; so the length of the document is limited only by the size of the file-storage medium in use. WordPerfect requires that only a portion of a long document be in RAM at any one time. Thus, if you have a storage medium capable of holding 1,000 pages of text, you can process a 1,000-page document with WordPerfect. (We'll discuss later why this might not be desirable.)

Merge Feature

The **Merge** feature of WordPerfect allows you to combine (merge) a "boiler plate" or template letter with a list of names and addresses, individualizing the letter for each addressee.

Figure 5.2
Two keyboards that can be used for word processing, replacing the
original keyboard. (Key Tronic KB5151 courtesy of Key Tronic; Computer Smartline Smart-board courtesy of WICO Corporation)

A Merge application requires two types of data: **constant information**
(the unchanging information contained in the template letter) and **variable
data** (consisting of parts that change from one letter to another). Merge must
be told where to find the variable data—in a data file, for example, or entered
from the keyboard—and it must be given a description of the variable data,
including the order of the information within each record of the file. Finally,
Merge must be told where in the template letter to place the variable data.

Speller and Thesaurus

The WordPerfect Speller enables you to proof a document on the screen. This
feature not only finds errors but also helps you correct them. The dictionary
contains over 100,000 words and allows you to add or delete words. Speller
can perform a phonetic analysis of a word and offer its "best guess" about the
correct word needed. In addition to performing the spelling check function,
Speller provides you with a word count.

Thesaurus contains about 10,000 words, among which you can find antonyms and synonyms for many words, thereby helping you find just the
right word. Up to three words and their references are displayed on a screen.

Additional Features

In addition to the preceding features, WordPerfect enables you to manipulate
columns of text, perform math within a document, automatically insert footnotes and endnotes, build a table of contents or an index, and make drawings
within the body of a document.

Starting WordPerfect

The manner in which you start WordPerfect depends on whether you are
using a diskette or hard disk microcomputer.

Diskette Systems

To start WordPerfect on a diskette, you first boot the computer using a DOS
system disk (this is probably the disk containing WordPerfect). You then enter

the date and time, if you want this information to appear in the directory entries of the files you create.

With a diskette system, you usually place your WordPerfect program diskette in drive A and the diskette that is to hold your document in drive B. To get WordPerfect to store files in the diskette in drive B, change the default drive to B and then tell DOS to execute the WordPerfect program in drive A. This is accomplished by entering the following commands:

```
A>B:
B>A:WP
```

The first command (B:) changes the default drive to B. The second command (A:WP) tells DOS to go to drive A and execute the file WP.EXE. WordPerfect now is able to automatically save any files to the diskette in drive B.

Hard Disk Systems

To start WordPerfect on a hard disk system, boot the computer and then tell DOS to activate the directory in which your WordPerfect program and data files reside. This accomplished by using the Change Directory (CD) DOS command (see Chapter 4); that is, if your WordPerfect directory is named WP, enter CD \WP. After you have activated the directory, you can start WordPerfect by entering WP at the DOS prompt. Any files that you create will now be saved to this activated directory.

If you have WordPerfect installed on hard disk and try to start it from diskette by using the diskette-based option discussed above, the program will first start executing from drive A. Once it has started, however, it looks on the hard disk for a directory called WP. If it finds a WP subdirectory containing WordPerfect, it will execute from that directory rather than from the diskette drive from which it was started. This insures the fastest execution speed possible.

Once you issue the WP command to start WordPerfect, the screen depicted in Figure 5.3 is displayed on your monitor.

The Note line indicates on which drive the WordPerfect files are located. If you start WordPerfect from a diskette and the files also reside in a directory called WP on the hard disk, this directory will be displayed instead of drive A. The * Please Wait * message informs you that the required WordPerfect files are being loaded by the computer. If you are using the Training version, an information screen appears (see Figure 5.4).

WordPerfect Screen

Once the WordPerfect files are loaded from disk, the screen depicted in Figure 5.5 appears on your monitor.

The dash in the upper left-hand corner of the screen is the cursor. The **status line** is the single line of information at the bottom of the screen; it is the twenty-fifth line on your screen. In this example, C:\WP\FILENAME indicates the name of the file that is being manipulated. This entry is absent when you are creating a document. It contains the file name only when you are editing an existing text file.

WordPerfect allows you to open two document files at one time and to manipulate both, a feature that will be discussed in detail later. The Doc 1 entry of the status line indicates that the first document is on the screen.

Figure 5.3
The WordPerfect copyright screen.

```
                    ┌─────────────────────────┐
                    │      WordPerfect        │
                    ├─────────────────────────┤
                    │      Version 4.2        │
                    └─────────────────────────┘




            (C)Copyright 1982,1983,1984,1985,1986
                     All Rights Reserved
                   WordPerfect Corporation
                     Orem, Utah  USA


        NOTE:  The WP System is using C:\WP


    * Please Wait *
```

Figure 5.4
Opening screen for the Training version of WordPerfect.

```
              WordPerfect 4.2 -- Training Version
              Copyright 1986 WordPerfect Corporation

This special training version is      The training version of
provided to help you get to know      WordPerfect has been limited in
WordPerfect.  It is protected by      the following ways:
Federal Copyright Law and
international trade agreements.        * Saved documents are limited in
                                         size to about 4000 characters;
You are allowed to copy and use
this software for demonstration       * Printed output occasionally
and training purposes.  You are         contains "*WPC";
not allowed to use copies of the
software, in whole or in part,        * Advanced printing features are
for any other purpose.                  not allowed;

WordPerfect Corporation retains       * LPT1 (PRN) is the only port
title to the software.                  that can be used for printing.


                 Press any key to continue
```

The Pg and Ln entries give the current page number and the line on which the cursor is located. You can see at a glance where you are in a document.

The Pos indicator tells the position of the cursor in a line of text and also provides other information. Notice that the Pos indicator contains the value of 11 even though the cursor appears to be in position 1 on the screen. The position displayed on the screen is the position of the line in which this character will appear on the printed document. The various characteristics of the printed document will be covered later in this chapter.

When the position indicator appears as Pos, the Caps Lock key is off; but if it appears as POS, the Caps Lock Key is on, and only upper-case characters will appear on the screen. The number that follows Pos also informs you of the status of other features. It tells you whether or not the Boldface or Underline features (to be discussed in detail later) are invoked. If you have invoked Boldface, then the number appears in boldface. If Underline is invoked, then the number appears underlined. If both features are on, the number will be boldface underlined.

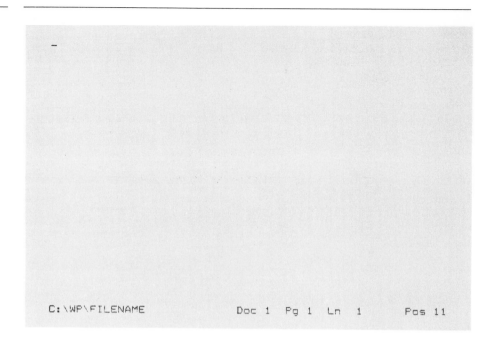

```
 -




















   C:\WP\FILENAME                    Doc 1  Pg 1  Ln  1          Pos 11
```

Text Window

The **text window** is composed of the twenty-four blank lines above the status line. When you first start WordPerfect, these lines are blank. As you enter text, the window fills with characters, from top down. The twenty-four displayable lines in the text window are the maximum amount of text that can be displayed on a standard monitor at any one time.

Entering and Canceling Commands

WordPerfect makes extensive use of the function keys in conjunction with the Ctrl, Shift, and Alt keys to enter commands. To ease the learning process, the WordPerfect Corporation designed a labeled template that fits over the function keys of your keyboard (a copy can be found in the back of this textbook).

To make the program as easy to use as possible, recent modifications to the WordPerfect program enable the user to issue commands in two or more ways. For example, if a typing error should happen to issue an unexpected command that results in the appearance of a "strange" screen or menu on your monitor, you can get out of the difficulty (or any such difficulty) by simply pressing the F1 (Cancel) key.

Help Feature

WordPerfect contains a built-in Help feature that can be invoked by pressing the Help key (F3). You can then get information about a command or function by entering the first letter of the command or by pressing the desired function key. Figure 5.6 depicts the Help screens that appear when the List Files (F5) command is issued.

Operating
WordPerfect

Entering a Document

You can type your document without worrying about the approach of the end of a line (as you would have to on a typewriter), because WordPerfect automatically moves a word that is too long for a line down to the next line via the

Figure 5.6
(a) The first help screen for the List Files (F5) command.
(b) The second help screen for the List Files (F5) command.

```
List Files (File Management)

    Lists all files on a disk or in a directory that match the filename
    template given (the default is *.* which means all files). The free
    disk space and current document size are also shown.

    You can move the block cursor to select any file using the arrow keys,
    Screen up/down, Page up/down or letters. Typing a letter activates the
    name search feature. You can type in some (or all) of a filename and
    the closest match will be found.

    Marking files: Pressing the "*" key marks or unmarks the file you are
    currently on and then moves you to the next entry. The Mark Text key
    will mark/unmark all the files in the current listing. All marked
    files can then be deleted, printed, copied or searched.

    Pressing the Print key will print the directory listing through the
    WordPerfect print queue.

               Type 1 for more help on List Files Options
```

(a)

```
List Files Options

1.   Retrieve: Bring file into WordPerfect.
2.   Delete: Delete all marked files or just the currently selected file.
         Empty directories can also be deleted.
3.   Rename: Change a file's name.
4.   Print: Print all marked files or just the file you are on.
5.   Text In: Retrieve a DOS text file.
6.   Look: Show contents of a file. You can scroll down through the file.
         If the entry is a directory, the files in that directory will be
         listed.
7.   Change Directory: Change default directory or create new directories.
8.   Copy: Copy all marked files or just the currently selected file to
         another disk or directory.
9.   Word Search: You list the word(s) to be found, and all the files which
         contain the word(s) will be shown.
     Ex.:  International   or   "WPCORP word*program";HP,LaserJet
           ; = logical AND      ?  matches one letter
           , = logical OR       *  matches one or more letters
```

(b)

word wrap feature. The only time you have to enter a **hard return** is at the end of a paragraph.

 To practice entering text, type in the two paragraphs that follow. Use the Tab key (located above the Ctrl key) to indent. Don't be concerned if the text on your screen does not look like that below, and don't correct errors that you make. We shall discuss how to delete text and correct errors later.

     A file is a collection of related information in the form of data or of instructions for manipulating that information. In other words, files can be either data files or program files. You keep track of files on a disk by name. Each file name must be unique; if you try to record a file using a name that already exists on the disk, the content of the previous file will be destroyed and replaced with the content of the new file.

     With a few exceptions, you can name your file anything you wish. Disk filenames can be 1 to 8 characters in length and can be followed by a filename extension that is preceded by a period and is 1 to 3 characters in length. For example, a student data file for grades might be called STUDGRAD.TXT.

Saving a Document (File) to Disk

There are two methods of saving a file to disk. The first returns you to the document, and the second enables you to start a new document or return to DOS.

SAVE

The SAVE (F10) command saves (stores) the current document in a file on disk. If the file is new, you are prompted to enter a file name. If the file is an old one that has been retrieved from disk, the name of the file is first displayed with a prompt. For example:

```
Document to be Saved: C:\WP\EXERCISE
```

Notice that the drive name is displayed along with the subdirectory, if any, and the file name. Press the ENTER key. You will now be asked if you want to overwrite the existing file with the new one:

```
Replace C:\WP\EXERCISE?(Y/N)N
```

     Respond with a Y. After the file has been saved, you are returned to the document and can resume editing. This procedure saves any changes that have been made to your document. It is advisable that you do this regularly while working on a file, even though WordPerfect does provide a backup facility (to be discussed later).

EXIT

If you want to save a file and then leave WordPerfect or create or edit another document, press the Exit (F7) key. You will then be asked if you want to save the file, to which you respond Y. After the file has been saved on disk, WordPerfect displays the following prompt:

```
Exit WP? (Y/N)N        (Cancel to return to document)
```

If you respond N, the existing document is erased from RAM, and you receive a blank screen ready for new text; if you answer Y, you are returned to DOS. If you issue the Cancel (F1) command, you are returned to your document.

Save your two-paragraph practice file using the Exit (F7) command and the filename INPUT1; but remain in WordPerfect. After entering the command, you should see a `saving INPUT1` message at the bottom of the screen. You now have a file called INPUT1 on your disk. Be sure to respond N to the prompt to leave WordPerfect.

IMPORTANT When you want to leave WordPerfect, always use the Exit command. Remove the WordPerfect program disk only when the DOS prompt (A>, B>, C>, or D>) appears on the screen. If you remove the program disk while the computer is running, you can destroy the disk.

If you turn off the computer without first properly exiting WordPerfect, unallocated clusters (sectors) are placed on the disk. If you consistently exit WordPerfect improperly, your diskette will eventually fill with these unallocated sectors, and you will receive a disk full error message.

Retrieving the File

To practice viewing a file in various ways, load the file EXERCISE from your disk. Use the Retrieve (Shift + F10) command to load the file. This file contains the Introduction to Word Processing portion of this chapter. You will be using this file to try out the various WordPerfect commands that control the cursor movement.

List Files

What do you do if you forget the name of the file that you want to retrieve? The List Files (F5) command solves this and other problems. The List Files (F5) command allows you to view a directory of all files on disk; find the files that contain a specific word or phrase; read or scan a document; retrieve a document to the screen; delete, rename, print, or copy a file; and retrieve an ASCII file.

When you first issue the List Files (F5) command, WordPerfect prompts you for the name of the disk and subdirectory to be displayed, with the current disk and subdirectory as the default. At this time you can change the directory by pressing the = key and entering the name of a new directory, or you can press the ENTER key to accept the current one. A screen like Figure 5.7 now appears on your monitor.

The top lines of the screen provide the date, time, disk/directory name, size of the document in memory, and amount of space available on disk. The middle portion contains, for each of the various files on disk, the name, size, date, and time of creation. Use the cursor keys to move the bar from one file to the next. The bottom two lines contain a menu of various tasks that can be performed.

To execute a command, move the bar to the file and then select a menu option. The various options are as follows:

Retrieve. This command allows you to issue the Retrieve command from the List Files screen rather than having to return to your document before issuing the command. *Never retrieve any WordPerfect program files*

```
01/01/80  00:01              Directory C:\WP\*.*
Document Size:        0                    Free Disk Space:   4890624

.  <CURRENT>    <DIR>                    ..  <PARENT>    <DIR>
WPPRINTE.FIL   <DIR>   11/28/86 22:53    ADVDOS    .      27265  02/05/87 21:39
APNDANOT.        1061   03/22/87 10:15    APNDANOT. BK!     1063  03/22/87 10:11
APPCADUT.        2821   03/22/87 11:55    BOOKEXER.         8661  01/16/87 19:48
CH7EX5    .       103   01/19/87 15:20    CH7EX5    .BK!     348  01/19/87 15:16
CH7EX6    .       319   01/19/87 15:25    CH7EX6    .BK!     280  01/19/87 14:46
CH9EX1A   .      4257   01/31/87 09:52    CH9NAMES.          784  01/28/87 18:35
CHAP15    .     39524   01/01/80 04:12    CHAP15    .BK!   39524  01/01/80 04:12
CHAP20    .     36267   03/18/87 15:20    CHAP20    .BK!   36266  03/18/87 14:32
CHAP21    .     55615   01/01/90 05:44    CHAP22    .      48193  01/01/80 04:13
CHAP22    .BK!  48193   01/01/80 00:25    CHAP22A   .      48033  03/07/87 00:30
CHAP23    .     37092   01/01/80 04:19    CHAP23    .BK!   37071  01/01/80 00:04
CHAP24    .     36944   01/01/80 00:05    CHAP24    .BK!   36933  01/01/80 00:14
CHAP25    .     40791   01/01/80 04:21    CHAP25    .BK!   40792  01/01/80 00:07
CHAP3CHN.        5268   02/08/87 10:44    CHAP3CHN. BK!     5267  02/08/87 10:02
CHAP4     .     65767   01/19/87 14:29    CHAP4     .BK!   65768  01/15/87 19:52
CHAP4DOS.       53589   03/15/87 12:41    CHAP4DOS. BK!   49914  02/11/87 20:18
CHAP5     .     51956   01/19/87 14:32    CHAP5     .BK!   51931  01/19/87 14:25
CHAP6     .     31769   01/16/87 20:35    CHAP7     .      39970  02/11/87 21:36

1 Retrieve; 2 Delete; 3 Rename; 4 Print; 5 Text In;
6 Look; 7 Change Directory; 8 Copy; 9 Word Search; 0 Exit: 6
```

Figure 5.7
The List Files screen.

(any file that starts with WP or any file with a .COM or .EXE file extension), because you can damage them and ruin your copy of the program.

Delete. This command displays the message Delete filename? Y/N N. If you depress the Y key, the file is deleted; otherwise, it remains on the disk.

Rename. This command allows you to rename the indicated file. Simply enter the new name at the prompt New Name:_.

Print. This command sends the indicated file to the printer.

Text in. This command allows you to load any ASCII (DOS) file at the cursor location.

Look. This command allows you to view a file without loading it into RAM, by displaying it a page at a time to the screen. The message Press any key to continue _ is displayed at the bottom of your screen (and doing so returns you to the file directory). You can use cursor commands to scroll through the file, but you cannot make changes to the file.

Change Dir. This command allows you to access files from another directory or disk. WordPerfect will then use the indicated directory or disk for saving or retrieving files.

Figure 5.8
Various functions of the
numeric key pad that are
supported on IBM and IBM-
compatible computers.

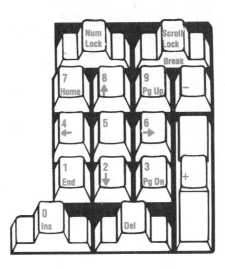

Copy. This command allows you to copy the indicated file to another
file, disk, or directory.

Word Search. This command allows you to display all files in the
current directory that contain a word or phrase that matches a pattern
that you provided.

Moving around the Document

Cursor movement commands move the cursor over the text in the text window. The cursor movement commands of WordPerfect are executed by using
the ten-key numeric keypad (see Figure 5.8).

Pressing the Up-arrow key moves the cursor up one line, and pressing
the Down-arrow key moves the cursor down one line. Other commands are
not quite so obvious, but with a little practice they, too, become almost second
nature.

Cursor Movement Commands

Simple Movement

Up arrow	Moves the cursor up one line
Right arrow	Moves the cursor to the right one position
Left arrow	Moves the cursor to the left one position
Down arrow	Moves the cursor down one line

Horizontal Movement

Ctrl + Right arrow	Moves the cursor to the first character of the next word to the right
Ctrl + Left arrow	Moves the cursor to the first character of the next word to the left
End	Moves the cursor to the end of the line

Home, Right arrow	Moves the cursor to right edge of the current screen
Home, Left arrow	Moves the cursor to the left edge of the current screen
Home, Home, Right arrow	Moves the cursor to the extreme right edge of the document
Home, Home, Left arrow	Moves the cursor to the extreme left edge of the document

Vertical Movement

Home, Home, Up arrow	Moves the cursor to the beginning of the file
Home, Home, Down arrow	Moves the cursor to the end of the file
PgUp	Moves the cursor to the first line of text on the previous page
PgDn	Moves the cursor to the first line of text on the next page
–	Moves the cursor up one screen (24 lines) of text
+	Moves the cursor down one screen (24 lines) of text
Ctrl + Home #	Moves the cursor to the top of the page having the given number

A feature of WordPerfect's cursor movement is that the cursor stays in the same relative position on a line as you move from one line to the next or from one screen to the next. For example, if your cursor is at position 41 and you begin to move the cursor down the page, the cursor stays in position 41. Should the next line be shorter, the cursor moves to the right-most position of that line. If a blank line intervenes (for example, between paragraphs), the cursor moves to position 10 on the blank line (the first position within your document) and upon reaching the next line moves back to position 41.

The Ctrl + Home # command merits some additional discussion. This command positions the cursor at the top of the indicated page number (#). For example, if you want to move the cursor to the top of page 10, you enter the keystrokes Ctrl + Home (whereupon you receive the prompt Go to _); you then enter 10 and press ENTER. After the repositioning message disappears from the top of the screen, you are at the top of page 10.

Page Breaks

WordPerfect allows you to see where a page break will appear when the file is printed. A **soft page break** occurs when one page is full and another page is about to begin. To indicate a soft page break, WordPerfect places a line of dashes (-------) across the screen. This line appears after the 54th line of text on the screen, but it does not become part of your document. It is placed on the screen only to mark the breaks between pages and to aid you in keeping "widow" or "orphan" lines out of your document. A **widow** is the first line of a paragraph that appears alone at the bottom of a page. An **orphan** is the last line of a paragraph that appears alone at the top of a page.

A **hard page break**, caused by entering the command Ctrl + ENTER, becomes part of the document. A hard page break occurs on a page at any place you have issued the Ctrl + Enter command. After this command, the cursor moves to the next page. WordPerfect uses a line of equal signs (= = = = = = = =) across the screen to indicate a hard page break. A hard page break can be deleted from a document by positioning the cursor to the line immediately above the row of equal signs and depressing the Del key.

Reforming a Paragraph

When you edit a document, you delete text from some lines and insert text in others. This deletion and insertion of text gives a line a ragged appearance. WordPerfect automatically issues a reform command to realign the text within the left- and right-hand margins whenever you press an Up or Down cursor key.

Editing Text

After text has been entered, you will want to correct spelling and grammatical errors, delete unwanted words, and smooth punctuation. Many times, however, you will detect typing errors as soon as you make them. WordPerfect, because it combines the input and editing modes, makes it easy for you to correct errors while entering text. You simply move the cursor back to the error and correct it. In contrast, some other word processing packages require you to shift manually from input mode to edit mode.

Editing a document can take place in *real time* or *batch* mode. Real-time editing corrects an error as soon as it occurs; batch-mode editing may involve printing out the document and proofreading for errors. For efficiency, word processing experts recommend that, rather than correcting your errors as they occur, you complete the document and then go back and correct errors—in other words, they recommend using the batch mode. If you're not interested in becoming an expert word processor but simply want to have as error-free a document as possible, go ahead and correct the errors as they occur.

Regardless of which editing method you prefer, you will eventually want to print out the rough draft of your document and mark any errors for correction. You should print out the document rather than proofing it on the screen, because you're still too intimately involved with the work on the screen to see even obvious errors. This also can occur with printed output, but less often because you can take more time and review the document away from the computer.

After you have marked the corrections on the document, it is a fairly easy task to make changes using the following WordPerfect commands: cursor movement commands to move through the document, commands to insert new text into the body of the document, and commands to delete unwanted text.

Inserting Text

With WordPerfect, you can insert new text into a document in two ways: with the insert option (the WordPerfect default) or the typeover option.

Insert Option. The **insert** option of WordPerfect is the default. To insert text into a document, simply place the cursor at the desired location and enter the new characters. These appear to the left of the cursor. Existing text is moved to the right on the same line. If text extends beyond the right-hand margin, it will be reformed as soon as you issue a vertical cursor movement command.

Assume that you want to insert the word *black* before the word *cat* in the sentence, The cat ran up the tree. Since the insert option is the WordPerfect default, position your cursor under the *c* in *cat* and enter the word *black* (followed by a space). Here is the way the screen will look, character by character:

```
The bcat ran up the tree.
The blcat ran up the tree.
The blacat ran up the tree.
The blaccat ran up the tree.
The blackcat ran up the tree.
The black cat ran up the tree.
```

You can see that the existing text is moved to the right as you enter each character. If the text overruns the right-hand margin, remember that it will be reformed when a vertical cursor movement command is used.

ENTER Key and Space Bar in Insert Mode. The ENTER key and the Space Bar both play a role in editing data. When pressed, the ENTER key signals the end of a paragraph by inserting a hard carriage return, and any text to the right of the cursor is moved to the next line. The ENTER key can also be used to insert one blank line—each time it is pressed—between existing lines of text.

The Space Bar can be used to slide existing text to the right in a line. Each time it is pressed, any existing text moves to the right one position.

Typeover Option. Sometimes you want to insert text and don't want any of the existing text to remain on the line. You can accomplish this by pressing the Ins key to turn on the **typeover** option. WordPerfect now displays the message Typeover on the status line where the filename usually appears. You return to the insert option by pressing the Ins key again. What happens if you change the preceding practice sentence from "up the tree" to "down the street"? (You don't want to keep any of the "old" text in this example.) Shown below is the line *before, during,* and *after* you add the new phrase in typeover mode.

Before:

```
The black cat ran up the tree.
```

During:

```
The black cat ran do the tree.
The black cat ran do the tree.
The black cat ran dowthe tree.
The black cat ran downhe tree.
```

After:

```
The black cat ran down the street._
```

The ENTER key inserts blank lines in a document in either mode. Remember, you can delete hard carriage returns by pressing the Del key when the cursor is positioned on a blank line.

You'll quickly become accustomed to the differences in the two modes and begin to favor one over the other. The option that you use most is a matter of personal choice.

Deleting Text

WordPerfect allows you to delete text one character at a time, one word at a time, part of a word at a time, part of a line at a time, a line at a time, and the rest of a page. Look before you delete. WordPerfect is somewhat forgiving with the Delete commands, because deleted text from only the last three delete commands can be restored using the Undelete command. The Undelete feature will be discussed after the Delete commands.

Deleting One Character at a Time. WordPerfect provides two commands for deleting material one character at a time. The Del key deletes the character at the cursor position, and the Backspace key deletes the character to the left of the cursor position.

The following example illustrates the use of the Del key. The cursor is placed under the *t* of *cat*, and the Del key is pressed. At once, only the *ca* remains, and the cursor now appears under the blank between *ca* and *ran*.

Before:

```
The black cat ran down the street.
```

After:

```
The black ca_ran down the street.
```

The second example illustrates the use of the BackSpace key in deleting text. The cursor is positioned under the *t* of *cat*, the Backspace key is pressed. Only the *ct* remains, and the cursor still appears (as before) beneath the *t*.

Before:

```
The black cat ran down the street.
```

After:

```
The black ct ran down the street.
```

All text is moved to the left automatically as characters are deleted.

Role of Codes When Deleting Characters. As mentioned previously, WordPerfect embeds special codes in text to tell the monitor how to display text, to tell the printer how text is to be printed, and to accomplish any number of other special tasks. When you are deleting text one character at a time and one of these special codes is encountered, WordPerfect responds with a message such as

```
Delete [name of code]? (Y/N)N
```

To delete this code, enter a Y. If you want to leave the embedded code, simply press N or ENTER.

Rejoining a Split Paragraph. The Del command can be used to rejoin a split paragraph. A split paragraph occurs when you inadvertently press ENTER and insert one or more hard carriage returns. In the example below, two hard carriage returns are embedded after the word *for*. To delete them requires that you first position the cursor one space to the right of *for* and then press the Del key twice. The paragraph is now rejoined:

Before:

```
    A file is a collection of related information in
the form of data or of instructions for _


manipulating that information. In other words, files
can be either data files or program files. You keep
track of files
```

After:

```
    A file is a collection of related information in
the form of data or of instructions for manipulating
that information. In other words, files can be either
data files or program files. You keep track of files
```

Deleting One Word at a Time. WordPerfect allows you to delete one word at a time. Simply position the cursor beneath any character of a word and press Ctrl + Backspace. This deletes the entire word and any trailing space to the next word. WordPerfect automatically closes up the text in the line.

In the example below, the word *ran* is deleted. The cursor is placed beneath the *r*. The Ctrl + Backspace command is issued. The cursor is now located beneath the *d* of *down*.

Before:

```
The black cat ran down the street.
```

After:

```
The black cat down the street.
```

Deleting Part of a Word. WordPerfect also allows you to delete the right- or left-hand portion of a word. The Home, Del command sequence is used to delete any characters in a word to the right of the cursor. In the example that follows, the characters *ack* of the word *black*, along with the trailing blank, are deleted. The cursor is first placed beneath the *a*, and then the Home, Del command is issued.

Before:

```
The black cat ran down the street.
```

After:

```
The blcat ran down the street.
```

The Home, Backspace command sequence deletes any characters in a word to the left of the cursor. In the example that follows, the characters *bl* of the word *black* are deleted. The cursor is first placed beneath the *a*, and then the Home, Backspace command is issued.

Before:

```
The black cat ran down the street.
```

After:

```
The ack cat ran down the street.
```

Deleting a Line or a Portion of a Line. You use the Ctrl + End command to delete the rest of a line (and any embedded codes) to the right of the cursor or to delete an entire line.

The example that follows illustrates the deletion of text from the cursor position to the end of the line via the Ctrl + End command sequence. The portion of the sentence beginning with the word *ran* will be deleted when the cursor is positioned beneath the *r* and the Ctrl + End command is issued.

Before:

```
The black cat ran down the street.
```

After:

```
The black cat _
```

The Ctrl + End command deletes an entire line of text when the cursor is at the beginning of the line. If the line is part of a paragraph and contains a **soft carriage return** (automatically placed within the document by the word-wrap feature), the text is moved up one line, replacing the deleted line. When a line that contains a hard carriage return (inserted by pressing ENTER) is deleted, a blank line (holding the carriage return) remains. The carriage return itself must be deleted by pressing the Del key.

In the next example, the second line is to be deleted. The cursor must be placed at the beginning of the second line. Then the Ctrl + End command is issued. Only the first and third lines of text remain, and the second line is now blank (containing only the hard carriage return). After pressing the Del key, the text is reformed.

Before:

```
The black cat ran down the street.
It was chased by a big dog.
The cat ran up a tree to escape.
```

After:

```
The black cat ran down the street.
The cat ran up a tree to escape.
```

Deleting to the End of the Page. WordPerfect allows you to delete text from the cursor position to the end of the current page by issuing the Ctrl + PgDn key sequence. Both codes and text are deleted. When the Ctrl + PgDn command is issued, the following message appears on the status line of your screen:

```
Delete Remainder of Page (Y/N)N
```

Enter a Y to delete the text, or if you change your mind, choose the default N by pressing ENTER.

Summary of Delete Commands

Del	Deletes character at cursor
Backspace	Deletes character to left of cursor
Ctrl + Backspace	Deletes the word at the cursor location
Home, Del	Deletes portion of a word from cursor location to end of word
Home, Backspace	Deletes portion of a word from cursor location to the beginning of word
Ctrl + End	Deletes to the end of the line
Ctrl + PgDn	Deletes to the end of the page

Restoring Deleted Text

WordPerfect saves the last three pieces of text that have been deleted. A deletion, in this sense, is any group of characters that is erased between two moves of the cursor. There is no limit to the number of characters in any of these three deletions, and any of the delete commands are included.

When you want to retrieve deleted text, you first move the cursor to the location where you want the text reinserted; then press the F1 (Cancel/Undelete) key to display the retrieve menu:

```
Undelete: 1 Restore; 2 Show Previous Deletion: 0
```

The last piece of text to be deleted is now highlighted in your document at the cursor location. If this is the correct piece of text, press the 1 key; otherwise, press the 2 key to display the previous deleted text, and so on. The 0 cancels the operation.

Remember, the location of your cursor plays an important role in the text restoration process. If you suddenly realize that the cursor is not at the proper location, press the 0 or ENTER key to end this restore session.

Enter the following sentence: *The black cat ran up the street.* Now, delete the word *black* and the word *the.* Position the cursor to the *c* of *cat.* Now press the Cancel/Undelete (F1) key. The undelete menu is displayed:

```
Undelete: 1 Restore; 2 Show Previous Deletion: 0
```

The word *the* (the last word to be deleted) is highlighted. Tell WordPerfect to show the previous deletion by pressing the 2 key. The word *black* (highlighted) now appears in the appropriate location. To restore this word, simply press the 1 key.

Line Spacing

Up to this point we have used only single spacing. For readability, however, you may want to double- or even triple-space a document. WordPerfect provides this ability through the Line (Shift + F8) command. Once you enter this command, the following menu appears in the status line:

```
1 2 Tabs; 3 Margins; 4 Spacing; 5 Hyphenation; 6 Align Char: 0
```

The 4 key indicates the current spacing with a message/prompt such as

```
[Spacing Set]1
```

Enter a new number to change the spacing: 2 for double spacing and 3 for triple spacing. Once you enter the appropriate value and press ENTER, the entire document is reformed to this new spacing—except for areas in which you have previously entered other Spacing commands.

It is important to note that when you issue the Spacing command, a code is embedded within the text at the cursor location to tell WordPerfect how to display and print the text. Only the text following the cursor is affected by the spacing command; if you want the entire document respaced, be sure to position the cursor at the beginning of the document.

Likewise, once the spacing for the entire document has been changed, a portion (for example, a paragraph) can be spaced differently by moving the cursor to the desired paragraph and resetting the spacing. The rest of the document is now reformed to the new spacing. You next position the cursor at the beginning of the next paragraph and issue a spacing command to return to the previous spacing. The document now has the first portion and the last portion with one spacing and the middle portion with another.

 Try the Spacing command on the INPUT1 file that you created earlier. Load it into RAM (making certain that the cursor is at the beginning of the document); then issue the Line (Shift + F8) command and enter a 2 to switch to double spacing. Below is a partial listing of the file after the Spacing command has been executed. The margins may be different from yours.

```
A file is a collection of related information in the

form of data or of instructions for manipulating that

information. In other words, files can be either data

files or program files. You keep track of files on a
```

Issue the Save (F10) command to save the re-formed INPUT1 file.

Printing the Document

You are now ready to print your INPUT1 document. WordPerfect enables you to print a file that resides either in RAM or on disk; you are not required to save the file to disk before you can print. The Print command is evoked by the Shift + F7 keystrokes. Once the Print command has been given, the following menu is displayed:

```
1 Full Text; 2 Page; 3 Options; 4 Printer Control; 5 Type-through; 6 Preview; 0
```

To begin the print operation depress the 1 key. After the `* Please Wait *` message is displayed on the screen, your document will be printed. Notice that the text on your screen has a ragged right-hand margin and that the printed text has a smooth right-hand margin (**right-justification**). This smooth right-hand margin is one of the print defaults of WordPerfect. We'll see later how to turn this off.

A printed document (see Figure 5.9) appears as a result of a number of WordPerfect defaults. Some are the following: all margins are one inch, there are fifty-four printable lines of text per page, all documents are single spaced, and pica pitch (ten characters per inch) is in effect. How to change these print defaults will be discussed in a later chapter

Figure 5.9
WordPerfect preset print default.

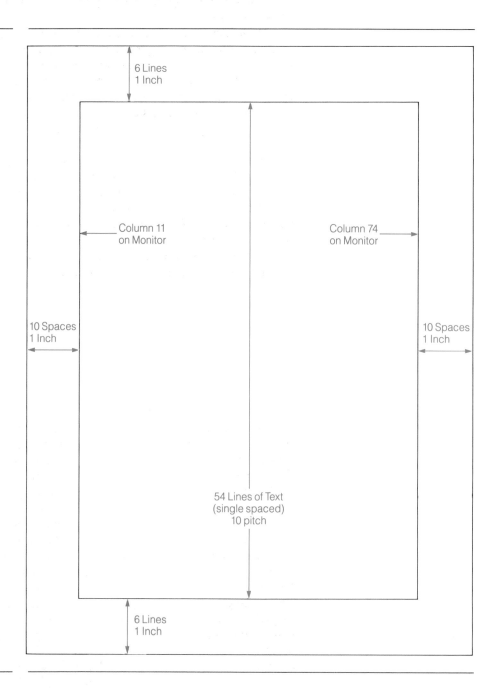

6 Lines
1 Inch

Column 11
on Monitor

Column 74
on Monitor

10 Spaces
1 Inch

10 Spaces
1 Inch

54 Lines of Text
(single spaced)
10 pitch

6 Lines
1 Inch

Chapter Review

Word processing involves entering, saving, changing, and printing documents and written correspondence. Computerized word processing, which greatly eases this process, has undergone a revolution from difficult-to-use programs for mainframe computers, through large, specialized, and expensive dedicated word processing systems using minicomputers, to the inexpensive, adaptable, and easy-to-use word processing software packages for microcomputers that have appeared in the last decade. These systems have made computerized word processing affordable for just about anyone who has the need.

A large number of such packages are on the market. One of the most popular is WordPerfect, which comes with Speller/Thesaurus, Merge, and Math capabilities. These features provide a comprehensive word processing software system.

WordPerfect is a command-driven word processing package. These commands involve using the function keys alone or in conjunction with the Ctrl, Shift, and Alt keys. When you start WordPerfect, you first see a clear screen with a status line, which contains information about the location of the cursor and also provides an area for displaying prompts or menus to the user.

The area above this status line is called the entry window. Twenty-four line "chunks" of text that are being entered or edited are displayed in this window.

Cursor movement commands allow you to move the cursor in the document. The simple, horizontal, and vertical cursor movement commands provide you with flexibility in moving around a document.

Editing is the process of making changes to an existing document. Changes can be made in insert or typeover mode. Insert moves existing text to the right. Typeover simply replaces existing characters with new characters. Other editing commands include commands for deleting text, breaking paragraphs, and changing the line spacing.

Key Terms and Concepts

constant information (Merge)	reform
cursor movement	revision
data entry window	right-justification
dedicated word processor	Samna III
deleting text	soft carriage return
desk-top publishing	soft page break
Electric Pencil	Speller
enter/return	Stand-alone word processor
hard return	status line
hard page break	text window
insert	typeover
line editor	variable data
line spacing	virtual file allocation
logged device	widow
mag typewriter	word processing
Merge	WordPerfect
orphan	word wrap

Chapter Quiz

Multiple Choice

1. Which of the following is not used for word processing?
   a. Line editor
   b. Typewriter
   c. Dedicated word processor
   d. Microcomputer with WordStar
   e. All of these are used for word processing.
   f. None of these is used for word processing.

2. Which of the following statements about WordPerfect is(are) false?
   a. It was originally developed for the CP/M operating system.
   b. It allows a document to be as large as the amount of available RAM.
   c. It is tremendously popular word processing package.
   d. It requires that you store a document before you can print it.
   e. All of the above statements are true.

3. Which of the following statements is false?
   a. WordPerfect is used for entering, editing, and printing documents.
   b. WordPerfect can be used for generating synonyms.
   c. The Merge allows you to personalize a "form" letter.
   d. All of the above statements are true.

4. Select the following WordPerfect command(s) that affect one word at a time:
   a. Left arrow
   b. →
   c. Ctrl + Backspace
   d. Ctrl + End
   e. Ctrl + Right arrow
   f. Ctrl + Left arrow

5. Which of the following is not typically contained on the status line?
   a. file name
   b. page number
   c. amount of available RAM
   d. line number

True/False

6. Word processing can be accomplished with either a typewriter or a computer.

7. When using word processing software, you must first carefully plan how your document is going to appear.

8. WordPerfect limits document size to the amount of available RAM memory.

9. A command-driven word processing package forces you to have the menu on the screen at all times.

10. The Enter/Return key is pressed at the end of each line in a paragraph.

Answers

1. e 2. b&c 3. e 4. c,e,&f 5. c 6. t 7. f 8. f 9. f 10. f

Exercises

1. Define or describe each of the following:
   a. virtual file allocation   e. status line
   b. word wrap   f. page break
   c. hard carriage return

2. List the three types (levels) of computers that have had word processing developed for them.

   a.

   b.

   c.

3. A _line editor_ allows you to change only one line at a time.

4. A computerized word processing software package allows you to create a document without much prior planning. This process is called _Composing_ at the keyboard.

5. _Stand-alone WP_ word processors are minicomputers that perform only word processing.

6. Word processing software for _microcomputers_ has resulted in much lower priced word processing systems.

7. _____ file word processing packages allow you to have a file as large as the amount of available storage on your disk.

8. The feature that automatically moves a word that will not fit on the current line down to the next line is called _Word wrap_.

9. The _Enter_ key is pressed only at the end of a paragraph.

10. The line at the bottom of the data entry window is called the _Status_ line.

11. _Cursor_ movement commands move the cursor over the text.

12. The line of dashes (--------) in a document is called a _soft pagebreak_.

13. A(n) _Widow_ line occurs when the first line of a new paragraph appears by itself at the bottom of the page.

14. A(n) _Orphan_ line occurs when the last line of a paragraph appears by itself at the top of the page.

15. The WordPerfect command _____ is used to reform a paragraph so that it will fit in new margins.

16. The WordPerfect command _CTRl + End_ is used to delete one line of text from a document.

17. The WordPerfect command _Line (Shift + F8)_ is used to change the line spacing in a document.

18. The _Exit (F7)_ command is used to exit WordPerfect properly.

19. WordPerfect uses a line of ___ *= signs* ___ to indicate hard page break.

20. The go to a specific page command is _____ .

Computer Exercises

1. Following is a summary of the cursor movement and scrolling commands covered in this chapter. Load the file called BOOKEXER and practice using these commands with that file.

Cursor Movement Commands

Simple Movement Commands

Up arrow	Moves the cursor up one line
Right arrow	Moves the cursor to the right one position
Left arrow	Moves the cursor to the left one position
Down arrow	Moves the cursor down one line

Horizontal Movement Commands

Ctrl + Right arrow	Moves the cursor to the first character of the next word to the right
Ctrl + Left arrow	Moves the cursor to the first character of the next word to the left
End	Moves the cursor to the end of the line
Home, Right arrow	Moves the cursor to the right edge of the current screen
Home, Left arrow	Moves the cursor to the left edge of the current screen
Home, Home, Right arrow	Moves the cursor to the extreme right edge of the document
Home, Home, Left arrow	Moves the cursor to the extreme left edge of the document

Vertical Movement Commands

Home, Home, Up arrow	Moves the cursor to the beginning of the file
Home, Home, Down arrow	Moves the cursor to the end of the file
PgUp	Moves the cursor to the first line of text on the previous page
PgDn	Moves the cursor to the first line of text on the next page
–	Moves the cursor up one screen (24 lines) of text
+	Moves the cursor down one screen (24 lines) of text

When you have finished experimenting with the commands, change the spacing to double spacing and reform the document. When this is finished, issue a F10 command and save the file.

Other Commands

Tab	Move cursor to the next tab stop.
Save (F10)	Save the file to disk.
Exit (F7)	Leave WordPerfect or clear screen.
Retrieve (Shift + F10)	Retrieve a file from disk for editing.
List Files (F5)	List the files in this directory or on this disk.
Hard Page Break (Ctrl + Enter)	Insert a page break that will always appear at this position.
Typeover (Ins)	Switch between insert or typeover mode.
Undelete/Cancel (F1)	Restore text from the last three delete commands or cancel a command.
Print (Shift + F7)	Direct the output to the printer.

2. Below is a summary of delete commands covered in this chapter.

Summary of Delete Commands

Del	Deletes character at cursor
BackSpace	Deletes character to left of cursor
Ctrl + BackSpace	Deletes the word at the cursor location
Home, Del	Deletes portion of a word from the cursor to the end of the word
Home, BackSpace	Deletes portion of a word from the cursor to the beginning of the word
Ctrl + End	Deletes to the end of the line
Ctrl + PgDn	Deletes to the end of the page

Clear the WordPerfect screen and retrieve the file called EXER1B. Delete the underlined words in the paragraphs below that are found in the file. Correct any spelling errors. Notice that as you make changes to the text it automatically reforms as you use cursor movement commands.

One of the <u>most</u> important aspects of <u>microcomputer</u> computerized word proacessing is that the original document does not not haav to be carefooly planed. Ruther, wurdprocessing allows yu to compose a dokumint wile sitting ut the keyboard.

Line editors were the originul word processors. <u>They wer really grat for secretaries</u> Line editors are software development aids that allow a pgraogrammer to make a change(s) to a line of program code.

From the days that line editurs weere made avaluble to komputer programers for making unline chaunges to pograms, usirs huv been taking adnatage of the kompooter to perform basic editing functions such as <u>making hay while entering data, to perform basic editing functions such moving, copying</u>, inserting, and deleting tixt.

Save the file back to disk using the Save (F10) command.

3. Clear the WordPerfect screen. Enter the following text and save it in a file called CH5EX3. After you have saved the text, print it out. Once the file is saved, review the printout and make any necessary corrections. Insert a hard page break after the first paragraph. Exit WordPerfect.

One major difference among microcomputer-based word processing packages is how they handle document size. Some packages limit the size of the document to the amount of available RAM, making ten to sixteen pages the effective maximum. In contrast, what could be referred to as a "virtual file" allocation word processing packages contain only about six to twelve pages of a document in RAM at one time, saving the remainder on disk.

A later trend in microcomputer word processing software was the introduction of supplementary writing aid programs such as spelling checkers, grammar checkers, and thesauruses. Some word processing software comes with these options built in, while others make them installable at additional cost. Add-on programs compatible with many word processing packages are also available from third-party vendors.

Chapter 6

More on Printing, Saving, and Other WordPerfect Features

Chapter Objectives

After completing this chapter, you should be able to:

Discuss the various ways to save a file

Discuss how WordPerfect creates and saves a file

Discuss the various print options that are available in the print options menu

Discuss the margin commands

Discuss the centering command

Discuss the tab commands

In the last chapter, you were introduced to a number of WordPerfect commands for entering and editing text. This chapter considers how WordPerfect saves files and how it uses various files. In addition, the Print command and its various options are covered in detail. **(If you are using the student version of WordPerfect, Print features marked in this book with an asterisk are not available.)** Other commands include the margin commands, centering, and tabs.

Saving Files

If you remember, WordPerfect has two methods for **saving files**, the first of which involves simply issuing the Save command (F10). This command can be issued any time, and it is especially important that you use the command periodically (every ten minutes or after entering about two pages of text) when you are entering or editing large documents. If you do not save your documents periodically and a power failure occurs, all of your work is lost.

The second way to save a file is to first issue the Exit (F7) command. Then WordPerfect asks whether or not you want to save the file. You might not want to save a ''quick and dirty'' document (such as a letter) to disk, or you may have messed up a document to the point that you do not want to save it. In such a situation, all you have to do is respond N to the prompt; WordPerfect then asks if you want to exit WordPerfect. If you respond with an N, the screen, along with RAM memory is cleared, and you can start a new document.

The reason WordPerfect can exit from a document without affecting the original file is that when you retrieve a document, it is loaded into a temporary file. Thus, when you make changes in the document, you are really entering data and making changes only in that temporary file. When you save your document, this temporary file becomes permanent, replacing the old file on disk.

Backup Feature of WordPerfect

As you might have gleaned from the preceding discussion, saving your file to disk from time to time can save you a tremendous amount of mental distress and work if something goes wrong. WordPerfect provides two *automatic* backup facilities to aid those people who have difficulty in remembering to save documents to disk periodically.

The backup feature of WordPerfect is not a default option. You must specifically tell WordPerfect that you want to use a backup option. Invoking the backup option as well as changing defaults is accomplished by using the WordPerfect **Set-up Menu**.

Set-up Menu

The **Set-up Menu** is accessed by starting WordPerfect (from DOS) with the command WP/S. The /S tells WordPerfect to display the Start-up Menu rather than going directly to a clear screen.

```
                    Set-up Menu

  0 - End Set-up and enter WP

  1 - Set Directories or Drivers for Dictionary and Thesaurus Files
  2 - Set Initial Settings
  3 - Set Screen and Beep Options
  4 - Set Backup Options

  Selection: _

  Press Cancel to ignore changes and return to DOS
```

Figure 6.1
The Initial Settings menu invoked from the Set-up Menu.

```
Change Initial Settings


Press any of the keys listed below to change initial settings


    Key                 Initial Settings


Line Format         Tabs, Margins, Spacing Hyphenation, Align Character

Page Format         Page # Pos, Page Length, Top Margin, Page # Col Pos, W/O

Print Format        Pitch, Font, Lines/Inch, Right Just, Underlining, SF Bin #

Print               Printers, Copies, Binding Width

Date                Date Format

Insert/Typeover     Insert/Typeover Mode

Mark Text           Paragraph Number Definition, Table of Authorities Definition

Footnote            Footnote/Endnote Options

Escape              Set N

Screen              Set Auto-rewrite

Text In/Out         Set Insert Document Summary on Save/Exit



Selection: _



Press Enter to return to the Set-up Menu
```

Option 1 allows you to tell WordPerfect where to find the various dictionary files that it needs for Speller and Thesaurus. If you are using a computer with two disk drives, enter a B: in front of each file. For example, when you are prompted for the location of the first file with LEX.WP, you must change this entry to B:LEX.WP. If you are using a hard disk, make certain that the complete path C:\WP\LEX.WP is entered for each file. If the first file is correct, simply press ENTER until you are returned to the Set-up Menu.

Option 2 allows you to configure WordPerfect to your needs. A menu (see Figure 6.1) with options that you can change is displayed on your screen. Each of the options in bold display can be changed by issuing the appropriate commands (found in Appendix B) from the keyboard. (Do not now make any changes to these initial settings; this textbook assumes that the defaults are in effect.)

Option 3 (see Figure 6.2) allows you to tailor WordPerfect for your monitor. The menu shown below is displayed. You must either make a change or press ENTER to take the existing value of each selection.

Option 4 allows you to select the appropriate backup option. Upon selection of this option, the screen depicted in Figure 6.3 is displayed.

Figure 6.2
Various WordPerfect screen
and audio options available.

```
        Set Screen Options


              Number of rows: 25

              Number of columns: 80

              Hard return displayed as ascii value: 32

              Display filename on status line? (Y/N) Y


        Set Beep Options


              Beep when search fails? (Y/N) N

              Beep on error? (Y/N) N

              Beep on hyphenation? (Y/N) Y
```

Leave the 0 for the timed backup, but enter a Y for the original backup prompt. Now, when you save a file, a backup will be placed in a file called FILENAME.BK!. From the explanation on the screen, you can see that you do *not* want to use one filename for more than one document, even with different extensions, because this would cause the backups of the various documents to be stored in the same backup file.

How WordPerfect Handles Files with the Backup

Let's examine how WordPerfect handles these various files when it is performing tasks for you. The three basic files that WordPerfect deals with are (1) your original document file, which is stored on disk; (2) a backup of the file which it automatically creates (after the first tile is originally created and then edited and saved); and (3) a temporary file that it creates and to which any changes are made.

The Original File

WordPerfect *never* works directly on a file when you are editing, although it does work directly on a file that you are creating. During editing, WordPerfect creates a temporary file which it uses to store the original file, to enter new text, and to edit the text. When you issue a Save command, WordPerfect stores the edited data from the temporary file in the original file that you retrieved from disk when you started this session.

Backup Files

After telling WordPerfect to create **backup files**, you will find files on your disk with the .BK! extension. These are the backup files that were automatically created for you by WordPerfect. The content of the backup file is identical to

Figure 6.3
The backup screen that ex-
plains the various Word-
Perfect backup options.

```
    Set Timed Backup


    To safeguard against losing large amounts of text in the event of a power or

    machine failure, WordPerfect can automatically backup the document on your

    screen at a chosen time interval and to a chosen drive/directory (see Set-up

    in the WordPerfect Installation pamphlet).  REMEMBER--THIS IS ONLY IN CASE OF

    POWER OR MACHINE FAILURE.  WORDPERFECT DELETES THE TIMED BACKUP FILES WHEN YOU

    EXIT NORMALLY FROM WORDPERFECT.  If you want the document saved as a file you

    need to say 'yes' when you exit normally.



    Number of minutes between each backup: 0




    Set Original Backup


    Wordperfect can rename the last copy of a document when a new version of the

    document is saved.  The old copy has the same file name with an extension of

    ".BK!".  Take note that the files named "letter.1" and "letter.2" have the

    same original backup file name of "letter.bk!".  In this case the latest file

    saved will be backed up.



    Backup the original document? (Y/N) N
```

the content of your document before the last save command was executed. So
the automatic backup is always one generation old. At the end of a session,
the backup file is automatically deleted when you save your document and is
replaced with the original file.

Because a backup file is not directly available to WordPerfect, it cannot
be edited or accessed by a Retrieve command. Instead, the backup file can be
copied to another file or renamed, without the .BK! file extension. After that it
can be retrieved with the Retrieve command.

Temporary Files

When you open a file to make changes to an existing document, you are not
really entering data or making changes to that file; instead, WordPerfect is
placing the data and/or copying the data into a **temporary file** in RAM. If there

is not enough room in RAM, the extra text is placed in an overflow file on the WordPerfect disk called {WP}.TV1. This explains why you can totally "botch" your file and Exit, knowing that your original file remains safe and unbotched.

How WordPerfect Handles Files

It is important that you understand exactly how WordPerfect creates and saves a file and then lets you retrieve and edit it. In the discussion that follows, assume that you want to create a file called REPORT.

Creating Files

To create the file called REPORT, you type the text for the document. This text is actually placed in the temporary file in RAM. After you save the file to disk using the name REPORT, the REPORT file appears in the disk directory.

Editing Files

When you retrieve the REPORT file for editing, WordPerfect opens a temporary file in RAM and copies into it the original file from disk. If there is not enough room in RAM, it places any overflow into the {WP}.TV1 file on the WordPerfect disk. Any changes that you now make to the REPORT text are actually made to the temporary file in RAM.

When you finish the session and issue a Save command, the REPORT file on disk becomes the backup file REPORT.BK!, the temporary RAM file becomes the new REPORT file, and both files are saved.

Using Files Subsequently

You now have two files: REPORT, which is the latest version, and REPORT.BK!, which was the version that existed before your latest WordPerfect session.

What happens at your next session? Again, you retrieve REPORT, and a temporary RAM file is created to receive any changes you make. Then, when you save the newly edited file at the end of this session, the (now two-generation-old) REPORT.BK! file is automatically deleted. The old REPORT file becomes the new REPORT.BK! file, and the newly edited RAM file becomes the new REPORT file.

Suppose, though, that you somehow manage to destroy seventy percent of your current document, but you discover this before you issue the Save command. What do you do? Since the destruction has occurred only to the temporary RAM file, not to the original, you simply issue the Exit (F7) command without saving. The original file remains unchanged.

However, suppose that you do not realize before you issue the Save command that you have destroyed seventy percent of the file. Then you open the file later to make additional changes and discover the damage. What do you do then? At this point many people panic and destroy everything; the one thing you do not want to do is issue any type of save command, because that will destroy the only remaining good copy of the file—the .BK! file.

To restore the file, issue the Exit (F7) command but do *not* save the file. You get a clear screen. Now, issue the List Files (F5) command, move the bar to REPORT.BK!, take option 8, and copy the REPORT.BK! to a file called TEST. You can now retrieve TEST.

Figure 6.4

The Reveal Codes screen used to find embedded codes within text.

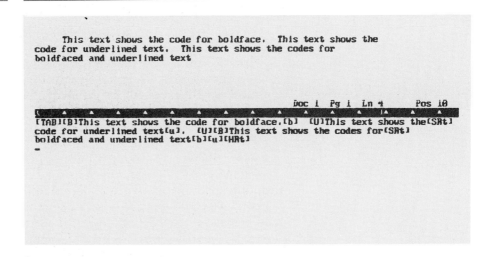

Why not name the REPORT.BK! file REPORT? If you did and you subsequently destroyed this copy of the file, you would no longer have a source of backup. By giving the new copy the name TEST, you still have the file REPORT.BK! as backup if anything happens to the new file.

Even though WordPerfect automatically provides a backup, you should periodically copy important files to another disk. This protects you when you have one of those days when absolutely nothing goes right and you destroy not only your original but also the backup copy in a moment of panic.

When you check to make certain that a disk has enough room for a document, remember that you are possibly dealing with *three* disk files. There must be enough room on the disk for the original file, the temporary file overflow (if needed), and the backup file.

WordPerfect Codes

When you are entering text and issuing commands that tell WordPerfect what to do with that text, WordPerfect is embedding **codes** ("invisible" commands) that tell the monitor how to display text, tell the printer how to print text, or tell WordPerfect the characteristics of the text so that it can properly handle it. These codes are not usually visible to the user but, at times, can make their presence known. For instance, you press the right-pointing arrow to move the cursor from one character to the next, but the cursor does not move. You probably have come across one of these hidden codes. They can be made visible by moving the cursor to the area of the problem and entering the **Reveal Codes command** (Alt + F3). WordPerfect then displays a screen like that in Figure 6.4.

Notice that your screen is divided into two parts. The top portion contains the actual text (three lines above and three lines below the current cursor location); the bottom portion contains the text and any embedded codes. They are separated by the status line and a line of triangles (representing the **tab stops**). The codes are surrounded by brackets [ ].

In this example, soft carriage return [SRt] codes can be seen at the ends of two lines on the bottom portion of the screen. The hard carriage return at the end of the paragraph is visible as [HRt]. Finally, there is a [TAB] code at the beginning of the paragraph, used to mark the paragraph indent command.

You can edit the codes in the lower portion of the Reveal Codes screen just as you would edit regular text. For example, assume that you want to get rid of the [TAB] code. First move the cursor one space to the left of [TAB] and then press the Del key. [TAB] disappears, and that line of text moves flush left. The Reveal Codes screen disappears and you are returned to your text when you press the ENTER key.

The Reveal Codes function provides easy editing of the often rather complex instructions that you have issued. You'll be making extensive use of these codes and, no doubt, of the ability that WordPerfect gives you to edit codes and correct errors.

Printing Files

Chapter 5 showed you how to print a file with what could be termed the "quick and dirty" method, which assumes that fanfold paper is mounted in the printer. However, you may want your output printed on good single-sheet rag bond paper, or you may not want to print the complete document, or you may want to print only "this" page, or you may want to print the page number on every page. The Print (Shift + F7) command enables you to give complete printing instructions to WordPerfect.

When WordPerfect prints a file, the character position that is number ten on the screen automatically becomes position number ten on the paper. Thus WordPerfect automatically gives you a ten-character left-hand margin on the printed output. This margin can be expanded simply by positioning the paper farther to the left in the printer.

After the Print (Shift + F7) command is issued, the print menu appears at the bottom of your screen:

```
1 Full Text; 2 Page; 3 Options; 4 Printer Control; 5 Type-Thru 6 Preview: 0
```

NOTE WordPerfect usually provides the zero (0) entry of a menu as the default. If you press the ENTER key, you are usually returned to the document or to a higher-order menu.

Option 1. This "quick and dirty" method takes note of all print options that you have previously defined and prints the entire document accordingly.

Option 2. Only the page on which the cursor resides is printed.

*Option 3. The Print Options Menu (see Figure 6.5) is displayed. This menu enables you to specify (1) which printer to use and (2) the number of the number of copies you want. The binding width option (3) tells WordPerfect how much space you want it to add (in tenths-of-an-inch) to the left-hand margin for binding the finished document. Any printer changes specified here are temporary and will only affect this print operation.

*Option 4. The Print Control Menu (see Figure 6.6) is displayed. The numeric entries of this menu let you select the printer to be used and the font, number of copies, and binding width. The alphabetic commands control the order and priority of print jobs and let you start and stop a print job.

Option 1 of the Printer Control Menu displays the same menu as option 3 of the Print Menu (see Figure 6.5), but the Print Menu option is temporary whereas this option remains in effect until you exit WordPerfect.

Option 2 of the Printer Control Menu lists the printers for which Word-Perfect has been configured. Up to six printers can be specified, and the "active" printer (the one to which output is directed) is changed with this option. It is important that you have the correct printer specified; otherwise, strange

Figure 6.5
Print Options Menu.

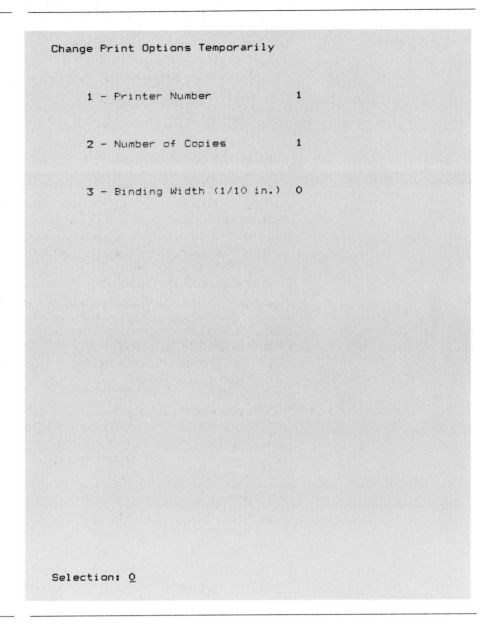

```
Change Print Options Temporarily


    1 - Printer Number          1


    2 - Number of Copies        1


    3 - Binding Width (1/10 in.)  0

















Selection: 0
```

characters will appear on your paper, or the entire document may (maddeningly) be printed with only one line on a sheet of paper.

*Option 3 of the Printer Control Menu enables you to add or change printers. The library of printer drivers must be present on the WordPerfect program drive before new printers can be added.

WordPerfect has its own queuing method for printing files. A **queue** is another word for a waiting line. Many word processing packages can accept printing instructions for only one document at a time, and before instructions for printing another document can be given, the previous document must be finished. WordPerfect creates a queue (waiting line) of documents to be printed. If printing of the current document is not finished, a document for which you issue the Print command is placed at the end of the waiting line. Any documents nearer the front of the line must print before WordPerfect prints the added document.

Figure 6.6
Printer Control Menu.

```
   Printer Control
                                        C - Cancel Print Job(s)

   1 - Select Print Options           D - Display All print Jobs
   2 - Display Printers and Fonts     G - "Go" (Resume Printing)
   3 - Select Printers                P - Print a document
                                       R - Rush a print job

   Selection Q                        S - Stop printing



   Current Job


   Job Number: n/a                     Page Number:  n/a
   Job Status: n/a                     Current Copy: n/a
   Message:     The print queue is empty


   Job List


   Job Document              Destination        Forms and Print Options




   Additional jobs not shown: 0
```

On the Printer Control Menu, the alphabetic commands, the current job information, and the job list either contain information about print jobs or control how jobs in the queue are handled. Novices with WordPerfect usually need to be concerned only about the Stop printing and Resume Printing commands.

Printing multiple files requires that you issue multiple Print commands. For each Print command issued, WordPerfect prompts you for the name of the file and adds that to the queue for later printing. After all of the files that you want to print have been added to the queue, simply press the ENTER key.

When you exit this menu, you are returned to the document rather than to the Print Menu. Returning to the Print Menu requires that you again enter the Print (Shift + F8) command.

After you have made any changes via the print menu at the bottom of the screen (other than issuing a Print command through option 4), simply press the 1 key to print the document. Provided that the changes made were appropriate, your document should print correctly.

Special Text Entry Commands

Center Command

WordPerfect, like most other word processing packages, automatically centers a line of text via the **Center** (Shift + F6) **command**. Assume that you want to center the heading "Section Title" on the screen. Position the cursor to the desired line, enter the Center (Shift + F6) command (the cursor now moves to the center position of the line), enter the text, and press the ENTER key when you are finished. You'll then have a line that looks like this:

```
                          Section Title
```

Boldface Command

The **boldface command** results in dark, heavy print like that appearing here in the words "boldface command." Boldface characters are generated in ways that depend on your printer. Letter-quality printers usually type each letter four times to achieve the dark character; dot matrix printers usually make two, three, or four passes over the text, moving the print head slightly on each pass to fill in the areas between the dots.

Boldfacing is achieved by using the Bold (F6) command: The first F6 command turns the boldface feature on; the second turns it off. To **boldface this text**, enter the Bold (F6) command and type the words **boldface this text**. Then enter another Bold (F6) command to terminate the boldface printing. The text now appears as boldface print on screen.

Underline Command

The **underline command** underscores every character of text as well as the spaces between words.

Letter-quality printers usually print a letter and then its underscore, without moving the print head. Dot matrix printers usually make two passes: the first to print the text and the second to print the underscore.

The type of monitor that you have also determines how these characters are displayed to the screen. A monochrome monitor displays the underline, but a color monitor may show "highlighted" text.

Underlining is achieved by using the Underline (F8) command: The first F8 command turns the underline feature on; the second turns it off. To under-line this text, enter the Underline (F8) command and type the words underline this text. Then enter another Underline (F8) command to terminate the under-lining. The text now appears as underlined print on screen.

Flush Right

The **flush right command** aligns text against the right-hand margin. It can be used to position dates, headings, and other pieces of data against the right margin. The Flush Right (Alt + F6) command, when issued, jumps the cursor to the right-hand margin. Then type the text and press the ENTER key when you are finished. An example of flush right text follows:

```
                          Fred Chalmer's Grocery Store
```

Overstrike

The **overstrike command** allows you to print one character and then print another character on top of it. This enables you to place diacritical marks—accents (´ or `), circumflexes (^), macrons (¯), and tildes (˜), for example—over words.

This command is achieved by pressing the Super/Subscript (Shift + F1) keys and selecting the Overstrike option. Next the backspace key is pressed, and the overstrike character is entered. Although the first of the two characters does not appear on the screen, it will appear on the printout.

Assume that you want to type the Spanish phrase *Voy a pasar un año en España*, which means *I'm going to spend a year in Spain*. First type *Voy a pasar un an*, which takes the cursor one space past the character over which the tilde is to be placed. Then enter the Super/Subscript (Shift + F1) command, select the overstrike option, type the tilde (̃) and the text *o en Espan*, enter the Super/Subscript (Shift + F1), select overstrike, and type ̃a.

Your line on the screen should now look like this: Voy a pasar un a˜o en Espa˜a. The tildes will print over the appropriate *n*'s, even though they are not visible on the screen. To verify that they are present, issue a Reveal Codes command.

Combining Commands

Any of the commands discussed above can be combined. For example, you can have **boldfaced, <u>underlined text</u>** simply by turning both features on before typing the text and both features off at the desired location. The features do not have to be turned on and off in any particular order; just remember to turn them off. If you do forget, it will be quickly obvious.

You may forget which features you have turned on or off. If your text does not appear the way you want it in your document, use the Reveal Codes (Alt + F3) command. Centering codes are represented by [C] and [c], Boldface codes are [B] and [b], and Underline codes are [U] and [u]. Once the beginning code is deleted, the text on your screen returns to normal.

You can also delete codes with other edit commands. When you are deleting one character at a time and come to an embedded code, WordPerfect displays a message on the status line:

```
Delete [Bold]? N
```

The name of the code is contained between brackets, and the default is no.

Date

The **Date command** accesses the system date information that you entered and changes it so that it is presented in a format such as January 7, 1987. This command requires that you enter the system date manually or have a clock/calendar in your computer. The date command, invoked via the Date (Shift + F5) command, displays the following menu:

```
Date: 1 Insert date; 2 Format; 3 Insert Function: 0
```

Option 1 inserts the date at the cursor location. Option 2 allows you to build your own date format scheme and, to facilitate this process, displays the Format menu in Figure 6.7. Using the options provided in the date format menu, you can indicate to WordPerfect exactly how you want the date and time displayed in your document. WordPerfect does, however, place a 29-character limit on the format pattern.

Option 3, the Insert Function, enables you to "date stamp" a document. Then, no matter when you print or retrieve the document, the current date and time will be inserted. For example, if you type a document on January 7, 1989 and then print it two days later, the printout will be dated January 9, 1989.

Figure 6.7
The date format menu.

```
Date Format


    Character    Meaning

        1        Day of the month

        2        Month (number)

        3        Month (word)

        4        Year (all four digits)

        5        Year (last two digits)

        6        Day of the week (word)

        7        Hour (24-hour clock)

        8        Hour (12-hour clock)

        9        Minute

        0        am/pm

        %        Include leading zero for numbers less than
                 10 (must directly precede number)



    Examples:  3 1, 4        = December 25, 1984

               %2/%1/5 (6)   = 01/01/85 (Tuesday)

Date Format: 3 1, 4
```

Margin Commands

The WordPerfect Line Format (Shift + F8) command enables you to reset the right- and left-hand margins. The default margins are a left-hand margin of 10 and a right-hand margin of 74. The values may be 0 through 250. The new margins you set begin at the current cursor location; if the cursor is not at the beginning of a line, a [HRt] is inserted in the text by WordPerfect to place the margins at the beginning of a line. Once you issue the Line Format (Shift + F8) command and choose option 4 from the menu, the following prompt is displayed:

```
[Margin Set] 10 74 to Left = _
```

The first number, 10, is the current setting for the left-hand margin, and the second number, 74, is the current setting for the right-hand margin. To change the left-hand margin, enter a new value and press the ENTER key. A prompt similar to that below will appear.

```
[Margin Set] 10 74 to Left = 10 Right = _
```

 After you enter a new value for the right-hand margin and press the ENTER key, the new margins are in effect. These margins will remain in effect until new ones are entered. To change the margins for another part of your document, position the cursor at the beginning of a new line and repeat the process. Since embedded codes are used, various margins can be used in various parts of the document without interfering with each other.

Assume that the following text (the Input1 file) is part of a document:

```
A file is a collection of related information. This
information can be in the form of data or instructions
for manipulating that information. In other words,
files can be either data files or program files. You
keep track of files on a disk by their names. Each
filename must be unique (different) from any other
filename.
```

Now suppose that you want the left-hand margin to be in column 20, and the right-hand in column 65. You position the cursor to the beginning of the line, issue the Line Format (Shift + F8) command, and set the margins to 20 and 65. You should see the following:

```
A file is a collection of related information.
This information can be in the form of data or
instructions for manipulating that
information. In other words, files can be
either data files or program files. You keep
track of files on a disk by their names. Each
filename must be unique (different) from any
other filename.
```

Indent

From time to time you might want to reset the left-hand margin for only a single paragraph of text. For example, it is a convention to indent a long quote five spaces into the document from the left-hand margin. This is accomplished by using the Left Indent (F4) command. The **Left Indent command** resets the left-hand margin to the next tab stop. The default tab stops occur every five spaces and operate like those on a typewriter. You have already used them in indenting the first line of a paragraph.

Assume that you want to change the left-hand margin for only the following paragraph.

```
A file is a collection of related information. This
information can be in the form of data or instructions for
manipulating that information. In other words, files can be
either data files or program files. You keep track of files
on a disk by their names.
```

To accomplish this you must perform the following tasks: first, position the cursor to the beginning of the line, issue the Left Indent (F4) command, and move the cursor to reform the paragraph.

```
        A file is a collection of related information.
This information can be in the form of data or
instructions for manipulating that information. In
other words, files can be either data files or program
files. You keep track of files on a disk by their
names.
```

The current left-hand margin for the above paragraph is at the second tab location (column 20). To reset the left-hand margin to column 30 (the fourth tab location) requires entering the Left Indent (F4) command four times. The changed text can be seen below:

```
                A file is a collection of related
        information. This information can be in the
        form of data or instructions for manipulating
        that information. In other words, files can
        be either data files or program files. You
        keep track of files on a disk by their names.
```

L/R Indent

Occasionally, you might want to indent both the left- and right-hand margins for a single paragraph. This task involves using the **L/R Indent** (Shift + F4) **command**. Assume that you have the following paragraph:

```
        A file is a collection of related information. This
information can be in the form of data or instructions for
manipulating that information. In other words, files can be
either data files or program files. You keep track of files
on a disk by their names.
```

To indent both margins requires positioning the cursor at the beginning of the first line of the paragraph, issuing the L/R Margin command (Shift + F4) and pressing the cursor key. The finished product can be seen below:

```
        A file is a collection of related
        information. This information can be in the form
        of data or instructions for manipulating that
        information. In other words, files can be either
        data files or program files. You keep track of
        files on a disk by their names.
```

Notice that both the left- and right-hand margins have moved inward five spaces.

Margin Release

The Margin Release (Shift + Tab) command moves the cursor one tab stop to the left each time you issue it; it is used to create a **hanging paragraph**, in which the first line begins at the left margin and the remaining lines are indented. It can even move the cursor beyond the current left-hand margin. Each time the command is issued, a code is inserted at the cursor location. You can issue Margin Release (Shift + Tab) commands until the left-most tab stop is reached. Assume that you want to edit the following paragraph from the Input1 file:

```
        A file is a collection of related information.
This information can be in the form of data or
instructions for manipulating that information. In
other words, files can be either data files or
program files. You keep track of files on a disk by
their names.
```

If you want to create a hanging paragraph (see the following example) in which the first line begins at the current left-hand margin and the remainder of the lines are indented, you must first issue an Indent (F4) command and then issue the Margin Release (Shift + Tab) command. The indent ends when you press the ENTER key.

```
A file is a collection of related information. This
    information can be in the form of data or
    instructions for manipulating that information.
    In other words, files can be either data files
    or program files. You keep track of files on a
    disk by their names.
```

Tabs and Resetting Tabs

The previous chapter mentioned that each of the triangles beneath the status line on the Reveal Codes screen represents a tab stop. The tab stops in WordPerfect work the same way on a typewriter, except that the cursor (rather than the entire carriage) is repositioned to the next tab. The cursor is moved from one tab stop to another by pressing the Tab key.

You may want tab stops at only two or three locations, since one tab stop every five positions may be too many for a particular application. You can clear all tab stops from the ruler line below by entering the Line Format (Shift + F8) command. The menu below is then displayed:

```
    1 2 Tabs; 3 Margins; 4 Spacing; 5 Hyphenation; 6 Align Char: 0
```

Select option 1 or 2. WordPerfect now displays the following information about the current tab stops:

```
L....L....L....L....L....L....L....L....L....L....L....L....L....L....L....
0123456789012345678901234567890123456789012345678901234567890123456789
         20        30        40        50        60        70        8
Delete EOL (Clear tabs); Enter number (set tab); Del (clear tab);
Left; Center; Right; Decimal; .= Dot leader; Press EXIT when done.
```

Each L represents one tab stop on the ruler line, and as you can see, there is one tab stop every five positions. The menu is the two lines at the bottom. The Exit (F7) command is issued when all changes are finished.

To delete all of the tab stops, enter the Delete EOL (Ctrl + End) command. This command is usually executed before the new tab stops are entered, which cuts down on the number of Tab keystrokes. Once the Delete EOL command has been issued, only periods remain in the ruler line. You can now issue the Cancel (F1) command to return to your document, or you can create new tab stops. To create new tabs, simply move the cursor to the appropriate location and type t (tab). Assume that you have set tab stops at positions 15 and 30. Now, if you enter the two columns of text below, you will see the following:

```
Men's               125.00
Women's             35.00
Boy's               5.00
Sports              123.50
```

Notice that the columns are oriented toward alphabetic text; that is, the text aligns at the left-hand side of the column, and the numbers do not align on the decimal points.

Aligning columns of numbers is accomplished by using the **Tab Align** (Ctrl + F6) **command**. This command lines up text or numbers vertically on a character such as a decimal point. Once the tab stops have been set, position the cursor to the first line in the document, issue the Format Line (Shift + F8), and take option 6 (Align Char;). WordPerfect now gives you a prompt:

```
Align char = .
```

The decimal point (period) is the default alignment character (therefore this command is not needed when you want to align numbers). You can change this character as often as you wish. To realign the preceding example, each line has to be entered again: Enter the information at the first tab, then position the cursor to the second tab by issuing the Tab Align (Ctrl + F6) command, and then enter the numeric text.

```
Men's               125.00
Women's              35.00
Boy's                 5.00
Sports              123.50
```

Notice that the numbers align on the decimal point. You also may have noticed that Align char = . appears on your screen as a reminder. Typed text moves to the left until the alignment character is entered (a . in this case) or until the Tab, Tab Align, or ENTER key is pressed. Text typed after the Tab Align command is inserted normally.

Chapter Review

WordPerfect provides you with two ways to save a file to disk: (1) Save the document to disk and return to the same document and (2) issue the Exit command, which allows you to save the document and either exit Word-Perfect or clear RAM and the screen.

When you are editing a file using WordPerfect, you are not dealing directly with that file but rather with a temporary file that WordPerfect has copied from the original file. Temporary files residing in RAM and, if necessary, an overflow file provide for good error handling. If you really mess up the file that you are editing, all that you have to do is issue the Exit (F7) command. The original file remains intact, and the messed-up file is erased.

Another handy feature provided by WordPerfect is the backup file, identified by its .BK! file extension. The backup file holds the contents of the file that existed on disk before the last save was executed. If you mistakenly erase your original file, you can recreate it by using the Copy command contained in the List Files feature.

The Print command (Shift + F7) allows you to print the file currently in memory. This command provides you with tremendous flexibility in how a document is printed. For instance, it allows you to determine which printer to use as well as how many copies of the document to print. You can print only the page where the cursor is located. You also have control over which files to be printed, cancelled, or rushed to printing.

WordPerfect provides the ability to center, boldface, or underline text. A code at the beginning of the text turns the selected feature on, and another code at the end of the text turns it off. Two or more of these codes can be used together.

WordPerfect also provides you with a number of commands that are used for resetting margins. (1) The Format Line (Shift + F8) command enables you to reset both the left- and right-hand margins. (2) The Left Indent (F4) command resets the left-hand margin to the next tab stop only for the current paragraph. (3) The L/R Indent (Shift + F4) indents both the left- and right-hand margins of a paragraph by one tab stop.

A number of ways to position or rearrange data are provided by Word-Perfect. (1) The Center (Shift + F6) command automatically centers any text between the right- and left-hand margins. (2) You can use the Tab (Shift + F8, 1) command to set tab stops in a way that is similar to tab stops on a typewriter or for creating columns of data. (3) Tabs can be set for text or numeric data. (4) The Tab Align (Ctrl + F6) command is used to align the decimal points of numerals.

Key Terms and Concepts

align characters
backup files
boldface command
Center command
codes
Date command
exiting
flush right command
hanging paragraph
Left Indent command
L/R Indent command

margin commands
overstrike command
queue
Reveal Codes command
saving files
Set-up Menu
Tab Align command
tab stops
temporary files
underline command

Chapter Quiz

Multiple Choice

1. The key sequence for the Print command is:
   a. F7
   b. Shift + F7
   c. F10
   d. Shift + F10

2. Which of the following commands is not a save command?
   a. Exit
   b. Save
   c. Terminate
   d. All of the above are save commands.

3. Which of the following is *not* a margin command?
   a. Format Line
   b. Left Indent
   c. Center
   d. L/R Indent
   e. All of the above are margin commands.

4. Which of the following is not an option provided in the print option menu?
   a. Change the printer number.
   b. Print only this page.
   c. Print the entire document.
   d. Change the font.
   e. All of the above are print options.

5. Which of the following commands must be reissued for each paragraph from Line Format when resetting margins?
   a. Center
   b. Left Indent
   c. Tabs
   d. L/R Indent
   e. Margins

True/False

6. If you really mess up a file that you are editing, the safest thing to do is to issue the Exit command.

7. A major problem in using tabs is that the decimal points do *not* easily align in a straight column.

8. A .BK! file can be changed by using the Retrieve command.

9. The printer can be interrupted simply by pressing the Cancel command.

10. The Center command centers text between the left- and right-hand margins.

Answers

1. b   2. c   3. c   4. f   5. b&d   6. t   7. t   8. f   9. f   10. t

Exercises

1. Define or describe each of the following:
   a. temporary files   d. L/R Indent
   b. backup files   e. tab stops
   c. tab align command

2. The _____ command saves the file and exits WordPerfect.

3. The _____ command saves the file and returns you to your document.

4. The _____ command allows you to abandon a file being created or edited.

5. When you are working with large documents, it is a good idea to use the _____ command to avoid retyping them.

6. Special effects commands require you to issue _____ special effects commands.

7. You can interrupt any file that is printing by issuing the _____ command.

8. If you are editing an existing file, the file that you are actually making the changes to is the _____ file in RAM.

9. The _____ command as well as the Print command allows you to initiate the printing of a file.

10. The _____ or _____ command is used for setting the right-hand margin.

11. _____, _____, or _____ command is used for setting the left-hand margin.

12. The _____ command is used to underline text.

13. The _____ command is used to center text.

14. The _____ command is used to clear all tabs from the ruler line.

15. The _____ symbol is used to set a tab.

16. The _____ command is used to move the cursor to the next tab location.

17. The _____ command is to indicate that numeric information is being entered and directs WordPerfect to align the numbers on the decimal point.

18. The _____ command is used to reset the left-hand margin of only one paragraph.

19. Backup files automatically created by WordPerfect have a _____ file extension.

20. Pressing the _____ key cancels any WordPerfect command.

Computer Exercises

Below is a summary of the WordPerfect commands covered in this chapter.

Save (F10)	Save a file to disk.
Exit (F7)	Save a file and either exit or start a new document.
Cancel (F1)	Undelete/Cancel command to restore deleted text or cancel a command.

Reveal Codes (Alt + F5)	Examine embedded codes that appear in a document.
Print (Shift + F7)	Print a document.
Center (Shift + F6)	Center text on a line.
Boldface (F6)	Boldface text.
Underline (F8)	Underline text.
Flush right (Alt + F6)	Right-justify text on a line.
Date (Shift + F6)	Convert the system date to various formats.
Line Format (Shift + F8)	Set margins and tabs.
Indent (F4)	Indent the left-hand margin for a single paragraph.
L/R Indent (Shift + F4)	Indent both the left- and the right-hand margins for a single paragraph.
Margin Release (Shift + Tab)	Create a paragraph with a hanging indent.
Tab Align (Ctrl + F6)	Align numbers by a decimal point or text by any character.

1. Load the BOOKEXER file and then use the Exit command to clear the screen. Remain in WordPerfect.

2. Print out the entire BOOKEXER file, which is on the disk.

3. Print out only page two from the BOOKEXER file.

4. Using the BOOKEXER file, perform the following tasks:
   a. Position the cursor to the beginning of the file. Set the left-hand margin to 15. Set the right-hand margin to 65.
   b. Position the cursor to the second paragraph of page 2. Indent the left-hand margin two tab stops.
   c. Reset the left margin to 10 and the right margin to 74. Reform the document.
   d. Position the cursor to the second paragraph of page 3. Issue a L/R Indent command and reform the paragraph.
   e. Use the Reveal Codes command to examine the beginning of the second paragraph of page 2. Note the [Indent] codes that have been embedded by WordPerfect.

      Set the document for double spacing. Reset the margins to 25 for the left-hand and 60 for the right-hand.

      Use the Exit (F7) command to quit the document. Do not save the file.
   f. Reload the BOOKEXER file. Notice that the file is still in its original condition.

      Position the cursor to the second paragraph. Issue two Indent commands. Notice how the document has changed. Use the Exit to quit the file.

5. Clear the screen. Use the Center command to center the following text on separate lines.

WordPerfect
Using Centering Commands
Using Decimal Tabs

Delete all tab stops from the ruler line. Enter tab stops in columns 25 and 50. Enter the two columns of numbers below using only the Tab command; then, using the Tab Align command, reenter the columns of numeric data. The first column is placed with the decimal in position 25. The second column is placed with the decimal in position 50.

```
     12.76           7.65
    134.50            .531
  1,965.75          10.50
     12.65           9.6
```

Notice how the decimals are now lined up. Save the file under the name CH6EX5.

6. Type the following letter using the conventions that appear below:
   a. Use the Center command to center the text *Acme Computing*.
   b. Use the Flush Right command to enter today's date.
   c. Store the document to a file called CH6EX6.

```
                        Acme Computing

                                           January 15, 1988


Laura Miller
2117 Emerson
Bloomington, Il 61701


Dear Ms. Miller:

Thank you for submitting your application and
resume for the applications programmer/analyst
positions advertised for our data processing
department. After all of the resumes have been
screened we shall contact you about your status.
This process is expected to be completed by
March 25, 1988.

Sincerely yours,



Lucky Luciano
```

7. Enter the following table. Before starting, however, remove all tab stops and create new tab stops at positions 15, 40, 55, and 70. Use the Boldface and Center commands to center the title data, and use the Tab Align command for entering the numeric data. Note how the numbers move to the left until the decimal points are entered and afterward move to the right.

Ed's Microcomputer Shop
Projected Profit Margin

	1	2	3
Sales	325,000.00	347,588.00	371,745.00
Cost	195,000.00	208,553.00	223,047.00
Margin	130,000.00	139,035.00	148,698.00

Save the document to disk using the name `CHGEX7`.

8. Using the steps described at the beginning of this chapter, tell WordPerfect to use the backup file option.

Chapter

7

Special WordPerfect

Print Features

After completing this chapter, you should be able to:

Discuss WordPerfect's special Page Format commands

Discuss WordPerfect's special Print Format commands

Discuss WordPerfect's Print to Disk feature

This chapter introduces you to WordPerfect's format/print features that enable you to accent your document with page headings, footings, and a justified or ragged right-hand margin, among other things.

Page Format

The **Page Format** (Alt + F8) **command** allows you to control the appearance of the text on the printed page. This command embeds codes into the document at the cursor location. After this command has been issued, the Page Format screen appears (see Figure 7.1) on your monitor.

Page Number Position

The **Page Number Position** option provides nine alternatives for positioning page numbers on the output. When you select option 1, the menu depicted in Figure 7.2 appears on your monitor.

Most of these menu selections are self-explanatory, but options 4 and 8 merit discussion. These options, used when you intend to bind the output in pamphlet or booklet form, cause even-numbered page numbers to occur on the left and odd-number page numbers on the right.

When the page number is at the top of the page, it prints on line seven. WordPerfect uses position 10 for the left corner page-number, position 42 for the center, and position 74 for the right corner. After you have made your selection, you return to the Page Format menu.

New Page Number

The **page numbering** of a document is automatically controlled by Word-Perfect. From time to time, however, you may want to alter this automatic numbering. For example, you may be working on a report that is composed of different files—part one residing in a file called REPORT1, say, and part two in REPORT2. Suppose that part one has ten pages, and you want the two parts to be numbered sequentially. The first page of REPORT2 should then be numbered page 11.

Entering a **new page number** is a two-step process: (1) enter the new page number and (2) specify its format. To accomplish this, place the cursor at the beginning of the REPORT2 file, enter the Page Format (Alt + F8) command, and select option 2. At that time the prompt New Page #: _ appears at the bottom of the screen. Enter the new page number, in this case 11. After you press the Enter key, WordPerfect asks you to select **numbering style** with the prompt Numbering Style: 1 Arabic; 2 Roman; 0 (Arabic numbers are 1, 2, 3, and so forth; Roman numerals are i, ii, iii, iv, and so forth.) You can use Roman numerals for paginating the preface, foreword, table of contents, and so on. Select the Arabic option.

As soon as you change the page number, the new number appears on the status line. When you print out REPORT1, its pages will be numbered 1 to 10; then when you print REPORT2, WordPerfect will start the first page of this document with 11 instead of 1. Subsequent pages are numbered consecutively, based on the initial value that you entered.

NOTE When you use page numbers, WordPerfect subtracts two lines from the available 54 lines: one for the page number and one to keep a blank line between the text and the page number line. This leaves you with 52 printable lines (assuming single spacing). The soft page breaks shown on your screen accurately depict where the printed breaks will occur as long as you do not incorporate headers and footers.

Figure 7.1
The Page Format screen contains various options that you can use to format text on a printed page.

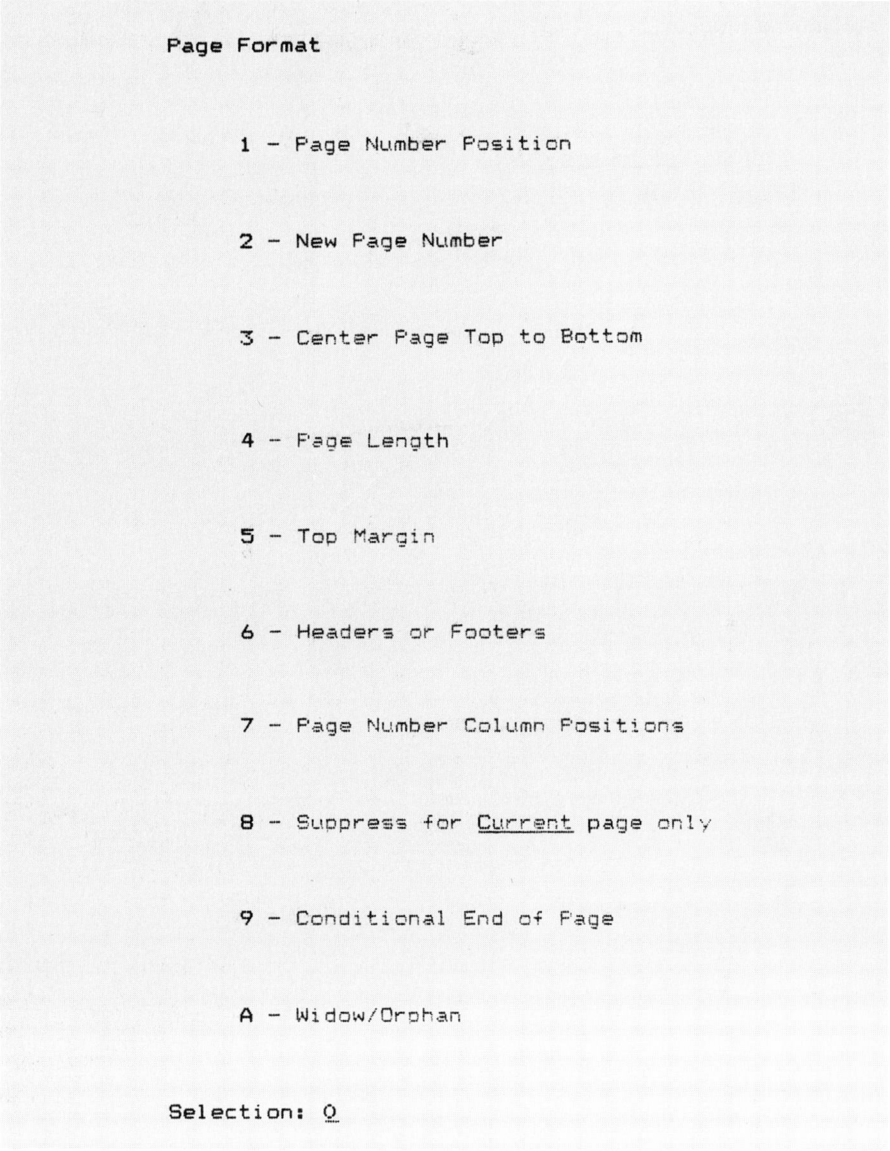

```
        Page Format


            1 - Page Number Position


            2 - New Page Number


            3 - Center Page Top to Bottom


            4 - Page Length


            5 - Top Margin


            6 - Headers or Footers


            7 - Page Number Column Positions


            8 - Suppress for Current page only


            9 - Conditional End of Page


            A - Widow/Orphan


     Selection: 0
```

Center Page Top to Bottom

The **center page** option centers information vertically on the printed page by inserting the same number of blank lines before and after the text. It is used to center short letters, figures, or tables. Make certain that you position the cursor at the beginning of the page before entering this command. Only the page on which the code is embedded is centered.

Page Length

WordPerfect assumes that a standard page (8½ by 11 inches) contains 66 lines, of which 54 contain text. This provides for one-inch (6-line) margins at the top and bottom. Upon selecting the **page length** option, you are shown the menu depicted in Figure 7.3.

Figure 7.2
Page Number Position
screen.

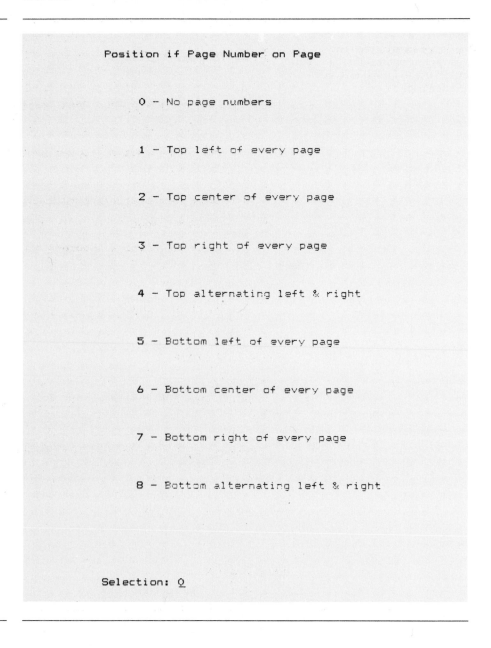

```
          Position if Page Number on Page


              0 - No page numbers


              1 - Top left of every page


              2 - Top center of every page


              3 - Top right of every page


              4 - Top alternating left & right


              5 - Bottom left of every page


              6 - Bottom center of every page


              7 - Bottom right of every page


              8 - Bottom alternating left & right




          Selection: 0
```

If you want to have more printed lines on each page, select option 3. In the figure, the cursor is placed beneath the page length; but since you want to leave this as is, press the Enter key. Now, change the 54 to whatever value you desire. The value that you enter is the number of lines of text that will appear on every page from this point on in your document.

In counting lines of text, WordPerfect includes headers, footnotes, one line of footer text, and page numbers in the total number of text lines.

NOTE The top margin is not affected by this command. It will still continue to occupy the same amount of space (default of one inch).

Top Margin

The default size of the **top margin** is one inch or six lines (twelve half-lines). The Top Margin option of the Page Format command is used to change this

Figure 7.3
Page Length screen.

```
Page Length


    1 - Letter Size Paper: Form Length = 66 lines (11 inches)
        Single Spaced Text lines = 54 (This includes lines
        used for Headers, Footers and/or page numbers.)


    2 - Legal Size Paper:  Form Length = 84 lines (14 inches)
        Single Spaced Text Lines = 72 (This includes lines
        used for Headers, Footers and/or page numbers.)


    3 - Other (Maximum page length = 108 lines.)

Current Settings


    Form Length in Lines (6 per inch): 66


    Number of Single Spaced Text Lines: 54




Selection: 0
```

setting beginning at the cursor location. Since the top margin is not shown on the screen, you must use Reveal Codes (Alt + F3) to see the top margin code.

Upon selecting Top Margin, the prompt Set half-lines (12/inch_ from 12 to _ is displayed at the bottom of the screen. If you want a margin of two-thirds of an inch instead of one-inch, you enter 8 in response to the prompt. This now places the page number on line 5 instead of line 7.

If you are hand-feeding your paper to the printer, WordPerfect assumes that you have not already positioned the paper one inch down from the print head. When printing starts, it will move the paper up one inch.

Headers or Footers

Headers and **Footers** are lines of text that are printed in the top and bottom margins, respectively. You need to enter these commands only once, at the beginning of the file; the headers and/or footers will be repeated as specified.

Figure 7.4
Header/Footer screen.

```
Header/Footer Specification


    Type                           Occurrence

    1 - Header A                   0 - Discontinue

    2 - Header B                   1 - Every Page

    3 - Footer A                   2 - Odd Pages

    4 - Footer B                   3 - Even Pages

                                   4 - Edit



    Selection: 0                   Selection: 0
```

The default is *no* header or footer. To create a header or footer, position the cursor at the top of the page on which you want the header or footer to start. Upon selecting the Headers or Footers option, the screen depicted in Figure 7.4 is displayed on your screen.

You first specify the header or footer you want (the first two options are headers and the second two are footers) and then tell WordPerfect how it is to position the text by selecting from the Occurrence menu. WordPerfect now clears the screen so you can enter the header or footer text. Any special features such as bold, center, underline, or flush right can be used. The status line of the header/footer text-entry screen contains the prompt Press EXIT when done along with the line and position data. When you are finished entering the header or footer, press the Exit (F7) key.

WordPerfect provides control over printing headers and footers. It prints headers beginning with the first text line of the page and automatically subtracts the header lines plus a blank line from the total number of text lines. Therefore, if you have a one-line header, two lines are subtracted from the total lines (assuming the 54 line default); thus 52 text lines are actually printed from your document.

The first line of footer text is printed on the last text line of the page. A blank line is automatically inserted to separate the text from the footer. Any additional footer lines are printed in the bottom margin.

If you discover an error in a header or footer line, move the cursor to the line in the document that holds the [Hdr/Ftr] code. Use the Reveal Codes (Alt + F3) to locate the code, and position your cursor to the right of the code. You are now ready to correct the error. After you issue the Page Format (Alt + F8) command and select the Header/Footer option, the Header/Footer Specification menu is displayed on the screen. Select the appropriate header or footer and take option 4, the Edit command. The footer is now displayed on the header/footer entry screen. Make your changes and save them using the Exit (F7) command.

You may not want to have a header appear on the first page of your document, but you may want the footer to print there. In this case, you must place the header code anywhere after the end of the first line of the first page but before the first line of the second page. The footer must be specified before the last line of the first page. This results in the header line(s) printing at the top of the second page, rather than at the top of the first page.

Figure 7.5
The Page Number Column
Position screen.

```
      Reset Column Position for Page Numbers


      (L = Left Corner,  C = Center, R = Right Corner)



         1 - Set to Initial Settings (In tenths of an inch)
                L=10 C=42 R=74



         2 - Set to Specified Settings


   Current Settings


        L=10 C=42 R=74












      Selection: 0
```

The ^B (Ctrl + B) command sequence is used in the header or footer text line to include the page number in the header or footer. For example, the following sequence would cause WordPerfect to place the header and the appropriate page number at the top of every page of printed text in a file:

```
Four Software Tools Page ^B
```

Placing page numbers in a header or footer now presents a problem: If you previously told WordPerfect to print the page number, it will print every page number twice, once in the header and again at the bottom of each page. You must now tell WordPerfect, via the Format Print (Alt + F8), not to number the pages.

Page Number Column Position

This option allows you to tell WordPerfect the left corner, center, or right corner positions in which to place the page number. This is especially helpful if you are using 12 pitch rather than 10 pitch, because the right-hand margin changes to 89 using 12 pitch (elite) type. When you select this command, the screen depicted in Figure 7.5 is displayed on your screen.

To accept the current settings, press the Enter key. To return the current settings to the WordPerfect defaults, select option 1. To enter your own settings, select option 2 and, using the conventions shown, enter your own.

Suppress for Current Page Only

This option allows you to turn off any page formatting for a page. First position the cursor to the very top of the page and then select this option. The screen depicted in Figure 7.6 is then displayed on your screen.

To suppress more than one of these options, concatenate (join) them with plus (+) signs.

Conditional End of Page

The **conditional end of page** command specifies that if a page break occurs within a certain number of following lines, a hard page break will occur. After entering the command, you must tell WordPerfect how many lines from the cursor location are to be "page-break protected" with the prompt `Number of lines to keep together = _`. This command is useful for protecting text such as tables from being split by page breaks. For example:

```
              Inflation During the 80s

                   1980          9.9%
                   1981          8.5%
                   1982          6.0%
                   1983          4.5%
```

In this example, the cursor is placed at the beginning of the text to be protected. The Page Format (Alt + F8) is issued and the conditional end of page command is selected. A 6 is now entered to tell WordPerfect to protect the next six lines from page breaks. This command gives you better control over how page breaks appear in a document; it can be used any number of times in a document.

Widow/Orphan

A **widow** occurs when only the first line of a paragraph appears at the bottom of a page. An **orphan** occurs when the last line of a paragraph appears at the top of a page. The Widow/Orphan option tells WordPerfect to avoid widow and orphan lines in a document if the cursor is at the beginning, or from the cursor location onward. After entering this command, the `Widow/Orphan Protect? (Y/N): N` prompt appears at the bottom of the screen. Enter Y to start the protection.

You typically use the conditional end of page feature of WordPerfect to protect tables, and you use this option to protect the first and last lines of paragraphs. This option can also be turned on and off within your document any number of times.

*Print Format

The Print Format (Ctrl + F8) command embeds codes that give you control over the appearance of the text on the printed page. After this command has been issued, the screen depicted in Figure 7.7 appears on your monitor.

Pitch

This option enables you to change the **pitch** (the number of characters printed per inch—ten is the default) and the **font** (the style of print used to generate

Figure 7.6
The Suppress Page Format
for *Current* Page Only screen.

```
Suppress Page Format for Current Page Only


To temporarily turn off multiple items, include a "+" between menu entries.

For example 5+6+2 will turn off Header A, Header B, and Page Numbering

for the current page


    1 - Turn off all page numbering, headers and footers


    2 - Turn Page numbering off


    3 - Print page number at bottom center (this page only)


    4 - Turn off all headers and footers


    5 - Turn off Header A


    6 - Turn off Header B


    7 - Turn off Footer A


    8 - Turn off Footer B


Selection(s): 0
```

characters), beginning at the cursor location. The various fonts and pitches that are available for your use are determined by the fonts provided by WordPerfect for the printer you are using.

Some sample pitches and fonts for a Star printer can be seen in Figure 7.8. When you select this option, you first change the pitch, and then you can change the font if you want to. If you are in doubt about which fonts are supported by WordPerfect for your printer, print the PRINTER.TST and PRINTER2.TST files.

When you change the pitch and/or the font, you may be employing larger or smaller characters; as a result, your line of text may no longer fit properly on the line. The solution to this problem is to change the margins at the same place in the document that you enter the pitch or font change.

Proportional Spacing. A popular font that usually requires a letter-quality printer is proportional spacing. **Proportional spacing** inserts increments of

Figure 7.7
The Print Format menu.

```
Print Format


        1 - Pitch                         10

            Font                          1


        2 - Lines per Inch                6


    Right Justification                   On

        3 - Turn off

        4 - Turn on


    Underline Style                       5

        5 - Non-continuous Single

        6 - Non-continuous Double

        7 - Continuous Single

        8 - Continuous Double


        9 - Sheet Feeder Bin Number       1


        A - Insert Printer Command


        B - Line Numbering                Off


    Selection: 0
```

space equally between words in a line. This gives the text a finished, professional appearance similar to that of typesetting. To start proportional spacing, you enter a 13* for most printers.

Lines per Inch

You can change the number of lines printed per vertical inch: The default is six and can be changed to eight.

Care should be exercised in using this command because using both 6 and 8 lines per inch on the same page may cause your printer to think it has reached the end of the page prematurely. This causes problems with page breaks. If you select this option to set 8 lines per inch, you will also want to tell WordPerfect to print more than 54 lines of text per page; for example, you would probably want to set the page length to 84 and the number of text lines to 72.

WordPerfect Printer Test Document

| In this document each word associated with a feature is printed
| with that feature (e.g., bold, superscript, subscript, and
| strikeout). Overstrike is sometimes used to build new characters
| like ≠ ä ˣ. This paragraph is redlined. Redline will print a
| vertical bar or a plus symbol in the left margin.

Text can be centered   or flushed right.
If a feature described does not appear on your printout,
your printer may not have that capability.

Continuous_____Double_underlining   Continuous
Non-Continuous   Double_underlining   style
Continuous   Single underlining   underlines
Non-Continuous   Single underlining   tabs.
WordPerfect has left, center, right, and decimal aligned tabs.
Centered tabs center on the tab stop, not between the margins.
Several types will be demonstrated with dot leaders included.
      Left Aligned   Centered. . . . . Decimal.aligned
      Left   Center $4.50

1   At this point, each line will   within columns. There are two
2   be numbered in the left margin.   types of columns, parallel and
3   The column feature allows text   newspaper. This is an example
4   to be right and left justified   of newspaper columns.
5
6   This document has been printed in 10 pitch with font 1. In the
7   next few lines, pitches and fonts will be changed as specified.
8   If your printer changes pitch when only a font change was
9   specified, your printer may be pitch/font specific, meaning the
10   pitch can only be changed with the font.

      This is 12 pitch in font 1. You may notice that the margins are
      a little different for this block of text. For one-inch margins
      12 pitch, the margins should be set at 12 and 89.

This is 15 pitch in font 1. For one inch-margins 15 pitch, use
15 and 112. This paragraph is also printed in eight lines per
inch. Unless your printer prints 15 pitch in condensed print,
the lines may look too close with this character size.
      This is 10 pitch in font 2.
This is 13* pitch in font 3. Font three is usually a proportionally
spaced font in WordPerfect. Notice the asterisk after the pitch
which specifies PS.
      This is 10 pitch in font 4.
            This is 10 pitch in font 5.
            This is 10 pitch in font 6.
This is 10 pitch in font 7.
This is 10 pitch in font 8.

Advance up and down move text up or down 1/2 line.

Advance down   Text on a regular line   Advance up   Normal

      For More Available Features, Refer To Printer2.tst

                              1

Auto page number is centered above.   This is a footer.

Figure 7.8   Sample fonts supported by WordPerfect.

Right Justification

This option spaces the printed text so that the right-hand margin is either even (right justified) or ragged. The command is embedded at the cursor location. The default is right justification on. Right justification should be on when you are using the proportional spacing font.

Underline Style

This option provides you with four alternatives for presenting underlined text. Continuous single is the default. Monochrome monitors show a true underline on the screen, whereas color monitors show underlined text in a different color.

The single and continuous single options use the single underscore (_), whereas the noncontinuous double and the continuous double options use the double underscore (=) (but single and double underscoring appear the same on the screen). The continuous options underscore blanks, and the noncontinuous methods do not. Samples of the underscore options appear below:

5. Noncontinuous Single

    <u>ID</u>   <u>Name</u>   <u>Hours</u>   <u>Gross Pay</u>

6. Noncontinuous Double

    <u>ID</u>   <u>Name</u>   <u>Hours</u>   <u>Gross Pay</u>

7. Continuous Single

    <u>ID   Name   Hours   Gross Pay</u>

8. Continuous Double

    <u>ID   Name   Hours   Gross Pay</u>

Sheet Feeder Bin Number

Some letter-quality printers have sheet feeders with multiple bins for feeding single sheets of paper to the printer automatically. This allows you to have different sized paper in each bin. The default is 1. If you change the bin number, the printer begins using that bin at the cursor location; therefore, this code must be entered at the beginning of a page.

Insert Printer Command

This option embeds codes at the cursor location that control special functions of a printer or typesetter. As are other codes, they are invisible on the screen. These codes are the decimal equivalents of **escape codes**, sequences of characters that give a command to the printer and can be found in an appendix of your printer manual. Any code less than 32 decimal or greater than 126 must be entered in angle brackets <>.

When this command is invoked, the Cmnd: _ prompt appears at the bottom of the screen. You can now enter, for instance, the command <27>4. This command activates italic print on an Epson FX printer. The <27> repre-

Figure 7.9
The Line Numbering menu

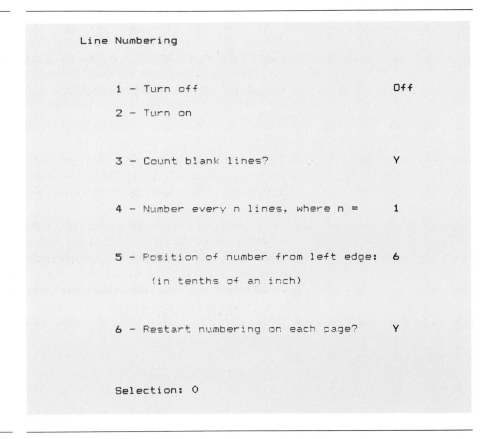

Figure 7.9
The Line Numbering menu

sents the decimal value of the Escape command. Since most printer-oriented commands begin with an Escape, they are referred to as escape codes.

Line Numbering

This option prints line numbers at the beginning of each line of text in your document, starting at the cursor location. When the command is invoked, WordPerfect displays the menu depicted in Figure 7.9 on your screen.

The entries in the right-hand column are the defaults. You can decide whether or not you want to include the blank lines, and you can specify the location of the line number and whether or not to restart the numbering on each page.

*Print to Disk

The **print to disk** feature enables you to direct output that would normally go to the printer to a disk file. The contents of the disk file appear exactly as if it had been printed. To accomplish this, however, you must tell WordPerfect to assume that one of its defined printers is, instead, a disk file. This option is desirable when you wish to send a report without embedded WordPerfect codes over telephone.

Sending output to a disk file requires the following steps: (1) Invoke the Print (Shift + F7) command, (2) select the Printer Control menu (4), (3) take the Select Printers option (3), (4) press the Right or Left arrow key until you reach the printer definition you want to use for print to disk, and (5) press the Enter key. The screen displays the following:

```
Printer Port
     0 - LPT 1    1 - LPT 2    2 - LPT3
     4 - COM 1    5 - COM 2    6 - COM 3    7 - COM 4
     8 - Device or File Pathname
```

You now take option 8 and enter the name of the disk file that is to take the printout. WordPerfect now displays the following:

```
Type of forms
     1 - Continuous
     3 - Sheet Feeder
Selection: 1
```

Press the Enter key to take the default, which is 1. Now issue the Exit (F7) command to leave the Select Printers menu. Now, when you are ready to print, select the number of the printer that you defined to have the disk file output.

WordPerfect also has a default printer number (6) that it reserves for this task. Printer 6 is a DOS Text printer, and sending any files to it will delete all codes except carriage returns and line feeds. The output will be placed in a file called DOS.TXT.

Chapter Review

WordPerfect enables you to control how information will appear on the page and provides flexibility in how the document will be printed. Some of the Page Format commands enable you to control page numbering, centering, length, and the top margin; insert headers and/or footers; insert conditional end of page commands; and control the occurrence of widow and orphan lines.

Other special printing features can be obtained by using the Print Format command. Options from this menu allow you to control the pitch and font, right justification, underlining style, and line numbering.

The last command covered was the print to disk feature of WordPerfect. This feature allows you to specify a receiving file on disk and then direct output to that file by issuing a print command.

Key Terms and Concepts

center page	Page Format command
conditional end of page	page length
escape codes	page numbering
font	page number position
footer	pitch
header	print to disk
new page number	proportional spacing
numbering style	top margin
orphan	widow

Chapter Quiz

Multiple Choice

1. Which is the default for page numbering?
   a. Bottom center of every page
   b. No page numbers
   c. Top alternating left and right
   d. None of the above

2. The key sequence for invoking the Print Format command is
   a. Ctrl + F8
   b. Ctrl + F7
   c. Shift + F8
   d. Ctrl + F8
   e. None of the above

3. Which command is used to avoid widow and orphan lines?
   a. Print Format
   b. Print
   c. Page Format
   d. Conditional end of page
   e. None of the above

4. Which of the following command(s) may not work properly on a dot matrix printer?
   a. Headers or Footers
   b. Widow/orphans
   c. Proportional spacing
   d. Pitch
   e. All will work well.

5. Which command(s) are used to place one or more lines of text at the top and/or bottom of each page?
   a. Conditional Page
   b. Top Margin
   c. Headers/footers
   d. Suppress for current page only

True/False

6. The cursor does not play any role in issuing Print Format and Page Format commands.

7. The default file used for receiving output from the Print command is PRINT.TXT.

8. WordPerfect does not allow you to change a header line; you must first delete the header and then reenter it.

9. WordPerfect allows you to center information both horizontally on a line and vertically on a page.

10. The ^B command is used to include the page number in a header or footer line.

Answers

1. b 2. e 3. c 4. c 5. c 6. f 7. f 8. f 9. t 10. t

Exercises

1. Define or describe each of the following:
   a. font   d. conditional end of page
   b. header line   e. underline style
   c. footer line

2. The _____ key sequence invokes the Page Format command.

3. The _____ key sequence invokes the Print Format command.

4. The default for the number of text lines on a page is _____ lines.

5. The features invoked using Print Format and Page Format commands are not visible until the document is _____ .

6. Many format commands must be entered at the _____ of a document.

7. The number of headers and footers that you can specify is _____ .

8. The top margin, unless otherwise specified, has _____ lines.

9. The default pitch in WordPerfect is _____ CPI.

10. The _____ style of numbering usually appears in a preface.

11. The _____ command allows you to initialize the page counter to a value other than 1 when printing a document.

12. When you specify a page number and print a document, _____ lines of text will print.

13. When you change the page length the _____ remains unchanged.

14. When printing letters or short memos, the _____ command makes the document appear more balanced.

15. When you are printing a large document, the _____ command is useful in starting the page numbering with a value other than 1.

16. Widow and orphan lines can be avoided by using the _____ command.

17. When _____ is used on a header or footer line, it results in page numbers appearing.

18. The column in which the page number is to be printed can be changed by using the _____ command.

19. The _____ command can result in erroneous page breaks.

20. The _____ command allows you to print a document with either a smooth or ragged right-hand margin.

Computer Exercises

Summary of Commands

Page Format (Alt + F8)	This command allows you to determine how information will appear on each page.
Print Format (Ctrl + F8)	This command allows you to determine how information will appear on the printed page.

1. Retrieve the BOOKEXER file. If you move the cursor to examine the file, be sure to move it back to the beginning of the document before starting this exercise.
   a. Tell WordPerfect to center the page number at the bottom of each page. Print the document. Compare this with the printout of this file

from the previous chapter. Notice that there are two fewer lines of text per page.

b. Change the page length to 58. Decrease the top margin by two lines. Print the document and compare this to the previous printout.

c. Turn off page numbering. Create the following header:

BOOKEXER

Tell WordPerfect to print this header at the top of each page. Now create a footer that prints the word Page followed by the page number. Print the document and compare this printout with those from the two previous exercises.

d. At the beginning of the document, tell WordPerfect to turn on widow/orphan protect. Again, print the document.

e. Tell WordPerfect to use 5 as the beginning page number. Print the file. Is the new numbering in effect?

2. Use the Reveal Codes command to examine the codes now embedded at the beginning of your document. Identify which code was used for each task above.

3. Clear the screen and load the CH6EX7 letter. Center this letter vertically on the page and print.

4. Retrieve the CH6EX7 file. Place a conditional end of page to protect the table at the bottom of the page. Print the document.

* 5. Retrieve the BOOKEXER file. Turn off right-justification and print the document using 12 pitch. Change the left-hand margin to 12 and the right-hand margin to 84 and print the document again. Notice that 12 pitch "packs" more text per line.

* 6. Print the BOOKEXER file using the following font specifications. Exit without saving the file to disk, after you have printed the document.
   a. For paragraph 1 of page 1 use font 1 and 12 pitch.
   b. For paragraph 2 of page 1 use font 2 and 10 pitch.
   c. For paragraph 3 of page 1 use font 2 and 12 pitch.
   d. For paragraph 4 of page 1 use font 3 and 10 pitch.
   e. For paragraph 5 of page 1 use font 3 and 12 pitch.
   f. For paragraph 6 of page 1 use font 4 and 10 pitch.
   g. For paragraph 1 of page 2 use font 4 and 12 pitch.
   h. For paragraph 2 of page 2 use font 7 and 10 pitch.
   i. For paragraph 3 of page 2 use font 7 and 12 pitch.
   j. For paragraph 4 of page 2 use font 8 and 10 pitch.
   k. For paragraph 5 of page 2 use font 8 and 12 pitch.

* 7. Print the BOOKEXER using 15 pitch at 8 lines per inch. The page length must be set to 72, text lines to 66, left-hand margin to 15, and right-hand margin to 100. Print and then save the document.

8. Use the Reveal Codes command to display the codes from exercise 1e. Delete these codes. Your text should now appear as the original.

9. Print out the BOOKEXER document with each line numbered. Numbering should start over on each page.

10. Print the BOOKEXER to a file called CH10EX10. Exit WP and use the Pipe command to view the CH10EX10 file. It should have the text from the BOOKEXER file.

*These exercises cannot be done with the educational version of WordPerfect.

Chapter
8

WordPerfect Block
and Find

Chapter Objectives   *After completing this chapter, you should be able to:*

Discuss how to handle blocks of text using bold, underline, center, redline and strikeout, cut, and copy commands

Discuss how various previously covered commands can be used with marked blocks of text

Discuss some new commands that require the block feature

Discuss the Move command

Discuss the Search command

Discuss the Replace command

Discuss the split-screen feature

Discuss the rectangle feature and related commands

Discuss what actions to take when you receive a disk full error message.

Discuss the line draw capability of WordPerfect

This chapter introduces you to the block commands, the Search command, the split-screen feature, the line draw feature, and the rectangle feature of WordPerfect. The Block command enables you to mark off parts of a document and perform various tasks with them, such as move them to another position within the document, perform special formatting, and cut or copy the marked text. The Search command allows you to locate text and replace it with other text.

Block Command

Using the Block command involves first marking the text be included in the block and then issuing a command to tell WordPerfect what to do with the marked text.

Marking a Block of Text

A **block** of text can be any group of characters, words, sentences, paragraphs, or pages of text. Before WordPerfect can execute command against a block of text, it must know what is contained in the block.

To mark a block, position the cursor at the beginning of the text to be included in the block and issue the Block (Alt + F4) command. The message Block on then flashes on and off in the status line. Now move the cursor to the end of the block. As you move the cursor over the text to be included in the block, the text changes to reverse video on your screen (a process many times referred to as painting).

You can use any of the pointer positioning commands to enlarge the block (or to make it smaller). For instance, the Right arrow extends the block one character at a time to the right, and the Down arrow extends the block one line at a time. After you have defined the block, you can issue any command that can use blocked text (see Figure 8.1).

Using Blocks with Previously Covered WordPerfect Commands

A number of commands that have been covered previously can now be used with Block, including boldface, underline, centering, overstrike and redline, and case change.

Bolding, Underlining, and Centering Blocks. Have you ever forgotten to press the Bold command before you typed the text? You no doubt found that inserting the Bold command after the text was entered had no effect whatsoever. Getting the text boldfaced seemed to require you to retype the text. But there is an easier way: Mark the text as a block and then issue the Bold command.

For example, how would you boldface the words *Stand alone word processors* in the following example?

```
     Stand alone word processors are computers whose
sole task is word processing.
```

You first have to position the cursor under the *S* of *Stand*. Now, issue the Block (Alt + F4) command (Block on now flashes on the status line), paint to the right four words, and issue the Bold (F6) command. The text now appears as follows:

Figure 8.1
WordPerfect commands with
which you can use the block
commands.

Bold	Replace
Center	Save
Delete	Sort
Flush Right	Spell
Mark Text	Super/Subscript
Move	Underline
Print	Upper/Lower Case (Switch key)

        Stand alone word processors are computers whose
sole task is word processing.

This same sequence of steps is used for underlining or centering text. If you want to both boldface and underline some text, you must first mark the text and issue one of the special feature commands. Then you must issue two Go to (Ctrl + Home) commands to rehighlight the block of text before you issue the command for the other feature.

If you want to center a block of text, WordPerfect displays the message [Center]? (Y/N) N; simply press Y to **center block**.

Deleting Blocks of Text. Up to now you have been able to delete text only in a rather rigid format. For instance, you can delete a character, part of a word, a word, part of a line, an entire line, or to the end of the page. With the Block command, however, you can delete any marked text by pressing the Del key. Suppose that you want to delete the last sentence in this paragraph:

        In the early 1960s IBM introduced the mag
typewriter, which used a magnetic tape cartridge for
sequential access to documents that had been stored
on the tape. This was hailed as a dramatic advance
because it allowed a user not only to store and then
retrieve a document, but also to make immediate
insertions, deletions, and corrections on the
original without having to change the entire document
manually.

Performing this task requires you to position the cursor at the *T* of the word *This*, invoke the Block (Alt + F4) command, paint the text to be deleted, press the Del key, and respond Y to the prompt [Delete block]? (Y/N) N. You should see the following text:

        In the early 1960s IBM introduced the mag
typewriter, which used a magnetic tape cartridge for
sequential access to documents that had been stored
on the tape.

Save Block. Using the Save (F10) command with a block saves it to a separate file on disk. It is convenient to place an often used portion of a document on disk and retrieve it whenever it is needed.

Saving a block requires the following steps: (1) marking the text via the Block command; (2) issuing the Save (F10) command, at which time Word-Perfect responds with the `Block Name:_` prompt; (3) enter the name you want for the file and press the Enter key; (if the file already exists, the message `Replace (filename)? (Y/N) N` appears); and (4) issue another <u>Block (Alt + F4)</u> command to turn off the block feature.

You may want to add a block of text to the end of a disk file via the Append feature of WordPerfect. Issue the <u>Move (Ctrl + F4)</u> command after the text has been marked and select the Append option. When WordPerfect displays the `Append to: _` prompt, enter the name of the file to which you want the text added and press the Enter key. The text is then added to the end of the specified file.

Print Block. The **Print Block** command lets you print a portion of a document that is longer than the current page, while not printing the entire document. To print a block of text, mark the block and then issue the Print (Shift + F7) command. WordPerfect now displays the prompt `Print Block? (Y/N) N`. Press the Y key to start printing. Turn off the block feature with another Block (Alt + F4) command.

New WordPerfect Commands that use the Block Feature

Move. This **Move** command provides you with great flexibility in cutting or copying chunks of text and moving them from one place in a document to another. It also allows you to delete the original text—which can consist of a sentence, paragraph, page, or block of text. Using the Move feature of WordPerfect is a two-step process that first requires you to indicate which text is to be moved or copied and then to indicate where the text is to be copied or moved. The Move command, invoked by pressing the Ctrl + F4 keys, displays the following menu (only the Move part is of interest now):

```
Move 1 Sentence; 2 Paragraph; 3 Page;Retrieve 4 Column; 5 Text; 6 Rectangle:0
```

The Move (Ctrl + F4) command executes at the current cursor location for a sentence, paragraph, or page of text. After you have indicated to WordPerfect the amount of text that you want moved by pressing the appropriate key, the affected text changes to reverse video on your screen and the following menu is displayed:

```
1 Cut; 2 Copy; 3 Delete: 0
```

The **cut** option removes the highlighted text from your document and places it in a temporary file.

The **copy** option leaves the original text in your document but also copies it to a temporary file. The highlighted text in the document returns to regular video and is left unchanged. The copy feature works much as a duplicating machine might, leaving the original intact.

The **delete** option removes the marked text from your document without saving it to a temporary file (this text can, however, be restored via the Undelete command).

After you have indicated a cut or copy operation to WordPerfect, you must now position the cursor to the place in your document that you want to receive the block. You again issue the Move (Ctrl + F4) command and this time use the Retrieve portion of the menu. To perform a regular retrieve, press the 5 key, and the marked text is copied, beginning at the cursor.

The following example shows how the Move command (cut option) is used to move the second sentence to a new position behind the third sentence. The original order is as follows:

```
     This is the first sentence. This is the second
sentence. This is the third sentence. This is the
fourth sentence.
```

To mark the second sentence, position the cursor anywhere in that sentence. Enter the Move (Ctrl + F4) command, and the Move menu is displayed at the bottom of your screen. Select the *Sentence* option (placing the sentence in reverse video), and then take the *Cut* option. The highlighted text is now deleted from the paragraph and saved to a temporary file, and WordPerfect knows what type of operation is to be performed. After reforming, the text appears like that below.

```
     This is the first sentence. This is the third
sentence. This is the fourth sentence.
```

You now move the cursor to the *T* at the beginning of the fourth sentence. Issue the Move (Ctrl + F4) command and select the *Text* option from the menu. The text is now moved and should look like the following:

```
     This is the first sentence. This is the third
sentence. This is the second sentence. This is the
fourth sentence.
```

The next example shows the use of the *Copy* option of the move feature. The same sequence of commands are executed except that the *Copy* option instead of *Cut* is selected.

Before:

```
     This is the first sentence. This is the second
sentence. This is the third sentence. This is the
fourth sentence.
```

After:

```
This is the first sentence. This is the second
sentence. This is the third sentence. This is the
second sentence. This is the fourth sentence.
```

Rectangular or Columnar Blocks. You may want to move a **rectangular** or columnar **block** of text in a highlighted area, rather than the entire text. The regular block moves transfer all of the text, from the beginning of the marked area to the end of the marked area, no matter how wide the line or lines happen to be. For rectangular blocks, however, you specify the width of the text block to be moved. The beginning and ending locations of the cursor determine the upper left-hand and lower right-hand corners of the rectangular block of text.

Position the cursor at the upper left-hand corner of the text to be moved. Enter the Block (Alt + F4) command, paint the text (the entire lines are painted), and place the cursor in the lower right-hand corner. Even though the entire text looks as though it is painted, subsequent commands will reduce the area.

After you have painted the block, issue the Move (Ctrl + F4) command and select the Cut/Copy Rectangle option from the following menu:

```
1 Cut Block; 2 Copy Block; 3 Append; 4 Cut/Copy Column; 5 Cut/Copy Rectangle:0
```

The area of text denoted by the original upper left-hand and lower right-hand cursor positions is now highlighted on the screen, and the following menu is displayed.

```
1 Cut; 2 Copy; 3 Delete: 0
```

Only the highlighted text is affected by your choice of operation. All text outside the highlighted area remains unchanged. When you retrieve the text, be sure to use the Rectangle option; otherwise, the text from the last *regular* Move command will be restored to the cursor location rather than the text from the rectangle just marked. Also make certain that there is enough room in the area that is to receive the block. If there is not enough room, existing text will be moved to the right, and the document will look like a mess.

 In the next example, assume that Col1 is to be moved to the right of Col 2:

```
Col1        Col2
Col1        Col2
Col1        Col2
Col1        Col2
```

In this case, the cursor must be moved under the C of the first Col1, and the Block (Alt + F4) command is issued. The blocked area is now extended to include the last Col1. Notice that all of the lines in both columns appear in reverse video. Issue the Move (Ctrl + F4) command, and select the Cut/Copy Rectangle option. Now only Col1 is highlighted. Tell WordPerfect to execute a Cut command. Your screen will show the following:

```
Col2
Col2
Col2
Col2
```

Now position your cursor at the location that you want to place the text— in this case, to the right of Col2. Enter the Move (Ctrl + F4) command and select the Rectangle option. The following will then appear on your screen:

```
Col2        Col1
Col2        Col1
Col2        Col1
Col2        Col1
```

Redline and Strikeout. These options provide the ability to mark text within a document to draw attention to added text or to text that you think should be deleted. The **redline** feature marks a line(s) of text by placing a vertical bar in the left margin next to any indicated text. You invoke the redline feature by issuing the Mark Text (Alt + F5) command. WordPerfect displays the following menu:

```
1 Outline; 2 Para #; 3 Redline; 4 Short Form; 5 Index; 6 Other Options: 0
```

Now select the Redline option by pressing the 3 key. A + sign is displayed on the status line to the right of the position number, and you can now type the text that you want to be redlined. When you are finished, again enter the Mark Text (Alt + F5) command and press 3; then move the cursor off the redlined text. The + sign disappears.

```
¦        This is an example of a text residing in a
¦ paragraph that has been marked via the redline (Alt
¦ + F5) command.
```

The **strikeout** command causes a dash (–) to be printed over every character in a portion of text, indicating to someone that the marked text is not supposed to be there.

To use the strikeout command, invoke the Block (Alt + F4) command, paint the desired text, and then issue the Mark Text (Alt + F5) command and take the Strikeout (4) option. Although the dashes do not appear on the screen, they can be seen to the right of the cursor position indicator as you move the cursor through the marked text.

```
Text marked via the strikeout command.
```

To remove redline marks or delete all strikeout text, issue the Mark Text (Alt + F5), take the Remove (4) option, and answer Y to the prompt.

Superscript/Subscript. The **superscript** or **subscript** options allow you to print a character or a block of characters $\frac{1}{3}$ to $\frac{1}{2}$ line above (superscript) or below (subscript) the current line of text. This WordPerfect feature is useful in both the scientific and the academic environments.

These commands may not be supported (that is, the output cannot always be predicted) on dot matrix printers, but they are usually supported by most letter-quality printers. The Super/Subscript (Shift + F1) command displays the menu:

```
1 Superscript; 2 Subscript; 3 Overstrike; 4 Adv Up; 5 Adv Dn; 6 Adv Ln: 0
```

To subscript or superscript a character, simply make the appropriate selection and enter the character. If you want to subscript or superscript more than one character, first mark the text with the Block (Alt + F4) command; then issue the Super/Subscript (Shift + F1) command and tell WordPerfect whether or not the text is a Superscript or Subscript.

Superscripts and subscripts do not appear on the screen. To see how the text will print, you must issue the Reveal Codes (Alt + F3) command.

Simple subscript: A_2

Simple superscript: 2^2

Multiple subscript: $Chromium_{Dioxide}$

Multiple superscript: A^{23}

Case Conversion. Have you ever entered text only to find later that the characters are all in upper case? The only way to correct this has been to erase the text and retype it. WordPerfect has a **case conversion** feature that allows you to correct such errors. For example, suppose that the following text appears in your document:

    STAND ALONE WORD PROCESSORS ARE COMPUTERS WHOSE
SOLE TASK IS WORD PROCESSING.

To convert the text to lower case, use the Switch (Shift + F3) command, which displays the following menu:

Block: 1 Uppercase; 2 Lowercase: 0

The steps involved in switching the case of the characters are (1) block the text that you want to change (beginning with the *T* of *STAND*), (2) issue the Switch (Shift + F3) command, (3) select the appropriate option (lowercase), and (4) turn off the Block command with another Block (Alt + F4). The text should now appear like the following:

    Stand alone word processors are computers whose
sole task is word processing.

Disk Full Errors

If you fail to check the status of your diskette, you may receive a Disk full – Strike any key to continue message when you try to save a file. This means that there is not enough disk space for both the text and the changes that you've made to the file. If you leave WordPerfect at this point, you lose the entire document and any editing that you have done. The most important thing to remember is not to panic!

If you are using the backup option of WordPerfect, remember that not only is your original file on disk, but the BK! backup file is on disk as well. Use the List Files (F5) command and delete any unwanted files from your disk to make room (BK! files are likely candidates). Then try the Save command again.

Unless your document is extremely large, it resides completely in RAM; so another option is to replace the data diskette with a blank, formatted diskette and save the file. In a hard disk environment, save the file to a diskette in drive A.

If a disk full message appears while you are printing, you must print the file from Printer Control or List Files. You cannot print from the screen via a Print command, since this option creates a separate print file on disk and, as a result, takes up even more disk space.

Search and Replace Commands

The Search and the Replace commands enable you to locate (or to locate and change or delete) a word or phrase wherever it appears in your document. The primary limitation is that the phrase can be no longer than 60 characters.

Search

The Search (F2) command allows you to locate the first and all subsequent occurrences of a word or phrase. When the command is entered, the cursor moves to the right of the first occurrence of the word or phrase.

First, the Search (F2) command is issued to WordPerfect, which responds with the prompt ⟶ Srch _ in the status line. Then you enter the desired word or phrase (up to sixty characters) and issue the Search (F2) command to initiate the search. The cursor will appear to the right of the first occurrence of the desired text in the file; to find the next occurrence, enter the Search (F2) command twice. The search operation has ended when you see the * Not Found * message displayed in the status line.

The regular search command is a forward search. This means that the search starts at the current cursor location and moves toward the end of the file. You can also use a reverse search, which starts at the current cursor location and moves toward the beginning of the file. The **Reverse Search** (Shift + F2) works in the same manner as the forward search.

In addition to finding desired text, the Search command can also find embedded codes. For example, if you are interested in finding the next hard carriage return, simply press the Enter key to obtain the prompt ⟶ Srch _. This time the search string is [HRt].

You can also return the cursor to the position it had before the last Search (F2) command was executed by entering the Goto (Ctrl + Home) command twice.

Replace

The Replace (Alt + F2) command is used to find a word or phrase and then replace it with another word or phrase. When the Replace command is initially entered, you receive the prompt w/Confirm? (Y/N) N. If you respond N, every occurrence of the old word or phrase is replaced automatically. If you respond Y, WordPerfect will stop at each occurrence of the found word or phrase and prompt you with Confirm? (Y/N) N. Y replaces and moves to the next occurrence; N leaves the old word or phrase and moves the cursor to the next occurrence.

The search and replace process is as follows. Press Alt + F2. Answer the confirm prompt. Then WordPerfect prompts ⟶ Srch: _. Enter the text that you want to replace and press the F2 key. You are prompted: Replace with: _. Type the replacement text and again press the F2 key. The search and replacement process proceeds as you indicated, either automatically for all of the document that follows the initial cursor location or with confirmation after each find.

The search and replace character strings can also be embedded codes.

Some clarification is needed for special types of operations. If you want to find complete words such as *dog* rather than *dogma* or *dogmatic*, you must enter spaces before and after the word you want. Lower-case characters can be used to search for either upper-case or lower-case characters, whereas upper-case characters can be used to search only for upper-case characters.

Wild Card. The WordPerfect Search/Replace command also enables you to search for special character strings using the so-called **Wild Card** technique. For example, assume that you want to locate any word in your document that begins with the character *d* and has *g* as the third character. Such a search would locate words such as dig, dog, dug, dogmatic, and digital. To issue such a Search/Replace command requires that you enter the following criteria at the Search/Replace prompt:

```
d^V^Xo
```

The ^V (Ctrl + V) indicates to WordPerfect that it should get ready for a special command. The ^X (Ctrl + X) tells WordPerfect that this character can be any character. Your Search/Replace command can now proceed.

Dual Document Capabilities

The **dual document capability** differentiates WordPerfect from many other word processing packages in its ability to give you access to two documents at one time, enabling you to type information into or to edit both documents by simply flipping from one document to the other.

This ability to handle two documents at one time is supported by the **window** and **switch window** features of WordPerfect. The Screen (Ctrl + F3) command displays the menu that offers you the option of determining how many lines of text are to be included in window 1 (the current window). Once the Screen (Ctrl + F3) option is selected the following menu is displayed.

```
0 Rewrite; 1 Window 2 Line Draw; 3 Ctrl/Alt Keys; 4 Colors 5 Auto Rewrite: 0
```

Choosing the Window option displays the prompt `# of Lines in the Window: 24`. The default window size is 24 lines (a window cannot be smaller than 2 lines). If you wish to have equal-sized windows, enter a window size of 12. You will now have a screen with a tab line in the middle (see Figure 8.2) with the cursor active in the upper window. There are two status lines, one for the upper window and one for the lower.

To make the cursor jump from one window to the other, use the Switch (Shift + F3) command. This switch capability enables you to mark blocks of text by using the Block (Alt + F4) command to cut or copy text in one window and then jumping to the document in the other window to place the text there. The status lines always tell in which document the cursor resides.

Any WordPerfect command that you execute in one window works independently from the other window. A Save command executed in one window does not affect the document displayed in the other window.

You can *close* the inactive window (the one in which the cursor does not reside) by issuing a Screen (Ctrl + F3) command, taking the Window option, and then entering a screen size of 24 lines. The current window size becomes 24 lines. When you try to exit WordPerfect, however, you are first prompted to save the document displayed in the active window and, having done that, you are prompted to save the document in the other window before you can exit.

Assume that you want to incorporate the part of content of one file into that of another file. The retrieve command does not work well in this case because WordPerfect appends the entire content of the second file at the cursor location in the first file. Therefore, you must retrieve the first file (Doc 1), create a window, jump to the second window (Doc 2), and retrieve the other file. You can now mark the desired portion of the file for a block cut or copy operation, activate the first window (Doc 1) by a switch command, and move the content to the cursor location.

Line Draw Capabilities

Another feature that sets WordPerfect apart from many other word processing packages is its ability to draw lines around text. The **Line Draw** feature, available through the Screen (Ctrl + F3) command, allows you to use the

Figure 8.2
The split-screen feature of
WordPerfect allows you to
have a document open in the
top window and another
document open in the bot-
tom window.

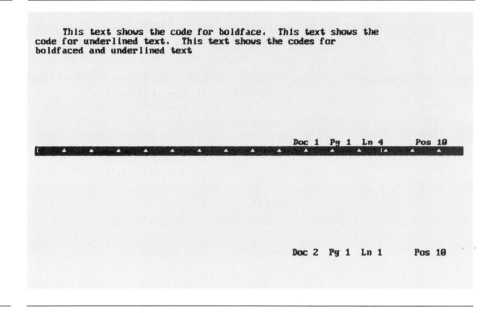

arrow keys to draw boxes, graphs, and other illustrations using DOS graphics
characters. This feature permits you to draw on a clear screen or around and
over text.

 For example, assume that you had typed the following information on
the title page of a history report.

```
The Mexican War
by
Tim Duffy
```

Also assume that you want to draw a box around the text to make it stand out.
Use the Line Draw option from the menu presented by the Screen (Ctrl + F3)
command. First position the cursor at the beginning of the box and issue the
Screen (Ctrl + F3) command; the following menu is displayed.

```
1 ¦ 2 ¦¦ 3 *; 4 Change; 5 Erase; 6 Move: 1
```

The first line type is the default option. Drawing the box requires selecting option 1 and then using the arrow keys to create the four corners
and complete the rectangle. When you are finished, execute the Exit (F7)
command.

```
┌─────────────────────┐
│   The Mexican War   │
│         by          │
│      Tim Duffy      │
└─────────────────────┘
```

Chapter Review

Block commands enable you to mark an area of text in a document and then to move the marked material, copy it to another position in the document, delete it, save it to a file on disk, or change its display characteristics.

Before you can issue block manipulation commands, you must mark the desired text by issuing a Block (Alt + F4) and painting with cursor movement commands. A block can consist of one or more characters, words, phrases, sentences, paragraphs, or pages.

The Move (Ctrl + F4) command enables you to select a default option of sentence, paragraph, or page to be cut or copied from your document. The desired entity to be cut or copied is determined by the cursor location. If you want to manipulate a unit of text other than a sentence, paragraph, or page, you can first mark the text as a block and then issue the Move command.

Most block commands, which are used to mark chunks of text for later manipulation, are of little use when you want to move only a column or rectangle of text. Before you can move a rectangle of text that is embedded in other text, you must paint the desired text by placing the cursor at the beginning of the text, issuing the Block (Alt + F4) command, and moving the cursor to the end of the desired text; then you issue the Move (Ctrl + F4) command. All of the text between the beginning and ending cursor locations is painted. After you tell WordPerfect that you want to execute the Rectangle or Column option, the rectangle or column of text is all that is painted—and cut or copied.

One of the real benefits of using block commands is that they allow you to store often-used pieces of text to disk for later use. This feature saves you a tremendous amount of time retyping the same text from one document to the next. Unless you use the **Append** command, data that you save to an existing file will destroy the data that is currently in that file and replace it with the marked block of text.

WordPerfect provides you with two ways to find text: The first merely locates text, which can then manipulate or change in any way you please; the second finds the text and replaces it with other text that you have previously chosen.

From time to time you will forget to check on the available amount of disk storage remaining on a diskette. When you try to save a file and receive a Disk Full error, you can use the List Files (F5) command to delete unwanted files to free enough disk space to save your file; or you can replace the full disk with a blank, formatted disk and save to the new disk, since the temporary file is usually completely contained in RAM.

Finally, the Line Draw feature of WordPerfect enables you to place boxes and other drawings on your document around existing text.

Key Terms and Concepts

Append command	redline
block	Replace
case conversion	Reverse Search
center block	Save block
copy	Search
cut	Strikeout
delete	subscript
dual document capability	superscript
Line Draw	Switch window
Move	Wild Card
Print block	window
rectangular block	

Chapter Quiz

Multiple Choice

1. Which of the following commands is not used for a defined block of text?
   a. Save
   b. Delete
   c. Center
   d. Indent
   e. All of the above commands are for blocks.

2. Which of the following commands are used for rectangle block mode?
   a. Sentence
   b. Paragraph
   c. Page
   d. Retrieve
   e. None of the above

3. Which of the following statements is false?
   a. When a block is moved into the current document, it is placed at the current cursor location.
   b. When a block is written to disk, it is placed at the end of existing data in that file via the Append option.
   c. The cut option causes two copies of the blocked text to appear in a document.
   d. All of the above statements are true.
   e. Both a and c are false.

4. Which of the following commands are extremely important when you receive a disk full error message?
   a. Block delete
   b. List Files
   c. Copy
   d. Cut
   e. None of these are really important.

5. Which of the following is not an option in the Replace command of WordPerfect?
   a. Search backwards.
   b. Ignore upper and lower case.
   c. Search only for whole words.
   d. Search for embedded codes.
   e. All of the above are options for the find and replace.

True/False

6. A block must be marked before you are allowed to use the append command.

7. The first files to delete after you receive a disk full error message are the files with a .BK! extension.

8. When using WordPerfect for finding text, you are unable to move the cursor back to the location of the previous find.

9. Only one status line is displayed on the screen when a window option is in effect.

10. WordPerfect allows only one type of line in a drawing.

Answers

1. d 2. e 3. c 4. b 5. e 6. t 7. t 8. f 9. f 10. f

Exercises

1. Define or describe each of the following:
   a. block   d. replace
   b. superscript/subscript   e. line drawing
   c. block write

2. The command to mark a block of text is _Alt + F4_.

3. A block of text is painted using _pointer positioning_ commands.

4. The command that creates a copy of a block of text is the _Copy_ option of the Move command.

5. The command that moves a block of text to another location in a document and erases the original is the _Cut_ option of the Move command.

6. The command that is used to place WordPerfect in column block mode is the _____ option of the Move command.

7. The block delete command is _Delete_.

8. The command that is used to print text slightly above or below the current line is the _____ command.

9. The command that is used to record a marked block of text to disk is _____.

10. The command used to display the directory of your default disk is _____.

11. The command used to delete files while you are still entering or editing text in your document can be found as part of the _____ option.

12. Unless a block of text is first marked, only _____ character at a time is affected by the Super/Subscript command.

13. The Block command is accessed by pressing the _Alt + 4_ keys.

14. The Search forward command is accessed by the _____ keys, and the Search backward command is accessed via the _____ keys.

15. The _____ command is used to move back to the prior cursor location in a Search command.

16. You can move from one window to the other by executing the _Move_ command.

17. The minimum number of lines for a window is _2_.

18. The maximum number of characters that can be included in a search string is _60_.

19. WordPerfect provides the ability to draw _____ different types of lines.

20. The _____ command enables you to change upper-case text to lower-case text and vice versa.

Computer Exercises

Below is a summary of the new WordPerfect commands covered in this chapter.

Command	Description
Block (Alt + F4)	Mark a block of text in a document for use with another command.
Move (Ctrl + F4)	This command is used to cut or copy a unit or block of text to another position in a document.
Redline/strikeout (Alt + F5)	This command marks text in a document.
Super/Subscript (Shift + F1)	This command prints superscripts and subscripts and spaces them properly.
Case Conversion (Shift + F3)	This command converts upper case to lower case and vice versa.
Search (F2)	Finds specified character strings in a document.
Replace (Alt + F2)	Finds and replaces character strings in a document.
Screen (Ctrl + F3)	Creates a window on your screen and specifies the number of lines in it.
Switch (Shift + F3)	Allows you to move the cursor from one window to the other.

1. Retrieve the following list of names and addresses from the disk file called CH8EX1. Using the block commands, arrange the names and addresses in alphabetical order by last name. Save the sorted names and addresses to a file called CH8EX1A.

Reza Ghorbani
4033 N. Wolcott
Chicago, Il. 60712

Debbie Acklin
408 E. Monroe
Bloomington, Il. 61701

Harvey Posio
1013 Hillcrest
San Diego, Ca. 94307

Juan Decesario
1214 Flores
Miami, Fl. 12562

Arthur Adams
115 Ginger Creek Ct.
Bloomington, Il. 61701

Russell Davis
707 Vale St.
Bloomington, Il. 61701

Fred Ficek
1215 Tamarack
Normal, Il. 61761

2. Using the same file of names and addresses, arrange them in order by zip code. Save the sorted names and addresses to a file called CH8EX2.

3. Retrieve the file called BOOKEXER. Using the block commands, save the first paragraph to a file called CH8EX3A. Save the third paragraph to a file called CH8EX3B. Append the fifth paragraph to the CH8EX3A file. Quit the BOOKEXER file using the Exit command without saving the file. Open a file called EXER4C. Retrieve the PARAx files that you just created in order. Be sure to position the cursor to the end of a "chunk" of text, before retrieving the next file. Using the file delete commands, delete the PARAx intermediate files. Save the file.

4. Retrieve the BOOKEXER file. Locate each occurrence of the term *word processing*. Locate each occurrence of the word *program* and change it to *pogrom*. Experiment with other find commands using the BOOKEXER document. When you are finished, exit without saving the file.

5. Retrieve the CH8EX5 file. Using the Rectangle command, place the second column of names beneath the first. Save the finished product to a file called CH8EX5A.

```
Reza Ghorbani        Debbie Acklin
Harvey Posio         Juan Decesario
Arthur Adams         Russell Davis
Fred Ficek
```

6. Clear the screen and retrieve the CH8EX6 file. You will find text like that listed below. Using the block command, perform each indicated task on the appropriate line. For example, the first line "Center this text" should be centered using the Block + Center commands. Save your work to the file CH8EX6A. Print out the entire file.

```
Center this text
Center and boldface this text
Center and underline this text
Center, boldface, and underline this text
Underline this text
Boldface and underline this text
Right justify this text
Underline and right justify this text
Delete this text
CONVERT THIS TEXT TO LOWER CASE
convert this text to upper case
```

Use the block command to print only the first five lines of the changed CH8EX6 file.

WordPerfect

Productivity Aids

Chapter Objectives

After completing this chapter, you should be able to:

Discuss the Speller

Discuss the Thesaurus

Discuss Merge

Discuss the primary merge file (letter template)

Discuss requirements of data files used by Merge

WordPerfect has productivity aids that make the user's life easier: Speller, which checks the spelling in WordPerfect documents; Thesaurus, which helps you find synonyms and antonyms for words; and Merge, which (among other things) enables you to generate personalized form letters. The examples presented use the README.WP file found in the training version of WordPerfect.

Speller

The Speller option helps you proofread a document that is on your screen by comparing every word in your document with the words contained in the Speller dictionary. Some of its features are the following:

1. A main dictionary that contains over 100,000 words
2. The ability to create and maintain a personal dictionary for words that are not in the main dictionary.
3. The ability to tell WordPerfect to check spelling on a page, in a block, or in an entire document.
4. The ability to find alternative spellings by a phonetic or pattern look-up.
5. The detection of double occurrences of words (for example, the the) and to delete the second occurrence.
6. The automatic detection of nonwords in the document.
7. A count of the words that were checked for spelling in the text.

WordPerfect contains a number of files that it uses in performing a spelling check:

Main dictionary (LEX.WP).   The LEX.WP file contains the main dictionary file, which holds over 100,000 words. The dictionary, because of its large size, is on a separate disk.

Supplemental dictionary ({WP}LEX.SUP).   The {WP}LEX.SUP file contains words that you add to WordPerfect's dictionary, such as words that are related to your specific discipline. It can be edited directly by WordPerfect. It is this file that is searched if WordPerfect cannot find a word in the main dictionary file.

Speller utility (SPELL.EX).   The SPELL.EX file contains the utility that allows you to modify and create dictionaries by adding, correcting, or deleting words.

The method of starting Speller depends on whether you are using a diskette-based or a hard-disk–based computer.

 Diskette-based System.   When you are using a diskette-based system, you first Retrieve the document to RAM. Then remove the data disk from the disk drive (usually drive B) and replace it with the Speller (dictionary) diskette. Issue the Spell (Ctrl + F2) command to start the spelling check. You must leave the speller disk in drive B while the proofreading of your document is in process.

Hard-Disk–based System.   When you are using a hard-disk–based system, you must first Retrieve the document to RAM. Issue the Spell (Ctrl + F2) command to start the spelling check.

This method assumes that both dictionaries are in the same directory as your WordPerfect files. If WordPerfect is unable to find the dictionary files, it displays a message in the status line similar to the following:

```
Main dictionary not found. Enter name: C:\WP\LEX.WP
```

If the dictionary files are in a subdirectory or another directory, you must change to that directory.

Once the Speller command has been given, the following menu appears at the bottom of your screen:

```
Check: 1 Word; 2 Page; 3 Document; 4 Change Dictionary; 5 Look Up; 6 Count
```

If you want to check only the word or page at the current cursor location, select option 1 or 2, respectively. Option 3 (the option most frequently selected) checks spelling of the entire document.

When you select option 4, a message similar to that below is displayed.

```
Enter new main dictionary name: LEX.WP
```

You can now enter the name of a separate main dictionary of your own creation for WordPerfect to use in its spelling check. For instance, if you were a medical student, you might want to use a dictionary of medical terms.

After you have chosen the new main dictionary, WordPerfect asks if you want to use a new supplementary dictionary:

```
Enter new supplementary dictionary name: {WP}LEX.SUP
```

Again, if you want WordPerfect to use a new supplementary dictionary, simply enter its name.

Option 5, the Look Up option, helps with words you don't know how to spell by looking for words in the main dictionary that include a particular pattern of letters. The words found are displayed at the bottom of the screen.

Option 6, the Count option, counts the words in your document without taking the time for a spelling check. When the Count is finished, the number is displayed at the end of the document.

Once the proofing process has started, the message * Please Wait * is displayed at the bottom of your screen and stays there until WordPerfect encounters a group of characters in your document that it cannot find in its dictionary. At that time, your screen splits into two parts, with text from your document at the top with the suspect word highlighted in reverse video, and speller information at the bottom (see Figure 9.1). Let's examine the lines at the bottom of the screen:

```
Not Found! Select Word or Menu Option (0=Continue):0
1 Skip Once; 2 Skip; 3 Add Word; 4 Edit; 5 Look Up 6 Phonetic
```

The Not Found! message at the bottom of your screen is not relevant if suggestions for replacing the suspect word are displayed. Type the letter of the correct suggestion, and any occurrence of that word in your document is corrected. If the correct spelling is not displayed on the screen but options A through X appear, depress the Enter key to display the next screen of suggestions.

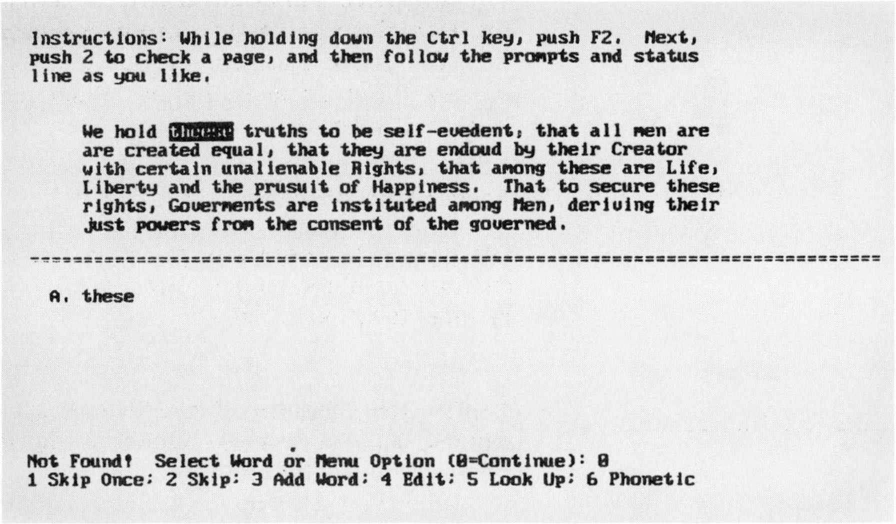

Figure 9.1
The spelling screen of
WordPerfect, showing the
suspect word and suggested
words for the README.WP
test file.

```
Instructions: While holding down the Ctrl key, push F2.  Next,
push 2 to check a page, and then follow the prompts and status
line as you like.


    We hold ███████ truths to be self-evedent, that all men are
    are created equal, that they are endoud by their Creator
    with certain unalienable Rights, that among these are Life,
    Liberty and the prusuit of Happiness.  That to secure these
    rights, Gouerments are instituted among Men, deriuing their
    just powers from the consent of the governed.

-=============================================================================

    A. these





Not Found!  Select Word or Menu Option (0=Continue): 0
1 Skip Once; 2 Skip; 3 Add Word; 4 Edit; 5 Look Up; 6 Phonetic
```

A suspect word is not always misspelled; WordPerfect may simply not have your particular word in its dictionary. In this case, you can take the Skip Once or Skip option. With the Skip option WordPerfect asks you no further questions about that word during the current proofing session. The Add Word option adds the word to the supplementary dictionary and the Speller then resumes the proofing session.

If the suspect word is indeed incorrect and WordPerfect does not have a correction in its dictionary, the Edit option must be selected to correct the suspect word. Once the Edit option is selected, the message Press Enter when done appears at the bottom of the screen, and the cursor appears beneath the suspect word. You can now manually correct the spelling. When you are finished, use the Enter key to continue the proofing session.

You may have misspelled a word in such a way that WordPerfect cannot make any suggestions. You may select the Look Up option to provide the pattern of characters to be used in finding the correct spelling for the suspect word once the message Word Pattern: _ is displayed at the bottom of the screen. If the correct word is not located, select the Edit option or go to Webster's unabridged, and correct it manually.

WordPerfect provides wildcard characters for the Look Up operation. You can represent a single letter, of which you are uncertain, by a question mark (?) and more than one letter by an asterisk (*). For example, if you enter the character string *p?ck*, the words *pack, peck, pick, pock,* and *puck* are displayed on the screen. The Look Up character string *pack** generates *pack, package, packaged,* and so on.

The Phonetic option tells WordPerfect to look up all words in the main dictionary that sound like the suspect word. If the correct spelling now appears, the word can be corrected automatically; otherwise, it must be corrected via the Edit option.

You may from time to time have to use a word that contains numeric characters. When WordPerfect encounters such a word, it displays the following message:

```
1 2 Skip; 3 Ignore words containing numbers; 4 Edit
```

When option 3 is selected, any words containing numbers will be ignored for the remaining portion of the proofing session.

One handy feature of the Speller is that it can locate double occurrences of a word (for example, the the). When a **double word** is found, the menu below is displayed.

```
DoubleWord! 1 2 Skip; 3 Delete 2nd; 4 Edit; 5 Disable double word checking_
```

Options 1 and 2 resume the proofing session. The Delete 2nd option automatically deletes the second occurrence of the double word in your document and resumes the proofing session.

Thesaurus

The Thesaurus feature of WordPerfect offers synonyms and antonyms for a word so that you can convey the exact meaning you want.

Starting the Thesaurus

The method used to start Thesaurus depends on whether you are using a diskette-based computer or a hard-disk–based computer.

Diskette-based System. If you are using a diskette-based system, you must first Retrieve the document to be checked to RAM. Then remove the data disk from the disk drive (usually drive B) and replace it with the Thesaurus diskette. Position the cursor at the word you want to look up and issue the Thesaurus (ALT + F1) command. You must leave the Thesaurus disk in drive B while looking for synonyms and antonyms.

Hard-Disk–based System. When you are using a hard-disk–based system, you must first Retrieve the document to RAM. Position the cursor at the word you want to look up and issue the Thesaurus (ALT + F1) command.

This method assumes that the TH.WP thesaurus dictionary is in the same directory as your WordPerfect files. If WordPerfect is unable to find the thesaurus dictionary file, it displays a message similar to the following:

```
Thesaurus not found. Enter name: TH.WP
```

If the thesaurus file is in a subdirectory or another directory, you must change to that directory.

Retrieve the README.WP file from the student revision of WordPerfect. Once the Thesaurus (ALT + F1) command is executed, the thesaurus screen appears on your monitor (see Figure 9.2). Four lines of text with the desired word highlighted appear at the top; three columns for holding information appear below. Depress the space bar at any time to return your document.

Three items play important roles in using Thesaurus. The **headword** is a word that can be looked up in the thesaurus. The **reference** is a word or phrase found under a headword. A reference preceded by a bullet (•) is a headword. A **subgroup** is a group of words that have the same connotation. Subgroups are numbered under the headword.

The displayed list of synonyms is divided into lists of nouns, verbs, and adjectives to make it easy for you to choose an appropriate word. You can tell WordPerfect to replace the word automatically by selecting option 1 of the thesaurus menu and entering the letter next to the desired word.

Figure 9.2
Thesaurus screen for the
word *fools* of the document
README.WP.

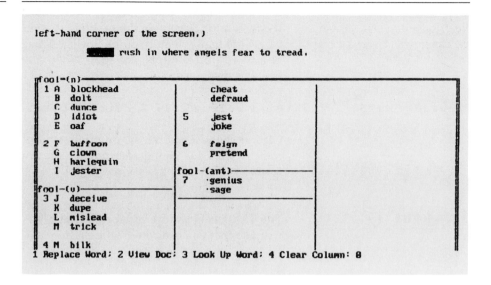

Synonyms and antonyms can also be examined by selecting that alphabetic option. Using Figure 9.2, for example, if you want to examine the word *blockhead* and then want additional terms for the provided word *idiot*, press the D key; an additional column of terms appears for the word *idiot* (see Figure 9.3).

You can have only three columns of terms on the screen at one time. When the third column is filled, any additional terms overlay that column. You can erase columns from right to left either by entering the Clear Column command or by pressing the Backspace or Del key.

From time to time, more terms are provided by the thesaurus than can be displayed on the screen in the column. You can view other subgroups of terms by pressing the Up Arrow, Down Arrow, Pg Up, and Pg Dn keys.

You can look up words in four ways. (1) Position the cursor at the desired word and enter the Thesaurus (ALT + F1) command. (2) Enter the desired word from the Look Up Word option of the thesaurus menu. (3) Enter the character next to a headword while using the thesaurus. (4) Move the cursor to the word while using the View Doc option and again enter the Thesaurus (Alt + F1) command.

To replace the word in your document, select the Replace Word option from the thesaurus menu. WordPerfect now displays the prompt `Press letter for word _` and waits for you to enter the letter of the desired headword. That word now replaces the word in your document.

Merge

Despite technological advances, most communication is still conducted via the written word, and writing letters is still extremely important to the business community. Writing the same letter to 100 different people, however, poses some real problems for the typical business environment. In many situations, it is important to modify each letter so that it appears to have been typed individually for the recipient. People do not like "Dear Customer" letters.

Without Merge, it is possible to save every letter to a separate file and change the name and address of the recipients before printing. However, if various references within the body of the letter also have to be changed, this result is a lot of additional work.

Figure 9.3
Additional suggestions from the thesaurus for the word *idiot* in the README.WP file.

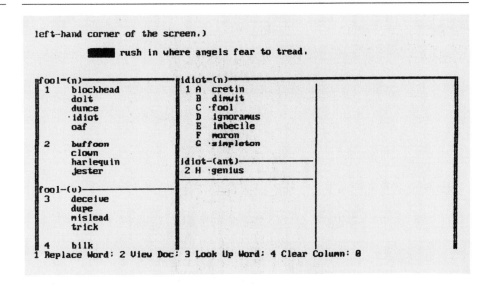

```
left-hand corner of the screen.)
          ███ rush in where angels fear to tread.

┌fool-(n)──────────┬idiot-(n)─────────┬──────────────┐
│  1    blockhead  │ 1 A   cretin     │              │
│       dolt       │   B   dimwit     │              │
│       dunce      │   C  ·fool       │              │
│      ·idiot      │   D   ignoramus  │              │
│       oaf        │   E   imbecile   │              │
│                  │   F   moron      │              │
│  2    buffoon    │   G  ·simpleton  │              │
│       clown      │                  │              │
│       harlequin  │idiot-(ant)───────│              │
│       jester     │ 2 H  ·genius     │              │
│                  │                  │              │
│fool-(v)──────────│                  │              │
│  3    deceive    │                  │              │
│       dupe       │                  │              │
│       mislead    │                  │              │
│       trick      │                  │              │
│                  │                  │              │
│  4    bilk       │                  │              │
└──────────────────┴──────────────────┴──────────────┘
1 Replace Word: 2 View Doc: 3 Look Up Word: 4 Clear Column: 0
```

With WordPerfect's Merge and a letter-quality printer, each letter in a bulk lot can look as though it were individually typed. See Figures 9.4 and 9.5 for examples of such letters; notice that the only differences between the two letters are the names and addresses of the recipients.

As its name implies, **Merge** is capable of combining (merging) files. Usually two files are needed. The **primary file** (sometimes called the template letter) contains the text to be included in all letters and the instructions for placing the individualizing data. The **secondary file** contains the variable, individualizing data to be used to make each letter unique (this is referred to as the *data file*). These two files can be viewed as a data processing program composed of three parts: input, processing, and output. The data file is the input to the template; the template is, in effect, a computer program containing instructions on what to do with the input data file; and the output consists of the individualized letters for each recipient listed in the data file.

Primary (Template) File

The easiest way to understand the process of creating a merge application is to begin with the primary file or letter template (see Figure 9.6). Notice that there are a number of codes—a single character following a control (^) character—embedded in the text of the template letter. These codes are used to pass information from the data file to the Merge option as well as to provide more information about how to perform any given task. The template letter is typed as a regular document file. The letter in Figure 9.6 contains a number of ^Fn^ codes that tell Merge where to put information in the document. These codes are entered by using the Merge Codes (Alt + F9) command and selecting the F option from the merge menu. WordPerfect now tells you via the Field Number? _ prompt to enter the field number. Notice that a space is inserted between the F1, F2, and F3 entries. In this example, the codes are defined as follows:

^F1^, the first variable field, contains the salutation of the recipient.

^F2^, the second variable field, contains the first name of the recipient.

^F3^, the third variable field, contains the last name of the recipient.

Figure 9.4
Individualized letter produced by Merge.

```
ACME Computing
533 Gold Avenue
Downs, Il 61777

January 1, 1980

Mr. Roy Seegler
223 Flora Way
Normal, Il 61761

Dear Mr. Seegler:

Thank you for submitting your application and resume for the
applications programmer/analyst positions advertised for
our data processing department. After all of the resumes
have been screened, we will contact you about your status.
This process is expected to be completed by March 15, 1987.

Thank you for considering job opportunities at ACME Comput-
ing.

Sincerely yours,


Lucky Luciano
```

^F4^, the fourth variable field, contains the address of the recipient.

^F5^, the fifth variable field, contains the city, state, and zip code of the recipient.

^D, the date code, inserts the system date during the merge operation.

Secondary (Data) File

Figure 9.7 shows the data file NAMES, which contains the pieces of data that were placed into the variable fields in the form letter in Figure 9.6 to create the individualized letters reproduced in Figures 9.4 and 9.5.

Figure 9.5
The same letter as in Figure 9.4, with a different name and address, produced in the same merge run.

```
ACME Computing
533 Gold Avenue
Downs, Il 61777

January 1, 1980

Ms. Laura Miller
2117 Emerson
Bloomington, Il 71701

Dear Ms. Miller:

Thank you for submitting your application and resume for the
applications programmer/analyst positions advertised for
our data processing department. After all of the resumes
have been screened, we will contact you about your status.
This process is expected to be completed by March 15, 1987.

Thank you for considering job opportunities at ACME Comput-
ing.

Sincerely yours,


Lucky Luciano
```

Figure 9.6
The primary (template) file
LETTER used in creating the
two personalized letters in
Figures 9.4 and 9.5.

```
ACME Computing

533 Gold Avenue

Downs. Il 61777


^D


^F1^ ^F2^ ^F3^

^F4^

^F5^


Dear ^F1^ ^F3^:


Thank you for submitting your application and resume for the

applications programmer/analyst positions advertised for our data

processing department.  After all of the resumes have been

screened. we will contact you about your status.  This process is

expected to be completed by March 15, 1987.


Thank you for considering job opportunities at ACME Computing.


Sincerely yours,




Lucky Luciano
```

Figure 9.7
The data file NAMES used in creating the personalized letters in Figures 9.4 and 9.5.

```
Mr.^R

Roy^R

Seegler^R

223 Flora Way^R

Normal, Il 61761^R

^E

Ms.^R

Laura^R

Miller^R

2117 Emerson^R

Bloomington, Il 61701^R

^E

Mrs.^R

James^R

Bonzer^R

1714 S. Western^R

Bloomington, Il 61701^R

^E

Mr.^R

Norman^R

Backles^R

253 E. Loucks^R

Peoria, Il 61603^R

^E
```

The following rules must be observed when you are creating a secondary (data) file to be used by Merge:

1. Each piece of information, called a field, must be terminated by a Mrg R (F9) command. When you give this command, the ^R is placed at the end of the field.

2. When multiple pieces of data (lines) are contained in a field, enter a hard carriage return to start the next line. The ^R does not have to appear at the end of each line.

3. When you have finished entering the fields for one record, you indicate the end of Merge by entering a Mrg E (Shift + F9) command. When this command is issued, the ^E appears. The Mrg E command can be entered on a separate line or at the end of the last field following the Mrg R (F9) command.

4. Fields for which you do not have information (blank fields) still must be marked by a Mrg R command. A line appears with an ^R but no text.

5. Once a secondary (data) file has been created, it can be used with any number of primary file templates.

Merging

Once you have completed and saved the template letter and the data file, you can begin the merge operation. To start the merge operation, clear the screen and then issue the Merge/Sort (Ctrl + F9) command. The following menu is displayed in the status line:

`1 Merge; 2 Sort; 3 Sorting Sequences: 0`

 Select the Merge option from the menu; WordPerfect asks you for the primary file name with the prompt `Primary file: _.` Enter the file name LETTER and press the Enter key. WordPerfect then asks you for the secondary file name with the prompt `Secondary file: _.` Enter the file name NAMES and press the Enter key. The merge operation now starts. While it runs, WordPerfect displays the message `* Merging *` at the bottom of your screen. When the message disappears, the merge operation is finished.

A separate letter for each record contained in the secondary file is now in RAM. To print the letters, enter the Print (Shift + F7) command and select the Full Text option. After the letters are printed, you can either save them to disk or erase them from RAM via the Exit (F7) without executing a save command.

Other Merge Features

The power of Merge is not limited to producing simple, repetitive letters. Its other abilities include typing data from the keyboard, issuing prompts to the user, and printing directly to the printer.

In the previous example, the primary file received all of its data from the secondary file. But you may have an application for which you want to enter all or some data directly from the keyboard. In this situation, you use a ^C to tell Merge that this data is to be entered by the user. Of course, if all of your variable fields are defined with a ^C, you do not need a secondary file. You can enter the ^C either manually or by selecting the Merge Codes (Alt + F9) command and selecting the C option from that menu.

Now, when the merge operation begins, WordPerfect automatically stops at the first ^C and waits for you to enter the data for this field. When you have finished entering the data, issue the Mrg R (F9) command to continue the merge until it reaches the next ^C field indicator. You can stop a merge at this time by entering a Merge E (Shift + F9) command.

If you have a number of ^C fields in your document, you may not remember what information is required for a given field. In this situation, you can use the ^O command to provide yourself with a prompt, which appears on the status line. First the ^O command is issued, then the text of the message is entered, and finally, a closing ^O command is again issued.

For example, the entry ^O Enter Amount Due^O ^C embedded in a primary file document results in the appearance of `Enter Amount Due` in the status line as a prompt for the type of data to enter. When you have finished entering the data, issue a Mrg R (F9) command to continue.

Figure 9.8
Primary file for generating
mailing labels using the data
file shown in Figure 9.7.

```
                                    (Blank line with print codes)
^F1^ ^F2^ ^F3^

^F4^

^F5^

                                    (Blank line)

^T^N^P^P
```

Automatic Printing

Instead of using the two-step merge and print process, WordPerfect can provide **automatic printing** of the merge-generated documents. This is accomplished by embedding the command ^T^N^P^P at the end of the LETTER primary file. Although all of the letters are printed immediately, WordPerfect can handle only the current merge operation; thus no other commands can be executed until the operation is finished.

The ^T sends all text that has been merged to this point to the printer. The ^N tells WordPerfect that when one letter (record) has been printed, it should check to see if any record from the secondary file still remains. The first ^P instructs WordPerfect to look at the primary file of the name you specified. The final ^P tells WordPerfect that the end of the code has been reached.

Mailing Labels and Envelopes

The data file in Figure 9.7 can be used for other applications. For example, after the letters have been written, this file can be used to address a mailing label or an envelope for each individual. The primary file depicted in Figure 9.8 contains instructions for generating mailing labels. Figure 9.9 contains the mailing labels that were generated.

To create mailing labels that can be automatically printed requires entering the line of merge codes on the last line of the document. The first line of the text has control codes embedded for the following changes:

1. Page length set to 6 lines
2. Text length set to 6 lines
3. Top margin set to 0
4. Left margin set to 5 and right margin set to 35

This method also assumes that you are using standard labels, one across, that are 3.5 inches wide and 15/16 inches high. Each standard-sized mailing label has five lines, and one additional line is required to get the next label to print in the proper position on the label; you must keep track of six different lines. A blank line precedes the name and address, and two blank lines follow them.

But what if you want to print envelopes instead of labels? Printing envelopes requires that you place enough blank lines before the name and address to print it in the middle of the envelope and that you indent the text to a

Figure 9.9
Examples of mailing labels
generated by the combined
use of the files shown in
Figures 9.7 and 9.6.

```
Mr. Roy Seegler
223 Flora Way
Normal, Il 61761



Ms. Laura Miller
2117 Emerson
Bloomington, Il 71701



Mrs. James Bonzer
1714 S. Western
Bloomington, Il 61701



Mr. Norman Backles
253 E. Loucks
Peoria, Il 61603
```

column farther to the right than print position 10. You can use the same primary file that you use in printing labels, but you must enter the following print settings on the first line of the document:

1. Top margin set to 0
2. Left margin set to 5 and right margin set to 35
3. Issue the single sheet command

You also must position the envelope in the printer to the line at which you want printing to begin.

Chapter Review

The Speller option allows you to check the spelling of any document file quickly. The two dictionaries used by this spelling checker are the main dictionary and the supplemental dictionary. The Speller option provides an easy-to-follow menu that gives alternative actions that can be performed on a suspect word. In addition, the appropriate part of the document is displayed (with the suspect word in reverse video) so that you can see the word in context.

The Thesaurus option helps you find synonyms and antonyms for the word at the current cursor location. Up to three columns of headwords can be displayed on the screen. The word at the cursor location can be replaced automatically when a better word is located.

Merge allows you to individualize form letters by creating a primary (constant) letter that combines variable and constant text. The individualizing (variable) set of data is found in the secondary file and is composed of fields and records. Each record, which is followed by ^E, corresponds to all data needed to mail a letter to a particular recipient. Each field of the record is terminated by ^R and may consist of more than one line of text.

The constant text stays the same from one letter to the next. The variable data are read by Merge and placed in the variable fields of the primary file. These variable data areas within the template provide the individualization.

Besides identifying the variable fields, which are contained inside circumflexes (ˆ), the primary file tells Merge which data field is to be used in filling the blanks of the primary file. The variable fields must remain in the same order from one record to the next within the file.

After developing the primary file, a user's second task is to build a data file composed of records of the data to be merged. This file can be used by any number of primary files. For instance, the same secondary file can be used to generate addresses on labels or to address envelopes.

Once the merge operation has been performed, WordPerfect can be told to send the output to the printer. This entire process can be automated so that information is sent immediately to the printer. WordPerfect is, however, unable to accept commands while Merge is executing.

Key Terms and Concepts

automatic printing
double word
headword
main dictionary
Merge
primary file

reference
secondary file
subgroup
supplementary dictionary
Thesaurus

Chapter Quiz

Multiple Choice

1. Merge allows you to do which of the following?
   a. Automatically place today's date in a letter
   b. Send messages to the operator
   c. Enter variable information from the keyboard
   d. Prepare personalized form letters
   e. All of the above

2. The primary file does NOT contain which of the following?
   a. Constant information
   b. Field numbers
   c. The data file
   d. Merge commands
   e. For a letter template, all of the above

3. Which of the following merge commands is (are) minimally required in a primary file?
   a. ˆFnˆ
   b. ˆD
   c. ˆR
   d. ˆE
   e. All of the above

4. Which of the following is NOT a rule for entering Merge data files?
   a. Each record must have the same number of fields.
   b. The fields for each record must be arranged in the same order.
   c. The character used between fields is the comma (,).
   d. If a field has an embedded comma, you must enclose that field with double quotes (").
   e. All of the above are true.
   f. Only *a* and *b* are true.

5. Which of the following merge commands is not used for printing?
   a. ^Fn^
   b. ^T
   c. ^N
   d. ^P
   e. None of the above

True/False

6. The same data file can be used for a number of merge applications.

7. The command used to tell Merge which primary file to use in a merge operation is ^P.

8. Primary files for Merge can contain messages to the operator as well as data to fulfill a task.

9. Once you have issued the Thesaurus command, you can find information related to only one word (the one at the cursor location).

10. It is usually advisable to set the top margin to zero (0) when printing mailing labels.

Answers

1. e 2. c 3. a 4. f 5. a 6. t 7. t 8. f 9. f 10. t

Exercises

1. Define or describe each of the following:
   a. primary file   c. constant data
   b. secondary file   d. variable data

2. The file holding the text of the letter to be merged is called a _____.

3. The text that does not change from one letter to another is called the _____ text.

4. The variable fields are surrounded by _____.

5. The merge command _____ is used to tell Merge to look to see if there is another record remaining in the secondary file.

6. A _____ can be used to replace the word at the cursor location when you are using the Thesaurus option of WordPerfect.

7. The merge command _____ is used to tell Merge to display a message on the screen.

8. Each record in a Merge secondary file must end with a _____.

9. Each field in a Merge data file must end with a _____.

10. The speller command _____ can be used to find a word by using wild card characters.

11. The speller command _____ is used to find words that sound like the suspect word.

12. The merge commands can be entered by using the Merge Codes (Alt + F9) command or by holding down the _____ and pressing the appropriate letter key.

13. A standard mailing label can typically hold _____ lines of text.

14. Special print commands must be entered on the _____ line of the primary file document.

15. You can use the merge command _____ to enter data from the keyboard.

Computer Exercise

Enter the following names and addresses in a secondary file called NAMES.SEC. Enter the data so that they can be used by Merge.

Name and Address Data

Sal	Last	First	In	Address	City	St	Zip
Mr.	Ghorbani	Reza	R.	4033 N. Wolcott	Chicago	Il	60712
Ms.	Ghorbani	Ann	B.	4033 N. Wolcott	Chicago	Il	60712
Mr.	Acklin	Douglas	C.	408 E. Monroe	Bloomington	Il	61701
Ms.	Walters	Barbara	A.	1981 Crestlawn	Arlington	Va	13411
Mr.	Adams	Arthur	V.	115 Ginger Creek Ct.	Bloomington	Il	61701
Mr.	Davis	Russell	B.	707 Vale St.	Bloomington	Il	61701
Ms.	Acklin	Debbie	C.	408 E. Monroe	Bloomington	Il	61701
Mr.	Posio	Harvey	B.	1013 Hillcrest	San Diego	Il	94307

Create the following letter as the primary file for a merge application in which you are to use the file that you have just entered. The items that appear in bold print in the letter are to be read in from the file. Name the file Letter.PRM

```
Gold Department Store
123 Lotus Avenue
Micro, Ca, 53211

Name
Address
City, St, Zip

Dear Sal Last Name

We at the Gold Department Stores would like to take
this opportunity to invite you to attend the grand
opening of our new store in your town this Saturday,
Sal Last Name we have been informed that you are in-
terested in using microcomputers, One of the features
of our new store is that it offers a complete depart-
ment dealing with microcomputers, We are sure that it
will meet your computer needs for years to come,

We look forward to seeing you this Saturday,

Sincerely yours,

Minnie Micro, President
```

Use the same data file and create a merge template to generate the mailing labels for each of the individuals who received a letter.

Chapter

10

Advanced Features

of WordPerfect

After completing this chapter, you should be able to:

Discuss the footnoting and endnoting processes

Discuss the math feature of WordPerfect

Discuss the sort feature of WordPerfect

Discuss the macros feature of WordPerfect

This chapter introduces you to a number of advanced features found in WordPerfect that are not found in most other word processing packages—the endnoting/footnoting, math, sort, and macro features—which provide you with tremendous flexibility in creating reports or term papers.

Footnotes/Endnotes

One topic of concern to anyone who wants to create a scholarly document is page size when **footnotes** (citations indicating the source of material used) are placed at the bottoms of pages (see Figure 10.1). Some of the problems involve how many lines of text should be placed on a particular page, how many footnotes occur on the page, and how many lines of print are needed for the footnotes. In a manual environment, these are critical concerns, and making a wrong decision results in having to retype the entire page. One solution often used to avoid these problems is to place the notes at the end of the document (**endnotes**).

WordPerfect automatically takes care of creating footnotes and endnotes and provides a professional looking printed page. It keeps track of numbering, inserts the footnote or endnote in the proper position, and keeps track of the number of text and footnote lines to print on each page.

Footnotes or endnotes can be created by positioning the cursor at the place in the text where the note number should go and issuing the Footnote (Ctrl + F7) command. The following menu is then displayed at the bottom of your screen:

```
1 Create; 2 Edit; 3 New #; 4 Options; 5 Create Endnote; 6 Edit Endnote: 0
```

Creating a Note

Option 1 and option 5 are used to create a footnote and endnote, respectively. When one of these options is selected, WordPerfect automatically inserts the proper footnote/endnote number in your document. A blank screen now appears on your monitor, on which you enter the text for the footnote or endnote. The status line provides information about the position and line number of the footnote. When you have finished entering the note, issue the Exit (F7) command; you are then returned to your document. You can now see the footnote/endnote number. Don't worry that the number does not appear as a superscript. This is taken care of when the document is printed. Remember, WordPerfect automatically inserts the footnote/endnote number, so do not try to enter it.

 The text of the footnote or endnote does not appear on the screen but, rather, has been inserted into the body of the text in RAM as part of a footnote/endnote code. For example, if you typed the following paragraph and wanted to insert the footnote text following that paragraph, your document would appear on the screen with the 1, but the footnote would not be visible.

```
Roussey echoes many of the above views.1 He indicates
that many firms are currently using the microcomputer
and spreadsheet software to computerize the working
trial balance. Micros may also be used in statistical
sampling, keeping track of fee estimates, budgets,
time control audit programs, and standard audit
forms.

        Roussey, R., "Microcomputers and the Auditor,"
Journal of Accountancy, December 1983, p. 106.
```

According to many critics, these maxi models have various

problems which inhibit their effective use by university

planners. The first problem is cost. The CAMPUS model, for

instance, cost the University of Minnesota over $100 to run one

ten-year simulation for the school of business.⁷⁶

Other criticsm includes: The high turnover of

administrators coupled with the complexity of the models does not

result in proper understanding and effective use being made of

the models by most administrators.⁷⁷ The cost of implementing

the models is high due to the need for outside technical

assistance and data conversion constraints imposed by the models'

data dictionary requirements.⁷⁸ The appetitie for data of these

models, because of their complexity, is overwhelming.⁷⁹

The problems of cost and complexity pervade current college

and university simulation models. The complexity factor means it

takes too long to learn how to use them effectively. "Maxi-

Models" are designed to simulate as many aspects as possible of

the institution for purposes of long-range planning. A narrower,

---

⁷⁶David C. Cordes, "Project Prime: A test Implementation of
the CAMPUS Simulation Model," Managing the University: A Systems
Approach, ed. Paul W. Hamelman (New York: Praeger Publishers,
1972), p. 207.

⁷⁷"Let's End the Confusion About Simulation Models," p. 49.

⁷⁸John Shephard, "Resource Requirements Prediction Model-1
(RRPM-1)," p. 207.

⁷⁹William F. Massy, "Reflections of the Application of a
Decision Science Model to Higher Education," Decision Sciences 9
(April 1978):362-369.

To view the footnote entry, you must issue the Reveal Codes (Alt + F3) command (see Figure 10.2). The entry [Note:Foot,1;[Note #]Rous-sey,R,, "Microcomputers and the Auditor," [U] Jo,,,] represents the footnote code that has been embedded in the paragraph. Notice that the complete text of the footnote is not visible in the Reveal Code screen. Although only about the first 45 characters are displayed in the code, this is enough to let you determine whether or not this is the correct footnote.

Editing a Note

Once you have located the correct footnote or endnote using either the number of that note or the Reveal Codes command, you can edit that footnote or endnote using the respective Edit or Edit Endnote option on the Footnote

Figure 10.2
Control codes that are
embedded in a document to
keep track of the footnote/
endnote.

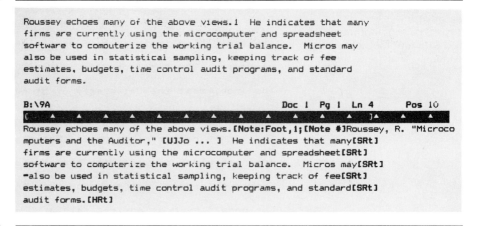

```
Roussey echoes many of the above views.1  He indicates that many
firms are currently using the microcomputer and spreadsheet
software to computerize the working trial balance.  Micros may
also be used in statistical sampling, keeping track of fee
estimates, budgets, time control audit programs, and standard
audit forms.

B:\9A                                    Doc 1  Pg 1  Ln 4      Pos 10
[    ^    ^    ^    ^    ^    ^    ^    ^    ^    ^    ^    ]^    ^    ^
Roussey echoes many of the above views.[Note:Foot,1;[Note #]Roussey, R.  "Microco
mputers and the Auditor," [U]Jo ... ]  He indicates that many[SRt]
firms are currently using the microcomputer and spreadsheet[SRt]
software to computerize the working trial balance.  Micros may[SRt]
-also be used in statistical sampling, keeping track of fee[SRt]
estimates, budgets, time control audit programs, and standard[SRt]
audit forms.[HRt]
```

menu. Once selected, you are prompted for the note to be edited by a F t n
#? _ or E n d n #? _ prompt. Enter the appropriate note number, or if the
default is correct, simply press the ENTER key. The edit option allows you to
make any changes to an existing note by temporarily placing the edit screen
with the note over your document (see Figure 10.3). When you have finished
making changes to the note, issue the Exit (F7) command to return to your
document.

Deleting a Note

The process for deleting a footnote/endnote from the text of a document is the
same as that for deleting any other embedded code. Place the cursor at the
position in your document that contains the code and press either the BACK-
SPACE or the DEL key. WordPerfect now responds with the prompt D e l e t e
[N o t e]? (Y/N) N. Press the "Y" key to delete the note. Any notes that
follow in your document are automatically renumbered by WordPerfect.

Changing a Note Number

From time to time you may have a document that you want to break up into
one or more files. For instance, you may start out writing a report and find
that it should be broken into three logical parts or chapters. If you have used
footnotes or endnotes, you may also want the footnote numbering to start
over in each logical section. This requires using the New # option of the
Footnote menu.

To execute this command, position the cursor to the left of the footnote
number in your document. Then issue the Footnote (Ctrl + F7) command and
select the New # option. WordPerfect now prompts you with the message
F t n #?. Enter the new number, and all following footnotes are automatically
renumbered.

Options

The options listed on the Footnote menu give you control over exactly how
WordPerfect should print the footnotes/endnotes. Once the footnote or endnote option is selected, a menu of customizing options is displayed on your
screen (see Figure 10.4). For most applications, WordPerfect's defaults are all
that you need for footnote/endnote applications.

Figure 10.3
An existing note accessed via
the Edit command of the
Footnote menu.

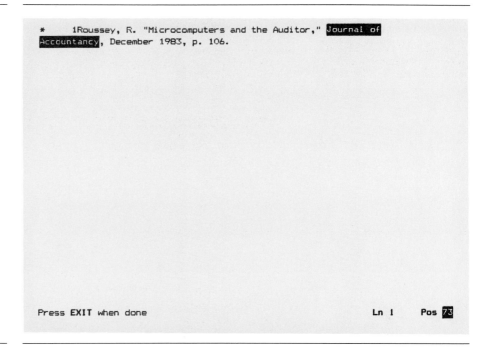

One option that you might want to change is option 7, which defaults to a one-line separation between the text of a page and the footnotes. You may be required to have a 2-inch line between the text and the footnote(s). If you respond with a 1 after taking option 7, a line will be printed before any footnotes.

Math

WordPerfect enables you to perform arithmetic in the body of a document. Using the Math feature, you can perform addition, subtraction, multiplication, and division and do calculations across or down columns.

The tab feature of WordPerfect plays a critical role in mathematical operations. Any column that is to be added must begin at a numeric tab stop, which is defined using the tab key. The Math default provides for calculating subtotals, totals, and grand totals *down* tab columns.

Subtotals

Assume that you want to place the numbers 125.00, 35.00, 5.00, and 123.50 in a **math column** and generate a total with decimal alignment at column 30. You first have to clear all tabs and set a new tab in position 30. You then turn on the Math feature by issuing the Math (Alt + F7) command and select the Math On option. Now enter each number by moving the cursor to the correct column with the tab key (do *not* use the Tab Align command). Tell WordPerfect to place the total at the bottom of the column by entering a plus (+) sign (do *not* use the plus sign on the number pad). Tell WordPerfect to calculate the total. Turn the Math feature off. Once the Math (Alt + F7) command is given, the following menu is displayed.

`1 Math On; 2 Math Def; 3 Column On/Off; 4 Column Def; 5 Column Display: 0`

Figure 10.4
The Options menu selections
from the Footnote (Ctrl + F7)
command.

```
    Footnote Options


         1 - Spacing within notes              1

         2 - Spacing between notes             1

         3 - Lines to keep together            3

         4 - Start footnote numbers each page  N

         5 - Footnote numbering mode           0

         6 - Endnote numbering mode            0

         7 - Line separating text and footnotes 1

         8 - Footnotes at bottom of page       Y

         9 - Characters for notes              *

         A - String for footnotes in text      [SuprScrpt][Note]

         B - String for endnotes in text       [SuprScrpt][Note]

         C - String for footnotes in note            [SuprScrpt][Note]

         D - String for endnotes in note       [Note].


       For options 5 & 6              For option 7:

          0 - Numbers                    0 - No line

          1 - Characters                 1 - 2 inch line

          2 - Letters                    2 - Line across entire page

                                         3 - 2 in. line w/continued strings


    Selection: 0
```

 A step-by-step method of accomplishing these tasks follows:

Set the tab stop.

1. Select the Line Format (Shift + F8) command.
2. Select the Tab command from this menu.
3. Erase all tab stops with an Erase Line (Ctrl + End) command.
4. Enter a new tab stop at column 30.
5. Use the Exit (F7) command to return to the document.

Use the math commands.

1. Select the Math (Alt + F7) command.
2. Activate the Math feature by selecting the Math On option. The Math On indicator now appears in place of the file name on the status line.
3. Press the tab key, enter 125.00, and press the ENTER key. Notice that even though you enter a Tab command, the number is entered as though this were a Tab Align command.
4. Press the tab key, enter 35.00, and press the ENTER key.
5. Press the tab key, enter 5.00, and press the ENTER key.
6. Press the tab key, enter 123.50, and press the ENTER key twice.

7. Press the tab key, enter + (do *not* use the plus [+] key on the numeric key pad).

8. Select the Math (Alt + F7) command.

9. Calculate by selecting the Calculate command. A `* Please Wait *` message appears for a few seconds on the status line, and shortly the answer appears to the left of the plus (+) sign.

10. Turn off the Math feature by issuing a Math (Alt + F7) command and selecting the Math Off command. The Math On indicator is now replaced by the file name in that status line.

Notice that the Math Definition and the Math On options of the Math command operate as toggles. A **toggle** is either in an on or off state: Issuing a command once turns a feature on, and issuing the command again turns the feature off. Once an option is turned on, the prompt takes the opposite value it had before, to prompt you to turn off the option.

IMPORTANT You must be in the range of your document in which the math feature is invoked (the Math indicator appears on the status line) when you issue a Calculate command to calculate arithmetic operations after data has been changed. If you try to issue a Calculate outside the math range, you will see Math Def as the second option rather than Calculate.

You should now have a column of numbers that appear as follows:

```
125.00
 35.00
  5.00
123.50

288.50+
```

The plus sign tells WordPerfect to include any numbers above in the total.

Multiple Columns

Entering a single column of numbers is a straightforward task. Multiple columns of numbers in which you intermix text and numerals, however, require other options of the Math feature.

To generate the table below requires performing a number of tasks.

Dpt	Employee	Total Hours	Gross Pay	Net Pay
1	Adams, Sam	40.00	260.00	163.80
1	Johns, Peter	40.00	233.75	147.26
1	Kent, John	40.00	260.00	163.80
1	Lester, Ned	40.00	220.00	138.60
1	Smith, Luther	40.00	260.00	163.80
1	Dix, Yvonne	40.00	300.00	189.00
1	Hunt, Mary	40.00	289.25	182.23
1	Jones, Anthony	40.00	279.50	176.09
1	Lora, Kathy	40.00	260.00	163.80
1	Sahara, Ohmar	40.00	220.00	138.60
	Total	400.00+	2,582.50+	1,626.98+

The first thing that you have to do is clear the tab stops and enter new tabs at positions 17, 19, 44, 55, and 66 (refer to the previous example for help on setting tabs). Before you turn on the Math feature, you must first provide some additional information to WordPerfect about the characteristics of the data in each column.

Unless told otherwise, WordPerfect assumes that each column is to hold numeric information. This means that when you tab to a text column the message Align char. = . appears at the bottom of the screen. We have to tell WordPerfect that the first two columns contain text information by issuing the Math (Alt + F7) command and then selecting Math Def option. The screen depicted in Figure 10.5 now appears on your monitor.

WordPerfect allows you to define up to 24 columns (hence the letters A through X). The entries below each of these marked columns give information about how data will be handled. WordPerfect allows you to define four column types: Calculation (0), Text (1), Numeric (2), and total (3). It also allows you to decide what character to use to represent a negative number and defaults to a left parenthesis. [)]. It also assumes that you want two characters to the right of the decimal point.

As you can see, for each column defined, defaults are a numeric column, negative numbers represented by parentheses, and two digits to the right of the decimal point.

This exercise requires five columns, one for each tab stop entered. The first two columns are text data; therefore, the entries for columns A and B must be changed to text (1). To make these changes, move the cursor right and left or up and down, using the cursor movement keys. When you have made the necessary changes for columns A and B, issue the Exit (F7) command to return to the document.

Now turn on the Math feature and enter the data for the appropriate column. Remember, you must move the cursor from one column to the next using the tab key; do not use the Tab Align command.

When you have finished entering the columns of data, press the ENTER key twice to place a blank line between the detail data and the line that will shortly hold the totals. Use the tab key to position the cursor beneath the numeric columns and enter a plus sign (+). Remember, use only the upper case +; do not use the + on the cursor movement pad. Issue the Math (Alt + F7) command and select the Calculate option. Your totals should now look like those in the example. Since you are finished with issuing math commands, select the Math feature and turn Math off.

Totals and Subtotals

Now assume that you want to make some changes to your document. For example, instead of having just one total at the bottom of each column, generate a **subtotal** for each department and then generate a total for both departments. The subtotal (+) fields add any numbers that are in a column after the last + (subtotal) entry. The **Total** (=) entry combines all subtotals. Neither the + nor the = indicators appear on the printed document. They serve only as visual reminders of the command that you have entered telling WordPerfect how to handle arithmetic at this location in the document.

Insert three blank lines after the last department 1 employee. Tab twice and then position the cursor, using the Space Bar, and enter the word Subtotal. Use the tab key and enter the two required plus signs.

Figure 10.5
The screen accessed via the Math Def option of the Math command. You can determine what type of text will be contained in each defined column.

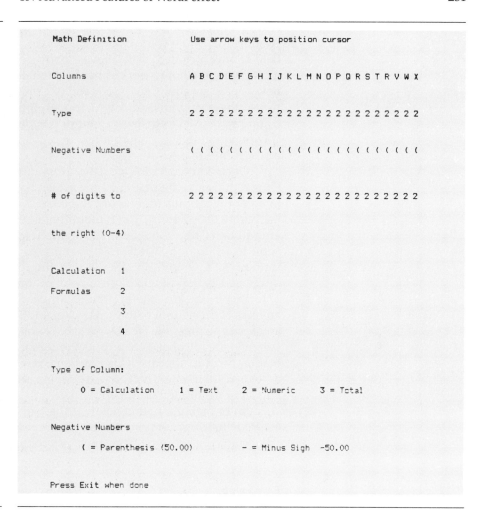

```
Math Definition              Use arrow keys to position cursor


Columns                      A B C D E F G H I J K L M N O P Q R S T R V W X


Type                         2 2 2 2 2 2 2 2 2 2 2 2 2 2 2 2 2 2 2 2 2 2 2 2


Negative Numbers             ( ( ( ( ( ( ( ( ( ( ( ( ( ( ( ( ( ( ( ( ( ( ( (


# of digits to               2 2 2 2 2 2 2 2 2 2 2 2 2 2 2 2 2 2 2 2 2 2 2 2


the right (0-4)


Calculation    1
Formulas       2

               3

               4


Type of Column:

     0 = Calculation    1 = Text    2 = Numeric    3 = Total


Negative Numbers

     ( = Parenthesis (50.00)          - = Minus Sigh  -50.00


Press Exit when done
```

Subtotals in turn can be combined by using an equal sign (=) for that field. After making the required changes, your document should appear like that below:

Dpt	Employee	Total Hours	Gross Pay	Net Pay
1	Adams, Sam	40.00	260.00	163.80
1	Johns, Peter	40.00	233.75	147.26
1	Kent, John	40.00	260.00	163.80
1	Lester, Ned	40.00	220.00	138.60
1	Smith, Luther	40.00	260.00	163.80
	Subtotal		1,233.75+	777.26+
2	Dix, Yvonne	40.00	300.00	189.00
2	Hunt, Mary	40.00	289.25	182.23
2	Jones, Anthony	40.00	279.50	176.09
2	Lora, Kathy	40.00	260.00	163.80
2	Sahara, Ohmar	40.00	220.00	138.60
	Subtotal		1,348.75+	849.72+
	Total		2,582.50=	1,626.98=

Formulas

Assume that you want to change the previous application so that the pay rate field is now included. This allows you to generate a new gross pay field by multiplying the hours worked by the pay rate. Delete all tab stops and create new ones at positions 17, 44, 55, and 66. You must now tell WordPerfect how to use these columns via the Math Def option of the Math command. The columns are used as follows: Column A contains text (1) data, columns B and C contain numeric (2) information, and column D contains a calculation/formula (0) information.

Once you have indicated that column D is a calculated column, Word-Perfect moves to the middle of the screen (see Figure 10.5) and waits for you to enter the formula (only four can be specified at one time) that you want to use across the columns. The four arithmetic operations that can be performed are addition (+), subtraction (−), multiplication (*), and division (/). Since we want to indicate to WordPerfect that it is to multiply hours by pay rate, the formula B * C is used. In other words, the content of this row of column B is multiplied by the content of this row of column C.

When you are entering the data, make certain that the Math indicator appears at the bottom of the screen. Again, the tabs are automatically aligned any time you press the tab key. Be sure to enter a Tab command to position the cursor at the calculated column; as the cursor arrives at that column, an exclamation point (!) appears. This is a visual reminder that this entry will appear as soon as you enter the Calculate command; the exclamation point will not appear in the printed document.

Enter the information below using tab stops at positions 17, 44, 55, and 66. Redefine your columns so that column B is now a numeric column. Enter the formula for column D (the gross pay column).

Employee	Hours	Pay Rate	Gross Pay
Dennison, John	25	3.45	86.25!
Baird, Ken	13	4.50	58.50!
Ayers, Charlie	34	3.75	127.50!
Nichols, Michelle	35	4.65	162.75!
Total			435.00+

When you are using formulas, you can use total calculated fields by entering the subtotal (+) command.

Sort Feature

You will often encounter a situation in which you have entered information into a document in order only to find that you really need that information presented in a different order. The **Sort** feature of WordPerfect makes it easy to change the order of a set of data. This data set can be either on the screen or in a data file on disk. The result of the sort can replace the data currently on the screen or it can be put on a separate file on disk.

Only simpler sorts are covered in this textbook. Instructions for the more complicated sorts can be found in the WordPerfect documentation.

The WordPerfect Sort feature permits sorting of select lines, paragraphs, or secondary merge records (data files). The Sort command is invoked by entering the Merge/Sort (Ctrl + F9) command. After you issue the Merge/Sort command, the following menu is displayed at the bottom of the screen.

1 Merge; 2 Sort; 3 Sorting Sequences: 0

Figure 10.6

Sort-by-line screen that lets you control exactly how a sort is to execute.

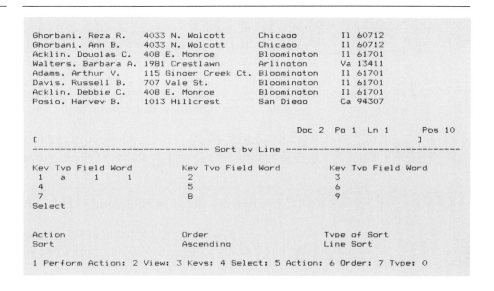

Once you issue the Sort command, WordPerfect asks what you want to sort with the prompt `Input File to sort: (Screen)`. As you can see, the default (Screen) sorts the document that appears on the screen. After you have selected the input file, WordPerfect questions you about the output file with the prompt `Output file for sort: (Screen)`. Again, the default is the document on the screen.

This method assumes that the entire document is to be sorted. One method of limiting a sort is first to use the Block (Alt + F4) command to mark the portion of the document that you want sorted and then to issue the Sort command. Assume that you have the following names and addresses:

Name and Address Data

Name	Address	City	St	Zip
Ghorbani, Reza R.	4033 N. Wolcott	Chicago	Il	60712
Ghorbani, Ann B.	4033 N. Wolcott	Chicago	Il	60712
Acklin, Douglas C.	408 E. Monroe	Bloomington	Il	61701
Walters, Barbara A.	1981 Crestlawn	Arlington	Va	13411
Adams, Arthur V.	115 Ginger Creek Ct.	Bloomington	Il	61701
Davis, Russell B.	707 Vale St.	Bloomington	Il	61701
Acklin, Debbie C.	408 E. Monroe	Bloomington	Il	61701
Posio, Harvey B.	1013 Hillcrest	San Diego	Ca	94307

To sort only the names and addresses you must block all the relevant lines, starting with the Reza Ghorbani line and ending with the Harvey Posio line. After the Sort command has been executed, Figure 10.6 appears on the monitor.

The Sort command creates a window on the screen. The upper window shows the document, and the lower window contains information about the Sort keys as well as the Sort menu in the status line. Note also that the Sort menu is viewed as Doc 2 by WordPerfect.

Let's examine the menu options:

Perform Action. This is the command that starts the sort operation.

View.   This command moves the cursor to the upper window and enables you to scroll through the document to ascertain exactly what areas are involved in the sort. The message `Press EXIT when done` appears at the bottom of the screen. When the Exit (F7) command is issued, control is returned to the Sort menu.

Keys.   This option enables you to define the order in which the information is to be sorted. A **key** is the entity (field, line, or word) by which the data are to be sorted. When you are determining priority, key1 has the highest priority, key2 the next priority, key3 has the next priority, and so on. This feature lets you specify a sort by first name in last-name column. In this case, the last name is key1 and the first name is key2. If you add a third field (for example, department), department becomes key1, the last name is key2, and the first name is key3.

Any key must be composed of alphanumeric or numeric data. Alphanumeric fields (designated by "a") may contain both alphabetic characters and numbers; numeric fields (designated by "n") may contain only numbers. Alphanumeric fields that contain numeric information (for example, zip codes, phone numbers, or social security numbers) must all be the same length. Numeric fields, on the other hand, can be any length.

When sorting, WordPerfect needs to know the exact location of each key. In these examples, WordPerfect is always dealing with lines of text. In other types of sorts, it may be dealing with other units of text.

A line of text ends with a hard carriage return code [Hrt] or soft carriage return code [Srt]. Lines are counted from top to bottom but can be counted from bottom to top by using negative numbers when sorting a secondary Merge file.

Select.   This command allows you to create a select statement with logic symbols.

Action.   The options are Select and Sort or Select Only (selection is performed only if a select statement exists).

Order.   The options are an ascending or descending sort order.

Type.   This option allows you to specify a Line, Paragraph, or Merge sort.

In this example, all that you have to do is to take the Perform Action option. The blocked area of text now appears as follows:

Name and Address Data

Name	Address	City	St	Zip
Acklin, Douglas C.	408 E. Monroe	Bloomington	Il	61701
Acklin, Debbie C.	408 E. Monroe	Bloomington	Il	61701
Adams, Arthur V.	115 Ginger Creek Ct.	Bloomington	Il	61701
Davis, Russell B.	707 Vale St.	Bloomington	Il	61701
Ghorbani, Ann B.	4033 N. Wolcott	Chicago	Il	60712
Ghorbani, Reza R.	4033 N. Wolcott	Chicago	Il	60712
Posio, Harvey B.	1013 Hillcrest	San Diego	Ca	94307
Walters, Barbara A.	1981 Crestlawn	Arlington	Va	13411

Now let's assume that you want to sort the name and address data by first name within last-name column. Again, you must block the text, starting with the Ghorbani line and ending with the Posio line. This type of sort is, of course, a two-key sort: The key1 field is the last name, and the key2 field is the first name. Issue the Merge/Sort (Ctrl + F7) command. You are to perform the sort of the information on the screen rather than sending the sorted data to a separate disk file. The Sort menu again appears on the monitor.

You must now indicate to WordPerfect the order of the sorts. Since the information is already in last name then first name order, this does not present a problem. In this type of sort (line), WordPerfect assumes that a space indicates the end of one field and the beginning of another. The last name, in this example, is field 1 and the first name is field 2.

Providing this information to WordPerfect requires that you select the Keys option. The first field (last name) comes up as **a 1 1**. This means that the sort will be alphanumeric and will be based on the first word of this field (last name). Press the right arrow until the cursor is in key field 2. You now want to sort on the second word (first name), so your entry for the second key should now be **a 1 2**. Now issue the Exit (F7) command to return to the sort menu. All of the required information has now been provided to WordPerfect, so issue the Perform Action command. The information shown on your monitor should look like the following:

```
                         Name and Address Data
---------------------------------------------------------------------------
       Name                 Address              City          St  Zip
---------------------------------------------------------------------------

Acklin, Debbie C.       408 E. Monroe           Bloomington    Il  61701
Acklin, Douglas C.      408 E. Monroe           Bloomington    Il  61701
Adams, Arthur V.        115 Ginger Creek Ct.    Bloomington    Il  61701
Davis, Russell B.       707 Vale St.            Bloomington    Il  61701
Ghorbani, Ann B.        4033 N. Wolcott         Chicago        Il  60712
Ghorbani, Reza R.       4033 N. Wolcott         Chicago        Il  60712
Posio, Harvey B.        1013 Hillcrest          San Diego      Ca  94307
Walters, Barbara A.     1981 Crestlawn          Arlington      Va  13411
```

Notice that even though the first name is logically a second field, it is really the second word of the first field since WordPerfect requires a ^R to separate physical fields. This presents a problem when you are using address information. If you examine the above lines closely, you notice that street addresses become separate words. For instance, the address Ginger Creek Ct. is treated as three separate words by WordPerfect. This means that if you wanted to arrange these lines in name order by zip code, the zip codes would have to be moved inward (before the street address) before the sort could execute properly. After using a rectangle-move to move the state and zip information, your monitor appears as follows:

```
                         Name and Address Data
---------------------------------------------------------------------------
       Name              St  Zip        Address              City
---------------------------------------------------------------------------

Acklin, Debbie C.       Il  61701    408 E. Monroe           Bloomington
Acklin, Douglas C.      Il  61701    408 E. Monroe           Bloomington
Adams, Arthur V.        Il  61701    115 Ginger Creek Ct.    Bloomington
Davis, Russell B.       Il  61701    707 Vale St.            Bloomington
Ghorbani, Ann B.        Il  60712    4033 N. Wolcott         Chicago
Ghorbani, Reza R.       Il  60712    4033 N. Wolcott         Chicago
Posio, Harvey B.        Ca  94307    1013 Hillcrest          San Diego
Walters, Barbara A.     Va  13411    1981 Crestlawn          Arlington
```

Now, assume that you want to sort these lines first by zip code, then by last name, and finally by first name. This is called a multiple-level sort. Again, since all of this information is viewed as being in one field, the use of spacing is critical.

Upon selecting the Keys option, you usually want to delete any previous key settings. This is accomplished by pressing the DEL key for keys 2 through any that were previously defined. In the above example, the zip code entry, which is to be the key1 field, is actually the fifth word in the field; the last name is the key2 field and is the first word; and the first name is the key3 field and is the second word. After these entries are described via the Keys option, key1 should have the contents **a 1 5**, key2 should be **a 1 1**, and key3 should be **a 1 2**. Issue the Perform Action command, and you should see the following on your monitor:

```
                    Name and Address Data
----------------------------------------------------------------
        Name          St  Zip       Address           City
----------------------------------------------------------------
Walters, Barbara A.   Va  13411  1981 Crestlawn      Arlington
Ghorbani, Ann B.      Il  60712  4033 N. Wolcott     Chicago
Ghorbani, Reza R.     Il  60712  4033 N. Wolcott     Chicago
Acklin, Debbie C.     Il  61701  408 E. Monroe       Bloomington
Acklin, Douglas C.    Il  61701  408 E. Monroe       Bloomington
Adams, Arthur V.      Il  61701  115 Ginger Creek Ct. Bloomington
Davis, Russell B.     Il  61701  707 Vale St.        Bloomington
Posio, Harvey B.      Ca  94307  1013 Hillcrest      San Diego
```

Notice that the lines are arranged first in zip code order, then in last name order, and then in first name order.

Macros

WordPerfect has the ability to record an often-used string of keystrokes (called a **macro**) you enter, assign a name to, and then execute whenever you request it. Thus you need perform a common task once only; thereafter, you can ask WordPerfect to simply replay the stored keystrokes.

A macro can be created in four steps:

Begin the macro definition process.

Name the macro.

End the macro definition process.

Execute the stored macro keystrokes.

You begin the macro definition process by entering the Define Macro (Ctrl + F10) command. Once this command is executed, the prompt Define Macro: appears at the bottom of the screen. You now enter the macro name, which can be done in any of four ways:

1. Type a name of two to eight characters.
2. Press the ALT key and type any letter from A to Z.
3. Press the ENTER key. This bypasses the naming of the macro and is used when only one macro is needed. Unnamed macros cannot be saved to disk.
4. Type a name consisting of only one character.

If you define a macro using options 1 or 2, the macro can be retrieved from the disk whenever you are in WordPerfect. Options 3 and 4 create temporary macros that are erased when you exit WordPerfect. The name that you give a macro is important, because permanent macros are saved to the default disk as separate files using the names that you entered plus a .MAC file extension. When you later tell WordPerfect to execute a macro, it looks for this file on the default disk and, upon finding it, loads and executes the stored keystrokes.

Once the macro has been named, you are ready to record any keystrokes. When you have finished entering the keystrokes to be incorporated into the macro, issue another Define Macro (Ctrl + F10) to your document.

Build a Temporary Macro

Assume that you are in a word processing application in which you will be intermixing text and numeric information. You have projected that there will be about 15–20 of these numeric blocks. Each block requires that you place tab stops at positions 15, 40, 51, and 62, shift to 12 pitch, and turn Math on. This type of repetitious task is an ideal use of WordPerfect's macro feature.

Since the document will be generated at one sitting, there is no need to create a permanent macro. This application will demonstrate a **temporary macro**. The macro is built using the following steps.

1. Issue the Macro Define (Ctrl + F10) command to start the macro definition process. Prompt is Define Macro:.
2. Press the ENTER key; WordPerfect names the macro. (This is actually bypassing the unneeded naming process.)
3. Enter the following commands to be included in the macro:
   a. Enter the Line Format (Shift + F8) command, clear all the tabs using the Ctrl + End command, and enter tab stops at positions 15, 40, 51, and 62.
   b. Enter the Line Format (Shift + F8) command and change the right-hand margin to 90.
   c. Enter the Page Format (Alt + F8) command to change the pitch to 12 and leave the font the same.
   d. Enter the Math/Columns (Alt + F7) command, define column 1 as text, and turn Math on.
4. Issue another Define Macro (Ctrl + F10) command to end the macro definition process.

This macro is now ready for use. To invoke this macro, enter the Macro (Alt + F10) command and press the ENTER key when WordPerfect prompts you for the macro name. The Macro sets the tab, margin, and pitch, defines the math columns, and turns on the math feature. You can now enter the numeric columns in the usual fashion.

Permanent Macros

The preceding method of entering a macro is sufficient as long as you do not have to interrupt your data entry session. It does, however, require you to enter all the commands necessary to restore the previous WordPerfect settings for columns and to recalculate and reset the pitch and margin settings. The following steps create macros called COLMNON and COLMNOFF that will perform all the previous steps as well as the steps that return WordPerfect to its initial state.

COLMNON. The COLMNON macro sets new tab stops, margins, pitch settings, and math columns and turns the math feature on. It is created by the following steps.

1. Issue the Macro Define (Ctrl + F10) command to start the macro definition process. Prompt is `Define Macro:`
2. Type COLMNON and press the ENTER key. This creates a file called COLMNON.MAC on disk.
3. Enter the following commands to be included in the macro:
   a. Enter the Line Format (Shift + F8) command, clear all the tabs using the Ctrl + End command, and enter tab stops at positions 15, 40, 51, and 62.
   b. Enter the Line Format (Shift + F8) command and change the right-hand margin to 90.
   c. Enter the Print Format (Ctrl + F8) command to change the pitch to 12 and leave the font the same.
   d. Enter the Math/Columns (Alt + F7) command, define column 1 as text, and turn math off.
4. Issue another Define Macro (Ctrl + F10) command to end the macro definition process.

COLMNOFF. The COLMNOFF macro restores old tab stops, margins, and pitch settings, recalculates pitch and margins, and turns off the math feature. It is created via the following steps.

1. Issue the Macro Define (Ctrl + F10) command to start the macro definition process. Prompt is `Define Macro:`.
2. Type COLMNOFF and press the ENTER key. This creates a file called COLMNOFF.MAC on disk.
3. Enter the following commands to be included in the macro:
   a. Enter the Line Format (Shift + F8) command, clear all the tabs using the Ctrl + End command, and enter tab stops at positions 15, 20, 25, 30, 35, 40, 45, 50, 55, and 60.
   b. Enter the Line Format (Shift + F8) command and change the right-hand margin to 74.
   c. Enter the Print Format (Ctrl + F8) command to change the pitch to 10 and leave the font the same.
   d. Enter the Math/Columns (Alt + F7) command, issue the Recalculate command, and turn math off.
4. Issue another Define Macro (Ctrl + F10) command to end the macro definition process.

Now, when you want to enter one of the numeric blocks, you can issue the Macro (Alt + F10) command and enter the COLMNON macro name. This issues all of the commands necessary to prepare WordPerfect to build numeric columns. When you are finished, you enter the Macro (Alt + F10) command and enter the COLMNOFF macro name to recalculate and restore tabs and margins.

Another Macro

Assume that you have written a twenty-page term paper for one of your classes with forty-five different endnote quotations. While attending class the day before the assignment is due, you learn that footnotes, rather than end-notes, are required for the paper. If you were using another word processing package, this change would require a tremendous amount of effort. Word-Perfect, however, requires only that you enter the instructions necessary to change one of the endnotes to a footnote, store these in a macro, and then execute the macro enough times to change all of the endnotes to footnotes. The following steps are required.

1. Issue the Macro Define (Ctrl + F10) command to start the macro definition process.
2. Type FOOTNOTE and press the ENTER key. This creates a file called FOOTNOTE.MAC on disk.
3. Enter the following commands to be included in the macro:
   a. Issue the Footnote command (Ctrl + F7) and edit an endnote (option 6).
   b. Press the ENTER key to display the endnote.
   c. Issue the Delete (DEL) command and respond Y to delete the endnote number.
   d. Issue the Block command (Alt + F4) and paint the entire endnote (Home, Home, DownArrow).
   e. Issue the Move (Ctrl + F4) command and Cut (option 1) the end-note from the document.
   f. Issue the Exit (F7) command and return to the document.
   g. Issue the Footnote (Ctrl + F7) command and create a footnote (option 1).
   h. Issue the Move (Ctrl + F4) command and Retrieve the cut endnote (option 5).
   i. Exit (F7) the footnote screen.
4. Issue another Macro Define (Ctrl + F10) command to end the session.

Once the macro has been created and saved to disk you can automatically change all of your document's endnotes to footnotes by issuing the Escape (ESC) command and entering a number larger than the total number of end-notes in your document (make certain that it is larger than the total number of endnotes). Start the macro, and it will be repeated until there are no more endnotes to be changed. Once this macro is finished, your document is ready for printing.

This coverage of the Macro feature of WordPerfect barely scratches the surface of this powerful feature. To learn more, consult the WordPerfect documentation.

Chapter Review

This chapter introduces you to some of the advanced features of Word-Perfect. These include the footnoting/endnoting, math, sort, and macro features. The coverage of these features is introductory; if you need more information, you must consult the WordPerfect documentation.

The Footnote (Ctrl + F7) command provides the capability for entering footnotes or endnotes for quotations. Even though the text for a footnote appears at the bottom of a page and the text for an endnote appears at the end of a document, the actual text of a note is embedded in the text of a document. WordPerfect keeps track of the number of lines needed for a footnote and the number of lines needed for a text page, so that everything fits on a printed page. Endnotes, of course, are placed at the end of the document.

WordPerfect does an excellent job of keeping track of the footnote/endnote numbers. If other footnotes or endnotes are added or deleted from the document, the note numbers are automatically adjusted to reflect the addition or deletion.

The Math feature of WordPerfect allows you to enter columns or multiple columns (rows) of numeric information and perform arithmetic calculations on that data (addition, subtraction, multiplication, and division). Totals of columnar numbers can be either subtotals, or totals. The Math feature of WordPerfect requires that you tell it which columns contain text, numbers, or calculation (formula) data. To perform mathematical operations, the Math feature must be turned on, and to reflect a new formula or changes to numbers, the Recalculation operation must be specified.

The Sort operation allows you to sort lines, paragraphs, or secondary files of data. The most commonly used sort is the line/block sort. Once the range of the sort has been specified to WordPerfect, the order, field, and word number must be specified. Either an ascending or descending sort can be specified.

The macro feature of WordPerfect has the ability to store keystrokes entered from the keyboard and to ''replay'' them later, thus performing any number of tasks. A macro can be either temporary or permanent. A temporary macro is ''forgotten'' when you exit WordPerfect. A permanent macro is stored to a file with a .MAC file extension. Both temporary and permanent macros save many keystrokes in repetitious operations.

Key Terms and Concepts

Endnote	permanent macro
Footnote	Sort
Formulas	subtotal
key	temporary macro
macro	toggle
Math/Columns	Total

Chapter Quiz

Multiple Choice

1. Which of the following statements concerning footnote/endnotes is false?
   a. Footnotes are actually entered in a separate file and then combined with your document file at print time.
   b. A note when it is entered generates a hidden code.
   c. Footnotes are limited to a length of fifty characters.
   d. All of the above are true.
   e. All of the above are false.

2. Which of the following statements concerning footnotes/endnotes is true?
   a. A footnote can be changed to an endnote.
   b. Either a footnote or an endnote can be edited.
   c. You are limited to a maximum of two lines when entering a note.
   d. WordPerfect automatically reserves enough room at the bottom of a page for footnote text.

3. The Math feature of WordPerfect does *not* allow which of the following?
   a. Calculation of totals or subtotals

  b. Once numeric data has been changed a total is automatically regenerated to reflect the changed data.

  c. Specification of calculation formulas

  d. You to use the Tab command to move from one numeric column to the next.

  e. All of the above are true.

4. Which of the following statements is true concerning the Sort feature of WordPerfect?

  a. Sorts can include lines, paragraphs, or files.

  b. A sort can be either in descending or ascending order.

  c. A line sort requires that you first block the area of the document to sort.

  d. Multiple key sorts are allowed.

  e. All of the above are true.

5. Which of the following statements about macros is false?

  a. A macro is really composed of keystrokes that have been stored and that can be ''played back'' on demand.

  b. A macro can be either permanent or temporary.

  c. A permanent macro is stored in the text of your document.

  d. A macro is invoked by entering the Macro (Alt + F10) command.

  e. All of the above are true.

True/False

6. WordPerfect permits you to insert/delete footnotes or endnotes and automatically renumbers any following notes in your document.

7. You are allowed to restart the renumbering of notes in your text.

8. WordPerfect provides the square root math command.

9. A permanent macro actually resides on disk as a separate file.

10. Sending your output to the screen is dangerous when using the Sort feature of WordPerfect.

Answers

1. a & c 2. a, b, & d 3. b 4. e 5. c 6. t 7. t 8. f 9. t 10. f

Exercises

1. Footnotes are embedded in a _____ code in the text of your document.

2. An Endnote can be changed by selecting the _____ option from the Footnote (Ctrl + F7) menu.

3. The usual number of lines that WordPerfect keeps together for a footnote is _____ .

4. The _____ entry of the Footnote command allows you to place a two-inch line between the text and your footnotes.

5. Changing a footnote number requires selecting the _____ option from the Footnote menu.

6. The Math operator _____ is used for generating a subtotal.

7. The Math operator _____ is used for generating a grand total.

8. Formulas entered in WordPerfect can contain either _____ or _____ .

9. The Tab command acts like a _____ command when the Math On indicator appears at the bottom of your screen.

10. The command _____ generates an average.

11. A _____ command must be issued before WordPerfect knows that new totals are to be calculated to reflect changed data.

12. The Sort is activated by issuing the _____ command.

13. If you do not enter an output file, WordPerfect assumes that the output of the sort goes to the _____ .

14. The _____ option enables you to define the order of the sort.

15. The _____ command is used when you are performing a line sort to the screen.

16. _____ or fields can be specified in a sort command.

17. A _____ is really composed of stored keystrokes.

18. A permanent macro is stored to disk with a _____ extension on the file name.

19. Executing a permanent macro requires entering the Macro (Alt + F10) and then entering the _____ .

20. You can automatically repeat a macro by first entering a(n) _____ command and then telling WordPerfect how many times to execute the macro.

Computer Exercises

Below is a summary of the WordPerfect commands covered in this chapter.

Footnote/Endnote (Ctrl + F7)	Create a footnote/endnote and embed this text within the document.
Math (Alt + F7)	Allows you to perform mathematical operations within a document.
Sort (Ctrl + F9)	Allows you to sort lines, paragraphs, or files.
Define Macro (Ctrl + F10)	Allows you to create a macro.
Macro (Alt + F10)	Allows you to execute a saved macro.

1. Load the file named CH10EX1A and insert the footnotes indicated below. Print the file. Save this changed document to the file CH10EX1.

CHAPTER II

REVIEW OF THE RELATED LITERATURE

The review of the related literature is divided into four parts. The first part examines the concept of long-range planning and the use of Management Information System (MIS) and computer-based long-range planning systems in organizations. The second part examines the role of models and simulation in long-range planning. The third part examines computer-based planning systems in education and the fourth part deals with computer-based planning systems in business.

Long-Range Planning and MIS

The Problem

The quality of human life in the western world today is better than at any time in the history of man. However, as man's quality of life in the world has generally improved the problems facing western cultures have, paradoxically, also increased. Our cities are suffering from decay and bankruptcy. The populations of third world countries are increasing above predicted rates creating food distribution problems. Energy is being consumed at a faster rate and is becoming increasingly more expensive. Natural resources are quickly being depleted. Last, there are fears that technology is out of control.[1]

It is difficult to demonstrate the critical nature of many of the crises or impending crises. Without acceptance of such reality, it is difficult to motivate action toward plans and programs. Most of us are not aware of any plans or programs of a national or world scope for anticipatory action to link policy goals and ways of achieving the goals. Many of the efforts to generate a motivation for acceptance among society are thwarted by conflicting reports and actions.[2]

In the past decade, it was possible to categorize the frustrations and dilemmas as: (1) members of society had unprecedented needs, interests and urgencies; (2) established institutions and their instrumentalities were no longer capable of making appropriate and adequate responses; (3) technological progress had outdistanced our ability to cope; and (4) natural resources were scarce and on the verge of depletion in many cases with time being one of the most critically depleted resources.[3]

The above problems deal directly with man's inability, both as an individual or via his instrumentalities, to deal effectively with technological and societal change. Alvin Toffler's concept of future shock—the impact of the rate of change and the direction of that change on man's ability to cope has a direct bearing on our inability to solve problems which are the result of rapid changes in our society.[4]

Martin and Norman address this problem of our inability to cope with rapid change:

As the pace of technology quickens and its inventions become more and more devastating, so it becomes more dangerous to allow society to evolve by natural selection, if the law of the jungle prevails for the next

[1]Robert U. Ayres, *Uncertain Futures: Challenges for Decision Makers* (New York: John Wiley & Sons, 1979), pp. 57, 121, 188, 144.

[2]J. H. McGrath, "Perturbations in Society and Education," in "McGrath on Education, Schooling and Futurism," Normal, Illinois, Illinois State University, 1975, pp. 11–12. (mimeographed.)

[3]Ibid., p. 1.

[4]Alvin Toffler, *Future Shock* (New York: Random House, 1970), p. 3.

50 years and during this time we have the technical innovations that are now being predicted in, say, electronics and biochemistry alone, then society will be thrown into unspeakable turmoil. . . If we had a large amount of time in which to think about society and to text out the effects of changes that we could introduce, then we would be better able to guide the process. Slow evolution can be controlled evolution. The rate of technical change, however, is becoming too rapid. It is only too apparent that many institutions of today are failing to keep pace with the changes. We are not directing the technology it, to a major extent, is directing us.[5]

Futurism and Long-Range Planning

Futurism holds that a future deemed desirable can be achieved by systematically doing well the things that must be done. Futurology, the study of the future, is the science that offers methods and techniques for long-range planning.[6] According to Drucker, long-range planning is:

. . . the continuous process of making present entrepreneurial (risk-taking) decisions systematically with the best possible knowledge of their futurity, organizing systematically the efforts needed to carry out these decisions, and measuring the results of these decisions against the expectations through organized, systematic feedback.[7]

[5]James Martin and Adrian R. D. Norman, *The Computerized Society* (Englewood Cliffs, New Jersey: Prentice-Hall, Inc., 1970), pp. 437–438.
[6]McGrath, "Perturbations in Society and Education," p. 23.
[7]Peter F. Drucker, "Long-Range Planning Means Risk Taking," in *Long-Range Planning for Management*, ed. David W. Ewing (New York: Harper & Row, Publishers, 1972), p. 6.

2. Change the file that you created in exercise 1 above so that the footnotes begin with the number 50. Notice that WordPerfect automatically renumbers the footnotes.

3. Use the edit footnote feature of WordPerfect to change footnote 3 to the following:

   John Argenti, *Systematic Corporate Planning* (New York: Halsted Press, 1974), p. 53.

4. Retrieve the file CH10EX4A. This file contains the numbers for the document below. Your task is to enter the calculation columns as well as generate the required totals using the numeric information. Once you have completed this task, print the document and then save it to the file CH10EX4.

5. Retrieve the file CH10EX5A. This file contains name and address information. Perform a line sort to arrange the names in alphabetical order, first name within last name. Once you have completed this task, print the document and then save it to the file CH10EX5.

6. Retrieve the file CH10EX1 that you created in exercise 1. Create a permanent macro that changes all the footnotes to endnotes. Use the Esc command to execute your macro, changing all of the footnotes to endnotes in one session. Print the document and then save it to the file CH10EX6.

TOOL THREE

SPREADSHEETS USING VP-PLANNER

Chapter 11

Fundamentals of Spreadsheets and VP-Planner

Chapter Objectives   *After completing this chapter, you should be able to:*

Describe the concepts of spreadsheets and worksheets

Define and discuss common spreadsheet terminology

Discuss features that are common to many spreadsheet packages

Discuss the steps involved in using spreadsheet packages

Define and discuss the three parts of VP-Planner

Discuss the various aspects of the VP-Planner screen

Discuss the various means of manipulating the VP-Planner pointer (cursor)

Discuss the role of the various keys and their relationship to VP-Planner

Discuss various elementary features of the VP-Planner packages

Enter a VP-Planner worksheet

Introduction to Spreadsheets

The spreadsheet is the piece of software that has single-handedly caused American business to take the microcomputer seriously as a problem-solving tool. An electronic spreadsheet is simply the electronic equivalent of the accounting worksheet. Both the electronic worksheet and the accounting worksheet consist of a matrix composed of rows and columns. These rows and columns allow a person to organize information in an easy to understand format.

The terms *spreadsheet* and *worksheet* can be distinguished as follows: **spreadsheet** is the set of program instructions, such as VisiCalc or VP-Planner, that produces a worksheet; a **worksheet** is a model or representation of reality that is created using a spreadsheet software package. Spreadsheets can be used in completing any data manipulation involving numbers and text that is usually performed with pencil, paper, and calculator. Uses of spreadsheets in business include:

Budget preparation

Working trial balances

Business modeling

Sales forecasting

Investment analysis

Payroll

Real estate management

Taxes

Investment proposals

Electronic spreadsheet software greatly improves the user's accuracy, efficiency, and productivity. Once a worksheet has been prepared, other options ("what if" alternatives) can be easily considered simply by making the appropriate changes and instructing the spreadsheet to recalculate all entries to reflect these changes. This allows the user to spend more time on creative decision making.

Spreadsheet Syntax

Each spreadsheet package allows the user to identify a unique address or **cell** at the intersection of a row and a column. A **row** is on a horizontal axis; a **column** is on a vertical axis. Worksheet cells are referred to by their COL-UMN,ROW designation, and each may contain a label, a number, or a formula.

A **label** is alphanumeric text used to provide headings for the rows and columns, to make the worksheet easier to understand. Labels may be numeric (for example, quarters 1, 2, 3, or 4) or alphabetic (for example, the word *quarter*). A **number** is a numeric value entered in a cell; it may be either a constant or a variable—in which case it is the result of some type of mathematical calculation.

The **formula** contained in a cell creates relationships between values in other specified cells. For example, if the contents of cells E1, E2, E3, and E4 were to be added together, with the result to be placed in cell E7, the formula +E1+E2+E3+E4 would have to be placed in cell E7. Formulas used in cells can be more complex than just simple sums; they can contain financial calculations such as net present value or statistical expressions such as variance or standard deviation.

Understanding that formulas allow computations (based on the value in one cell) to determine values in other cells makes spreadsheets easy to use. It is imperative that anyone wishing to make effective use of spreadsheets be able to express relationships in terms of values—for example, gross margin = sales − cost of goods sold, or taxes = gross income × 35 percent. Once any such relationship has been defined and placed in a numeric format, any situation involving that relationship can be analyzed via an electronic worksheet.

One major strength of the electronic spreadsheet is that it presents and works with data in the familiar tabular format that is used to present or depict almost all data. A personal budget, for example, uses this tabular format: the budget categories are placed in a column, and the various time periods are placed as headings across the top row. Moreover, the spreadsheet is able to project and evaluate numerous alternatives to a single plan—the ubiquitous "what if" form of analysis—making it an important aid in decision making. The interrelationship of the cells enables the viewer to see immediately what effect changing the contents of one or more cells has on the rest of the worksheet.

Spreadsheets can be used in two basic ways: with your own worksheet, if you have a unique application or just have the time and want the practice (and if the application to be modeled is not very complex); or with a template. A **template** is much the same as an application program, except that someone has already done all the logical planning, designing, and implementing involved in building the template. Consequently, the individual using the template only has to enter some data and receive the results.

VisiCalc, an acronym for Visible Calculator, was the first spreadsheet introduced for microcomputers. It was designed by Dan Bricklin and Robert Frankston at a time when Bricklin was a student in the Harvard MBA program; he became interested in developing VisiCalc after growing tired of playing "what if" games in case studies that primarily required financial analysis. At the time, some software packages available for mainframe computers were capable of performing this type of manipulation, but they were difficult to use. One apocryphal story has Bricklin discussing the possible application of such a concept to the newly emerging microcomputers with one of his MBA professors, and being told that the idea would never be marketable.

Another person associated with VisiCalc is Dan Flystra, also a student in the MBA program at Harvard, who purchased the marketing rights to the product and founded Personal Software—later renamed VisiCorp (now defunct).

VisiCalc was originally designed to run on the Apple II computer and was responsible for many purchases of Apple computers by business. Since the introduction of the program, many different spreadsheet packages have been produced for microcomputers. Many of these reflect tremendous improvements in power and capability over the original VisiCalc.

Problem-solving Steps Using Spreadsheets

In approaching a problem, especially a complex problem, you should try to develop a plan for handling it as early in the process as possible. A lot of additional work can be avoided by prior planning; your end product will look better, and you will avoid redoing work. The planning process steps are: determining the purpose, planning, building and testing, and documenting.

Determining the Purpose. The first step is to determine exactly what the purpose or goal of the worksheet is. In other words, what do you want it to do for you? What inputs will be necessary to provide to the worksheet? What outputs do you want the spreadsheet to generate? Are printed reports needed to make the information the worksheet provides useful?

Planning. The second step is to plan a blueprint of your worksheet on paper. This blueprint should maintain the same rectangular format presented by the screen you are using and should include all screens that will have explanations to you or other users. Remember that you may only be using this spreadsheet once a year and may not remember all the nuances of your spreadsheet logic after such a long separation. You should also plan how you will manipulate your data.

Building and Testing. The third step is to build and test your worksheet. If you have planned everything properly, this should go smoothly. Testing the spreadsheet involves making sure that it manipulates the data correctly. A lot of things can go wrong—for instance, a formula might reference an incorrect cell, or it might be entered incorrectly—but a number of packages that you can process against a spreadsheet help in this process. Two of them, Spreadsheet Auditor and Docucalc, display the spreadsheet (as it appears on the screen), the cell values, and the corresponding formulas within cells used to manipulate data.

Documenting. The final step is to finish the documentation for using the worksheet. Some of this documentation is included within the worksheet itself, but a lot of other concepts may have to be covered to allow a user other than the worksheet's author to operate it effectively. In addition, limitations on inputs and outputs must be communicated, and if the worksheet is to be used as a template within an organization, its date of creation and its author's name and telephone number must be provided.

Introduction to VP-Planner

The **VP-Planner** software package has three logical and totally integrated parts: spreadsheet, data management, and graphing. **Integration** means that you do not have to leave the spreadsheet program, for instance, to get to the graphing or data management programs.

Parts of VP-Planner

Spreadsheet. The extremely powerful **spreadsheet** portion of VP-Planner manipulates the tabular accounting-like data. You can enter numbers, labels, or formulas into the worksheet. For example you can list twelve numbers in a column and define one cell to hold the sum of those twelve numbers; thereafter, when any one of these numbers is changed, the sum is automatically updated to reflect the change.

Data Management. The **data management feature** of VP-Planner allows you to sort, summarize, and extract (make reports) portions of the individual records contained in a file. The major difference between this type of data management and other types is that here the entire file is contained in a worksheet. It should be noted that VP-Planner also contains a three-dimensional data management feature that is beyond the scope of this textbook.

Graphics. The **graphics feature** allows you to take information that you have entered in a worksheet and display it graphically to the screen (assuming you have graphics screen capability) or to the printer. You can display information in the form of a pie chart, bar chart, stacked bar chart, line, or xy. A regular monochrome monitor, however, will not display a graph; rather, the computer will simply beep.

Figure 11.1
The VP-Planner Main Menu.

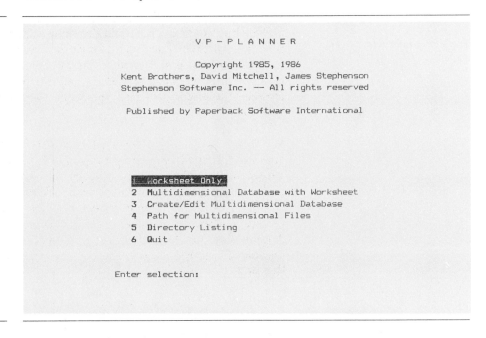

```
                V P - P L A N N E R

                Copyright 1985, 1986
   Kent Brothers, David Mitchell, James Stephenson
   Stephenson Software Inc. -- All rights reserved

       Published by Paperback Software International




              1 Worksheet Only
              2  Multidimensional Database with Worksheet
              3  Create/Edit Multidimensional Database
              4  Path for Multidimensional Files
              5  Directory Listing
              6  Quit


       Enter selection:
```

Starting VP-Planner

VP-Planner is a menu-driven software package, meaning that lists of options (*menus*) are displayed for you to choose from. VP-Planner allows you to make a selection by either entering the first character of the option at the keyboard or positioning the pointer using a right or left arrow key and then depressing ENTER.

Starting VP-Planner is a straightforward process. Simply boot the computer and then place the VP-Planner disk in disk drive A and your data disk in disk drive B and enter VP). The computer will then display the **VP-Planner Main Menu** (see Figure 11.1). At this time, either enter a 1 and/or depress the ENTER key. After some disk processing, the screen in Figure 11.2a will be displayed, and the directory of the disk in disk drive B will be read by the system.

VP-Planner Screen

At first, there may appear to be little on the worksheet screen, but looks in this case are deceiving. The following pieces are part of the worksheet screen: control panel, mode indicator, border, worksheet, pointer/cursor, error message area, and indicators.

Border. The **border** labels the rows and columns of your worksheet. The columns are labeled with letters of the alphabet (A, B, C, and so on), and the rows are labeled with numbers (1, 2, 3, and so on).

Worksheet. The **worksheet** contains whatever space is available to the user for problem solving. The worksheet has several key parts: cell, pointer, and window. As was noted earlier, a cell is the intersection point of a row and column and is referred to by its cell address COLUMN/ROW. For example, B5 refers to the cell located at the intersection of column B and row 5. A cell can contain either a label, a value, or a formula.

Figure 11.2a
The VP-Planner worksheet
screen.

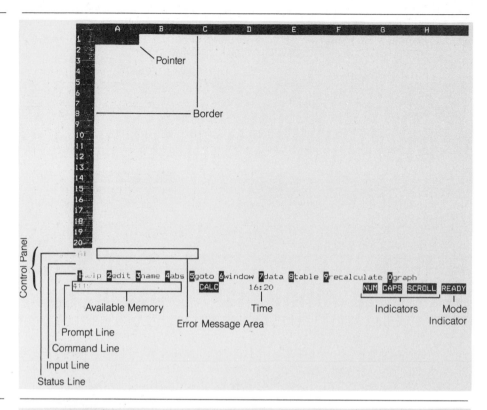

Figure 11.2b

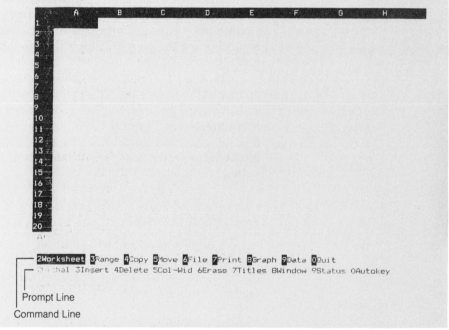

The **pointer**, also sometimes referred to as the cursor, is the reverse-video (light background with dark characters) bar. Its width is dependent on the width of the cell being referenced. The contents of the referenced cell are displayed in the status line of the control panel.

The full-blown VP-Planner worksheet is large compared to many other spreadsheet packages. It contains 256 columns (A, B, C, D, . . . IV) and 9,999 rows for a grand total of 2,559,744 cells. How large a piece of paper would you need to hold this size spreadsheet? If each cell were one-quarter-inch high and one-inch wide, a piece of paper that could hold all of these rows and columns would have to be 208.3 feet high and 21.3 feet wide. The VP-Planner worksheet is, indeed, large.

It goes without saying that all these cells cannot be displayed at one time on your small display screen. Instead, only small, rectangular sections of these 2,559,744 cells can be displayed at one time. The display, referred to as the **window** always has 20 rows; the number of columns displayed depends on the column width. Your worksheet, however, consists of only 64 columns and 256 rows. This gives you a total of 16,384 cells to use in building a worksheet.

Control Panel. The **control panel** is contained in the four lines immediately below the row border and consists of (1) the status line, (2) the input line, (3) the command line, and (4) the prompt line. The **status line** tells where you are, displaying the cell address, data format (if any), and the cell contents; information is given about how the data in that particular cell are being processed by VP-Planner and about where the cell contains a label, a value, or a formula.

The **input line** corresponds to a "scratch" area that contains any data you happen to enter. It also contains any preentered information destined for the cell location given in the status line. This information is not placed in either the cell or the status line until the ENTER key is pressed.

The **command line** displays currently available function keys or "/" commands from the Main Menu. These are used to make a menu of options for performing various operations on your worksheet. The Main Menu can be invoked any time by entering the slash (/) command. Each of these commands can then be executed in one of three ways: highlighting the desired menu option with the pointer (pointing) and depressing the ENTER key, entering the first letter of the desired menu option, or pressing the indicated function key.

The **prompt line** contains further options or an explanation of a specific command when a VP-Planner Menu is displayed (see Figure 11.2b). It also contains various indicators used by VP-Planner, which will be discussed later.

Mode Indicator. The **mode indicator**, at the far right of the prompt line, displays status information about what VP-Planner is doing. Some mode indicators you will be seeing in this textbook are:

READY—VP-Planner is waiting for you to tell it to do something.

VALUE—You are entering a number or formula to be contained in a cell.

LABEL—You are entering text information to be contained in a cell.

EDIT—You are changing the contents of a cell via the edit feature of VP-Planner.

POINT—You are pointing to a cell or to a range of cells.

MENU—You have a menu displayed before you and are selecting from it.

HELP—You are using the VP-Planner help feature.

ERROR—Something went wrong, and VP-Planner is waiting for you to depress the ENTER or ESC key to acknowledge the error.

WAIT—VP-Planner is calculating the spreadsheet or performing a read/write operation and cannot accept more commands.

FIND—VP-Planner is using its data management feature to perform a find operation.

Available Memory. The amount of unused RAM is the number displayed in the **available memory**. This number represents the amount of unused memory, measured in K (1,024 bytes), that is available for use in a worksheet.

Current Time. The **current time** of day is displayed here. Remember, for this time to be correct, you must respond to the T I ME prompt when you boot the computer system.

Error Message Indicator. **Error messages** appear in the lower left-hand corner of the screen and give a brief explanation of what has gone wrong. They are accompanied by a beep from the computer when a VP-Planner rule has been broken. After you have read the message and wish to return control to the worksheet, simply depress the ESC or ENTER key.

Indicators. The IBM keyboard does not tell you whether the SCROLL LOCK, CAPS LOCK, or NUM LOCK keys are on or off. The VP-Planner **indicators** for each of these provide this information. If one of these keys is on, a message in reverse video will be displayed in the lower right-hand corner of the screen. A fourth indicator is CALC, which will be discussed in a later chapter.

Navigating Around the VP-Planner Worksheet

Because VP-Planner was designed specifically for the IBM PC, it makes full use of all the keys on the keyboard—an especially important feature when it comes to moving the pointer quickly around the worksheet. Most pointer movement commands are accomplished by using the ten-key pad found on the right-hand side of the keyboard, and VP-Planner automatically places these keys in cursor movement mode rather than in numeric mode. The movement keys work as follows:

>   The **down arrow** moves the pointer down one cell position (down one row).
>
>   The **up arrow** moves the pointer up one cell position (up one row).
>
>   The **right arrow** moves the pointer to the right one cell position (to the right one column).
>
>   The **left arrow** moves the pointer to the left one cell position (to the left one column).
>
>   The **PG UP key** moves the pointer up twenty lines (one page) in its present column.
>
>   The **PG DN key** moves the pointer down twenty lines (one page) in its present column.
>
>   The **HOME key** moves the pointer to cell position A1.
>
>   The **END key**, when entered prior to an arrow key, positions the pointer in the same direction as the arrow key at the next nonblank boundary cell. For example, a worksheet will typically have blocks of cells with data, followed by blocks of blank, empty cells that are in turn followed by other cells with data. If the pointer is in a blank/empty region and the END key is depressed, followed by an arrow key, the pointer will be moved to the first nonblank cell. If the same command sequence is entered again, the pointer moves to the last nonblank cell in that block. Entering the same command sequence moves the pointer to the next nonblank area. When there are no longer any nonblank cells remaining in one direction of pointer movement, one of VP-Planner's

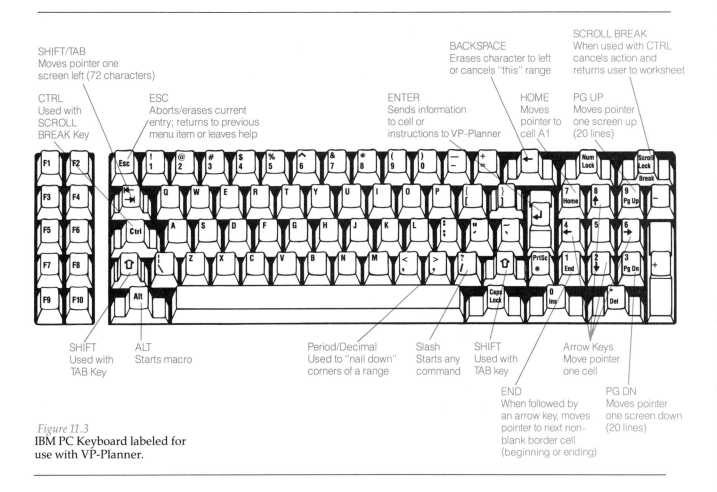

SHIFT/TAB
Moves pointer one
screen left (72 characters)

CTRL
Used with
SCROLL
BREAK Key

ESC
Aborts/erases current
entry; returns to previous
menu item or leaves help

BACKSPACE
Erases character to left
or cancels "this" range

SCROLL BREAK
When used with CTRL
cancels action and
returns user to worksheet

ENTER
Sends information
to cell or
instructions to VP-Planner

HOME
Moves
pointer to
cell A1

PG UP
Moves pointer
one screen up
(20 lines)

SHIFT
Used with
TAB Key

ALT
Starts macro

Period/Decimal
Used to "nail down"
corners of a range

Slash
Starts any
command

SHIFT
Used with
TAB key

Arrow Keys
Move pointer
one cell

END
When followed by
an arrow key, moves
pointer to next non-
blank border cell
(beginning or ending)

PG DN
Moves pointer
one screen down
(20 lines)

Figure 11.3
IBM PC Keyboard labeled for
use with VP-Planner.

boundaries will have been reached (for example, row 9999 or column IV).

The **TAB key**, located above the CTRL key, moves the pointer to the right one screen (seventy-two characters) at a time. The TAB plus the **SHIFT key** moves the pointer to the left one screen (seventy-two characters) at a time.

The above keys move or skip the cursor across the worksheet. In contrast, the **SCROLL LOCK key** causes the worksheet to move under the cursor, rather than causing the cursor to move across the spreadsheet.

How VP-Planner Uses Other Keys

Figure 11.3 shows where the various special purpose keys are located on the IBM PC keyboard and what they are used for. The remaining special purpose keys work as follows:

The **ESC key** is used to back out of a command sequence, if you are in a menu. If you are entering data in a cell, anything that appears on the entry line is simply erased when you depress ESC, and the original contents of the cell (if any), are left unchanged.

The **CTRL key** plus the **SCROLL BREAK** key is used to cancel any action taking place and return the user to the worksheet. This key sequence can be used to cancel printing, sorting, or any other VP-Planner operation.

The **ALT key** lets you give letter keys alternative meanings. If you find yourself repeating certain sequences of keystrokes, you can have VP-Planner save these keystrokes in a **keyboard macro**; then you can direct VP-Planner to execute them, by depressing the ALT key along with the coded one-letter name.

The **ENTER key** tells VP-Planner that you have finished typing and want to send the information to the cell or give VP-Planner an instruction.

The **BACKSPACE key** deletes the character to the left of the pointer and can also cancel the current range.

The **function keys** are the ten keys lying together on the left-hand side of the keyboard. They are used to perform specially defined VP-Planner functions with only one keystroke. The ten function keys perform the following tasks:

F1	HELP	Displays a help screen
F2	EDIT	Edits the contents of a cell
F3	NAME	Displays defined range names
F4	ABS	Defines a cell as an absolute value
F5	GOTO	Moves the pointer to a cell
F6	WIND	Jumps from one window to another
F7	QUERY	Performs the last query sequence
F8	TABLE	Performs the last table sequence
F9	CALC	Recalculates all the formulas in the worksheet
F10	GRAPH	Generates the graph last defined

Data Entry

Data entry is the process of placing values, labels, or formulas into the individual cells of a worksheet. A label cell can be printed or listed onto the screen, but it cannot be involved in a calculation. Therefore, you could say that the type of data stored in a cell dictates how that cell can be manipulated. The spreadsheet software must have some indication of the type of data you wish to store in a cell, and it is forced to make certain assumptions.

If you begin entering data of an alphabetic character within a cell, the spreadsheet will assume that you wish to enter **label data**. When VP-Planner encounters alphabetic data, it automatically places a single quote (') at the beginning. This presents a problem when you are entering formula-related information because the formula's reference to the cell location must start with an alphabetic character. The problem is solved by placing a + symbol before the cell location, so VP-Planner recognizes the entry as a formula rather than as a label.

Numeric information is entered simply by typing the digits that they are composed of. (A negative number is represented by preceding the number with a minus sign (−); no such convention is needed if the number is positive.) This, however, presents a problem when you wish to have **numeric data** treated as a label. For example, how could the years *1984* and *1985* be presented to VP-Planner as labels rather than numbers? VP-Planner uses a very simple technique: in order to present *1984* as a label, all you need to do is place a single quote (') before the value to be treated as a label. For example in this case, you would enter the characters '1984 and VP-Planner would treat *1984* as a label.

Formulas explaining how numeric data are to be manipulated are entered as they would be processed. A formula is comprised of operands and operators. In the formula +A4 − B4, the + and − are operators. An operator tells VP-Planner what task to perform. The cell references (A4 and B4) are the operands. An operand is either a cell reference or a number to be acted upon by VP-Planner.

If the formula is entered properly, the spreadsheet will perform the operation; otherwise, an error message will be displayed in the lower left-hand corner of the screen, and the computer will beep. If this happens, the formula must be edited or reentered.

Entering Formulas

Operators. Formulas tell VP-Planner what mathematical manipulations you wish it to perform on specific cell contents. The operations VP-Planner can perform are invoked by using the following symbols in a formula:

- ^ Exponentiation
- * Multiplication
- / Division
- + Addition
- − Subtraction

Thus, to divide the contents of cell C3 by the contents of cell D3, you would enter the formula +C3/D3.

Precedence (Order of Operations). The order in which calculations are executed is called **precedence**. Operations are always performed in the following order, left to right within a formula:

Exponentiation is performed first

Then any multiplication and division, in the order that they occur

Then any addition and subtraction, in the order that they occur

For example, the formula +A7/A1+B3*D4^3 would result in the following:

1. The contents of cell D4 are raised to the third power.
2. The contents of cell A7 are divided by the contents of cell A1.
3. The contents of cell B3 are multiplied by the result of step 1.
4. The result of step 2 is added to the result of step 3.

Parentheses and Precedence. Parentheses can be used to override the above order of operations. At the most general level, operations inside parentheses are performed before those outside; within the parentheses, however, the order of operations is the same. When multiple sets of parentheses are used, the operations within the innermost set are executed, followed by those within the next set.

For example, the formula +C3 − (A3+D3) would result in the following:

1. The contents of cell A3 are added to the contents of cell D3.
2. The result of step 1 is subtracted from the contents of cell C3.

For a more complex example, the formula $+D3*D4+(C7+E4^3*F6 -(G6/F7+D3^2)+A1)$ would result in:

1. The $(G6/F7+D3^2)$ would be performed first because these operations reside in the innermost set of parentheses.
   a. The contents of cell D3 are raised to the second power.
   b. The contents of cell G6 are divided by the contents of cell F7.
   c. The result of step 1a is added to the result of step 1b.
2. The formula now logically appears as $+D3*D4+(C7+E4^3*F6 -Step1+A1)$, and the next part of the formula to be executed would be $(C7+E4^3*F6-Step1+A1)$.
   a. The contents of cell E4 are raised to the third power.
   b. The result of step 2a is multiplied by the contents of cell F6.
   c. The contents in cell C7 are added to the result of step 2b from which is subtracted the result of step 1, and to which is added the contents of A1.
3. The formula now logically appears as $+D3*D4+Step2$.
   a. The contents of cell D3 are multiplied by the contents of cell D4.
   b. The result of step 3a is now added to the result of step 2 to obtain the final result.

Circular References

One problem that almost all users of a spreadsheet like VP-Planner encounter when entering formulas is the circular reference. A **circular reference** is a formula in a cell that, directly or indirectly, refers back to that same cell. A circular reference in a worksheet is indicated when a CIRC message appears at the bottom of the screen. When the circular reference is corrected, the CIRC message disappears. A circular reference would appear on the screen if the following formula appeared in cell B12:

    @SUM(B1.B12)

The circular reference appears because cell B12 is an operand in the operation as well as the cell designated to hold the answer. A cell cannot be both.

Built-in Functions

Built-in functions are processes or formulas that have already been programmed into the spreadsheet software package. These functions save the user a tremendous amount of effort and tedium in writing all the statements needed to perform some type of mathematical manipulation. In the VP-Planner spreadsheet package, a function is designated by the @ symbol. To sum the values contained in cells A3, B3, C3, D3, and E3 and place the result in cell G3, the following formula would be required in cell G3: @SUM(A3.E3). Although there are many others, some of the more common VP-Planner functions are:

Mathematical
    Absolute value, arc cosine, arc sine, arc tangent, cosine, log,
    exponent, pi, random, round, integer, sine, square root, tangent
Logical
    True, false, if/then/else

Financial
>Internal rate of return, net present value, future value of an annuity, present value, payment

Statistical
>Average, minimum, maximum, standard deviation, variance

Correcting Errors on the Worksheet

There are basically five correction methods (plus one start-over method) for dealing with errors you've made while using the VP-Planner package:

1. If you make an error while typing something in the "scratch" area of the control panel, use the BACKSPACE key to erase the mistake, and then retype any deleted data.

2. If you have entered something in the worksheet that you want to replace with other data, move the pointer back to that cell, type the new data, and hit ENTER. The new entry will take the place of the old.

3. If you have entered data in a cell of the worksheet that you want to blank out, position the pointer to that cell, and depress the key sequence /RE, and hit ENTER to erase the contents of that one cell.

4. If you start to enter data for a cell and then change your mind, simply depress the ESC key, and the data will not be entered in the cell. If you are inside a menu, you can depress the ESC key to get the previous level. If you want to return to the worksheet, depress CTRL and BREAK simultaneously.

5. Suppose a cell that has an error in it contains a very long formula or label. You don't want to reenter all of the information because you will more than likely commit some other type of error in doing so. In this type of situation, you should depress the **EDIT key F2**. The EDIT key places the cell contents on the entry line, as well as on the status line. You can now use the following keys and perform "word processing" on the cell contents displayed on the entry line.

    HOME   Places the cursor at the beginning of the line

    END   Places the cursor at the end of the line

    DEL   Deletes the character under the cursor

    BACKSPACE   Deletes the character to the left of the cursor

    ESC   Returns the user to the worksheet without changes

    CTRL + BREAK   Stops what is being done and returns you to the worksheet in ready mode

    [arrow key]   Moves the cursor in the direction of the arrow

    To insert information on a line, position the cursor one position to the right of where you wish the new information to go, and start typing.

6. If everything is totally wrong and you have a complete mess on your hands, you may just wish to start over with a new worksheet, erasing what's already on the screen. To erase the current worksheet, enter the following commands: /Worksheet Erase Yes. This will erase the screen and RAM. You cannot recall anything, so use this command sequence carefully.

Getting Help

From time to time, you may forget where you are in a menu structure (see Appendix D for VP-Planner command structure) or may not understand how a particular command operates. Since VP-Planner has over 110 built-in commands, it's reasonable to assume that you will not be acquainted with all of them.

To aid you in remembering (or in becoming acquainted for the first time with) these commands, VP-Planner provides a built-in tutor, known as the **help facility**, which you can activate by pressing the F1 key. The help facility displays information about the current menu options available to you or about the current command you are working on; it is made context-sensitive by the position of the pointer in a menu or a command sequence from a menu. To get out of help and back to the worksheet, simply press the ESC key.

Entering a Sample VP-Planner Worksheet

Let's assume that a friend of yours named Ed owns a grocery store with the following departments: Deli, Bakery, Liquor, Grocery, Produce, and Meat. It's the end of the year and Ed would like to compare the sales of the various departments for last year and this year, keeping track of the overall change in sales (either positive or negative) and of the percentage change in sales for each of the departments.

Since Ed knows you are enrolled in a course that covers VP-Planner, you have been honored with a request to help him prepare a spreadsheet to perform the data manipulation. After carefully examining the problem, you decide that a worksheet like the following will present the information in an understandable format:

```
COMPSALS


    Department          Last Year        This Year          Change        % Change
Deli                       700.00           575.00         (125.00)           -18%
Bakery                   1,000.00         1,100.00          100.00             10%
Liquor                   1,200.00         1,400.00          200.00             17%
Grocery                  2,500.00         2,900.00          400.00             16%
Produce                    950.00         1,000.00           50.00              5%
Meat                     1,500.00         1,410.00          (90.00)            -6%


Store Total              7,850.00         8,385.00          535.00              7%
```

In the course of this project, the following learning objectives in the use of VP-Planner will be accomplished:

1. Introduction to pointer movement
2. Entering labels (text)
3. Use of the @Sum function
4. Entering VP-Planner formulas
5. Changing column width for an entire worksheet
6. Global data format changes
7. Use of the copy command
8. Use of the range format command
9. Use of the range erase command
10. Justification of text within a cell
11. Printing a worksheet

Format of Instructions. In accomplishing these objectives, you will have to perform a number of processing steps, which are detailed on the following pages. Any time you see a letter followed by a number (for example, B4), it signifies that you are to go to that cell location and enter the following data or execute the following instruction.

After you have finished entering the data or instruction, depress the ENTER key or an arrow key. Depressing the ENTER key takes the information from the entry line and places it in the cell, leaving the pointer on that cell. The pointer can then be moved to another cell via the appropriate arrow key.

To accomplish the same task with one less keystroke, simply depress an arrow key when you are finished entering data on the entry line. This action both enters the data in the cell and moves the pointer to the next cell location.

VP-Planner allows you to enter menu commands by using the pointer to point to a command, entering the first character of a command, or by pressing the appropriate function key. Remember that the appropriate function keys to press are displayed on the prompt line of the control panel. Whenever a function key can be used, it will be included within parentheses after the first character of the command (for those who prefer to use the function keys instead of pointing to a command or entering the first character of that command). Do not enter both the first character of a command and the function key. For example, if you wished to enter the command / File Retrieve, it would be represented as follows:

/—Brings up the Main Menu for VP-Planner.

F (F6)–Selects the File option. This option is selected any time you wish to read or write data onto a disk.

R (F2)—Executes the Retrieve command to load a worksheet from the disk in drive B.

You can press either the F key to invoke the File option, or you can press the F6 function key to invoke the File option on the Main Menu. You cannot, however, press both keys. Likewise, you can press either the R key to invoke the Retrieve option of the File Menu, or you can press the F2 key to perform the same task.

Step-by-Step Instructions for VP-Planner Sample Worksheet–COMPSALS

1. Enter row and column labels. Don't worry if some of the labels won't fit in a cell. That will be taken care of later.

    B1   COMPSALS

    B3   Department

    C3   Last Year

    D3   This Year

    E3   Change

    F3   % Change

    B5   Deli

    B6   Bakery

    B7   Liquor

    B8   Grocery

    B9   Produce

    B10   Meat

    B12   Store Total

2. Change the column width to 12 for the whole worksheet (global). VP-Planner brings up a blank worksheet with a column width of 9.

/—Brings up the Main Menu for VP-Planner.

W (F2)—Selects the desired Worksheet selection from the Main Menu. You may select from a menu in either of two ways: (1) you can move the pointer with arrow keys to the selection and depress ENTER; or (2) you can enter the first letter of the option desired. You will notice that, as you move the pointer along the options, the prompt line changes from option to option. This gives the user additional information about each option.

G (F2)—Tells VP-Planner that the command to be entered will affect the entire worksheet.

C (F4)—Signifies that the Col-Wid command has been selected from the menu.

12—Changes the column width from 9 to 12 positions.

ENTER—Tells VP-Planner to execute the command.

3. Enter totals for the Last Year and This Year columns. Don't enter the commas or decimal points as presented above. You'll tell VP-Planner what to do with these numbers later.

C5	700
C6	1000
C7	1200
C8	2500
C9	950
C10	1500
D5	575
D6	1100
D7	1400
D8	2900
D9	1000
D10	1410

4. At C12, demonstrate the use of the @SUM command.

C12 [by manual pointer movement] @SUM(—Enters the beginning of the formula.

C5 [by manual pointer movement]—Positions the pointer at cell C5.

.—Marks the beginning of the range.

C10 [by manual pointer movement]—Positions the pointer at cell C10—the last cell to be summed.

)—Stops the process with a).

ENTER—Executes the sum function.

The above steps will produce the value 7850 in cell C12. The use of the @SUM function introduces the use of a function and illustrates VP-Planner's ability to point to data and then enter that pointed address into a formula. The @SUM function also introduces the concept of a **range**. As you no doubt noticed, the pointed range (adjacent cells included in the operation) appeared in reverse video. This convention allows a user to see exactly which cells will be included in an operation.

Note carefully what happens on the screen as you total the This Year column.

5. At D12, use the @SUM command to add the numbers in the This Year column.

> D12 [by manual pointer movement] @SUM(—Enters the first part of the formula.
>
> D5 [by manual pointer movement]—Positions the pointer at cell D5.
>
> . —Marks the beginning of the range.
>
> D10 [by manual pointer movement]—Positions the pointer at D10.
>
>) —Stops the process with a).
>
> ENTER—Executes the sum function.

The above steps will produce the value 8385 in cell D12.

6. Use a global change to put two positions to the right of the decimal point and to allow for commas between the hundreds and thousands digits.

> / —Brings up the Main Menu for VP-Planner.
>
> W (F2)—Selects the Worksheet option from the Main Menu (see task 2 above).
>
> G (F2)—Tells VP-Planner that the command to be entered will affect the entire worksheet.
>
> F (F2)—Tells VP-Planner that the format (the manner in which data are presented on the worksheet) is to be selected.
>
> , (F5)—Tells VP-Planner that commas are to be placed where you would logically expect them. Negative numbers will be contained in parentheses. A fixed number of decimal places can also be specified.
>
> 2—Tells VP-Planner that two decimal positions will be displayed.
>
> ENTER—Tells VP-Planner to execute the instruction.

7. At E5, calculate the change between This Year and Last Year (using the pointer method).

> + —Indicates to VP-Planner that a formula is to be entered.
>
> D5 [by manual pointer movement]—Positions the pointer at cell D5.
>
> − —Indicates to VP-Planner that the next cell is to be entered.
>
> C5 [by manual pointer movement]—Positions the pointer at cell C5.
>
> ENTER—Executes the command and places the result in cell E5.

You can use the pointer when entering a cell location in a formula. This works well when you don't remember the exact location.

8. Copy (replicate) this formula for the rest of the cells in the column. Copying the formula into the other cells in the column can save a

tremendous amount of time and can eliminate typing errors. Make sure that the pointer is at E5.

> /—Brings up the Main Menu.
>
> C (F4)—Selects the Copy option.
>
> ENTER—Establishes the sending area. You only want to copy the contents of this cell (E5).
>
> Down Arrow to E6—Positions the pointer at the first cell in the range, to receive the formula contained in E5.
>
> .—Indicates to VP-Planner that this is the first cell to be referenced in a range—"nailing down" the beginning.
>
> Down Arrow to E12—Positions the pointer at the last cell in the range to receive the formula contained in E5.
>
> ENTER—Tells VP-Planner to execute the Copy command.

Don't worry about the garbage in E11. You'll get rid of that later. You will notice that the other cells now have answers in the change column that correspond to those at the beginning of this lesson. Move the pointer from one cell to another in the column. Notice that the cell addresses have been changed automatically by VP-Planner. This ability to change cell locations automatically during a copy or move is referred to as **relative addressing**.

9. Enter the formula to calculate the percentage change. You'll change the format of the column later. Position pointer to cell F5.

> +E5/C5—Places this formula in cell F5.
>
> ENTER—Executes the sum function.

You should have the value (0.18) in cell F5.

This method demonstrates that you are not required to point if you know the cell addresses. The pointing method, although impressive at first, can actually result in extra work for a worksheet user. This is especially true if the cell locations are far away on the worksheet.

10. Copy this formula for the rest of the column, after first positioning the pointer at cell F5.

> /—Invokes the Main Menu.
>
> C (F4)—Selects the Copy command.
>
> ENTER—Establishes cell F5 as being the only cell holding data to be copied to other cells.
>
> Down Arrow to F6—Positions the pointer at the first cell that is to receive the formula to be copied.
>
> .—Indicates to VP-Planner that this is the first cell to be referenced in a range.
>
> Down Arrow to F12—Positions the pointer at the last cell in the range that is to receive the formula from cell F5.
>
> ENTER—Tells VP-Planner that the range has been established and that the command is to be executed.

11. To get rid of the two entries at E11 and F11, position the pointer at F11.

> /—Invokes the Main Menu.
>
> R (F3)—Selects the Range option from the Main Menu. The Range option should be used whenever you wish to per-

form operations on only a part of the worksheet, rather than on all of it.

E (F4)—Tells VP-Planner that you wish to erase the contents of a range of cells beginning with F11—not the entire worksheet.

Back Arrow—Moves the pointer to the last cell in the range (E11).

ENTER—Tells VP-Planner that the range has been established and that the command is to be executed.

Your worksheet should now look as follows:

```
            B              C           D           E           F
 1COMPSALS
 2
 3Department  Last  Year   This  Year  Change      % Change
 4
 5Deli               700.00      575.00   (125.00)       (.18)
 6Bakery           1,000.00    1,100.00     100.00         .10
 7Liquor           1,200.00    1,400.00     200.00         .17
 8Grocery          2,500.00    2,900.00     400.00         .16
 9Produce            950.00    1,000.00      50.00         .05
10Meat             1,500.00    1,410.00    (90.00)       (.06)
11
12Store Total      7,850.00    8,385.00     535.00         .07
```

12. Format column F for percentages, beginning with position F5.

/—Invokes the Main Menu.

R (F3)—Selects the Range option from the Main Menu.

F (F2)—Selects the Format to change a portion of the worksheet.

P (F8)—Tells VP-Planner that you wish to use the Percent format to display data within a range.

0—Tells VP-Planner that there are to be no positions to the right of the decimal.

ENTER—Marks cell F5 as the beginning of the range.

Down Arrow to F12—Marks the rest of the cells in the range.

ENTER—Tells VP-Planner that the range has been established and that the data format is now to be changed to percent.

13. Position the pointer at F3 to right-justify the column labels.

/—Invokes the Main Menu.

R (F3)—Selects the Range option from the Main Menu. You only want to right-justify one row of labels (a range).

L (F3)—Selects the Label Prefix command.

R (F3)—Tells VP-Planner to right-justify the label within the cell and start the range with cell F3.

Back Arrow to B3—Establishes the range of cells whose labels are to be right-justified.

ENTER—Tells VP-Planner to right-justify the labels within the marked range of cells.

14. Save the worksheet onto disk, using the name COMPSALS.

   /—Brings up the Main Menu.

   F (F6)—Selects the File option. This option is selected any time you wish to read or write data onto a disk.

   S (F3)—Executes the Save command to save a worksheet to the disk in drive B.

   COMPSALS—Responds to VP-Planner prompt for the file name. If the file has already been saved before, VP-Planner will ask if you want to cancel or replace: CANCEL would result in the command being canceled; REPLACE would overwrite the old file with the present worksheet in RAM.

15. Print the worksheet.

   /—Brings up the Main Menu.

   P (F7)—Selects the Print option.

   P (F2)—Tells VP-Planner that the output is to go to the printer.

   R (F2)—Tells VP-Planner that you wish to tell it what part of the worksheet is to be printed. (Remember, there are 524,288 cells.)

   A1 [by manual pointer movement]—Gives the first cell location (upper left-hand corner).

   .—Tells VP-Planner that a range is to be established.

   F12 [by manual pointer movement]—Gives the last cell location (lower right-hand corner).

   ENTER—Tells VP-Planner that the range has been established.

   G (F8)—Tells VP-Planner to begin printing.

   P (F4)—Tells VP-Planner to go to the top of the next page.

Saving and Retrieving Worksheet Files

The first time that you work on a worksheet, VP-Planner prompts you to enter a name for the worksheet when you issue the command to save it to disk. Any worksheet file that you save to disk has the .WKS file extension. The following commands are used to save a worksheet to disk:

   /—Brings up the Main Menu for VP-Planner.

   F (F6)—Selects the File option from the Main Menu. This option is selected any time that you wish to save or load a worksheet from disk.

   S (F3)—Executes the Save command to save a worksheet to the disk in drive B.

The worksheet file can now be loaded at a later time and changes can be made to that worksheet. Use the following commands to load a worksheet:

   /—Brings up the Main Menu for VP-Planner.

   F (F6)—Selects the File option from the Main Menu.

   R (F2)—Selects the Retrieve option to read a worksheet file from the disk in drive B. You can now either manually enter the name of the worksheet to be loaded or simply "point" to the appropriate worksheet file using the pointer and then depressing the ENTER key.

One you finish making any changes to the worksheet, you must again save it to disk. Since you indicated the name of the worksheet to VP-Planner when you loaded it, when you issue the Save command VP-Planner displays that name as the default. By pressing the ENTER key, you accept that default. If you wish to enter another name, the current name disappears as soon as you press any other alphabetic or numeric key. If you press the ENTER key to accept the default name, VP-Planner displays the following menu:

```
Cancel   Replace   Backup
```

The Cancel command tells VP-Planner to stop this operation and returns you to Ready mode.

The Replace command tells VP-Planner to go ahead and save the contents of this worksheet to disk. This process destroys the original worksheet file and replaces it with the new worksheet.

The Back-up command saves this worksheet out to disk with a file extension of .BAK and also writes the worksheet out to a disk file with a .WKS file. The Back-up command, therefore, results in two disk files being created.

Once you have saved a file to disk, you may want to verify that it actually was stored properly. You can verify that a worksheet was stored properly in two ways. First, you can simply reload the worksheet file from disk using the / File Retrieve commands. Second you can use the List command from the File Menu. Issuing the / File List command results in a menu display from which you select the appropriate type of file that you wish to have displayed. In this case, you would enter the following commands:

/—Brings up the Main Menu of VP-Planner.

F (F6)—Selects the File option of the Main Menu.

L (F7)—Selects the List option of the File Menu.

W (F2)—Tells VP-Planner to display all of the worksheet files (those files with a .WKS file extension) to the screen, as follows:

```
In directory B:\   (347136 bytes free on disk)
FUNCTION WKS    2183    86 06 22    COMPSALS WKS   4756   86 06 23
EDCHECK   WKS    3205    86 06 23
```

```
Press any key to continue.
```

Your worksheet should now look exactly like the worksheet at the beginning of this lesson. If it doesn't, you have done something wrong. Compare the contents of each cell with the contents listed below:

B1:	'COMPSALS
B3:	''Department
C3:	''Last Year
D3:	''This Year
E3:	''Change
F3:	''% Change
B5:	'Deli
C5:	700
D5:	575
E5:	+D5−C5
F5:	(P0) +E5/C5
B6:	'Bakery
C6:	1000
D6:	1100

E6:	+D6 − C6
F6:	(PO) +E6/C6
B7:	'Liquor
C7:	1200
D7:	1400
E7:	+D7 − C7
F7:	(PO) +E7/C7
B8:	'Grocery
C8:	2500
D8:	2900
E8:	+D8 − C8
F8:	(PO) +E8/C8
B9:	'Produce
C9:	950
D9:	1000
E9:	+D9 − C9
F9:	(PO) +E9/C9
B10:	'Meat
C10:	1500
D10:	1410
E10:	+D10 − C10
F10:	(PO) +E10/C10
B12:	'Store Total
C12:	@SUM(C5..C10)
D12:	@SUM(D5..D10)
E12:	+D12 − C12
F12:	(PO) +E12/C12

Chapter Review

One of the most frequently used microcomputer applications in business is the electronic spreadsheet, which allows an individual to manipulate any data/information that can be placed in a row-and-column format. Most spreadsheet software packages have a number of features in common, including the ability to copy formulas or text, delete rows or columns, load worksheets from disk, insert rows or columns, change the format of data presentation, move text or formulas from one location to another, print the worksheet, save the worksheet, freeze portions (titles) of the worksheet, and split the screen.

Two of the most popular spreadsheet packages are VisiCalc and Lotus 1-2-3. VisiCalc was originally built for the Apple II microcomputer, and Lotus 1-2-3 was originally built for the IBM PC. Both software packages resulted in dramatically increased sales for their respective machines when they were first introduced. A package that has emerged to challenge 1-2-3's supremacy in the marketplace is VP-Planner. VP-Planner is a look-alike product that works exactly the same as 1-2-3 and improves on many features of the original package.

When you are using a spreadsheet package you must follow a number of logical steps in planning, developing, and testing your worksheet, in order to ensure that the problem is properly modeled.

The VP-Planner spreadsheet package is a menu-driven, integrated package composed of the functional parts of spreadsheet, graphics, and data management. Its screen consists of a control panel, border, mode indicator, special indicators, error message indicator, and worksheet area. Various keys of the keyboard are used to move the pointer around the worksheet area.

You can enter data and correct errors by making changes in the control panel area. After data are entered or changes made, they will be reflected in the appropriate cell if you press an arrow key or the ENTER key. Arithmetic manipulation of numeric data contained in cells can be accomplished by entering a formula or by telling VP-Planner to use one of its built-in functions. A detailed example of worksheet formation involves the practical application of many of these functions.

Key Terms and Concepts

ALT key	label data
available memory	left arrow
BACKSPACE key	mode indicator
border	number
built-in functions	numeric data
cell	PG DN key
circular reference	PG UP key
column	pointer
command line	precedence
control panel	prompt line
CTRL + SCROLL BREAK keys	range
current time	relative addressing
data entry	right arrow
data management feature	row
down arrow	SCROLL LOCK key
EDIT key F2	SHIFT key
END key	spreadsheet
ENTER key	status line
error messages	TAB key
ESC key	TAB + SHIFT keys
formula	template
function keys	titles
graphics feature	up arrow
help facility	VisiCalc
HOME key	VP-Planner
indicators	VP-Planner Main Menu
input line	VP-Planner spreadsheet
integration	VP-Planner worksheet
keyboard macro	window
label	worksheet

Chapter Quiz

Multiple Choice

1. Which of the following terms is not related to a worksheet:
   a. Row
   b. Column
   c. DOS prompt
   d. Pointer
   e. Border
   f. All of the above terms are related to a spreadsheet

2. Which of the following items is not allowed in a cell:
   a. Formula
   b. Label
   c. Function
   d. Number
   e. All of the above are allowed in a cell
   f. None of the above are allowed in a cell

3. Which of the following names is not related to spreadsheet software triumphs:
   a. Mitch Kapor
   b. Dan Bricklin
   c. VisiCalc
   d. Steve Jobs
   e. VP-Planner

4. Which of the following keystrokes does not result in cursor movement:
   a. Arrow key
   b. PG UP
   c. ALT
   d. TAB
   e. END + an arrow key
   f. All of the above result in cursor movement

5. Which of the following items is not found in the control panel:
   a. Input line
   b. Prompt line
   c. Error line
   d. Status line
   e. All of the above are part of the control panel
   f. None of the above is part of the control panel

True/False

6. Integrated packages allow you to pass information from one part to another without any real difficulty.

7. The mode indicator is used to show the current status of the worksheet.

8. A cell is referenced by using the ROW/COLUMN designation.

9. The built-in functions in VP-Planner always start with a @ character.

10. When entering a formula, you need only enter the cell location and an operation symbol—for example, A2-B7.

Answers

1. c 2. e 3. d 4. c 5. c 6. t 7. t 8. f 9. t 10. f

Exercises

1. Define or describe each of the following:
   a. built-in function   f. mode indicator
   b. VP-Planner data management   g. indicators
   c. VP-Planner graphics   h. EDIT key F2
   d. VP-Planner Main Menu   i. precedence
   e. control panel   j. on-line help

2. A spreadsheet is the software, while a(n) _____ is the work area.

3. Any cell can be referenced by referring to its corresponding _____ _____ and _____ .

4. List each of the types of contents a cell may have.
   a.

   b.

   c.

5. A(n) _____ is similar to a prepackaged program. You enter the data, and it computes the results.

6. List the steps involved in using a spreadsheet to solve a problem.
   a.

   b.

   c.

   d.

7. List the three integrated parts of VP-Planner.
   a.

   b.

   c.

8. List the four parts of the VP-Planner control panel.
   a.

   b.

   c.

   d.

9. The _____ indicator is used to identify the current status of the VP-Planner package.

10. The part of your worksheet that is visible on your screen is referred to as the _____ .

11. The second line of the control panel is the _____ line.

12. Explain the use of each of the following cursor movement keys:
    a. Arrow key

    b. PG UP

    c. PG DN

    d. END

    e. HOME

    f. TAB

13. The _____ key is used to quit an instruction or back up a step in the menu.

14. The two keys _____ and _____ are used to stop any spreadsheet process or function.

15. A cell that contains text automatically has a(n) _____ placed in it.

16. Why is the concept of precedence important in entering formulas? Explain how VP-Planner evaluates a formula and executes it using precedence. How can this order of precedence be changed?

17. Why are built-in functions so useful? List some functions that you might find useful, and beside each function list an application of it.
    a.

    b.

    c.

    d.

18. Explain how the use of each of the following keys changes when the EDIT mode is entered by pressing the F2 key.
    a. HOME

    b. DEL

    c. BACKSPACE

    d. END

    e. ESC

    f. Arrow keys

19. The four keystrokes _____ , _____ , _____ , and _____ are used to erase the entire worksheet.

20. Practice using the on-line help facility, which is activated by pressing the F1 key.

Computer Exercises

1. Use the / File Retrieve command to load the worksheet file called CALENDAR, which contains an appointment calendar for keeping track of various appointments. Practice moving the pointer around the worksheet using the following commands.

Part I

    a. Use the various arrow keys to move the pointer.
    b. Press the HOME key.
    c. Press the PG DN key twice.

d. Press the PG UP key three times; notice the beep.
   e. Position the pointer at 8:00.
   f. Press the END key, followed by the down arrow key.
   g. Press the same two keys again; the pointer should be at row 256.
   h. Press the END key, followed by the right arrow key; the pointer should be at cell BL256.
   i. Press the END key, followed by the up arrow key. You should now see "end of column" at cell BL1. Notice that there is a single quote mark in front of the text. This single quote tells VP-Planner that the contents of this cell are text data. Although you can enter the single quote, VP-Planner automatically places it in the cell for you.
   j. Press the HOME key.
   k. Press the TAB key twice.
   l. Press the SHIFT and TAB keys together.
   m. Position the pointer at cell A5. This cell contains the VP-Planner function @TODAY. This function is used to get the date that you entered when you started VP-Planner. If you did not enter a date, this cell contains 01-Jan-80 (the DOS default).

Part II

   a. Press the SCROLL LOCK key.
   b. Use the various arrow keys to move the pointer.
   c. Press the PG DN key twice.
   d. Press the PG UP key once.
   e. Press the TAB key twice.
   f. Press the SHIFT and TAB keys together.

2. Use the / File Retrieve command to load the worksheet file called PAYMENT, which is a template that allows you to enter the amount of a loan, the interest rate, and the number of years for the loan. It then automatically calculates the amount of the payment and the total amount paid over the life of the loan.

   Before you do anything to the worksheet, let's explore some of its features. There are two areas in this worksheet: the first area will hold information about various loans, and the second contains the information about a loan that you are permitted to change. If you try to change any cells, the computer merely beeps and displays the error message "Protected Cell." Press ESC to continue. The cells containing a "U" can be changed (cells A7–A10, B19, and B20).

   You are therefore allowed to change the loan amount, the interest rate, and the life of the loan in years. Enter the loan amounts without using dollar signs or commas. For example, if a loan is for $10,000, enter it as 10000. The current interest rate is 12 percent, expressed as a decimal (.12). The final field that you are allowed to change is the length of the loan, which is currently set for 4 years. These two variables appear at the bottom of the screen.

   Notice that as soon as you change the contents of one field the worksheet automatically recalculates itself.

   Enter information about the following loans:

   a. $10,000 at 12 percent for 4 years
   b. $15,000 at 12 percent for 4 years
   c. $25,000 at 14 percent for 6 years
   d. $80,000 at 16 percent for 20 years
   e. $120,000 at 13 percent for 15 years

3. Use the / File Retrieve command to load the worksheet file called ERRORS, which contains a number of mistakes that you should correct.

   a. Reenter the following mistakes:
      twilve
      cumpany

   b. Use the F2 Edit command to remedy the following errors:
      The dog jumpd ovr the lasy cat
      The childrun sat at hoam

   c. Use the / Range Erase command to delete each of the following:
      xxxxxxxxx
      ****
      \ \ \ \ \ \ \ \ \ \

4. You are to create a student's budget schedule that will subtract total expenses from total income for a 4½-month period (one semester) and set net cash amounts for each month. In addition, the schedule should provide monthly totals for income and expense items, with grand totals as depicted in the example below.

   The dollar figures, along with the budget categories in the example below, are only illustrative. You are to pick categories and supply amounts appropriate to your particular situation. You are to use formulas or the Sum function to calculate column and row totals as well as the net cash amount.

SCHOOL YEAR BUDGET

TERM: FALL   YEAR: 198__
NAME:

INCOME	AUGUST	SEPTEMBER	OCTOBER	NOVEMBER	DECEMBER	TOTAL
WORK	150	300	300	300	150	1200
AWARDS	50	100	100	100	50	400
ALLOWANCE	25	50	50	50	50	225
OTHER	5	10	10	10	10	45
EXPENSES						
TUITION	250	500	500	500	250	2000
BOOKS	75	150	150	150	25	550
HOME	25	100	100	100	100	425
CLOTHING	40	80	80	80	40	320
FOOD	40	90	90	90	40	350
TRANSPORT	20	35	35	35	100	225
OTHER	20	35	35	35	35	160
TOTALS						
INCOME	230	460	460	460	260	1870
EXPENSES	470	990	990	990	590	4030
NET CASH	−240	−530	−530	−530	−330	−2160

Save the worksheet to a file called CH9EXR4.

5. You are the manager of a car dealership. You have five salespeople working for you. Your boss has requested that you take the last two years of sales information for each sales rep and determine the difference between the two years in sales dollars. Your boss has requested the information in the following format:

Sales Rep.	Last Year	This Year	Change	% Change
Harry	125,000	178,000		
Sally	190,000	260,000		
Ben	76,000	68,000		
Marge	98,000	153,000		
Felix	230,000	198,000		
Carol	78,000	163,000		
Totals	797,000	1,020,000		

You are to enter the formulas that will calculate the Change and % Change column entries. Place a total at the bottom of any column containing numeric information.

Set the worksheet column width to 12.

Save the worksheet to a file called CH11EXR5.

6. The band leader has asked you to help in the record-keeping for the high-school band members' fund-raising drive. The band members are selling candy (at $3.00 per can) to pay for a trip to Washington, D.C. The band leader has accounting information concerning the number of cans of candy checked out by each member and about the money turned in by each member. You have been asked to determine how much, if anything, each member owes and to provide any information you can on totals.

Band Member	Cans Taken	Money Received	Balance Due
Diane Collins	40	120.00	
Melvin Davis	30	66.00	
Jack Gibson	50	140.00	
Darlene Posio	25	60.00	
Chris Peterson	45	120.00	
Joan Rushing	30	90.00	
Totals	220	596.00	

Save this worksheet file to disk using the name CH11EXR6.

7. The head of the accounting department is interested in a comparative income statement for the last two years and has asked you to prepare the financial statement using the information below. You have been asked to ascertain the dollar change between the various income statement entries, as well.

```
                          ACE Inc.

                 Income Statement (unaudited)

              Last Year    This Year    Change

      INCOME

      Sales          150,000      175,000
      Cost            90,000      115,000

      Margin          60,000       60,000

      EXPENSES

      Materials       20,000       18,000
      Supplies         3,000        3,100
      Payroll         15,000       16,000
      Utilities          700          720
      Misc.              900          850
      Rent             6,000        6,000

      Total

      NET INCOME
```

Don't worry too much about getting the headings exactly centered. Save this worksheet to a file called CH11EXR7.

Chapter

12

More on Ranges,

Copying, Formatting,

Printing, and

Functions

Chapter Objectives   *After completing this chapter, you should be able to:*

Discuss in greater detail the concept of range

Discuss the range column-width feature of VP-Planner

Discuss in detail VP-Planner's copy conventions

Discuss in detail VP-Planner's format conventions and the differences between a range format and a global format

Explain in detail the various options available under the Print Menu

Discuss in greater detail VP-Planner's built-in functions

In Chapter 11, you were introduced to a number of different VP-Planner commands, some of which had virtually self-explanatory names. The concept of a range and the Copy, Format, and Print commands, however, must be covered in more detail. These commands give a VP-Planner user additional power to simplify actions and to determine how output will appear.

Range

When you are using VP-Planner, a statement or a process you wish to perform may require your indicating a range of cells to VP-Planner. A **range** is any specially designated single cell or rectangular group of cells on a worksheet; it is defined by pointing to the cells with the pointer or by typing the addresses of cells at the opposite corners of the range. Remember that a cell is a rectangle and therefore has only four corners.

Figure 12.1a displays a valid range containing three cells:

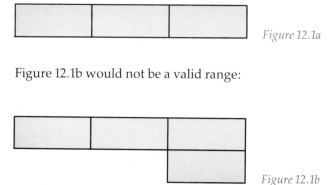

Figure 12.1a

Figure 12.1b would not be a valid range:

Figure 12.1b

You can give the cell locations of any pair of cells on opposite corners in defining a range to VP-Planner. For example, if you had a range containing a number of cells and having as its four corners the cells A, B, C, and D; to define the range, you would only have to give the cell addresses of two opposite corners, in whichever order you like—A and C, B and D, D and B, or C and A. Given any of these cell addresses, VP-Planner will define the same range as is depicted in Figure 12.2:

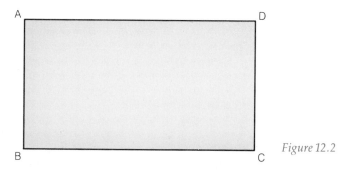

Figure 12.2

From time to time a worksheet will contain range settings from a previous session with VP-Planner that you no longer desire, such as print settings. You may wish to cancel a previous print range and specify another. Any range in any VP-Planner command can be cancelled by depressing the BACKSPACE key. The new range can now be entered.

The Copy Command

The **Copy command**, which takes information that has been entered in one or more cells and copies it to other cells on the worksheet, can save you many keystrokes and much time when building a worksheet. You will probably remember using the Copy command as part of your work on the sample COMPSALS worksheet in Chapter 11, but you may not yet understand everything that it was doing. The Copy command involves setting up a **sending** cell or cells that contain the data to be copied and then setting up a **receiving** set of cells to which the data will be copied. The following steps are required:

1. Select the Copy command from the Main Menu.

2. Indicate to VP-Planner which cells are to be in the "From" range—that is, which cells hold data to be copied onto other cells. If only one cell is involved, simply hit the ENTER key; if a range of cells is involved, extend the range (the two periods [. .] indicate that the beginning of the range is already fixed) and then move the pointer to the last cell in the range (or enter the cell address) and depress the ENTER key.

3. Indicate to VP-Planner which cells are to be in the "To" range—that is, which cells are to receive data currently held in the "From" cells. If only one cell is involved, simply hit the ENTER key. If a range of cells is involved, **nail down** the beginning of the range with a period (.), and then move the pointer to the last cell in the range (or enter the cell address) and depress the ENTER key.

WARNING Make certain that your "From" cell range does not overlap your "To" cell range. If this happens, VP-Planner simply overwrites the previous contents of cell(s), and the previous contents are irretrievably lost.

As was noted in Chapter 11, VP-Planner automatically changes the cell references in a formula it is copying to reflect the new cell location of the formula. This is an example of the concept of relative addressing. Other text data are copied from one cell to another exactly as they appear. For example, if a cell having the label *Year* in it were copied to another cell, the receiving cell would also contain *Year*; and if the text in the sending cell is right justified, the text in the receiving cell will also be right justified.

The Copy command contains a time-saving feature you can use when copying a range of cells. Imagine that you wish to copy a range of cells two cells (columns) wide by twenty rows deep. You would establish the "From" range as before—by entering the cell addresses or by pointing—and VP-Planner would then be informed that the sending range consists of two columns and twenty rows. When you tell VP-Planner the "To" range, however, you can simply identify the address of the upper left-hand cell of the receiving range (or point to this cell) and hit the ENTER key. Because VP-Planner retains in memory what the sending data looks like, it assumes that you want it to move the whole range and does so.

Formatting

The VP-Planner spreadsheet package uses the FORMAT command to control the manner in which numeric information appears in a cell. As you have already seen, you can either **format** the entire worksheet via the **Worksheet Global Format** option or format a specific part of the worksheet via the **Range Format** series of commands. It is important to note that the Range Format takes precedence over the Worksheet Global Format, so any cell containing data not specifically formatted using the / Range Format command can be changed using the / Worksheet Global Format command.

Cell data can be formatted using the global or range options in various ways, including the following:

Fixed—This option displays a fixed number of decimal places (0–15), specified by the worksheet user. Examples: 10, 10.5, −120.00.

Scientific—This option displays data in the exponential scientific notation format. The worksheet user specifies the number of decimal places in the multiplier (0–15). The exponent is expressed as a power of 10 (E) from +99 to −99. Examples: 1.35E +11, −7.5E −19.

Currency—This option places a dollar sign ($) before each numeric cell entry, and commas after the thousand and million places in each entry large enough to have them. Negative numbers are placed in parentheses. The user indicates how many positions to the right of the decimal are desired. Examples: $13.50, ($6.75), $1,050.

,—This option is identical to the Currency option, except that no dollar signs are used.

General—This option, the default numeric display, suppresses trailing zeros after a decimal point. Extremely large or small numbers are displayed in exponential notation format. Examples: 17.66, −4.3, 2.4 +10.

+/−—This option displays a horizontal bar graph in which the number of symbols is the integer part of the value. + signs are used to represent positive integers, and − signs are used to represent negative integers; if the value is zero, a . is displayed. For example:

$$6 = + + + + + +$$
$$4 = + + + +$$
$$-3 = - - -$$
$$10 = + + + + + + + + + +$$
$$-5 = - - - - -$$
$$3.5 = + + +$$

Percent—This option displays the numeric entry in a cell as a percentage (%). The user must specify how many decimal positions are desired. The value contained in the cell is the decimal equivalent multiplied by 100 and followed by a percent sign. Examples: 45%, 12.5%, −23%.

Date—This option requests you to enter the format of date display desired from among the following seven possibilities:

1 = D-MMM-Y	Day-Month-Year	(Example: 19-Jun-86)
2 = D-MMM	Day-Month	(Example: 19-Jun)
3 = MMM-Y	Month-Year	(Example: Jun-86)
4 = M/D/Y	Month/Day/Year	(Example: 06/19/86)
5 = D/M/Y	Day/Month/Year	(Example: 19/06/86)
6 = Y M D	Year-Month-Day	(Example: 86 06 19)
Time	Hour:Minute	(Example: 17:50)

Text—This option displays the formula—rather than the result of the formula—in a cell. Example: +D3/C3.

1—Same as Currency option, but this option uses the custom format 1 specified with / Worksheet Global Default Custom command.

2—Same as , (comma) but uses the custom format 2 specified with / Worksheet Global Default Custom command.

Remember that the General format option is the default format used by VP-Planner to start a spreadsheet, and that the default column width used by VP-Planner is nine positions wide. You can determine other default values used by VP-Planner by entering the command / Worksheet Status.

The Print Command

When you want to get something out of the computer or off disk so that you can examine it at your leisure, the **Print command** is an invaluable aid. On the other hand, if you don't undersand how it generates output, the command can also be frustrating to use. The Print command allows you to print the whole worksheet or parts (ranges) of it. The output can be sent directly to a printer or placed in a disk file, from which it can later be used by a word processing program. The worksheets displayed in this book were originally created using VP-Planner, then saved to disk, and then accessed using WordStar's read file (^KR) command.

After you select the Print option from the Main Menu, VP-Planner prompts you to tell it whether you want the output to go to a printer (the Print option) or onto a disk file (the File option). If you select the File option, you will be asked to enter the file name to which VP-Planner will add the extension .PRN. This is important to remember, because if you wish to access the file later, the file name you specify must include the .PRN extension.

Print Menu

At this point, the following **Print Menu** will be displayed in the control panel by VP-Planner:

Range   Line   Page   Options   Clear   Align   Go   Quit   Status

Let's examine in turn what each of these options does.

Range. The **Print Range option** is selected to tell VP-Planner which part of the worksheet is to be printed. You can enter the cell addresses of two opposite corners of the range that is to be printed, or you can use the pointer to identify the range to VP-Planner.

Line. The **Line option** tells the printer attached to your computer to advance the paper one line. This command is useful when you wish to leave some blank space between ranges that are being printed out.

Page. The **Page option** advances the paper in the printer to the top of the next page. It is useful if you wish to have printed output start on a new sheet of paper. After VP-Planner is finished printing the range of cells that you indicated, it stops the printer at that location. To advance the page in the printer, simply take the Page option.

Options. The Options selection invokes the **Options Menu** (shown below), which allows you to place headings, footings, borders, and so forth on the printout:

```
Header  Footer  Margins  Borders  Setup  Page-Length  Other  Quit
```

Options contained in this menu enable you temporarily to override defaults set by VP-Planner for printing information. These overrides remain in effect until you change them or restart VP-Planner. If you save your spreadsheet and then call it back, VP-Planner will remember the overrides because they will have become part of the worksheet file.

Header/Footer. These options allow you to enter one line of text to be used as a heading or footing for each page of printout generated. You will be prompted for the text and can place up to 240 characters on the line. In either a heading or footing line, the following special characters can be used to give printing instructions to VP-Planner:

#—Numbers the pages beginning with 1

¦—Splits heading/footings into sections as follows:

The first is left-justified

The second is centered

The third part is right-justified

@—Prints today's date

For example, in the footing of the sample worksheet COMPSALS, you could place the following text:

```
Page# ¦ COMPSALS ¦ @
```

This would develop a footing with the word *Page* and the page number in the first (left-justified) section. The word COMPSALS would appear in the center part of the footing, its text centered. The date would appear in the third (right-justified) section.

VP-Planner always leaves two blank lines between the worksheet and any headings and footings. Headings and footings can be suppressed by selecting Options Other Unformatted, and they can be reinstated by selecting Options Other Formatted.

Margins. This option, which allows you to change the current margins (left, right, top, and bottom), is especially important if you have a dot matrix printer and wish to print the worksheet using compressed print so that you get more characters per line. The maximum value allowed for resetting the right-hand margin is 255 characters.

Borders. This option allows you to specify horizontal or vertical borders that will be displayed on each page of a printed report. For example, you may have a worksheet that develops a loan amortization table and generates one line of output for each month of the loan; the Borders option could be used in this case to print column headings on each page. All you have to do is select the row or column (depending on where you want the labels), and then specify the range of cells containing the desired text. To clear the borders, you would enter the commands /PRINT PRINTER CLEAR BORDERS. The Borders option, to work properly, must have the print range specified differently. When using borders, do not specify any border cells in the print range. Specify them separately in the border range. Otherwise the border cells print twice on the first page. See Figure 12.3.

Figure 12.3

Border Range ⟶

Print Data Range ⟶

```
              Interest              12.00%
              Loan Amount           $1,200
              Months                    20
              Beginning Date       May-85

                 TOTAL                                BALANCE
     DATE     PAYMENT     PRINCIPAL     INTEREST     OUTSTANDING
     May-85     66.50       54.50         12.00        1145.50
     Jun-85     66.50       55.04         11.46        1090.46
     Jul-85     66.50       55.59         10.90        1034.87
     Aug-85     66.50       56.15         10.35         978.72
     Sep-85     66.50       56.71          9.79         922.01
     Oct-85     66.50       57.28          9.22         864.73
     Nov-85     66.50       57.85          8.65         806.88
     Dec-85     66.50       58.43          8.07         748.45
     Jan-86     66.50       59.01          7.48         689.44
     Feb-86     66.50       59.60          6.89         629.84
     Mar-86     66.50       60.20          6.30         569.64
     Apr-86     66.50       60.80          5.70         508.34
     May-86     66.50       61.41          5.09         447.43
```

Setup. This option tells your printer which escape code to use for printing the data. For example, for Epson FX or Epson-compatible printers, condensed printing (17.16 cpi) can be obtained by entering \015 as the setup string. In order to get back to Pica (10 cpi) printing, you would have to enter /PRINT PRINTER OPTIONS SETUP, followed by \027\018. If you wished to print in Elite (12 cpi), you would enter \027\077 to turn elite on; to turn it off, you would enter \027\080. Depending on the set-up string, you can print in 10, 12, or 17.1 character pitch.

Page Length. This option, which allows you to tell VP-Planner how many lines are on a page of paper, becomes important when you use something other than 11-inch paper.

Other. This option displays the following menu:

```
As-Is   Cell Fmla   Fmt'd   Unfmt   Page #   No Page #   R/C #s   Stop R/C #s   BackPrn
```

As-Is. This option prints the output exactly as it appears on the screen. This is the default.

Cell Fmla. This option prints one cell per line and displays the cell contents (text or formula).

Fmt'd. This option restores any footings, headings, or page breaks that might have been suppressed.

Unfmt. This option overrides any footings, headings, or page breaks, printing the output without any of these.

Page #. This option prints the page number on each page.

No Page #. This is the default option. It turns off the page number feature.

R/C #s. This option prints the row and column labels of the border on the top and side of each page printed (see below).

Stop R/C #s. This is the default option. It turns off the row/column labeling feature.

BackPrn. This option enables or disables background printing of worksheets or graphs. The default setting is *disabled*. This feature allows VP-Planner to be printing a long worksheet, but still allows you to make changes on the worksheet.

	A	B	C	D	E	F
1		COMPSALS				
2						
3		Department	Last Year	This Year	Change	% Change
4						
5		Deli	700.00	575.00	(125.00)	-18%
6		Bakery	1,000.00	1,100.00	100.00	10%
7		Liquor	1,200.00	1,400.00	200.00	17%
8		Grocery	2,500.00	2,900.00	400.00	16%
9		Produce	950.00	1,000.00	50.00	5%
10		Meat	1,500.00	1,410.00	(90.00)	-6%
11						
12		Store Total	7,850.00	8,385.00	535.00	7%

Clear. As print specifications are entered, VP-Planner stores them in RAM and uses them for any printing operations, and in addition stores them to your worksheet file when the file is saved onto disk. Occasionally, you may not want these various print settings to be stored in memory; by selecting the **Clear option**, you can return all print options to their default values. This option results in the following menu being displayed.

```
All   Range   Borders   Format
```

All. Resets all print settings to the default values.

Range. Cancels the print range.

Borders. Cancels the border range.

Format. Cancels margins, page length, and set-up string and returns them to their default values.

Align. The **Align command** is used when VP-Planner has lost track of where it is on a sheet of paper—for example, when a user turns the knob on the printer platen to roll the paper forward, rather than using the Line or Page options. When this happens, position the paper in the printer to the top of a new sheet and execute the Align command; VP-Planner will immediately assume that it is at the top of a new page.

Go. The **Go option** tells VP-Planner to send the designated range as output to the printer or to the named disk file, after which control is returned to the Print Menu. This allows you to print other parts of the worksheet if you desire. If the printer is not on line, VP-Planner will try to print and find that it can't; it will then beep and display an error message. You must depress the ESC key to continue. If you are storing data onto a disk file, the Go command tells VP-Planner to put the information in the file.

What happens if you forget to enter the set-up string or print the wrong range? To stop printing, depress both the CTRL and the BREAK keys; this will interrupt the printer and return control to the Print Menu. Use the page command to go to the top of the next page, or position the paper to the top of the next page manually and enter the Align command.

Quit. The **Quit option** tells VP-Planner to terminate the print session and returns you to ready mode in the worksheet. When storing output data onto a disk file, you must use this command to close the file properly. If you do not, no data will be in the file when you try to access it later. When storing data onto a disk file, you must go through the following steps:

1. Name the file.
2. Establish the range and any options.
3. Enter the Go command to store data onto the disk file.
4. Enter the Quit command to close the disk file.

Status. This command displays a screen showing the current temporary and default settings (see below).

```
PRINT STATUS               Current drive and path: B:\

   Print range:            all: A1..A1              CONFIGURATION FILE
   Text width:             9
   Page length:            66                       Auto LF        OFF
   Margins:                                         Interface      PAR1
      Left                 4                         Print Wait     OFF
      Right                76                        Page length:   66
      Top                  2                         Margins:
      Bottom               2                            Left     4      Top      2
                                                        Right    76     Bottom   2
   Borders:                                         Default drive and path:
    Top Rows               none                         B:\
    Left Columns           none                     .DIM file access from:
    Border width:          0                            none specified
                                                    .DBF file access from:
   Header                                              none specified
   Footer                                          Video: Hercules
   Printer Set-up:                                 Printer Set-up:

   Print Content:          As Displayed
   Page Numbering:         OFF
   Formatting:             ON
   Row-Col Numbering:      OFF
   Background Print:       OFF                      Press any key to continue
```

When a blank worksheet is started or when the Clear option is taken, VP-Planner institutes or restores all permanent default settings (those not included in the Print Options submenu).

VP-Planner and the Print Line Counter

The VP-Planner software package has an internal line counter for keeping track of the current printer position on a page. As it prints each line of a worksheet, VP-Planner automatically adjusts this line counter. Three of the Print Menu commands—Line, Page, and Align—also affect this counter. The Line command not only issues a line feed for the printer, but it also increments the internal VP-Planner line counter by a value of 1. The Page command tells the printer to go to the top of the next page and sets the line counter back to a beginning value. The Align command just resets the line counter back to its beginning value.

You should be able to tell from the above discussion that you will not want to manually adjust the position of the paper within the printer; VP-Planner has no way of knowing that you have moved the paper. It remembers only the current line counter value. When you manually position the paper at the top of the next page and try to print another worksheet, you will receive a ten line gap wherever VP-Planner "remembers" to issue a page break command to the printer. To solve this problem, issue a CTRL + BREAK command and return to the Print Menu. Then, manually move the paper to the top of the next page and issue an Align command. The line counter will be reset, and you will be ready to start printing.

You have probably noticed that VP-Planner works differently based on whether or not a footer line is specified. It advances to the top of the next page when a footer line is specified. If no footer line is specified, you must manually issue a Page command to advance to the next page.

VP-Planner Functions

You have already used the VP-Planner function @SUM to take the place of a number of other, longer instructions. Functions save time and increase accuracy because they reduce the number of keystrokes and the chance for error. A function contains a preprogrammed set of instructions that you issue by using what VP-Planner refers to as a **function call** (this involves naming the function) and then telling VP-Planner where to find the data to act on.

A typical VP-Planner function consists of the following parts:

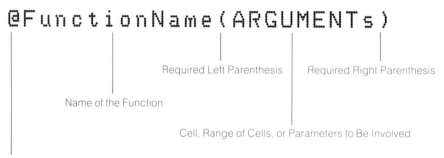

Some VP-Planner functions that are used frequently in business and education are listed below.

Date Functions:

@DATE (year,month,day)—Places the date for any day since 1/1/1900

@DAY (date)—Gets the day number from this date

@MONTH (date)—Gets the month number from this date

@YEAR (date)—Gets the year number from this date

@TODAY—Gets the date from the DOS date register

Statistical Functions:

@COUNT (list)—Counts the number of entries in the specified list (range)

@SUM (list)—Sums the values of all cell contents in the list (range)

@AVG (list)—Averages the values of all cell contents in the list (range)

@MIN (list)—Finds the smallest value from the cells listed in the range

@MAX (list)—Finds the largest value from the cells listed in the range

@STD (list)—Finds the standard deviation from the values of the cells listed in the range

@VAR (list)—Finds the variance from the values of the cells listed in the range

Miscellaneous Functions:

@IF (cond,x,y)—Indicates that, if the condition is true, the value in x or the formula in x will be used; otherwise, the value in y or the formula in y will be used

@ROUND (x,n)—Indicates that number x will be rounded to n decimal positions: if the next position has a value of 5 or greater, the digit n will be rounded up; if that position has a value of 4 or less, the digit n will remain unchanged

Functions can be **nested**—meaning that one function references another function. Suppose, for example, that you wish to get the number of the month from the system date (DOS). You could do this by using the nested function statement @MONTH(@TODAY), which uses the output of the @TODAY function as input to the @MONTH function.

Another example of nesting would be the statement @ROUND(@AVG (F3..F6),1), which averages the numbers in the range F3 to F6 and then rounds the results to one decimal place. When using nested functions, you must make certain that the number of left-hand parentheses equals the number of right-hand parentheses. If the numbers don't match, VP-Planner will cause the computer to beep at you, indicating an error.

VP-Planner Sample

FUNCTION

Worksheet

Suppose you are taking an introductory class in statistics, and early in the semester the teacher asks that you examine the characteristics of four sets of numbers. For each set of numbers, you are to calculate the average, the standard deviation, and the variance; you are also to give the high, the low, the sum, and the number of entries for each set of numbers. You are aware that VP-Planner would be an ideal aid in performing this homework assignment. The sets of numbers are:

1. 9, 12, 7, 5, 2, 1, 3, 4, and 8
2. 8, 36, 16, 9, 4, 0, and 12
3. 1, 16, 4, 9, 36, 25, 16, 23, and 17
4. 69, 60, 59, 65, 56, 77, 81, 91, and 85

After careful analysis, you conclude that the worksheet below will solve the problem.

```
FUNCTION
     27-Aug-86
Homework assignment for Business Statistics:
Examine the statistical characteristics of four sets of numbers.
                    Set 1          Set 2          Set 3          Set 4
                       9              8              1             69
                      12             36             16             60
                       7             16              4             59
                       5              9              9             65
                       2              4             36             56
                       1              0             25             77
                       3             12             16             81
                       4                            23             91
                       8                            17             85

            =================================================================
        Sum:          51             85            147            643
    Average:        5.67          12.14          16.33          71.44
 Stand. Dev.:        3.4          10.86          10.26          11.83
   Variance:       11.56         117.84         105.33         140.02
    Maximum:          12             36             36             91
    Minimum:           1              0              1             56
      Count:           9              7              9              9
```

In doing this project, you will practice the following skills:

1. Using the @TODAY and @DATE date functions
2. Changing the column width of one column
3. Using the F2 Edit function for correcting errors
4. Using statistical functions
5. Using the @ROUND function
6. Using nested functions
7. Copying a single-column range to multiple columns
8. Handling blank cells and cells with a blank on functions

Be sure that you enter the date when you start VP-Planner. It will become important later on. If you have already entered the date and there is material on the worksheet screen, you can erase it by typing:

/

W   Worksheet
E   Erase
Y   Yes

VP-Planner Sample

FUNCTION

Spreadsheet

1. Enter the name of the worksheet.

   A1 FUNCTION

2. "Stamp" the worksheet with today's date at cell A3, using the `@TODAY` function.

```
A3 @TODAY
ENTER
```

In this sample worksheet, the `@TODAY` function caused 31582 to be placed in the cell, signifying that 31,582 days have elapsed since January 1, 1900. That number must now be converted to a more useful format.

You could also enter today's date manually, using the `@DATE` (yy,mm,dd) function. In this example, you would enter `@DATE(86,6,19)`. You would receive the same result of 31582 in cell A3, however, and you would still need to format that cell in order for the information to become useful.

3. Change the number in cell A3 to a standard business format.

/—Gets the Main Menu.

R (F3)—Selects the Range option.

F (F2)—Selects the Format option.

D (F9)—Selects the Date command from Format.

ENTER—Selects the first option of date (DD-MM-YY).

ENTER—Executes the command.

4. You will notice that ********* (VP-Planner's overflow indication) now appears in cell A3, indicating that the cell is not wide enough to display the data. This generally happens after some type of data manipulation; it does not happen with standard text data. In order to get rid of this error, you must change the width of column A to 15—a size large enough for labels that are to be entered later.

/—Gets the Main Menu.

W (F2)—Selects the Worksheet option.

C (F5)—Selects the Col-Wid command.

S (F2)—Selects the Set command.

15—Enters the new desired column width for this column.

ENTER—Executes the instruction.

5. Enter the text data exactly as it appears below (you'll correct any errors later).

```
A5    Homework assignment for Business
      Statistics:
A6    Examine the statistical characteristics
      of fours sets of numbers.
B8    ^Set 1
C8    ^Set 2
D8    ^Set 3
E8    ^Set 4
A19   "Sum:
A20   "Average:
A21   "Stand. Dev.:
```

```
A22    "Variance
A23    Maximum
A24    "Minimum:
A25    "Count:
```

The ˆ character is found above the 6 key and is used to tell VP-Planner to center the data within the cell. It is one of three commands that tell VP-Planner how to position data within a cell. The three are:

'   Left-justify text within the cell

"   Right-justify text within the cell

ˆ   Center text within the cell

Notice that text data and manipulated data are handled differently by VP-Planner. Text data are allowed to overflow their cell boundaries. For example, if you went to cell B6 and entered "new text," the words would appear in the middle of the text that was entered in A6.

6. You probably noticed that the text you entered above contains three errors: cell A6 says *fours* instead of *four*; cell A22 does not have a : mark after *Variance*; and cell A23 is not right-justified and lacks a : mark. You could correct these errors by reentering all of the data, but to be more efficient you could also use the Edit function (invoked by the F2 key) as part of the following procedure:

A6 [by manual pointer movement]—Positions the pointer to cell A6.

F2—Displays the contents of cell A6 on both the status line and the entry line and positions the pointer at the end of the line. The text is now available to the user for manipulation.

Back Arrow to *s* of *fours*—Moves the pointer to the *s* of *fours*.

DEL—Erases the *s*.

ENTER—Tells VP-Planner to change the data within the cell.

A22 [by manual pointer movement]—Positions the pointer at cell A22.

F2—Displays the contents of cell A22 for editing, with the pointer at the end of the line.

:—Enters the : at the end of the line.

ENTER—Tells VP-Planner to change the data within the cell.

A23 [by manual pointer movement]—Positions the pointer at cell A23.

F2—Displays the contents of cell A23 for editing, with the pointer at the end of the line.

HOME—Moves the pointer to the beginning of the line, under the ' mark.

DEL—Deletes the single quote (').

"—Tells VP-Planner to right-justify the contents of the cell.

END—Moves the pointer to the end of the text within the cell.

:—Enters the : mark at the end of the line.

ENTER—Tells VP-Planner to change the data within the cell.

7. Enter the four sets of numbers.

B9	9	C9	8	D9	1	E9	69
B10	12	C10	36	D10	16	E10	60
B11	7	C11	16	D11	4	E11	59
B12	5	C12	9	D12	9	E12	65
B13	2	C13	4	D13	36	E13	56
B14	1	C14	0	D14	25	E14	77
B15	3	C15	12	D15	16	E15	81
B16	4			D16	23	E16	91
B17	8			D17	17	E17	85

8. Enter the total line for cell B18.

   \=—Repeats the equal sign throughout the cell.

   ENTER—Tells VP-Planner to enter the data in the cell.

   The backslash (\) located above the ALT key is used by VP-Planner as the repeat indicator. Any character(s) that appear after the backslash will be repeated throughout the cell. For example, \ABC would place ABCABCABC in the cell.

9. Copy the total line to the cell locations of C18, D18, and E18. Leave the pointer at cell B18.

   /—Gets the Main Menu.

   C (F4)—Selects the Copy command.

   ENTER—Establishes cell B18 as the only cell in the "From" range.

   C18 [by manual pointer movement]—Positions the pointer at cell C18 (the beginning of the "To" range).

   .—Nails down the beginning of the range.

   E18 [by manual pointer movement]—Positions the pointer at the last cell in the "To" range.

   ENTER—Tells VP-Planner to execute the copy instruction.

10. Enter the statistical functions for column B.
    a. Enter the @SUM function at B19 by pointing.

    B19 @SUM(—Enters the first part of the @SUM function.

    B9 [by manual pointer movement]—Positions the pointer at cell B9 (the beginning of range).

    .—Nails down the beginning of the range.

    B17 [by manual pointer movement]—Positions the pointer at the end of the range.

)—Enters the right parenthesis.

    ENTER—Tells VP-Planner to execute the command, and places the result in cell B19.

    This method demonstrates using the pointer to point addresses to a VP-Planner function. In addition to entering the locations via pointing, you can also just give the locations directly to VP-Planner.

    b. Enter the @AVG function at B20 by directly entering the cell addresses of the cells involved.

    B20 @AVG(B9.B17) ENTER

    Since you already know the cell locations from having pointed out the @SUM locations, you now need enter only the cell location at the beginning of the range and the cell location at the end of the range. To execute the command, just depress the ENTER key.

c. Enter the remaining functions, either by pointing or by entering the cell addresses directly. Remember, only enter the formulas for column B; you'll be copying these to the other columns later.

@STD—Standard Deviation

@VAR—Variance

@MAX—Maximum

@MIN—Minimum

@COUNT—count

11. You can now see that the average, standard deviation, and variance entries all have six decimal positions; having this many positions to the right of the decimal point can be distracting to anyone wishing to use the information in report form. You could use the /Range Format command to change the output format of these three cells, but this is also an excellent opportunity to use nested functions. You will use the Edit feature of VP-Planner and add the @ROUND function to the three cells containing average, standard deviation, and variance entries. First, position the pointer at cell B20.

F2—Invokes VP-Planner's Edit mode.

HOME—Positions the pointer at the beginning of the line.

@ROUND(—Inserts @ROUND(at the beginning of the existing line.

END—Positions the pointer at the end of the line.

,2)—Tells VP-Planner that you only want two positions to the right of the decimal.

ENTER—Tells VP-Planner to enter the data in the cell.

Instead of seeing 5.666666 in cell B22, you should now see 5.67.

12. Repeat the steps in task 11 to change the entries in cells B21 and B22.

13. Copy the formulas for the calculations from column B to columns C, D, and E. Position the pointer at B19.

/—Invokes the Main Menu.

C (F4)—Selects the Copy command.

B25 [by manual pointer movement]—Positions the pointer at the end of the "From" range.

ENTER—Tells VP-Planner that the "From" range has been completely defined.

C19 [by manual pointer movement]—Positions the pointer at the first cell in the "To" range.

.—Marks the beginning of the "To" range.

E19 [by manual pointer movement]—Positions the pointer at the last cell in the "To" range.

ENTER—Tells VP-Planner that the "To" range has been completely defined, and tells it to execute the command.

The reason you didn't have to give cell E25 as the last address has to do with how VP-Planner remembers your definition of the "From" range. You defined the range as one column wide and going from cell B19 to cell B25. VP-Planner is thus informed that the

"From" range consists of seven rows of cells. Once you tell VP-Planner in a Copy command where to put the first cell of the "From" range column, it will assume that you also wish to copy the rest of the cells in that column.

You gave three cells as the columns to receive the range. Each of these cells was in a different column, so VP-Planner assumed that you wanted three copies of the "From" range—one for each column.

14. Examine the results of the calculations on the screen. Notice that column C has two blank entries and that the count is indeed equal to 7. VP-Planner is capable of determining when to include a cell in a calculation, and when not to, based on its contents or lack of them. Now what will happen if you make a change in cell C16? Position your pointer at C16.

> SPACE—Adds a character space.

> ENTER—Tells VP-Planner to enter the "data" in the cell.

Notice that, even though there isn't a value in C16, the results of the calculations on the screen have been altered dramatically. Note also that a single quote (') appears in cell C16. Go back to cell C16 and enter the command / Range Erase. The results of the various statistical evaluations immediately return to their original values.

When using ranges that contain so-called blank cells, you should make certain that they really are blank. The single quote (') warns you that the contents of this cell will not work properly in any type of numeric calculation.

15. Save the worksheet using the file name FUNCTION.

> /—Gets the Main Menu.

> F (F6)—Takes the File option.

> S (F3)—Takes the Save command.

> FUNCTION—Enters the name FUNCTION as the file name.

16. Print the file, and put the date, page, and name of the file in a footing.

> /—Invokes the Main Menu.

> P (F7)—Selects the Print option.

> P (F2)—Directs the output to the printer.

> R (F2)—Selects the Range command.

> A1 [by manual pointer movement]—Positions the pointer at A1.

> .—Nails down the beginning of the print range.

> F25 [by manual pointer movement]—Positions the pointer at F25 (the end of the range), allowing all text to print.

> ENTER—Indicates to VP-Planner that the range has been established.

> O (F5)—Selects the Options Menu entry from the Print Menu.

> F (F3)—Selects the Footer command from the Options Menu.

> Page #¦FUNCTION¦@—Tells VP-Planner to divide the footing into three parts, as follows: the page number left-justified in the left-hand part; the name of the file, FUNC-TION, centered in the middle part; today's date right-justified in the right-hand part.

> ENTER—Submits the footing to VP-Planner.

Q (F9)—Terminates the Options Menu, and returns to the
Print Menu.

G (F8)—Prints the worksheet.

Q (F9)—Quits and returns to the worksheet.

Your worksheet should now appear exactly like that at the beginning of this
Sample Worksheet. If it doesn't, compare your cell contents to these:

FUNCTION Cell Contents

```
A1: 'FUNCTION
A3: (D1) @TODAY
A5: 'Homework assignment for Business Statistics:
A6: 'Examine the statistical characteristics of four
sets of numbers.
B8: ^Set 1
C8: ^Set 2
D8: ^Set 3
E8: ^Set 4
B9: 9
C9: 8
D9: 1
E9: 69
B10: 12
C10: 36
D10: 16
E10: 60
B11: 7
C11: 16
D11: 4
E11: 59
B12: 5
C12: 9
D12: 9
E12: 65
B13: 2
C13: 4
D13: 36
E13: 56
B14: 1
C14: 0
D14: 25
E14: 77
B15: 3
C15: 12
D15: 16
E15: 81
B16: 4
D16: 23
E16: 91
B17: 8
D17: 17
E17: 85
B18: \=
C18: \=
D18: \=
```

```
E18:   \=
A19:   "Sum:
B19:   @SUM(B9..B17)
C19:   @SUM(C9..C17)
D19:   @SUM(D9..D17)
E19:   @SUM(E9..E17)
A20:   "Average:
B20:   @ROUND(@AVG(B9..B17),2)
C20:   @ROUND(@AVG(C9..C17),2)
D20:   @ROUND(@AVG(D9..D17),2)
E20:   @ROUND(@AVG(E9..E17),2)
A21:   "Stand. Dev.:
B21:   @ROUND(@STD(B9..B17),2)
C21:   @ROUND(@STD(C9..C17),2)
D21:   @ROUND(@STD(D9..D17),2)
E21:   @ROUND(@STD(E9..E17),2)
A22:   "Variance:
B22:   @ROUND(@VAR(B9..B17),2)
C22:   @ROUND(@VAR(C9..C17),2)
D22:   @ROUND(@VAR(D9..D17),2)
E22:   @ROUND(@VAR(E9..E17),2)
A23:   "Maximum:
B23:   @MAX(B9..B17)
C23:   @MAX(C9..C17)
D23:   @MAX(D9..D17)
E23:   @MAX(E9..E17)
A24:   "Minimum:
B24:   @MIN(B9..B17)
C24:   @MIN(C9..C17)
D24:   @MIN(D9..D17)
E24:   @MIN(E9..E17)
A25:   "Count:
B25:   @COUNT(B9..B17)
C25:   @COUNT(C9..C17)
D25:   @COUNT(D9..D17)
E25:   @COUNT(E9..E17)
```

Chapter Review

A range is any "box" of data cells that has four 90° angles. Various commands allow you either to point out a range of cells to be affected by a later command or to specify addresses of two opposite corners of the range, thereby identifying it.

The Copy command is used to copy the contents of one or more cells (the sending area) and place this in a receiving area of one or more other cells. There are two parts to the Copy command: specifying the sending area (the "From" range), and specifying the receiving area (the "To" range). Both areas are ranges that you can denote by giving the cell addresses or by using the pointer to point them out.

The Format command can be used in either a range or global manner. The Range option formats only a portion of the worksheet, whereas the Global option formats the entire worksheet not currently under a Range command format. A number of format options are available, including fixed, currency, date, percent, or scientific.

The Print command allows you to specify exactly how you wish to print all or part of your worksheet—the range to be printed, and any options that you desire, such as margins, headings, or footings—and then lets you tell VP-Planner to print.

The built-in functions of VP-Planner may be simple or compound (the so-called nested functions, produced when one function is used as input to another function). A worksheet using a number of statistical functions can accommodate many of the spreadsheet concepts involved in these various commands.

Key Terms and Concepts

Align command	Margins option
Borders option	nailing down
Clear option	nested functions
Copy command	Options Menu
Footer option	Other option
Format	Page-Length option
Format Currency option	Page option
Format Date option	Print command
Format Fixed option	Print Menu
Format General option	Print Range option
Format Percent option	Print Status option
Format Scientific option	Quit option
Format Text option	Range
Format , option	Range Format
Format +/− option	receiving ("To" range)
function call	sending ("From" range)
Go option	Setup option
header option	Worksheet Global Format
Line option	

Chapter Quiz

Multiple Choice

1. Which of the following statements about ranges is false:
   a. A range must be either a rectangle or a square.
   b. A range can be defined by "pointing."
   c. A range can be defined by giving the cell addresses of two opposite corners.
   d. A range can be defined by pointing to the first cell and entering the address of the second cell.
   e. All of the above methods can be used to define a range to VP-Planner.

2. Which of the following statements about the Copy command is false:
   a. The first item to be defined is the sending cell/range.
   b. The second item to be defined is the receiving cell/range.
   c. The receiving range can overlap with the sending range without losing data.
   d. The receiving range can be larger than the sending range.
   e. All of the above statements are true.

3. Which of the following steps is not involved in printing a worksheet to a file:
   a. Name the file.
   b. Establish the range and any options.

   c. Issue the Go command.
   d. Take the Quit command to close the file.
   e. All of the above are necessary.

4. Which of the following is not available using the Print Menu:
   a. Specify the right margin.
   b. Specify the page length.
   c. Specify the subtotal point.
   d. Specify the heading and/or footing for each page.
   e. Specify the set-up string for printing.
   f. All of the above are print commands.

5. Which of the following statements is true for functions:
   a. It is difficult to nest functions.
   b. The character used to denote a function is *.
   c. The date functions are of relatively little use.
   d. The function @MONTH(@TODAY) is used to get the month of the year when the date was entered after the boot process.

True/False

6. Functions can save you, the user, a tremendous amount of time.

7. Ranges are typically entered by using three cell addresses.

8. You can print a worksheet without specifying the print range.

9. The set-up string allows you to print in 10, 12, or 17.1 cpi.

10. Print footings allow you to print out the page number, today's date, and some text data.

Answers

1. d 2. c 3. e 4. c 5. d 6. t 7. f 8. f 9. t 10. t

Exercises

1. Define or describe each of the following:
   a. range   f. Align command
   b. Range Format   g. Line option
   c. Global Format   h. Page option
   d. Set-up string   i. nested function
   e. footing

2. When using the Copy command, you must first define the _____ _____ range and then define the _____ _____ range.

3. When the receiving range overlaps the sending range, some data will be _____ .

4. A(n) _____ format affects the entire worksheet, while a(n) _____ format affects only an area of the worksheet.

5. The _____ places a $ sign and any needed commas in a number.

6. Before the worksheet or a part of the worksheet can be printed out, the print _____ must be defined to VP-Planner.

7. In addition to dumping output to a printer, VP-Planner can also place it in a(n) _____ .

8. The _____ selection under the Options Menu allows you to change the print pitch.

9. The _____ command allows you to define *top of page* to VP-Planner.

10. The _____ command moves the paper a small increment, while the _____ command moves the paper to the top of the next page.

11. How does the role of the Quit command differ in creating printer output from its role in creating disk output?

12. What is the advantage of nesting functions?

13. List the functions you consider to be useful at this time.

14. When a number will not fit in a cell, VP-Planner fills that cell with _____ .

15. The _____ character tells VP-Planner to repeat the text across the cell.

Computer Exercises

1. In this exercise, you are to prepare a payroll register. Enter the formulas that would be necessary to prepare the register shown below. The Net Pay is calculated by subtracting the appropriate deductions and taxes from the Gross Pay figure that has been previously calculated. The deductions and taxes, for the sake of simplicity, are assumed to be 37%. The overtime rate = rate * 1.5. Set column A to a width of 20. Set the remaining columns to a width of 11. Your worksheet will not appear so crowded.

Employee	Total Hours	Rate	Overtime Hours	Overtime Rate	Gross Pay	Net Pay
Jones, Anthony	40.00	6.50	2.00	9.75	279.50	176.09
Adams, Sam	40.00	6.50		9.75	260.00	163.80
Smith, Luther	40.00	6.50		9.75	260.00	163.80
Hunt, Mary	40.00	6.50	3.00	9.75	289.25	182.23
Lora, Kathy	40.00	6.50		9.75	260.00	163.80
Kent, John	40.00	6.50		9.75	260.00	163.80
Lester, Ned	40.00	5.50		8.25	220.00	138.60
Sahara, Ohmar	40.00	5.50		8.25	220.00	138.60
Johns, Peter	40.00	4.25	10.00	6.38	233.75	147.26
Dix, Yvonne	40.00	7.50		11.25	300.00	189.00
TOTALS					$2,582.50	$1,626.98

Save your worksheet file using the name CH12EXR1.

2. A teacher friend has asked your assistance in developing a worksheet for calculating grades. Your friend has developed the following criteria for the worksheet:

    a. It is important to have the worksheet stamped with today's date.

    b. The total possible points are to appear at the top of each column.

    c. The average, high grade, low grade, standard deviation, and variance statistics are to be calculated using VP-Planner functions.

    d. The % of Total Points entry is to be calculated by dividing the total possible points by the average.

The following information contains the format for the worksheet:

    a. You must set column A to a width of 15.

    b. Set the rest of the columns to a width of 11.

    c. You must also use the @TODAY function to "date-stamp" the worksheet in cell A1.

    d. The ¦ character is found above the ALT key.

    e. Set column B to a width of 1.

```
10-Feb-85

                              Grading Template

                        ¦
          NAME          ¦ Exam I   Anot. Bib.   Exam II
POSSIBLE POINTS         ¦   150        45         130
- - - - - - - - - - - - ¦- - - - - - - - - - - - - - - - - - - - -
                        ¦
Student 1               ¦   113        44         110
Student 2               ¦   116        42          90
Student 3               ¦   129        42          85
Student 4               ¦   133        44         125
Student 5               ¦   121        42          76
Student 6               ¦   139        41         115
Student 7               ¦   116        42          75
Student 8               ¦   130        39         120
Student 9               ¦   127        42          95
Student 10              ¦   120        42         115
- - - - - - - - - - - - ¦- - - - - - - - - - - - - - - - - - - - -
                        ¦
Average                 ¦   124        42         101
% of Tot. Pnts.         ¦ 82.93%    93.33%      77.38%
High Grade              ¦   139        44         125
Low Grade               ¦   113        39          75
Std. Deviation          ¦     8         1          18
Variance                ¦    65         2         312
```

Save this worksheet file using the CH12EXR2.

3. Print out your CH12EXR2 worksheet file. Specify a heading that has "Introduction to Microcomputers" as the text to appear at the top of the page. Specify a footing that has the page number, name of the worksheet

file, and the date at the bottom of the page. Refer to the print command structure in Appendix B, if you have questions about how to get to a command.

4. Print out your CH12EXR1 worksheet file. Specify a condensed print setup so that the worksheet will print on one page of paper. Refer to the print structure chart in Appendix B. You will also have to expand the right-hand column to a width of 120.

5. Print out your CH12EXR2 worksheet to a disk file called TEST. Leave VP-Planner and access the TEST.PRN file with your word processing software, or use the DOS TYPE command to make sure that you created the file properly. Remember that VP-Planner has placed the .PRN extension on the file.

Chapter

13

Maintaining and
Enhancing Your
Worksheets

Chapter Objectives

After completing this chapter, you should be able to:

Explain the concept of range names

Discuss the Range Column-Width command

Discuss adding and deleting rows and columns

Discuss the use of the Move command

Discuss the use of the Sort command

Discuss the use of the Titles option

Discuss the differences in relative and absolute addressing

Discuss the merits of mixed cell addresses

Discuss the use of absolute range names

Discuss automatic versus manual worksheet recalculation

Discuss in greater detail the @PMT, @ROUND, *and* @IF *functions*

Explain the use of the @DATE *function and its use in arithmetic manipulation*

Once you have finished a worksheet, you are usually still not finished with it. There may be minor errors that you wish to correct, or enhancements that you wish to add to your worksheet to give it a more professional appearance.

This chapter will cover the following topics: range names, adding and deleting rows and columns, moving, sorting, titles, absolute versus relative addressing, manual versus automatic recalculation, and more on the functions @IF, @PMT, and @DATE.

Range Names

By now, you have used ranges extensively in formatting, copying, and printing information from worksheets. One problem with using ranges is that you must always keep track of the cell addresses of two opposite corner cells in each range; to help avoid this problem, VP-Planner has a feature that allows you to give a **range name** to a range of cells and thereafter refer to that range by the given name.

Let's reexamine the procedure involved in setting up function formulas for the FUNCTION worksheet you practiced on in Chapter 12. Every time you wanted to add a function in column B of the worksheet, you either had to point to the cell locations in the range or had to enter the previously recorded cell locations. Another alternative is to give the cell range a name like COLB; then every time VP-Planner requests a range, you can simply use COLB (short for column B).

Another advantage of using range names is that they make a worksheet self-documenting and, therefore, more readable. This can be very helpful when you are setting up formulas to refer to a range name rather than merely a cell location. If you come back to a worksheet later, a formula using range names will make much more sense.

Name Menu

To give a range a name, you must invoke the Range option from the Worksheet Menu (which is invoked from the Main Menu), and select the Name option from the Range Menu. You then receive a menu that looks as follows:

Create   Delete   Labels   Reset   Show

Create. The **Create option** is used to give a name to a range of cells or to redefine the location of the named range. The range name can be one to fourteen characters in length (including special characters and spaces); VP-Planner recommends that you use only A–Z, 0–9 and the dash (–), without using spaces. After you select the Create option, you are prompted for the name you wish to give the range. You are then prompted to define the range to VP-Planner (by pointing or by typing in the actual addresses).

At this point, you can use the F5 key (GOTO) to reference a range name or a cell address. You are not restricted in the number of times that you include a cell in different named ranges. When the worksheet is saved, the range names are also saved.

Delete. The **Delete option** is used to allow VP-Planner to drop a named range from memory. The contents of the individual cells involved remain unchanged. After you select this option, you are prompted to enter the name of the range to be deleted or to point to the range to be deleted on the prompt line.

Labels. The **Labels option** is very similar to the Create option, except that the name for the range is taken directly from an adjacent label entry. You must make certain that the label to be used as the range name does not contain more than fourteen characters.

For example, assume that you have two adjacent entries like those shown below. Position your pointer at cell D3, and enter the commands / Range Name Labels. Depress the ENTER key (or if there are multiple cells involved, indicate the end of the range). You must now tell VP-Planner whether the named cells are right, down, left, or up with respect to the labels.

```
   D3             E3
¦Sales  ¦  $100,00¦
```

Each entry is treated as a separate range name. You cannot delete them in one step, as you can create them; instead, you have to delete them individually or use the reset option.

Reset. The **Reset option** makes VP-Planner drop from its memory all range names that have been assigned.

Show. The **Show** command generates a report of all range names that you have created in your worksheet and displays it to the screen. A report of range names that were created for the FUNCTION worksheet is shown below. As you can see, each range name appears on a separate line along with the upper-right corner cell address and the lower-left corner cell address. If you wish to make a printed copy of the report, simply use the Print Screen feature of VP-Planner (SHIFT + PrtSc) to dump each screen to the printer. Once you have the report printed, you can examine it in length.

```
Currently defined named ranges:

COLB            B9..B17
DATA            B9..E17
HEADING         B8..E8
PRINT           A7..E25
STATS           A19..A25


        Press any key to continue.
```

Naming Instructions

The steps needed to give the numbers in column B of the FUNCTION worksheet the range name COLB are as follows:

/—Gets the Main Menu.

R (F3)—Takes the Range option and displays the Range Menu.

N (F5)—Takes the Name option of the Range Menu and displays the Name Menu.

C (F2)—Takes the Create option of the Name Menu.

COLB—Specifies the range name to be used.

B9 [by manual pointer movement]—Points to the first cell in the COLB range.

.—Nails down the beginning of the range.

B17 [by manual pointer movement]—Points to the last cell in the COLB range.

ENTER—Tells VP-Planner to execute the command.

You can now enter functions simply by referring to the range name, COLB. For example, you could enter the @SUM function as @SUM (COLB), without having to enter the cell addresses or pointing. You can also copy this formula to the other columns, in which case VP-Planner keeps track of the range but not the range name.

Range Column Width

Many times after you have set global column-width size you have a number of adjacent columns that you wish to set to common column width other than the original width. For example, in the worksheet below, you may wish to change the column width of all the columns containing numbers from 5 to 10. Rather then using the / Worksheet Col-Wid command, it is much easier to use the / Range Col-Wid command. This means that instead of entering four different commands, you only have to enter one single series of commands.

	A	B	C	D	E	F	G	H
1	FUNCTION							
2								
3	23-Jun-86							
4								
5								
6		Set 1	Set 2	Set 3	Set 4			
7		9	8	1	69			
8		12	36	16	60			
9		7	16	4	59			
10		5	9	9	65			
11		2	4	36	56			
12		1	0	25	77			
13		3	12	16	81			
14		4		23	91			
15		8		17	85			
16		=====================						
17	Sum:	51	85	147	643			
18	Average:	5.67	12.1	16.3	71.4			
19	Stand. Dev.:	3.4	10.9	10.3	11.8			
20	Variance:	11.6	118	105	140			
21	Maximum:	12	36	36	91			
22	Minimum:	1	0	1	56			
23	Count:	9	7	9	9			

The commands are as follows:

/—Brings up the Main Menu of VP-Planner.

R (F3)—Selects the Range option of the Main Menu.

C (F10)—Selects the `Col-Wid` command.

S (F2)—Selects the Set option.

B7 [by manual pointer movement]—Positions the pointer at cell B7.

.—Marks the beginning of the range.

E7 [by manual pointer movement]—Positions the pointer at cell E7.

ENTER—Establishes the range.

9—Establishes the column width.

ENTER—Executes the command.

The changed worksheet can now be seen as follows:

```
              A           B        C        D        E             F
 1FUNCTION
 2
 3       23-Jun-86
 4
 5
 6                      Set  1   Set  2   Set  3   Set  4
 7                          9        8        1       69
 8                         12       36       16       60
 9                          7       16        4       59
10                          5        9        9       65
11                          2        4       36       56
12                          1        0       25       77
13                          3       12       16       81
14                          4                23       91
15                          8                17       85
16                      ====================================
17          Sum:           51       85      147      643
18      Average:         5.67    12.14    16.33    71.44
19   Stand. Dev.:         3.4    10.86    10.26    11.83
20      Variance:       11.56   117.84   105.33   140.02
21      Maximum:           12       36       36       91
22      Minimum:            1        0        1       56
23        Count:            9        7        9        9
```

Another use of the / Range Col-Wid command is to "hide" columns of the worksheet so that they will not appear either on the screen or on a printout (you can also hide a single column with the / Worksheet Col-Wid command). Suppose, for example, that you had a worksheet like the one below. You decide that you want to print the worksheet to compare the first year's earnings with the last year's earnings, and you decide that you do not wish to see the information for year 2 or year 3. This means that you do not wish to have columns H or I appear on the printout.

	F	G	H	I	J	K
1						
2						
3						
4		1	2	3	4	
5		--------	--------	--------	--------	
6	Sales	260,000	296,400	337,896	385,201	
7	Cost	130,000	148,200	168,948	192,601	
8		--------	--------	--------	--------	
9	Margin	130,000	148,200	168,948	192,601	
10						
11	Expenses:					
12	Advertising	68,200	45,748	50,684	57,780	
13	Salaries	26,000	29,640	33,790	38,520	
14	Supplies	3,900	4,446	5,068	5,778	
15	Clerical	4,000	4,240	4,494	4,764	
16	Other Costs	10,000	10,500	11,025	11,576	
17		--------	--------	--------	--------	
18	Total Expenses	112,100	94,574	105,062	118,419	
19		--------	--------	--------	--------	
20						
21	Income b/f Taxes	17,900	53,626	63,886	74,182	
22	Income Taxes	8,950	26,813	31,943	37,091	
23		--------	--------	--------	--------	
24	Net Income	8,950	26,813	31,943	37,091	
25		=========	=========	=========	=========	

To accomplish this task all that is required is to place the pointer anywhere in column H. Enter the / Range Col-Wid command, extend the range through column I, and enter a 0 for the column width when prompted. The following worksheet will now appear:

	F	G	J	K	L	M
1						
2						
3						
4		1	4			
5		--------	--------			
6	Sales	260,000	385,201			
7	Cost	130,000	192,601			
8		--------	--------			
9	Margin	130,000	192,601			
10						
11	Expenses:					
12	Advertising	68,200	57,780			
13	Salaries	26,000	38,520			
14	Supplies	3,900	5,778			
15	Clerical	4,000	4,764			
16	Other Costs	10,000	11,576			
17		--------	--------			
18	Total Expenses	112,100	118,419			
19		--------	--------			
20						
21	Income b/f Taxes	17,900	74,182			
22	Income Taxes	8,950	37,091			
23		--------	--------			
24	Net Income	8,950	37,091			
25		========	========			

When you set a column to a width of zero, it is still part of the worksheet, but it is not visible on the screen. As a matter of fact, if you pass the pointer through this "invisible" column, the pointer actually disappears from the screen, and the information from that cell is visible in the status line of the control panel. You can make a hidden column reappear on the screen by simply placing the pointer in that column and respecifying a new column width greater than zero.

Adding and Deleting Rows and Columns

From time to time, you may also wish to add or delete one or more rows or columns on the worksheet. This task simply involves pointing to where you wish to add or delete the row or column. The pointer plays a major role in this process. Columns are added to the *left* of the pointer position, and rows are added *above* the pointer position.

WARNING Make certain that there are not important areas of the worksheet off screen that may be affected by deleting a row or column. Remember, the entire column or row will be completely destroyed—not just what appears on the screen.

 Let's add a column to the COMPSALS worksheet, which currently appears as follows:

	B	C	D	E	F
1	COMPSALS				
2					
3	Department	Last Year	This Year	Change	% Change
4					
5	Deli	700.00	575.00	(125.00)	-18%
6	Bakery	1,000.00	1,100.00	100.00	10%
7	Liquor	1,200.00	1,400.00	200.00	17%
8	Grocery	2,500.00	2,900.00	400.00	16%
9	Produce	950.00	1,000.00	50.00	5%
10	Meat	1,500.00	1,410.00	(90.00)	-6%
11					
12	Store Total	7,850.00	8,385.00	535.00	7%

First, position the pointer where the addition or deletion is to take place. For example, if you want to add a column between present columns B and C, place the pointer anywhere in column C. Then issue the following commands:

/—Gets the Main Menu.

W (F2)—Takes the Worksheet option.

I (F3)—Takes the Insert option from the Worksheet Menu.

C (F3)—Tells VP-Planner that you wish to insert a column.

ENTER—Executes the command.

The pointer in column C appears in reverse video. This means that the range is only one column wide. When you depress the ENTER key, the old column C will become the new column D. If you had wished to add two rows, you would have depressed the right arrow one time and then the ENTER key.

The COMPSALS worksheet now looks as follows:

	B	C	D	E	F	G
1	COMPSALS					
2						
3	Department		Last Year	This Year	Change	% Change
4						
5	Deli		700.00	575.00	(125.00)	-18%
6	Bakery		1,000.00	1,100.00	100.00	10%
7	Liquor		1,200.00	1,400.00	200.00	17%
8	Grocery		2,500.00	2,900.00	400.00	16%
9	Produce		950.00	1,000.00	50.00	5%
10	Meat		1,500.00	1,410.00	(90.00)	-6%
11						
12	Store Total		7,850.00	8,385.00	535.00	7%

Now let's add two rows between the Deli and Bakery lines. First, position the pointer anywhere on the Bakery line; then issue the following commands:

/—Gets the Main Menu.

W (F2)—Takes the Worksheet option from the Main Menu.

I (F3)—Takes the Insert option from the Worksheet Menu.

R (F2)—Tells VP-Planner to insert a row.

Down Arrow—Extends the range to two rows.

ENTER—Tells VP-Planner to add the rows.

The COMPSALS worksheet now appears as follows:

B	C	D	E	F	G
1 COMPSALS					
2					
3 Department		Last Year	This Year	Change	% Change
4					
5 Deli		700.00	575.00	(125.00)	-18%
6					
7					
8 Bakery		1,000.00	1,100.00	100.00	10%
9 Liquor		1,200.00	1,400.00	200.00	17%
10 Grocery		2,500.00	2,900.00	400.00	16%
11 Produce		950.00	1,000.00	50.00	5%
12 Meat		1,500.00	1,410.00	(90.00)	-6%
13					
14 Store Total		7,850.00	8,385.00	535.00	7%

You are now free to use these new rows and columns to enter new departments and to enter summary information for sales from two years ago.

Deleting rows and columns involves essentially the same process, except that you mark the actual ranges (rows or columns) to be deleted instead of inserted.

Moving Cell Contents

You may want to add or delete a column or row from your worksheet, only to discover that another area of your worksheet would be disastrously affected by such an action. This is the time to use VP-Planner's **Move feature**, which allows you to relocate cell contents without disturbing other areas of your worksheet. The Move feature automatically retains all functional relationships of any formulas; it works by specifying sending and receiving areas on the worksheet (much like the copy statement—except that the sending contents are then destroyed).

WARNING Make certain that the receiving range does not overlap any valuable cells in your worksheet. All cells in the receiving range will be destroyed, and you will not be able to retrieve the data contained in them.

Suppose that you have a loan amortization worksheet that looks like the following one:

	A	B	C	D	E	F
2	Interest		12.00%			
3	Loan Amount		$1,200			
4	Months		20			
5	Beginning Date		May-85			
6						
7				TOTAL	BALANCE	
8	DATE	PRINCIPAL	INTEREST	PAYMENT	OUTSTANDING	
9	May-85	54.50	12.00	66.50	1145.50	
10	Jun-85	55.04	11.46	66.50	1090.46	
11	Jul-85	55.59	10.90	66.50	1034.87	
12	Aug-85	56.15	10.35	66.50	978.72	
13	Sep-85	56.71	9.79	66.50	922.01	

Imagine that you want to center the information contained at the top of the worksheet in order to give it a more balanced look. To perform this task, which involves moving the information contained in eight cells one column to the right, you would have to execute the following steps:

/—Invokes the Main Menu.

M (F5)—Selects the Move option from the Main Menu.

A1 [by manual pointer movement]—Positions the pointer at A1 to establish the beginning of the "From" range.

.—Nails down the beginning of the "From" range.

C5 [by manual pointer movement]—Positions the pointer to the ending cell in the "From" range.

ENTER—Tells VP-Planner that the "From" range has been defined.

B1 [by manual pointer movement]—Positions the pointer at the beginning of the "To" range.

ENTER—Tells VP-Planner to move the cell contents.

The worksheet would now appear as follows:

	A	B	C	D	E	F
2		Interest		12.00%		
3		Loan Amount		$1,200		
4		Months		20		
5		Beginning Date		May-85		
6						
7				TOTAL	BALANCE	
8	DATE	PRINCIPAL	INTEREST	PAYMENT	OUTSTANDING	
9	May-85	54.50	12.00	66.50	1145.50	
10	Jun-85	55.04	11.46	66.50	1090.46	
11	Jul-85	55.59	10.90	66.50	1034.87	
12	Aug-85	56.15	10.35	66.50	978.72	
13	Sep-85	56.71	9.79	66.50	922.01	

Sorting

From time to time, you may want to rearrange data in a particular order. Some spreadsheets allow you to perform such a task via the Move statement; VP-Planner, however, contains a **Sort command**. This feature allows a worksheet to be constructed in a way that is logical for the individual building it, and then to be accessed by another user and rearranged in a manner that is logical for that person's application.

Sort Menu

The Sort command is found in the Data Menu, which is invoked from the Main Menu. When the Sort option is selected, the following menu is displayed:

Data-Range Primary-Key Secondary-Key Reset Go Quit

Data Range. The **Data Range option** allows you to mark the area to be sorted—an operation that must occur before a sort can take place. Column headings and total lines are not included in the data range. It is wise to save a worksheet before you perform a sort; then if you really mess things up, you can just reload the worksheet from disk.

Primary Key. The **Primary Key option** allows you to select the column you want the data range to be sorted by. Since the entire range has been described to VP-Planner, all you have to do is point to the column; VP-Planner will then prompt you to select the sort order, in either ascending or descending order.

Secondary Key. The **Secondary Key option** allows you to arrange data within the primary key when the sort is executed. For example, in a sort of name and address data, you could establish City as the primary key and Last Name as the secondary key; the data would then be sorted by city, and within each city would be sorted by last name.

Reset. The **Reset option** is selected to make VP-Planner drop from its memory all the sort parameters you've given it.

Go. The **Go option** is the command that tells VP-Planner to execute the sort.

Quit. The **Quit option** returns you to your worksheet and ready mode.

When you have a large worksheet, you may wish to set up a number of sorts for different data ranges. In this type of application, it is advisable to use the Reset before the next sort. This is especially important when you are going from an application that has both primary and secondary sort keys to an application that has only a primary sort. Unless you tell VP-Planner to reset the sort parameters, it still remembers the secondary key. In this type of situation, you would receive a `Key column outside of sort range` error message.

 ### *Worksheet Practice with the Sort Command*

Load in the `CH12EXR1` worksheet you created in Chapter 12, and try some experiments with the Sort command. The loading process is accomplished via the following commands:

/—Gets the Main Menu.

F (F6)—Selects the File option.

R (F2)—Selects the Retrieve option.

`CH12EXR1`—Identifies the name of the worksheet.

ENTER—Tells VP-Planner to get the worksheet.

You should now have the following worksheet loaded (since the entire worksheet will not normally fit on one page, spaces have been deleted to make it fit here):

	A	B	C	D	E	F	G
1		Total		Overtime	Overtime	Gross	
2	Employee	Hours	Rate	Hours	Rate	Pay	Net Pay
3							
4	Jones, Anthony	40.00	6.50	2.00	9.75	279.50	176.09
5	Adams, Sam	40.00	6.50		9.75	260.00	163.80
6	Smith, Luther	40.00	6.50		9.75	260.00	163.80
7	Hunt, Mary	40.00	6.50	3.00	9.75	289.25	182.23
8	Lora, Kathy	40.00	6.50		9.75	260.00	163.80
9	Kent, John	40.00	6.50		9.75	260.00	163.80
10	Lester, Ned	40.00	5.50		8.25	220.00	138.60
11	Sahara, Ohmar	40.00	5.50		8.25	220.00	138.60
12	Johns, Peter	40.00	4.25	10.00	6.37	233.75	147.26
13	Dix, Yvonne	40.00	7.50		11.25	300.00	189.00
14							
15	TOTALS					$2,582.50	$1,626.98

Once the worksheet has been loaded, you must tell VP-Planner how to sort the information, by invoking the Main Menu and selecting the Data option from it. The following steps should now be taken:

S (F4)—Takes the Sort option from the Data Menu.

D (F2)—Selects the data range to define the area of the worksheet to be sorted.

A4 [by manual pointer movement]—Positions the pointer at A4 (the cell with the contents "Anthony Jones").

.—Nails down the beginning of the range.

G13 [by manual pointer movement]—Positions the pointer at cell G13 (the cell with the contents "189.00").

ENTER—Tells VP-Planner that the data range is defined.

P (F3)—Selects the Primary Key option.

A4 [by manual pointer movement]—Positions the pointer at A4 (the cell with the contents "Anthony Jones"). Actually, the pointer could just as well be placed anywhere in column A inside the data range.

ENTER—Tells VP-Planner to accept this information.

A—Tells VP-Planner to perform the sort in ascending order.

ENTER—Indicates to VP-Planner that the sort order has been completed.

G—Tells VP-Planner to perform the sort.

Your worksheet should now look like the one shown below:

	A	B	C	D	E	F	G
1		Total		Overtime	Overtime	Gross	
2	Employee	Hours	Rate	Hours	Rate	Pay	Net Pay
3							
4	Adams, Sam	40.00	6.50		9.75	260.00	163.80
5	Dix, Yvonne	40.00	7.50		11.25	300.00	189.00
6	Hunt, Mary	40.00	6.50	3.00	9.75	289.25	182.23
7	Johns, Peter	40.00	4.25	10.00	6.37	233.75	147.26
8	Jones, Anthony	40.00	6.50	2.00	9.75	279.50	176.09
9	Kent, John	40.00	6.50		9.75	260.00	163.80
10	Lester, Ned	40.00	5.50		8.25	220.00	138.60
11	Lora, Kathy	40.00	6.50		9.75	260.00	163.80
12	Sahara, Ohmar	40.00	5.50		8.25	220.00	138.60
13	Smith, Luther	40.00	6.50		9.75	260.00	163.80
14							
15	TOTALS					$2,582.50	$1,626.98

This information is ideal if you're looking for a payroll listing of employees in the company. What happens, though, if you want to group individuals in alphabetic order by department? On this worksheet, doing so would involve adding a column to the left of the Employee column to contain the department number and setting the Dpt. column to a width of four positions and changing the format to zero decimal positions.

First, position the pointer anywhere in column A and add a column as follows:

/—Invokes the Main Menu.

W (F2)—Selects the Worksheet option.

I (F3)—Selects the Insert option.

C (F3)—Selects the Column option.

ENTER—Executes the Insert command.

Next, position the pointer in new column A and change it to a width of 4.

/—Invokes the Main Menu.

W (F2)—Selects the Worksheet option.

C (F5)—Selects the Col-Wid option.

S (F2)—Selects the Set option.

4—Specifies the new width.

ENTER—Executes the command.

Next, position the cursor to cell A4 (the one to the left of "Sam Adams"). Change the format to zero positions to the right of the decimal.

/—Invokes the Main Menu.

R (F3)—Selects the Range option.

F (F2)—Selects the Format option.

F (F2)—Selects the Fixed option.

0—Identifies the number of decimal positions.

ENTER—Executes the command.

A13 [by manual pointer movement]—Positions the pointer at the end of
          the range.

          ENTER—Tells VP-Planner to execute the command.

     Enter the Dpt. heading and the following department numbers to your
worksheet:

	A	B	C	D	E	F	G	H
1			Total		Overtime	Overtime	Gross	
2	Dpt.	Employee	Hours	Rate	Hours	Rate	Pay	Net Pay
3								
4	1	Adams, Sam	40.00	6.50		9.75	260.00	163.80
5	2	Dix, Yvonne	40.00	7.50		11.25	300.00	189.00
6	2	Hunt, Mary	40.00	6.50	3.00	9.75	289.25	182.23
7	1	Johns, Peter	40.00	4.25	10.00	6.37	233.75	147.26
8	2	Jones, Anthony	40.00	6.50	2.00	9.75	279.50	176.09
9	1	Kent, John	40.00	6.50		9.75	260.00	163.80
10	1	Lester, Ned	40.00	5.50		8.25	220.00	138.60
11	2	Lora, Kathy	40.00	6.50		9.75	260.00	163.80
12	2	Sahara, Ohmar	40.00	5.50		8.25	220.00	138.60
13	1	Smith, Luther	40.00	6.50		9.75	260.00	163.80
14								
15		TOTALS					$2,582.50	$1,626.98

More sort instructions must now be issued to tell VP-Planner exactly how to
sort information in the data range, including giving a new sort range to VP-
Planner (remember, a field outside the old range has been added), specifying
a new primary key, and specifying a secondary key. (Since the data range has
not changed dramatically and both a primary and a secondary key sort will be
executed, the Reset command does not have to be executed.) These tasks
require the following steps:

     /—Invokes the Main Menu.

     D (F9)—Selects the Data option.

     S (F4)—Selects the Sort option from the Data Menu.

     D (F2)—Selects the Data Range option.

     BACKSPACE—Cancels the existing range.

     A4 [by manual pointer movement]—Positions the pointer at the left of
          the cell with "Sam Adams" in it.

     .—Nails down the beginning of the range.

     H13 [by manual pointer movement]—Positions the pointer at the end of
          the range.

     ENTER—Tells VP-Planner that the range has been established.

     P (F3)—Selects the Primary Key option.

     BACKSPACE—Cancels the existing range.

     A4 [by manual pointer movement]—Positions the pointer at cell A4
          (any other cell in column A inside the data range would do just as
          well).

     ENTER—Tells VP-Planner that the Primary Key range has been estab-
          lished.

     ENTER—Tells VP-Planner to sort in ascending order (default).

S (F4)—Selects the Secondary Key option.

B4 [by manual pointer movement]—Positions the pointer at cell B4 (any other cell in column B within the data range would do just as well).

ENTER—Tells VP-Planner that the Secondary Key range has been established.

A—Tells VP-Planner to sort in ascending order.

ENTER—Tells VP-Planner that the order of the sort is specified.

G (F6)—Tells VP-Planner to sort the worksheet.

Your worksheet should now look as follows:

	A	B	C	D	E	F	G	H
1			Total		Overtime	Overtime	Gross	
2	Dpt.	Employee	Hours	Rate	Hours	Rate	Pay	Net Pay
3								
4	1	Adams, Sam	40.00	6.50		9.75	260.00	163.80
5	1	Johns, Peter	40.00	4.25	10.00	6.37	233.75	147.26
6	1	Kent, John	40.00	6.50		9.75	260.00	163.80
7	1	Lester, Ned	40.00	5.50		8.25	220.00	138.60
8	1	Smith, Luther	40.00	6.50		9.75	260.00	163.80
9	2	Dix, Yvonne	40.00	7.50		11.25	300.00	189.00
10	2	Hunt, Mary	40.00	6.50	3.00	9.75	289.25	182.23
11	2	Jones, Anthony	40.00	6.50	2.00	9.75	279.50	176.09
12	2	Lora, Kathy	40.00	6.50		9.75	260.00	163.80
13	2	Sahara, Ohmar	40.00	5.50		8.25	220.00	138.60
14								
15		TOTALS					$2,582.50	$1,626.98

Save this worksheet to a file called PAYSORT, as follows:

/—Invokes the Main Menu.

F (F6)—Selects the File option from the Main Menu.

S (F3)—Selects the Save option.

PAYSORT—Keys in the new worksheet name.

ENTER—Saves the file to disk.

Titles

By this time, you have surely noticed that it is inconvenient to work with large spreadsheets, like PAYROLL, whose width exceeds the display on the screen—especially when you are interested in gross pay and net pay information for an employee. You can see the net or gross pay numbers on the screen, but you can't see the employee names. You may have wished you could freeze a column of data or a row of text to act as labels for an off-screen row or column. VP-Planner, like many spreadsheet packages, has a feature that provides this capability (it is referred to as the **Titles option**).

When you are using the Titles option, the pointer again plays an important role. Any columns to the left of the pointer or any rows above the pointer that appear on the screen can be frozen to act as labels. You cannot move the pointer into a title area by using the arrow keys. In order to get the pointer into the titles area, you must press the F5 key and then enter the address of the cell. This causes two copies of the title cells to be displayed on the screen.

Titles Menu

The Titles command is invoked from the Worksheet Menu. It presents a menu consisting of the following options:

```
Both   Horizontal   Vertical   Clear
```

Both.   The Both option freezes the rows above the pointer and the columns to the left of the pointer, creating a fixed border of headings for vertical and horizontal scrolling through the worksheet.

Horizontal.   The Horizontal option freezes the rows above the pointer, creating fixed headings for vertical scrolling through the worksheet.

Vertical.   The Vertical option freezes the columns to the left of the pointer, creating fixed line labels for horizontal scrolling through the worksheet.

Clear.   The Clear option causes any rows or columns that have been frozen to return to unfrozen status. (Note that in order for a cell to be frozen on the screen it must appear on the screen at the time that the Titles option of the Worksheet Menu is selected. If a cell does not physically appear on the screen, it cannot be frozen on the screen.)

Titles Instructions

Using the Titles command to freeze the employee names would require the following steps:

> HOME—Positions the pointer at cell A1.
>
> C1 [by manual pointer movement]—Positions the pointer at cell C1.
>
> /—Gets the Main Menu.
>
> W (F2)—Selects the Worksheet option.
>
> T (F7)—Selects the Titles option.
>
> V (F4)—Selects the Vertical Titles option.

When you move the pointer to the Net Pay column, the Employee column will remain on the screen and your display will look as follows:

	A	B	E	F	G	H
1			Overtime	Overtime	Gross	
2	Dpt.Employee		Hours	Rate	Pay	Net Pay
3						
4	1	Adams, Sam		9.75	260.00	163.80
5	1	Johns, Peter	10.00	6.37	233.75	147.26
6	1	Kent, John		9.75	260.00	163.80
7	1	Lester, Ned		8.25	220.00	138.60
8	1	Smith, Luther		9.75	260.00	163.80
9	2	Dix, Yvonne		11.25	300.00	189.00
10	2	Hunt, Mary	3.00	9.75	289.25	182.23
11	2	Jones, Anthony	2.00	9.75	279.50	176.09
12	2	Lora, Kathy		9.75	260.00	163.80
13	2	Sahara, Ohmar		8.25	220.00	138.60
14						
15	TOTALS				$2,582.50	$1,626.98
16						
17						
18						
19						
20						

Relative and Absolute Addressing

As you have already seen, a formula can be copied across a row or down a column, and VP-Planner will automatically adjust the formula placed in each cell to reflect its new location and the location of any participating cells. This is the concept behind **relative addressing**. But what happens if you don't want VP-Planner to change a formula automatically to reflect a new cell location? How do you tell VP-Planner, without directly entering a different formula in each cell, to refer to only one cell in a series of calculations?

Let's examine a concrete application of this question. How would you find out what percentage each individual's gross pay was of the total gross pay in the CH10EXER1 worksheet? You could insert a column between the Gross Pay and Net Pay columns, but how could you enter a formula and copy it to the other cells in the column in such a way that it would always refer to the contents of the total gross pay cell in calculating the percentage?

The first possibility, manually entering the required formula for each row in the column, is feasible with the few employees that are currently in the worksheet, but it would be a tremendous amount of work if you were dealing with 100 employees. The easiest way to solve the problem is to use a technique referred to as **absolute addressing**.

An absolute cell reference is easy to distinguish from a relative cell reference because it appears with one or more dollar signs ($) in the cell reference— for example, A1, $A1, or A$1.

Let's begin by examining why the relative addressing feature of VP-Planner is inappropriate for this application.

 Load the worksheet file PAYSORT, if it is not already on your screen.

1. Position the pointer anywhere in column H (Net Pay), and insert the new column, using the following instructions:

/—Gets the Main Menu.

W (F2)—Selects the Worksheet option.

I (F3)—Selects the Insert option from the Worksheet Menu.

ENTER—Executes the Insert command.

2. Enter the column headings.

```
H1 % of Total
H2 ^Gross
```

Center (^) the second line of the heading.

3. At cell H4, enter the formula for calculating the percentage of total gross pay, using the relative addressing convention.

```
H4  +G4/G15
```

When you depress ENTER, you should see 0.10 as the cell contents.

4. Set the column to a percentage format with one decimal position.

/—Invokes the Main Menu.

R (F3)—Selects the Range option.

F (F2)—Selects the Format option from the Range Menu.

P (F8)—Selects the Percent format.

1—Sets the number of decimal positions to one.

ENTER—Tells VP-Planner that this part of the command is finished.

H13 [by manual pointer movement]—Positions the pointer at the last cell in the range.

ENTER—Tells VP-Planner that the range has been defined and that the command is to be executed.

5. Copy this formula to the rest of the cells in the column.

H4 [by manual pointer movement]—Positions the pointer at cell H4.

/—Invokes the Main Menu.

C (F4)—Selects the Copy command option.

ENTER—Indicates to VP-Planner that cell H4 is the only "From" cell.

H5 [by manual pointer movement]—Positions the pointer at cell H5, the beginning of the "To" range.

.—Nails down the beginning of the "To" range.

H13 [by manual pointer movement]—Positions the pointer at the last cell in the "To" range.

ENTER—Tells VP-Planner to execute the Copy command.

You should now see the following worksheet (with more spaces) on your screen:

	A	B	C	D	E	F	G	H	I
1			Total		Overtime	Overtime		Gross % of Total	
2	Dpt.	Employee	Hours	Rate	Hours	Rate	Pay	Gross	Net Pay
3									
4	1	Adams, Sam	40.00	6.50		9.75	260.00	.10	163.80
5	1	Johns, Peter	40.00	4.25	10.00	6.38	233.80	ERR	147.29
6	1	Kent, John	40.00	6.50		9.75	260.00	ERR	163.80
7	1	Lester, Ned	40.00	5.50		8.25	220.00	ERR	138.60
8	1	Smith, Luthe	40.00	6.50		9.75	260.00	ERR	163.80
9	2	Dix, Yvonne	40.00	7.50		11.25	300.00	ERR	189.00
10	2	Hunt, Mary	40.00	6.50	3.00	9.75	289.25	ERR	182.23
11	2	Jones, Antho	40.00	6.50	2.00	9.75	279.50	ERR	176.09
12	2	Lora, Kathy	40.00	6.50		9.75	260.00	ERR	163.80
13	2	Sahara, Ohma	40.00	5.50		8.25	220.00	ERR	138.60
14									
15		TOTALS			15.00		$2,582.55		$1,627.01

Obviously something is drastically wrong with this worksheet. What happened? When VP-Planner copied the formula +G4/G15 to the other cells in the column, it automatically changed the formula for each cell as it proceeded down the column; as a result, cell H5 contains the formula +G5/G16, and cell H6 has the formula +G6/G17. But cells G16 and G17 do not contain any numeric values—hence the error message ERR.

VP-Planner did not want to use the contents of the total gross pay cell for each of the calculations after the Copy command was used because no absolute cell references are contained in the original formula entered at H4.

Go to cell H4, and enter the formula +G4/G15. Then use the instructions contained in step 5 above to copy the formula to the other cells in the column. Afterward, your screen should have a display like the following:

	A	B	C	D	E	F	G	H	I
1			Total		Overtime	Overtime		Gross % of Total	
2	Dpt.	Employee	Hours	Rate	Hours	Rate	Pay	Gross	Net Pay
3									
4	1	Adams, Sam	40.00	6.50		9.75	260.00	10.1%	163.80
5	1	Johns, Peter	40.00	4.25	10.00	6.38	233.80	9.1%	147.29
6	1	Kent, John	40.00	6.50		9.75	260.00	10.1%	163.80
7	1	Lester, Ned	40.00	5.50		8.25	220.00	8.5%	138.60
8	1	Smith, Luther	40.00	6.50		9.75	260.00	10.1%	163.80
9	2	Dix, Yvonne	40.00	7.50		11.25	300.00	11.6%	189.00
10	2	Hunt, Mary	40.00	6.50	3.00	9.75	289.25	11.2%	182.23
11	2	Jones, Anthony	40.00	6.50	2.00	9.75	279.50	10.8%	176.09
12	2	Lora, Kathy	40.00	6.50		9.75	260.00	10.1%	163.80
13	2	Sahara, Ohmar	40.00	5.50		8.25	220.00	8.5%	138.60
14									
15		TOTALS			15.00		$2,582.55		$1,627.01

The dollar signs in the amended formula tell VP-Planner that it is to leave this part of the formula exactly the same as it copies it from one cell to another. Relative addressing will not affect any part of the formula containing dollar signs.

In the above example, the formula containing the absolute cell reference had a cell address of G15. As was noted earlier, you can also use addresses like $A1 or A$1. Since this type of cell reference has elements of absolute addressing and relative addressing, it is referred to as a **mixed cell address**. The relative part of a mixed cell address will change; the absolute part will remain the same. For example:

$A1 (**$ column row**). The absolute address portion of this reference is the column portion of the reference, so the row can change within the address, but the column must remain as A. This formula could be read as "any row in column A."

A$1 (**column $ row**). The absolute address portion of this reference is the row portion of the reference, so the column can change within the address, but the row must remain as 1. This formula could be read as "any column in row 1."

It is important to be aware that mixed cell addresses cannot be used with range names. If absolute addresses are desired for range names (for example, $COLB), the range name will be treated as though both the column and the row portions of the address are absolute—that is, it will be wholly an **absolute range name**.

Automatic Versus Manual Worksheet Recalculation

Each time you press the ENTER key, VP-Planner automatically recalculates the entire worksheet. This is not a problem when the worksheet is small, but when the worksheet is large and involves many calculations it can become very time-consuming.

To avoid this problem, VP-Planner has the ability to turn off its **automatic recalculation** feature, allowing the user to tell it when to recalculate. This is accomplished by entering the following command sequence:

/—Invokes the Main Menu.

W (F2)—Selects the worksheet option.

G (F2)—Selects the Global option from the Worksheet Menu.

R (F5)—Selects the Recalculation option from the Global Menu.

M (F6)—Executes the Manual command.

If you make changes to any cell after this **Manual Recalculation** option has been selected, VP-Planner tells you by displaying a CALC message at the bottom of your screen next to the indicators area. To get VP-Planner to recalculate the worksheet, you must depress the F9 function key.

If you save the worksheet file onto disk, the manual recalculation setting is saved in the worksheet file. If you wish to reset the spreadsheet to automatic, all you need do is enter the above commands replacing the M with an A (for Automatic).

More on Functions

@PMT

VP-Planner has incorporated a financial function that is a true time-saver. The @PMT(principal,interest,periods)—payment per period— function calculates the payment of a loan or mortgage based on the three pieces of information: principal, interest, and number of periods. Using this function allows you to avoid entering the following formula:

```
Prin*Inter/12/(1-1/(1+Inter/12)^Periods)
```

@IF *and Logical Operators*

The @IF function allows VP-Planner to check for certain conditions and then take actions based on the results of the check. The format of the @IF function is @IF(condition,true,false). The "condition" portion of the function allows you to set up an equation to check for specific results or cell contents; the "true" portion contains instructions that will be executed if the condition is true; the "false" portion contains instructions that will be executed if the condition is false.

The operators allowed in a VP-Planner @IF function are:

Relational:

=	equal to
<	less than
<=	less than or equal to
>	greater than
>=	greater than or equal to
<>	not equal to

Logical:

#NOT#	not (The opposite of any equation or relation must be the case before the true option is executed.)
#AND#	and (Both conditions must be true before the true option is executed.)
#OR#	or (Either action can be true for the true option to be executed.)

These operators can be used to set up a number of different conditions:

+B13=60#OR#D17<20   The value contained in cell B13 is equal to 60, or the value contained in cell D17 is less than 20.

+H14>0#AND#D19>1985   The value contained in cell H14 is greater than zero, and the value in cell D19 is greater than 1985.

#NOT#(YEAR=1985)   The value stored in the cell named YEAR is not 1985.

(B15-C10)=D3#AND#C5>D7   The value of cell B15 minus the value of cell C10 is equal to the value contained in cell D3, *and* the value contained in cell C5 is larger than the value contained in cell D7.

These new conditions also have places in the order of precedence discussed earlier. The complete listing of this order is as follows:

Operator	*The Operator Order of Precedence Meaning*	Level
^	exponentiation	7
−	negative	6
+	positive	6
*	multiplication	5
/	division	5
+	addition	4
−	subtraction	4
=	equal	3
<	less than	3
<=	less than or equal	3

Operator	*The Operator Order of Precedence Meaning*	*Level*
>	greater than	3
>=	greater than or equal	3
<>	not equal	3
#NOT#	logical not	2
#AND#	logical and	1
#OR#	logical or	1

@DATE *and Arithmetic*

You were introduced to some aspects of the @DATE function when you entered the FUNCTION worksheet. The information returned by the @TODAY and @DATE functions is numeric and represents the number of elapsed days since December 31, 1899. Thus, when VP-Planner displays a date via one of the three formats listed below, it is merely formatting numeric information for display. If you loaded the FUNCTION worksheet and looked in cell A3, you would see a number that corresponds to today's date. VP-Planner displays date information in one of the following formats:

1 = D-MMM-Y (Example: 19-Jun-86)

2 = D-MMM (Example: 19 Jun)

3 = MMM-Y (Example: Jun-86)

4 = M/D/Y (Example: 06/19/86)

5 = D/M/Y (Example: 19/06/86)

6 = Y M D (Example: 86 06 19)

Time (Example: 17:50)

Displaying a date is a two-step process: first, you get the data via the @DATE or @TODAY function, causing a number to appear on the screen and in the cell; second, you use the / Range Format commands on the cell to hold one of the above formats, causing a date display to appear on the screen.

The numeric method that VP-Planner uses to display dates can be very beneficial in manipulating dates. Since the date is really numeric, any arithmetic operations can be performed on it. To get the date for a week from today, for example, you simply add 7 to the existing numeric date. Or if you want to find out how many weeks there are between two dates, you can subtract the ending date from the beginning date, divide by 7, and round the result using the @ROUND or @INT functions, and find out how many intervening weeks there are.

With date arithmetic involving months, you must be careful. You can't simply convert a month to thirty days and expect it to work. Adding a number like 30.5 doesn't work well either, unless the period covered is small. The following method assumes that payment will occur on or before the twenty-eighth day of the month:

1. Add 31 to the previous date.

2. Subtract the current @DAY from the present number to bring you back to the present day of the prior month.

3. Add @DAY to the original number to move you forward to the proper day in the next month.

This allows you to advance from one month to the next, if the day of the month is 1 through 28.

You can also compare the value of the @TODAY function with another date already entered on the worksheet or with a date in a formula. To do this requires using the command @IF(@TODAY>@DATE(85,2,1),x,y). The x represents the action to be taken if the condition is true, while the y represents the action to be taken if the condition is false.

Worksheet Practice

A number of the topics discussed in this chapter are used in the next few pages to prepare two worksheets: the first worksheet involves generating a loan amortization table; the second serves as the basis for evaluating various automobile loan alternatives.

Loan Amortization Worksheet

The following loan amortization table requires you to enter the loan amount, the interest on the loan, the length of the loan in months, and the starting date of the loan. It will then generate a table that includes the amount of the payment, the month of the payment, the portion applied toward the principal, the portion applied to the interest, and the outstanding balance.

In doing this project, you will practice the following skills:

1. Using the @PMT function
2. Using the @IF function
3. Using date arithmetic
4. Using absolute addressing

The worksheet is as follows:

```
Interest            12.00%
Loan Amount         $1,200
Months                  20
Beginning Date     May-85

        TOTAL                           BALANCE
DATE    PAYMENT  PRINCIPAL INTEREST OUTSTANDING
May-85   66.50     54.50     12.00     1145.50
Jun-85   66.50     55.04     11.46     1090.46
Jul-85   66.50     55.59     10.90     1034.87
Aug-85   66.50     56.15     10.35      978.72
```

To present the information in the above format, you'll obviously have to use some form of absolute addressing to allow each line of formulas to refer to the data at the top of the worksheet. In addition, you'll have to use date arithmetic to advance the date month by month from one line to the next; you'll have to use the @PMT function for easy calculation of the payment (you could place this piece of information at the top also); and later you'll have to use the @IF function to generate the worksheet properly.

The various column amounts are calculated as follows:

The payment is calculated via the @PMT function.

The interest is calculated by multiplying the outstanding balance by the interest rate, and dividing that result by 12 (interest for one month).

The principal is calculated by subtracting the interest amount from the payment amount.

The new outstanding balance is calculated by subtracting the amount of the payment applied toward the principal from the old outstanding balance.

Now let's go through the individual tasks involved in creating this worksheet.

1. Set the global column width to 10.

    /—Invokes the Main Menu.

    W (F2)—Selects the Worksheet option of the Main Menu.

    G (F2)—Selects the Global option of the Worksheet Menu.

    C (F4)—Selects the Col-Wid option.

    10—Specifies the new column width.

    ENTER—Tells VP-Planner to execute the command.

2. Enter label information in the appropriate cells.

    ```
    A2  Interest
    A3  Loan Amount
    A4  Months
    A5  Beginning Date
    A8  ^DATE
    B7  ^TOTAL
    B8  ^PAYMENT
    C8  ^PRINCIPAL
    D8  ^INTEREST
    E7  ^BALANCE
    E8  ^OUTSTANDING
    ```

3. Enter the loan information.

    ```
    C2  .12
    C3  1200
    C4  20
    C5  @DATE(85,5,1)
    ```

4. Format cell C2 for percentage, with two decimal positions.

    C2 [by manual pointer movement]—Positions the pointer at cell C2.

    /—Invokes the Main Menu.

    R (F3)—Selects the Range option.

    F (F2)—Selects the Format option from the Range Menu.

    P (F8)—Selects the Percent option.

    ENTER—Takes the default of two decimal positions.

    ENTER—Tells VP-Planner to format only this cell.

5. Format cell C3 for currency, with zero decimal positions.

    C3 [by manual pointer movement]—Positions the pointer at cell C3.

    /—Invokes the Main Menu.

    R (F3)—Selects the Range option.

> F (F2)—Selects the Format option from the Range Menu.
>
> C (F4)—Selects the Crncy option.
>
> 0—Tells VP-Planner the number of decimal positions.
>
> ENTER—Tells VP-Planner to accept the decimal position information.
>
> ENTER—Tells VP-Planner to format only this cell.

6. Format cell C4 for whole months.

> C4 [by manual pointer movement]—Positions the pointer at cell C4.
>
> /—Invokes the Main Menu.
>
> R (F3)—Selects the Range option.
>
> F (F2)—Selects the Format option from the Range Menu.
>
> F (F2)—Selects the Fixed format option.
>
> 0—Specifies the number of decimal positions.
>
> ENTER—Tells VP-Planner to accept the decimal position information.
>
> ENTER—Tells VP-Planner to format only this cell.

7. Format cell C5 for the date.

> C5 [by manual pointer movement]—Positions the pointer at cell C5.
>
> /—Invokes the Main Menu.
>
> R (F3)—Selects the Range option.
>
> F (F2)—Selects the Format option from the Range Menu.
>
> D (F9)—Selects the Date option.
>
> 3 (F4)—Selects the (MMM-Y) option.
>
> ENTER—Tells VP-Planner to format only this cell.

The information on the first line of the schedule also represents the first payment. As a result, the formulas in this row will be a little bit different from those in subsequent rows.

8. Copy the beginning date onto the schedule.

> A9 [by manual pointer movement]—Positions the pointer at cell A9.
>
> + C5—Tells VP-Planner to refer to the contents of cell C5 and place them here also. (If the contents of cell C5 change, the contents of this cell will also change.)
>
> ENTER—Tells VP-Planner to execute the command.

9. Format cells A9 and A10 for the date.

> A9 [by manual pointer movement]—Positions the pointer at cell A9.
>
> /—Invokes the Main Menu.
>
> R (F3)—Selects the Range option.
>
> F (F2)—Selects the Format option from the Range Menu.
>
> D (F9)—Selects the Date option.
>
> 3 (F4)—Selects the (MMM-Y) option.
>
> Down Arrow—Includes cell A10.
>
> ENTER—Tells VP-Planner to execute the command.

10. Enter the formula to calculate the monthly payment in cell B9.

```
@PMT(C$3,C$2/12,C$4)
```

The first parameter above provides the address of the cell containing the principal; the second parameter provides the address of the cell containing the interest; the third parameter provides the address of the cell containing the number of periods. Since each of these pieces of information must be referenced in each row, absolute addressing is required; the absolute portion of each parameter freezes the location to a particular row. The formula can now be copied correctly.

11. Enter the formula to calculate the interest portion of this payment in cell D9.

```
+C$3*C$2/12
```

The amount must be divided by 12 to provide the amount of interest for this particular month rather than for the whole year.

12. Enter the formula to calculate the amount of the payment applied toward the principal in cell C9.

```
+B9-D9
```

13. Enter the formula to calculate the outstanding balance in cell E9.

```
+C3-C9
```

14. Format the entire worksheet for two decimal positions.

/—Invokes the Main Menu.

W (F2)—Selects the Worksheet option.

G (F2)—Selects the Global option from the Worksheet Menu.

F (F2)—Selects the Format option from the Global Menu.

F (F2)—Selects the Fixed command.

ENTER—Takes the default and reformats the worksheet.

15. Copy the payment and principal formulas (which will stay the same) to the next line. (The cells will contain the correct results after the next steps are finished.)

B9 [by manual pointer movement]—Positions the pointer at cell B9.

/—Invokes the Main Menu.

C (F4)—Selects the Copy command.

C9 [by manual pointer movement]—Positions the pointer at the last cell in the "From" range.

ENTER—Tells VP-Planner that the "From" range has been established.

B10 [by manual pointer movement]—Positions the pointer at the beginning of the "To" range.

ENTER—Tells VP-Planner to copy the formulas.

16. Enter the formula to advance the date incrementally in cell A10.

    ```
    +A9+31-@DAY(A9+31)+@DAY(A9)
    ```

    This command provides you with the ability to advance the date by the proper increment from one month to the next, as long as the loan begins on day 1 through 28. This formula can now be copied to the rest of the rows.

17. Enter the new formula for calculating the interest in cell D10.

    ```
    +E9*C$2/12
    ```

    You now have a formula that can be easily copied to other rows.

18. Enter the new formula for calculating the outstanding balance in cell E10.

    ```
    +E9-C10
    ```

    You now have a formula that can be easily copied to other rows.

19. Copy the formulas contained in row 10 down enough rows. (Enough rows depends on the maximum number of periods that you wish to allow in a loan; you'll copy this one down forty rows. Remember, the more rows you have, the longer your worksheet will take to recalculate.)

    A10 [by manual pointer movement]—Positions the pointer at cell A10.

    /—Invokes the Main Menu.

    C (F4)—Selects the Copy option command.

    E10 [by manual pointer movement]—Positions the pointer at the last cell in the "From" range.

    ENTER—Tells VP-Planner that the "From" range has been defined.

    A11 [by manual pointer movement]—Positions the pointer to cell A11, the first cell in the "To" range.

    .—Nails down the beginning of the "To" range.

    PgDn [twice]—Moves the pointer down the worksheet forty rows.

    ENTER—Tells VP-Planner to copy the formulas and recalculate the worksheet.

Now sit back and watch VP-Planner do all the work! When you look at your worksheet, everything seems to have worked until about row 29—when negative numbers suddenly begin popping up in the worksheet. What happened? The loan was completely paid, but VP-Planner wasn't aware of it, so the balance went from positive to negative.

Somehow, you have to indicate to VP-Planner to take appropriate action when the balance is completely paid to get rid of the negative numbers. Let's review the logic and determine which are the critical formulas.

On examination, the two most important calculations seem to be the outstanding balance and the payment. When the outstanding balance equals a few cents or less, that means that the loan is paid off. (The outstanding balance never comes out to exactly zero because of rounding errors.) All other calculations are based on the contents of either the outstanding balance or payment entry; so if you can get these fields to zero out, the other fields will also contain zeros.

To examine the contents of a cell and check for a value, you must use the @IF function.

20. Change the method of recalculation from automatic to manual to save waiting time.

> /—Invokes the Main Menu.
>
> W (F2)—Selects the Worksheet option.
>
> G (F2)—Selects the Global option from the Worksheet Menu.
>
> R (F5)—Selects the Recalculation option from the Global Menu.
>
> M (F6)—Selects the Manual command.

21. Position your pointer at cell E10, and either reenter the formula or use the Edit feature to enter changes. Your new formula should now look like the following:

```
@IF(E9<=1,0,@ROUND(+E9-C10,2))
```

This formula can be translated as: if the result of the old balance is just a few cents, put a zero in this cell; otherwise, calculate the new rounded outstanding balance.

22. You also have to do something to make the payment column stop printing. Position your pointer at cell B10, and either enter the new formula or use the Edit feature to enter changes.

```
@IF(E9<=1,0,@PMT(C$3,C$2/12,C$4))
```

This formula can be translated as: if the contents of the outstanding balance cell are just a few cents, place a zero in the payment cell; otherwise, execute the payment function.

23. Copy these new formulas onto the rest of the worksheet, using the commands from step 19 above.

24. Tell VP-Planner to recalculate the worksheet, by pressing the [F9] CALC function key.

25. Center the information at the top of the spreadsheet to give it a more balanced appearance.

> A2 [by manual pointer movement]—Positions the pointer at cell A2.
>
> /—Invokes the Main Menu.
>
> M (F5)—Selects the Move command.
>
> C5 [by manual pointer movement]—Positions the pointer at cell C5, to establish the "From" range.
>
> ENTER—Tells VP-Planner that the "From" range is defined.

> B2 [by manual pointer movement]—Positions the pointer at
> the beginning of the "To" range.
>
> ENTER—Executes the Move instruction.

26. Save the worksheet under the name LOANAMOR. You should now have a worksheet that looks like the following:

	A	B	C	D	E	F
1						
2		Interest		12.00%		
3		Loan Amount		$1,200		
4		Months		20		
5		Beginning Date		May-85		
6						
7		TOTAL			BALANCE	
8	DATE	PAYMENT	PRINCIPAL	INTEREST	OUTSTANDING	
9	May-85	66.50	54.50	12.00	1145.50	
10	Jun-85	66.50	55.04	11.46	1090.46	
11	Jul-85	66.50	55.59	10.90	1034.87	
12	Aug-85	66.50	56.15	10.35	978.72	
13	Sep-85	66.50	56.71	9.79	922.01	
14	Oct-85	66.50	57.28	9.22	864.73	
15	Nov-85	66.50	57.85	8.65	806.88	
16	Dec-85	66.50	58.43	8.07	748.45	
17	Jan-86	66.50	59.01	7.48	689.44	
18	Feb-86	66.50	59.60	6.89	629.84	
19	Mar-86	66.50	60.20	6.30	569.64	
20	Apr-86	66.50	60.80	5.70	508.84	
21	May-86	66.50	61.41	5.09	447.43	
22	Jun-86	66.50	62.02	4.47	385.41	
23	Jul-86	66.50	62.64	3.85	322.77	
24	Aug-86	66.50	63.27	3.23	259.50	
25	Sep-86	66.50	63.90	2.59	195.60	
26	Oct-86	66.50	64.54	1.96	131.06	
27	Nov-86	66.50	65.19	1.31	65.87	
28	Dec-86	66.50	65.84	.66	.03	
29	Jan-87	.00	-.00	.00	.00	
30	Feb-87	.00	.00	.00	.00	
31	Mar-87	.00	.00	.00	.00	
32	Apr-87	.00	.00	.00	.00	

Car Loan Evaluation Worksheet

In doing this project, you will practice the following skills:

1. Using mixed cell addressing
2. Observing the effects of copying mixed cell addresses

A friend of yours, Sandy, is trying to decide which vehicle to purchase, and a major part of the decision-making process involves the size of the monthly payment. Sandy wishes to finance the purchase over four years. The vehicles being considered, along with the amount to be financed, are as follows:

Conversion van	$18,000
Toyota pickup	8,000
Chrysler LeBaron	10,000
Ford Thunderbird	11,000

Sandy has also visited a number of financial institutions to find the interest rate offered. They are:

Credit Union	11%
Car Manufacturer	15.5%
Bank 1	12.5%
Bank 2	13%

The following worksheet allows you to present the above information in a tabular format to assist your friend's decision-making process.

```
                        Sandy's Loan Evaluation
                   Amount      Credit        Car
                   Financed    Union        Manuf.      Bank 1      Bank 2
                               11.0%        15.5%       12.5%       13.0%
Conversion van     $18,000     465.22       505.53      478.44      482.89
Toyota pickup      $8,000      206.76       224.68      212.64      214.62
Chrysler LeBaron   $10,000     258.46       280.85      265.80      268.27
Ford Thunderbird   $11,000     284.30       308.93      292.38      295.10


Number of Years                4
```

The @PMT function is perfect for this application. Mixed cell addressing, combining absolute and relative addressing, will also be useful.

Entering the worksheet involves a number of steps.

1. Position the pointer in column A, and change the width of column A to 20.

> /—Invokes the Main Menu.
>
> W (F2)—Selects the Worksheet option.
>
> C (F5)—Selects the Col-Wid command from the Worksheet Menu.
>
> S (F2)—Sets the column width.
>
> 20—Specifies the new width.
>
> ENTER—Executes the command.

2. Enter the label data.

```
C1    Sandy's Loan Evaluation
B2    Amount
C2    "Credit
D2    "Car
B3    Financed
C3    "Union
D3    "Manuf.
```

```
E3   "Bank 1
F3   "Bank 2
C4   .11
D4   .155
E4   .125
F4   .13
A5   Conversion van
A6   Toyota pickup
A7   Chrysler LeBaron
A8   Ford Thunderbird
B5   18000
B6   8000
B7   10000
B8   11000
A12  Number of Years
B12  4
```

3. Format the percentages. Begin by positioning the pointer at cell C4.

    /—Invokes the Main Menu.

    R (F3)—Selects the Range option.

    F (F2)—Selects the Format option from the Range Menu.

    P (F8)—Selects the Percent format.

    1—Specifies the number of desired decimal positions.

    ENTER—Submits the decimal positions to VP-Planner.

    F4 [by manual pointer movement]—Extends the range to cell F4.

    ENTER—Executes the format change.

4. Format the amount financed to currency. Begin by positioning the pointer at cell B5.

    /—Invokes the Main Menu.

    R (F3)—Selects the Range option.

    F (F2)—Selects the Format option from the Range Menu.

    C (F4)—Selects the Crncy format.

    0—Specifies the number of desired decimal positions.

    ENTER—Submits the decimal positions to VP-Planner.

    B8 [by manual pointer movement]—Extends the range to cell B8.

    ENTER—Executes the format change.

5. Set the worksheet format to two decimal positions.

    /—Invokes the Main Menu.

    W (F2)—Selects the Worksheet option.

    G (F2)—Selects the Global option.

    F (F2)—Selects the Format option from the Global Menu.

    F (F2)—Selects the Fixed option.

    ENTER—Changes the worksheet format.

6. Format the length of loan cell to fixed with 0 decimal positions. Begin by positioning the pointer to cell B12.

    /—Invokes the Main Menu.

> R (F3)—Selects the Range option.
>
> F (F2)—Selects the Format option of the Range Menu.
>
> F (F2)—Selects the Fixed option.
>
> 0—Specifies the number of desired decimal positions.
>
> ENTER—Submits the decimal positions to VP-Planner.
>
> ENTER—Executes the format change.

7. Enter the @PMT function for cell C5.

```
@PMT($B5,C$4/12,$B$12*12)
```

       The principal entry, $B5, keeps VP-Planner returning to column B of "this" row. The interest entry, C$4, keeps VP-Planner returning to "this" column of row 4. It is divided by the twelve months of the year. The periods entry, B12, keeps VP-Planner returning to cell B12. It is multiplied by the twelve monthly payments.

8. Copy this formula to the rest of the worksheet. Begin by positioning the pointer to cell C5.

> /—Invokes the Main Menu.
>
> C (F4)—Selects the Copy Command.
>
> ENTER—Establishes the "From" range.
>
> .—Nails down the beginning of the "To" range.
>
> F8 [by manual pointer movement]—Moves the pointer to the end of the "To" range.
>
> ENTER—Executes the Copy command.

9. Save this worksheet to the file CARLOANS.

Cell Contents Listing for Amortization Worksheet

```
B2:  'Interest
D2:  (P2) 0.12
B3:  'Loan Amount
D3:  (C0) 1200
B4:  'Months
D4:  (F0) 20
B5:  'Beginning Date
D5:  (D3) @DATE(84,5,1)
B7:  ^TOTAL
E7:  ^BALANCE
A8:  ^DATE
B8:  ^PAYMENT
C8:  ^PRINCIPAL
D8:  ^INTEREST
E8:  ^OUTSTANDING
A9:  (D3) +D5
B9:  (F2) @PMT(D$3,D$2/12,D$4)
C9:  (F2) +B9-D9
D9:  (F2) @ROUND(+D$3*D$2/12,2)
E9:  (F2) @ROUND(+D3-C9,2)
A10: (D3) +A9+31@DAY(A9+31)+@DAY(A9)
B10: (F2) @IF(E9<=1,0,@PMT(D$3,D$2/12,D$4))
C10: (F2) +B10-D10
```

```
D10:  (F2)  +E9*D$2/12
E10:  (F2)  @IF(E9<=1,0,@ROUND(+E9-C10,2))
A11:  (D3)  +A9+31@DAY(A9+31)+@DAY(A9)
B11:  (F2)  @IF(E10<=1,0,@PMT(D$3,D$2/12,D$4))
C11:  (F2)  +B11-D11
D11:  (F2)  +E10*D$2/12
E11:  (F2)  @IF(E10<=1,0,@ROUND(+E10-C11,2))
A12:  (D3)  +A9+31@DAY(A9+31)+@DAY(A9)
B12:  (F2)  @IF(E11<=1,0,@PMT(D$3,D$2/12,D$4))
C12:  (F2)  +B12-D12
D12:  (F2)  +E11*D$2/12
E12:  (F2)  @IF(E11<=1,0,@ROUND(+E11-C12,2))
```

Cell Contents Listing for Car Loan Worksheet

```
C1:  'Sandy's Loan Evaluation
B2:  'Amount
C2:  "Credit
D2:  "Car
B3:  'Financed
C3:  "Union
D3:  "Manuf.
E3:  "Bank 1
F3:  "Bank 2
C4:  (P1) 0.11
D4:  (P1) 0.155
E4:  (P1) 0.125
F4:  (P1) 0.13
A5:  'Conversion van
B5:  (C0) 18000
C5:  @PMT($B5,C$4/12,$B$12*12)
D5:  @PMT($B5,D$4/12,$B$12*12)
E5:  @PMT($B5,E$4/12,$B$12*12)
F5:  @PMT($B5,F$4/12,$B$12*12)
A6:  'Toyota pickup
B6:  (C0) 8000
C6:  @PMT($B6,C$4/12,$B$12*12)
D6:  @PMT($B6,D$4/12,$B$12*12)
E6:  @PMT($B6,E$4/12,$B$12*12)
F6:  @PMT($B6,F$4/12,$B$12*12)
A7:  'Chrysler LeBaron
B7:  (C0) 10000
C7:  @PMT($B7,C$4/12,$B$12*12)
D7:  @PMT($B7,D$4/12,$B$12*12)
E7:  @PMT($B7,E$4/12,$B$12*12)
F7:  @PMT($B7,F$4/12,$B$12*12)
A8:  'Ford Thunderbird
B8:  (C0) 11000
C8:  @PMT($B8,C$4/12,$B$12*12)
D8:  @PMT($B8,D$4/12,$B$12*12)
E8:  @PMT($B8,E$4/12,$B$12*12)
F8:  @PMT($B8,F$4/12,$B$12*12)
A12  Number of Years
B12  4
```

Chapter Review

After a worksheet has been created, you will probably want to make a number of improvements to it. One of these, making cell formulas self-documenting and easier to read, can be accomplished easily by the use of range names. A single cell or a range of cells can be given a name and accessed under that name in such applications as calculations, uses of the Copy command, and printing a portion of your worksheet.

Other common changes involve adding or deleting rows or columns. These procedures can be accomplished quickly, but you must be careful not to produce an adverse affect on an unseen portion of your worksheet by deleting a row or column

Still another method of improving a worksheet is to use the Move command, which allows you to achieve a more balanced appearance on your screen and to move items to make a worksheet easier and more logical to use for a particular application.

The Sort feature included with VP-Planner enables you to arrange data in an order that is logical for any given application. Another handy (and more common) feature is the Titles feature, which allows you to freeze column or row headings on the screen so that they are visible no matter where you are in the worksheet. This makes it much easier to track information in large spreadsheets.

The ability to reference a single cell over and over, even when the formula is copied down a column, is often useful. In VP-Planner, this is called absolute addressing. An entire address can be absolute, or only the row or column can be; the latter is referred to as a mixed cell address.

Because the worksheet automatically recalculates itself when any cell's contents are changed, long delays can often result in a large worksheet after a simple change has been made. In such a case, you can direct VP-Planner to recalculate the worksheet only when the F9 key has been pressed. This option is known as manual recalculation.

The @IF function allows you to imbed logic within the worksheet that enables the function to perform one action if the logic is satisfied and perform another if it is not.

Key Terms and Concepts

absolute addressing
absolute range name
#AND#
automatic recalculation
$columnrow
column$row
Create option
Data Range option
@DATE
Delete option
Go option
@IF
Labels option
manual recalculation

mixed cell address
Move feature
#NOT#
#OR#
@PMT
Primary Key option
Quit option
range name
relative addressing
Reset option
@ROUND
Secondary Key option
Sort command
Titles option

Chapter Quiz

Multiple Choice

1. Which of the following statements is false about range names:
   a. Range names can be used to enhance readability.
   b. Range names make cell formulas self-documenting.
   c. Using range names in formulas is better than using cell addresses.
   d. A range name created via the Label option takes its name from the contents of an adjacent cell.
   e. All of the above statements are true.
   f. All of the above statements are true except d.

2. Which of the following statements is false about the Sort command:
   a. It is safest to save your worksheet before you do any sorting.
   b. Three levels of sorts or keys can be specified.
   c. All or part of a worksheet can be sorted.
   d. The Sort command allows you to rearrange data quickly within the worksheet.
   e. None of the above statements is false.

3. Which of the following statements is false about an absolute address:
   a. It can have both the column and row absolute—CR.
   b. It can have only the column portion absolute—$CR.
   c. It can have only the row portion absolute—C$R.
   d. It can actually be a range name—$EXPENSES.
   e. All of the above responses are correct.

4. Which of the commands below allows you to freeze portions of the worksheet so that they can be used as column or row headings on the screen:
   a. Titles
   b. Labels
   c. Borders
   d. Legend
   e. None of the above responses is correct

5. Which of the commands below allows you to transfer information physically from one position in the worksheet to another, altogether different area:
   a. Copy
   b. Transfer
   c. Move
   d. Transport
   e. None of the above responses is correct

True/False

6. Using manual recalculation slows down the operation of the spreadsheet.

7. The Titles command allows only horizontal text to be frozen on the screen.

8. Relative addressing is used whenever you wish a formula that is to be copied down a column or across a row to refer to the identical cell.

9. It is impossible to create a mixed range name by using a mixed cell address.

10. The function @IF allows you to quickly imbed sophisticated logic within your worksheet.

Answers

1. e   2. b   3. e   4. a   5. c   6. f   7. f   8. f   9. t   10. t

Exercises

1. Define or describe each of the following:
   a. range name   d. absolute address
   b. titles   e. mixed cell address
   c. manual recalculation   f. date arithmetic

2. One of the greatest benefits of range names is that they allow a cell formula to be self- _____ .

3. Positioning the pointer at a word (cell) and then making that word the range name is accomplished via the _____ option of the Range Menu.

4. The Create and Delete commands reside in the _____ Menu.

5. The column to the _____ of the pointer or the _____ _____ above the pointer will be added.

6. If you delete a row or a column, all of the _____ in that row or column will be deleted.

7. The _____ command destroys the sending area, while the _____ command leaves the sending area intact.

8. A(n) _____ key will have information sorted in order inside a(n) _____ key.

9. The Sort option is found in the _____ Menu.

10. Before you use the Sort command, it is probably wise to _____ _____ your worksheet file.

11. The _____ command allows you to freeze rows and/ or columns on the screen for use as headings.

12. _____ addressing allows cell references to change as they are copied. _____ addressing maintains all or part of the cell address from one cell to the next.

13. _____ cell addressing allows one part of the cell address to change while keeping the other part intact.

14. _____ recalculation enables you to avoid waiting for long spreadsheets to recalculate each time a cell is changed or a new cell is entered.

15. The function key _____ is pressed when you wish VP-Planner to recalculate a worksheet while you are in manual recalculation mode.

16. The message _____ appears at the bottom of the screen when a change has been made to the contents of some cell during manual recalculation mode.

17. The _____ function allows you to imbed logic in your worksheet.

18. The logical operators _____ , _____ , and _____ allow you to specify how comparisons are to interact.

19. The operators $<$, $>$, and $<=$ are referred to as _____ operators.

20. The @DATE function is extremely useful because it allows you to perform _____ to advance the date from one month to the next.

Computer Exercises

1. Ed has been approached to invest in a microcomputer store that will specialize in selling relatively low-cost microcomputers. Ed has done an excellent job of collecting information about this proposed business venture. He is interested in modeling the next four years of business activity. He wants a worksheet built to present information in two basic areas—an input area and an income statement area—as appears below.*

   The following criteria must be applied to the worksheet:

   1. The input area will start in column A. Column A should be set to a width of 25.

   2. The income statement will start in column F.

   3. Sales are expected to be 300 units the first year.

   4. Rent for each year is $7,500 per year.

   5. Salaries are equal to 10% of sales (commission sales).

   6. Supplies are 1.5% of sales.

   7. Clerical costs are $4,000 the first year, and 6% more each additional year.

   8. Advertising costs are $50,000 plus 7% of sales the first year; $25,000 plus 7% of sales the second year; and 5% of sales in subsequent years.

```
INPUT AREA
UNITS SOLD (YEAR 1)          300
COST PER UNIT              $650
ANNUAL SALES GROWTH       15.00%
ANNUAL PRICE REDUCTION     7.00%
PRODUCT MARGIN            40.00%
```

---

*Adapted from Arthur Andersen & Co. materials.

ED'S MICROCOMPUTER SHOP
Projected Financial Statements

	1	2	3	4
Sales	325,000	347,588	371,745	397,581
Cost	195,000	208,553	223,047	238,549
Margin	130,000	139,035	148,698	159,032
Expenses:				
Advertising	72,750	49,331	18,587	19,879
Salaries	32,500	34,759	37,174	39,758
Rent	7,500	7,500	7,500	7,500
Supplies	4,875	5,214	5,576	5,964
Clerical	4,000	4,240	4,494	4,764
Other Costs	10,000	10,500	11,025	11,576
Total Expenses	131,625	111,544	84,357	89,441
Income b/f Taxes	(1,625)	27,491	64,341	69,591
Income Taxes	0	13,746	32,170	34,796
Net Income	(1,625)	13,746	32,170	34,796

9. There is a 50% tax rate.

10. Other costs are $10,000 the first year, and 5% more each additional year.

11. An @IF statement must be set up to check for a positive income b/f taxes.

12. The following range names will be used:

Units Sold	Units
Costs per Unit	Cost
Annual Growth	Growth
Annual Price Reduction	Ann.red
Profit Margin	Margin
First Year Sales	Sales
Year 1 Net Income	Year1
Year 2 Net Income	Year2
Year 3 Net Income	Year3
Year 4 Net Income	Year4

13. Column F will be set to a width of 16.

14. The global column will be set to a width of 11.

15. For year 1, the following sales formula will be used:

    ```
    $UNITS*($COST/(1-$MARGIN))
    ```

16. For years 2–4, the following sales formula will be used:

    ```
    +SALES*(1+$GROWTH)*(1-$ANN.RED)
    ```

17. The following cost formula for year 1:

```
SALES*(1-$MARGIN)
```

18. Generate a range name report on your screen. Use the PrtSc feature to dump to paper.

Save this worksheet to a file called CH13EXR1.

2. Retrieve the worksheet CH12EXR2. You just received word that your teacher friend forgot to include a student named Student 5a in the list. This individual's scores are 100 for Exam I, 41 for Anot.Bib., and 113 for Exam II. Add this individual to the existing grading worksheet, making any changes that are necessary. Store the changed worksheet to a file named CH13EXR2.

3. Retrieve the CH11EXR5 file. Use the VP-Planner Sort command to place the rows of the worksheet in order by the name of the sales representatives. Don't include any total or heading lines in the sort. Save the sorted worksheet to a file called CH13EXR3.

4. You are now to add a column to replace the existing column A in the CH11EXR5 file. This column should have a heading of "Dept." The two different sales forces in the business are the new car sales staff (1) and the preowned car sales staff (2). Sally, Marge, and Harry are in the Dept. 1 cells. Sort the file with Dept. as the primary key and Sales Rep as the secondary key. Place the result in a file called CH13EXR4.

5. Retrieve the CH12EXR2 worksheet. To the right of the worksheet enter a Final Percentage column as depicted below. Take the students' total earned points and divide them by the total possible points to calculate the current percentage grade.

27-Aug-86

Grading Template

NAME		Exam I	Anot. Bib.	Exam II	Final %
POSSIBLE POINTS		150	45	130	325
Student 1		113	44	110	82.15%
Student 2		116	42	90	76.31%
Student 3		129	42	85	78.77%
Student 4		133	44	125	92.92%
Student 5		121	42	76	73.54%
Student 6		139	41	115	90.77%
Student 7		116	42	75	71.69%
Student 8		130	39	120	88.92%
Student 9		127	42	95	81.23%
Student 10		120	42	115	85.23%
Average		124	42	101	82.15%
% of Tot. Pnts.		82.67%	93.33%	77.69%	
High Grade		139	44	125	
Low Grade		113	39	75	
Std. Deviation		8	1	18	
Variance		65	2	312	

Save this worksheet using the name CH13EXR5.

6. Develop a loan amortization schedule for a 15-year mortgage. The principal is $20,000. The interest rate is 13.5%. You select the beginning date. Each line in the amortization schedule should have the month, payment amount, principal reduction amount, amount applied toward interest, and the remaining outstanding balance. (Remember that you must multiply the periods (years) by 12 when dealing with months.)

   In solving this problem and looking at the worksheet, you must use the Horizontal Titles option to keep the column headings on the screen. You must also design the worksheet so that it quits calculating and outputing negative numbers when the principal is completely paid.

   Print this worksheet using the Borders option. This will print the column headings at the top of each page of the printout, making the output more readable. Save this worksheet under the name CH13EXR6.

7. Develop a worksheet that allows users to investigate a number of different principal amounts plotted against a number of different interest rates for home mortgages. Start with principal amounts of $20,000, $40,000, $60,000, $80,000, $100,000 and $120,000. Use interest rates of 11.5%, 12.5%, 13%, 14%, 14.5%, 15%, and 15.5%. Refer to the Car Loan Evaluation Worksheet for ideas. The loans are all for 25 years. Save this file using the name CH13EXR7.

8. Load the CH12EXR1 worksheet containing the payroll information. Sort it alphabetically by rate of pay—that is, so that rate of pay is the primary key and last name is the secondary key. Save this file using the name CH13EXR8.

9. Load the CH13EXR6 worksheet file. Change the column containing the monthly payment to a width of zero and print the worksheet.

Professional Use

of Worksheets

After completing this chapter, you should be able to:

Describe a template and cover the steps involved in creating templates

Discuss the VP-Planner Window command

Discuss the technique of worksheet and cell protection

Discuss the use of the Data Fill command

Discuss the technique of sensitivity analysis and how this technique is accomplished in VP-Planner through the use of data tables with one or two variables

This chapter will cover the following topics: template design, cell protection, windows, data fill, and use of VP-Planner tables in sensitivity analysis.

Templates

After you have designed a worksheet, other people may also wish to use it. When this happens, whoever originally designed the worksheet (or someone else in the firm) will have to spend some additional time on the worksheet converting it to a template. A **template** is a prewritten worksheet that guides a person step-by-step through a particular application.

The steps in designing a worksheet, which were covered in Chapter 11, apply to a template as well, but other factors are also important. Because often the only person who uses a worksheet is the person who originally created it, such a worksheet does not need to have a template's capacity to address a number of similar concerns faced by many different users.

Another major difference between templates and worksheets is in the matter of documentation. The usual documentation supplied inside a worksheet is a memory-triggering device for the worksheet's author. The amount of documentation needed for a template is much greater, since an individual with little understanding of the application and no understanding of spreadsheet software may be required to use it. In addition, there must be written documentation to augment documentation in the template itself.

Writing good spreadsheet templates is similar to generating third-party applications programs like those discussed in Chapter 2. The person who develops a template is engaged in building a generalized set of instructions capable of solving various specific instances of a general type of problem. Not everyone can (or will want to) design and develop templates.

Planning

A template can be viewed as a system or application program with three functional parts: input, processing, and output. A good template should: (1) require the user to input the data to be processed in a structured format, (2) process that data correctly, and (3) provide some way to get the results (output) to the user in an easy-to-use format.

The physical areas of the template should be divided to reflect these three functional parts. A good template will have one or more input screens that allow easy entry of the data. If a specific manual data form is used to capture information, it should also appear as part of the input screen so that users can simply fill in blanks that are familiar to them. An input area commonly has a lot of label entries to provide this form-like appearance. Making a good input screen is similar to designing a good form: information is entered from the top downward and from left to right; numeric information and alphanumeric information are not indiscriminately mixed; as much as possible, information should be entered in rows or columns, but not both.

The processing area of the template should be in an area completely separate from the input and output screen(s). A good template locks the user out of making changes to template formulas, by utilizing worksheet or cell-locking features provided by the spreadsheet software. Protecting cells makes it much more difficult for a user to change a formula erroneously.

Although any templates you build using this book will probably combine the calculation and output areas into one area, many of the calculations referred to above utilize a special VP-Planner feature called a macro. Macros are beyond the scope of this book, but they are used in many sophisticated templates.

The output or report area should also be completely separate. The reports should have range names, which can then be used to direct the spreadsheet quickly to print reports that are needed by the user. Report and column headings should be descriptive of the use of their contents. The @TODAY function should be used to date the various reports, so a user can keep track of when various reports were run.

Implementing Template Functions in the Design

The three separate functions discussed above can be readily implemented in a rectangular format, making it easy to keep track of the various functional areas and allowing better utilization of RAM memory.

Each input area is designed as a screen for the user. The user can move easily from one input area to another either by depressing the TAB key or by depressing a paging key; each screen also has an instruction identifying the appropriate key to depress to continue from one page to the next. The number of columns that appear on a screen is, of course, determined by the width of the various columns. The user is prompted on how to move from one functional area (input, processing, or output) to another by screen prompts. If you get lost on the worksheet of the template, you can always return to cell A1 by depressing the HOME key.

On-line documentation providing instructions to the user often appears in the "home" position (cell A1). This documentation, called a **help screen**, can easily be created by giving column A the same width as the screen. Multiple help screens can then be stacked on top of one another, and the user can move from one to another by pressing the PG UP or PG DN keys.

The first help screen typically contains identifying information about the template, such as the name of the template, what kind of processing is performed by it, who created it, and a telephone number to call if things go wrong in processing the data. Most important, it includes the revision number and date of the last update or revision. To ensure that this help screen appears as soon as the template is loaded into memory, you need only place the pointer in the "home" position before the template is saved. The pointer always appears in a worksheet at the same location it was in when the save operation was performed.

It is important that you not stack reports. Reports require different column widths to present various pieces of information attractively. When you vary column width, the width changes for the entire column within the worksheet. Since column widths cannot be one width in one part of a column and another width in another part of the same column, the best course is to place reports side by side.

Designing the Logic

Obtaining an in-depth understanding of the application to be modeled is the key to incorporating the correct logic. If the individual who builds the template does not have the proper understanding, the template will be of questionable value at best.

The structured walkthrough, a method used extensively in testing the logic of an application program, can be applied to the construction of templates. In a **structured walkthrough**, the individual who designed the logic explains it to coworkers who are responsible for making certain that the logic is correct, straightforward, and easy to understand. In addition to using the structured walkthrough approach, the template builder should sit down with potential users and go through the logic. This will allow them to find any mistakes in logic and also to suggest changes for input screens or output reports. Active user involvement at this point can save expensive changes later: it is much easier to incorporate changes at the design step than to do so after all of the logic is hard-coded within the template.

Developing the Template

This step is the one at which the logic that has been developed is implemented using the syntax of the spreadsheet package. Developing the template involves entering instructions by means of the spreadsheet software package. Error-trapping at this step is critically important.

By this point, the individual entering the template should have an intimate knowledge of what the expected results are. A simple application is used to test the incorporation of the logic. This process of verifying the logic and results of a template, known as **testing**, allows you to verify that you've entered the formulas correctly and that the results generated by the template are reasonable. The term *reasonable* implies that you have some idea of what the results should look like.

You can also increase confidence in a template by building in redundancy features. For example, if you have to sum or "foot" several columns of numbers, you should also "crossfoot" the individual rows and sum those totals. The sum of the crossfooted totals should be the same as the sum of the footed totals.

For large template applications, the automatic recalculation feature should be switched to manual recalculation. This will save users a tremendous amount of time while using the template. Instructions must be included, however, to let the template novices know how to make the template recalculate.

Final Testing

Final testing should be a joint effort between the individual(s) who constructed the template and the people who will eventually be its day-to-day users. It is important to involve users who have an in-depth understanding of the application to which the template will be applied in the final testing. They often detect minor errors that have escaped the developers or raise nuances of the application that the developers did not properly understand.

In addition to enlisting users to test templates, you may want to try one of a number of software packages on the market that are designed to examine the logic of a worksheet or template. Two such packages are Spreadsheet Auditor and Docucalc. These packages examine your worksheet and print formulas in the relative locations where they appear on the screen, and keep track of the various range names used in a worksheet or template. They are also useful in locating a cell containing a circular reference.

Final Documentation

The documentation manual that is to accompany the template must now be finished. The process of documentation is an ongoing task; it is *not* one of the last things done. Much of the documentation is identical to what appears inside the template itself. The final documentation should include:

1. Purpose of the template
2. Identifying characteristics
   a. Author(s)
   b. Revision number and date
   c. Phone number for assistance
3. Copies of the input screens and any explanations about what each data field represents
4. Copies of any reports that are generated by the system
5. Any explanatory text needed for clarifying how information is processed within the template
6. Formatted listings of all formulas

One extremely important piece of internal documentation is the prompt(s) directing the user to save the completed worksheet that was built using the template. If the user were to save the worksheet back to the original template file, it would destroy the template. To avoid having this happen, you must put very explicit instructions to the user to save the worksheet to a different file. Backing up a template is critical. Many harmful things can happen: it can be overwritten; it can inadvertently be erased; the diskette containing it can be lost. The steps required to backing up a template, therefore, must be emphasized to the user.

One rule of thumb to keep in mind is that many people will not bother to read the written documentation. Consequently, as much documentation as possible should be placed in the template itself.

Support and Maintenance

When the template is "finished," it is not necessarily really finished. What happens if an error is found? Who provides the answers to any questions that arise from users? Who is responsible for making revisions to a template and sending those out to the user community? One or more people will have to be responsible for maintaining and supporting the templates. You can now begin to see why template preparation and support have been equated with programming: they require skill, effort, and lots of time.

Windows

When you are using a large worksheet, regardless of whether or not it is a template, you will frequently want to be able to see two or more pieces of the worksheet at one time—for instance, the data input area and the data output area. This is accomplished in most spreadsheet packages via windows. **Windows** allow you to split the screen vertically or horizontally, giving you different views of the same worksheet and allowing you to see the input area and the output area on the screen at the same time. A maximum of six windows can be defined in VP-Planner. When you make a change in one part of the screen, the result is automatically reflected in the other half. If the changes are not reflected immediately in the other window(s), they will change as soon as you move the pointer to that window.

The pointer position determines where the screen is going to split. If you want a horizontal window, the screen will split above the pointer, and the pointer will appear in the top window. If you want a vertical window, the screen will split to the left of the pointer, and the pointer will appear in the left-hand window. To jump from one window to the other requires depressing the F6 function key. The F6 key moves the pointer from the window where it

Figure 14.1a
A screen with a horizontal
window.

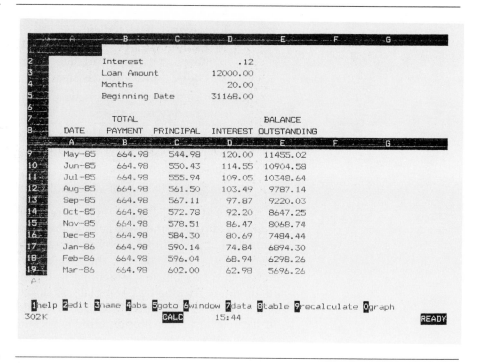

is currently located to the other window. The pointer moves from one window to the next, top down and left to right.

If you wish to follow along with a computer, the following example requires you to load the worksheet file LOANAMOR and then position the pointer anywhere on row 9 of the worksheet.

To obtain a split screen or window, enter the following commands:

/—Invokes the Main Menu.

W (F2)—Selects the Worksheet option.

W (F8)—Selects the Window command from the Worksheet Menu.

H (F2)—Selects the Horizontal command of the Windows Menu.

Your screen should now contain the same representation as that in Figure 14.1a. You can add a vertical window like that in Figure 14.1b by executing the following commands:

F6—Moves the pointer from the top window to the bottom window.

E9—[by manual pointer movement]—Positions the pointer in cell E9.
  (Actually the pointer can be placed anywhere in column E.)

/—Brings up the Main Menu.

W (F2)—Selects the Worksheet option.

W (F8)—Selects the Window command from the Worksheet Menu.

V (V3)—Selects the Vertical command from the Windows Menu.

Let's examine the Windows Menu below.

```
Horizontal   Vertical   Sync   Unsync   Clear
```

Figure 14.1b
A screen with both a horizontal and a vertical window.

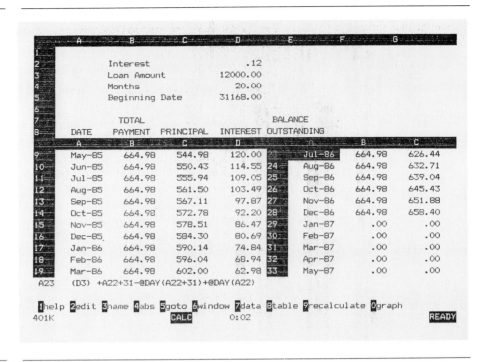

Horizontal. This option creates a horizontal window above the present pointer position and causes the pointer to appear in the upper window.

Vertical. This option creates a vertical window to the left of the present pointer position and causes the pointer to appear in the window to the left.

Sync. This option causes the contents of like windows to move synchronously, so that horizontal windows keep the same rows on the screen, and vertical windows keep the same columns on the screen.

Unsync. This option produces separate movement of the visible parts of the worksheet within any windows. The worksheet can only be moved when the pointer is in the appropriate window. This is the VP-Planner default.

Clear. This option is used to remove any windows and revert the display to a single screen.

It should be emphasized that only one worksheet resides in memory, and any changes made within a window will alter the worksheet currently in memory. All windows are saved with a file.

Synchronizing Windows

When synchronization is turned on, multiple windows will be synchronized vertically or horizontally depending on the following factors:

Vertical Synchronization. Up-and-down movement (vertical synchronization) requires that windows

1. Have their upper left-hand corners lined up horizontally.
2. Contain the same number of rows.

Horizontal Synchronization. Left-and-right movement (horizontal synchronization) requires that windows

1. Have their upper left-hand corners lined up vertically.
2. Contain the same number of columns.

Figure 14.2 represents a screen that has been divided into the maximum six windows with the Synchronous option of the Windows Menu selected. The windows are numbered 1–6. Windows 1, 2, and 3 are synchronized vertically, for up-and-down movement. Notice that the upper left-hand corners are lined up horizontally and that they have the same number of rows.

Windows 4 and 5 are synchronized horizontally, for side-to-side movement. Notice that the upper left-hand corners are lined up vertically and that they contain the same number of rows.

Window 6 is not synchronized, since the left-hand corner of this window neither lines up vertically nor does it have the same number of rows as the other like windows.

Worksheet and Cell Protection

After you've spent many hours building a template, you don't want to risk having someone inadvertently erase a critical formula while using the template. Such an action can totally destroy a template and may require many hours of effort to be spent in trying to determine what went wrong.

Protecting the Worksheet

The VP-Planner spreadsheet package allows you to safeguard a template against this danger by using VP-Planner's protection feature. Either a range of cells or the entire worksheet can be protected. **Cell protection** guarantees that the contents of a cell cannot easily be changed by a user; if a change is attempted, the computer beeps and displays a "protected cell" error in the status line.

Worksheet protection is obtained by giving the following commands:

/—Invokes the Main Menu.

W (F2)—Selects the Worksheet option.

G (F2)—Selects the Global option from the Worksheet Menu.

P (F6)—Selects the Protection command from the Global Menu.

E (F2)—Selects the Enable option.

The entire worksheet is now protected: it is impossible to change the contents of any cell. Although this is desirable for the template's calculation area, it is not at all desirable for the template's input areas. In order to allow data entry in the input areas, the protection must be disabled for those cells. What command can you use for this?

As you have probably already realized, any command you intend only for selected cells must go through the Range option of the Main Menu. Disabling protection is no exception:

/—Invokes the Main Menu.

R (F3)—Selects the Range option.

U (F8)—Selects the Unprotect option.

_•_ [by pointing or by entering the cell addresses]—Establishes the range.

ENTER—Tells VP-Planner to execute the command.

Figure 14.2
Adjacent windows move in
synchronized mode.

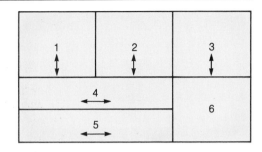

The unprotected cells can be differentiated from the protected cells in the following manner. When the pointer is on an unprotected cell, a U, along with the current cell contents, can be seen in the status line of the control panel. The U indicates that this is an unprotected cell.

To further illustrate the use of worksheet protection, load the file COMP-SALS. Issue the appropriate commands above to enable global protection. Now you can no longer make any worksheet changes. When you try to press the ENTER key, a **protected cell** error message appears at the bottom of the screen. To get rid of the error message, simply press the ESC key. Your screen should look something like the one below.

```
          B            C            D            E          F
 1COMPSALS
 2
 3   Department  Last Year   This Year      Change  % Change
 4
 5Deli            700.00      575.00    (125.00)      -18%
 6Bakery        1,000.00    1,100.00     100.00        10%
 7Liquor        1,200.00    1,400.00     200.00        17%
 8Grocery       2,500.00    2,900.00     400.00        16%
 9Produce         950.00    1,000.00      50.00         5%
10Meat          1,500.00    1,410.00     (90.00)       -6%
11
12Store Total   7,850.00    8,385.00     535.00         7%
```

Now that the entire worksheet has been protected, any areas designated for change must be unprotected by using the / Range Unprotect command. After examining the worksheet above, you decide to only unprotect the cells containing sales information for column D (This Year). A user does not need access to any of the other cells: the headings don't have to be changed, sales for last year are history, formulas merely reflect changes in the designated cells, and the various department names do not have to be changed. Using the Unprotect command key sequence (above) unprotects the indicated cells in column D.

Once these cells have been unprotected, look at the contents of the status line. You will notice that a U appears in any recently unprotected cell. Now change the sales of the Deli department from 575 to 1,000. Notice that even though other cells are still protected and therefore unavailable to you, VP-Planner still uses the contents of the cell that you changed to generate a new worksheet.

Unprotecting the Worksheet

If someone finds an error that you wish to correct, how do you reverse the above actions? First, you must remove the global protection by entering the commands:

/—Invokes the Main Menu.

W (F2)—Selects the Worksheet option.

G (F2)—Selects the Global option from the Worksheet Menu.

P (F6)—Selects the Protection command from the Global Menu.

D (F3)—Selects the Disable option.

You can now enter information in any cell on the spreadsheet, although the cells in the previously unprotected range areas still contain a U. In order to get rid of the Us, those cells must have the / Range Unprotect command reversed by using a / Range Protect command as follows:

/—Invokes the Main Menu.

R (F3)—Selects the Range option.

P (F7)—Selects the Protection option.

_•_ [by pointing or by entering the cell addresses]—Establishes the range.

ENTER—Tells VP-Planner to execute the command.

Utilizing the Data Fill Feature

VP-Planner has a feature called **Data Fill** that allows a user to set up a range and then fill it with numbers. This is especially helpful if you wish to have a number of columns that will represent, for example, the years 1976 to 1990. Rather than manually entering each of these numbers, you can describe the range, start the initial cell with a value of 1976, specify an incremental value of 1 for each of the other cells in the range, and specify a maximum value (or ending value). Upon depressing the ENTER key, you will see that the cells of the range are filled with the appropriate numbers. If you now examine the contents of the cells, you will notice that there are numbers in each cell, meaning that you are now able to left-justify or center the contents of these cells using the Label Prefix command. If centered or left-justified cells are desirable, all you will have to do is to convert them to labels rather than edit the contents of each cell you just filled.

The command steps for the above application are as follows (remember, you want the years 1976 to 1990 in the cells B4 to P4):

/—Invokes the Main Menu.

D (F9)—Selects the Data option.

F (F2)—Selects the Fill command.

B4.P4 [by pointing or address entering]—Establishes the beginning and ending of the range.

ENTER—Tells VP-Planner to accept the range.

1976—Enters 1976 as the beginning value in the range (START).

ENTER—Enters 1 (default) as the step or incremental amount from one cell to the next.

ENTER—Takes 9999 (default) as the ending value.

The range now fills quickly with numbers. You are not limited to entering only whole numbers for the starting value or increment. The only real limitation is that the constant values cannot be greater than the default. If, for example, you wanted to fill a range starting with the value 10000, only the contents of the first cell containing the 10000 would print; since 10000 is greater than 9999, the other values will not appear within the range.

The maximum value of 2047 can be changed by entering another constant or formula. For example, the function @DATE (86,1,1) could be specified as the initial value and incremented with a step value of 5 and an ending value of 50,000. In this case VP-Planner does not stop when the original 9999 default has been reached.

The Data Fill feature has many labor-saving uses in building worksheets; it can be especially useful in conjunction with tables.

VP-Planner and Sensitivity Analysis

After a worksheet model has been created, most spreadsheet packages offer plenty of room for you to ask "what if" questions and to change one or more basic assumptions that were used in building the original worksheet. For example, you may have an application that used a rate of inflation of 4 percent; you can easily see what the effect would be on the worksheet of changing the rate of inflation to 5, 6, or 10 percent.

Sensitivity analysis is the process of asking these various "what if" questions with a view to determining the impact a change will have on a model. The process of sensitivity analysis is made much easier when the worksheet has been designed with basic assumptions as part of the input area. These entries can be quickly changed and the results tracked simply by entering a single piece of information, rather than by changing a formula in a cell.

The only problem encountered with most spreadsheet packages in asking "what if" questions is the matter of keeping track of the changes generated by the worksheet. In order to compare results properly, you either have to keep track of the changes manually or have to print the worksheet after each important change. While it remains relatively easy to ask the "what if" questions, the process can become so time-consuming that important alternatives are not examined.

VP-Planner solved the problem involved in asking multiple "what if" questions by incorporating a feature known as a Table. A **Table** allows either one or two inputs to be varied, and then generates a table detailing the results. The Table feature allows you to examine many more "what if" questions than are possible using other spreadsheets.

The table-generating process is similar to running a lot of different pieces of information through a worksheet and keeping track of the results. VP-Planner takes a set of values that you have given it and substitutes them one at a time. All you have to do is tell VP-Planner where the "what if" values are in the worksheet for the one or two assumptions you want varied and where to put the results of these questions.

Several pieces of data must be supplied to VP-Planner in building the table: the cell or formula(s) against which the "what if" questions are to be asked, the assumption(s) to be changed, the "what if" values to be used, and the extent or range of the table. Changes in the input to the formula or modeled cell can be made and new results generated by pressing the F8 table function key—without redefining the table to VP-Planner (see Figure 14.3).

The top row of the table depicted in Figure 14.3 contains the formulas or the cell references that contain the formulas to be examined using a variety of what-if questions. The left-hand column contains values to be used for the various what-if questions. You manually supply the cell reference of the value to be varied. VP-Planner then generates the answers in the results area.

Figure 14.3
Parts of a one-assumption
data table.

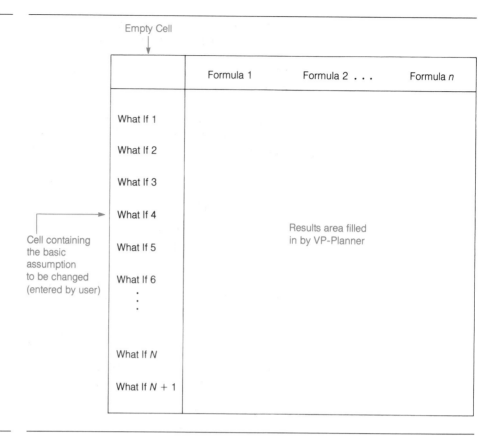

WARNING No cell involved in a table can be protected, whether it is the modeled cell, the basic assumption cell, a cell containing a value to be substituted, or the receiving area for the "what if" results.

Sensitivity Analysis Changing One Basic Assumption

Some of the concepts covered in this chapter can be illustrated by adapting the car loan worksheet from Chapter 11. In generating this worksheet, you will try to make it as flexible as possible and will follow good worksheet construction methods. The purpose of the worksheet is to evaluate the effect of a variety of interest rates on monthly payments of a car loan. You'll need three pieces of data as input: the principal of the loan, the interest rate, and the number of months of the loan.

In doing this project you will practice the following skills:

1. Establishing an input area
2. Establishing an output/report area
3. Using the Data Fill command
4. Setting up a single-variable table
5. Using the Window command
6. Using the Text Format command

The input and output areas, which are to begin at cells A1 and F1, respectively, should appear as follows:

```
Cost of a Car Loan at a Variety
         of Interest Rates

Please enter the following
characteristics of the loan:

After you have entered the data,
press the [F8] key to generate the
new table.

Press the [F6] key to move to the
other window.

Be sure to enter the interest as a
decimal. Ex. 12% is entered as .12

Principal              $5,000
Interest                12.0%
Months                    40

                   INPUT AREA

Loan Principal         $5,000
Payment                152.28

             Payment
             +J2

       10.0%  147.50
       10.5%  148.69
       11.0%  149.88
       11.5%  151.08
       12.0%  152.28
       12.5%  153.49
       13.0%  154.70
       13.5%  155.92
       14.0%  157.14
       14.5%  158.37
       15.0%  159.61
       15.5%  160.85
       16.0%  162.09
       16.5%  163.35
       17.0%  164.60
       17.5%  165.87
       18.0%  167.14
       18.5%  168.41
       19.0%  169.69
       19.5%  170.97
       20.0%  172.26

                   OUTPUT AREA
```

The output area will eventually also contain the data table.

The cell +J2 references the cell of the worksheet against which you'll be performing the sensitivity analysis. That cell, of course, is the one containing the payment function, so you'll be asking "what if" questions about the effect of changes in interest rates on a car payment.

The basic assumption to be changed is the interest rate. Cell C17 contains this piece of information. The first column contains the twenty-one values of the basic assumption (interest rate) that are to be substituted into the worksheet one at a time. VP-Planner will process the worksheet twenty-one times—one time for each different interest rate value.

The range of the table includes both columns. The top row of the range contains the +J2 entry; the bottom row contains the 20.0%. The second column contains the results of the various "what if" questions about each change in the interest rate.

A number of steps are involved in entering the worksheet, apart from enhancements.

1. Format the spreadsheet for Fixed, with two decimal positions.

2. Enter label information.

```
A1    Cost of a Car Loan at a Variety
B2    of Interest Rates
A4    Please enter the following
A5    characteristics of the loan:
A7    After you have entered the data,
A8    press the F8 key to generate the
A9    new table.
A11   Press the F6 key to move to the
A12   other window.
A14   Be sure to enter the interest as a
A15   decimal. Ex. 12% is entered as .12
A17   Principal
A18   Interest
A19   Months
H1    Loan Principal
H2    Payment
```

3. Enter the principal amount of 5000 in cell C17. Format the cell for currency, with 0 decimal positions.

4. Enter the interest rate of .12 in cell C18. Format the cell for percent, with 1 decimal position.

5. Enter the number of months (40) of the loan in cell C19. Format the cell for no decimal positions.

6. At cell location J1, format the cell for currency with 0 decimal positions and display the contents of the principal entry by entering the following formula:

   ```
   +C17
   ```

7. Enter the following payment function at cell J2:

   ```
   @PMT(C17,C18/12,C19)
   ```

8. Prepare the interest/payment table.

   a. Enter the identifying text.

   ```
   I6 Payment
   ```

b. Enter the cell that contains the information to be modeled (in this case, the payment formula).

I7 +J2

The result of the @PMT function is now copied onto cell I7. This is the part of the worksheet that will be modeled and undergo the various "what if" analyses.

c. Change the number to a formula. This will avoid confusing the cell to be modeled with results in the table, and it will also quickly show the modeled cell location on the table. First, position the pointer at cell I7.

/—Invokes the Main Menu.

R (F3)—Selects the Range option.

F (F2)—Selects the Format option of the Range Menu.

T (F10)—Selects the Text command from the Format Menu.

ENTER—Executes the command and displays the +J2 formula.

d. Use the Data Fill option to place in a single column the interest rates that are to be used in the various "what if" analyses by the @PMT function formula. Begin by positioning the pointer at cell H8.

/—Invokes the Main Menu.

D (F9)—Selects the Data option.

F (F2)—Selects the Fill option of the Data Menu.

H8.H28 [by entering the cell addresses or by using the pointer]—Indicates the range to be filled.

ENTER—Establishes the range.

.1—Identifies the beginning value (10%).

ENTER—Tells VP-Planner to accept the value.

.005—Specifies the incremental value.

ENTER—Tells VP-Planner to accept the incremental value.

ENTER—Accepts the default maximum size.

e. Format the column for percent, with 1 decimal position.

f. Build the table.

/—Invokes the Main Menu.

D (F9)—Takes the Data option.

T (F3)—Selects the Table option from the Data Menu.

1—Specifies the number of variables (basic assumptions) to be changed.

H7.I28 [by pointing or by entering addresses]—Establishes the range of the table. (Notice that the formula reference in cell I7 is part of the table range; this cell contains the basic assumption to be modeled.)

ENTER—Establishes the range of the table.

C18—Identifies the cell containing the basic assumption data (in this case, the interest data) that will be varied within the formula or part of the worksheet contained in cell I7.

ENTER—Causes a WAIT message to appear in the upper right-hand corner for a few seconds, and then generates the table.

9. Create the window. First, depress the left arrow key until column H is in the middle of the screen. Next, move the pointer back to column H. Next, enter the following instructions:

/—Invokes the Main Menu.

W (F2)—Selects the Worksheet option.

W (F8)—Selects the Windows option from the Worksheet Menu.

V (F3)—Creates a vertical window to the left of column H.

10. Move the left window to cell A1 by depressing the HOME key. The input area is now in the left part of the screen, and the payment table is now in the right part of the screen. You can jump from one screen to the other by pressing the F6 Window function key.

11. Position the pointer in the input area, and enter 10000 as the new principal amount.

12. Recalculate the table by depressing the F8 Table function key.

13. Jump back to the table part of the screen and examine the new table.

You now want to introduce one or two enhancements to the above worksheet. Besides modeling the monthly payment, you must model the grand total paid and the total interest paid for each possible interest amount, if you are to create the worksheet that appears below.

The above changes require that you perform a number of additional tasks.

14. Enter label information.

```
H3 Total Amount
H4 Total Interest
```

15. Enter two new formulas.

```
J3  +J2*C19     (payment amount × number of periods)
J4  +J3−C17     (total amount paid − principal)
```

16. Add these two formulas to the table.
    a. Enter new labels.

```
J5 Grand
K5 Total
J6 Total
K6 Interest
```

    b. Enter the formula or worksheet locations to be modeled, using the table feature for sensitivity analysis.

```
J7  +J3
K7  +J4
```

    c. Format the formula locations to text, using the commands found in step 8c above.

d. Redescribe the table to VP-Planner. The only part that will change is the width of the table, which can be expanded by pressing the right arrow key twice. All the other parameters stay the same. You do not have to recreate the Interest column.

/—Invokes the Main Menu.

D (F9)—Takes the Data option.

T (F3)—Takes the Table option of the Data Menu.

1—Specifies that the table will have one variable.

Right Arrow [twice]—Extends the range to the right two columns. The range is now H7..K28.

ENTER—Establishes the range.

ENTER—Accepts the input cell (interest) as the assumption to be varied.

After a few seconds the table will have completed its recalculations and will show the two columns that have been added. This illustrates that even though you are limited to using one variable as the basic assumption, you can model a number of areas on the worksheet that are affected by the changed variable.

17. Use the F6 key to switch screens and change the principal amount. Then use the F8 key to recalculate the table.

18. Save the worksheet using the name 1TABLE.

With a principal amount of $5,000, the new table would look as follows:

	H	I	J	K	L
1	Loan Principal		$5,000		
2	Payment		152.28		
3	Total Amount		6091.12		
4	Total Interest		1091.12		
5			Grand	Total	
6		Payment	Total	Interest	
7		+J2	+J3	+J4	
8	10.0%	147.50	5900.16	900.16	
9	10.5%	148.69	5947.56	947.56	
10	11.0%	149.88	5995.19	995.19	
11	11.5%	151.08	6043.04	1043.04	
12	12.0%	152.28	6091.12	1091.12	
13	12.5%	153.49	6139.42	1139.42	
14	13.0%	154.70	6187.95	1187.95	
15	13.5%	155.92	6236.70	1236.70	
16	14.0%	157.14	6285.67	1285.67	
17	14.5%	158.37	6334.87	1334.87	
18	15.0%	159.61	6384.28	1384.28	
19	15.5%	160.85	6433.92	1433.92	
20	16.0%	162.09	6483.78	1483.78	
21	16.5%	163.35	6533.86	1533.86	
22	17.0%	164.60	6584.16	1584.16	
23	17.5%	165.87	6634.68	1634.68	
24	18.0%	167.14	6685.42	1685.42	
25	18.5%	168.41	6736.38	1736.38	
26	19.0%	169.69	6787.55	1787.55	
27	19.5%	170.97	6838.94	1838.94	
28	20.0%	172.26	6890.55	1890.55	

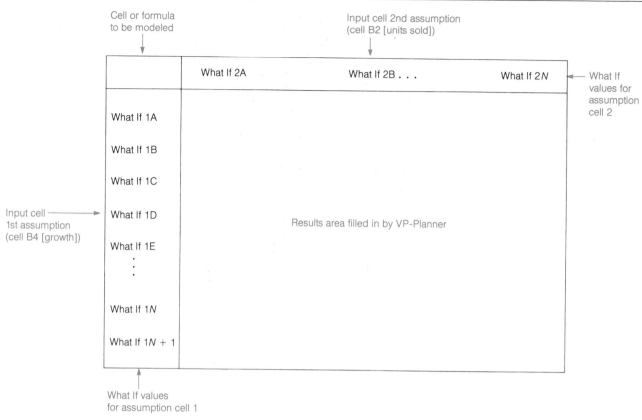

Figure 14.4
Parts of a two-assumption data table.

 Since the information at the top of the page runs into the table, it might be desirable to move the table a number of rows down. This would have no effect whatsoever on the table. VP-Planner would adjust all of the information that you have previously given it to reflect the table's new location on the worksheet.

Sensitivity Analysis Changing Two Basic Assumptions

Now that you've had a chance to read about templates and about the need for separate areas for input and output, you probably understand why some of the criteria used in building Ed's analysis worksheet were required in Chapter 12. You are now going to use the prevously assigned worksheet to create a table that allows two basic assumptions to be changed (see Figure 14.4).

Two of Ed's chief concerns are the effect of the number of units sold each year and the effect of annual sales growth on net income. He wants to be able to model net income based on these two assumptions. You are now going to create a table that will have the percentage-growth "what if" numbers along the left-hand column and the number-of-units-sold-each-year "what if" numbers along the top.

Your spreadsheet is divided into two parts: the input area and the balance sheet area. The input area starts at cell A1 and should currently look as follows:

```
INPUT AREA
UNITS SOLD (YEAR 1)          300
COST PER UNIT                $650
ANNUAL SALES GROWTH          15.00%
ANNUAL PRICE REDUCTION       7.00%
PRODUCT MARGIN               40.00%
```

The income statement starts at cell H1 and should currently look as follows:

ED'S MICROCOMPUTER SHOP

Projected Financial Statements

	1	2	3	4
Sales	325,000	347,588	371,745	397,581
Cost	195,000	208,553	223,047	238,549
Margin	130,000	139,035	148,698	159,032
Expenses:				
Advertising	72,750	49,331	18,587	19,879
Salaries	32,500	34,759	37,174	39,758
Rent	7,500	7,500	7,500	7,500
Supplies	4,875	5,214	5,576	5,964
Clerical	4,000	4,240	4,494	4,764
Other Costs	10,000	10,500	11,025	11,576
Total Expenses	131,625	111,544	84,357	89,441
Income b/f Taxes	(1,625)	27,491	64,341	69,591
Income Taxes	0	13,746	32,170	34,796
Net Income	(1,625)	13,746	32,170	34,796

You are going to want the sensitivity analysis table beginning in column L to appear as follows (some spaces in the table have been ommitted so that it will fit on one page):

UNITS SOLD (YEARx)

	+YEAR2	125	150	175	200	300	425
	10%	(17,456)	(11,499)	(5,542)	207	12,121	27,013
	15%	(16,102)	(9,874)	(3,647)	1,290	13,746	29,315
ANNUAL	20%	(14,748)	(8,250)	(1,751)	2,374	15,370	31,616
SALES	25%	(13,394)	(6,625)	72	3,457	16,995	33,918
GROWTH	30%	(12,040)	(5,001)	1,020	4,540	18,619	36,219
	35%	(10,687)	(3,376)	1,967	5,623	20,244	38,521

Nine steps are involved in creating this table.

1. Load the spreadsheet containing the income statement and input area (CH13EXR1).

2. Position the pointer at cell L1 using the TAB key.

3. Enter label information.

```
01   ED'S MICROCOMPUTER SHOP
N2   Annual Sales Growth/Units Sold Analysis
05   UNITS SOLD (YEARX)
L9   ANNUAL
L10  SALES
L11  GROWTH
```

4. Enter the part of the worksheet to be modeled (net income for year 2) at cell location M6. This marks the beginning of the table. For this to work, you must have given the net income figures the range names specified in Chapter 13.

```
+YEAR2
```

5. Change the contents of cell M6 to text to avoid confusion.

6. Enter the quantity-sold "what if" numbers.

```
N6  125
06  150
P6  175
Q6  200
R6  300
S6  425
```

7. Enter the percent-growth "what if" numbers, using the Data Fill command.

/—Invokes the Main Menu.

D (F9)—Selects the Data option.

F (F2)—Selects the Fill command from the Data Menu.

M7.M12 [by pointing or by giving the cell addresses]—Establishes the range.

ENTER—Tells VP-Planner to accept the range.

.10—Identifies the beginning value.

ENTER—Accepts the beginning value.

.05—Specifies the step increment.

ENTER—Accepts the increment entered.

ENTER—Accepts the default and executes the command.

8. Format the table for percent, with zero decimal positions. Begin by positioning the pointer at cell M7.

/—Invokes the Main Menu.

R (F3)—Selects the Range option.

F (F2)—Selects the Format option.

P (F8)—Selects the Percent option.

> 0—Indicates the number of positions to the right of the decimal.
>
> ENTER—Tells VP-Planner to accept the command.
>
> .—Nails down the pointer at cell M7.
>
> M12 [by manual pointer movement]—Positions the pointer at cell M12.
>
> ENTER—Tells VP-Planner to accept the range.

9. Build the table.

> /—Invokes the Main Menu.
>
> D (F9)—Selects the Data option.
>
> T (F3)—Selects the Table option from the Data Menu.
>
> 2—Tells VP-Planner that two basic assumptions will be used.
>
> M6.S12 [by pointing or by giving addresses]—Establishes the table range.
>
> ENTER—Tells VP-Planner to accept the range.
>
> GROWTH—Identifies the first assumption range name (or you may give B4 as the address). The first assumption is always the vertical set of numbers.
>
> ENTER—Tells VP-Planner to accept the address of the first assumption.
>
> UNITS—Identifies the range name of the second assumption (or you may give cell B2 as the address).
>
> ENTER—Tells VP-Planner to accept the second assumption and to complete the table with the results of the "what if" analyses that have been performed. (This process, you will notice, takes much longer with two assumptions than with only one.)

10. Save the worksheet using the name 2TABLE.

You can model any of the year 2, year 3, or year 4 net incomes. All you have to do to recalculate the table is change the cell to be modeled in the upper left-hand corner of the table and depress the F8 Table function key. Year 1 does not work well because it is the basis of the assumptions.

You can always test your table by checking inside it for the net income for the year modeled inside the table. If you can't find the net income for the modeled year inside the table, either you have used different net income or you have specified a wrong assumption cell.

Cell Contents of Car Loan Sensitivity Analysis

Input Screen:

```
A1:  'Cost of a Car Loan at a Variety
B2:  'of Interest Rates
A4:  'Please enter the following
A5:  'characteristics of the loan:
A7:  'After you have entered the data,
A8:  'press the F8 key to generate the
A9:  'new table.
```

```
A11:  'Press the F6 Key to move to the
A12:  'other window.
A14:  'Be sure to enter the interest as a
A15:  'decimal. Ex 12% is entered as .12
A17:  'Principal
C17:  (C0) 5000
A18:  'Interest
C18:  (P1) 0.12
A19:  'Months
C19:  (F0) 40
```

Table for Sensitivity Analysis:

```
H1:   'Loan Principal
J1:   (C0) +C17
H2:   'Payment
J2:   (F2) @PMT(C17,C18/12,C19)
I6:   'Payment
I7:   (T) +J2
H8:   (P1) 0.1
I8:   147.50394651
H9:   (P1) 0.105
I9:   148.68900829
H10:  (P1) 0.11
I10:  149.87970957
H11:  (P1) 0.115
I11:  151.07604023
H12:  (P1) 0.12
I12:  152.27798989
H13:  (P1) 0.125
I13:  153.48554786
H14:  (P1) 0.13
I14:  154.69870319
H15:  (P1) 0.135
I15:  155.91744466
H16:  (P1) 0.14
I16:  157.14176077
H17:  (P1) 0.145
I17:  158.37163974
H18:  (P1) 0.15
I18:  159.60706954
H19:  (P1) 0.155
I19:  160.84803787
H20:  (P1) 0.16
I20:  162.09453215
H21:  (P1) 0.165
I21:  163.34653957
H22:  (P1) 0.17
I22:  164.60404703
H23:  (P1) 0.175
I23:  165.8670412
H24:  (P1) 0.18
I24:  167.13550849
H25:  (P1) 0.185
I25:  168.40943505
```

```
H26:  (P1) 0.19
I26:  169.68880679
H27:  (P1) 0.195
I27:  170.97360939
H28:  (P1) 0.2
I28:  172.26382827
```

Cell Contents of Ed's Computer Shop Sensitivity Analysis

Input Screen:

```
A1:  'INPUT AREA
A2:  'UNITS SOLD (YEAR 1)
B2:  300
A3:  'COST PER UNIT
B3:  (C0) 650
A4:  'ANNUAL SALES GROWTH
B4:  (P2) 0.15
A5:  'ANNUAL PRICE REDUCTION
B5:  (P2) 0.07
A6:  'PRODUCT MARGIN
B6:  (P2) 0.4
```

Balance Sheet:

```
H1:  'ED'S MICROCOMPUTER SHOP
G2:  'Projected Financial Statements
G4:  1
H4:  2
I4:  3
J4:  4
G5:  ' --------
H5:  ' --------
I5:  ' --------
J5:  ' --------
F6:  'Sales
G6:  +$UNITS*($COST/(1-$MARGIN))
H6:  +G6*(1+$GROWTH)*(1-$ANN.RED)
I6:  +H6*(1+$GROWTH)*(1-$ANN.RED)
J6:  +I6*(1+$GROWTH)*(1-$ANN.RED)
F7:  'Cost
G7:  +G6*(1-$MARGIN)
H7:  +H6*(1-$MARGIN)
I7:  +I6*(1-$MARGIN)
J7:  +J6*(1-$MARGIN)
G8:  ' --------
H8:  ' --------
I8:  ' --------
J8:  ' --------
F9:  'Margin
G9:  +G6-G7
H9:  +H6-H7
I9:  +I6-I7
J9:  +J6-J7
```

```
F11:  'Expenses:
F12:  'Advertising
G12:  50000+G6*0.07
H12:  25000+H6*0.07
I12:  +I6*0.05
J12:  +J6*0.05
F13:  'Salaries
G13:  +G6*0.1
H13:  +H6*0.1
I13:  +I6*0.1
J13:  +J6*0.1
F14:  'Rent
G14:  7500
H14:  7500
I14:  7500
J14:  7500
F15:  'Supplies
G15:  +G6*0.015
H15:  +H6*0.015
I15:  +I6*0.015
J15:  +J6*0.015
F16:  'Clerical
G16:  4000
H16:  +G16*1.06
I16:  +H16*1.06
J16:  +I16*1.06
F17:  'Other Costs
G17:  10000
H17:  +G17*1.05
I17:  +H17*1.05
J17:  +I17*1.05
G18:  ' _____
H18:  ' _____
I18:  ' _____
J18:  ' _____
F19:  'Total Expenses
G19:  @SUM(G12..G17)
H19:  @SUM(H12..H17)
I19:  @SUM(I12..I17)
J19:  @SUM(J12..J17)
G20:  ' _____
H20:  ' _____
I20:  ' _____
J20:  ' _____
F22:  'Income b/f taxes
G22:  +G9-G19
H22:  +H9-H19
I22:  +I9-I19
J22:  +J9-J19
F23:  'Income Taxes
G23:  @IF(G22<0,0,G22*0.5)
H23:  @IF(H22<0,0,H22*0.5)
I23:  @IF(I22<0,0,I22*0.5)
J23:  @IF(J22<0,0,J22*0.5)
```

```
G24:  ' _____
H24:  ' _____
I24:  ' _____
J24:  ' _____
F25:  'Net Income
G25:  +G22-G23
H25:  +H22-H23
I25:  +I22-I23
J25:  +J22-J23
G26:  ' ========
H26:  ' ========
I26:  ' ========
J26:  ' ========
```

Sensitivity Table:

```
O1:   'ED'S MICROCOMPUTER SHOP
N2:   'Annual Sales Growth/Units Sold Analysis
O5:   'UNITS SOLD (YEARx)
M6:   (T) +YEAR2
N6:   125
O6:   150
P6:   175
Q6:   200
R6:   300
S6:   425
M7:   (P0) 0.1
N7:   -17455.78125
O7:   -11498.9375
P7:   -5542.09375
Q7:   207.375
R7:   12121.0625
S7:   27013.171875
M8:   (P0) 0.15
N8:   -16101.953125
O8:   -9874.34375
P8:   -3646.734375
Q8:   1290.4375
R8:   13745.65625
S8:   29314.679688
M9:   (P0) 0.2
N9:   -14748.125
O9:   -8249.75
P9:   -1751.375
Q9:   2373.5
R9:   15370.25
S9:   31616.1875
M10:  (P0) 0.25
N10:  -13394.296875
O10:  -6625.15625
P10:  -71.9921875
Q10:  3456.5625
R10:  16994.84375
```

```
S10:  33917.695313
M11:  (P0) 0.3
N11:  -12040.46875
O11:  -5000.5625
P11:  1019.671875
Q11:  4539:625
R11:  18619.4375
S11:  36219.203125
M12:  (P0) 0.35
N12:  -10686.640625
O12:  -3375.96875
P12:  1967.3515625
Q12:  5622.6875
R12:  20244.03125
S12:  38520.710938
```

Chapter Review

A template is used when a number of different people will want to make use of the same worksheet. Because many of these future users are likely not to know too much about either computers or spreadsheets, built-in directions and documentation are necessary.

The process of building a template is very similar to programming: the problem to be solved must be well defined, and the logical processes involved in solving the problem and the physical layout of the worksheet must be planned. The input, processing, and output portions of the template should be separated, and help screens with directions on how to use the worksheet must be included for the user. A structured walkthrough should be conducted in order to catch any errors in logic or items that the developer has overlooked. The template must be properly tested, and final documentation must be developed. When the template is released for use, someone must be assigned to provide support and maintenance in case of problems.

Windows split the display screen either vertically or horizontally, providing you with two different but simultaneous views of the same worksheet. Windows are frequently used with templates.

When you are building a template, you do not want unknowledgable users to destroy a part of the worksheet inadvertently. VP-Planner allows you to protect the entire worksheet to prevent any changes being made to a cell; if a change is attempted, the computer merely beeps. Cells that are used as input cells can be returned to unprotected status, in which case they will appear in high-intensity video.

The Data Fill command is used to fill a range rapidly with numbers that change by some incremental value. This command can easily develop column headings for the years 1985–2000, for example, saving you a lot of data entry work.

Sensitivity analysis is the process of asking a number of "what if" questions. Various changes can be entered in a worksheet to see what effect they have on other values. For instance, if you are interested in what effect inflation has on a worksheet, you may enter a number of different values to determine the consequences of various rates of inflation. In order to do this, you have to enter the value and then note the effect of the change. The data table feature of VP-Planner automates this process, allowing a table of values to be created and defined to VP-Planner; VP-Planner can then be directed to note the impact of each change and to fill in the table with the data resulting from changes in the targeted cell.

Key Terms and Concepts

cell protection	Sync
Clear	Table
Data Fill	template
help screen	testing
Horizontal	Unsync
protected cell	Vertical
sensitivity analysis	windows
structured walkthrough	worksheet protection

Chapter Quiz

Multiple Choice

1. Which of the following is not a separate part of a template:
   a. Input screen
   b. Processing area
   c. Output area
   d. Planning area
   e. All of the above are parts of a template

2. Which of the following is not a step in developing a template:
   a. Planning
   b. Walkthrough
   c. Designing logic
   d. Testing
   e. Documenting
   f. All of the above are steps in developing a template

3. Which of the following statements about worksheet and cell protection is false:
   a. In building an input area, the designer first protects the worksheet and then "unprotects" the input area.
   b. It is possible to change the contents of a protected cell by holding down the CTRL key.
   c. When a protected worksheet has been unprotected, the input area cells must be protected in order to make them look right.
   d. The worksheet is protected via an option off the Worksheet Menu, while the input area is unprotected via an option off the Range Menu.
   e. All of the above statements are true.

4. Which command is used to enter numeric information quickly into a range of cells when each subsequent cell is to be changed by a fixed, incremental value:
   a. simple data entry
   b. Step Fill
   c. Data Fill
   d. Step Increment
   e. None of the above

5. Sensitivity analysis involves:
   a. Asking a number of "what if" questions
   b. Entering each separate value to determine the impact
   c. Using the Data Table feature of VP-Planner
   d. All of the above are correct
   e. None of the above is correct

True/False

6. Template documentation will typically appear only in an instruction manual.

7. Column A is typically used for help screens.

8. The process of reviewing the logic of the template is called a walkabout.

9. Windows can be used to split the screen either vertically or horizontally.

10. Input cells in a protected template appear in high-intensity video.

Answers

1. d 2. f 3. b 4. c 5. d 6. f 7. t 8. f 9. t 10. f

Exercises

1. Define or describe each of the following:
   a. template   d. window
   b. help screen   e. worksheet protection
   c. structured walkthrough   f. sensitivity analysis

2. List the differences between a regular worksheet and a template.
   a.

   b.

   c.

3. List the three functional areas of a template.
   a.

   b.

   c.

4. The _____ data table is recalculated by pressing the F8 key.

5. The _____ involves the developer of a template explaining it to potential users. This ensures all design considerations have been addressed.

6. The process of verifying the logic and results of a template is known as _____ .

7. One of the primary advantages of using the structured walkthrough is to catch _____ .

8. A software package used to verify the logic and results of a template is _____ or _____ .

9. List the items that should be included in the final documentation.
   a.

   b.

   c.

d.

e.

10. _____ allow you to split the screen either vertically or horizontally, giving you two views of the same worksheet.

11. When newly created, a horizontal window appears _____ the pointer, and a vertical window appears to the _____ of the pointer.

12. Using vertically synchronized windows, windows move _____ at the same time.

13. The cell _____ allows you to prohibit a user from changing an important cell.

14. The _____ allows you to set up a range and then fill it with numbers.

15. The number _____ is the upper limit default for the Data Fill command.

16. The process of asking a number of "what if" questions is known as _____ .

17. The VP-Planner _____ is used in sensitivity analysis.

18. After a worksheet has been protected, the input area must be _____ _____ .

19. The VP-Planner table feature allows you to vary either _____ or _____ variables.

20. The number entered in response to the _____ prompt of the Data Fill command determines the increment from one cell to the next.

Computer Exercises

1. Develop a sensitivity analysis template for examining the impact of a number of interest rates on the principal of a house mortgage. Use the principles of good template design in developing your worksheet. There should be separate areas for the input and for the sensitivity table. Use the manual recalculation mode. Use a principal of $90,000. The interest rates should start at 8 percent and go to 17 percent by half-percent increments. There should be a 20-year mortgage. This means that you either have to enter the number of months in 20 years or have to enter 20*12 in the payment formula. Use the Window feature so that you can see both the input and the sensitivity table on the screen at the same time. Save the template to a worksheet file called CH14EXR1.

2. Develop an expanded mortgage sensitivity analysis table that will track not only the payment but the grand total of loan payments and total interest payments at the various interest rates above. Also examine mortgage principals of $75,000, $60,000, $120,000, and $150,000. Save this template to a worksheet file called CH14EXR2.

3. Perform a two-assumption sensitivity analysis on the CH11EXR1 worksheet. Instead of varying units sold and sales growth, vary cost per unit and annual price reduction. Save this worksheet onto a file called CH14EXR3.

4. Load the worksheet file, PAYMENT. This worksheet already has all cells but the input cells protected. Try to change any cells other than the high intensity cells. You will receive a Protected cell error message at the bottom of the screen. Unprotect the worksheet and do a range protect on the input cells. You can now make any changes that you wish to the worksheet. Now protect the worksheet and change the protection on the input cells so that new data can be entered.

Chapter

15

Graphing with

VP-Planner

Chapter Objectives   *After completing this chapter, you should be able to:*

Discuss in detail the various options contained in the Graph Menu

Discuss the steps involved in building a graph

Discuss the various types of graphs that can be constructed by VP-Planner

Discuss the method of saving graph settings for later use

Discuss additional items for graphs, such as Titles and Legends

This chapter is divided into two parts: the first deals with the various options provided in the Graph Menu, and the second deals with building graphs.

The information presented in Chapters 13 and 14 demonstrates how VP-Planner can be used to manipulate information arithmetically through the use of formulas for processing data that have been entered on the worksheet. The worksheet is automatically updated and completely recalculated whenever information is entered in a cell, allowing you to play a number of "what if" games to see how a change will affect the rest of the worksheet.

These characteristics alone may satisfy your needs when a worksheet containing small amounts of data is being used, but what happens when you have large amounts of data or when you cannot make sense of the small amount of data that is in the worksheet? The answer lies in the old maxim "a picture is worth a thousand words": VP-Planner allows you, with only a small amount of effort, to depict the data that have been entered in a worksheet on the screen, in the form of a graph.

If you wish to use this feature, your IBM PC computer must have either a color graphics board and a color (or regular) monitor or a board that makes it possible to display graphics on a monochrome monitor. If you don't have this hardware (see Figure 15.1), your computer will only beep when you try to display the graph.

If your computer has both a monochrome monitor and a color monitor attached to it, VP-Planner will use the monochrome monitor to display the worksheet, and the color monitor to display the graph.

Steps in Building a Graph and Printing the Graph

The process of building a graph using VP-Planner involves the following simple, easy-to-follow steps:

1. Selecting and loading in a worksheet file from disk, or using the current worksheet
2. Selecting the graphing menu via the command sequence / Graph
3. Selecting the type of graph to be used (line, bar, XY, stacked bar, or pie)
4. Telling VP-Planner which data ranges are involved in the graph (up to six ranges of data can be depicted in a graph)
5. Telling VP-Planner to include any labels or extra information
6. Displaying the graph on the screen
7. Making any changes in the graph
8. Printing the graph with the Print command

After you become accustomed to using the Graph option, you can go through this process easily in 3 to 5 minutes.

You can also enter "what if" changes in your data and automatically regraph the new information via the **F10 Graph key**, without going back through the Graph Menu.

Graph Menu

The **Graph Menu** is invoked by entering a / Graph command sequence. Unless you wish to add information to a "naked" graph, you can build the entire graph from this menu, without entering any submenus; the submenus allow you to dress up a graph with meaningful, descriptive data. Appendix D includes a chart of the graph command structure.

Figure 15.1
(a) Hercules graphics board; *(b)* Monochrome screen with Hercules graphics board.

The Graph Menu that appears on your screen when you depress the command sequence / Graph is as follows:

Type Reset View Print Save Options Name Quit Look X A B C D E F

Type

The **Type option** of the Graph Menu allows you to select the type of graph you wish to display from the following menu:

Line Bar XY Stacked Bar Pie

Line. The standard one-dimensional **line graph** presents the data on the **Y (vertical) axis** and the label of the data on the **X (horizontal) axis**. Up to six lines (sets of data) can be depicted. When graphing multiple sets of data, VP-Planner automatically uses different data point symbols for each set of data.

Bar. The standard one-dimensional **bar graph** (when multiple data ranges are used) places the bars for each data point from the data ranges side by side. Different shadings are used for each data range.

XY. An **XY graph** is a two-dimensional graph with a set of data points referenced on both the X-axis and the Y-axis. For example, if you want to graph a company's profits compared to inflation over a period of years, you would select this option.

Stacked Bar. A **stacked bar graph** stacks multiple ranges of data on top of each other instead of next to one another. Different shadings are given to each range of data to differentiate among them.

Pie. The **Pie chart**, as the name implies, is a circle divided into wedges; it is used to depict a single data range. Because of its nature, the pie chart cannot depict multiple data ranges.

Reset

The **Reset option** selects the Reset Menu for the graphing function. The options of the Reset Menu allow you to cancel either the entire graph or portions of it. The Reset Menu options are as follows:

```
Graph X  A B C D E F  Quit
```

Graph. The Graph command allows you to cancel the entire graph. If this option is taken, the entire graph will have to be respecified to VP-Planner.

X. The X command allows you to cancel the labeling of the graph's horizontal axis.

ABCDEF. The ABCDEF commands allow you to cancel one or more data ranges of a graph. If you cancel all of them, VP-Planner acts as though you do not have a graph specified.

Quit. The Quit command returns you to the Graph Menu.

View

The **View command** allows you to display the currently specified graph on the monitor, after which you can depress any key on the keyboard to return to the Graph Menu.

You can also obtain a display of a graph, showing the specified settings, while you are in the worksheet in ready mode. To do so, simply depress the F10 Graph Function key. You can return to the worksheet by depressing any key.

Print

The **Print command** allows you to ''dump'' the graph that you have created to the printer. When you enter this command, VP-Planner redisplays the graph to the screen. After the graph has been completely displayed, it starts printing. When the print process is finished, you are returned to the Graph Menu.

It is important to note that VP-Planner will only be able to print graphs on printers that have a graphics chip installed. Furthermore, your printer's graphics chip must be compatible with the IBM family of graphics chips for printers. If your graph does not print out properly the first time, turn off the printer and then turn it back on. This resets any special print commands that may still be active within your printer. If the graph still does not print properly, you will have to use another printer for generating a hard copy of the graph.

Save

The **Save command** is used to store the currently specified graph onto a disk file. Such a file is referred to by VP-Planner as a "graph" or "picture" file and contains a .PIC extension.

Options

The **Options** selection allows you to dress up a graph with various options. When this option is selected the following menu is displayed:

```
Legend  Format  Titles  Grid  Scale  Color  B&W  Data-Labels  Quit
```

Legend. The **Legend option** displays a menu that allows you to specify characters for the legend to be used to represent the various ranges of data. Up to nineteen characters can be shown, but as few as possible should be selected. The following menu is displayed:

```
A  B  C  D  E  F
```

You now select the appropriate data range, and VP-Planner displays the current legend for it. If you wish to change the legend, enter the new characters; if you wish to leave it unchanged, depress the ENTER key. The legend is displayed beneath the X-axis title entry.

Format. The **Format option** is used to change how the specified graph is displayed—that is, what characters are used to represent the displayed data points and how those data points are connected on the graph. The following menu is displayed when this option is selected:

```
Graph  A  B  C  D  E  F  Quit
```

Graph. By selecting this option, you can determine how the data are to be presented on the graph. The following menu is displayed:

```
Lines  Symbols  Both  Neither
```

> *Lines.* This command will connect each data point within a range with a line.
> *Symbols.* This command will display each data point in a data range with the same character or symbol.
> *Both.* This command uses both lines and symbols in representing data points in a data range.
> *Neither.* This command uses neither lines nor symbols, requiring the legends for data points to be specified in legend option commands.

ABCDEF. This command option allows you to select a data range. When you have done so, VP-Planner prompts you in exactly the same way it does when you select the Graph option in this menu.

Quit. This command returns you to the Options Menu.

Titles. The **Titles option** enables you to label the graph with up to two lines of text; these will appear at the top of the graph. The Titles option can also be used to enter a one-line text label for each axis. When you select the Titles option, you will be presented with the following menu:

```
First   Second   X-Axis   Y-Axis
```

First. This command allows you to enter the first line of text that is to be placed at the top of the page.

Second. This command allows you to enter the second line of text that is to be placed (below the first line) at the top of the page.

X-Axis. This command allows you to enter one line of text to be displayed along the X (horizontal) axis.

Y-Axis. This command allows you to enter one line of text to be displayed along the Y (vertical) axis.

Grid. The **Grid option** allows you to choose grid lines for display on a graph. When selected, it displays the following menu:

```
Horizontal   Vertical   Both   Clear
```

Horizontal. This command places horizontal grid lines on the graph when it is displayed. Grid lines can be used to make the relative size of plotted points clearer.

Vertical. This command places vertical grid lines on the graph when it is displayed.

Both. This command places both horizontal and vertical grid lines on a graph when it is displayed.

Clear. This command clears any grid lines from the display.

Scale. The **Scale option** allows you to set the scaling and format of a graph for either the X- or Y-axis. When you have selected the axis, the following menu of options will be displayed:

```
Automatic   Manual   Lower   Upper   Format   Quit
```

Automatic. With this option, the scaling on the graphs is automatically calculated by VP-Planner so as to keep the entire graph visible on the display.

Manual. With this option, you select the scaling.

Lower/Upper. These options must be used if the Manual command was selected. They allow you to select the upper- and lower-scale limits, giving you more control over how data are presented. Small differences can be made to seem much greater.

Format. This option allows you to decide how numeric data will be used with scaling. When the graph is displayed, the numbers will appear in the selected format.

Quit. This option returns you to the Options Menu.

Color/B&W. The Color option displays the information in colors that have been preselected by VP-Planner. The B&W option displays the data in standard black-and-white, with cross-hatching on the bars.

Data/Labels. The Data option allows you to specify a range of cells whose contents will be used to label the data points of a data range (A–F). First choose the range (A–F); then specify the cells to be included in the range; then, for line and XY graphs, select the alignment of the labels in relation to the data points (Centered, Left, Above, Right, Below), using the Labels option. Select the **Quit option** when you are finished, and you will return to the Graph Menu. The next time the graph is displayed, the cell contents of the specified range(s) will be displayed as data points.

Name

The **Name option** allows you to load in a graph file that was previously saved using the Save option of the Graph Menu, reset the graph options to those saved in this file, and then draw the graph using the specified features. When selected, the name option displays the following menu:

```
Use   Create   Delete   Reset
```

Use. The **Use command** allows you to make graph file settings that are contained in RAM memory current by entering the name or by pointing to the file with the pointer. The selected graph will then be displayed.

Create. The **Create command** allows you to save part of a worksheet (range) for graphing, rather than saving the entire worksheet to another graph in RAM. If a portion of a spreadsheet is saved, it can later be accessed via the Use command.

Delete. The **Delete command** is used to delete any graph settings contained in memory. To do this, enter the graph name and depress ENTER or point to the graph and depress ENTER.

Reset. The **Reset command** erases all named graphs from the computer's memory.

Quit

The **Quit option** returns you to the Main Menu of VP-Planner.

Look

The **Look command** allows you to view a graph contained in a .PIC file on screen.

X

The **X command** defines a range of the worksheet to be used for a horizontal label of the graph. When you take the X option, you must give the addresses of or point to the cell(s) containing the label information. Often, these are row or column labels from the worksheet.

ABCDEF

The **ABCDEF commands** are used to specify up to six data ranges to be depicted on your graph. The first data range must be labeled A, the second B, and so on. You can enter the cell addresses or point to the cells to be included in each data range; then depress the ENTER key when you have finished.

VP-Planner remembers each data range you specify; to respecify an existing range, reselect it and specify a new data range to be graphed. If you wish to cancel a data range, you must use the Reset option. VP-Planner requires you to define at least one data range, regardless of the type of graph that has been selected.

Generating Graphs

Simple Bar Graphs

The first exercise below is to generate a simple bar graph using the "This Year" information contained in COMPSALS worksheet. The graph you produce should look like the graph shown in Figure 15.2.

1. Load in the COMPSALS worksheet.

    /—Gets the Main Menu.

    F (F6)—Selects the File Menu.

    R (F2)—Selects the Retrieve command.

    COMPSALS—Identifies the worksheet (or you can point to the worksheet name).

    ENTER—Executes the command.

2. Select the Graph Menu and tell VP-Planner to generate a bar graph.

    /—Gets the Main Menu.

    G (F8)—Selects the Graph Menu.

    T (F2)—Selects the Type option from the Graph Menu.

    B (F3)—Tells VP-Planner to generate a bar chart.

3. Establish the X-axis label range (department names).

    X (F10)—Indicates that the X-axis label range is to be specified.

    B5 [by manual pointer movement or address entry]—Positions the pointer at cell B5.

    .—Nails down the beginning of the range.

    B10 [by manual pointer movement or address entry]— Positions the pointer at the last cell in the label range.

    ENTER—Tells VP-Planner that the range is established.

4. Establish the "This Year" column as the A data range.

    A—Tells VP-Planner that you wish to specify the A data range.

    D5 [by manual pointer movement]—Positions the cursor at the beginning of the "This Year" data.

    .—Nails down the beginning of the range.

    D10 [by manual pointer movement]—Positions the pointer at the last cell to be included in the A data range.

    ENTER—Tells VP-Planner that the A data range is established.

5. Execute the View command (V) to display graph on screen. Depress any key to return to the Graph menu.

6. Print the graph.

    P (F5)—Selects the Print command.

Figure 15.2
Simple bar graph of the "This Year" information from the COMPSALS worksheet.

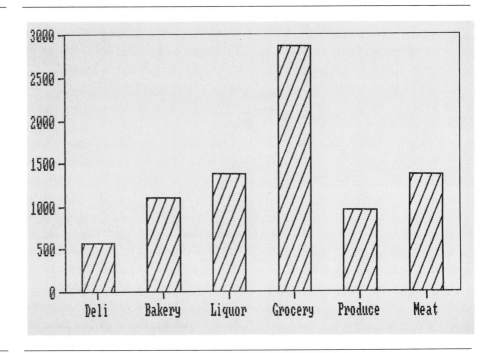

![Entering Titles icon] **Entering Titles**

Although the graph in the just-completed exercise looks okay, if you want it to mean anything at a later date, you should probably put some descriptive labels on it. VP-Planner allows you to put a two-line title at the top of the graph and a one-line title on each axis of the graph. In this exercise, you will place the following labels on the bar chart (see Figure 15.3):

Line 1	Ed's Supermarket
Line 2	1985 Sales
X-axis	Departments
Y-axis	Dollar Sales

Placing these labels on the graph involves the following steps:

1. The Options selection from the Graph Menu allows you to place the labels on the bar chart.

   O (F7)—Selects the Options Menu from the Graph Menu.

   T (F4)—Selects the Titles option from the Options Menu.

   F (F2)—Selects the First line option.

   Ed's Supermarket—Specifies the title.

   ENTER—Tells VP-Planner to accept the title.

   T (F4)—Selects the Titles option.

   S (F3)—Selects the Second line option.

   1985 Sales—Specifies the title.

   ENTER—Tells VP-Planner to accept the title.

   T (F4)—Selects the Titles option.

Figure 15.3
Bar graph of 1985 COMPSALS
sales, with graph and axis
titles in place.

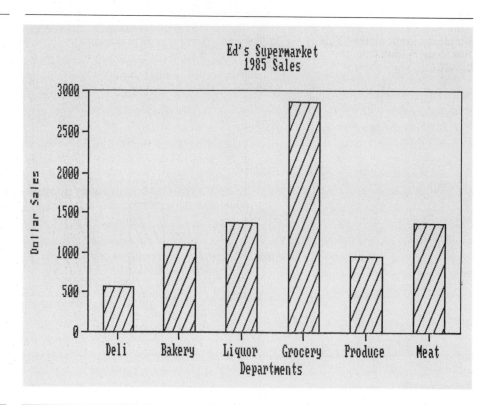

> X (F4)—Selects the X-axis title option.
>
> Departments—Specifies the title.
>
> ENTER—Tells VP-Planner to accept the title.
>
> T (F4)—Selects the Titles option.
>
> Y (F5)—Selects the Y-axis title option.
>
> Dollar Sales—Specifies the title.
>
> ENTER—Tells VP-Planner to accept the title.
>
> Q (F10)—Quits the Options Menu and returns to the Graph Menu.

2. View the graph by depressing the V option. Your graph should now look like the one in Figure 15.3.

3. Depress any key to return to the Graph Menu.

4. Save the graph's settings onto the worksheet, so it can easily be retrieved later.

> N (F8)—Selects the Name option of the Graph Menu.
>
> C (F3)—Selects the Create option.
>
> 1985SALE—Names the group of graph settings.
>
> ENTER—Tells VP-Planner to accept these graph settings.

If you want to take a look at this graph again, you don't have to reenter all the keystrokes; you just tell VP-Planner to load 1985SALE as the settings to generate a graph. These graph settings are also saved to a worksheet file when a save operation is performed.

Figure 15.4
Bar graph of 1984 COMPSALS
sales, with graph and axis
titles in place.

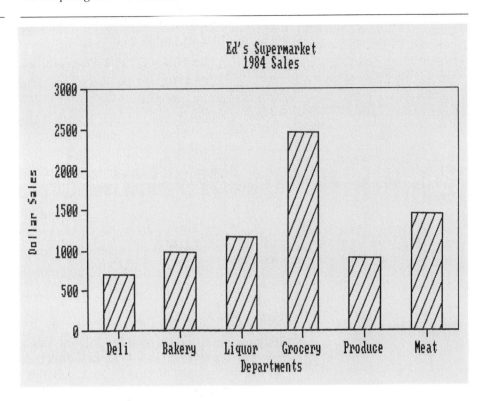

Figure 15.4
Bar graph of 1984 COMPSALS
sales, with graph and axis
titles in place.

Changing Data Ranges

The current graph settings contain instructions for creating a graph of the 1985
sales for Ed's Supermarket. To graph the 1984 sales, the A data range and the
second line of the worksheet title must be changed. You have to change the A
data range to the Last Year column, and put "1984 Sales" in the second title
line. The remaining graph specifications can be left unchanged.

The steps involved in performing this task are as follows:

1. Get to the Graph Menu.

2. Change the A data range.

> A—Selects the A option from the Graph Menu.
>
> BACKSPACE—Cancels the existing range.
>
> C10 [by pointer movement or address entry]—Establishes the
> first cell in the A range.
>
> .—Nails down the beginning of the range.
>
> C5 [by pointer movement or address entry]—Establishes the
> end of the A range.
>
> ENTER—Tells VP-Planner to accept the A data range.

3. Change *1985* to *1984* in the second title line.

> O (F7)—Selects the Options Menu from the Graph Menu.
>
> T (F4)—Selects the Titles option.
>
> S (F3)—Selects the Second line option, causing 1985 Sales
> to be displayed.

>   Right Arrow—Moves the pointer under the *5* in *1985*.
>
>   4—Identifies the new character to be inserted.
>
>   ENTER—Tells VP-Planner to accept the changed title.
>
>   Q (F10)—Quits the Options Menu and returns to the Graph Menu.

4. View the changed graph, using the View command (V) from the Graph Menu. The graph should now look like the one shown in Figure 15.4.

5. Depress any key to return to the Graph Menu.

6. Save these worksheet settings for later use.

>   N (F8)—Selects the Name option from the Graph Menu.
>
>   C (F3)—Selects the Create option.
>
>   1984SALE—Names the group of graph settings.
>
>   ENTER—Tells VP-Planner to execute this command.

Side-by-Side Bar Graphs

You now have two bar graphs showing sales for the years 1984 and 1985. Ed, however, wants to be able to make a direct comparison between the two years via one bar graph. Because you saved the settings of the 1985SALE bar graph, all you have to do is load in those graph settings and change them in accordance with Ed's request. The following steps are required:

1. Get to the Graph Menu.

2. Replace the current graph settings with those contained in 1985SALE (and stored in the spreadsheet).

>   N (F8)—Selects the Name option from the Graph Menu.
>
>   U (F2)—Selects the Use option from the Names Menu, enabling you to replace graph settings with previously stored settings.
>
>   1985SALE—Specifies the graph settings to be stored.
>
>   ENTER—Tells VP-Planner to execute the command.

3. The graph 1985SALE is now displayed on the screen. Depress any key to return to the Graph Menu.

4. Establish the B range as the numbers in the Last Year column.

>   B—Tells VP-Planner to expect the B data range.
>
>   C5 [by pointer movement or address entry]—Establishes the beginning of the B data range.
>
>   .—Nails down the beginning of the range.
>
>   C10 [by pointer movement or address entry]—Establishes the end of the B data range.
>
>   ENTER—Tells VP-Planner to accept the B data range.

5. Change the second title line of the graph.

>   O (F7)—Selects the Options Menu.
>
>   T (F4)—Selects the Titles option.
>
>   S (F3)—Selects the Second line option.
>
>   Right Arrow—Positions the pointer under the *S* in *Sales*.
>
>   Ins—Press the INS key for insert mode.

Figure 15.5
Side-by-side bar graphs of
COMPSALS sales.

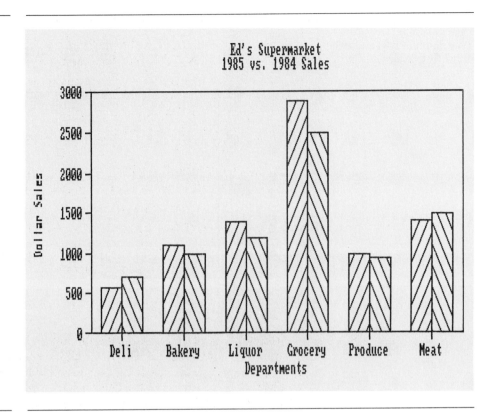

vs. 1984—Identifies new characters to be inserted.

ENTER—Accepts the new second title line.

Q (F10)—Quits the Options Menu and returns to the Graph Menu.

5. View the graph, using the V command. It should now look like the graph shown in Figure 15.5.

6. Depress any key to return to the Graph Menu.

7. Print the graph.

8485SALE—Names the graph.

ENTER—Tells VP-Planner to execute the save command.

8. Save these graph settings for later use.

N (F8)—Selects the Name option from the Graph Menu.

C (F3)—Selects the Create option from the Name Menu.

8485SALE—Specifies the name of the graph settings to be saved.

ENTER—Records these settings to the worksheet.

Converting to Line Graphs

Ed would also like to see the bar graph information depicted as a line graph. The following steps are involved:

1. From the Graph Menu, change the graph type.

T (F2)—Selects the Type option from the Graph Menu.

L (F2)—Tells VP-Planner to generate a line graph.

Figure 15.6
**Line graph of 1984 and 1985
COMPSALS sales.**

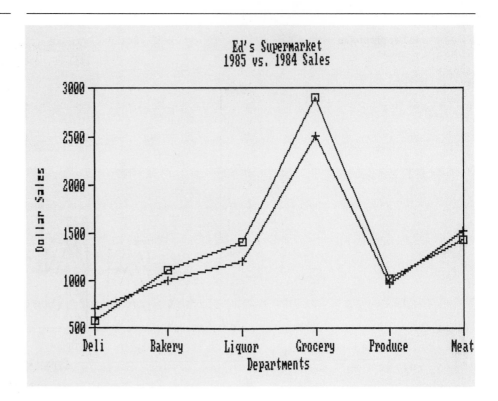

Figure 15.6
**Line graph of 1984 and 1985
COMPSALS sales.**

2. View the graph, using the V command. It should now look like the graph shown in Figure 15.6.

Entering Legends

Now Ed's confused because he can't tell the difference between 1985 and 1984 on the line graph. You will solve this problem by providing a legend that tells what symbols represent what data ranges.

The following steps are involved when you begin from the Graph Menu:

1. Add the legends.

   O (F7)—Selects the Options Menu.

   L (F2)—Selects the Legend option.

   A (F2)—Selects the A data range to hold the first legend text.

   1985 Sales—Identifies the text of the legend.

   ENTER—Tells VP-Planner to accept the legend.

   L (F2)—Selects the Legend option.

   B (F3)—Selects the B data range to hold the second legend text.

   1984 Sales—Identifies the text of the legend.

   ENTER—Tells VP-Planner to accept the legend.

   Q (F10)—Leaves the Options Menu and returns to the Graph Menu.

Figure 15.7
Line graph of 1984 and 1985
`COMPSALS` sales, with accompanying legend.

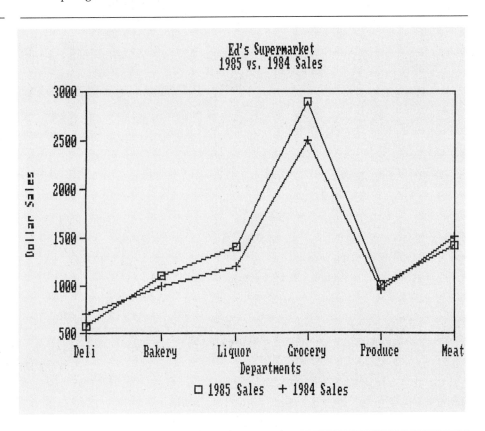

2. View the graph, using the V command. It should now look like the graph shown in Figure 15.7.

3. Depress any key to return to the Graph Menu.

4. Save these graph settings.

    N (F8)—Selects the Name option from the Graph Menu.

    C (F3)—Selects the Create option from the Names Menu.

    `8485LINE`—Names the graph settings.

    ENTER—Tells VP-Planner to save the graph settings.

5. Print the graph.

Reconverting to Bar Graphs

Ed is very impressed with VP-Planner and now wants the double bar graph to include a legend for its bars. You need to take the following steps:

1. Get to the Graph Menu.

2. Select a new graph type.

    T (F2)—Selects the Type option from the Graph Menu.

    B (F3)—Tells VP-Planner to create a bar graph.

3. View the graph, using the V command. It should now look like the graph shown in Figure 15.8.

Figure 15.8
Bar graph of 1984 and 1985
COMPSALS sales, with ac-
companying legend.

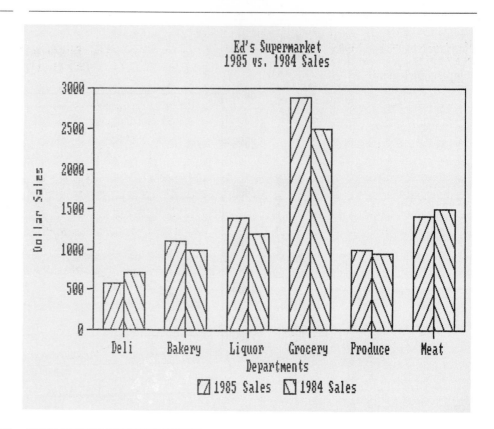

 ### Pie Charts

Ed wants more. You will try to satisfy him by putting the original bar chart information about 1985 sales into the form of a pie chart. This involves the following:

1. Get to the Graph Menu.
2. Reset the graph settings to 1985SALE.

    N (F8)—Selects the Name option from the Graph Menu.

    U (F2)—Selects the Use command, telling VP-Planner which graph settings to use.

    1985SALE—Specifies the settings to use.

    ENTER—Tells VP-Planner to change the settings of the current graph.

3. Get to Graph Menu and change the graph type.

    T (F2)—Selects the Type option from the Graph Menu.

    P (F6)—Tells VP-Planner to draw a pie chart.

4. View the graph, using the V command. It should now look like the graph shown in Figure 15.9. VP-Planner remembers all of the titles from the 1985SALE graph settings.

5. Print the graph.

Figure 15.9
Pie chart of 1985 COMPSALS
sales.

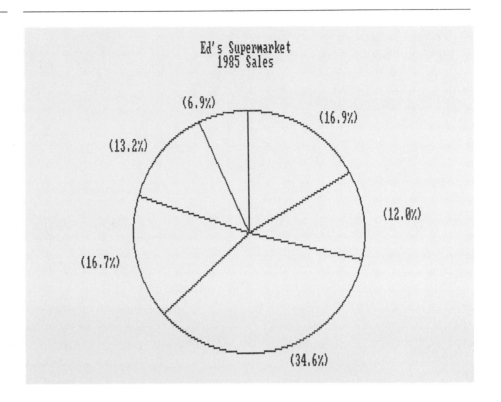

 Stacked Bar Charts

Ed would now like a stacked bar graph showing the combined sales of each department for the years 1984 and 1985. Once you have reached the Graph Menu, the steps are as follows:

1. Get the settings from the 8485SALE graph that you stored previously.

   N (F8)—Selects the Name option from the Graph Menu.

   U (F2)—Selects the Use option from the Name Menu.

   8485SALE—Specifies the graph settings to use.

   ENTER—Puts the graph on the screen.

2. Depress any key to get to the Graph Menu.

3. Select a new graph type.

   T (F2)—Selects the Type option from the Graph Menu.

   S (F5)—Tells VP-Planner to generate a stacked bar graph.

4. Enter a new second title line for the graph.

   O (F7)—Selects the Options Menu from the Graph Menu.

   T (F4)—Selects the Title option from the Options Menu.

   S (F3)—Selects the Second title line.

Figure 15.10
Stacked bar graph of 1984 and
1985 COMPSALS sales.

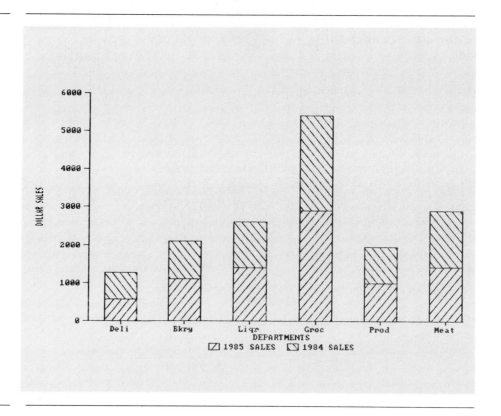

Right Arrow—Moves the pointer under the *v* of *vs*.

DEL [three times]—Deletes the word *vs*.

Ins—Places VP-Planner in insert mode.

+ —Identifies the character to be added.

ENTER—Tells VP-Planner to accept the changed second line.

Q (F10)—Quits the Options Menu and returns to the Graph Menu.

5. View the graph, using the V command. It should look like the graph shown in Figure 15.10.

6. Depress any key to return to the Graph Menu.

7. Resave the worksheet file so that VP-Planner remembers the various named graph settings.

XY Graphs

Up until now, Ed has been requesting only one-dimensional graphs—graphs in which only Y data points are plotted. Now Ed has come up with an application that requires you to plot a set of Y data points against a set of X data points. Ed has accumulated seven years of profit figures that he would like to compare to each year's rate of inflation. To build such a graph, you must use the XY option from the Type Menu. Ed's figures are listed below.

This information has been entered in a worksheet called PROFITS. The cell that contains *1985* is cell A6. Either load or create this worksheet. At this point, the following steps must be performed to get the XY graph:

```
                    PROFIT
                              Inflation
       Year       Profit       Rate
       1985          70        3.5%
       1984          65        4.0%
       1983          50        4.0%
       1982          15        8.0%
       1981          20        6.0%
       1980         -50        9.8%
       1979          90        9.0%
```

1. Get the Graph Menu.

    /—Gets the Main Menu.

    G (F8)—Takes the Graph option.

2. Select the graph type.

    T (F2)—Selects the Type option of the Graph Menu.

    X (F4)—Tells VP-Planner to generate an XY graph.

3. Tell VP-Planner the A data range.

    A—Selects the A data range option from the Graph Menu.

    B6 [by manual pointer movement]—Positions the pointer at the first A range cell.

    .—Nails down the beginning of the range.

    B12 [by manual pointer movement]—Positions the pointer at the end of the range.

    ENTER—Submits the A data range to VP-Planner.

4. Tell VP-Planner the X data range.

    X—Selects the X data range option from the Graph Menu.

    C6 [by manual pointer movement]—Positions the pointer at the first X range cell.

    .—Nails down the beginning of the range.

    C12 [by manual pointer movement]—Positions the pointer at the end of the range.

    ENTER—Submits the X data range to VP-Planner.

5. Enter the titles for the graph.

    O (F7)—Selects the Options Menu.

    T (F4)—Selects the Titles option.

    F (F2)—Selects the First line.

    Ed's Supermarket—Identifies the first line title.

    ENTER—Submits the title to VP-Planner.

    T (F4)—Selects the Titles option.

    S (F3)—Selects the Second line.

    Profits Compared to Inflation '79-'85—Identifies the second title line.

    ENTER—Submits the title to VP-Planner.

    T (F4)—Selects the Titles option.

    X (F4)—Selects the X-axis title.

    Inflation—Identifies the X-axis title.

Figure 15.11
XY graph comparing profits
to inflation over a seven-year
period.

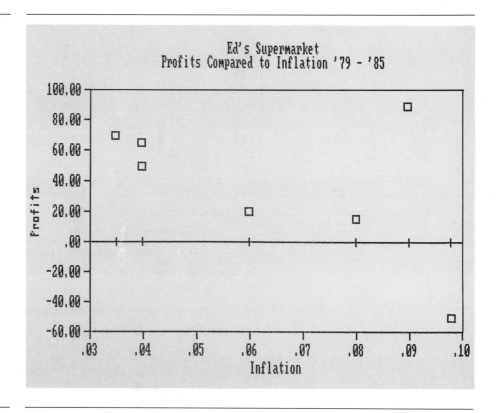

 ENTER—Submits the title to VP-Planner.

T (F4)—Selects the Titles option.

Y (F5)—Selects the Y-axis title.

Profits—Identifies the Y-axis title.

ENTER—Submits the title to VP-Planner.

6. Tell VP-Planner not to connect the data points with lines.

F (F3)—Selects the Format option.

G (F2)—Selects the Graph option.

S (F3)—Selects the Symbols-only option.

Q. (F9)—Quits the Format Menu and returns to the Options Menu.

Q (F10)—Quits the Options Menu and returns to the Graph Menu.

7. View the graph, using the V command. It should now look like the graph shown in Figure 15.11.

8. Depress any key to return to the Graph Menu; then print the graph.

Formatting the X and Y Numeric Scaling.

9. Change the format of the X and Y numeric scaling—the manner in which the scale numbers are displayed.

O (F7)—Selects the Options Menu.

S (F6)—Selects the Scale option.

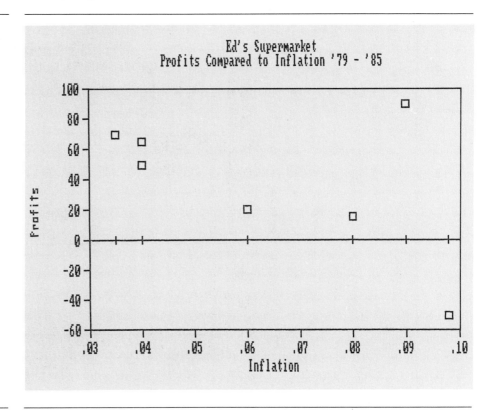

Figure 15.12
Reformatted XY graph comparing profits to inflation over a seven-year period.

Y (F3)—Specifies the Y scale as the scale to be changed.

F (F6)—Selects the Format option from the Scale Menu.

F (F2)—Selects the Fixed option of the Format Menu.

0—Enter a zero.

ENTER—Changes the format to zero decimal positions.

Q (F7)—Quits the Scale Menu and returns to the Options Menu.

Q (F10)—Quits the Options Menu and returns to the Graph Menu.

10. View the graph, using the V command. It should now look like the graph shown in Figure 15.12.

11. Print the graph.

Labeling Graph Data Points

XY graphs can sometimes be rather hard to read. The data points represented are not properly labeled because the X option (typically used for labeling the X-axis) is used for plotting a set of data points. This can be eliminated through the use of the Data Labels feature of VP-Planner. Using the Data Labels feature involves the following steps:

1. Establish the Data Labels.

O (F7)— Selects the Options Menu.

D (F9)—Selects the Data Labels option of the Options Menu.

Figure 15.13

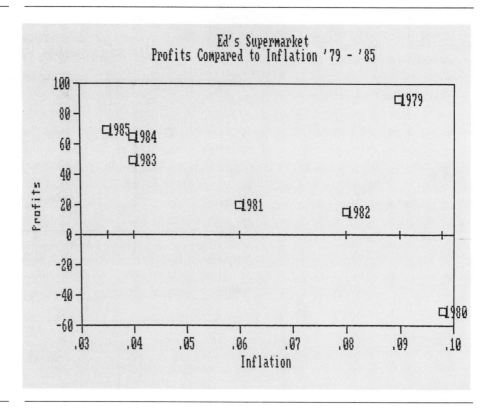

A (F2)—Selects the A data range option.

A6 [by manual pointer movement]—Positions the pointer at the first A range cell.

.—Nails down the beginning of the range.

A12 [by manual pointer movement]—Positions the pointer at the end of the range.

ENTER—Submits the A Data Labels range to VP-Planner.

R (F5)—Tells VP-Planner to place the labels to the right of the data point representation (square).

Q (F8)—Quits the Data Labels Menu.

Q (F10)—Quits the Options Menu.

2. Tell VP-Planner to display the graph shown in Figure 15.13.

Chapter Review

To build a graph using VP-Planner, you must do the following: (1) select a worksheet file that contains information you wish to graph; (2) obtain the Graph Menu; (3) select the type of graph you want, and identify the pieces of data to be included; (4) enter any additional titles, labels, and legends; (5) view the graph on the screen; (6) make any further changes or enhancements.

The VP-Planner package allows you to develop the following graphs: line, bar, XY, stacked bar, and pie. Each of these graphs, except the XY graph, is one-dimensional—meaning that only one set of data points interacts across an unchanging X-axis. If you wish to graph two sets of data points against each other, you must use an XY graph.

Each of the graph selections, except the pie chart, can use more than one set of Y data points. Each subsequent set of data points produces an additional line or bar, depending on the type of graph selected. The pie chart, by its very nature, is only able to plot one set of data points at a time.

After a graph has been finished, the settings for that graph can be saved onto an area of the worksheet by using the Name option of the Graph Menu. At this point, another graph, termed the "current" graph, can be built. You can make the graph settings you previously saved become the current graph by entering the Name option and specifying which group of graph settings is to be used. The graph itself can be saved, too, but it (unlike the graph setting) is saved to disk as a separate file. A graph can be printed by using the Print command.

Key Terms and Concepts

ABCDEF commands	Print command
bar graph	Quit option
Create command	Reset command
Delete command	Save command
Format option	Scale option
F10 Graph key	stacked bar graph
Graph Menu	Titles option
Grid option	Type option
Legend option	Use command
line graph	View command
Look command	X command
Name option	X (horizontal) axis
Options	XY graph
Pie chart	Y (vertical) axis

Chapter Quiz

Multiple Choice

1. Which of the following graph types can only have one set of Y data points:
   a. Line
   b. Bar
   c. Pie
   d. Stacked bar
   e. XY
   f. All of the above can have more than one set of Y data points

2. Which of the following is not considered to be a title:
   a. The two lines at the top of the graph
   b. X-axis title
   c. Y-axis title
   d. Legends
   e. All of the above are titles

3. ABCDEF are:
   a. Grades assigned for this exercise
   b. X-axis data points
   c. Y-axis data points
   d. Data point labels
   e. None of the above responses is correct

4. Which of the following is not a feature of Print:
   a. Exists as a separate program
   b. Allows you to specify up to four fonts in a graph
   c. Allows you to batch-print graphs
   d. Displays all graph files on your data disk
   e. None of the above is a feature of Print

5. Which of the following statements is not true about the name feature of the Graph Menu?
   a. The stored graph settings are all active.
   b. The "current" graph settings can be saved onto the worksheet using this option.
   c. When the worksheet is saved onto disk, any graph settings are also saved.
   d. You can delete select graph settings individually or all at once.
   e. All of the above statements are true.

True/False

6. Print is one of the nonintegrated features of VP-Planner.

7. Once a set of graph settings is selected via the Use option of the Name Menu, the graph built with these settings is automatically displayed on the screen.

8. It is possible to reset selected parts of a graph or the complete graph.

9. Using legends allows you to distinguish among the various sets of Y data points.

10. The XY graph is the only VP-Planner graph type that allows you to create a two-dimensional graph.

Answers

1. c & e   2. d   3. c   4. e   5. a   6. f   7. t   8. t   9. t   10. t

Exercises

1. Define or describe each of the following terms:
   a. X-axis
   b. Y-axis
   c. legend
   d. scaling

2. List the steps involved in building and then printing a graph.
   a.

   b.

   c.

   d.

   e.

   f.

g.

h.

3. VP-Planner automatically places the extension _____ on the file of any graph that is saved onto disk.

4. The _____ option allows you to label each set of Y data points, in order to make a graph more readable.

5. Graph settings can be saved onto the worksheet using the _____ _____ option of the Graph Menu.

6. The _____ command of the Graph Menu enables you to see the graph.

7. The _____ command is used when you wish to delete a portion of all of the current graph settings.

8. The _____ command is used to store a graph onto disk.

9. Any range can be canceled by pressing the _____ _____ key.

10. The format in which numeric data appears on a graph can be controlled by using the _____ option.

11. The _____ axis is usually enlisted to produce labels across the bottom of the graph.

12. Explain the difference between a one-dimension graph and a two-dimensional graph.

13. _____ bar charts combine entries into one set of Y data points, whereas _____ bar charts allow you to see differences immediately by comparing bars.

14. _____ allows you to specify a number of graphs to be printed and then leave to do whatever you want.

Computer Exercises

In building the following graphs, feel free to refer to the graph command structure in Appendix D. This will help you greatly in locating the various graph commands.

1. Retrieve the CH11EXR5 worksheet file.
   a. Generate a pie chart, using the This Year column data.
   b. Generate a bar graph, using the same data. Save these graph settings to a named area called TYEAR.
   c. Compare the two years of sales, using a line graph. Save these graph settings to a named area called TYLYSALE.
   d. Generate a bar graph of the named graph TYEAR, using all the stored graph settings, but change the column to be graphed to Last Year.
   e. Generate a line graph of the named graph TYLYSALE, and enter legends at the bottom of the graph. Save these settings to a named area called LEGENDS. Print the graph.

f. Using the TYLYSALE settings, change the graph type to a bar graph. Print the graph.

    g. Enter the following headings:

1st	FRED'S AUTO SALES
2nd	YEARLY SALES COMPARISON
X-Axis	Sales Reps
Y-Axis	Dollar Sales

    h. Print the graph.

    i. Save the graph settings to a named area BARTITLE.

    j. Exit from the Graph Menu. Change the contents of cells in the sales range. View the graph by depressing the F10 key.

    k. Resave the worksheet file. This will also save the named graphs.

2. Retrieve the CH11EXR7 worksheet file.

    a. Graph the expenses for each year, using a line graph. Enter appropriate headings, labels, and legends. Print the graph.

    b. Generate a pie chart for each year's expenses. Print them. Save the graph settings using the names PIE1 and PIE2. You will have to reset the B data range to accomplish this.

Chapter Objectives

After completing this chapter, you should be able to:

Discuss the basic concepts of VP-Planner data management

Discuss how data management fields and records are handled

Discuss the various options of the data management menu

Discuss how to define a data base to VP-Planner

Discuss how to set up a Criterion range

Discuss how to locate or find records in the data base

Discuss how the Output and Extract commands interact

Discuss how the Unique and Delete commands work

Discuss how the data base statistical functions work

Discuss the External menu commands

Discuss how to access a dBASE file

Discuss the Browse command

The data management feature of VP-Planner, sometimes referred to as data base, is the third integrated function of VP-Planner. The data management feature of VP-Planner is accessed by issuing the / Data command. Once the Data Menu is displayed, either of the two VP-Planner data management features can be accessed. The first, Query, is used for building and manipulating VP-Planner data bases (tables). The second, External, is used to access dBASE files and to load all or part of a dBASE file into the worksheet. Once the dBASE data have been loaded into the worksheet, they can be manipulated like any other VP-Planner data base by using the / Data Query commands.

VP-Planner Data Management Versus dBASE III

The first difference between VP-Planner's low-level data base and dBASE's is in how the two software packages store data. dBASE stores data in a disk file, whereas VP-Planner stores records in a worksheet. The data in a dBASE application are not visible to a user; instead, file manipulation commands are issued to access or list the information contained in a file. In contrast, VP-Planner's information, since it is contained in a worksheet, is directly visible to the worksheet user.

A **VP-Planner data management file** is composed of one or more rows containing one or more columns. This method of file storage sets certain limitations on VP-Planner data management files, the most important of which is that file size is limited by the amount of available RAM memory on the computer. A computer with 512K or even 640K of RAM might not be enough for a large data file.

A VP-Planner data base can only be accessed sequentially. If a view of the file in some other order is desired, the data base must be rearranged using VP-Planner's sort feature. Unfortunately, the sort feature is extremely slow with larger data bases. A data base with 2,000 records, for example, can take hours to sort.

Data management in VP-Planner operates in **immediate mode**—that is, commands are issued from the keyboard. dBASE provides the ability to incorporate file manipulation commands in separate programs and thereafter to manipulate files via the stored instructions. A security problem exists with VP-Planner data management files (but not with dBASE files) because all the data are immediately available to a user. Fields cannot be hidden from a user via programmed command files.

The concepts of *record* and *field* also differ in the two systems. A **VP-Planner record** does not have to have the length and data characteristics of its component field(s) described: it is simply a row on a worksheet. The **fields** are columns in the row in which data are stored; a one-line heading at the top of each column functions as the **field name**.

Because of these limitations, VP-Planner's data management capabilities are somewhat limited. However, VP-Planner does an excellent job with small files dealing with fairly simple applications, and its Data Management function is easy to use because it does not involve a separate syntax and can readily be incorporated into existing worksheets.

Introduction to VP-Planner Data Management

Ed has requested the development of a check register application to record his checks, keep track of the balance, and help him in reconciling his checkbook. He also wants to be able to track the checks by budget category and by tax deductibility, and Ed has requested that the application be placed on VP-Planner.

After examination of the application, the following worksheet is designed to solve his problem.

Each row (record) of the worksheet holds information about a check that has been written. The information is divided into six fields of data: check number (NO.), the date the check was written (DATE), check payee (PAYEE), check amount (AMOUNT), budget category (BUDGET), and tax deductibility (TAX). The name of the application, PERSONAL CHECK REGISTER, and the current checkbook balance are at the top of the worksheet.

```
PERSONAL CHECK REGISTER


                              BALANCE        338.89

------------------------------------------------------------------------

  NO.    DATE            PAYEE             AMOUNT     BUDGET    TAX

        08-Feb-85  Deposit Paycheck       1,850.00
  858  09-Feb-85  Jewel Supermarket        (45.60)    food
  859  10-Feb-85  Stroink Pathology Lab    (30.00)    med       x
  860  10-Feb-85  Harjak Motors            (45.55)    car
  861  11-Feb-85  Jean's Flowers           (15.00)    fun
  862  11-Feb-85  Dr. Theobald             (30.00)    med       x
  863  11-Feb-85  St. Joseph's Hospital    (35.00)    med       x
  864  13-Feb-85  Osco Pharmacy            (12.73)    med       x
  865  15-Feb-85  Illinois Power           (79.84)    util
  866  15-Feb-85  Osco Pharmacy            (20.00)    med       x
  867  15-Feb-85  Jewel Supermarket        (75.34)    food
  868  16-Feb-85  Ed Curry Plumbing       (115.00)    rep
  869  16-Feb-85  General Telephone Co.    (45.24)    util
  870  16-Feb-85  Braden Auditorium        (47.00)    fun
  871  17-Feb-85  Jewel Supermarket        (22.75)    food
  872  17-Feb-85  Illinois Power - Gas    (114.00)    util
  873  21-Feb-85  Bloomington Federal Bank (710.00)   mtge
  874  21-Feb-85  Osco Pharmacy            (18.00)    med       x
  875  21-Feb-85  Home Sweet Home Mission  (50.00)    char      x
```

It is important to be aware that VP-Planner treats the column headings as field names. Column headings play a critical role in data management and are used in just about all steps of data manipulation. Where more than one line of headings occur, only the last line can be used by VP-Planner.

Load the file EDCHECK, or follow the set of instructions given below.

The first step in building the worksheet is to set the various column widths. Use the column widths given below. Remember, the column width commands are: / Worksheet Col-Wid Set. After you've reset the column widths, enter the appropriate headings in row 4; then enter the identifying information.

Column	Width	Heading
A	5	NO.
B	10	^DATE
C	25	^PAYEE
D	10	^AMOUNT
E	2	
F	9	BUDGET
G	9	TAX

A1   PERSONAL CHECK REGISTER
C2   "BALANCE
D2   @SUM(D5.D23)
A3   Enter dashes for this cell, and copy across to the other cells.

You must now place the above checkbook entries (records) in the worksheet.

VP-Planner Data Base Commands

VP-Planner's data base manipulation commands are accessed through the Data option of the Main Menu.

VP-Planner Query Menu Commands

Query Menu

The Query option of the Data Menu provides the actual data base capability. The **Query Menu** contains the following options:

Input Criterion Output Find Extract Unique Delete Reset Quit

Input. The **Input option**, which must be selected before you choose any data base manipulation commands, is used to define the limits of the data base to VP-Planner. The first row of the data base contains the field labels for VP-Planner. (VP-Planner treats upper- and lower-case characters the same in labels.)

Criterion. The **Criterion Range option** determines selection or search criteria for extracting or finding information in the data base. The range will have at least two rows: one for the heading, and one for the selection or search criteria. The first criterion row has one or more column headings copied from the first row of the data base; it is usually better to copy these headings into the criterion range than to enter them manually. Any imbedded blanks included in the data base labels but not included in criterion labels, or vice versa, will adversely affect a search. The second row, which is left blank, is the row where the various search or selection criteria are entered.

Output. The **Output Range option** is used in defining the area that is to hold "reports" of information that meets the conditions established in the criterion range.

Find. The **Find command** moves the pointer (which is expanded to appear over an entire record) to the first record that meets the condition(s) established in the criterion range. Any other records that meet the criteria can also be accessed by depressing the up and down arrow keys. The down arrow key moves the pointer to the next record below the pointer's present position that meets the criteria, and the up arrow moves the pointer to the next record above the pointer's present position that meets the criteria. When the last record that meets the criteria has been accessed, the computer will beep. You can move the pointer to the first or last record in the data base by depressing the HOME or END key, respectively. Depressing the right or left arrow keys moves the cursor within the pointer. Depressing the ENTER or ESC key cancels the search and returns you to the Query Menu.

Extract. The **Extract command** creates the reports in the output range by extracting records from the data base and copying them into the report area.

Unique. If there are several records with the characteristics specified in the criterion range, the **Unique option** allows you to have only one of each grouping copied into the output area.

Delete. The **Delete command** removes records that meet the criteria established in the criterion range, and then it compresses the data base (removes any blank rows).

Reset. When selected, the **Reset option** clears any previously established input, criterion, and output specifications.

Quit. The **Quit option** takes you out of the Query Menu and returns you to ready mode.

Building a Data Base and Accessing Information

The steps in building a data base and accessing information from it are as follows:

1. The data base (range) must be described in VP-Planner, and the headings row must be included in the range. This is accomplished via the Input option.
2. The criterion range must be built, and the search criteria must be specified to VP-Planner.
3. If an output report is desired, the output range has to be defined; but if you just wish to locate records via the Find command, it does not.

The headings included in the criterion and output ranges must be very similar to the headings contained in the input range because the output range headings will determine which fields are copied from the input range. If a field heading is not specified, the information in that field will not be copied from the input to the output range.

Use the following commands to describe your data base to VP-Planner:

/—Invokes the Main Menu.

D (F9)—Selects the Data option.

Q (F5)—Selects the Query option from the Data Menu.

I (F2)—Defines the input range of the data base.

A4.G23 [by entering cell addresses or by pointing]—Establishes the range of the data base

ENTER—Tells VP-Planner to accept the data base range.

Q (F10)—Quits the Query Menu.

The Criterion Range

For simple types of search (a **simple find**), the criterion range will consist of two rows: the first row holds the appropriate criterion range headings (**field names**); the second contains the search criteria, in the form of values or formulas.

Building the criterion range begins with copying the column headings contained in row 4 to another location on the worksheet (row 25). Then you must establish the criterion range by entering the following commands:

/—Invokes the Main Menu.

D (F9)—Takes the Data option.

Q (F5)—Selects the Query option from the Data Menu.

C (F3)—Selects the Criterion option.

A25.G26 [by entering the cell addresses or by pointing]—Establishes the criterion range.

ENTER—Tells VP-Planner to execute the command.

Q (F10)—Quits the Query Menu.

In order to locate all the records in the medical budget category, you must first set up a search criterion like the following:

NO.	DATE	PAYEE	AMOUNT	BUDGET	TAX
				med	

To find the desired records, enter the / Data Query Find commands, and use the up arrow and down arrow keys to locate the records. Then depress the ENTER or ESC key when you are finished and want to return to the Query Menu.

To locate all tax deductible records, use a / Range Erase command on the budget cell and place an *x* in the tax criterion cell. The following criterion is appropriate:

NO.	DATE	PAYEE	AMOUNT	BUDGET	TAX
					x

Since the input range and the criterion range have already been established, and since the Find instruction has already been executed, a shortcut can be taken. Instead of finding these records by entering the / Data Query Find commands, you can simply depress the **F7 Query function key** and move the pointer as specified above.

Now erase the contents of the tax criterion cell, using the / Range Erase command, and locate all the records that contain an amount greater than $100. This task requires the following criterion range:

NO.	DATE	PAYEE	AMOUNT	BUDGET	TAX
			+D5<-100		

You will notice that a 0 appears in the tax entry cell, indicating that the condition for cell D5 is false. This doesn't give you much information; it would be more meaningful to have a display of the search formula used for the entire search than to have the result of the comparison for a single cell. Change the formula to text via the / Range Format Text command. Press the F7 Query function key.

Now find any checks that have an amount greater than $100 and belong to the mortgage budget category. The following criterion range is called for:

NO.	DATE	PAYEE	AMOUNT	BUDGET	TAX
			+D5<-100	mtge	

The formula happens, in this case, to go in the column (field) being searched, but it could just as easily be placed in any other field. The next criterion range example (shown below) locates any record that has a check amount greater than $100. The search formula has been placed in the Payee field, but VP-Planner knows that you are looking for the check amount, since the column specified in the search is the Amount (column D).

Before you enter the following criterion range, make certain that you erased the budget and amount criterion fields:

NO.	DATE	PAYEE	AMOUNT	BUDGET	TAX
		+D5<-100			

VP-Planner also allows you to use the following **wild card characters** in the search criteria:

> *—Finds entries that contain the same value to the left of the asterisk. For example, *for** would find *fortune, formula,* and *fortuitous.*

> ?—Finds entries that contain the same value at every position besides the question mark. For example, *c?t* would find *cat, cut,* and *cot.*

> ˉ—Finds entries that do not contain the same value at every named position. For example, ˉ*ll** finds *formula, cat,* and *ignoramus*—but not *Ilium.*

Find any record that has an entry in the Payee column starting with *Il.* The following criterion range is needed:

NO.	DATE	PAYEE	AMOUNT	BUDGET	TAX
		Il*			

Find any record having a budget entry other than *med.* The appropriate criterion range is as follows:

NO.	DATE	PAYEE	AMOUNT	BUDGET	TAX
				~med	

Find any record having a nonempty budget entry that does not start with the letter *m.* Use the following criterion range:

NO.	DATE	PAYEE	AMOUNT	BUDGET	TAX
				~m*	

The above examples all illustrate how a simple search or a search using an **"and" condition** can be performed. Establishing a search with an **"or" condition** requires adding an additional row to the bottom of the criterion range after the Criterion option is selected. Before you can return to performing a simple search, the criterion range must be reduced by one row.

Find all records that have either a *med* budget designation and an amount greater than $25 or a *util* budget designation and an amount greater than $100. The criterion range is expressed as follows:

NO.	DATE	PAYEE	AMOUNT	BUDGET	TAX
			+D5<-25	med	
			+D5<-100	util	

What happens if you want to initiate a new search that can be ordered in a one-line criterion range, but you forget to shrink the criterion range from three rows back to two? After entering the criterion range and pressing the F7 key, you will find that every record in the data base is selected. This is because a blank row tells VP-Planner to do so. You must shrink the criterion range back to two rows to avoid this problem.

Output and Extract

The Output and Extract options of the Query Menu allow a user to compile a list of records that correspond to certain predetermined criteria. The process of compiling the report is performed by the Extract command; but before records can be extracted, an area of the worksheet known as the output region must be defined to contain them.

The output region is formed by copying or entering the labels of the fields that you desire to have in your report. For example, you can copy the labels from the criterion region and use them for the output region; then you take the Output option from the Query Menu and define the output range to VP-Planner as the line of field headings. Any rows under the row of field headings that are needed to hold the desired records are automatically added to the output range.

After the output range has been defined, the Extract option can be used to instruct VP-Planner to search the data base in accordance with the criteria established in the criterion range and to place any records meeting those criteria in the output range. Any time the Extract command is executed, all records currently in the output range are erased; only the field headings remain from one extraction to another. The size of the output range is tracked by VP-Planner, and the only limit on it is the number of rows remaining beneath the Output headings that have been defined to VP-Planner. If 1,000 rows remain, room remains for 1,000 records in the output range.

After the output range has been defined to VP-Planner and an extraction command has been executed, other criteria can be entered with the worksheet in ready mode. A new extraction can then be executed simply by depressing the F7 Query function key. If you want to create a hard copy listing of these various reports, you can command VP-Planner to print out the output range between extraction commands.

On the worksheet, create an output range that contains the existing headings from the criterion range. It will also start in row 29.

First, copy the criterion headings.

/—Invokes the Main Menu.

C (F4)—Selects the Copy option.

A25.G25 [by entering the addresses or by pointing]—Establishes the "From" range.

ENTER—Tells VP-Planner that the "From" range is established.

A29 [by entering the address or by pointing]—Establishes the "To" range.

ENTER—Tells VP-Planner to execute the move.

Erase any existing criteria entries. Now, place *food* in the budget criterion cell.

1. Tell VP-Planner the output range.

    /—Invokes the Main Menu.

    D (F9)—Selects the Data option.

    Q (F5)—Selects the Query option of the Data Menu.

O (F4)—Selects the Output option of the Query Menu.

A29.G29 [by pointer movement or address entry]—Establishes the range of the output range.

ENTER—Tells VP-Planner to accept the output range definition.

2. Shrink the criterion range by one row.

C (F3)—Selects the Criterion option.

Up Arrow—Shrinks the criterion range to two rows.

3. Create the Output report by taking the Extract option (E) from the Query Menu.

You should now see the following criterion and output ranges on your screen:

NO.	DATE	PAYEE	AMOUNT	BUDGET	TAX
				food	

NO.	DATE	PAYEE	AMOUNT	BUDGET	TAX
858	09-Feb-85	Jewel Supermarket	(45.60)	food	
867	15-Feb-85	Jewel Supermarket	(75.34)	food	
871	17-Feb-85	Jewel Supermarket	(22.75)	food	

At this point, you can select the Quit option of the Query Menu and afterward enter new selection criteria for output records. Then you can direct VP-Planner to extract the desired records and place them in the output area by depressing the F7 Query function key.

You may wish to see only records of tax deductible payments. To get this listing, erase any existing criterion range entries with the Range Erase command. Then enter an x in the tax criterion cell, and press the F7 Query function key. You should now see the following criterion and output ranges on your screen:

NO.	DATE	PAYEE	AMOUNT	BUDGET	TAX
					x

NO.	DATE	PAYEE	AMOUNT	BUDGET	TAX
859	10-Feb-85	Stroink Pathology Lab	(30.00)	med	x
862	11-Feb-85	Dr. Theobald	(30.00)	med	x
863	11-Feb-85	St. Josephs Hospital	(35.00)	med	x
864	13-Feb-85	Osco Pharmacy	(12.79)	med	x
866	15-Feb-85	Osco Pharmacy	(20.00)	med	x
874	21-Feb-85	Osco Pharmacy	(18.00)	med	x
875	21-Feb-85	Home Sweet Home Mission	(50.00)	char	x

As you can see, the Extract feature of VP-Planner data management offers a user tremendous power to obtain different views of records contained in a data base. You can use as simple or complex criteria as you desire for extracting records.

Several large accounting firms have used VP-Planner's Extract option to examine a company's checking account during an auditing engagement. They can take the computerized records containing the checking account information and pass them to a VP-Planner worksheet. The data management feature can then be used to extract the various groupings of records that the auditors feel should be examined. Using this feature drastically reduces the amount of time that must be spent on certain parts of an audit.

Unique and Delete

Two other searches are provided by the data management option of VP-Planner. The first, Unique, enables the user to print only nonduplicate records into an output range; the other, Delete, allows a user to remove any records from a data base that meet certain criteria.

 Unique. Ed has lost his listing of budget categories and would like a new listing based on the budget entries contained in the data base. This is an excellent application for the Unique command, which will only allow one occurrence of a budget category in a list.

For this application, redefine the output range to contain only the budget category. This requires Range Erasing of any existing output range, followed by replacement with a single budget field. You should also erase any entries in the criterion range: all records are to be included in this search. Now you are ready to redefine the output range as the budget field. Select the Unique option on the Query Menu. Your worksheet criterion and output areas should look as follows:

```
NO.   DATE          PAYEE          AMOUNT   BUDGET   TAX

BUDGET

food
med
car
fun
util
rep
mtge
char
```

The blank entry above is the result of the blank budget field entry of the deposit. As you see, none of the budget entries is duplicated.

Delete. The Delete option is used to remove any unwanted or unneeded records from the data base. When executed, the Delete command automatically compresses the remaining records in the data base, removing all gaps and blank records (rows) in the data base.

The criteria for the records to be deleted must be placed in the criterion range. It is usually safest to review records with the extract command before deleting them. When you are certain that the Extract command has worked properly, you can feel sure that the Delete command will work, too.

Ed wrote a check to the Braden Auditorium for concert tickets. Unfortunately for Ed, the auditorium is sold out for the concert and has returned Ed's check. Ed would now like to remove the unwanted check and adjust the balance for his worksheet.

Just so you're entirely safe, give your output area the same headings as the criterion range by copying the headings from the latter. You must also redefine the output range to VP-Planner, using the Query Menu option, in order to hold the entire heading line.

Now, go to the payee field of the criterion range and enter *Bra** to select the Braden Auditorium check for extraction. Invoke the Query Menu and give the Extract command to VP-Planner. You should now have the following information in your criterion and output ranges:

NO.	DATE	PAYEE	AMOUNT	BUDGET	TAX
		Bra*			

NO.	DATE	PAYEE	AMOUNT	BUDGET	TAX
870	16-Feb-85	Braden Auditorium	(47.00)	fun	

When the check to be deleted from the data base is displayed, you can take the Delete option on the Query Menu. VP-Planner then asks if you want to cancel the command or delete records, and you affirm the Delete option. The before and after views of the data base are displayed below.

Before:

PERSONAL CHECK REGISTER

BALANCE   338.89

NO.	DATE	PAYEE	AMOUNT	BUDGET	TAX
	08-Feb-85	Deposit Paycheck	1,850.00		
858	09-Feb-85	Jewel Supermarket	(45.60)	food	
859	10-Feb-85	Stroink Pathology Lab	(30.00)	med	x
860	10-Feb-85	Harjak Motors	(45.55)	car	
861	11-Feb-85	Jean's Flowers	(15.00)	fun	
862	11-Feb-85	Dr. Theobald	(30.00)	med	x
863	11-Feb-85	St. Josephs Hospital	(35.00)	med	x
864	13-Feb-85	Osco Pharmacy	(12.79)	med	x
865	15-Feb-85	Illinois Power	(79.84)	util	
866	15-Feb-85	Osco Pharmacy	(20.00)	med	x
867	15-Feb-85	Jewel Supermarket	(75.34)	food	
868	16-Feb-85	Ed Curry Plumbing	(115.00)	rep	
869	16-Feb-85	General Telephone Co.	(45.24)	util	
870	16-Feb-85	Braden Auditorium	(47.00)	fun	
871	17-Feb-85	Jewel Supermarket	(22.75)	food	
872	17-Feb-85	Illinois Power - Gas	(114.00)	util	
873	21-Feb-85	Bloomington Federal Bank	(710.00)	mtge	
874	21-Feb-85	Osco Pharmacy	(18.00)	med	x
875	21-Feb-85	Home Sweet Home Mission	(50.00)	char	x

After:

PERSONAL CHECK REGISTER

BALANCE   385.89

NO.	DATE	PAYEE	AMOUNT	BUDGET	TAX
	08-Feb-85	Deposit Paycheck	1,850.00		
858	09-Feb-85	Jewel Supermarket	(45.60)	food	
859	10-Feb-85	Stroink Pathology Lab	(30.00)	med	x

```
860 10-Feb-85 Harjak Motors              (45.55)   car
861 11-Feb-85 Jean's Flowers             (15.00)   fun
862 11-Feb-85 Dr. Theobald               (30.00)   med        x
863 11-Feb-85 St. Josephs Hospital       (35.00)   med        x
864 13-Feb-85 Osco Pharmacy              (12.79)   med        x
865 15-Feb-85 Illinois Power             (79.84)   util
866 15-Feb-85 Osco Pharmacy              (20.00)   med        x
867 15-Feb-85 Jewel Supermarket          (75.34)   food
868 16-Feb-85 Ed Curry Plumbing         (115.00)   rep
869 16-Feb-85 General Telephone Co.      (45.24)   util
871 17-Feb-85 Jewel Supermarket          (22.75)   food
872 17-Feb-85 Illinois Power - Gas      (114.00)   util
873 21-Feb-85 Bloomington Federal Bank  (710.00)   mtge
874 21-Feb-85 Osco Pharmacy              (18.00)   med        x
875 21-Feb-85 Home Sweet Home Mission    (50.00)   char       x
```

Check 870 has been deleted from the data base, the data base has been compressed, and the checkbook balance has been updated.

VP-Planner Statistical Functions for Data Base

In designing the data management facility for VP-Planner, it was decided to include **statistical functions** for manipulating numeric data in a data base. These functions are similar in nature to the regular VP-Planner statistical functions and contain the same names with a leading @D to denote that they are data base statistical functions, but they were adapted for use in a data base. The VP-Planner statistical data base functions are:

```
@DCOUNT
@DAVG
@DMIN
@DMAX
@DSTD
@DVAR
```

Each of these functions has the following format:

```
@Function Name(Input Range,Offset,Criterion Range)
```

The input range is typically the same size as the data base. Keep in mind that if you plan to copy these formulas you may have to provide absolute cell references.

The Offset tells VP-Planner which field to use from the data base in the function. A 0 tells VP-Planner to use the first column; 1 tells VP-Planner to use the second column.

The criterion range portion of the formula gives the location of the criterion range specifying the criteria to be used in generating the statistics.

 Ed wants some summary statistics about his checking account activity. Specifically, he wants information about number of checks written, average check amount, high check amount, and low check amount, and he wants the summary to be in the following form:

```
Criterion      CHECK STATISTICS
AMOUNT         Number of Checks              17
               Average Amount           -86.12
               Highest Check Amount       -710
               Smallest Check Amount    -12.79
```

To accomplish this, you must erase the existing criterion and output ranges. The new criterion range will consist of *Criterion* and *AMOUNT*, the latter entry telling VP-Planner that all entries from offset column 3 are to be used in the calculations.

Enter the following information in the designated cells:

```
A25 Criterion
C25 CHECK STATISTICS
A26 AMOUNT
C26 Number of Checks
C27 Average Amount
C28 Highest Check Amount
C29 Smallest Check Amount
D26 @DCOUNT(A5..G22,3,A25..A26)
D27 @DAVG(A5..G22,3,A25..A26)
D28 @DMIN(A5..G22,3,A25..A26)
D29 @DMAX(A5..G22,3,A25..A26)
```

Format cells D26 to D29 for fixed decimals with two positions to the right of the decimal point.

You must begin the Input range at cell A5 in order to avoid including the deposit record in the areas to be examined by the functions. You must also reverse the @DMIN and @DMAX functions, since you are dealing with negative numbers. The Criterion range must be referenced in each formula to establish which parts of the column are to be included. Format the receiving cells to hold two decimal positions.

The checkbook worksheet should now appear as follows:

```
PERSONAL CHECK REGISTER

                              BALANCE        385.89

------------------------------------------------------------------------

NO.    DATE          PAYEE              AMOUNT       BUDGET    TAX
       08-Feb-85  Deposit Paycheck     1,850.00
858  09-Feb-85  Jewel Supermarket        (45.60)     food
859  10-Feb-85  Stroink Pathology Lab    (30.00)     med       x
860  10-Feb-85  Harjak Motors            (45.55)     car
861  11-Feb-85  Jean's Flowers           (15.00)     fun
862  11-Feb-85  Dr. Theobald             (30.00)     med       x
863  11-Feb-85  St. Josephs Hospital     (35.00)     med       x
864  13-Feb-85  Osco Pharmacy            (12.79)     med       x
865  15-Feb-85  Illinois Power           (79.84)     util
866  15-Feb-85  Osco Pharmacy            (20.00)     med       x
867  15-Feb-85  Jewel Supermarket        (75.34)     food
868  16-Feb-85  Ed Curry Plumbing       (115.00)     rep
869  16-Feb-85  General Telephone Co.    (45.24)     util
871  17-Feb-85  Jewel Supermarket        (22.75)     food
872  17-Feb-85  Illinois Power - Gas    (114.00)     util
873  21-Feb-85  Bloomington Federal Bank (710.00)    mtge
874  21-Feb-85  Osco Pharmacy            (18.00)     med       x
875  21-Feb-85  Home Sweet Home Mission  (50.00)     char      x

Criterion      CHECK STATISTICS

AMOUNT         Number of Checks           17
               Average Amount            -86.12
               Highest Check Amount     -710
               Smallest Check Amount     -12.79
```

The / Data External DBase Menu is used for building, accessing, and retrieving information from dBASE data files. Either dBASE II or dBASE III files can be built, accessed, and manipulated. Once the DBase command is issued, the menu below is displayed.

Since the objective of this portion of the chapter is to show you how to load and manipulate dBASE files rather than build them (which is covered in the dBASE portion of the textbook), some of the commands will be covered in a summative fashion. If you desire to build a dBASE file using VP-Planner, please refer to the software documentation manual.

```
TotRetr  AllStore  Define  Browse  RetrTbl/Cell  StoreTbl/Cell  Quit
```

TotRetr

The TotRetr option is used to transfer data that have been specified in a / Data External DBase Create, / Data External DBase Define Table, or / Data External DBase Define Join command.

WARNING The TotRetr command affects *all* dBASE-file tables on a current worksheet. In most cases, it's preferable to limit retrieval to the current table or cell. Please refer to the / Data External DBase RetrTbl/Cell command discussed later.

Once this command has been issued, data will be transferred from dBASE files to all defined cells in the current worksheet.

AllStore

The AllStore option transfers all data in the current worksheet defined with the / Data External DBase Create, the / Data External Define Table, or the / Data External DBase Define Join command to one or more dBASE files.

Define

The Define option is used to determine the criteria used for transferring data from a dBASE file (a file with a .DBF file extension) and a worksheet file. When this option is selected, the following submenu is displayed.

```
CreateFile  Table  Join  OneCell  (Define)
```

CreateFile. The CreateFile option is used to create a dBASE file. Since this topic is covered in the appropriate dBASE chapter, please refer to the software documentation.

Table. The Table option is used to define the criteria for retrieving a dBASE file to be placed in your worksheet. In executing this command, the pointer again plays an important role. The location of the pointer determines the physical location of the table that will be holding the dBASE records on the worksheet. Once the Table command has been issued, a menu containing the .DBF files is displayed. Make your selection by using the pointer to select the appropriate file, or by manually entering the appropriate file name.

For example, suppose that you wish to create a data base table beginning in cell A5. Before you invoke the Main Menu, you must move the pointer to cell A5. You can now issue the / Data External DBase Define Table command. When the listing of data base files is displayed, point to the PAYMAST file and depress the ENTER key. The line below now appears in your status line.

    RT;PAYMAST.DBF;

The RT indicates that this is a retrieve table definition, and the PAYMAST.DBF is the selected file.

Once the file has been selected, the appropriate fields from the file must be selected in the following fashion:

1. Use the left/right arrow keys to view the field names of the file.

2. Press the up arrow key to select the desired fields in the sequence that you want to appear in the worksheet. Each field selected is displayed on a line above the selection line as below:

RT;PAYMAST.DBF;EMPLOY:ID,EMP:NAM,PAY:RATE,YTD:GROSS,

   The RT indicates that this command is involved in setting up a retrieve table definition. The PAYMAST.DBF is the name of the file selected. The EMPLOY:ID, EMP:NAM, PAY:RATE, and YTD:GROSS entries are the names of the fields selected from the file structure.

3. When all desired fields have been selected, depress the ENTER key. This results in the following prompt appearing on the screen:

    Specify selection criteria: #

4. Depress the ENTER key if you want to load information from marked fields for all records in the file.

   You may wish to limit which records will be accessed. In that case, the following rules apply:

   a. The # symbol represents the record-number field. Use the left and right arrow keys to see the names of the other fields.

   b. Use the arrow key to select a field on which to impose selection criteria.

   c. Enter the selection criteria. You can use a literal criterion, a cell address, a range name, or a value.

   i. Selection criteria for numeric fields must be numeric.

   ii. Selection criteria for text fields or for logical fields must be enclosed in quotes.

   iii. Selection criteria for dBASE III date fields must be valid date numbers.

   iv. Expressions that are permitted as selection criteria are:

Expression		*Examples*
Relational operators	<	less than
	>	greater than
	=	equal to
	<>	not equal to
	<=	less than or equal to
	>=	greater than or equal to
	$	contains "string"
Numeric data	23	10.5
Text	"Peoria"	"61701"

Date	18352	62572
Cell reference	A1	IV221
Logical operators	.AND.	
	.OR.	
	.NOT.	

Sample criteria expressions

EMP:NAM="Jones"—Reads records whose EMP:NAM field contains "Jones".

EMP:NAM$"illia"—Reads records in which the string "illia" appears in the EMP:NAM field.

YTD:GROSS>1000—Reads records whose YTD:GROSS field contains an amount greater than 1000.

#>3. and .#<20—Read record numbers 4 through 19.

d. Press the down arrow key (or enter a new field name manually) to move back down to select another field name.

e. Repeat the above steps until all selection criteria are included. When you are finished, depress the ENTER key.

If all records from the selected file are not desired, the selection process then involves two additional steps: (1) selecting the appropriate selection field(s), and (2) entering the selection criteria expressions.

If you wished to only load those records whose YTD:GROSS field had an amount greater than 500, you need the following cell definition entry key strokes after defining which fields to include:

When you see the prompt Specify selection criteria: #, press the right arrow until the YTD:GROSS field is displayed on the screen. When the YTD:GROSS field name is visible, press the up arrow. Your cursor is now on the status line, and you can enter the >500 criterion. You should now see the following status line:

RT;PAYMAST.DBF;EMPLOY:ID,EMP:NAM,PAY:RATE,YTD:GROSS;YTD:GROSS>500

Your screen should now appear like the one below:

```
      A          B            C            D        E         F
 1
 2
 3
 4
 5PAYMAST    EMPLO       EMP:NAM        PAY:RATYTD:GROSS
```

Notice that the file name as well as all of the field names appear beginning in cell A5. The field names are centered automatically by VP-Planner within the cell. VP-Planner has also adjusted the width of each cell to correspond with the field size of each selected data base field.

WARNING You cannot copy cell A5, the cell with the data base file definition criteria to another cell. If this cell is included in a Copy command, VP-Planner will issue an error message. When you depress the ESC key, fields other than cell A5 will be copied.

It should be noted that if you wish to make changes in the selection criteria all that you have to do is position the pointer to the cell containing the definition/selection criteria (in this case cell A5), depress the F2 key to enter Edit mode, and make any necessary changes.

The cell definition is now complete and can be executed by in any of three ways:

1. Issuing the / Data External DBase TotRetr command.

2. Issuing the Total command from / Data External Define command menu.

3. Issuing the / Data External DBase RetrTbl/Cell command with the worksheet pointer on the defining cell (the cell in the upper left-hand corner) of the worksheet data base table.

Issue the / Data External DBase RetrTbl/Cell command, and your worksheet should appear like that below:

	A	B	C	D	E	F
1						
2						
3						
4						
5	PAYMAST	EMPLO	EMP:NAM	PAY:RAT	YTD:GROSS	
6		2 2870	Frank Terler	3.80	670.00	
7		3 4463	Edward Mockford	4.90	775.00	
8		4 4679	Kenneth Klass	4.90	780.00	
9		5 4908	Richard Payne	4.45	556.00	
10		6 5323	Pamela Rich	6.00	780.00	
11		7 5432	Alan Monroe	5.20	1340.00	
12		8 5649	Toni McCarthy	5.20	667.00	
13		10 5998	Paul Mish	4.90	887.00	
14		11 6324	Mark Tell	5.50	980.00	
15		12 8345	Thomas Momery	4.70	580.00	

Only those records with a YTD:AMOUNT field greater than 500 are loaded into the table.

Join. The **Join** command is used when you wish to create a table of records from a dBASE file that match, record-for-record, one or more fields in an existing data base table on the worksheet.

This option works much the same way as the Table option discussed previously. The difference is that with this option you match data in another dBASE file. This means that for a given record to be retrieved, the data contents in one or more selected fields must match the entries in the corresponding field(s) of at least one record in a previously defined worksheet data base table. When a data match is found, the record is retrieved and entered in the new Join table.

The fields to be matched must be of the same data type (text, numeric, date, and so on.) Matches are one-to-one correspondence only. This means that only the *first* data match encountered between a record in the retrieved file and a record in the existing worksheet data base table will appear in the Join table.

Steps in Joining a Table

1. Define the retrieval criteria for the first dBASE file using the Define Table command. Issue the Q command to return to ready mode.

2. Place the pointer in the first cell to the *right* of the last label defined for the first dBASE file in your worksheet.

3. Issue the / Data External DBase Define Join command.

4. Define the second file's retrieval criteria in the same way as the first, using the left and right arrow keys to view the field names and the up arrow key to select fields.

5. Define the selection criteria in the same way as described in the Define Table command discussed previously. Here, however, you must also match a field in the same file to a field of like data in the first file. In other words, you can use the cell address of a **field label** from the first file as a parameter of the selection criteria for the second file.

OneCell (Define). The OneCell option is used to set the criteria for retrieving a single value from an existing relational data base file. To obtain more information about this command, please refer to the software documentation manual.

Browse

The **Browse** command is used to literally browse the records of a selected dBASE file. While you are browsing a dBASE file with VP-Planner, you can edit, delete, or add new records to the file.

WARNING While you are in browse mode, never restart the computer, turn it off, or remove data disks. You can seriously damage your files in this fashion. Always exit the Browse screen and return to the worksheet before you stop VP-Planner.

The following browse conventions are used:

Pointer Movement.

Up and down arrow keys move the pointer up and down one record, respectively.

The ENTER key has the same affect as the down arrow key, but also moves the cursor to the first character in the next record.

The PG DN and PG UP keys scroll through the file a screen at a time.

WARNING Any changes you've made to a record are written to the file on disk when you scroll it off the screen.

The HOME key moves the pointer to the first record in the file.

The END key moves the pointer to the last record in the file.

The left and right arrow keys move the cursor one character to the left or right, respectively, within a record.

The CTRL key plus a right or left arrow moves the cursor to the first character in the next field in the direction of the arrow key.

The TAB key jumps the cursor to the right one-half screen at a time (toward the end of a record). The SHIFT + TAB keys jump the cursor to the left one-half screen at a time (toward the beginning of the record).

Record Editing. Move the cursor to the data base record that you wish to change and simply type the new data over the old. When editing a numeric field, enter only digits, decimal points, and/or a minus sign. Attempts to enter an incorrect data type are prevented by VP-Planner.

Adding Records. Records can only be added to the end of the file. To add records you must, therefore, move the cursor past the end of the file. VP-Planner will now respond with the prompt `Do you wish to add records? (Y/N)` If you respond with N, the cursor returns to the last record. If you respond with Y, a new, blank record is added to the end of the file. You now enter the new data into this blank record. Be sure to leave the first character of the record blank (this character position is used to indicate that a record has been deleted).

Deleting Records. To delete a record, move the cursor to the appropriate record and then move the cursor to the column labeled "DELETED" and type an asterisk (*). This is how records are marked for deletion by dBASE. Records marked with an asterisk are ignored by VP-Planner retrieval commands and by most dBASE commands. To "undelete" a record, place the cursor at the asterisk and press the Space Bar.

Locating a Character String. To locate a character string issue the command CTRL + F. Type the character string that you want VP-Planner to search for and then depress the ENTER key. The cursor will move to the first occurrence of the Find string after the current record. To find subsequent occurrences of the Find string, press CTRL + N. To find previous occurrences of the Find string, press CTRL + B.

Return to the Worksheet. To save your changes and return to the worksheet, press ESC. To return to the worksheet without saving changes to the disk, press CTRL + Break.

RetrTbl/Cell

The RetrTabl/Cell command retrieves values from dBASE file specified by a defining cell—that is, a cell defined for dBASE file access via one of the three following commands:

```
1. / Data External  DBase  Define  Create
2. / Data External  DBase  Define  Table
3. / Data External  DBase  Define  Join
```

This command retrieves a single table or value from a dBASE file. It executes a one reference-cell definition only.

StoreTbl/Cell

The StoreTbl/Cell command saves worksheet data to a dBASE file as specified by a current defining cell (`/DEDDC`, `/DEDDT`, or `/DEDDJ`).

Use this command to save a single table or value to a dBASE file. That is, execute only one defining cell reference only. (This command contrasts greatly with the AllStore command, which saves all defined cells and tables to their respective dBASE files.) To execute this command the cursor must be moved to the defining cell. When the command is executed, data from the defining cell are saved to the named dBASE file.

Quit

The Quit command quits the DBase submenu and returns VP-Planner to Ready mode.

Sample Worksheet Using dBASE Files

The following sample worksheet demonstrates how VP-Planner can access a dBASE file. The first part of the sample worksheet involves loading a dBASE file PAYMAST.DBF into the worksheet. The second part involves joining the original PAYMAST.DBF file with the PAYTRANS.DBF file. The third part involves using the regular data management feature of VP-Planner to manipulate this data. Some other data base commands are also covered.

The completed worksheet should look like the following:

	A	B	C	D	E	F	G
1							
2							
3							
4							
5	PAYMAST	EMPLO	EMP:NAM	PAY:RAT	YTD:GROSS	PAYTRANS	HOURS
6	1	456		.00	.00	1	29
7	2	2870	Frank Terlep	3.80	670.00	2	20
8	3	4463	Edward Mockford	4.90	775.00	3	29
9	4	4679	Kenneth Klass	4.90	780.00	4	45
10	5	4908	Richard Payne	4.45	556.00	5	35
11	6	5323	Pamela Rich	6.00	780.00	6	40
12	7	5432	Alan Monroe	5.20	1340.00	7	39
13	8	5649	Toni McCarthy	5.20	667.00	8	23
14	9	5789	Connie Reiners	3.35	450.00	9	38
15	10	5998	Paul Mish	4.90	887.00	10	43
16	11	6324	Mark Tell	5.50	980.00	11	40
17	12	8345	Thomas Momery	4.70	580.00	12	0

Step-by-Step Instructions for Sample Data Base Worksheet—Data Base

1. Position the pointer to cell A5 and to enter the definition criteria.

    /—Brings up the Main Menu for VP-Planner.

    D (F9)—Selects the Data option of the Main Menu.

    E (F7)—Selects the External option of the Data Menu.

    D (F3)—Selects the DBase option.

    D (F4)—Selects the Define option of the External Menu.

    T (F3)—Selects the Table option of the Define Menu.

    PAYMAST [by manual pointer movement]—Selects the file PAYMAST.

    ENTER—Tells VP-Planner to select this file. You should now have RT ; PAYMAST.DBF ; on the status line.

    Up Arrow—Tells VP-Planner to include the EMPLOY:ID field in the selection criteria.

    Right Arrow—Tells VP-Planner to advance to the next field.

    Up Arrow—Tells VP-Planner to include the EMP:NAM field in the selection criteria.

Right Arrow—Tells VP-Planner to advance to the next field.

Up Arrow—Tells VP-Planner to include the `PAY:RATE` field in the selection criteria.

Right Arrow—Tells VP-Planner to advance to the next field.

Up Arrow—Tells VP-Planner to include the `YTD:GROSS` field in the selection criteria.

ENTER—Tells VP-Planner that you are finished selecting fields to be included in the table.

ENTER—Tells VP-Planner that you do not wish to specify any selection criteria. This results in all records appearing in the table.

You should now have the screen depicted below on your monitor:

```
        A           B           C                   D           E               F
1
2
3
4
5PAYMAST      EMPLO         EMP:NAM          PAY:RATYTD:GROSS
```

2. Load the data from the dBASE file into the indicated location on your worksheet.

R (F6)—Selects the `RetrTbl/Cell` entry from the `DBase` Menu.

You should now have the screen depicted below on your monitor:

```
        A           B               C               D           E           F
1
2
3
4
5PAYMAST      EMPLO           EMP:NAM          PAY:RATYTD:GROSS
6           1    456                          .00          .00
7           2  2870  Frank  Terler           3.80       670.00
8           3  4463  Edward  Mockford        4.90       775.00
9           4  4679  Kenneth  Klass          4.90       780.00
10          5  4908  Richard  Payne          4.45       556.00
11          6  5323  Pamela  Rich            6.00       780.00
12          7  5432  Alan  Monroe            5.20      1340.00
13          8  5649  Toni  McCarthy          5.20       667.00
14          9  5789  Connie  Reiners         3.35       450.00
15         10  5998  Paul  Mish              4.90       887.00
16         11  6324  Mark  Tell              5.50       980.00
17         12  8345  Thomas  Momery          4.70       580.00
```

3. Specify the criteria for joining the `PAYTRANS` file with the `PAYMAST` file.

Q (F8)—Quits the `DBase` Menu and returns the worksheet to ready mode.

F5 [by manual pointer movement]—Positions the pointer to cell F5. This cell will contain the Join criteria.

/—Brings up the Main Menu for VP-Planner.

D (F9)—Selects the Data option of the Main Menu.

E (F7)—Selects the External option of the Data Menu.

D (F3)—Selects the DBase option.

D (F4)—Selects the Define option of the External Menu.

J (F4)—Selects the Join option of the Define Menu.

PAYTRANS [by manual pointer movement]—Selects the file PAYTRANS.

ENTER—Tells VP-Planner to select this file. You should now have RT ; PAYTRANS.DBF ; on the status line.

Right Arrow—Tells VP-Planner to advance to the next field.

Up Arrow—Tells VP-Planner to include the HOURS field in the selection criteria.

ENTER—Tells VP-Planner that you are finished selecting fields to be included in the table.

Right Arrow—Tells VP-Planner to advance to the next field.

Up Arrow—Tells VP-Planner to include the EMPLOY:ID field in the selection criteria for the Join operation. The status line should now have the following text:

RJ;PAYTRANS.DBF;HOURS;EMPLOY:ID_

=B5—Tells VP-Planner that it is to match records when the contents of the EMPLOY:ID field of the PAYTRANS file matches the EMPLOY:ID of the PAYMAST file. Your status line now looks like RJ;PAYTRANS.DBF;HOURS; ID=B5_

ENTER—Tells VP-Planner that you are finished specifying selection criteria for the Join operation.

Your worksheet should now look like the following:

	A	B	C	D	E	F	G
1							
2							
3							
4							
5	PAYMAST	EMPLO	EMP:NAM	PAY:RAT	YTD:GROSS	PAYTRANS	HOURS
6	1	456		.00	.00		
7	2	2870	Frank Terler	3.80	670.00		
8	3	4463	Edward Mockford	4.90	775.00		
9	4	4679	Kenneth Klass	4.90	780.00		
10	5	4908	Richard Payne	4.45	556.00		
11	6	5323	Pamela Rich	6.00	780.00		
12	7	5432	Alan Monroe	5.20	1340.00		
13	8	5649	Toni McCarthy	5.20	667.00		
14	9	5789	Connie Reiners	3.35	450.00		
15	10	5998	Paul Mish	4.90	887.00		
16	11	6324	Mark Tell	5.50	980.00		
17	12	8345	Thomas Momery	4.70	580.00		

4. Join the two files.

R (F6)—Selects the R e t r T b l / C e l l to tell VP-Planner to join the files in the table.

Your worksheet should now appear like the one below:

	A	B	C	D	E	F	G
1							
2							
3							
4							
5	PAYMAST	EMPLO	EMP:NAM	PAY:RAT	YTD:GROSS	PAYTRANS	HOURS
6		1	456	.00	.00	1	29
7		2	2870 Frank Terlep	3.80	670.00	2	20
8		3	4463 Edward Mockford	4.90	775.00	3	29
9		4	4679 Kenneth Klass	4.90	780.00	4	45
10		5	4908 Richard Payne	4.45	556.00	5	35
11		6	5323 Pamela Rich	6.00	780.00	6	40
12		7	5432 Alan Monroe	5.20	1340.00	7	39
13		8	5649 Toni McCarthy	5.20	667.00	8	23
14		9	5789 Connie Reiners	3.35	450.00	9	38
15		10	5998 Paul Mish	4.90	887.00	10	43
16		11	6324 Mark Tell	5.50	980.00	11	40
17		12	8345 Thomas Momery	4.70	580.00	12	0

You can now manipulate this worksheet just like any other. For example, you can create a Gross Pay column that is calculated by multiplying the hours worked by the pay rate. Once this formula is entered, it can be copied down the rest of the column.

Another option that is available is using the above table in regular VP-Planner data management discussed at the beginning of this chapter. Once the dBASE data is loaded into the worksheet, it can be manipulated or accessed in allowable VP-Planner method.

Using the DBase *Browse Command*

One simple-to-use feature of VP-Planner is the Browse command. The following example shows how the PAYMAST.DBF file is accessed using the VP-Planner Browse command. This example assumes that you are in ready mode.

/—Brings up the Main Menu for VP-Planner.

D (F9)—Selects the Data option of the Main Menu.

E (F7)—Selects the External option of the Data Menu.

D (F3)—Selects the DBase option.

B (F5)—Selects the Browse command.

PAYMAST [by manual pointer movement]—Selects the file PAYMAST. You should see on your monitor a display labeling the fields with

Figure 16.1

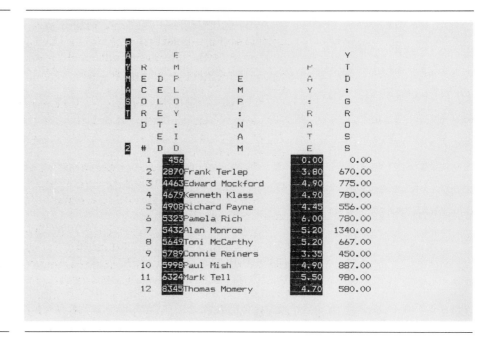

alternating high intensity and regular intensity field columns (see Figure 16.1). Refer to the previous discussion of the Browse command for entering, editing, and saving the file.

Chapter Review

The third part of VP-Planner is data management. A VP-Planner data base is held entirely in a worksheet; there is no disk input/output involved, as there is in dBASE. A row is equal to a record, and a column is equal to a field of data. The data base portion of the spreadsheet must be identified for VP-Planner.

Column headings play the important role in data management by acting as field names for the various fields in a record. They are also essential in setting up the criterion range. Any heading in a criterion range must be almost identical to the field name heading, since any difference will result in a beep from the computer, signifying that no match was found.

The criterion range is an area set up to determine which records are to be located, extracted, or deleted. At a minimum, the criterion range consists of two rows: the first contains the headings, and the second is used for establishing which records from the data base are to be used. An "and" condition is specified by entering selection criteria in more than one criterion field on the same line; an "or" condition is established by expanding the criterion range by one or more rows. If any row is left blank, VP-Planner will select all records in the worksheet.

After the Find command has been selected, the F7 Query function key can be used to locate records in the data base. VP-Planner highlights the selected record with an expanded pointer that appears over the entire record. The cursor within the pointer can be moved via the arrow keys.

Three wildcard characters are used in establishing criteria: the asterisk (*) works similarly to the way it does in DOS; the question mark (?) also works as it does in DOS; the tilde (˜) is a negation symbol, selecting any character string in the specified column that does not match the string it accompanies.

The output range and the Extract command work together. The output range is set up to hold any records that have been extracted from the data base; records are extracted if they meet the criteria established in the criterion range. The output range also requires field names that are very similar to the data base field names.

The final data base commands are Unique and Delete. The Unique command reports only unique occurrences of the contents of a data field. The Delete command deletes records from the data base that meet the criteria established in the criterion range.

The VP-Planner package also provides a complete set of functions for use with a data base. These functions all start with @D and are therefore easily distinguishable from other functions. These, too, are tied to the criterion range.

The VP-Planner spreadsheet package has the ability to directly load data from dBASE II and dBASE III data files. The entire file, selected fields, or selected records/fields based upon selection criteria can be loaded.

The dBASE access commands occur under the External option of the Data Menu. The DBF command is then entered. A menu containing the commands needed to manipulate a dBASE file now appears.

Before a dBASE file can be loaded into VP-Planner, the pointer must be positioned to a cell that will hold the selection criteria and also act as the upper left-hand cell of the table to which the dBASE data will be loaded. Once the selection criteria have been entered, VP-Planner automatically adjusts the column width of any table columns to the width of the data base field that will be occupying that location. It also places the field heading on the same line as the criterion cell and automatically centers the heading in the cell.

In addition to loading dBASE files into the worksheet, you also have the ability to view a file directly using the Browse command.

Key Terms and Concepts

"and" condition	"or" condition
Browse command	Output Range option
Criterion Range option	Query function key F7
data management file	Query Menu
Define command	Quit option
Delete command	Reset option
External command	simple find
Extract command	statistical functions
fields	Unique option
field label	VP-Planner record
field name	wild card characters
Find command	*
immediate mode	-
Input option	?
Join command	

Chapter Quiz

Multiple Choice

1. Which of the following statements is true about VP-Planner data management:
   a. The file is contained on disk.
   b. Disk I/O is common.

    c. A file is limited in size to 35,000 records.
    d. The entire file must be contained in RAM.
    e. Indexes are used to speed data retrieval.
    f. All of the above statements are true.

2. Which of the following statements is false about VP-Planner data management:
    a. A record is contained in a spreadsheet row.
    b. A field is contained in a spreadsheet column cell.
    c. The amount of RAM memory can limit the number of records in the data base.
    d. The column headings are used as field names.
    e. All of the above statements are true.
    f. None of the above statements is true.

3. What is the minimum number of data management "pieces" that have to be defined to find a record in the data base:
    a. The input and the criterion ranges
    b. The input range, the criterion range, and the output range
    c. The input and the output ranges
    d. The input and the extract ranges
    e. The delete and the output ranges
    f. None of the above responses is correct

4. Which commands are used together for creating reports using records from a data base:
    a. Unique and Delete
    b. Output and Unique
    c. Output and Extract
    d. Output and Find
    e. Output and Criterion
    f. None of the above responses is correct

5. VP-Planner data management provides:
    a. Password protection
    b. Random access
    c. Disk file storage
    d. Fast sorting for large files
    e. The ability to store complex programs for manipulating data
    f. None of the above responses is correct

True/False

6. Data Management in VP-Planner is in immediate mode. This means that commands are entered from the keyboard.

7. If a line in the criterion range is blank, all records from the data base are selected.

8. It does not matter if upper- and lower-case characters are used differently in the field name than in the criterion range.

9. If five fields are listed in the input range, all five field names must appear in the criterion range headings.

10. The Delete command provides an "unerase" ability to restore records that have been mistakenly erased.

Answers

1. d 2. e 3. a 4. c 5. f 6. t 7. t 8. t 9. f 10. f

Exercises

1. Define or describe each of the following:
   - a. VP-Planner data management file
   - b. record
   - c. field
   - d. field name
   - e. query range
   - f. output range

2. A spreadsheet row is used to contain a data base _____.

3. A spreadsheet column is used to contain a data base _____ _____.

4. A data base with 2,000 records takes _____ hours to sort.

5. Field names are defined by column _____.

6. The data base is defined by using the _____ command.

7. The _____ range determines which records are selected or deleted.

8. The output and _____ are usually used together.

9. List the steps you would have to perform if you wished simply to find records.
   - a.

   - b.

10. A blank line in the criterion range results in _____ from the data base being selected.

11. The _____ command results in all data base settings being erased.

12. The _____ command is used to generate a report of each "type" within a field.

13. The _____ command is used to erase unwanted records from the data base.

14. The wild cards and their functions are:
   - a.

   - b.

   - c.

15. Two lines under the criterion range headings are used for _____ _____ condition searches.

16. The dBASE commands are accessed by issuing the _____ from the Data Menu.

17. The dBASE Menu _____ command is used to directly access a dBASE file.

18. The _____ command is used to combine one or more dBASE commands into one table.

19. The _____ keys and _____, respectively, are used for moving from one field to the next and for including a field in the selection criteria for building a table reference cell.

20. When using the _____ command do not take diskettes out of the disk drive. This could result in damage to your data.

Computer Exercises

1. Set up a name and address data base like the following:

```
         Name  and  Address  Data  Base

------------------------------------------------------------------------

    Last        First     In      Address              City         St     Zip
Ghorbani      Reza       R.   4033 N. Wolcott       Chicago        Il    60712
Ghorbani      Ann        B.   4033 N. Wolcott       Chicago        Il    60712
Acklin        Douglas    C.   408 E. Monroe         Bloomington    Il    61701
Walters       Barbara    A.   1981 Crestlawn        Arlington      Va    13411
Adams         Arthur     V.   115 Ginger Creek Ct.  Bloomington    Il    61701
Davis         Russell    B.   707 Vale St.          Bloomington    Il    61701
Acklin        Debbie     C.   408 E. Monroe         Bloomington    Il    61701
Posio         Harvey     B.   1013 Hillcrest        San Diego      Ca    94307
Pietrowiak    Ben        A.   3334 N. Foster        Normal         Il    61761
Acklin        Sandy      C.   408 E. Monroe         Bloomington    Il    61701
Ficek         Fred       R.   1215 Tamarack         Normal         Il    61761
Decesario     Juan       C.   1214 Flores           Miami          Fl    12562
```

Use the following column widths and labels (you can center the labels using the / Range LabelPrefix command after they have been entered):

A	12	Last
B	10	First
C	2	In
D	1	
E	20	Address
F	1	
G	15	City
H	2	St
I	1	
J	6	Zip
C1		Name and Address Data Base

Create the data base, using the above data. Be sure to start each address with a single quote ('); if you do not, VP-Planner will try to treat the entry as a number rather than as an alphanumeric address. When you have created the data base, save to CH16EXR1 then copy the headings and create the criterion range.

a. Find any records with a 94307 zip code.

b. Find any records with a zip code greater than 70000.

c. Find any records with a last name of Acklin.

d. Find any records that do not have an Il state designation.

e. Establish an output area, and then extract any records outside of zip code 61701.

f. Extract any records with a last name of Ghorbani.

g. Extract any records from Normal.

h. Extract any records outside Illinois.

i. Extract only records with a unique last name.

j. Fred Ficek moved. Delete this record, but first extract it to make sure that the selection criteria have been properly given to VP-Planner.

2. This exercise involves first creating a VP-Planner dBASE table using the data found in the INVENTRY.DBF file. The table definition should be placed in cell A6. The table should contain the following fields from all records: INVID, NAME, ONHAND, and PRICE. Once the file has been loaded into your worksheet, your screen should look like the one below. It should have about 100 records.

	A	B	C	D	E
1					
2					
3					
4					
5					
6	INVENTRY	INVID	NAME	ONHAN	PRICE
7	1	3625a1	crt lamp	13	149.00
8	2	4545a1	ready files set	30	39.50
9	3	8093a1	serial microbuffer	45	379.00
10	4	6137a1	IBM nylon cartridge ribbon	47	5.95
11	5	6582 a1	computer vacuum	85	139.00
12	6	3970-8a1	multi-purpose back shelf	25	110.00
13	7	4400a1	workstations	9	699.00
14	8	4430a1	workstations	5	650.00
15	9	4440	triangle extension	15	185.00
16	10	4442	rectangle extension	100	175.00
17	11	4444	copyholder	55	99.00
18	12	4446	wristrest	35	39.00
19	13	4838	footrest	120	35.00
20	14	4858a1	manager's chair	8	549.00

Add the label EXTENSION to the right of the PRICE label. In the cell below enter the formula to multiply the on-hand cell by the price cell. Now copy this formula to the other cells. You must now create a data management data base using the Query Menu. Remember, you cannot copy the information contained in cell A6. After the data base has been defined to VP-Planner, perform the following tasks:

a. Find those records with an ONHAND greater than 50.

b. Find any records with a rest in the NAME field.

c. Extract those records that have an extension over $5,000.

3. Join the file INVTRANS.DBF to the INVENTRY table in your worksheet. The INV:NUMBER field is the INVTRANS field that is used to match with the INVID entry in cell B6. The Units field is the only field to be joined to the original table.

4. Use the Browse command to examine the PAYMAST file. Place your name, pay rate, and year-to-date in the 456 record. Add a friend's record to the end of the file.

Chapter
17

Spreadsheet Macros

After completing this chapter, you should be able to:

Discuss the concept of macros

Discuss the steps involved in building a macro

Discuss the placement of macros in the worksheet

Discuss special macro commands

Discuss errors and error correction in macros

Discuss some simple macros

Introduction
to Macros

The macro feature of the VP-Planner package sets it apart from all other spreadsheets. Macros enable you, with a minimum of effort, to automate just about any part of your worksheet. They enable you to store keystrokes as text in a cell and then execute those stored keystrokes by pressing the Alt key and one other key. A macro, more or less, is simply a repository of keystrokes.

A **macro** is only a cell of text that has a special name (range name); it is created by entering the keystrokes (or their representation) in a cell. With some of the advanced commands, macros can be made to resemble programs. A macro is capable of containing complex logic that controls how a worksheet executes and of building a menu from which users can select the operations or tasks that they want to perform. Some of these advanced commands are similar to BASIC's IF-THEN-ELSE, GOTO, and GOSUB commands.

Macros in VP-Planner can have global effects on a worksheet and should be used with care. Complex macros are not recommended for the spreadsheet novice, but you do not have to know everything about VP-Planner to use simple ones.

Complex macros that contain control logic may be easier to create if you have some programming background. It doesn't matter what language you have used. Prior programming experience enables you to solve a problem using a structured approach. Simple macros, however, can be created and used by any individual who understands how a spreadsheet's menu structure works.

If you are seated at a computer, prepare for the following example by loading (retrieving) the worksheet file COMPSALS. Set the global format of the worksheet to General.

Suppose you want to create a macro that will format the current cell to contain currency data with two positions to the right of the decimal. Before you create the macro, let's review the keystrokes you would use from VP-Planner to accomplish this task:

/	Invokes the Main Menu
R	Selects the Range option from the Main Menu
F	Selects the Format to change a portion of the worksheet
C	Tells VP-Planner that you want to use the Currency format to display data within a range
ENTER	Tells VP-Planner that you want to take the default of two positions to the right of the decimal point
ENTER	Tells VP-Planner that this is the only cell in the range

As you can see, the task of formatting a single worksheet cell to currency with two decimal positions requires six keystrokes. These keystrokes can be placed in a single cell and then executed. Position your pointer to any unused cell in your worksheet, such as H23, to enter the macro. The content of this cell appears below:

```
'/rfc~~
```

You enter this macro into a cell of the worksheet exactly the same way that you would enter any other label. First, you type the label prefix (', ", or ^). Otherwise, the "/" executes immediately to tell VP-Planner to display the Main Menu in the control panel. Any macro that begins with a nontext character must contain a label prefix (typically '). If it doesn't, VP-Planner will start to execute the commands.

The next four characters (commands) represent the keystrokes used to create this desired format. /RFC is the same keystroke shorthand that you've seen before. It means / Range Format Currency. The two characters at the end of the macro are called *tildes*. Each represents one ENTER keystroke. In the preceding macro, the ENTER key is to be pressed twice. It does not matter whether the keystrokes are entered in upper or lower case.

Once you have entered a macro into a worksheet cell, you must give it a special range name before it can be executed. The pointer is positioned to the cell containing the macro instructions, and the / Range Name Create command is issued. A VP-Planner macro name must consist of two characters. The first character is always a backslash (\), which tells the spreadsheet that a macro name is to be built. The second character is a letter. Name the cell containing your macro \F (abbreviation for Format). Be sure to press the ENTER key to tell VP-Planner that this is the only cell in this range.

You can now execute this macro by positioning the pointer to any numeric cell in the COMPSALS worksheet that you want to format and then issuing the keystrokes ALT + F. This means that the ALT key and the alphabetic F key must be held down at the same time. The ALT followed by any letter tells VP-Planner that it should find the macro with that name and execute it. If there is no macro with that name, the computer will beep, indicating that VP-Planner cannot find that macro. You now see that the format for the content of the cell has changed.

Special Keys

By now you may have noticed that the ENTER key could not be stored in a cell as a macro command without using some other special representation, in this case the tilde (˜), to signify this keystroke. Many keys must have special key representations before they can be used in spreadsheet macros. These special keys are divided into three groups: function keys, pointer positioning keys, and other special keys. Below is a complete list of the special key representations recognized by VP-Planner for use in macros:

Function Keys

{EDIT}	Edits content of current cell [F2]
{NAME}	Displays a list of range names in the worksheet [F3]
{ABS}	Converts relative reference to absolute [F4]
{GOTO}	Jumps cursor to cell coordinates [F5]
{WINDOW}	Moves the cursor to the other side of the window [F6]
{QUERY}	Repeats most recent query operation [F7]
{TABLE}	Repeats most recent table operation [F8]
{CALC}	Recalculates worksheet [F9]
{GRAPH}	Redraws current graph [F10]

Pointer Positioning Keys

{UP}	Moves pointer up one row
{DOWN}	Moves pointer down one row
{LEFT}	Moves pointer left one column
{RIGHT}	Moves pointer right one column
{PGUP}	Moves pointer up 20 rows
{PGDN}	Moves pointer down 20 rows
{HOME}	Moves pointer to cell A1
{END}	Used with an Arrow or Home key

Other Special Keys

{DEL}	Used with {EDIT} to delete a single character
{ESC}	Used to evoke the Esc command
{BS}	Used to move the cursor via the Backspace key
{?}	Causes the macro to pause and wait for keyboard input; the macro resumes executing when you press the ENTER key
	Represents one ENTER keystroke

Representations such as these are used for all of the special keys on the IBM PC keyboard. The name of the key is always enclosed in braces. If you enclose in braces a phrase that is not a function or key name, VP-Planner returns the error message:

```
Unrecognized key name {...}
```

An important special key representation is {?}, which is similar to BA-SIC's INPUT command. When VP-Planner encounters a {?} in a macro, it pauses and waits for the user to enter data from the keyboard. Once data are typed in and the ENTER key is pressed, the data are stored in the current cell.

Building More Macros

You are now going to build a macro that can be used to save an existing worksheet, COMPSALS, to disk. You must issue the following commands from the keyboard every time you want to save a worksheet: / File Save Enter (accept the default file name) Replace.

Position the pointer to an unused cell (H25) in your worksheet. Now enter the following character string: '/FS˜R. Make certain that there are no embedded blanks in the macro. A blank causes the macro to stop executing. Press the ENTER key. You should now have a cell with the following content:

```
'/fs˜r
```

Use the / Range Name Create command and give this cell the name \S. Issue an Alt + S command from the keyboard to execute the macro. The worksheet should now be saved to disk. The worksheet just saved contains the macros that you have created.

Next, you are going to build a macro that can be used to insert columns in the worksheet. You must issue the following commands from the keyboard each time you want to insert a row in a worksheet: / Worksheet Insert Column Enter.

Position the pointer to an unused cell (J25) in your worksheet. Now enter the following character string: '/WIC˜. Make certain that there are no imbedded blanks in the macro. Press the ENTER key. You should now have a cell with the following content:

```
'/wic˜
```

Use the / Range Name Create command and give this cell the name \C. After you position the pointer where you want to insert a column, issue an Alt + C command to execute the macro.

Most macros can be stored initially in a single cell, but some complex macros require more than one cell. Any other cells in a column that make up the macro are automatically included in the macro. A macro continues to execute instructions in a top-down, left-to-right fashion until it comes to a blank or a blank cell. There can be no embedded blanks between the commands in a cell (except label data). The blank cell tells the spreadsheet that this is the end of the macro.

Examining a Sample Macro

 Load the MACROSAL worksheet from the student disk. There appears to be nothing in it, but a macro called B is on the disk. This macro will build the COMPSALS worksheet that was used earlier. Execute it using the Alt + B command. After executing the macro, you should see the worksheet below:

```
                    COMPSALS

Department          LastYear       ThisYear        Change        % Change
Deli                 700.00         575.00       (125.00)         -17.9%
Bakery             1,000.00       1,100.00        100.00           10.0%
Liquor             1,200.00       1,400.00        200.00           16.7%
Grocery            2,500.00       2,900.00        400.00           16.0%
Produce              950.00       1,000.00         50.00            5.3%
Meat               1,500.00       1,410.00        (90.00)          -6.0%

Store Total        7,850.00       8,385.00        535.00            6.8%
```

You can view the macro used to generate the worksheet by pressing the F5 (GoTo) function key and typing and entering the range name MACROS. As you can see in the following macro used to build the COMPSALS worksheet, a macro can consist of more than one cell (as long as the cells are in a column). This macro appears to be composed of three columns, but really it consists only of the entries in the middle column. Notice also that the macro shown below has blank lines between some of the entries. These blank lines have been included to make the document more readable. A "real" macro would not have blank rows.

```
\B      '{goto}b1~                        The following 14 cells
                                          provide for entering row
                                          and column headings.

        'COMPSALS{down}{down}
        'Department{right}
        'LastYear{right}
        'ThisYear{right}
        'Change{right}
        '% Change{right}
        '{goto}b5~Deli{down}
        'Bakery{down}
        'Liquor{down}
        'Grocery{down}
        'Produce{down}
        'Meat{down}{down}
        'Store Total~{goto}c5~
```

```
'/wgc12~                          Sets the global column
                                  width to 12.
'700{right}                       Enter the dollar sales for
                                  each department.

'575{down}
'1100{left}
'1000{down}
'1200{right}
'1400{down}
'2900{left}
'2500{down}
'950{right}
'1000{down}
'1410{left}
'1500{down}{down}
'@sum(c5.c10)~                    Sum last year's sales.
'/c~{right}~                      Copy this formula to the
                                  ThisYear column.

'/wgf,~                           Set the global format to
                                  the comma (,).

'{goto}e5~+d5-c5~                 Go to cell E5 and enter the
                                  formula for the dollar
                                  change.

'/c~e6.e12~                       Copy this formula down the
                                  column.

'{right}+e5/c5~                   Position the pointer to
                                  cell E5 and enter the
                                  percent change formula.

'/c~f6.f12~                       Copy this formula down the
                                  column.

'{goto}f11~/re{left}~             Position the pointer to
                                  cell F11 and erase the
                                  garbage.

'{goto}f5~/rfp1~f5.f12~           Position the pointer to
                                  cell F5 and format this
                                  column for percent display.

'/rlrf5.c3~                       Right justify the column
                                  headings.

'/pprb1.f12~gpq                   Print the worksheet,
                                  advance the page, and quit
                                  the print menu.

'/fsnewmacro~r                    Save the file to a new
                                  worksheet called NEWMACRO.
```

The leftmost and rightmost columns document the macro. The \B entry serves only to alert the user that the entries to the right contain keystrokes for the B macro. It can, however, be used with the / Range Name Label Right command to give the macro a range name. In this instance, you can position the pointer on the cell that contains the \B entry, issue the / Range Name Label command, indicate that the range is to the right of the pointer, and press the ENTER key. This takes the \B range name and uses it to name the cell to the right of the pointer location. The macro is now named \B. The remark helps not only to name the macro but also to locate it on the worksheet.

The rightmost column explains the task performed by the macro instructions in each cell. These are not part of the macro, their function is solely to make the macro easier to understand and to change.

Rules for Entering Macros

The following rules apply when entering macros:

1. Use a comment to name the macro. Place a backslash (\) in the cell to the left of the macro location followed by the one-character name of the macro. Remember, you can use only letters. Do not use the same character twice. Enter a single quote before the backslash (/).

2. Name the cell by using the / Range Name Create or, because the name of the macro is already in a cell, use the / Range Name Label Right command.

3. Do not embed blanks in a macro (blanks within a label are permitted). A blank causes a macro to stop.

4. Multiple cells can be used to contain a macro as long as they are in the same column. Again, the rule about blanks applies; a blank cell in a column may cause the macro to terminate.

5. Unless an alphabetic character or brace ({) is the first character in a macro, it must be preceded by a label prefix (usually '). When you are entering numbers, for example, they must be preceded by the single quote (').

6. A cell containing a macro can have a maximum of 240 characters (the limit for any cell). A macro is much more readable, however, if you keep the number of macro commands in a cell confined to a small portion of an automated task.

Placement of Macros

You do not usually want to place macros inside your worksheet model. Keeping macros outside the active area helps keep you from erasing them accidentally. You usually place worksheet macros to the lower right of your main model in an unused area of the worksheet—in the lower right-hand corner because this area of the worksheet is not affected when you delete rows or columns. This arrangement is depicted in Figure 17.1, in which the worksheet is divided into four quadrants or areas.

Many users adopt a standard cell location in worksheets for starting macros. This prevents confusion in locating them for later maintenance. The easiest way to keep track of the location of macros, however, is to give the macro area of your worksheet a range name like MACROS. This allows you to use the GOTO [F5] function key. When you press the [F5] key, you can type in MACROS, and the spreadsheet will place the pointer in the upper left-hand corner of that range.

Macro Documentation

When you write a macro, remember that you are performing a process that is very similar to programming. Good programmers place remark statements inside program code to remind themselves, and to inform others, which

Figure 17.1
Quadrants of the worksheet.

Area of the worksheet that contains your "model"	Area of the worksheet affected by adding/ deleting rows
Area of the worksheet affected by adding/ deleting rows	Area of the worksheet that is "safe" for storing macros

task(s) are performed within a block of code. You should do the same with macros.

You can document your macros by placing explanatory text in the cell to the right of the macro instructions. Including these comments will make your macros easier to read. Your macros also will be easier to read if you make the column width of the macro column wide enough to display all macros completely. This makes the macro portions visible and lets you see the comments for every macro cell. This method will save you from wasting time later trying to figure out what you were trying to accomplish.

Entering Some Simple Macros

The following multiple-cell macro serves no useful purpose except for you to enter your first multiple-cell macro. Now, load the file COMPSALS from your data disk. Then move the pointer to cell G28 and enter the following macro. Be sure that you use the / Range Name Label Right to name the macro.

```
\R     {right}{right}{right}      Move the pointer to the right.
       {down}{down}{down}         Move the pointer down.
       {left}{left}{left}         Move the pointer to the left.
       {up}{up}{up}               Move the pointer up.
```

Press the TAB key one time. You can now execute this macro by issuing the Alt + R command. A rectangle of sorts appears on the screen. You can reexecute this command by issuing multiple Alt + R commands.

You can use the following macro to print the worksheet; it should begin in cell G37. Be sure to name the macro. Execute the macro.

```
\P    /ppc~a                        Select print option, clear, and align.
      rb1.f12~                      Tells what to print.
      om18~                         Select the left-hand margin.
      fPage #:COMPSALS:@~q          Tell VP-Planner to print a footer line.
      gpq                           Print the worksheet, advance to the next
                                    page, and quit.
```

The next macro is used to generate a bar chart that compares the sales of the various departments for the two years of sales information contained in the worksheet. It also places legends and titles, views the graph, and returns you to Ready mode. Be sure to name the macro. Now execute the macro.

```
\G    /gr~                          Select the Graph Menu and reset.
      tb                            Select the Bar Type.
      xb5.b10~                      Use Department names for X range.
      ac5.c10~                      Select Column B for A data range.
      bd5.d10~                      Select Column C for B data range.
      olaThis Year~                 Set Legend for A data range.
      lbLast Year~                  Set Legend for B data range.
      tfEd's Supermarket~           Enter title lines
      tsThis Year vs. Last Year's Sales~
      txDepartments~                Enter X and Y titles.
      tyDollar Sales~
      qvq                           Quit Options, View, and Quit Graph.
```

Planning for Macros

As you can see from the examples, macros often include a fairly large number of keystrokes. You also may try to incorporate a spreadsheet command that you do not know well. So you should properly plan your macro before you begin to enter it in the worksheet.

The easiest way to plan your macro is to manually enter the keystrokes that will accomplish the task that you want to perform. As you are entering the keystrokes, record them on a sheet of paper exactly as they occur.

Also, keep the entries for each step of a macro as small as possible. The preceding example places each portion of the commands in a separate cell. For example, the entry used to select the graph Type to Bar is one cell, the entries used to indicate the various Data Ranges are in other cells, and the entries for each of the *Others* options are also in separate cells. Keeping the cell entries small makes it easier to find errors later.

Errors in Macros

It seems that no matter how much care is taken entering a macro, errors will appear. Like other software that requires a user to supply the logic, macros will sometimes contain errors in logic or typing. Macros, unfortunately, do not have any error detecting logic. A macro will try to execute a misspelled word like {rihgt} and be unable to do so. Upon reaching such a word, your spreadsheet will display the error message:

```
Unrecognized key name {.......}
```

This means that you must be extremely careful when entering macros. Not even one character can be out of sequence. If this happens, VP-Planner will either produce strange results or just "hang up" and wait for you to do something.

One of the easiest characters to forget in entering a macro is the tilde (˜) used to represent the ENTER keystroke. Another problem with spreadsheet macros is that the cell references included in them are always absolute. They do not change when, for example, cells are moved about or deleted from the worksheet. This is easy to understand. Remember, macros are simply labels in the worksheet. Do labels change when they are moved from one cell to another in a worksheet? No. Only formulas containing cell references change.

This absolute quality of macros is a good reason for using range names. A range name remains associated with the same range even if the range is moved. Range names in macros (and other formulas) will follow the cells to which they apply if the macro is copied to another location. When cell references are used, they change when moved to a different cell location in the worksheet.

Macro Debugging

Just about any piece of software has errors in it when it is first written. No matter how much time you spend on an application, some error will usually get through. The process of finding and correcting these errors is known as **debugging**.

VP-Planner includes a useful tool that makes debugging easier: the STEP function. When VP-Planner is in the Step mode, all macros are executed one step at a time. To invoke the Step function, enter Alt F1. The mode indicator then changes to the message SST. The spreadsheet now will pause after every keystroke in the macro. After executing a keystroke, VP-Planner waits for you to press any key to execute the next command. Thus you can follow step by step with the macro as it executes. If you have text, such as a graph title, for example, you will have to press a key for each of the title's characters.

Once an error is found, get out of the macro and into the Ready mode by typing ESC one or more times (or CTRL + BREAK). When the mode indicator says READY, you can correct the erroneous part of the macro. You do this through the Edit mode by pressing the F2 function key, and you can use your editing keys to correct errors.

When you reexecute the macro, Step mode will still be on. To turn off Step mode, you have to enter the Alt + F1 command again.

Special Macro Commands

VP-Planner has a set of special macro commands that cannot be invoked from the keyboard—only from within a macro. These commands are programming oriented.

/XG, /XI, and /XQ

The /XGlocation command is similar to BASIC's GOTO command. It instructs the macro to continue executing, beginning with a particular cell location (usually a range name). This command is generally used with an /XI conditional test, which is discussed later.

You can easily add this command to the \R macro that "draws" a rectangle by using the pointer. To do this, however, you must give the top cell in the macro the range name Continue, using the / Range Name Create command. After you have done this, place the macro '/XGcontinue˜ in the last cell of the macro. Execute the macro.

Now that control is returned to the top cell of the macro (the Continue cell), a loop has been formed. Every time that control reaches the cell with the /XG command, the loop starts over. Since there is no way for control to leave this loop, it is called an **infinite loop**. The only way to stop this macro is to issue the break command (Ctrl + Break). An error message Ctrl-Break appears at the bottom of the screen. You must now press the Esc key to return to Ready mode.

The changed macro appears below:

```
                              ┌──────────── Cell named CONTINUE
\R    {right}{right}{right}     Move the pointer to the right.
      {down}{down}{down}        Move the pointer down.
      {left}{left}{left}        Move the pointer to the left.
      {up}{up}{up}              Move the pointer up.
      /xgcontinue~             Send control to Continue.
```

The /XI command is the equivalent of BASIC's IF-THEN-ELSE command. It enables you to build conditional tests in the middle of a macro. This very powerful tool can be used in a variety of interesting ways. The counter macro that follows is one example of the /XI function. Its /XQ command tells the macro to quit execution; this macro is frequently used with the /XI. For example, these two commands can be linked together to form a statement like the following:

```
'/xicount>10~/xq
```

This counter macro command tells the computer that if the content of the cell named Count is greater than ten, it should stop executing this macro. If this command were buried in a macro, it would perform this test and either continue or stop the execution of the macro. To add this command to the \R macro, you must embed the following command:

```
'/dfcount~count+1~~~
```

This statement uses the / Data Fill command of VP-Planner to increment a named range cell called Count by a value of one each time through the loop. We can now control the number of times the loop is executed by varying the value contained in the /XI macro command. For example, the following macro executes ten times.

```
\R    {goto}count~0~            Initialize count to 0.           11
      {right}{right}{right}     Move the pointer to the right.
      {down}{down}{down}        Move the pointer down.
      {left}{left}{left}        Move the pointer to the left.
      {up}{up}{up}              Move the pointer up.
      /xicount>10~/xq           If count > 10 quit, else loop.
      /dfcount~count+1~~~       Increment count by 1.
      /xgcontinue~
```

To enter this macro, make the following changes:

1. Delete the old macro name \R(/RND) and create a new \R macro name in the cell above (in this case G27).
2. Create a cell with the named range Count in cell K27.
3. Add the GoTo statement.
4. Add the /xi and the /df macro commands after inserting two rows.

/XC and /XR

The /XCrange and /XR commands are similar to BASIC's GOSUB and RETURN functions. /XC causes the macro to access a macro subroutine in a separate location. When that subroutine is finished, the /XR command causes processing to resume on the next line of the original macro. The /XC command is similar to the /XG command but offers a way to automatically return the macro to the point of departure. /XG, however, does not; it is an absolute GoTo to a different part of the worksheet.

/XNmessage˜range˜ /XLmessage˜range˜

/XNmessage˜range˜ and /XLmessage˜range˜ are input commands like {?}. They differ in that they allow a message to be displayed in the program's control panel before input is made. The message can contain up to thirty-nine characters.

The /XN command accepts only numeric entries. Numeric entries include @ functions and formulas as well as pure numbers. /XL accepts only labels, but it will accept a number that is entered in the cell as a label.

Both commands store input in the cell specified by the range. If a named range is used, the input will be stored there; otherwise, the input will be stored in the cell where the pointer is located.

Your current \R macro requires you to change the content of a cell in the macro if you want to alter the number of times that control is passed through the loop. The above /XN command gives you more control by prompting you to enter the number of passes via the keyboard.

Before you can do this, however, you must tell VP-Planner where to store this new piece of information called **Maximum**. This is done by creating a named range cell at location K28 and giving it the name **Maximum**. The following macro allows more control on the number of passes through the loop.

```
\R      {goto}count~0~                        Initialize count to 0.
        /xnEnter the number of passes: ~maximum~
        {right}{right}{right}                 Move the pointer to the right.
        {down}{down}{down}                    Move the pointer down.
        {left}{left}{left}                    Move the pointer to the left.
        {up}{up}{up}                          Move the pointer up.
        /xicount>maximum~/xq                  If count > Maximum quit, else loop.
        /dfcount~count+1~~~                   Increment count by 1.
        /xgcontinue~
```

Enter the macro using the following steps:

1. Create the named range Maximum at cell location K28.

2. Move the macro cells that appear under the GoTo down one cell.

3. Enter the /XN command. The character string following the /XN acts as the prompt to the user. When the user enters the number of passes, this information is placed in the cell called Maximum.

4. Change the /XI entry so that the comparison is made against the Maximum cell rather than the numeric constant 10.

/XM

This command enables you to create menus that appear while a macro is executing. Instead of the MENU mode indicator prompt, a CMD MENU mode indicator prompt is displayed. These menus look like the standard VP-Planner menus and enable you to make choices during the execution of a macro. They are also used during processing to give messages and warnings.

All VP-Planner menus are accessed by the /XMlocations commands. The Location in the /XM command points to a menu range, which can be up to eight columns wide and two rows deep. The entries in the first row of the menu range are called *menu options* and can contain up to eight options. When the menu is executed, these entries are displayed as menu options in the control panel (much the same as regular menu options). The second row of the menu range typically contains explanatory messages to clarify each menu option. Each message can contain a maximum of eighty characters.

One or more lines of macro code appear below each menu option explanatory message in the menu range. This code will run if, and only if, the preceding option is selected. The macro instructions follow the same rules as regular macros. That is, they execute top down and left to right, and terminate when a blank is encountered in a cell or when a blank cell is located.

One of the simplest uses for a menu is to allow the user to answer a yes/no question from within a macro. For example, the following macro, called the Quit macro (\Q), asks if you are sure that you want to exit from VP-Planner.

```
\Q      /xmquit~                          Go to named range Quit
    ┌──► Yes           No                 Menu Options
    │    Save worksheRemain in VP-Message lines
    │    /fs~r          /xq               Save file or stop
    │    /qy~                             Quit VP-Planner
    │
 Named range cell QUIT
```

After this macro is entered in your worksheet, it appears as follows:

```
        N              O              P            Q            R
---------------------------------------------------------------------------
¦ ¦Q        ¦ ¦/xmquit~      ¦            ¦ ¦Go to named range Quit ¦
¦ --------------+ -----------+ ---------+ - +----------------------¦
¦              ¦ ¦Yes        ¦ ¦No        ¦ ¦Menu Options           ¦
¦ --------------+ -----------+ ---------+ - +----------------------¦
¦              ¦Save workshe ¦Remain in VP ¦ - ¦Message lines       ¦
¦ --------------+ -----------+ ---------+ - +----------------------¦
¦              ¦ ¦/fs~r      ¦ ¦/xq       ¦ ¦Save file or stop      ¦
¦ --------------+ -----------+ ---------+ - +----------------------¦
¦              ¦ ¦/qy~       ¦            ¦ ¦Quit VP-Planner        ¦
---------------------------------------------------------------------------
```

Entering this macro requires the following steps:

1. Enter the name of the macro in cell N23.

2. The named range Quit is the cell containing Yes.

3. Since the menu entries are contained in adjacent cells, you must indicate to VP-Planner that they are ended. Do this by changing column Q to a width of one, and then enter comments in column R.

You are not required to use the /XQ command. Remember, if VP-Planner finds a blank or a blank cell while executing a macro, it assumes that the macro has ended. We can, therefore, simply omit the /XQ command. Upon locating a "null" or blank cell, the macro will stop.

The first line of the menu macro, /XMQuit˜, tells the macro to look for a menu beginning in the named range Quit. The actual menu is found in the second row of cells. This menu presents two choices, Yes and No, in the third row. Notice that the first choice is in column O, and the second choice is in column P. All /XM menus work this way: Each choice in the menu is presented in a different worksheet column.

The labels in row 3 are explanatory messages that accompany each menu option. In the preceding example, these messages seem to run together. This is because the first message is too long to be displayed completely in the cell. When the columns are widened, it is clear that the full message is there. They read:

```
Save worksheet and exit VP-Planner   Remain in VP-Planner
```

As with regular VP-Planner menus, you can select an option either by pointing or by entering the first letter of its name. (Make certain to choose names that begin with different letters. If two or more options in a menu have the same first letter and you try to select using the first letter, VP-Planner will give you the first entry that has this letter.)

Suppose that you select the Yes option. The macro will continue to process the macro's instructions contained in column O. The statements in this column instruct VP-Planner to save the worksheet file to the default name and quit from VP-Planner.

If you select the No option, the macro will continue processing in column P. This column cell contains a simple /XQ command that causes the macro to stop running.

If you create a menu that is too long for the control panel, VP-Planner will return the error message illegal menu. The same message is displayed if the menu has more than eight options. Similarly, the secondary messages associated with each menu option can contain up to eighty characters because the width of the display is only eighty characters.

Printing the Worksheet

Menu macros can be used to automate tedious tasks that are repeated frequently, such as printing. For example, you may want several different reports. Each one will require several steps to prepare the worksheet for printing: You must define the output range to be printed, align the paper, and specify any options such as borders, headers, footers, and margins.

Although the actual implementation of such a macro will vary greatly from application to application, the following macro can be used as a guide for automating this task. Two different reports are required: The first requires a report in order by department name, whereas the second report is in order by the dollar amounts in the Change column. The macro assumes that the print head is aligned at the top of a sheet of paper.

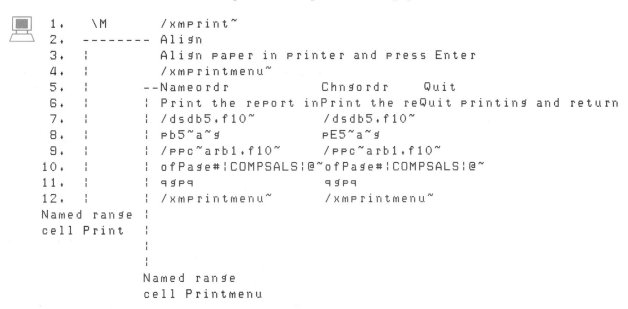

```
  1.   \M           /xmprint~
  2.   --------- Align
  3.   |           Align paper in printer and press Enter
  4.   |           /xmprintmenu~
  5.   |         --Nameordr          Chngordr      Quit
  6.   |         | Print the report inPrint the reQuit printing and return
  7.   |         | /dsdb5.f10~        /dsdb5.f10~
  8.   |         | pb5~a~g            pE5~a~g
  9.   |         | /ppc~arb1.f10~     /ppc~arb1.f10~
 10.   |         | ofPage#!COMPSALS!@~ofPage#!COMPSALS!@~
 11.   |         | qgpq               qgpq
 12.   |         | /xmprintmenu~      /xmprintmenu~
Named range |
cell Print  |
            |
            |
            |
         Named range
         cell Printmenu
```

There is not enough room to have the comment statements appear to the right of this macro. Instead, the lines of the macro have been numbered, and the following discussion of the macro commands refers to these line numbers.

Lines 1, 2, and 3. The \M is a remark statement indicating the name of the macro (M). The /XMprint‾ entry tells VP-Planner that a menu (/XM) located at the named range cell **Print** is to be executed. That menu appears immediately below the command. The menu consists of the two lines immediately below (lines 2 and 3). The objective of this menu is to give an instruction to the user to align the paper in the printer. The single option is contained in the first line and contains the word *Align*, which will be displayed on the entry line of the control panel. The second line (line 3) contains the text that further describes this entry to the user: an instruction to Align the paper in the printer and press the ENTER key to continue.

Lines 4, 5, and 6. Line 4 contains the /XM command, which tells VP-Planner to execute the menu found in the named range cell **Printmenu**. The Printmenu cell is located in line 5. Lines 5 and 6 contain the print menu that is displayed on the control panel. Line 5 contains the three menu options to be displayed in the entry line of the control panel. Each entry occupies one cell. Two reports can be generated, Nameordr and Chngordr, or the user can Quit the menu and return to Ready mode.

Line 6 contains an explanation of each menu entry. The explanation of the Nameordr menu entry is "Print the report in department name order." The explanation for the Chngordr menu entry is "Print the report in ascending order by amount of change." The explanation for the Quit entry is "Quit printing and return to Ready mode."

Line 7. Line 7 contains instructions to tell VP-Planner to issue the / Data Sort command and specify the sort range to consist of the cells B5.F10.

Line 8. Line 8 tells VP-Planner that the primary key is located in column B or column F and that the sort is to be in ascending order. It then tells the spreadsheet to execute the sort.

Line 9. Line 9 contains the instructions /PPC⁻A. The / invokes the VP-Planner main menu. The first P selects the print option; the second tells the spreadsheet to send the output to the printer. The C tells VP-Planner to access the Clear menu to clear the current print settings. The "⁻" tells the spreadsheet to take the first option of the Clear menu and clear all current print settings. The A tells VP-Planner to align the paper in the printer and take this print position as the Top of Page. The range to print is then specified for the spreadsheet.

Line 10. Line 10 contains the commands for making a footer line. The o selects the Options entry from the Print menu. The f selects the Footer option of the Options menu. The footer line is then entered.

Line 11. Line 11 contains the commands that tell VP-Planner to begin printing the worksheet. The Q tells the spreadsheet to quit the Options Menu. The G prints the worksheet. The P advances the paper to the top of the next page. The Q command quits the Print menu.

Line 12. This command tells VP-Planner to execute the menu found in the named range cell Printmenu.

Chapter Review

The macro feature of VP-Planner enables you to store representations of keystrokes in a worksheet cell and later execute those instructions. The representations of the instructions must be preceded by a single quote ('); otherwise, the spreadsheet package will immediately start executing the instructions instead of storing them as text data. Once the keystrokes have been entered properly, a one-character name (only alphabetic characters are allowed) that is preceded by a backslash (\) must be assigned to the cell with the keystrokes. The macro can now be executed by pressing the Alt key plus the alphabetic character.

Keystrokes are stored as they are used in entering a regular spreadsheet command, with the exception of a number of special commands such as the ENTER keystroke. A representation of such a keystroke (enclosed in braces {}) must be used for such a command.

Simple macros will reside in one cell, but complex macros can occupy a number of cells within a column. Try to limit the number of keystrokes stored in one cell of such a macro to those necessary to perform only a single task. If too many keystrokes are stored in a cell, it becomes difficult to make any changes, because the task being performed may be almost impossible to comprehend.

Macros should be placed in an area of a worksheet where they will not be harmed if you add or delete rows and columns. This "safe" area is usually in the lower right-hand quadrant of your worksheet. A complex macro in this reserved area will typically consist of three columns of text data: The first column contains the macro name, the second column the macro instructions, and the third column any explanatory remarks (documentation) about the instructions stored in a cell. Only the second column is actually used by the spreadsheet; the other columns are used for documentation by the user.

VP-Planner also provides some advanced macro commands that provide a tremendous flexibility to users. These include the /XG, /XI, /XQ, /XC, /XR, /XN, /XL, and /XM commands, which are divided into logical groupings. The /XG, /XI, and /XQ are used in loops to provide logic, branch control, and quit. The /XR and /XC commands are used for branching and then returning to the command following the initial branch instruction. The /XN and /XL commands are used to enter label or numeric information in a named range. The /XM command is used to build your own menus.

Key Terms and Concepts

debugging	Maximum
infinite loop	print
macro	printmenu

Chapter Quiz

Multiple Choice

1. Which of the following statements about macros is false?
   a. Only the first letter of a command needs to be entered.
   b. All macros are treated as label data.
   c. Only alphabetic keystrokes (with the exception of the /) are allowed in a macro.
   d. All macros must have names.

2. Which of the following statements about macro names is true?
   a. A macro name can contain up to 14 characters.
   b. A macro name can contain alphabetic or numeric characters.
   c. A macro name must have a slash (/).
   d. A macro name can contain only two characters, the second of which must be alphabetic.

3. Which of the following is not a special key representation to VP-Planner?
   a. {HELP}
   b. {EDIT}
   c. {CALC}
   d. {LEFT}
   e. All are valid special key representations.

4. Which of the following macro commands is used to exit from a macro?
   a. /XM
   b. /XI
   c. /XQ
   d. /XL

5. A macro stops when which of the following occurs?
   a. It encounters the /XQ command.
   b. It encounters a blank cell.
   c. It encounters the Stop command.
   d. It has executed for five minutes.

True/False

6. The only macro command that allows you to enter instructions across a row of cells is the /XM command.

7. There is no macro command equivalent to the IF-THEN-ELSE command.

8. The Step feature allows you to execute a macro five keystrokes at a time.

9. Numeric digits are the only characters that do not have to be preceded by a single quote within macros.

10. Range names are required by a number of special macro commands.

Answers

1. c 2. d 3. a 4. c 5. a&b 6. t 7. f 8. f 9. f 10. t

Exercises

1. The keystrokes contained within a macro must always start with a _____.

2. A macro name contains _____ characters.

3. A macro name always starts with a _____ and is followed by _____.

4. A macro executes from _____ to _____ in a cell.

5. One of the more common errors in building a macro is forgetting to enter the _____ command represented by a _____.

6. The _____ option of the Range Name submenu is frequently used for creating a macro name from existing text.

7. Once the macro has been named, it can be invoked by holding down the _____ key and then some other key.

8. Multiple cells can be used to contain a macro as long as they are in the same _____.

9. A cell containing a macro can store up to _____ keystrokes.

10. The special key {_____} is used to delete the character to the left of the current cursor location.

11. The special key {_____} causes the macro to pause until the ENTER key is pressed.

12. The area used for storing macros in a worksheet is the _____ quadrant.

13. The _____ feature is used for debugging a macro and enables you to examine the effect of each keystroke.

14. The debug feature is activated by pressing the _____ + _____ keys.

15. The macro command _____ requires two rows of your worksheet for holding additional options.

16. Once a macro has finished, you can invoke a menu via a _____ command.

17. The macro commands that reference a named range are the following:
    a.

    b.

    c.

18. The macro command that is the same as BASIC's GOTO is _____.

19. The spreadsheet _____ is used for incrementing a counter in your worksheet on every pass through a loop.

20. The _____ and _____ macro commands enable you to display a message and then accept information from keyboard.

Computer Exercises

1. To complete the following exercise, retrieve the CH12EXR1 (payroll) worksheet file. Create an area called MACROS that you will use to hold any macros you build. Be sure to position this area in the lower right-hand quadrant of your worksheet.
   a. Create a macro that you can use to add a blank row to receive a new employee.
   b. Create a macro that after you have positioned the pointer to the overtime rate cell for the new employee will automatically position to the same cell of the prior row and copy the formulas for the overtime rate, gross pay, and net pay cells to the new row.
   c. Save the worksheet file using the name CH17EXR1.

2. Retrieve the 2TABLE file. Create a macro that will print the input area, the financial statement, and the table. Each report should start on the top of the page. Be sure to change the setup string for printing the table; otherwise, it will be too wide to fit on a page.

3. Retrieve the CH13EXR5 file. Create a menu macro that allows you to arrange the gradebook worksheet in alphabetical order or in rank order by the final percentage. Four report options are also to be contained in the menu. Two of these options will print the entire gradebook worksheet in alphabetical order or in rank order by final percentage. The other two reports will be in the same order but will not include the summary information below the last student. After any item is selected from the menu and executed, your macro should return you back to the menu.

TOOL

FOUR

DATA BASE

MANAGEMENT

USING

dBASE III PLUS

Chapter
18

Introduction
to Data Base
and dBASE III Plus

After completing this chapter, you should be able to:

Discuss some of the basic concepts of data base

Discuss the steps involved in planning a file

Discuss some data base organization methods

Discuss in detail how indexes are created

Discuss the limitations of dBASE III Plus

Discuss the dBASE III Plus Assist feature

Discuss the parts of a dBASE III Plus screen

Discuss dBASE III Plus menu options

The term data base evokes different images for different people, but the concept is as nontechnical and as easy to envision as a filing cabinet in an office. The filing cabinet and its contents are the data base. Any time that the pieces of paper (data) pertaining to a specific function—such as customer addresses in the filing cabinet (data base)—are rearranged in a meaningful order (for example, alphabetically by last name), some sort of data management function is being performed. The data base itself doesn't do anything; it just holds information.

When a drawer of the filing cabinet is opened to find a record (for example, the record for customer Smith), the data base must be searched. The process of searching is actually a way to manage the data base. Data contained in a data base are typically stored in some order—alphabetically by last name, by city, or by zip code—to make the data base easier to manage.

Terminology

The **data base** holds information that is related to a specific application. In this context, the term is considered to be synonymous with *file*. This is especially true when dealing with dBASE.

A **record** relates to the entity that contains information about a specific business transaction in the data base. There are usually records in a data base.

A **field** holds information about one part of a transaction. For example, the LASTNAME field holds information about the last name of the individual who created the transaction. A record contains one or more fields.

Information from one or more fields is used to form a *key*, which is used to identify the records in a file. The record key makes the process of retrieving records from a file easier, and it plays an important part in the ordering of a file. Often the records in a file are placed in key order.

Commonly, several keys are used in a file. The primary key is the unique identifier for a particular record. The primary key in a data base is the physical record number. If a record occupies the fifth record location, it has the record number 5, which is the primary key for that record.

Data in a file are usually arranged in some order that is based on the contents of one or more fields; this order is known as the **secondary key**. For example, a file might be arranged in order by social security field or by name. You are not usually limited in the number of keys that you can develop for an application.

The following entries of a customer address data base file further illustrate these definitions:

Alfred A. Conant
2645 W. Hartford
Moosejaw, IL 61703
(309)367-8934

The preceding four lines constitute one record of the customer address data base file: Each line contains one or more fields of information about a customer in the data base. One important difference between human data base managers and computer data base management systems is that humans can easily differentiate the various fields of information, almost intuitively, whereas a computer has to have the information described in minute detail. For example, when arranging a series of records by customers' last names, a human being easily detects where the first-name and middle-initial parts of a name end and the last-name part of a name begins, but a computer must have detailed instructions.

Nor is a computer capable of telling the address line from the telephone line without help from the human being who sets up the data base. The fundamental difference between a human data manager and a computer is that the computer can't detect differences in data that are based on context. It is therefore necessary to structure a data base in a rigid enough way that the computer does not err when it tries to access and process a data base record.

What is this process of describing the data base to the computer? First, you must decide exactly what data should be stored; and to do this, you have to break the data down into meaningful units of information. For example, in the customer address data base, the following fields are needed for each record:

```
FIRST NAME
MIDDLE INITIAL
LAST NAME
ADDRESS
CITY
STATE
ZIP
PHONE
```

Thus it is desirable that every data base record be capable of holding all of these fields. Notice that there are eight fields of data for each record; the fact that there are only four lines of information does not mean that there are only four fields of data per record. If only one field is assigned per line, problems can surface later. For example, if you want the records to be ordered by last name, it would be extremely difficult for a computer to arrange records in last name order if you were working with whole-line fields. With the above arrangement, however, it is easy because every logical piece of data is also a complete and unique field of data on the record.

Learning to define the various meaningful items of information in a record is an important aspect of data base management. Given the proper data base structure, the information can be arranged or sorted by last name; and the data base can be searched for individuals in a given last-name range because the last-name field is isolated from the first-name and middle-initial fields. It therefore becomes a meaningful piece of data with which the computer can work.

In the example above, the computer is instructed that there are eight fields. The first field is FIRSTNAME, the second is MIDDLE INITIAL, the third is LASTNAME, and so on. If Chicago, Il 60603 is stored in the FIRSTNAME field, the computer will not object; it will store Chicago, Il 60603 as the first name and proceed from there. The user, therefore, must put the correct data in the appropriate field if the data are to be accessible.

The **structure** of the data base determines the manner in which the various pieces of information are arranged for each record, the type of characters (numeric or alphanumeric) that are used to store each field, and the number of characters that are required by each field.

Once the data base has been structured, it can be managed. This involves issuing instructions directing the computer to perform actions that include adding new records, changing existing records, sorting and arranging records into a new order for the user's convenience, searching the data base for specific types of records, printing data, and deleting data.

Certain operations are obviously desirable: From time to time, customers are added to the data base, it may occasionally be necessary to sort the records into some higher order (for example, alphabetically by last name within a city), or it may sometimes be advantageous to find all those records that meet certain criteria (for example, all records of customers who live in Peoria and have a 61603 zip code). Thus a provision must be included for updating old records when a customer moves or for deleting records of customers who die or move out of state.

The choice of field(s) to use as a key for a record depends on what type of processing you want to accomplish. If you want a report based on customers' names, you will probably want a key that combines the last and first names. If you want a report based on the customer's location, you will want a key that contains the last and first names and the city.

The concept of the computerized data base assigns to the computer the work of finding, replacing, and printing reports about specific types of records. It remains the responsibility of the user, however, to make certain that the information in the computer has been stored accurately.

Data Base Organization Methods

The way a data base is organized determines how fast data can be retrieved and how complex your interaction with the data base can be. It is important for you to know how the organization method affects the amount of time the system needs to process data. Some methods are much slower than others because they require large portions of a file to be read before a record is located. Some of the more common data base organization methods are discussed below.

List Structures

One organization method, called a **list structure**, links records together through the use of pointers. A **pointer** is a data item in a record that identifies the storage location of another record that is logically related. Records in a customer master file, for example, contain the names and addresses of every customer, and every record in this file has an identifying account number. During an accounting period, a customer may buy a number of items on credit on different days, and the company wants to maintain an invoice file of such transactions. A list structure can be used to show unpaid invoices at any given time. Every record in the customer file contains a field that points to the record location of the first invoice for that customer in the invoice file (see Figure 18.1). The first invoice record is linked to all later invoices for the customer. The last invoice in the chain is identified by a special character.

Hierarchical (Tree) Structures

Another organization method, called a **hierarchical (tree) structure**, arranges units of data in levels that graphically resemble an upside-down tree, with the root at the top and branches below. A hierarchical (tree) structure reflects a superior–subordinate (owner–owned) relationship. Below the single-root data component are subordinate elements called **nodes**, each of which in turn

Figure 18.1
List structure keeping track of unpaid invoices for a single customer.

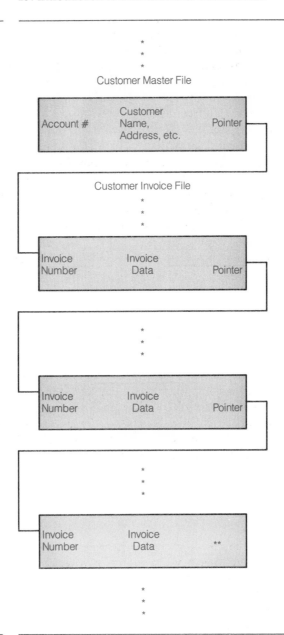

owns one or more other elements, or none. Each element (or branch) in this structure has a single superior (see Figure 18.2): The equal branches in a tree structure are not connected to each other.

Network Structures

A third data base organization method, called a **network structure**, differs from the tree in permitting the connection of the nodes multidirectionally (see Figure 18.3). In this system, each node may have several owners and may own any number of other data units. This data management software enables the extraction of information to begin at any record in a file.

Figure 18.2
Hierarchical (tree)
structure.

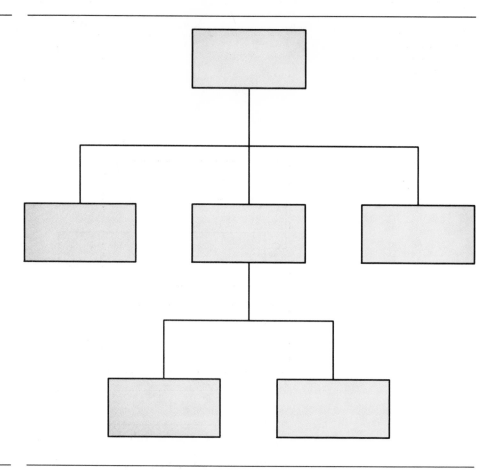

Figure 18.3
Network structure.

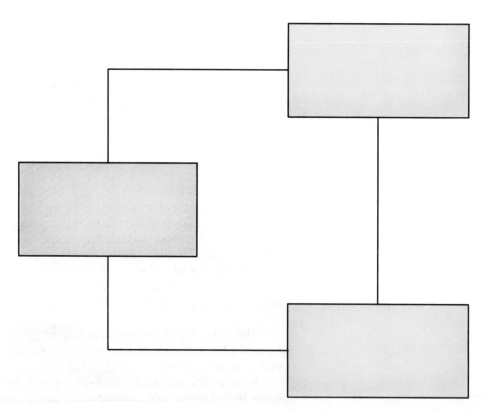

Course/Instructor Relation	
Course	Instructor
English 110	Meyer
Math 107	Garner
Spanish 115	Fiero
*	*
*	*
*	*

Course/Location Relation	
Course	Location
English 110	Stevenson 101
Math 107	Schroeder 223
Spanish 115	Stevenson 323
*	*
*	*
*	*

Other Relations
For example, course related to time of meeting, days of meeting, or hours of credit.

Relational Structures

Another data base organization method, a **relational structure**, consists of one or more tables on which data are stored in the form of relations. For example, relation tables can be used to link a college course with its instructor and the location of the class (see Figure 18.4). To find the name of the instructor and the location of an English class, you order a search of the course/instructor relation (which produces the name *Meyer*) and the course/location relation (which produces the class location, Stevenson 101). Many other relations are, of course, possible. Relational structures are a relatively new and very popular data base structure for microcomputer packages.

Indexing

An index enables you to keep track of the various relations in a relational data base environment and to access any record in a file quickly and easily; without it, the relational form of data base organization would not be possible. Thus any relational data base package must use an index for direct access to records.

The **index** contains one or more key fields for ordering a file. When you use an index, the physical record remains in the same physical position in the file, but the key of each record (along with its record number) is placed in the index, producing a file that has been logically reordered by one or more key fields.

The index has a treelike structure. Once a branch in the tree is chosen, you never have to go backward: Only the sub-branches of the chosen branch need to be considered.

In an index, information is held sequentially and in multiple data levels. Figure 18.5, for example, illustrates two levels, each of which divides its por-

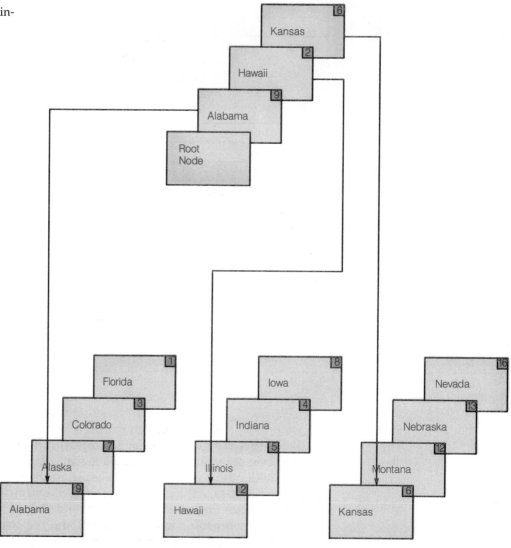

tion of the data into smaller parts at junctions or branching points called nodes.
The top level is the **root node**, at which every search for a particular record key
starts. The root node in Figure 18.5 has three keys: Alabama, Hawaii, and
Kansas. All alphabetic entries from Alabama to Hawaii are pointed to by the
lower-left node; all those from Hawaii to Kansas are in the middle node; and
all those from Kansas on are in the lower-right node.

Suppose the indexing program is required to find the record for Indiana.
The program first looks at the root node; and since Indiana is between Hawaii
and Kansas alphabetically, the program examines only the middle node. Because the tree in this case has two levels, Indiana is found in the next node
examined.

The index merely contains the location of the desired record(s) in the
data base file. After finding the address of the appropriate record, the data
base management software can access it from a hard disk in about two to three
seconds. Figure 18.6 illustrates this point.

Figure 18.6
Process dBASE follows in accessing an address found by indexing from a hard disk.

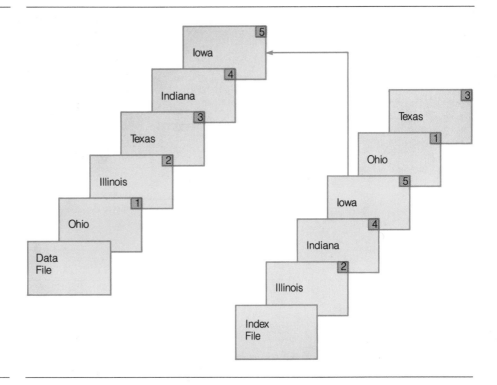

Accessing a relational data base record requires two steps. First, the index must be searched to find the location of the desired record in the file. Second, the desired record must be accessed in the file.

It is the subdivision of indexes that produces the ability to run through a file rapidly. Fast access to every key depends on the index tree's being in balance. As keys are added, the index grows and the nodes fill. When a node gets full, the data base management software splits it, creating two half-full nodes that can now accommodate additional records.

Indexing has the distinct advantage of being able to maintain data in several orders at the same time. Information about clients or customers can also be ordered simultaneously by last name, social security number, city, and state. Indexes can be used, therefore, to cross-reference a data file, giving a relational data base tremendous accessing power.

Suppose, for example, that you have to find out the classes in which Sam Thomas was enrolled at a college. Student information is in one file and class information is in another; each of these files has an index file. The program first looks at the student file, checking through the student index by name (see Figure 18.7). This leads (through several index levels not shown) to the index entry containing Sam Thomas's name and student ID (4417). The data base program now switches to the class file indexed by student ID (see Figure 18.8), searching for the first occurrence of 4417. This process points to record 1. The program is satisfied that no other classes for this individual exist, since the class index file is ordered in such a way that all 4417 class entries occur together in the class index file.

Because of its ability to index, the microcomputer is adequate for many data base needs. The advantage of indexing is that altering or retrieving information in the data base no longer entails sitting through a lengthy sort program; queries to the data base are answered quickly.

Figure 18.7
Index entries of the student file, containing name and student ID.

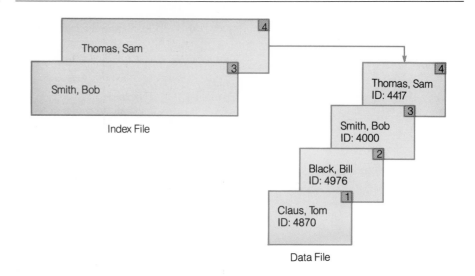

Figure 18.8
Index entries for student 4417 pointing to classes attended records.

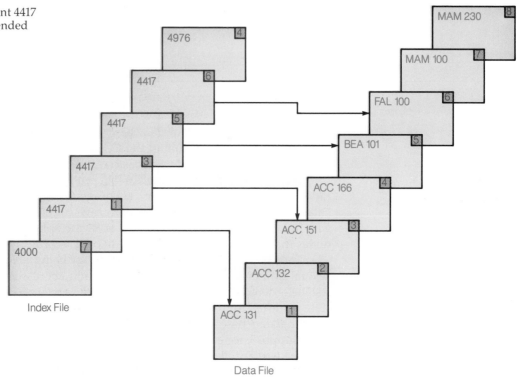

Sequential File Data Processing *versus Relational Data Base*

Relational file organization is much more efficient than sequential file organization and greatly improves computer performance. Users do not have to wait repeatedly for time-consuming file sorts to be performed, access to data is much quicker, and adding records to existing files is also quicker.

The following table illustrates some of the differences between sequential file organization and relational data base techniques.

	Sequential File Processing	Data Base (one index)
Building a file	Append newer record(s) after older records and sort when finished.	Append newer records after older records and update index.
Preparing for processing	Place records physically in ascending or descending order according to the contents of one or more fields.	Leave records in original order but generate an index of required key fields that point to the corresponding record on disk.
Accessing a record	Perform a sequential or binary search.	Use index to find location of record and go to that location on disk.
Adding a record	Append record and resort entire file.	Append record and update index.
Obtaining a different file order	Resort the file.	Use another index or generate a new index.

Introduction to dBASE III Plus

The dBASE package is the best-selling relational data base package on the market. The current version of dBASE (dBASE III Plus) evolved from dBASE II. Ashton-Tate originally developed dBASE II for 8-bit microcomputers that used the CP/M operating system. When IBM introduced the IBM PC, Ashton-Tate revised dBASE to run on the PC/MS DOS operating systems.

When Ashton-Tate first thought of developing dBASE II, it was envisioned as being a software package for the rather narrow market of systems developers rather than for the general public. The dBASE II developers, therefore, assumed that users would have certain programming and systems development skills not usually found in the general public. This resulted in a package that was not user friendly.

This lack of a user friendly interface was a problem when the package became tremendously popular and began to sell to users who were unskilled in programming. To overcome this total lack of user friendliness and to take advantage of the power of the IBM's 16-bit microprocessor, Ashton-Tate introduced the dBASE III package in 1984. This new dBASE III package had an ASSIST feature that provided a low-level user interface and the capacity for many more fields per record.

However, users demanded an even friendlier program with even more power. Ashton-Tate responded by introducing dBASE III Plus in the latter part of 1985. This version has the ability to network and a full-featured user interface. The new interface operates by menu selections and thereby avoids making the user enter instructions from a **dot prompt**. This means that a user can concentrate on solving a problem rather than spending time learning dBASE language rules.

Limitations of dBASE III Plus

Anyone who wants to use the full version of dBASE III Plus should be aware of the following limitations that the package places on an application: (1) The package requires an IBM PC or compatible 16-bit computer with a minimum of 256K of memory (more memory is faster); (2) the system should have either two 360K diskette drives or a hard disk and one diskette drive; (3) a limit of one billion records is placed on any file; (4) the maximum record size is 4,000 characters and 128 fields; (5) a character field can have a maximum length of 254 positions; (6) a numeric field is limited to 15 positions; (7) a memo field is limited to 4,096 positions; (8) no more than ten data base files can be open at one time; and (9) only seven indexes can be specified as active for a file at one time. Most applications are not affected by these limitations.

The version of dBASE III Plus covered in this and the following chapters is the student demonstration version. The only difference between the full version and the student version is that the student version limits file size to 31 records.

Modes of dBASE III Plus

The dBASE III Plus package provides you with three different modes. The first, Assistant mode, provides an easy to use menu-driven interface that enables you to issue commands without an in-depth understanding of dBASE. The second, Command mode, requires some understanding of dBASE because instructions are entered at the dot prompt (.) and does not display help menus for most commands. The third, Program mode (also referred to as batch mode), enables you to store instructions in a program file and execute all of them by issuing one command.

Starting dBASE III Plus

The manner in which you start dBASE III Plus depends on whether you are using a diskette or hard disk microcomputer.

Diskette Systems. To start dBASE III Plus on a diskette system requires you to boot the computer with the DOS system disk and then enter the date and time if you want to have this information in the directory of any files that you create.

You no doubt realize that when you use a diskette system, you usually place your program diskette in drive A and the diskette that is to hold your data files in drive B. To get dBASE III Plus to execute requires entering the command DBASE at the A> DOS prompt.

Once the necessary files contained in the first diskette are loaded, you are prompted to insert the second disk in the drive and press the ENTER key.

Hard Disk Systems. To start dBASE III Plus on a hard disk system requires that after turning on the system you tell DOS to activate the directory in which your dBASE III Plus program files reside. This is accomplished by using the Change Directory (CD) DOS command. If, for instance, your dBASE III Plus directory is named DB3PLUS, enter the command CD \DB3PLUS. After you have activated the directory, you can start dBASE by entering the command DBASE at the DOS prompt.

The Assistant Screen. Once you issue the DBASE command to start dBASE III Plus, the copyright screen (see Figure 18.9) is displayed on your monitor.

Figure 18.9
Copyright screen of dBASE
III Plus.

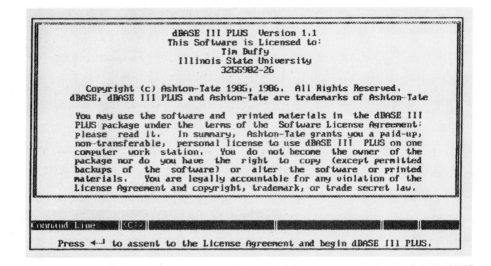

Figure 18.10
The dBASE III Plus screen
with the Assistant menu
activated.

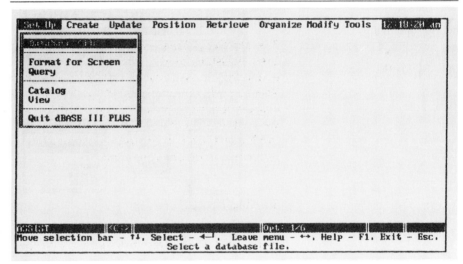

The copyright screen contains such information as the individual who purchased the package, the company at which this person works, the serial number of the package, and conditions of the copyright agreement. This screen disappears after a few seconds or when you press the ENTER key. At that time the Assistant menu is displayed (see Figure 18.10).

Whether you start dBASE from a hard disk or a diskette, the Assistant menu screen will be virtually identical. The Assistant menu provides, across the top of the screen, a number of options from which you can select. You select an option by either positioning the pointer (via the arrow keys) or entering the first character of the command. As you make selections, the pull-down menus change. For instance, the menu displayed when the Position option is selected (see Figure 18.11) is different from the Set Up menu that is automatically displayed by the Assistant (see Figure 18.10). Every option in the menu bar has its own pull-down menu with its own set of options (see Figure 18.12). And a pull-down menu may have a submenu with options.

Other components of the Assistant menu—the action line, status bar, navigation line, and message line—are discussed below.

Figure 18.11
Assistant screen after the
Position option has been
selected.

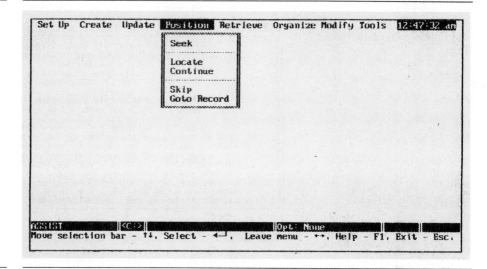

Figure 18.11
Assistant screen after the
Position option has been
selected.

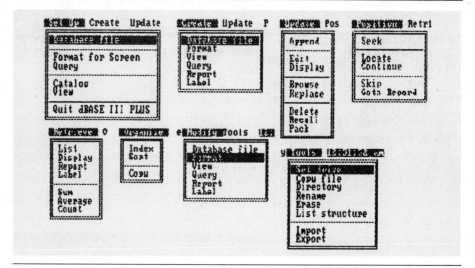

Figure 18.12
Various menus available from
the Assistant menu.

Action Line. The **action line** is the line above the bar near the bottom of the screen. It displays the command being generated by your menu or submenu selection.

Status Bar. The **status bar** is in reverse video near the bottom of your screen. The status bar displays information about the current status of dBASE III Plus; for instance, the current drive, the file (if any) in use, the current record number or the option from the menu or submenu in use, whether the Ins or Del option is in use (during the edit process), and the status of the CAPS LOCK key (**Caps** if the CAPS LOCK key is on).

Navigation Line. The **navigation line** appears just beneath the status bar and provides instructions for moving from one menu option to another or for moving from one submenu to another.

Message Line. The **message line** is beneath the navigation line and displays an explanation of the current menu option along with any action you are to take.

Leaving the Assistant Menu

If you make a mistake on a menu selection, you can back up one level by pressing the ESC key. If you are at the menu line, however, upon pressing the ESC key you leave the Assistant menu and drop to the so-called dot prompt mode. In dot prompt mode, no menus are displayed; rather, the dot prompt (.) appears on the action line. The status bar and the message line are also visible. The message line contains the prompt:

`Enter a dBASE III PLUS command.`

If you have pressed the ESC key by mistake, you can get back to the Assistant menu by entering the `ASSIST` **command** at the dot prompt and then pressing the ENTER key. The Assistant menu (see Figure 18.10) is redisplayed on the screen.

Leaving dBASE III Plus

It is important that you exit dBASE III Plus properly, because open files are not properly closed if you simply turn off the computer. If a file has had records added to it and is not closed properly, the end of file marker will be misplaced and records may be lost.

There are two ways to exit dBASE III Plus. Both methods return you to the DOS prompt after properly closing open files. The message `*** END RUN dBASE III PLUS` is displayed above the DOS prompt. The first involves selecting the Set Up option from the menu and then highlighting the `Quit dBASE III PLUS` option. The second involves dropping to dot prompt (.) by pressing the ESC key one or more times. Once you are at the dot prompt, enter the command `QUIT`.

The Help Facility

Help is available by highlighting any item in the Assistant menu or any submenu and then pressing the F1 function key. For instance, if you want help on the `CREATE` command, press the F1 key while that option is highlighted; a description of that command (see Figure 18.13) is displayed on your screen. Another way to obtain assistance is by responding Y to the prompt:

`Do you want some help? (Y/N)`

This prompt appears when you commit an error in entering a command at the dot prompt. Once you respond Y the Main Help Menu (see Figure 18.14) is displayed on your screen.

If you want information about a dBASE command, all you have to do is enter the `HELP` **command** at the dot prompt and press the ENTER key. The Help Main Menu appears on your screen. Select option 1, Getting Started, and enter the command about which you want additional information. For example, if you want information about the Report command, enter `REPORT` in the Message line, and after you press the ENTER key, information about that command is displayed on your screen (see Figure 18.15).

Note that when you are in Help mode, the Navigation line contains prompts about how to move from one screen to the next by pressing the PGUP or PGDN keys. It also instructs you to move to the previous menu by depress-

Figure 18.13
The Help screen for the
CREATE command.

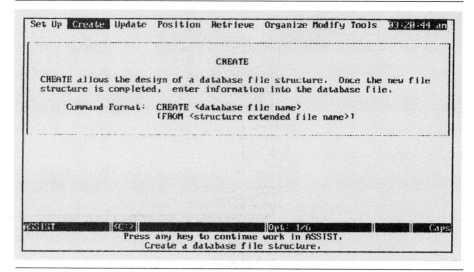

Figure 18.14
The Help Main Menu for the
REPORT command.

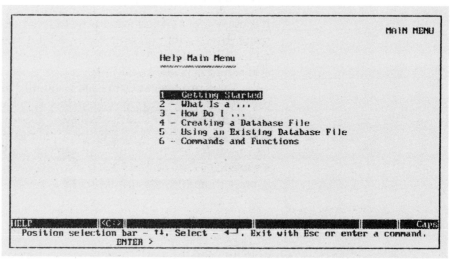

ing the F10 key or to exit to the dot prompt by pressing the ESC key. If you
want information about any other dBASE command, simply enter that command in the Message line.

You can save yourself one step by entering the HELP command and then
the command about which you want the information. To get the immediate
information about the REPORT command, enter the following command at
the dot prompt:

.HELP REPORT

Once the command is entered, the appropriate screen of information (see
Figure 18.15) is displayed on your monitor.

Leaving dBASE III Plus

When you have finished a dBASE III Plus session, you must remember to use
the QUIT **command**, which closes any files that might still be open. If a file
has had records added to it and is not closed properly, the end of the file

Figure 18.15
The Help screen generated for the REPORT command.

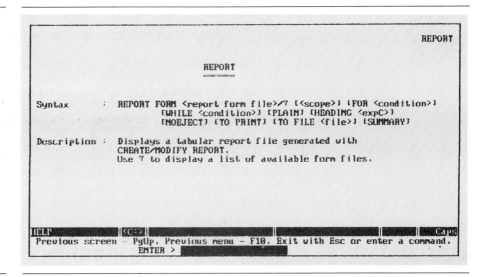

marker will be misplaced and records may be lost. To execute QUIT, you must move the Assistant pointer to the SET UP command and, once the Set Up menu is displayed, move the pointer bar to the Quit dBASE III PLUS selection and press the ENTER key.

If you wish to enter the QUIT command from the dot prompt, simply press the ESC key once or twice to receive the dot prompt on the Action line and then type QUIT and press the ENTER key. No matter which method you choose a message and the DOS prompt appears on your screen.

```
*** END RUN   dBASE III PLUS

C > _
```

Chapter Review

The term *data base* is usually taken to be synonymous with *file* when microcomputers are involved in processing data. A data base consists of records that hold information about some type of business entity or transaction. Each record is composed of pieces of data, called fields, that relate to the transaction.

When you are designing the format of the file to hold data, you must design it to handle future processing needs. This may mean separating name fields into lastname, firstname, and middle initial fields so that the computer can arrange the information in alphabetical order by last name.

A number of organizational methods are used to arrange data in a data base, including list structures, hierarchical (tree) structures, network structures, and relational structures. The relational structure has been favored by computer scientists because it is fairly easy to use. The indexing used by relational structures, however, proved difficult to implement properly until the microcomputer (with its independent power) was introduced.

The heart of the relational organization method is the index, which uses a treelike structure for holding record keys. The index allows you to access a record directly; it contains the field from each record indexed, along with the record's location on disk. The index is split into branches, and data are kept in sequence within a node of each branch. As a result, only a small portion of the index has to be searched to find the location of any record.

One of the greatest benefits of a relational data base is that a general understanding of how indexes work is all you need to know before using the index feature.

The index also enables you to use pieces of data to link one or more files together for processing. For instance, you may have to look up a record to get a piece of information that in turn enables you to access a record directly from a second file.

The dBASE III Plus package is a combination menu-driven and command-driven software package. The dBASE III Plus package places a number of limitations on files, including limitations on total records in a file, record size, number of fields in a record, and the number of active indexes.

DOS must be loaded before you start dBASE III, since room is severely restricted on the dBASE disk. The steps involved in starting dBASE III Plus depends on whether you are using a hard disk or a diskette system.

Key Terms and Concepts

action line
`ASSIST` command
data base
dot prompt
field
`HELP` command
hierarchical (tree) structure
index
list structure
message line

navigation line
network structure
nodes
pointer
`QUIT` command
record
relational structure
root node
secondary key
status bar
structure

Chapter Quiz

Multiple Choice

1. In which of the following data base organizations is a node owned by several higher nodes?
   a. Relational
   b. Hierarchical
   c. Network
   d. List structures
   e. None of the above

2. Which data storage entity is used to store information about a transaction?
   a. File
   b. Record
   c. Element
   d. Field
   e. None of the above

3. Which of the data base organizations makes use of tables to arrange data for access logically?
   a. Relational
   b. Hierarchical
   c. Network
   d. List structure
   e. None of the above

4. Which of the following statements about index structures is false?
    a. An index contains a number of branches.
    b. The field being indexed and the address on disk are stored for each record.
    c. Once a search is started for a record in an index, it will probably require going through several branches to find the desired record.
    d. Branches must be in balance (contain about the same number of entries) for searches to be efficient.
    e. All of the above statements are true.

5. In which data base organizations can ordered data be viewed as a table?
    a. Relational
    b. Hierarchical
    c. Network
    d. List structure
    e. None of the above

True/False

6. In discussions about managing data bases on microcomputers, *data base* and *file* usually mean the same thing.

7. A properly designed record layout allows you easily to order the file in a number of different ways.

8. Managing a data base includes such tasks as creating reports, adding, deleting, and changing records.

9. It is advisable to use the dBASE QUIT command to avoid data loss.

10. Even though data are not in the proper order in a relational data base, the index holds information that allows you to order the file logically.

Answers

1. c 2. b 3. a 4. c 5. a 6. t 7. t 8. t 9. t 10. t

Exercises

1. Define or describe each of the following:
    a. data base   d. root node
    b. index   e. relational structure
    c. pointer   f. status bar

2. The terms file and _data base_ are really the same when used in the context of microcomputers.

3. The _record_ is used to record information about a transaction.

4. A(n) _field_ holds one piece of information contained in a record.

5. In designing a record, it is important that the _index_ organize the fields properly for later processing.

6. The process of creating reports, adding records, deleting records, and changing records is called _structuring_ the data base.

7. The _hierarchical tree structure_ has a superior–subordinate relationship with data.

8. In the _network_ structure a node can be owned by a number of different nodes.

9. In the _hierarchial (tree)_ structure a node can be owned by only one superior node.

10. The _Relational_ structure uses tables to organize the records in the file logically.

11. Creating a new relation involves simply creating a new _table_.

12. The top node of an index is called the _root node_.

13. The index contains which two pieces of information about each record in an indexed file?

a. _Location_

b. _Field_

14. Data in an index are stored _sequentially_.

15. The field that identifies a record is called a(n) _key_.

16. The maximum number of records allowed in a dBASE III Plus file is _1 million_.

17. The line of the Assist menu that indicates the current disk drive and the name of the file in use is the _Status bar_ line.

18. The HELP command can be invoked by pressing the _F1 – function_ function key.

19. Before you turn off the computer you must issue the _Quit_ command to avoid data loss.

20. Exiting the Assistant menu is achieved by pressing the _ESC_ key.

Chapter

19

Building a File Using

dBASE III Plus

After completing this chapter, you should be able to:

Discuss how to issue commands to dBASE III Plus

Discuss how to create dBASE III Plus files

Discuss how to add and edit data

Discuss some elementary dBASE III Plus commands

This chapter introduces you to the **menu-driven** (default) and **command-driven modes** of dBASE III Plus and to the CREATE, USE, APPEND, LIST, and DIR commands. A disadvantage of the menu-driven mode for an experienced user is the amount of time that it takes to display menus and receive or execute instructions: Several menus may be displayed before one action can be accomplished, and control may have to be returned to previous menus before the next. However, menu-driven programs are useful for users without programming experience and when internal control is an important aspect of an application. Thus the Assistant menu mode is emphasized in this and the following chapters, although after you know the commands, you may prefer the command mode.

At the computer, start the dBASE III Plus program by the methods detailed in the previous chapter. You will then see the Assistant menu, which provides you with a list of alternatives and is an excellent tool for learning how to use dBASE.

The dBASE package also enables you to enter the command mode once you have mastered how commands are built by observing them on the Action line. This is accomplished by pressing the ESC key once or twice, which gives the dot prompt on the Action line:

The period (".") is the dBASE III Plus command mode prompt. This means that dBASE is now waiting for you to enter a command. Remember to press the ENTER key after each command to tell dBASE to execute your instruction.

Communicating with dBASE III Plus

In its command-driven mode, dBASE III Plus requires that you state the task you want to perform in a language that dBASE can understand. For example, suppose that you want to use the CUSTOMER file to list those who live in the state of Hawaii. This would require the following commands:

```
USE CUSTOMER
LIST FOR STATE = "Hawaii"
```

Before you can effectively communicate with dBASE II Plus in the command mode, you must learn some grammatical rules for constructing sentences in accordance with the syntax of dBASE's language. The parts of a dBASE sentence are

```
COMMAND  SCOPE  NOUN  CONDITION
```

The command portion of the sentence tells dBASE III Plus exactly what action to perform. Common commands include LIST, USE, DISPLAY, and REPORT. The *scope* portion of the sentence limits the range of the command, determining whether all or only a small part of the file is to be processed by the command. The noun is the object—a file, a field, or a variable—on which the command acts. The condition portion specifies the fields or files to be acted upon. A dBASE III Plus command need not have all four parts; it may consist of the command part alone.

The advantage of using the Assistant menu is that you do not have to concern yourself with the parts of a command. This menu-driven mode automatically constructs the commands on the Action line and then executes them for you. This ability of dBASE to build instructions and then execute them frees novices from the tedium of learning the dBASE language syntax and enables them to concentrate on solving problems.

Figure 19.1
The Tool option used to set the default drive to B and the dBASE command on the Action line that has been generated by the menu selections.

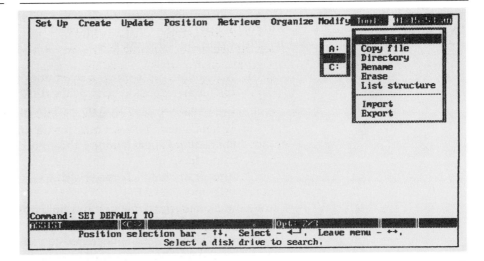

Figure 19.2
Example of a full-screen cursor menu.

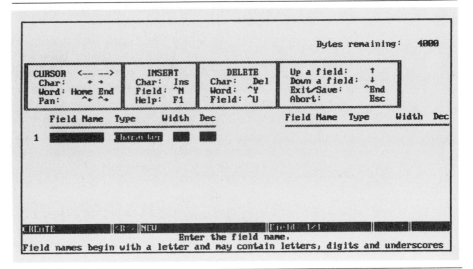

Setting the Default Drive

Unless told otherwise the dBASE program automatically assumes that data files are on the same disk as the dBASE III Plus program files. If you are using a diskette-based system, however, you will not want to record your data files on the limited disk space of the dBASE system disk. To record data files on a different disk, you select the Tools option from the Assistant menu and then press the ENTER key to obtain the Set-drive entry of this submenu (note that the Action line contains the entry (SET DEFAULT TO). Next, move the bar that indicates the next submenu to B: (see Figure 19.1) and press the ENTER key. Henceforth, commands entered without a drive specifier will operate on the assumption that the file resides in drive B.

Full-Screen Cursor Menus

The full-screen feature of dBASE enables you to move the cursor to various formatted locations on the screen. The dBASE III Plus package also offers full-screen menus (see Figure 19.2) that contain directions on how to use the cursor. This facility can be turned off by using the SET MENU ON/OFF command at the dot prompt. The ON displays the menus when dBASE goes into full-screen mode. The OFF results in no menus being displayed.

Creating a dBASE III Plus File

Before a file can be used by dBASE III Plus, you must provide some specific information about the file (its name) and the data fields (name, data type, and length), using the following rules:

1. A filename can contain a maximum of eight characters. Do not give the file an extension because the dBASE III Plus package automatically places a .DBF extension on all data base files.

2. A field name consists of a maximum of ten characters. Acceptable characters are the letters A through Z, the digits 0 through 9, and the underscore mark (_). The data to be stored in a field determine the type of the field: character string (C), numeric (N), logical (L), Memo (M), and Date (D).

   a. A *character string field* can hold any alphanumeric character (number, letter, or special character).

   b. A *numeric field* is restricted to numerals and the decimal point (.); the decimal point must be counted as part of the field length.

   c. A *logical field* will be marked Y (yes) or N (no) and is always only one position in length.

   d. A *Memo field* can hold a maximum of 4096 characters and is therefore ideal for containing large amounts of text data.

   e. A *Date field* contains eight positions and automatically has the slashes (/) in their correct locations; an empty Date field appears as __/__/__.

Once again, let's review the CUSTOMER data base application. The following ten data items will be used to compose a data record for each customer:

> First Name
>
> Middle Initial
>
> Last Name
>
> Address
>
> City
>
> State
>
> Zip
>
> Phone
>
> Amount Owed
>
> Payment Date

After deciding which pieces of information to store, you must decide the type of data to be stored in each field and how long each field should be. Character data will be used for all fields except for the amount owed and payment date fields. Why would you want to use character data for the zip field when a zip code is comprised of numeric digits? Zip codes are easier to store as character data for two reasons. First, a common rule of thumb is that data should be stored as character data unless they are to be used in calculations. Second, character data are easier to include in indexing.

The phone field is also character data because the area code appears between parentheses ( ) and a hyphen appears between the exchange and the number in that exchange. The only field that is numeric is the Amount owed field. It will have two positions to the right of the decimal point. The Payment date will use the Date field data type. The breakdown of field names, data types, and field lengths is as follows:

Figure 19.3
Select the disk drive on
which the file is to be created.

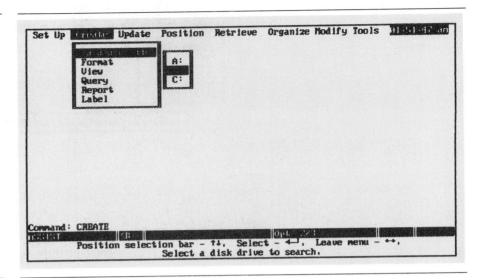

Field	Data Type	Field Length
FIRST	C	10
INITIAL	C	1
LAST	C	12
ADDRESS	C	25
CITY	C	15
STATE	C	2
ZIP	C	5
PHONE	C	13
Amount	N	8,2
Date	D	8

It is important not to use too many fields in a record or to define fields that are too large to hold the data. The size of the fields determines how much space they will take on disk. All fields are stored as described, and any unused field positions are filled with blanks. Thus, reserving too much room for a field wastes the disk storage space.

The CREATE command from the Assistant menu is used to build the template for a dBASE III Plus file. The Database file option from the CREATE command is then selected by pressing the ENTER key. dBASE now prompts you for the disk drive on which the file is to be created (see Figure 19.3) and then for the file name to be created (see Figure 19.4).

At this point, the cursor control menu is displayed at the top of the screen (see Figure 19.5). The status line contains important pieces of information: the name of the instruction being executed (CREATE), the name of the file (CUS-TOMER) and the disk on which is to be recorded (B:), and the fact that the pointer is on field 1 of 1 (no others have been created). In the upper right-hand corner of the screen is the number of bytes that remain for this record.

You can now define each field to dBASE. A field name can be up to ten characters and must start with an alphabetic character. After you have entered the field name, press the ENTER key. (Field names always appear in upper-case characters regardless of the status of the CAPS LOCK key.) The data type is the next information to be entered, and the default is character. Thus, for any character field, simply press the ENTER key. Next, enter the width and

Figure 19.4
Enter the file name of the file
to be created.

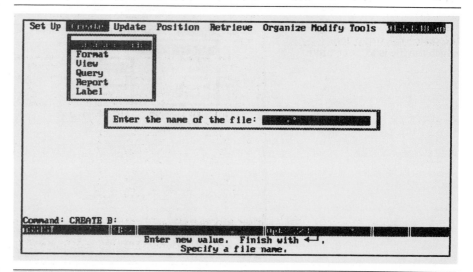

Figure 19.5
The Create screen that appears for a file to be created.

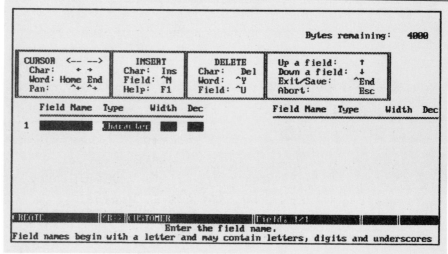

press ENTER. The only time you are prompted for decimal positions is when
the field has been defined as numeric.

You are now ready to define the next field. When you enter the last
payment date data type, the width is automatically assumed to be eight positions (see Figure 19.6).

Correcting errors that you spot is a straightforward process: Use the
cursor positioning keys on the key pad to move the cursor to the desired field
and reenter the data.

When you have finished defining the fields in the record, press ENTER
in response to the prompt for a field name, without entering any information.
You then receive a prompt to review the file (see below). When you press the
ENTER key again, the file definition is finished. Pressing any other key enables
you go back and make any needed changes.

```
Press ENTER to confirm. Any other key to resume. _
```

You now see the message Please Wait.... as dBASE records this information to the disk. It then asks

```
Input data records now? (Y/N) _
```

Figure 19.6
The completed Create screen
for the CUSTOMER.DBF file.

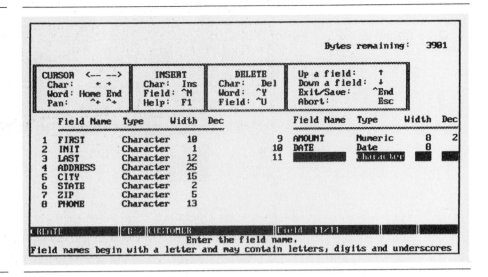

Type "Y" to enter the five records below:

```
                Name and Address Data Base
-----------------------------------------------------------------------

     Last       First     In       Address            City       St  Zip
 Ghorbani      Reza      R.  4033 N. Wolcott       Chicago       Il 60712
                             (312)245-0324         125.00     01/17/85

 Ghorbani      Ann       B.  4033 N. Wolcott       Chicago       Il 60712
                             (312)245-0324         250.00     03/23/85

 Acklin        Douglas   C.  408 E. Monroe         Bloomington   Il 61701
                             (309)663-8976          55.00     04/01/85

 Walters       Barbara   A.  1981 Crestlawn        Arlington     Va 13411
                             (703)237-3727          75.00     12/23/84

 Adams         Arthur    V.  115 Ginger Creek Ct.  Bloomington   Il 61701
                             (309)828-7290         357.00     03/15/85
```

The dBASE III Plus package clears the screen and places a blank record form on the screen (see Figure 19.7). The full-screen cursor menu appears at the top of the screen, the status line with the name of the file and the current record number at the bottom of the screen, and each field name in the left-hand column. Fill in the appropriate blanks. Each field appears in reverse video to indicate the field length. When you have reached the end of a field, the computer's bell rings, and the cursor automatically advances to the next field. If you finish entering data before the end of the field is reached, simply press the ENTER key. When the last field is filled or the ENTER key is pressed, a new blank form for the next record is displayed (see Figure 19.8).

When you enter numeric information, dBASE III Plus automatically right-justifies the number in the field when you press ENTER. If the number does not have decimal positions, you do not have to enter a decimal point; dBASE will automatically place it appropriately.

When the form has been filled with the data for the first record, it should look like Figure 19.8.

As each record is entered, dBASE raises the record number in the Status Bar of the screen. When you have finished entering all five of the records,

Figure 19.7
Blank record form for the
Customer file.

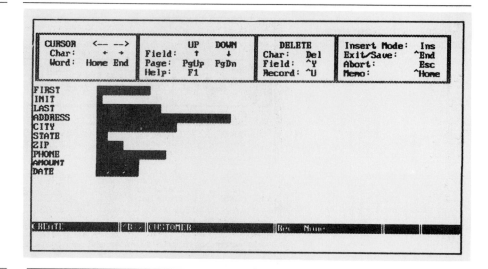

Figure 19.8
Filled-in form for the first
data record of the
CUSTOMER.DBF file.

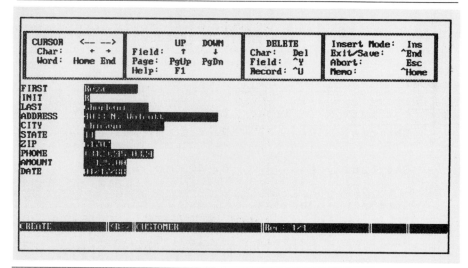

press ENTER when you are shown the first field of the next blank form. dBASE
then assumes that you have finished entering data and returns you to the
Assistant menu. You can now enter your next command. If you mistakenly
press the ENTER key, select the Update command from the Assistant menu
and press ENTER when the pointer is on the Append option. A new, blank
form is now displayed on the screen.

Activating
the Data Base

You have now created the CUSTOMER data base file and recorded five records in it. If you are still in dBASE and have not activated any other files, all
you have to do to add records to the CUSTOMER file is select the Update
option from the Assistant menu and press ENTER when the Append option
has been highlighted with the pointer.

If you quit dBASE and then later want to add records to the CUSTOMER
file, you must reenter dBASE and perform the following steps:

1. Select the Tools option of the Assistant menu, select the Set Drive
   option, and set the default drive to B: (assuming you are using a data
   disk in disk drive B).

Figure 19.9
Specifying a data base file to be opened.

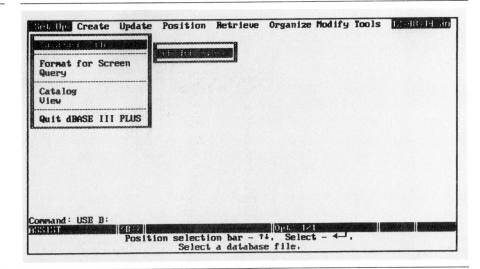

Figure 19.10
Specifying the data base file to open.

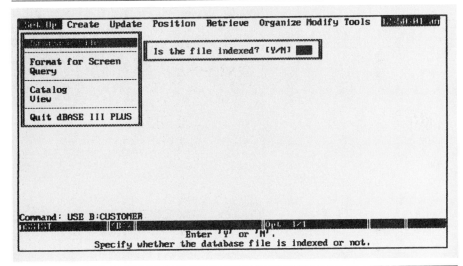

2. Select the Set Up option of the Assistant menu, specify the drive (press ENTER if step one has been performed), point to the file and press the ENTER key (see Figure 19.9), and respond N (in this case) to the prompt asking you whether or not the file is indexed (see Figure 19.10).

3. Select the Update option of the Assistant menu and press the ENTER key when the pointer has highlighted the **Append** option. A screen similar to that depicted in Figure 19.7 is displayed on your monitor. The only difference is that the Status bar contains the command APPEND rather than CREATE.

Once the file has been activated, you can look at the organization of the file by invoking the Tools option of the Assistant menu and then selecting the List structure option and entering N to the prompt Direct the output to the printer? (see Figure 19.11).

Once the LIST STRUCTURE command has executed, dBASE displays the message Press any key to continue work in ASSIST._. Press any key, and the Assistant menu appears on your monitor.

Figure 19.11
Output of the List structure
command for the
CUSTOMER.DBF
data base file.

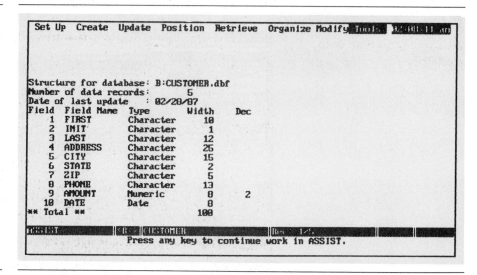

Figure 19.12
Assistant screen to implement the LIST command.

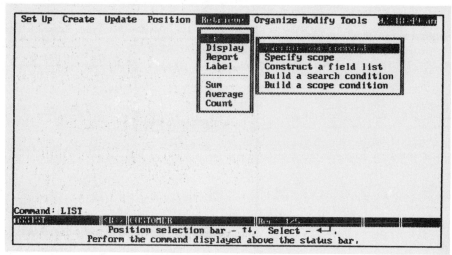

The dBASE package keeps track of the current number of records in the
file and includes the .DBF extension in the file name. If you remembered to
enter the date when you booted DOS, dBASE also keeps track of the date of
the last update; if you forgot to do so, the date will be 01/01/80. You can also
see the name, character type, and length of each field. The total bytes of
storage used by each record is at the bottom of the display.

The total number of bytes is one more than the sum of the individual
field sizes, to reserve a position for the delete indicator (*).

Now that you've looked at the structure of the data base, you should list
the content of the file to guarantee that you haven't done anything wrong.
Select the Retrieve option of the Assistant menu, position the pointer to the
List option, and press ENTER; then position the pointer to the Execute
the command line (see Figure 19.12) and press ENTER.

Once the command has been executed, the prompt Direct the
output to the printer? is displayed on the monitor. Simply press the
ENTER key to have the records displayed (see Figure 19.13). The prompt
Press any key to continue work in ASSIST._ is now at the
bottom of the screen. Once a key is pressed, you are returned to the Assistant menu.

Figure 19.13
Output of the LIST
command.

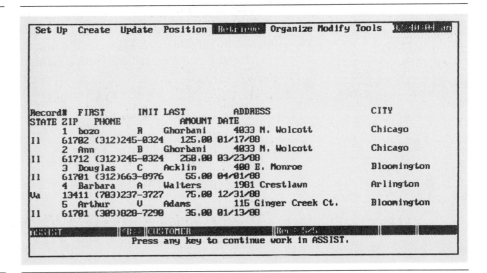

Figure 19.14
The Append screen.

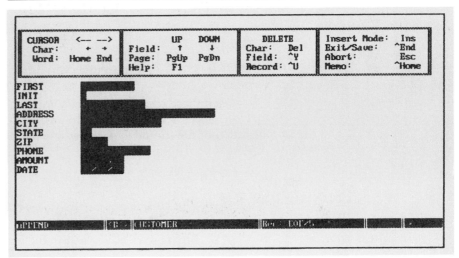

The LIST command starts at the beginning of your data file and lists all records to the screen. For readability, dBASE lists the names of the fields above the data, and it continues displaying records on the screen until the end of the file is reached. dBASE keeps track of where it is in a file by the use of a pointer, or record number, which is simply the file location of the current record being worked on by dBASE. The first record in a file is 1, the second is 2, and so forth.

Adding Records to the File

To add records to the data base file, select the UPDATE command from the Assistant menu, position the pointer to the APPEND command, press the ENTER key. Any records added to a file via the APPEND command are placed at the end of the existing file. When the APPEND command is executed, a number of actions are performed by dBASE: The screen is cleared and a blank record form is displayed, the record number in the Status bar is updated for the new record, and a blank entry screen (see Figure 19.14) is displayed on your monitor.

You can now enter more records, as you did after the file was initially created. The next blank record screen is automatically displayed when the last field of this record is filled, or when the ENTER key is pressed with the cursor in the last field of the record. You can indicate to dBASE III that you have finished by pressing ENTER when the first field of a blank form appears.

The following records can now be added to the existing CUSTOMER file:

```
         Last        First     In      Address              City        St  Zip
 Davis        Russell      B. 707 Vale St.        Bloomington      Il 61701
                           (309)662-1759        0.00              02/27/85

 Acklin       Debbie       C. 408 E. Monroe       Bloomington      Il 61701
                           (309)827-1395       35.00              03/21/85

 Posio        Harvey       B. 1013 Hillcrest      San Diego        Ca 94307
                           (619)271-9871     1250.00              04/03/85

 Pietrowiak   Ben          A. 3334 N. Foster      Normal           Il 61761
                           (309)452-9126       20.00              03/23/85

 Acklin       Sandy        C. 408 E. Monroe       Bloomington      Il 61701
                           (309)829-9901       35.00              02/25/85

 Ficek        Fred         R. 1215 Tamarack       Normal           Il 61761
                           (309)454-7123        0.00              04-05-85

 Decesario    Juan         C. 1214 Flores         Miami            Fl 12562
                           (305)719-1363       10.00              04-01-85
```

When these records have been entered, you can list the file via the RE-TRIEVE and LIST commands to ensure that you did not forget to enter a record. Your file should look something like the following:

```
Record#     FIRST        INITIAL LAST            ADDRESS            CITY
    STATE ZIP     PHONE           AMOUNT DATE
     1   Reza         R      Ghorbani      4033 N. Wolcott    Chicago
 Il    60712 (312)245-0324    125.00 01/17/85
     2   Ann          B      Ghorbani      4033 N. Wolcott    Chicago
 Il    60712 (312)245-0324    250.00 03/23/85
     3   Douglas      C      Acklin        408 E. Monroe      Bloomington
 Il    61701 (309)663-8976     55.00 04/01/85
     4   Barbara      A      Walters       1981 Crestlawn     Arlington
 Va    13411 (703)237-3727     75.00 12/31/84
     5   Arthur       V      Adams         115 Ginger Creek Ct. Bloomington
 Il    61701 (309)828-7290    357.00 03/13/85
     6   Russell      B      Davis         707 Vale St.       Bloomington
 Il    61701 (309)662-1759     35.00 02/27/85
     7   Debbie       C      Acklin        408 E. Monroe      Bloomington
 Il    61701 (309)827-1395     35.00 03/21/85
     8   Harvey       B      Posio         1013 Hillcrest     San Diego
 Ca    94307 (619)271-9871   1250.00 04/03/85
     9   Ben          A      Pietrowiak    3334 Foster        Normal
 Il    61761 (309)452-9126     20.00 03/23/85
    10   Sandy        C      Akclin        408 E. Monroe      Bloomington
 Il    61701 (309)829-9901     35.00 02/25/85
    11   Fred         R      Ficek         1215 Tamarack      Normal
 Il    61761 (309)454-7123      0.00 04/05/85
    12   Juan         C      Decesario     1214 Flores        Miami
 Fl    12562 (305)719-1363     10.00 04/01/85
```

Figure 19.15
An edit screen for record 10
of the Customer file.

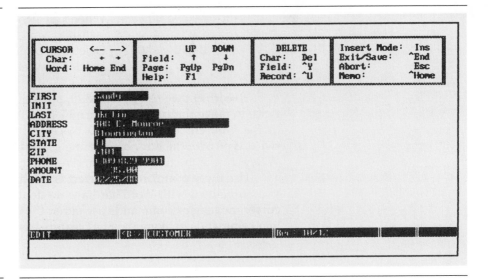

 Editing Records in the File

There should be twelve records in the file. Examine each record to make certain that there are no errors. Notice that in record 10 the last name is spelled incorrectly. This can be corrected via the EDIT command, which can be invoked from the Update option of the Assistant menu. Once the EDIT command has been invoked, a blank screen appears and the contents of the last record are displayed. You can now use the PGUP and PGDN keys to move backward and forward, respectively, in the file.

Once record 10 is located (see Figure 19.15) you can now use any of a number of commands to change the record.

You can advance the cursor to the next field by pressing the ENTER key. In addition to using the full-screen Cursor movement commands, you can also exercise cursor control with the following commands:

Cursor Control Key	dBASE Command	
	CTRL + A	Moves cursor one word to the left.
	CTRL + F	Moves cursor one word to the right.
←	CTRL + S	Moves cursor one position to the left.
→	CTRL + D	Moves cursor one position to the right.
↑	CTRL + E	Moves cursor up one line. At the top line it displays the prior record.
↓	CTRL + X	Moves cursor down one line. At the bottom line it displays the next record.
Del	CTRL + G	Deletes the character at the cursor position and moves the text one position to the left.
	CTRL + Y	Deletes the contents of an entire field.
	CTRL + W	Writes the changes back to the file. It then returns you to the Assistant menu.
PgUp	CTRL + R	Writes the current record to disk and displays the previous record.
PgDn	CTRL + C	Writes the current record to disk and displays the next record

| Ins | CTRL + V | Toggles between overwrite and insert mode. When you are in insert mode, the INS message is displayed in the Status bar. |
| | CTRL + U | Deletes or Undeletes a record. When a record is deleted a Del is displayed in the Status bar. |

To correct the error in record 10, press the ENTER or the down arrow key twice to move the cursor to the LAST field. You can then position the cursor to the *k* by entering CTRL + D twice or by pressing the right arrow key twice; type over the error by entering ck. Press the CTRL + END or CTRL + W keys to exit the EDIT process and return to the Assistant menu.

Use these commands to correct errors in your data base file. As those of you acquainted with WordStar have no doubt noticed, the full-screen EDIT cursor movement commands use either the cursor movement keys or Word-Star commands, making the EDIT feature easy to use for just about anyone.

dBASE III Plus
File Types

As was mentioned earlier, dBASE automatically places a .DBF file extension on any file that is generated via the CREATE command. In addition to .DBF files, dBASE also generates other files. Each of these files is discussed briefly below and will be introduced in more detail later.

Data Base Files

Date base files have a .DBF file extension and contain records that contain information about a business happening or transaction and are comprised of fields of data.

Memo Files. Memo files have a .DBT file extension and are capable of storing the large blocks of information found in the memo fields of a data base file. The information in a memo field is actually stored in a separate file.

Index Files. Index files have a .NDX file extension and provide dBASE with the abililty to appear to arrange information in a file without actually sorting it.

Format Files. Format files have a .FMT file extension and store custom screen forms or custom report forms.

Label Files. Label files have a .LBL file extension and are used for printing labels with the LABEL command.

Memory Files. Memory files have a .MEM file extension and are used to store the active memory variables to disk. A memory variable represents a temporary memory location that can hold the result of one or more computations.

Report Form Files. Report form files have a .FRM file extension and hold the parameters used to create a stored report form.

Text Files. Text files have a .TXT file extension and can hold data that have been copied from a data base file to this temporary file. This allows other applications packages (such as word processing packages) to access this data.

Catalog Files. Catalog files have a .CAT file extension and contain all of the names of a set of related data base files and their related files.

Query Files. Query files have a .QRY file extension and contain information about the conditions for displaying records from an existing data base file.

Screen Files. Screen files have a .SCR file extension and contain information about the screen layout of a custom data entry form.

View Files. View files have a .VUE file extension and are used for relating data base files with their related indexes, format fields, and other information defining the relationships among all these files.

Chapter Review

Before creating a dBASE file, you must plan the field name, the field length, and the type of data that is to be used for each field. The `CREATE` command from the Assistant menu is used to build a template for a data base file. Once the template is created, you can enter records immediately; the `APPEND` command is used to add records to the file later.

Accessing a file requires using the `SET UP` command from the Assistant menu (this issues a `USE` command). The Tools option of the Assistant menu is used to invoke the `LIST STRUCTURE` command to display the structure of the file to show the field names, data types and field size.

Listing the records to the screen requires selecting the Retrieve option from the Assistant menu and then selecting the Execute the command option. The field name along with each field's contents of all records are displayed to the monitor.

To change a record requires selecting the Update option of the Assistant menu and then positioning the pointer to the Edit option. The last record accessed is displayed to the screen. Full-screen cursor movement commands as well as WordStar cursor movement commands can now be used to position the cursor and to move from one record to the next within the file.

The `QUIT` command is used to leave dBASE II. The `QUIT` command is required any time that you have added records to an indexed file. If `QUIT` is not used, the records may not be added and the index will have to be rebuilt.

Key Terms and Concepts

dBASE III	`LIST`
menu-driven mode	`EDIT`
command-driven mode	`QUIT`
`CREATE`	full-screen editing
`USE`	record number
`APPEND`	`LIST STRUCTURE`

Chapter Quiz

Multiple Choice

1. Which is not a true statement about dBASE III Plus?
   a. The package can be used only in menu mode.
   b. No statements can be saved to a file and executed later.
   c. Once the dot prompt is reached, the Assistant menu cannot be reactivated.
   d. All of the above statements are false.

2. Which of the following commands enables you to place records in a data base file?
   a. USE
   b. CREATE
   c. LIST
   d. APPEND
   e. ADD

3. The LIST command is used for the following:
   a. Looking at records contained in a file
   b. Invoking a data base file
   c. Displaying the structure of a data base file
   d. Exiting the dBASE III program
   e. Making changes to a file

4. Which of the following commands enables you to make a change to an existing data base file?
   a. EDIT
   b. LIST
   c. USE
   d. CREATE
   e. QUIT

5. Which of the following are valid data types for use with dBASE III Plus?
   a. Character
   b. Numeric
   c. Memo
   d. Date
   e. Logical
   f. All of the above

True/False

6. The dBASE III Plus package in Assistant mode is menu driven.

7. The dBASE III Plus package uses the period (.) as the default user prompt.

8. It is advisable to use the QUIT command from the dot prompt or the QUIT dBASE III PLUS from the Set Up option of the Assistant menu to avoid data loss.

9. The dBASE III package EDIT command makes use of the cursor pad as well as WordStar-like commands for cursor manipulation.

10. The EDIT and APPEND commands use the full-screen feature of dBASE III Plus.

Answers

1. d 2. b&d 3. a&c 4. a 5. f 6. t 7. f 8. t 9. t 10. t

Exercises

1. Define or describe each of the following:
   a. command-driven   c. full-screen editing
   b. menu-driven   d. record number

2. The default mode for dBASE is the _____ menu.

3. A dBASE record can have up to _____ characters.

4. The _____ command is used to describe a record to dBASE.

5. A file is made available to dBASE by entering the _____ command.

6. The _____ gives the physical location of a record in a file.

7. The _____ should be used to exit dBASE.

8. The _____ command is used to look at the structure of a dBASE file.

9. The _____ command is used to add data to an existing data base file.

10. The APPEND and EDIT commands make use of the _____ screen editing feature of dBASE.

11. The EDIT command uses _____-like cursor movement commands.

12. The _____ edit command is used to save the changes to the current record and return control back to dBASE.

13. The _____ edit command deletes the contents of an entire field.

14. When you use the LIST STRUCTURE command, what pieces of information are provided before the field list?
    a.

    b.

    c.

15. List and describe three types of files used by dBASE III Plus.

Computer Exercises

1. Create a file called PAYMAST. It should have the following structure.

```
STRUCTURE FOR FILE:    A:PAYMAST .DBF
NUMBER OF RECORDS:     00012
DATE OF LAST UPDATE: 01/01/80
PRIMARY USE DATABASE
FLD        NAME        TYPE WIDTH      DEC
001        EMPLOYID     N    004
002        FIRSTNAM     C    010
003        LASTNAM      C    012
004        PAYRATE      N    006        002
005        YTDGROSS     N    009        002
**TOTAL**               00042
```

2. Enter the following records:

ID	NAME	RATE	GROSS
4908	Richard Payne	4.45	556.00
5789	Connie Reiners	3.35	450.00
5323	Pamela Rich	6.00	780.00
6324	Mark Tell	5.50	980.00
2870	Frank Terlep	3.80	670.00
4679	Kenneth Klass	4.90	780.00
8345	Thomas Momery	4.70	580.00

3. List the contents of the file by using the LIST command.

4. Add the records below:

5649	Toni McCarthy	5.20	667.00
5432	Alan Monroe	5.20	1340.00
5998	Paul Mish	4.90	887.00
4463	Edward Mockford	4.90	775.00
456		0.00	0.00

5. Use the EDIT command to correct any errors. Also use the EDIT command to place your name in the name area for record #12.

Chapter
20

dBASE III Plus
File Manipulation
Commands

After completing this chapter, you should be able to:

Discuss various dBASE III Plus file manipulation commands that can be issued from the Assistant menu and from the dot (.) prompt

Discuss pointer movement commands

Discuss the CREATE REPORT *command*

This chapter describes a number of dBASE III Plus commands used for file manipulation.

Access and Display Commands

The USE, LIST, and LIST STRUCTURE commands have already been introduced; the DISPLAY command, the ? character, and the RECNO( ) function have not.

Command Execution from the Assist Menu

Example 1   USE

The USE command makes a file available to the user. You can execute a USE command as follows:

1. Select the Tools option of the Assistant menu.
2. Select the Set Drive entry to set the default drive to B.
3. Select the Set Up option from the Assistant.
4. Select the Database file entry (note that the command Use now appears on the action line).
5. Select drive B (the default specified in the previous step; note that B: also appears on the action line).
6. Point to the customer file (note that USE B:CUSTOMER now appears on the action line).
7. Respond N to the prompt Is the file indexed? [Y/N].

The customer file is now activated and ready for use by dBASE.

Example 2   LIST STRUCTURE

If you want to examine the structure of the CUSTOMER file, you must select the Tools option of the Assistant menu and then select the LIST STRUC-TURE command (DISPLAY STRUCTURE now appears on the action line). Upon receiving the prompt Direct the output to the printer? [Y/N], enter an N. A list of the record structure is displayed (see Figure 20.1), allowing you to examine the structure of a record and providing information such as name of the file, number of records currently in the file, date of last update, names of the fields, data types of the fields, and field lengths. At the end of the structure report, the total number of bytes of storage occupied by each record is given.

Example 3   List

The LIST command enables you to display the contents of the CUSTOMER file on the screen. To execute a LIST command, select the Retrieve option of the Assistant menu (you will then see LIST on the action line); a submenu (see Figure 20.2) now appears. After you select the first option, execute the command, and respond N to the prompt Direct the output to the printer? [Y/N], the contents of the file CUSTOMER are displayed on your screen (see Figure 20.3).

Once the LIST command has finished executing, press any key to continue working in Assist mode.

The unmodified LIST command starts at the beginning of the file and lists all fields of each record. When a regular LIST command is executed,

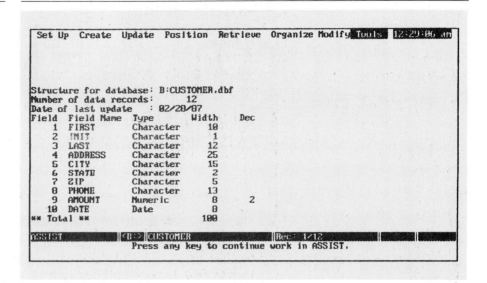

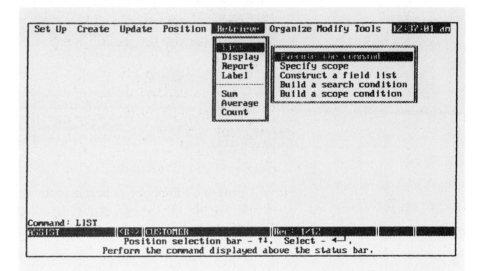

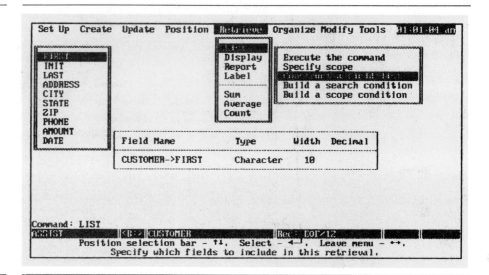

```
 Set Up   Create   Update   Position  Retrieve  Organize Modify Tools   01:01:04 am
                                    ┌─────────┐ ┌───────────────────────────┐
 ┌──────────────┐                   │ List    │ │ Execute the command       │
 │ FIRST        │                   │ Display │ │ Specify scope             │
 │ INIT         │                   │ Report  │ │ Construct a field list    │
 │ LAST         │                   │ Label   │ │ Build a search condition  │
 │ ADDRESS      │                   ├─────────┤ │ Build a scope condition   │
 │ CITY         │                   │ Sum     │ └───────────────────────────┘
 │ STATE        │                   │ Average │
 │ ZIP          │                   │ Count   │
 │ PHONE        │                   └─────────┘
 │ AMOUNT       │  ┌─────────────────────────────────────────────────────┐
 │ DATE         │  │ Field Name          Type        Width  Decimal       │
 └──────────────┘  ├─────────────────────────────────────────────────────┤
                   │ CUSTOMER->FIRST     Character    10                   │
                   └─────────────────────────────────────────────────────┘



 Command: LIST
 ASSIST          <B:> CUSTOMER                       Rec: EOF/12
           Position selection bar - ↑↓.   Select - ◄┘.   Leave menu - ←→.
              Specify which fields to include in this retrieval.
```

dBASE searches the entire file for records. The `LIST` command moves the pointer automatically to the beginning of the file, and when the search ends, the pointer is located at the last record.

Example 4 LIST field list

You can control which fields of records are listed by executing the `Construct a field list` option of the List submenu. The `Construct a field list` option enables you to determine which fields from records to list on the screen. For example, to list the first names, initials, and last names in the file, you use the following commands from the Assistant menu.

1. Select the `Retrieve` option of the Assistant menu.
2. Take the `List` option (`LIST` now appears on the action line).
3. Select the `Construct a field list` option of the List submenu; the fields in the `CUSTOMER` record are now displayed (see Figure 20.4).
4. Move the pointer with the up and down arrow keys to display the characteristics of each field in the middle of the screen.
5. Press the ENTER key to select field (the pointer automatically moves down to the next entry).

As each field is selected, dBASE adds that field name to the `LIST` command in the action line (see Figure 20.4). After all of the desired fields (`FIRST`, `INIT`, and `LAST`) have been selected, the action line should have the following content: `LIST FIRST, INIT, LAST.` Upon pressing a right- or left-arrow key, you are returned to the List submenu, and the `Construct a field list` entry is now in low-intensity video and unavailable for further selection. To execute the new `LIST` command, select the `Execute the command` entry with the pointer, press the ENTER key, and respond N to the prompt `Direct output to the printer? [Y/N]`. The records are now listed on the screen (see Figure 20.5).

Example 5 LIST Field List

To list the first names, initials, last names, and amounts for all the records, you use the same steps as described above but add the `AMOUNT` field. The

Figure 20.5

Output of the LIST command using selected fields.

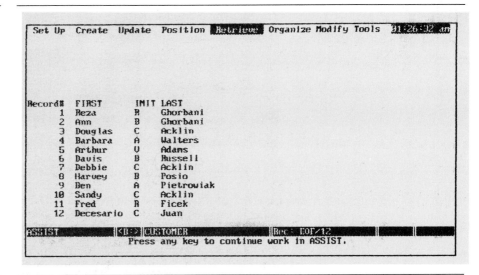

Figure 20.6

The LIST command with an additional field.

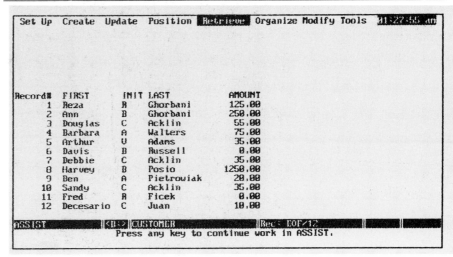

command that now appears on the action line is LIST FIRST, INIT, LAST, AMOUNT. The new output (see Figure 20.6) now includes the amount field.

Example 6   LIST NEXT

You can use the LIST command to display the next *x* number of records in a file by adding the NEXT **option** to the basic List command. First, however, since you are not including all records from the file in this command, you must reposition the pointer at the beginning of the file by means of the Assistant menu Position command. Once the Position command has been executed, select the Goto Record option and then the TOP command (see Figure 20.7). The pointer is now positioned at the beginning of the file.

You can now select the Retrieve option from the Assistant menu. Once the List option has been selected from this menu, select the Specify scope option of that submenu. A Scope submenu now appears on the screen, from which you select the NEXT option. An entry then appears that asks you to enter the number of records that you want to have listed on the screen (see Figure 20.8). Enter the number 5 and press the ENTER key. Now specify the FIRST, INIT, LAST, and AMOUNT fields to be included in the LIST

Figure 20.7
The Assistant screen for positioning the pointer at the beginning of the file.

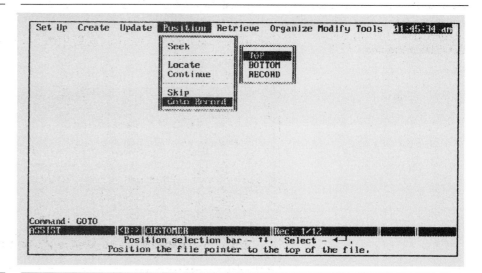

Figure 20.8
The Assistant screen for specifying the Scope.

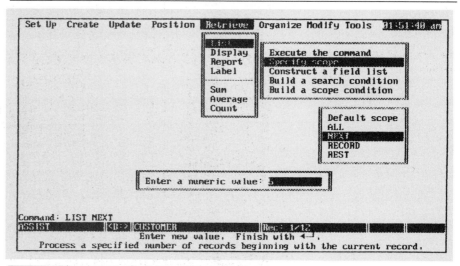

command by selecting the Construct a Field list option. Once you have finished this task, you are now returned to the List submenu and must now select the Execute the command option. Do not route the output to the printer. The first five records are displayed on your screen (see Figure 20.9).

Example 7   LIST While

You can also use the LIST command to display records that meet a certain criterion by entering the WHILE **parameter** and the selection criterion after the LIST command. For example, you might want to list all records that have an amount greater than $100. This is accomplished by selecting the Retrieve option from the Assistant menu and then executing the List command. Once the List submenu is displayed, select the Build a search condition option. This displays the record fields to the screen. Select the Amount field by positioning the pointer to that field (see Figure 20.10).

Once the field has been selected, a condition menu appears on the screen, and you must select (in this example) the > Greater Than option (see Figure 20.11). Then enter the value of 100 at the prompt Enter a nu-

Figure 20.9

Output of the LIST NEXT 5
RECORDS command.

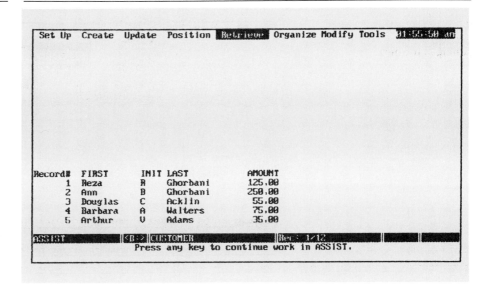

Figure 20.10

A field marked for a search
condition.

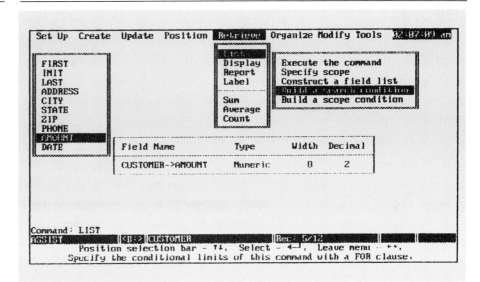

Figure 20.11

The condition screen.

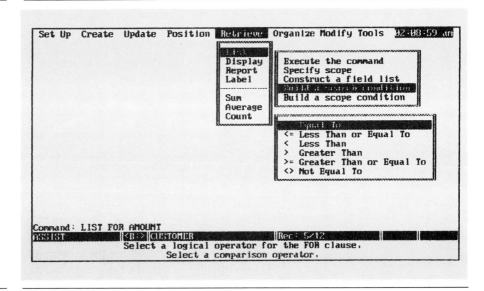

Figure 20.12
The More Conditions
prompt.

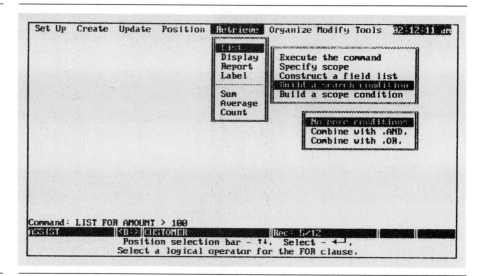

Figure 20.13
The records listed for the
command LIST FOR
AMOUNT > 100.

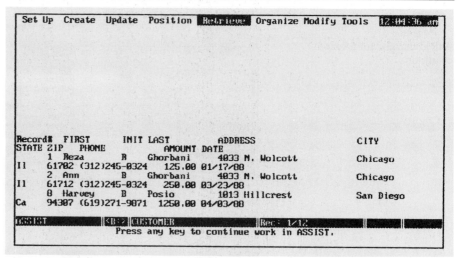

meric value: _. You now receive a prompt inquiring whether or not there are more conditions (see Figure 20.12) and should select the No more conditions entry (the command LIST WHILE AMOUNT > 100 is in the action line). Then select the Execute the command entry of the List submenu. Three records (see Figure 20.13) are now on the screen.

Example 8 LIST, with selection criteria and specified fields.

The LIST command probably generated more output than you need or want. To list only selected fields (in this case, the first and last names and the amount) of records that meet a criterion, you must position the pointer to the beginning of the file and select the Construct a field list option of the List submenu to specify the field list containing these fields; then take the Build a search condition option to enter your criterion. Once this has been done, you should see the command LIST FIRST, LAST, AMOUNT WHILE AMOUNT > 100 in the action line. List the records to the screen (see Figure 20.14).

Figure 20.14
List of specific fields for a
condition.

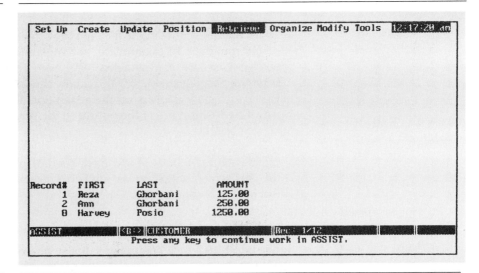

Figure 20.15
The result of a DISPLAY
command when the pointer
is located at the end of
the file.

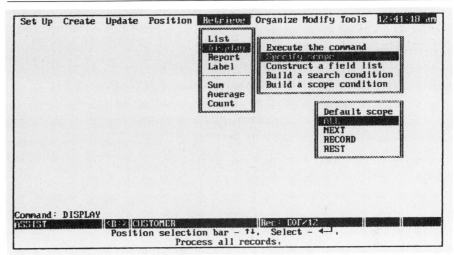

DISPLAY

The DISPLAY **command**, works similarly to the LIST command except that
only the record at the pointer location is displayed. The DISPLAY ALL command causes sixteen lines to appear on the screen. dBASE then gives a WAIT-
ING prompt, signifying that you may press any key to have the screen display
the next sixteen lines.

Unlike the LIST command, the DISPLAY command does not go immediately to the beginning of the data file; rather, it causes the display to begin
at the record at which the pointer is currently positioned. The DISPLAY
command is found in the Retrieve submenu.

Example 9   DISPLAY

If a DISPLAY command is issued after the pointer has moved to the bottom
of the file (for example, after a LIST command has been executed), no record
is displayed. In this example, the pointer is at the end of a file after execution
of the above list statement. Since it has reached end of file, no record is
displayed; only the field headings appear on the screen (see Figure 20.15).

Example 10   DISPLAY ALL

To list all the records in the file onto the screen in the same fashion that would result from the L I S T command, you must include the ALL **parameter**. This is accomplished by selecting Retrieve, then Display, then S r e c i f y s c o r e from the Display submenu, and finally the ALL option. The command D I S - PLAY ALL now appears on the action line. Select the E x e c u t e t h e c o m - m a n d option and direct the output to the screen (see Figure 20.16); press any key to continue.

When the D I S P L A Y A L L command is used, dBASE automatically stops (pauses) after 16 lines of text have been displayed on the screen. To display the next screen of text, press any key. This will continue until the end of file is reached.

Example 11   DISPLAY ALL field list

The D I S P L A Y A L L command can also be used to list specific files or records onto the monitor. For example, once the ALL scope has been specified, the fields first, last, and amount can be specified in the same manner as for the L I S T command. Once the process is completed, the command D I S P L A Y ALL FIRST, LAST, AMOUNT appears on the action line. Once the command is executed, the records are displayed to the monitor (see Figure 20.17).

The D I S P L A Y A L L command can use any of the field list, scope, or conditions options used by the L I S T command.

Crude reports can be generated by using the L I S T and D I S P L A Y A L L commands in two ways. First, you can issue a printer command by responding Y to the prompt D i r e c t o u t p u t t o t h e r r i n t e r? [Y / N]. This command, when executed, activates the printer, prints the output of the L I S T or D I S P L A Y A L L command, and then deactivates the printer. The second method is used from the dot prompt. You must issue a SET PRINT ON command to activate the printer, issue your command, and turn the printer off with a SET PRINT OFF command.

DIR

Example 12   DIR

The D I R **command** also can be used to list data base files onto the screen. The directory (DIR) command can be accessed from the Tools entry of the Assistant menu by selecting the D i r e c t o r y option. Once the directory option is se-lected, you are prompted for the drive to be used (the pointer automatically moves to the default drive); enter the appropriate drive. If you have selected drive B:, the prompt on the Action line is now D I R B :. You must now point to the type of file that you want displayed (in this case, . d b f) and press the ENTER key (see Figure 20.18). The files are now displayed on your screen.

Access and Display Commands Entered
from the Dot Prompt

The Assistant menu of dBASE III Plus enables you to create dBASE commands without knowing much about the dBASE language syntax. As you have seen in the preceding examples, dBASE shows the commands it is following in the action line; these commands are the same as those you would enter at the dot prompt. The commands for each of the above examples are given in this

Figure 20.16
Output of the DISPLAY ALL
command.

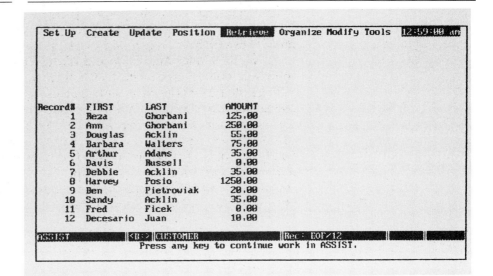

Figure 20.17
Output of the DISPLAY ALL
FIRST, LAST, AMOUNT
command.

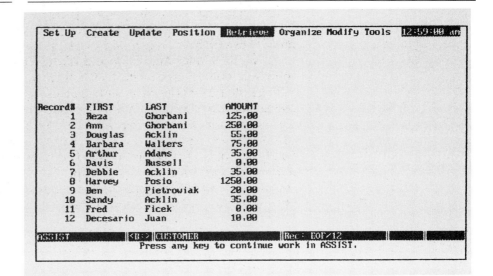

Figure 20.18
Screen for the DIR command.

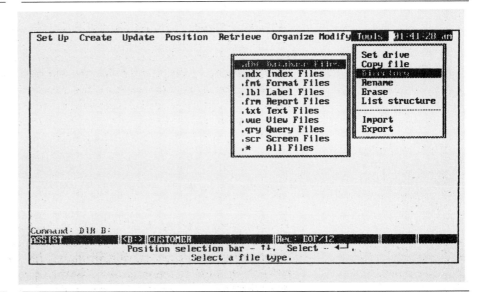

Figure 20.19
The dBASE screen with dot
prompt.

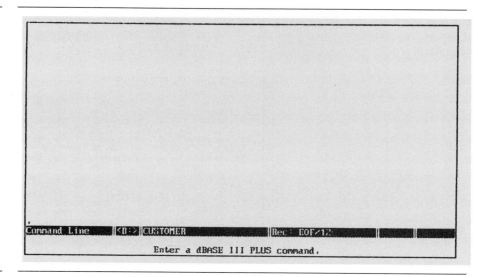

section. Since the output is very similar, only the commands issued at the dot
prompt are given.

To reach the dot prompt (.) press the ESC key one or more times. You
should now see a blank screen with the dot prompt on the action line (see
Figure 20.19).

The instructions required for each example are as follows:

Example 1

. `set default to b:`
. `use customer`

Example 2

. `list structure`

Example 3

. `list`

Example 4

. `list first, init, last`

Example 5

. `list first, init, last, amount`

Example 6

. `goto top`
. `list next 5 first, init, last, amount`

Example 7

. `list for amount > 100`

Example 8

```
. list first, last, amount for amount > 100
```

Example 9

```
. display
```

Example 10

```
. display all
```

Example 11

```
. display all first, last, amount
```

Example 12

```
. dir *.dbf
```

As you can see, the Assistant menu enables you to gradually construct your dBASE commands without much knowledge of the syntax, and the command mode (.) requires that you have a good understanding of how to form a dBASE command. As you get more and more acquainted with dBASE, you will probably spend more time at the dot prompt.

Some forms of the preceding commands just cannot be entered through the Assistant menu. For example, a version of the LIST/DISPLAY command(s) can be used to search for rather loose criteria. For instance, you might not know how to spell someone's name exactly, but you do know how the name starts. In this situation, it is best to use the **substring function ($)**. The following command could be translated as "list the first name and last name fields of any record that has the characters *Gho* in the last-name field."

```
. list first, last for 'Gho' $last
Record#  first     last
      1  Reza      Ghorbani
      2  Ann       Ghorbani
```

The following command generates a list of every record that has a capital *A* in the first-name field.

```
. list first, last for 'A' $first
Record#  first     last
      2  Ann       Ghorbani
      5  Arthur    Adams
```

The following command generates a list of every record that has the characters *ar* anywhere in the first-name field.

```
. list first, last for 'ar' $first
Record#  first     last
      4  Barbara   Walters
      8  Harvey    Posio
```

? and RECNO( ) Commands

The **? character** is used any time that you want some piece of information displayed on the screen. The RECNO( ) **function** is used to obtain the pointer location from dBASE. Using ? and RECNO( ) together produces a command to identify the location of the pointer and display that number on the screen, as follows:

```
. ? recno()
        5
```

Pointer Position Commands

Pointer positioning commands can be entered easily from the dot prompt. Entering them from the Assistant menu takes too many keystrokes for many users. A number of pointer position commands are included in dBASE. These commands activate (make available) records for dBASE processing; they include the GOTO, GO, GOTO TOP, GOTO BOTTOM, and SKIP commands. (Of course, such commands as LIST and DISPLAY also result in a change of the pointer position.)

GO and GOTO

The GO and GOTO **commands** can be used interchangeably. The following examples illustrate the joint use of the GOTO and DISPLAY commands to enable you to examine the content of a record. In each case, the DISPLAY command generates a display of the record pointed to by the GOTO command, as follows:

```
. goto 5
. display

Record#   FIRST        INITIAL LAST         ADDRESS              CITY
   STATE ZIP     PHONE               AMOUNT DATE
     5  Arthur      V       Adams          115 Ginger Creek Ct.Bloomington
    Il     61701  (309)828-7290    357.00 03/13/85

. goto 10
. display

Record#   FIRST        INITIAL LAST         ADDRESS              CITY
   STATE ZIP     PHONE               AMOUNT DATE
    10  Sandy       C       Acklin         408 E. Monroe        Bloomington
    Il     61701  (309)829-9901     35.00 02/25/85
```

The GOTO portion of a pointer position command (except in the cases of GOTO TOP and GOTO BOTTOM) can be implied simply by entering the desired record number after the dot prompt. For example, the following command sequence suffices.

```
. 2
. display first, last, amount
Record# FIRST        LAST         AMOUNT
     2  Ann          Ghorbani     250.00

. list next 4 first,last
Record# FIRST        LAST
     2  Ann          Ghorbani
     3  Douglas      Acklin
     4  Barbara      Walters
     5  Arthur       Adams
```

SKIP

The SKIP **command** advances the pointer one record forward in the file. It can be followed by a number (positive or negative): A positive number moves the pointer forward that number of records, and a negative number moves the pointer backward that number of record positions. When the Skip command is issued, the new pointer position is displayed on the screen. For example, with the pointer currently situated at record 5 (as the result of the preceding file manipulation), the unmodified SKIP command advances the pointer as follows:

```
. SKIP
Record no.       6
. display first,last,amount
Record# first       last       amount
      6 Russell     Davis       35.00
```

With the pointer currently located at record 6, the following SKIP command moves the pointer backward three records in the file:

```
. skip -3
Record no.       3
. display

Record# FIRST        INITIAL LAST         ADDRESS          CITY
    STATE ZIP    PHONE           AMOUNT DATE
    3 Douglas      C        Acklin        408 E. Monroe    Bloomington
  Il     61701 (309)663-8976     55.00 04/01/85
```

With the pointer located at record 3, the following SKIP command moves the pointer forward six records in the file:

```
. SKIP 6
Record no.       9
. display

Record# FIRST        INITIAL LAST         ADDRESS          CITY
    STATE ZIP    PHONE           AMOUNT DATE
    9 Ben          A        Pietrowiak    3334 Foster      Normal
  Il     61761 (309)452-9126     20.00 03/23/85
```

GOTO TOP

The GOTO TOP **command** positions the pointer at the first record in the file, as follows:

```
. GOTO TOP
. ?RENCO()
         1
```

The GOTO TOP command can also be used with the DISPLAY command to position the pointer at the beginning (top) of the file and display that record, as follows:

```
. goto top
. display first, last, amount
RECORD#    FIRST    LAST       AMOUNT
      1    Reza     Ghorbani    1.25
```

GOTO BOTTOM

The GOTO BOTTOM **command** positions the pointer at the last record in the file, as follows:

```
. GOTO BOTTOM
. ?RECNO()
```

```
        12
```

DATE

If you want to access the system date while you are in dBASE, use the DATE function. The date that you entered during the boot process is now displayed; or if you did not enter a date, 01/01/80 is displayed. The command and display are as follows:

```
. ? DATE()
03/13/87
```

End of File (EOF)

The **end of file (EOF) function** senses the end of the file—the location beyond the "last" record in the file. A sample EOF command follows:

```
. GOTO BOTTOM
. ? EOF ()
.F.
```

Notice that the value returned is F (false), meaning that the end of the file was not detected. This is because the pointer is now at the beginning of the last record. To activate the EOF function, a SKIP command must be issued to move the pointer past the last record.

```
. SKIP
Record no.        13
. ? EOF
.T.
```

Beginning of File (BOF)

The same technique applies to the **beginning of file (BOF) function**; as appears below, dBASE doesn't realize that it is actually at the top of the file until you try to access a record that isn't there.

```
. GO TOP
. ?bof()
.F.
. SKIP -1
  Record no.        1
. ?bof()
.T.
```

SUM

dBASE can be directed to perform arithmetic via the SUM **command**. For instance, if you want to know the grand total owed, you can find out by using

Figure 20.20
The Sum screen for summing the AMOUNT field.

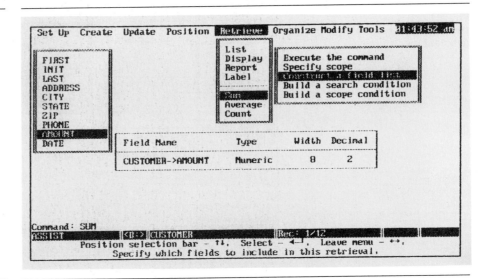

the Retrieve option of the Assistant menu. You now select the Sum option and then the Construct a field list option and point to any numeric fields that you want to sum (in this example, you can sum only the AMOUNT field). Once these commands have been given (see Figure 20.20) you are ready to execute the command.

Once control is returned to the Sum submenu, the command SUM AMOUNT appears on the action line. After the command is executed, the following message appears on your screen:

```
12 records summed
amount
1890.00
```

You might also be interested in knowing the grand total for customers that have a $100 or greater balance. To determine this, enter the search condition FOR AMOUNT > 100, after the AMOUNT field has been selected. After executing this command, you should see the following on your screen:

```
3 records summed
amount
1625.00
```

dBASE also enables you to generate the numeric average of a field within a data base file. For instance, you might want to know the average amount owed in the CUSTOMER file. This information can also be obtained via the Retrieve option of the Assistant menu. Now select the Construct a field list option and then select the appropriate numeric fields (in this example, only the AMOUNT field is numeric) and execute the command (see Figure 20.21).

Before the command is executed, the action line contains AVERAGE AMOUNT. Once the command is executed, the following data should be displayed on your screen:

```
12 records averaged
average
157.50
```

Figure 20.21
The Average screen of the
Assistant menu.

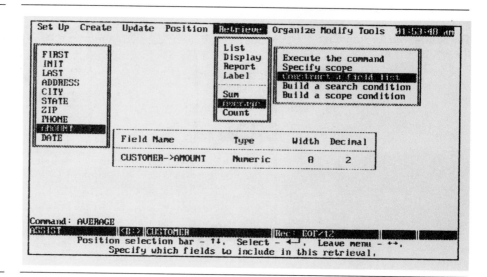

Record Alteration
Commands

You have already seen how to make changes in record by using the EDIT command. Other alterations can be made by using the REPLACE, DELETE, PACK, and RESTORE commands. The command-level dot prompt mode is used in the following examples. Although this mode provides maximum flexibility, the Assistant menu could be used in some of these examples.

REPLACE

Instead of accessing each record and displaying it for full-screen editing, you can use the REPLACE **command** to institute the change. For example, assume that Reza Ghorbani paid his bill in full. To change the amount in his record to zero, enter the REPLACE command shown below. A message telling you how many records were replaced will then be displayed. To verify that the REPLACE command has accomplished its task, enter the LIST command that follows it.

```
. replace amount with 0 for first = 'Reza'
      1 record replaced
. list first, last, amount
```

Record#	first	last	amount
1	Reza	Ghorbani	0.00
2	Ann	Ghorbani	250.00
3	Douglas	Acklin	55.00
4	Barbara	Walters	75.00
5	Arthur	Adams	357.00
6	Russell	Davis	35.00
7	Debbie	Acklin	35.00
8	Harvey	Posio	1250.00
9	Ben	Pietrowiak	20.00
10	Sandy	Acklin	35.00
11	Fred	Ficek	0.00
12	Juan	Decesario	10.00

This example limits the criteria for the replacement. If you want to change every record by the same amount, you can add the scope parameter ALL. For example, you could add five cents to each record's amount by issuing the

REPLACE command shown below. Clearly, if you need to make a change that will affect all the records in a file, or a large number of records, the REPLACE ALL command will do the job in significantly less time than the EDIT command requires. The following example illustrates how it works:

```
. replace all amount with amount + .05
     12 records replaced
. list first, last, amount

Record#   first       last            amount
      1   Reza        Ghorbani           0.05
      2   Ann         Ghorbani         250.05
      3   Douglas     Acklin            55.05
      4   Barbara     Walters           75.05
      5   Arthur      Adams            357.05
      6   Russell     Davis             35.05
      7   Debbie      Acklin            35.05
      8   Harvey      Posio           1250.05
      9   Ben         Pietrowiak        20.05
     10   Sandy       Acklin            35.05
     11   Fred        Ficek              0.05
     12   Juan        Decesario         10.05
```

You can easily return the file to its former status by issuing another REPLACE command.

```
. replace all amount with amount - .05
     12 records replaced
. list first, last, amount

Record#   first       last            amount
      1   Reza        Ghorbani           0.00
      2   Ann         Ghorbani         250.00
      3   Douglas     Acklin            55.00
      4   Barbara     Walters           75.00
      5   Arthur      Adams            357.00
      6   Russell     Davis             35.00
      7   Debbie      Acklin            35.00
      8   Harvey      Posio           1250.00
      9   Ben         Pietrowiak        20.00
     10   Sandy       Acklin            35.00
     11   Fred        Ficek              0.00
     12   Juan        Decesario         10.00
```

DELETE, PACK, and RECALL

From time to time, you will want to delete records from a data base file. This is a two-step process: (1) the record is marked for deletion via the DELETE command; and (2) the file is recopied, with all records that were marked for deletion left out and with all records packed together via the PACK command. The first step is sometimes referred to as *logical deletion*; although the record is marked, it is not removed from the file. Consequently, it can still be read and processed. The example that follows illustrates marking a record (record 7) for deletion. First the pointer is positioned at record 7; then part of the record is displayed to make certain that the desired record has been located; then the DELETE command is issued. The message displayed on the screen indicates that the record has been marked; the **delete indicator (*)** appears between the record number and the first field of the record. The command (with dBASE response) is as follows:

```
. 7
. display first, last
Record# first         last
      7 Debbie        Acklin
. delete
      1 record deleted
. display

Record#   FIRST         INITIAL LAST           ADDRESS           CITY
    STATE ZIP     PHONE                AMOUNT DATE
      7 *Debbie        C      Acklin          408 E. Monroe     Bloomington
    Il      61701 (309)827-1395      35.00 03/21/85
```

The asterisk (*) shows that the record has been marked for deletion, takes up one byte of storage on a dBASE record, and accounts for the extra position reserved for the fields in a record. In a listing of all the file records, the record marked for deletion is recognizable at once:

```
. list first, last, amount

Record#   first       last            amount
      1   Reza        Ghorbani          0.00
      2   Ann         Ghorbani        250.00
      3   Douglas     Acklin           55.00
      4   Barbara     Walters          75.00
      5   Arthur      Adams           357.00
      6   Russell     Davis            35.00
      7 *Debbie       Acklin           35.00
      8   Harvey      Posio          1250.00
      9   Ben         Pietrowiak       20.00
     10   Sandy       Acklin           35.00
     11   Fred        Ficek             0.00
     12   Juan        Decesario        10.00
```

Once a record has been marked for deletion, it can be undeleted (as long as a PACK command has not been issued) by using a RECALL **command.** If you want to undelete a record, you must first position the pointer at that record and then issue the RECALL command. To undelete all of the records in a file, enter a RECALL ALL command. Since the pointer is still on record 7 in the present case, a pointer positioning command does not have to be entered. After a RECALL command is entered, the number of records undeleted is displayed on the screen.

```
. 7
. recall
      1 record recalled
. display first ,last
Record# first         last
      7 Debbie        Acklin
```

Assume that record 13 is to be deleted from the file (you will first have to add it to the file using the APPEND command). The following steps have to be taken to delete record 13:

1. The pointer is positioned at record 13.

2. The record is displayed to ensure that the pointer is properly positioned.

3. The DELETE command is entered.

4. Part of the file is listed to ensure that the record has been marked.

5. The file is packed via the PACK command, physically removing the record.

6. Portions of each record are then listed to ensure that the record is gone.

On your screen, these steps appear as follows:

```
. 13
. display
Record#  FIRST      INITIAL LAST        ADDRESS              CITY
   STATE ZIP   PHONE           AMOUNT DATE
   13 Eric        C      Wild        207 S. Broadmore        Felix
   Kn    34762               0.00   /  /

      . delete
        1 record deleted
      . list first,last,amount

      Record#   first     last         amount
            1   Reza      Ghorbani        0.00
            2   Ann       Ghorbani      250.00
            3   Douglas   Acklin         55.00
            4   Barbara   Walters        75.00
            5   Arthur    Adams         357.00
            6   Russell   Davis          35.00
            7   Debbie    Acklin         35.00
            8   Harvey    Posio        1250.00
            9   Ben       Pietrowiak     20.00
           10   Sandy     Acklin         35.00
           11   Fred      Ficek           0.00
           12   Juan      Decesario      10.00
           13  *Eric      Wild            0.00
      . pack
        12 records copied
      . list first,last,amount

      Record#   first     last         amount
            1   Reza      Ghorbani        0.00
            2   Ann       Ghorbani      250.00
            3   Douglas   Acklin         55.00
            4   Barbara   Walters        75.00
            5   Arthur    Adams         357.00
            6   Russell   Davis          35.00
            7   Debbie    Acklin         35.00
            8   Harvey    Posio        1250.00
            9   Ben       Pietrowiak     20.00
           10   Sandy     Acklin         35.00
           11   Fred      Ficek           0.00
           12   Juan      Decesario      10.00
```

Figure 20.22
Options screen of the
CREATE REPORT command.

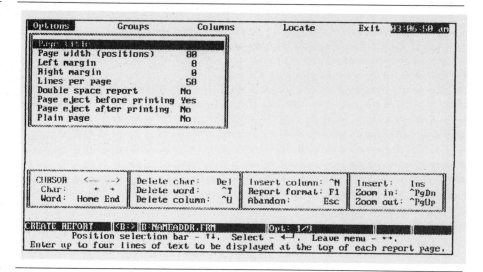

Figure 20.22 — Options screen of the CREATE REPORT command.

Report Template and the CREATE REPORT Command

Having data stored in a computerized file is not worth much by itself; for it to be useful in practical terms it must be placed in report form on paper. This is accomplished by using the CREATE REPORT command in dBASE. The CREATE REPORT command builds a **report template** on disk containing the report format, headings, and fields to be included in the report (see p. 526).

The template is created by filling in fields presented in dBASE screens that prompt you through the process. All you have to do is to respond to the prompts on each screen.

From the Assistant menu, enter the command CREATE and select the REPORT option from the submenu. dBASE now prompts you for the drive on which the report is to reside as well as the name of the report to be created. You must also have a data base file open; if you don't, dBASE will also prompt you for the name of the file to be used. Enter a report name of NAMEADDR.

The first screen displayed is the Options screen, which enables you to change a number of print options and enter the report heading (see Figure 20.22). When you select the Page Title option, a square box (see Figure 20.23) opens on the screen for the title. Enter the following title:

ABC COMPANY

CUSTOMER NAME AND ADDRESS REPORT

Don't worry about trying to center the information in the line; dBASE does this automatically when the report prints.

The next set of entries enables you to specify the width of the report, the number of positions in the right and left margins, the number of lines per page, whether or not you want the report double-spaced, printer eject options, and paper options.

When you have finished entering the title (see Figure 20.23), issue the End (Ctrl + End) command to return to the Options menu. Now position the bar to the Left Margin option and press the ENTER key. Pressing the ENTER key unlocks this entry: change the left margin to 2. Do the same for the right margin and set it to a width of 80. Press the right-arrow key to move to the next menu option (Groups).

Some of the maximum values for the Options screen entries are as follows:

1. Up to four lines of titles can be entered.

2. Up to 500 characters per line can be specified.

Figure 20.23
Report title box of the
Options screen.

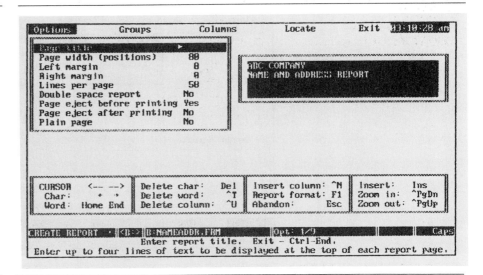

Figure 20.24
Groups screen of the
CREATE REPORT command.

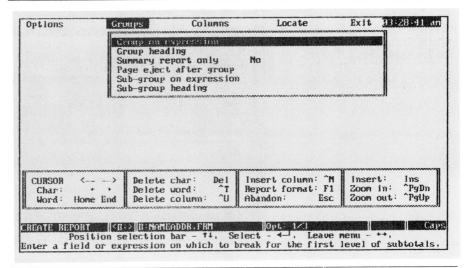

3. Default left margin is 8 characters.

4. Default right margin is 0 characters.

5. Default is single spacing for lines per page.

6. The default for Page Eject before Printing is Yes.

7. The default for Page Eject after Printing is No.

8. The default for Plain Page is No. If Yes, the page numbers and the system date are not printed. In such a situation the report heading is printed only on the first page of the printout.

The Groups screen (see Figure 20.24) enables you to establish subtotals for a report. Subtotals can be used only on a sorted or indexed file; and since NAMEADDR is not accessing a sorted or indexed CUSTOMER file, you do not want to enter any information about subtotals. Press the right-arrow key to advance to the Columns screen.

The Columns screen enables you to specify each field that you want to have printed on a line (see Figure 20.25). Use the top box to enter the names of the fields (unlock a field by pressing the ENTER key). If you have forgotten the field name, simply press the ENTER key to get into the Contents entry and press the F10 key. This results in a screen display of the fields for this file in a

Figure 20.25
The Columns screen.

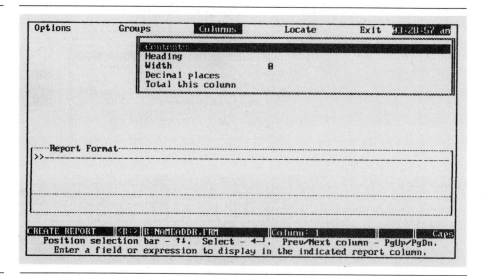

Figure 20.26
The dBASE F10 help facility
for fields. Both the field name
and information about the
data are displayed.

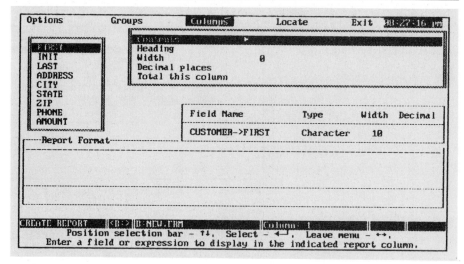

box in the left margin along with a description of the fields in a middle box (see Figure 20.26).

When the heading for that field is to be entered, a box appears in the middle of the screen and allows you to enter up to five lines of text (see Figure 20.27). The width of the field (if you want it set to a size other than that specified in the record structure) can also be entered. If you are entering information about a numeric field, you will also be prompted to state the number of decimal positions and whether or not dBASE should total that column in the report. The box at the bottom of the screen depicts the report format.

Enter the following information for the indicated fields:

```
Field      Heading    Total
FIRST
LAST       NAME
ADDRESS    ADDRESS
CITY       CITY
STATE      STATE
AMOUNT     AMOUNT     Y
```

Figure 20.27
Columns screen field-
heading box for a report
column heading.

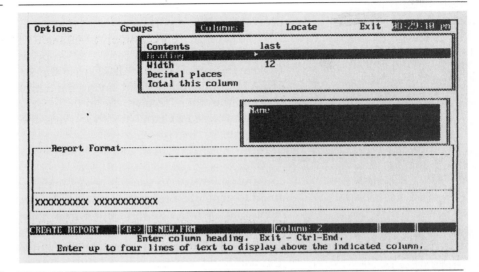

Figure 20.28
Completed Report Format
box of the Columns screen.

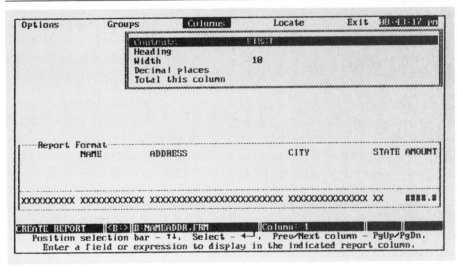

Should you make an error in entering a valid field name, dBASE will beep, display an error message at the bottom of the screen, and direct you to press any key to continue. If you can't remember the name of the field, press the F10 key (see Figure 20.26) for a listing of the valid field names for the file in use.

After you have entered a field and proceeded to the next field-definition box, dBASE shows you how the report will appear in the Report Format box (see Figure 20.28). dBASE takes the previously specified column headings and places them at the top of the box. The width of a character field is indicated by XXXXs and the width of a numeric field by ####.## (see Figure 20.28).

dBASE automatically takes the field length from the record and places that number in the Width entry for each field. If you want to trim a column, simply decrease the number. This results in rightmost truncation for character fields. For example, if a field width that was 25 is changed to 18, characters to the right of position 18 will not print on this line but will wrap to the next line. The only time that information does not wrap to the next line is when there are rightmost unused positions for this field in all records.

dBASE also automatically places one space between each column.

The Locate option of the REPORT command menu generates a screen containing all of the fields that are used by this report form. You can examine one of these fields by positioning the pointer to that field and pressing the ENTER key. The report window for that field is now displayed to the screen.

To save the report, simply issue the EXIT command from the REPORT command menu. You now receive a two-prompt menu: Save and Abandon. To save this report form to disk, select the Save option. To exit the REPORT CREATE command without saving the template to disk, select the Abandon option. You then receive the prompt Are you sure you want to abandon operation? [Y/N]. Press the Y key to return to the Assistant menu.

Printing a Report

You are now ready to use the report template and the REPORT FORM command to generate a report. First select the Retrieve option from the Assistant menu and then the Report option from this submenu. Indicate that the report template resides on the default drive (B: in this case). Select the NAMEADDR.FRM report form. At this time, you should see the following command on the action line: REPORT FORM B:NAMEADDR. Select the Execute the command option. If you respond Y to the prompt Direct the output to the printer? [Y/N], dBASE appends TO PRINT to the command on the action line; otherwise, the output is sent to the screen.

```
Page No.    1
04/15/87

                               ABC COMPANY
                    CUSTOMER NAME AND ADDRESS REPORT
             NAME          ADDRESS             CITY          ST    AMOUNT
Reza      Ghorbani    4033 N. Wolcott      Chicago       Il    125.00
Ann       Ghorbani    4033 No. Wolcott     Chicago       Il    250.00
Douglas   Acklin      408 E. Monroe        Bloomington   Il     55.00
Barbara   Walters     1981 Crestlawn       Arlington     Va     75.00
Arthur    Adams       115 Ginger Creek Ct. Bloomington   Il     35.00
Russell   Davis       707 Vale St.         Bloomington   Il     35.00
Debbie    Acklin      408 E. Monroe        Bloomington   Il      0.00
Harvey    Posio       1013 Hillcrest       San Diego     Ca   1250.00
Ben       Pietrowiak  3334 Foster          Normal        Il     20.00
Sandy     Acklin      408 E. Monroe        Bloomington   Il     35.00
Fred      Ficek       1215 Tamarack        Normal        Il      0.00
Juan      Decesario   1214 Flores          Miami         Fl     10.00
*** Total ***

                                                          1890.00
```

When dBASE executed the above command, it accessed the disk for the NAMEADDR.FRM file and loaded it. It then accessed the customer file.

Once you build a report template, you can use it over and over. You can also limit the records that are included in a report by use of the FOR parameter via the Build a search condition. For example, you may want to print an exception report containing only those customers whose balance is over $100. The following example illustrates such a report.

You enter the same commands as in the previous example. But instead of immediately telling dBASE to execute the command, select the Build a search condition option, select the AMOUNT field, select the > Greater Than option, enter 100, and press the ENTER key. Tell dBASE there are no more conditions. At this time you should see the following command on the action line: REPORT FORM B:NAMEADDR FOR AMOUNT > 100. Tell dBASE to execute the command, and the following report is generated.

```
Page No,    1
04/15/87
                              ABC COMPANY
                   CUSTOMER NAME AND ADDRESS REPORT
            NAME          ADDRESS           CITY      ST   AMOUNT
Reza     Ghorbani     4033 N, Wolcott     Chicago    Il    125,00
Ann      Ghorbani     4033 N, Wolcott     Chicago    Il    250,00
Harvey   Posio        1013 Hillcrest      San Diego  Ca   1250,00
*** Total ***
                                                          1625,00
```

You might also want to print a report of amounts owed by customers in a specific region. The following command entered at the dot prompt (.) produces a list of all customers who live in Bloomington and generates a grand total of the amount owed:

```
, report form nameaddr for city = 'Bloomington'
```

```
Page No,    1
04/15/87
                              ABC COMPANY
                   CUSTOMER NAME AND ADDRESS REPORT
            NAME          ADDRESS           CITY        ST   AMOUNT
Douglas  Acklin      408 E, Monroe       Bloomington   Il    55,00
Arthur   Adams       115 Ginger Creek Ct, Bloomington  Il    35,00
Russell  Davis       707 Vale St,        Bloomington   Il    35,00
Debbie   Acklin      408 E, Monroe       Bloomington   Il    35,00
Sandy    Acklin      408 E, Monroe       Bloomington   Il    35,00
*** Total ***
                                                            160,00
```

You could also specify the Build a search condition and specify the CITY field as the field to use in this operation. When prompted with Enter a character string (without quotes):, respond with Bloomington, press the ENTER key, tell dBASE there are no more conditions, and then tell it to execute the command.

To make changes to a report template requires selecting either the Create or Modify options of the Assistant menu and then the Report option. Once the drive and the template name have been specified, you can change any of the screen information.

Chapter Review

The dBASE III Plus package provides commands for manipulating data. The LIST command can be used to display (a) the contents of an entire file, (b) selected records that meet selection criteria, or (c) selected fields of records. The DISPLAY ALL command works like the LIST command except that it stops when it has displayed sixteen lines on the screen.

A number of pointer movement commands are provided, including the explicit and implied GO and GOTO commands and the SKIP command, which enable you to move forward or backward in the file, a record at a time or a number of records at a time.

The REPLACE command enables you to change one record, selected groups of records, or all records in the file at one time, in accordance with stated selection criteria. This provides you with another method, besides the EDIT command, for changing the field contents of records.

The substring command ($) is a powerful command that enables you to search for characters in a field of data. It can be used in conjunction with such commands as REPLACE and LIST DBASE.

The dBASE III Plus package does not automatically delete a record from a file when you issue the DELETE command. Instead, it only "logically" deletes the record, which means to mark it with dBASE's delete indicator, the asterisk (*), for future deletion. After a record has been marked for deletion, it can be undeleted by using the RECALL command. Physically removing a record from a file requires using the PACK statement following the DELETE. The PACK statement copies the entire file to a new location on disk, dropping any records marked for deletion.

The CREATE REPORT command enables you to generate a formatted report via a report template from information contained in a file. The CREATE REPORT feature provides a number of full-screen editing windows for you to use in describing the report, including screens for specifying report and column headings and any fields you want to print. The feature also generates totals for any numeric fields.

Key Terms and Concepts

CREATE REPORT command
DELETE command
delete indicator (*)
DIR command
DISPLAY command
end of file (EOF) function
FOR parameter
GOTO command
GOTO BOTTOM command
GOTO TOP command
LIST command
LIST STRUCTURE command
NEXT option

PACK command
RECALL command
RECNO function
REPLACE command
REPORT FORM command
report template
SKIP command
substring function ($)
SUM command
TO PRINT option
USE command
? character

Chapter Quiz

Multiple Choice

1. Which of the following dBASE command(s) can be used to change records in a file?
   a. LIST
   b. EDIT
   c. REPORT
   d. REPLACE
   e. CHANGE

2. If you use the SET PRINT ON command, reports could be generated using which of the following statements?
   a. LIST
   b. REPORT
   c. DISPLAY
   d. All of the above
   e. Only the REPORT

3. The report feature of dBASE III Plus enables you to do which of the following?
   a. Establish a report title
   b. Print column headings
   c. Number each page
   d. Print totals
   e. All of the above
   f. Only a, b, and c

4. Which of the following commands does not move the record pointer?
   a. SKIP
   b. GOTO BOTTOM
   c. GOTO TOP
   d. .5
   e. SKIP -5
   f. All of the commands move the record pointer.

5. Which of the following statements is true about the LIST and DISPLAY commands?
   a. The DISPLAY does not allow you to display selected fields.
   b. Both the LIST and DISPLAY prohibit arithmetic selection criteria.
   c. The DISPLAY shows the next 20 records and then pauses.
   d. The DISPLAY automatically lists all of the records in the file.
   e. None of the above statements is false.

True/False

6. The DISPLAY ALL command gives you more control than the simple LIST command.

7. The DELETE command physically removes a record from a file.

8. The RECALL command automatically unerases all deleted records within a file.

9. The DISPLAY command shows the record at the current pointer location.

10. The SUM command can be used to total numeric fields from a selected record.

Answers

1. b&d 2. d 3. e 4. f 5. c 6. f 7. f 8. f 9. t 10. t

Exercises

1. The command DISPLAY _____ will display all records in the file on the screen and pause after each sixteen lines.

2. The _____ command displays the record at the current pointer location.

3. List the pointer positioning commands:
   a.

   b.

   c.

   d.

4. The `GOTO` _____ places the pointer at the end of the file.

5. The _____ command can be used to move forward or backward in the file.

6. The _____ command is used to display the current record number.

7. The `GOTO` _____ command is used to position the pointer at the beginning of file.

8. The _____ command can be used to change records in the file.

9. The function _____ is used to find a character string in a field.

10. The _____ command is used to mark a record for deletion.

11. The _____ command is used to undelete a record.

12. The _____ command is used to remove records from a file that have been marked for deletion.

13. The _____ command is used to generate a total of a field from the records in a file.

14. The _____ command sends any output on the screen to the printer.

15. The _____ command is used to build a report template that can be used later.

Computer Exercises

The following exercises require using the `PAYMAST` file, created previously.

1. Look at the format of the data base records.

2. Look at the employee and pay rate of each record.

3. Look at only those employees with a gross of more than $850.

4. Total the gross pay field.

5. Total the gross pay field for those with a gross of more than $900.

6. Give Mark Tell a raise of .50.

7. Give everyone a raise of .25.

8. Go to record 5 and display it to the screen.

9. Delete and recall record 9.

10. Delete record 5.

11. Pack the file.

12. Use the $ function to find any record with a P in the first or last name.

13. Create the following report and print it out.

```
PAGE NO. 00001
04/13/87
                              PAYROLL SUMMARY
       ID          EMPLOYEE              PAY RATE        GROSS
     4908 Richard   Payne                  4.45         556.00
     5789 Connie    Reiners                3.35         450.00
     5523 Pamela    Rich                   6.00         780.00
     6324 Mark      Tell                   5.50         980.00
     2870 Frank     Terlep                 6.80         670.00
     4679 Kenneth   Klass                  4.90         780.00
     8345 Thomas    Momery                 4.70         580.00
     5649 Toni      McCarthy               5.20         667.00
     5432 Alan      Monroe                 5.20        1340.00
     5998 Paul      Mish                   4.90         887.00
     4463 Edward    Mockford               4.90         775.00
      456                                  0.00           0.00
     ** TOTAL **
                                                       8465.00
```

14. Use the report template you developed to generate a report for employees with a gross pay of more than $800.

Chapter 21

Ordering dBASE III Plus Files

After completing this chapter, you should be able to:

Discuss the dBASE III PLUS SORT *command*

Discuss the dBASE III PLUS INDEX *command*

Discuss locating records in sequential and random files

Discuss ordered reports

Discuss some miscellaneous file commands

Discuss the BROWSE *command*

This chapter introduces you to dBASE techniques that allow you to arrange, rearrange, and locate data in the manner most suitable to your application. The commands covered in this chapter include `SORT`, `INDEX`, `LOCATE`, `FIND`, `DELETE`, and `BROWSE`.

Arrangement
Commands

SORT

The `SORT` **command** is used to physically rearrange records in a file according to values contained in a specific field of each record. To do this, the sort does not rearrange the content of the file itself but specifies the order in which an output file will hold the original file's content. The `SORT` command has the following syntax:

```
SORT <field list> TO [<output file>]
```

The following are defaults for the SORT command. The TO file, which holds the output of the sort, has a .DBF file extension unless you specify another extension in the filename. Sorts are in ascending order (/A) unless you specify otherwise.

The `SORT` command has some general rules for its use. When you sort on multiple fields, the most important field is placed first. Up to ten fields can be specified. Place a comma between fields. You may not sort logical or memo fields.

Ascending order (the default setting) sorts the information in alphabetical order A to Z and in numeric order 0 to 9. If you specify descending order, alphabetic sorts are placed in order Z to A and numeric information in order 9 to 0.

Sorting the `CUSTOMER` file in zip code order requires setting the default drive to B: (if you have not already done so), activating the `CUSTOMER` file, selecting the `ORGANIZE` option of the Assistant menu, and then selecting the `SORT` option of this submenu (the action line now contains `SORT ON`). A listing of the fields contained in the `CUSTOMER` file, with information about each highlighted field, is now displayed on your screen (see Figure 21.1). Highlight the ZIP field, press the ENTER key, and then press the right arrow key to return to the Organize submenu. Select the default drive (B) to hold the sorted output file by pressing the ENTER key. You are now prompted for the name of the output file (see Figure 21.2). Enter the name `ZIPCUST` and press the ENTER key. The command `SORT ON ZIP TO ZIPCUST` has now been executed by dBASE, and the file `ZIPCUST` now holds the sorted information from the `CUSTOMER` file.

Once the sort starts the following lines appear at the bottom of your screen:

```
00%
100%              12 Records Sorted
```

The `SORT` command keeps you informed as to how much of the file has been sorted. When the sort is completed, the `100% xx Records Sorted` message is displayed on the screen. You now have two files: the original `CUSTOMER` file on disk, which remains unchanged, and the newly created `ZIPCUST` file, which contains the data from the `CUSTOMER` file arranged by the contents of the `ZIP` field. Because you have not changed the file specified via a `USE` statement, the `CUSTOMER` file remains active. You can confirm that its order has not changed by using the `RETRIEVE` com-

Figure 21.1

Field list for specifying key fields in a sort.

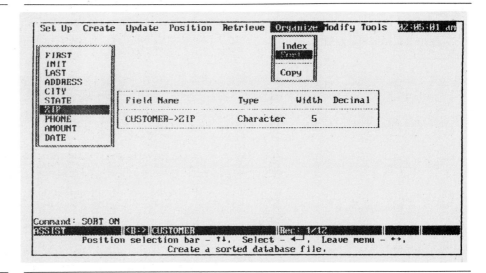

Figure 21.2

Screen for specifying the output file in a sort operation.

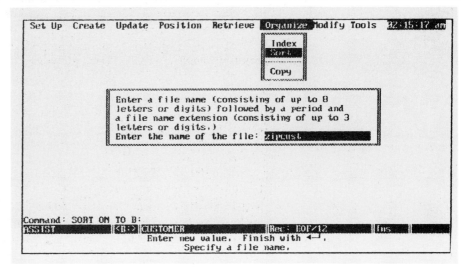

mand of the Assistant menu and listing the file by the fields FIRST, LAST, CITY, STATE, and ZIP (see Figure 21.3).

To verify that you have created the ZIPCUST file properly, issue the SET UP command from the Assistant menu, activate the ZIPCUST file, select the RETRIEVE command from the Assistant menu, specify the same fields, issue the LIST command, and execute (see Figure 21.4). Notice that the records are not in the same order as in the CUSTOMER file but are arranged by the contents of the ZIP field. This means that the record numbers are also different, having been changed to reflect their new locations in the ZIPCUST file.

The process of sorting information by two fields is just as straightforward. Suppose you want to sort the CUSTOMER file by name. When two customers have the same last name, you will want the first names to be in alphabetical order. In this case, the primary sort key (first field specified) is the last name, and the secondary sort key (second field specified) is the first name. Specify your sort fields in the manner previously indicated and place the output in the file ALPHNAME. Once the SORT command is executed, the information is placed in first-name within last name order. Activate the

Figure 21.3

Output of the unchanged CUSTOMER file via the LIST command.

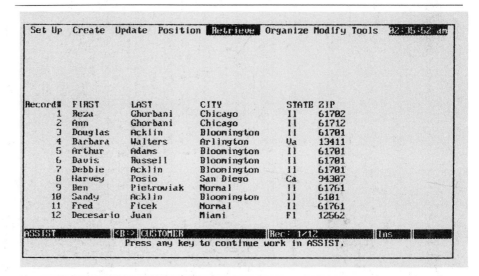

Figure 21.4

The sorted ZIPCUST file.

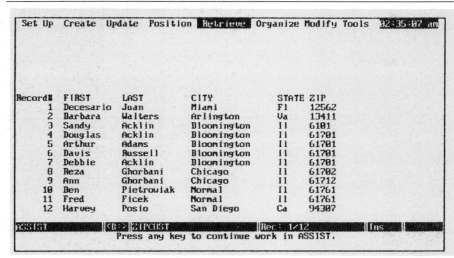

ALPHNAME file and list it in LAST, FIRST, CITY, STATE, and ZIP order (see Figure 21.5).

The dBASE command that created the ALPHNAME file is SORT ON LAST,FIRST TO B:ALLPHNNAME.

The SORT command is not usually the best way to arrange data within a file. Several restrictions apply to it:

1. It usually takes a lot of computer time. Although this is not evident with a small file such as CUSTOMER, an attempt to use SORT on a file containing 3,000 records you would make it obvious.

2. The SORT command generates a new file every time it is executed. This takes up a large amount of disk storage when you are dealing with large files.

3. The record numbers change from one file to another. The record number of a record in the unsorted file, will be useless to you in the sorted file.

Figure 21.5

Result of a LIST command
against the sorted
ALPHNAME file.

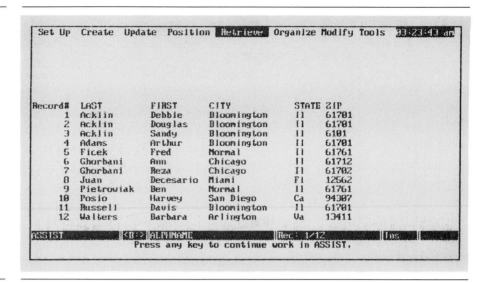

INDEX

The easiest way to overcome these shortcomings of the SORT command is
by using the INDEX **command**. This command can generate two types of
indexes: single field and multiple field.

Single-Field Indexes. A **single-field** index file is ordered by one field only.
The ordering of an indexed file is fundamentally different from that of a sorted
file: Instead of reordering the original data physically, as the SORT command
does, the INDEX command reorders it logically without moving records.
This is accomplished by using an Index Construct to create an index file in
which each specified field points to the appropriate record in the specified file.
The contents of the original file remain unchanged, with the same physical file
order and the same record numbers, whereas the index file created by the
INDEX command holds the logical order of the file.

To prepare for the following examples, activate the CUSTOMER file via
the SET UP command in the Assistant menu.

Logically arranging the CUSTOMER file in zip-code order requires selecting the ORGANIZE option of the Assistant menu, selecting the INDEX
option from the submenu, and responding with the field ZIP to the prompt
for entering an index expression. Now indicate that you want this index
placed on the default drive (in this example, B) by pressing the ENTER key.
Name the index file to be created (ZIP). The CUSTOMER file is now logically
arranged in ZIP field order, and the ZIP.NDX file is created on the default
drive.

Once the indexing process starts, the following information is displayed
on your screen:

```
00%
100% Indexed     12 Records Indexed
```

These steps generate the command INDEX ON ZIP TO ZIP in the
action line. The result is an index file called ZIP.NDX; each record in the
ZIP.NDX file contains the ZIP field for a record in the CUSTOMER file

Zip Code	Record Number
12562	00012
13411	00004
60712	00001
60712	00002
61701	00003
61701	00005
61701	00006
61701	00007
61701	00010
61761	00009
61761	00011
94307	00008

Figure 21.6
Information contained in the ZIP.NDX file: the zip code and the location of each record.

and also contains the number of the record with that particular zip-code value (see Figure 21.6). When the records are displayed, dBASE first accesses the ZIP.NDX file, which in turn points to the appropriate record from the CUS-TOMER file.

To activate the ZIP index requires a number of steps:

1. Use the SET UP option of the Assistant menu to select the CUS-TOMER file.

2. Indicate that the file is indexed by responding Y to the prompt Is the file indexed? [Y/N].

3. Point to the ZIP.NDX entry and press the ENTER key.

4. Press a right- or left-arrow key to activate the index (the command USE CUSTOMER INDEX ZIP appears on the action line).

5. Select the RETRIEVE option of the Assistant menu and take the LIST option.

6. Specify that the fields LAST, FIRST, CITY, STATE, ZIP, and AMOUNT be displayed.

7. Execute the command.

The information from the CUSTOMER file (see Figure 21.7) is now displayed.

When dBASE lists the records from an indexed file, it performs a number of tasks automatically. First, it goes to the ZIP.NDX file (see Figure 21.6) and finds zip 12562. It also finds that record 12 of the CUSTOMER file holds the data for this index entry. dBASE now accesses record 12 of the CUSTOMER file. It then moves to the second index entry and repeats the process until all index entries have been processed.

As you can see from this example, using the Assistant to create indexes and then invoke the file using that index requires a number of steps and even more keystrokes. Creating indexes and then verifying that you have created them correctly using the LIST command requires less time in command mode at the dot prompt (.). The remaining indexes will therefore be created using the command mode of dBASE III Plus.

Another bonus from using command mode is that after an index is created, it is automatically invoked by dBASE. This means that you do not have to issue a USE FILENAME INDEX command to list the records from the file for the created index.

To verify that the contents of the CUSTOMER file remain physically unchanged, you could issue the following commands:

```
. use customer
. list first,last,city,state,zip
```

Record#	FIRST	LAST	CITY	STATE	ZIP
1	Reza	Ghorbani	Chicago	Il	60712
2	Ann	Ghorbani	Chicago	Il	60712
3	Douglas	Acklin	Bloomington	Il	61701
4	Barbara	Walters	Arlington	Va	13411
5	Arthur	Adams	Bloomington	Il	61701
6	Russell	Davis	Bloomington	Il	61701
7	Debbie	Acklin	Bloomington	Il	61701
8	Harvey	Posio	San Diego	CA	94307
9	Ben	Pietrowiak	Normal	Il	61761
10	Sandy	Acklin	Bloomington	Il	61701
11	Fred	Ficek	Normal	Il	61761
12	Juan	Decesario	Miami	Fl	12562

Figure 21.7
The CUSTOMER file listed via the ZIP.NDX index.

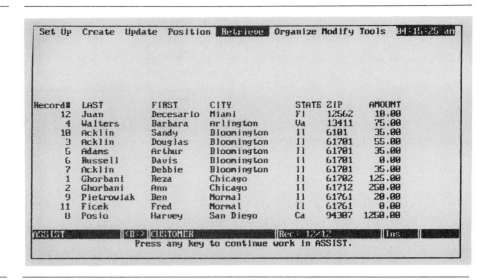

If you want to see the file arranged in logical order of last name, issue the INDEX and LIST commands:

```
. index on last to last
  12 records indexed
. list last, first, city, state, zip, amount
```

Record#	LAST	FIRST	CITY	STATE	ZIP	AMOUNT
3	Acklin	Douglas	Bloomington	Il	61701	55.00
7	Acklin	Debbie	Bloomington	Il	61701	35.00
10	Acklin	Sandy	Bloomington	Il	61701	35.00
5	Adams	Arthur	Bloomington	Il	61701	35.00
6	Davis	Russell	Bloomington	Il	61701	35.00
12	Decesario	Juan	Miami	Fl	12562	10.00
11	Ficek	Fred	Normal	Il	61761	0.00
1	Ghorbani	Reza	Chicago	Il	60712	0.00
2	Ghorbani	Ann	Chicago	Il	60712	250.00
9	Pietrowiak	Ben	Normal	Il	61761	20.00
8	Posio	Harvey	San Diego	Ca	94307	1250.00
4	Walters	Barbara	Arlington	Va	13411	75.00

Multiple-Field Indexes. A single-field index is inappropriate for many applications. For instance, what do you do if you want the file to appear in order by the first-name and last-name field contents? The INDEX command manages this task easily be enabling you to **concatenate** (join) fields in creating the index. The result is a **multiple-field index**. The first multiple-field index here will be created using the Assistant feature of dBASE, but others will be created at the dot prompt.

Reenter the Assistant mode by entering ASSIST at the dot prompt, and then press the ENTER key.

Once the file has been properly activated (it already is unless you have just started dBASE), perform the following steps:

1. Select the Organize option of the Assistant menu.

2. Enter the fields to be indexed (see Figure 21.8), the statement on the action line is now INDEX ON LAST + FIRST TO.

3. Press the ENTER key.

Figure 21.8
Screen used to concatenate
fields for creating the
LFNAME index file.

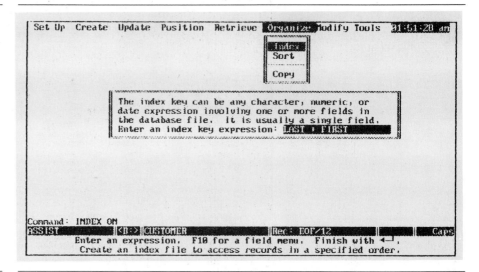

Figure 21.9
The listing of selected fields
from the Customer file in
alphabetical order via
the LFNAME index.

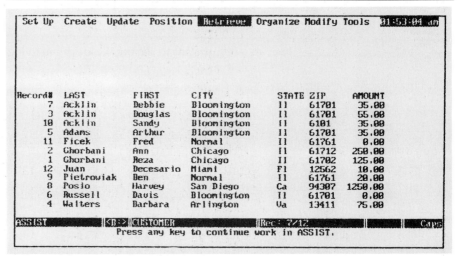

4. Indicate that the index file is to be placed on the default drive (in this case B:); the dBASE command on the action line is now INDEX ON LAST + FIRST TO B:.

5. Enter the index file name LFNAME and press ENTER. dBASE appends the file name to the command so that it becomes INDEX ON FIRST + LAST TO B:LFNAME. The file is now indexed by dBASE, and the message 100% Indexed   12 Records indexed appears at the bottom of your screen.

6. Use the Set Up option of the Assistant menu to activate the Customer file using the LFNAME index.

7. Press the left- or right-arrow key.

8. Use the Retrieve option of the Assistant menu, and then select the List option.

9. Construct a field list containing the LAST, FIRST, CITY, STATE, ZIP, and AMOUNT fields.

10. Execute the command.

A listing of the file in alphabetical order by last name (see Figure 21.9) is now displayed. You can see that within the last-name order the Acklin and the

Ghorbani records are now listed in alphabetic order by the first-name field contents.

The remaining examples of multiple-field index fields will be entered via command mode at the dot prompt. Notice that you do not have to enter the drive identifier in front of the index file name since dBASE automatically creates it on the default drive (in these examples drive B).

Extending the index order to three fields is done with the following INDEX command, which logically arranges the file in order by zip code, last name, and first name:

```
. index on zip + last + first to ziplfnam
  12 records indexed
. list last, first, city, state, zip, amount
```

Record#	LAST	FIRST	CITY	STATE	ZIP	AMOUNT
12	Decesario	Juan	Miami	Fl	12562	10.00
4	Walters	Barbara	Arlington	Va	13411	75.00
2	Ghorbani	Ann	Chicago	Il	60712	250.00
1	Ghorbani	Reza	Chicago	Il	60712	0.00
7	Acklin	Debbie	Bloomington	Il	61701	35.00
3	Acklin	Douglas	Bloomington	Il	61701	55.00
10	Acklin	Sandy	Bloomington	Il	61701	35.00
5	Adams	Arthur	Bloomington	Il	61701	35.00
6	Davis	Russell	Bloomington	Il	61701	35.00
11	Ficek	Fred	Normal	Il	61761	0.00
9	Pietrowiak	Ben	Normal	Il	61761	20.00
8	Posio	Harvey	San Diego	Ca	94307	1250.00

Assume that you now want to access the Customer file by last-name first-name order. You do not have to recreate the LFNAME index because it is still on the disk under the name LFNAME.NDX. All you have to do is type the name of the file and the name of the corresponding index to use in accessing the data. The commands are as follows:

```
. use customer index lfname
. list last, first, city, state, zip, amount
```

Record#	LAST	FIRST	CITY	STATE	ZIP	AMOUNT
7	Acklin	Debbie	Bloomington	Il	61701	35.00
3	Acklin	Douglas	Bloomington	Il	61701	55.00
10	Acklin	Sandy	Bloomington	Il	61701	35.00
5	Adams	Arthur	Bloomington	Il	61701	35.00
6	Davis	Russell	Bloomington	Il	61701	35.00
12	Decesario	Juan	Miami	Fl	12562	10.00
11	Ficek	Fred	Normal	Il	61761	0.00
2	Ghorbani	Ann	Chicago	Il	60712	250.00
1	Ghorbani	Reza	Chicago	Il	60712	0.00
9	Pietrowiak	Ben	Normal	Il	61761	20.00
8	Posio	Harvey	San Diego	Ca	94307	1250.00
4	Walters	Barbara	Arlington	Va	13411	75.00

You can also have the data sorted in some numerical order. The INDEX command operates only on character data, unless the created index refers exclusively to a numeric field of the original file. The data in an index are always stored as character data, not as numeric data; therefore, to create a

mixed data multiple-field index (an index that uses both numeric fields and character fields), the numeric fields in the original file must first be changed to character data using the `STR` **function**.

The following example illustrates the creation of an index ordered by the `AMOUNT` field only. The file can then be listed in ascending order by the amount owed. Keep in mind that the index entry is now character data, whereas the data in the original file remain numeric. The commands used and the list produced are as follows:

```
. use customer
. index on amount to amount
     12 records indexed
. list last, first, city, state, zip, amount
```

Record#	LAST	FIRST	CITY	STATE	ZIP	AMOUNT
1	Ghorbani	Reza	Chicago	Il	60712	0.00
11	Ficek	Fred	Normal	Il	61761	0.00
12	Decesario	Juan	Miami	Fl	12562	10.00
9	Pietrowiak	Ben	Normal	Il	61761	20.00
6	Davis	Russell	Bloomington	Il	61701	35.00
7	Acklin	Debbie	Bloomington	Il	61701	35.00
10	Acklin	Sandy	Bloomington	Il	61701	35.00
3	Acklin	Douglas	Bloomington	Il	61701	55.00
4	Walters	Barbara	Arlington	Va	13411	75.00
2	Ghorbani	Ann	Chicago	Il	60712	250.00
5	Adams	Arthur	Bloomington	Il	61701	35.00
8	Posio	Harvey	San Diego	Ca	94307	1250.00

Creating a mixed data multiple-field index that refers to one or more numeric field(s) requires the use of the `STR` (string) function: otherwise, an error message is displayed. The STR function works only if you provide the name of the field to be converted, the field length, and the number of positions to the right of the decimal point that are involved. To create an index using the zip code and amount fields, you would issue the following commands:

```
. index on zip + str (amount,8,2) to zipamoun
     12 records indexed
. list last, first, city, state, zip, amount
```

Record#	LAST	FIRST	CITY	STATE	ZIP	AMOUNT
12	Decesario	Juan	Miami	Fl	12562	10.00
4	Walters	Barbara	Arlington	Va	13411	75.00
1	Ghorbani	Reza	Chicago	Il	60712	0.00
2	Ghorbani	Ann	Chicago	Il	60712	250.00
6	Davis	Russell	Bloomington	Il	61701	35.00
7	Acklin	Debbie	Bloomington	Il	61701	35.00
10	Acklin	Sandy	Bloomington	Il	61701	35.00
3	Acklin	Douglas	Bloomington	Il	61701	55.00
5	Adams	Arthur	Bloomington	Il	61701	35.00
11	Ficek	Fred	Normal	Il	61761	0.00
9	Pietrowiak	Ben	Normal	Il	61761	20.00
8	Posio	Harvey	San Diego	Ca	94307	1250.00

Ancillary Commands. There are two versions of the DELETE and LIST commands to cover related to files. To delete files (such as the no longer needed CUSTZIP file), you can use the <u>DELETE FILE</u> **command**.

```
, delete file custzip,dbf
FILE HAS BEEN DELETED
```

You may sometimes want to list various families of files on the screen, which you can accomplish by using the <u>LIST FILES LIKE</u> **command**. You do not have to use an extension for data base files because when no extension is given, dBASE automatically inserts a .DBF extension. To list index files, however, you must use the **.NDX extension**. Wildcards can be used in LIST FILES LIKE commands such as the following:

```
, list files like *,ndx
ZIP       ,NDX      LAST      ,NDX      LFNAME    ,NDX
ZIPLFMAN,NDX        ZIPAMOUN,NDX        AMOUNT    ,NDX
   5120 bytes in       6 files,
330752 bytes remaining on drive,
```

```
, list files like *,Dbf
CUSTOMER,DBF         NEW,DBF        ALPHNAME,DBF
   3286 bytes in       3 files,
334848 bytes remaining on drive,
```

Managing Index Files. One of the major benefits of using index files is that they do not have to be constantly recreated as you add or delete records from them. You can specify as many as seven indexes in a USE statement. Any indexes that are specified following the INDEX portion of the USE statement are automatically **updated** when an APPEND, DELETE, or PACK command is executed against the file. For example, to make certain that all of the indexes created in this chapter are updated to reflect all future changes in the CUSTOMER file, you would issue the following command:

```
, use customer index ziplfnam,last,lfname,zipamoun,amount,zip
```

Any time a new record is appended or an indexed field is changed (via the EDIT or BROWSE commands), the appropriate indexes are automatically updated. Only the first index you specify, however, is **active**. In this example, the result is that the CUSTOMER file can be accessed only via the ZIPLFNAM index.

It is important to specify appropriate indexes after the file name when you are about to pack a file. The PACK command automatically recreates each of the specified indexes once the PACK statement has compressed the file; but if you do not specify the indexes before you pack the file, you will have to recreate each index separately. Should you forget to recreate any of the indexes and later try to use the old index to list the revised file contents, you will receive a RECORD OUT OF RANGE error message.

Reports Using Indexes. When you are generating a report, an index can be used to determine the order in which the data file will be used. For instance, to generate a report in zip code, last name, and first name order, you would use the following commands:

```
• use customer index ziplfnam
• report form nameaddr to print
```

Page No. 1
04/15/87

```
                         ABC COMPANY
                  NAME AND ADDRESS REPORT

            NAME          ADDRESS          CITY        STATE    AMOUNT
Decesario   Juan          1214 Flores      Miami       Fl        10.00
Barbara     Walters       1981 Crestlawn   Arlington   Va        75.00
Sandy       Acklin        408 E. Monroe    Bloomington Il        35.00
Debbie      Acklin        408 E. Monroe    Bloomington Il        35.00
Douglas     Acklin        408 E. Monroe    Bloomington Il        55.00
Arthur      Adams         115 Ginger Creek Ct. Bloomington Il    35.00
Davis       Russell       707 Vale St.     Bloomington Il         0.00
Reza        Ghorbani      4033 N. Wolcott  Chicago     Il       125.00
Ann         Ghorbani      4033 N. Wolcott  Chicago     Il       250.00
Fred        Ficek         1215 Tamarack    Normal      Il         0.00
Ben         Pietrowiak    3334 N. Foster   Normal      Il        20.00
Harvey      Posio         1013 Hillcrest   San Diego   Ca      1250.00
*** Total ***

                                                             1890.00
```

A report can also be easily generated using the "numeric" (actually, character) AMOUNT.NDX index file by entering the following commands:

```
• use customer index amount
• report form nameaddr to print
```

Page No. 1
04/15/87

```
                         ABC COMPANY
                  NAME AND ADDRESS REPORT

            NAME          ADDRESS          CITY        STATE    AMOUNT
Reza        Ghorbani      4033 N. Wolcott  Chicago     Il       125.00
Ann         Ghorbani      4033 N. Wolcott  Chicago     Il       250.00
Douglas     Acklin        408 E. Monroe    Bloomington Il        55.00
Barbara     Walters       1981 Crestlawn   Arlington   Va        75.00
Arthur      Adams         115 Ginger Creek Ct. Bloomington Il    35.00
Davis       Russell       707 Vale St.     Bloomington Il         0.00
Debbie      Acklin        408 E. Monroe    Bloomington Il        35.00
Harvey      Posio         1013 Hillcrest   San Diego   Ca      1250.00
Ben         Pietrowiak    3334 N. Foster   Normal      Il        20.00
Sandy       Acklin        408 E. Monroe    Bloomington Il        35.00
Fred        Ficek         1215 Tamarack    Normal      Il         0.00
Decesario   Juan          1214 Flores      Miami       Fl        10.00
*** Total ***

                                                             1890.00
```

Location Commands

Up to this point, you have used either the LIST or DISPLAY commands to locate a record. Both commands start at the beginning of a file and display all of the records that meet the specified search criteria. If you want to display only one relevant record at a time—rather than all of the relevant records at once—you can use either the LOCATE or SEEK command.

LOCATE

The LOCATE **command** is used to perform a sequential file search, starting at the beginning of the file and progressing through it until a "hit" occurs. (A hit occurs when a record's content meets the specified search criteria.) For example, assume that you want to find all the records of clients who live in the town of Normal. When you are setting up the criteria for a character field, make certain that you enter the characters exactly as they appear in the field. Accomplishing this would require the following statements:

```
. use customer
. locate for city = 'Normal'
Record =        9
. continue
Record =        11
. continue
End of locate scope
```

The dBASE program displays the record number of the first record in the file that meets the search criteria. Any number of simple or complex search criteria can be used to find records via the LOCATE command. The CON-TINUE **command** sends dBASE looking for the next record that meets the search criteria. This process continues until the last record in the file is processed, at which point the message End of locate scope is displayed. You can now use the EDIT command to examine any or all of the displayed record numbers.

The preceding example can also be executed from the Assistant menu, but then the information is not displayed together. The following discussion takes place from the Assistant.

SEEK

The SEEK **command** can be used only for accessing a **random file** (any dBASE file that has an index). Both the file and the index must be referenced in a USE statement before the SEEK command is issued.

The SEEK command operates differently from the LOCATE command. The LOCATE command results in a sequential search of the data file itself, whereas the SEEK command uses the index to find any record(s) that match the search criteria, and the entry in the index then points to the record location in the data file. Since the information in the index is all character data, the search criteria must be contained inside single quotes.

Again, the number of keystrokes in using the Assistant menu in conjunction with a SEEK command are many more than those required by the dot prompt. The following examples are executed at the dot prompt.

The SET HEADINGS OFF command turns off the field headings for a displayed record.

Assume that you are going to use the CUSTOMER file via the ZIP index. To find those records that have a 61761 zip code, you would use the following commands:

```
. use customer index zip
. set headings off
. seek '61761'
. display
     9  Ben          A Pietrowiak   3334 N. Foster              Normal
IL 61761 (309)452-9126      20.00
. skip
Record no.      11
    11  Fred         R Ficek        1215 Tamarack              Normal
Il 61761 (309)454-7123       0.00
. skip
Record No.       8
     8  Harvey       B Posio        1013 Hillcrest          San Diego
Ca 94307 (619)271-9871    1250.00
```

Notice that dBASE does not give the END OF FILE ENCOUNTERED message. When the SEEK command is executed, the first occurrence of zip code 61761 is found in the index file (see Figure 21.6), and dBASE positions the pointer to that record (in this case, record 9). After accessing this 61761 record, the only way to find out if there are any more 61761 records is to advance via the index to the next zip record. This is also a 61761 record. The second SKIP command advances you (via the index) to a 94307 zip code. Since the zip code found is no longer 61761, you know that there are no more 61761 records.

The SEEK 61761 command directs dBASE to find the first occurrence of the 61761 zip in the ZIP index. Unless the NO FIND **message** is displayed, dBASE positions the pointer at that record location. The record is displayed via the DISPLAY command. The next occurrence of the 61761 zip is located via the SKIP **command**, which positions the pointer at the next record that is pointed to in the ZIP index. This process is repeated until all of the 61761 zip codes have been located.

To use the AMOUNT index to find all customers in the CUSTOMER file who owe $35.00, you would need to issue the following commands:

```
. use customer index amount
. seek 35.00
. display
     5  Arthur       V Adams        115 Ginger Creek Ct.     Bloomington
IL 61701 (309)828-7290      35.00 01/13/88
. skip
Record no.       7
. display
     7  Debbie       C Acklin       408 E. Monroe            Bloomington
Il 61701 (309)827-1395      35.00 03/21/88
. skip
Record no.      10
. display
    10  Sandy        C Acklin       408 E. Monroe            Bloomington
Il 61701 (309)829-9901      35.00 02/25/88
. skip
Record no.       3
. display
     3  Douglas      C Acklin       408 E. Monroe            Bloomington
Il 61701 (309)663-8976      55.00 04/01/88
```

The following commands will also work:

```
. seek '     35.00'
. display
  6   Russell     B Davis              707 Vale St.              Bloomington
Il 61701 (309)662-1759        35.00 02/27/88
```

These examples illustrate that when you are using a single-field numeric index you do not have to be extremely careful in specifying search criteria. The same is not true, however, of specifications for a multiple-field relationship. An example of this type of application is to access the CUSTOMER file using the ZIPAMOUN index, as follows:

```
. use customer index zipamoun
. seek '6170135.00'
NO FIND
.? RECNO()
         13
```

Why was the NO FIND message displayed despite your having typed 61701 for the zip code and 35.00 for the amount? Remember, the amount field comprises eight positions, and the zip code field comprises five positions; each of these thirteen positions must be included in the search criteria if the search is to be successful. Notice also that the value returned by the RECORD function was 13 because no such records could be found. The following commands find any record with a zip code of 61701 and an amount-owed field of $35.00:

```
. seek '61701   35.00'
. display
  5   Arthur      V Adams            115 Ginger Creek Ct.      Bloomington
IL 61701 (309)828-7290        35.00 01/13/88
. skip
Record no.        7
. display
  7   Debbie      C Acklin           408 E. Monroe             Bloomington
Il 61701 (309)827-3195        35.00 03/21/88
. skip
Record no.        3
. display
  3   Douglas     C Acklin           408 E. Monroe             Bloomington
Il 61701 (309)663-8976        55.00 04/01/88
. skip
Record no.        1
. display
  1   Reza        R Ghorbani         4033 N. Wolcott           Chicago
Il 61702 (312)245-0324       125.00 01/17/88
```

As before, this process is continued until a record is displayed that does not meet the established criteria. The first SEEK command causes dBASE to find the first record that meets the criteria; the subsequent SKIP commands are used to determine whether any more records in the file exist that also meet the search criteria.

Aspects of random and sequential access can be combined to generate a listing of records that meet a certain criterion. Suppose that you want to list only those records in the file that have a zip code of 61701. If you use the L I S T command, dBASE will start at the beginning of the file and read through it sequentially to the end—a procedure that can consume a tremendous amount of time if you are dealing with a large file.

You can avoid this problem by using an index that incorporates the desired information in a continuous group. You tell dBASE to go to the beginning of the desired group of records via a SEEK command, and then you issue a L I S T command to list all records that meet the criterion. The statements that follow use the CUSTOMER file and the ZIP index. The beginning of the 61701 records is encountered, and all records are then listed as long as they match the 61701 zip code criteria. As soon as the characteristics of the records in the index no longer match the search criterion, the search is stopped. You would use the following commands:

```
    • use customer index zip
    • seek '61701'
    • list first, last, address, zip while zip = '61701'
  5   Arthur      Adams      115 Ginger Creek Ct.   61701
  6   Russell     Davis      707 Vale St.           61701
  7   Debbie      Acklin     408 E. Monroe          61701
 10   Sandy       Acklin     408 E. Monroe          61701
```

This very useful process of going randomly to a point in a file and then processing sequentially from that point is called **skip sequential processing**.

BROWSE

The BROWSE **command** enables you to change fields of records in a file rapidly. It is especially useful for a file that contains an index. Whereas the EDIT command displays complete records on one or more screens, the BROWSE command enables you to determine which field of each record you want displayed.

In posting payments from customers to the CUSTOMER file, you can have the payment information sorted in alphabetical order by last name. For this type of application, you need only the fields FIRST, LAST, and AMOUNT, because the FIRST and LAST fields enable you to determine whether you have the correct record, and the AMOUNT field enables you to enter the new balance after the payment is made.

Activate the Assistant menu and then do the following tasks: (1) invoke the CUSTOMER file with the LFNAME index; (2) select the Update option of the Assistant menu, point to Browse, and press the ENTER key. The entire record is now available to you (see Figure 21.10). Use the menu at the top of the screen for cursor movement.

The disadvantage of using the Assistant is that you are overwhelmed with data from the file. It would be much better if you were able to limit the number of fields that are displayed. This can be accomplished at the dot prompt using the BROWSE command, which has the following format (field names must be separated by a comma):

BROWSE FIELDS [list of fields]

The two necessary words are BROWSE and FIELDS; the list of fields to be displayed on the screen follows. To access the CUSTOMER file in alphabetical order, you would issue the following commands (see Figure 21.11):

Figure 21.10
The BROWSE command as it
is executed from the Assistant menu.

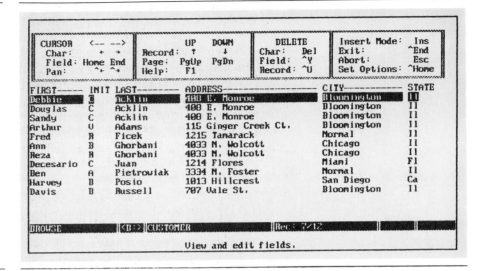

Figure 21.11
The BROWSE command
used against selected fields.

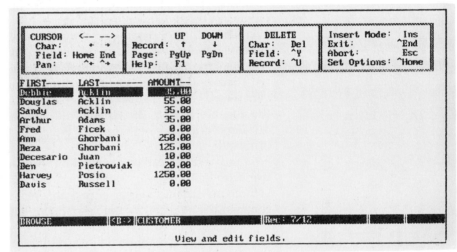

```
. use customer index lfname
. browse fields first,last,amount
```

The record number currently being changed is displayed at the top of the screen. The field names are displayed at the top of each display column. The first record displayed (in this case, record 3) is in reverse video. The cursor movement keys can be used to make changes. In this case, you want to move to the amount field, a task that requires entering two CTRL + F commands (you could also just hold down the right-arrow key). Each subsequent CTRL + F (or down arrow) command moves you to the AMOUNT field of the next record. Clearly, this method is much faster than the EDIT command in making scattered changes in a file.

Chapter Review

The dBASE package provides two ways to order records within a file: via the SORT command and via the INDEX command. The SORT command enables you to create a file in which the records are sorted by one or more specified fields. For large files it is a time-consuming command.

The INDEX command creates an index whose contents consist of the key field of each record and the location of each record on disk. The data file is left in its original order, whereas the index is arranged in the desired order. To access a record, dBASE first goes to the index file to find the location of the desired record and then goes to the identified location in the data file. An index file can be built using a number of fields and will produce the information in only one pass. For example, the file could be logically arranged in last-name first-name order with only one statement. The term *logically* is used to emphasize that the original file remains in its original order; only the index file is arranged to reflect the changed relationship.

When you are using multiple-field indexes, you often want changes in the data file to be reflected in every index. This is done by placing the names of any indexes that you want to be updated after the USE statement. Up to seven indexes can be specified. When a change is made that affects any of the specified indexes, the indexes will automatically be changed, too. Remember, however, that only the first index can be used with a SEEK command.

The dBASE package contains several commands that enable you to perform DOS-like actions. With them you can list files that meet certain criteria, or you can delete files from disk.

The REPORT command can be used with sorted or indexed files to generate reports that contain ordered data. With ordered files, the subtotal feature of the REPORT generator can be used.

Sequential files (sorted files without indexes) can be searched for relevant record via the LOCATE command. When the end of the file is reached, the END OF FILE ENCOUNTERED message is displayed on the screen. The next occurrence of that record type is located by issuing the CONTINUE command.

Indexed files can be searched for relevant records via the SEEK command. You must have specified the appropriate index on the USE statement beforehand. The next occurrence of that record type is located via the Skip command. If no record of the desired type is found in the entire file, the NO FIND message is displayed.

The BROWSE command enables you to change records by making use of the full-screen editing feature of dBASE. BROWSE differs from EDIT in enabling you to specify which fields to display on the screen. By using this command, you can quickly move through the file in an index file order and manually make changes to selected records.

Key Terms and Concepts

active index
BROWSE command
concatenation
CONTINUE command
DELETE FILE command
INDEX command
LIST FILES LIKE command
LOCATE command
mixed data index
multiple-field index
.NDX extension

NO FIND message
random file
SEEK command
SET HEADINGS OFF command
single-field index
SKIP command
skip sequential processing
SORT command
STR function
updating multiple indexes

Chapter Quiz

Multiple Choice

1. Which of the following statements about sorting is false?
   a. It takes more computer time than indexing.
   b. It takes up more disk space than indexing since an output file has to be created.
   c. A multiple key sort is simply impossible.
   d. You are allowed to sort on only one field at a time.
   e. All of the above statements are true.

2. Which of the following statements is false about indexing?
   a. The original file is left the same.
   b. The index file which "logically" orders the file is created.
   c. First the index must be accessed and then the data file, if the records are desired in indexed order.
   d. The index holds the contents of each data record.
   e. All of the above statements are true.

3. A version of the _____ command is used to list the files on disk.
   a. DISPLAY
   b. BROWSE
   c. LIST
   d. INDEX
   e. USE

4. Which of the following commands enable you to make changes in a record?
   a. BROWSE
   b. REPLACE
   c. EDIT
   d. All of the above
   e. None of the above

5. Which command is used to locate records in an indexed file?
   a. SEEK
   b. LOCATE
   c. SKIP
   d. CONTINUE
   e. None of the above

True/False

6. A file must be indexed before the LOCATE command can be used.

7. The SKIP command is used to find the next record that meets the search criteria for a sequential search.

8. An indexed file can be processed in sequential order by the indexed field.

9. When multiple indexes are specified, only the first index name can be used to find records.

10. Sorting files is usually faster than indexing them.

Answers

1. c 2. d 3. c 4. d 5. a 6. f 7. f 8. t 9. t 10. f

Exercises

1. Define or describe each of the following:
   a. Index
   b. multiple field index
   c. active index
   d. sequential file
   e. indexed file
   f. concatenation

2. Physically reordering the records within a file and creating a new file is done by using the _____ command.

3. The records in a file can be sorted in either _____ or _____ order.

4. The SORT command enables you to sort files using only one _____.

5. The _____ file contains both the key field contents and the record location.

6. Listing records from an indexed file requires going to the _____ file, which then points to the record _____ in the file.

7. Indexing a file usually takes _____ time than sorting a file.

8. Joining two or more fields to form one index is the process known as _____ .

9. Numeric fields can be included in an index, but they must first be converted to _____ characters.

10. The command _____ file custzip can be issued to erase the CUSTZIP file.

11. When several indexes follow the USE statement, only the _____ index can be used to find records.

12. When several indexes follow the USE statement, the PACK command will result in _____ index(es) being rebuilt.

13. An ordered report can be generated by using either a _____ or an indexed file.

14. Totals can be incorporated in a report only when a field is _____ .

15. The _____ is used to locate records via an index.

16. The _____ is used to locate records in a sequential file.

17. When you are using the SEEK command, the character string must appear inside _____ .

18. The _____ is used to find the next record in a sequential file search.

19. The _____ command enables you to display only desired fields when changing or updating records.

20. The BROWSE command makes use of the dBASE _____ screen editing feature.

Computer Exercises

The following exercises require the PAYMAST file, created previously:

1. Sort the file by last name.

2. Sort the file by gross pay.

3. Index the file by employee id. List the file.

4. Index the file by last name. List the file.

5. Index the file by gross pay. List the file.

6. Index the file by last name and first name. List the file.

7. Use the last-name index to list the file.

8. Find all the employees who have a gross pay of $780.00. Use the FIND command.

9. Use the LOCATE command to find all the employees that have a pay rate of $4.90.

10. Create a report using the last-name index.

11. Create a report using the gross-pay index.

12. Use the BROWSE command to examine selected fields of your records.

More on

dBASE Commands

After completing this chapter, you should be able to:

Discuss advanced dBASE III Plus report features

Discuss the label generation feature of the REPORT command

Discuss the steps involved in modifying a dBASE file

Discuss the various ways to create files of existing data

Discuss the manner in which data can be passed to and from other applications programs via the IMPORT and EXPORT commands

This chapter covers advanced uses of the REPORT command, introduces the MODIFY command, and demonstrates various ways that you can change existing files or create new ones.

Advanced Report Features

The reports that you have used thus far have been simple. Judging from them you might think that dBASE III Plus allows you only one line of print for each record selected from the file in use. If you know which commands to use, however, you can produce reports that contain more than one line for each record.

Subtotals

Another feature that you can now use in the report feature is the subtotal capability. **Subtotals** can be generated in the report feature in dBASE when the files have been ordered into groups via sorting or indexing. The process of generating subtotals for groups of records is referred to as a **control break** or **level break**.

Suppose you want to use the zip code index (invoke CUSTOMER file with zip index) to create a report that includes totals for each zip code area. In this case, you would not want each subtotal to generate a page break automatically. This report (named ZIPCUST.FRM) has the same format as the NAMEADDR report form, except that it includes the subtotal requirement. Thus, the original NAMEADDR.FRM report form can be copied to ZIPCUST.FRM and then modified using the MODIFY REPORT command.

To copy the NAMEADDR.FRM file and then invoke the MODIFY command requires the following steps:

1. From the Assistant menu invoke the Tools option and then select the Copy file.
2. Highlight the NAMEADDR.FRM file (see Figure 22.1).
3. Specify the ZIPCUST.FRM as the new file (see Figure 22.2).
4. Indicate that the ZIPCUST.FRM file is to be changed.
5. Select the Modify option of the Assistant menu and specify Report.
6. Indicate that the ZIPCUST.FRM file is to be changed.

The same steps can also be executed from command level at the dot prompt:

```
. copy file nameaddr.frm to zipcust.frm
    2048 bytes copied
. use customer index zip
. modify report zipcust
```

The Options screen is now displayed on the monitor (see Figure 22.3). All that you really have to change is the Groups screen, which you can invoke by pressing the right-arrow key. You now press the ENTER key and enter the name of the field ZIP for the Group on expression entry, establishing the field that is to be used for the subtotals. Position the pointer to the Group heading entry, press the ENTER key, and enter ZIP CODE TOTAL (see Figure 22.4). Take the defaults for the subtotal, since Summary report only would print only one line per zip code, and Page eject after group takes up too much paper for this application.

Figure 22.1
The file to be copied using
the Assistant is indicated.

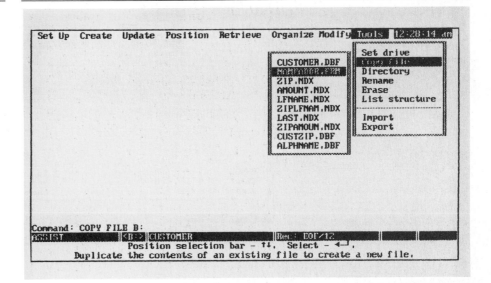

Figure 22.2
The name of the file to receive the NAMEADDR.FRM
contents is specified.

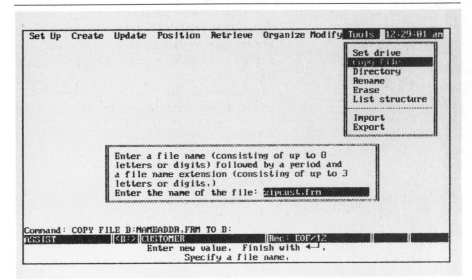

Figure 22.3
Options page of the
ZIPCUST.FRM report
template.

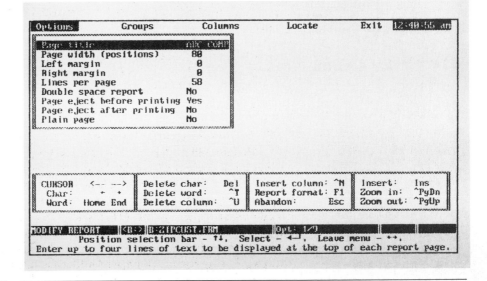

Figure 22.4
The changed entries for the
Groups screen of the
ZIPCUST.frm report
template.

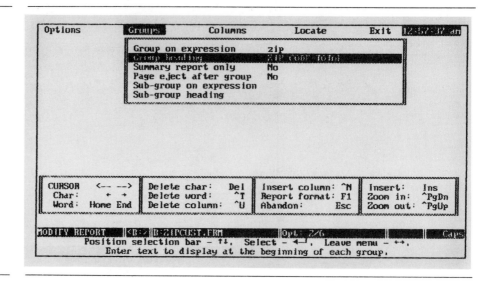

You are now finished with the changes for this example. If there are other things that you want to do, take the appropriate option. You may now save the changes to disk by selecting the Exit option and selecting Save. After the file has been saved to disk, you are returned to the Assistant menu. To print the report, select the Retrieve option, specify Report, specify the drive that the template resides on (b: in this example), tell dBASE to use the ZIPCUST.FRM template, and execute the command. The report is now generated, as follows:

```
Page No.        1
04/15/87


                          ABC COMPANY
                   NAME AND ADDRESS REPORT

            NAME            ADDRESS             CITY         STATE    AMOUNT
** ZIP CODE TOTAL 12562
Juan        Decesario  1214 Flores         Miami          Fl        10.00
** Subtotal **
                                                          10.00


** ZIP CODE TOTAL 13411
Barbara     Walters    1981 Crestlawn      Arlington      Va        75.00
** Subtotal **
                                                          75.00

** ZIP CODE TOTAL 6101
Sandy       Acklin     408 E. Monroe       Bloomington    Il        35.00
** Subtotal **
                                                          35.00

** ZIP CODE TOTAL 61701
Douglas     Acklin     408 E. Monroe       Bloomington    Il        55.00
Arthur      Adams      115 Ginger Creek Ct. Bloomington   Il        35.00
Davis       Russell    707 Vale St.        Bloomington    Il         0.00
Debbie      Acklin     408 E. Monroe       Bloomington    Il        35.00
** Subtotal **

** ZIP CODE TOTAL 61702
Reza        Ghorbani   4033 N. Wolcott     Chicago        Il       125.00
** Subtotal **
                                                         125.00
```

```
** ZIP CODE TOTAL 61712
Ann        Ghorbani   4033 N. Wolcott      Chicago      Il     250.00
** Subtotal **
                                                       250.00

** ZIP CODE TOTAL 61761
Ben        Pietrowiak 3334 N. Foster       Normal       Il      20.00
Fred       Ficek      1215 Tamarack        Normal       Il       0.00
** Subtotal **
                                                        20.00

** ZIP CODE TOTAL 94307
Harvey     Posio      1013 Hillcrest       San Diego    Ca    1250.00
** Subtotal **
                                                      1250.00

*** Total ***
                                                      1890.00
```

Notice that the zip code does not print on every line. Instead, a subtotal heading is printed for each group of records, thereby enabling you to keep track of the records included in each subtotal.

Multiple Line Reports

 Assume that you want to create a new multiple-line report with the following features.

1. Change the left-hand margin to 0. Enter the following headings:

```
                    ABC COMPANY
        CUSTOMER NAME AND ADDRESS REPORT
              IN ORDER BY ZIP CODE
```

2. Concatenate the first and last name fields on the report so there are no excess blanks between the two fields.

3. Place the address so that it will take up two lines in one column:

```
Address
City, State Zip
```

4. Place the phone number next to the address field, followed by the amount field.

5. Print only a final total.

After these features have been integrated into the NEWLIST.FRM template file, the report can be generated.

Use the CREATE command of the Assistant menu to create the report NEWLIST on the B drive. When the Options screen is displayed, set the left margin to 0, enter the specified headings, and issue the CTRL + END command (see Figure 22.5). Now issue the COLUMNS command to display the first field definition screen on your monitor.

Concatenating Fields. dBASE provides alternatives for concatenating fields of data on a report. The first method involves the plus sign (+). For example, a report field might be specified as .FIELD1 + FIELD2. When fields are concatenated using the plus sign, the second field is added to the end of the

Figure 22.5
Options screen for the
NEWLIST.FRM report.

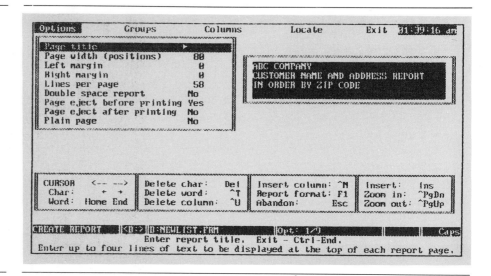

first field. If there are any blanks in the first field, they also appear, which results in two columns of data in this field of the report (one for each field). If you change the field size from the default (the combined size of both fields), information that does not fit in the new column width wraps to the next line of the report in the same field.

The second method involves getting rid of lower-order spaces (those spaces that appear in the unused rightmost portion of a field) via the TRIM function. For example, a report field might be specified as TRIM(FIELD)+ ' '+FIELD2. The TRIM function deletes any lower-order blanks in FIELD1. The + sign is used to concatenate fields—in this case, a blank is joined to the FIELD1 contents, and the contents of FIELD2 are joined to the first field. Again, if you change the field size from the default (the combined size of both fields) information that does not fit in the new column width wraps to the next line of the report in the same field.

The third method of concatenating fields provides more control over how information wraps within a column from one line to the next. If your column width is set the same as the first field, that width determines the number of characters that fit. Any extra characters for this column of the current line wrap to the next line. This might result in having the contents of a field appear on multiple lines within a column on a report. You can control this break by using the semicolon. Whenever dBASE encounters a semicolon, it assumes that this is the end of the data to be printed in the column for the current line; any leftover data are moved to the next line. For example, a report field might be specified as ADDRESS+ ';'+LOCATION. This results in the contents of the field ADDRESS appearing on the first line of a column for this record and LOCATION CONTENTS appearing on the next line of the same column for this record.

Enter the following information for the field contents screen of field 1: TRIM(FIRST)+' '+LAST. Enter the column heading of NAME and change the 23 column width to 18 (see Figure 22.6). Press the PGDN key to go to the next column.

Fill in the following information for the field contents of field 2: AD-DRESS +';'+ TRIM(CITY)+', '+STATE+' '+ZIP. Enter the column heading of ADDRESS and change the column width to 25 (see Figure 22.7). In this field definition entry, the ADDRESS field reserves twenty-five

Figure 22.6
Contents of the Column screen for specifying the concatenated name field.

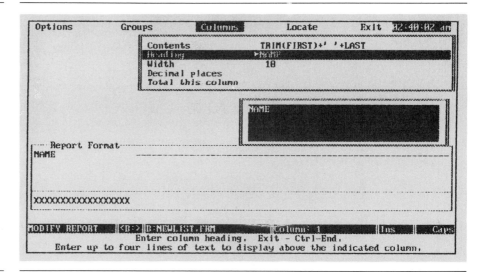

Figure 22.7
Definition screen for the Address column.

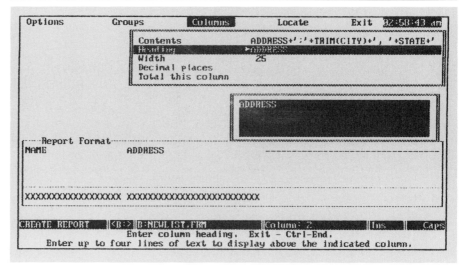

print positions, the semicolon tells dBASE that any following data should begin on the next line, and the CITY, STATE, and ZIP fields are concatenated to the ADDRESS field. The TRIM function deletes any lower-order blanks, the '', '' results in a comma and a space being placed after the trimmed city name, the " " after the state places a space after the state abbreviation. Remember, the comma is not stored in the CITY field. Press the PGDN key to go to the next columns definition screen.

Fill in the following information for the field contents of field 3: PHONE. Enter TELEPHONE as the column heading and leave the field width as it appears. Press the PGDN key to go to the next column definition screen.

Fill in the column screen for the fourth field AMOUNT. Enter the AMOUNT as the heading (see Figure 22.8), and take the defaults for this field. Review the design and SAVE the file to disk.

Using the Assistant menu, send the report to the printer. Your report should look like this:

Figure 22.8
The definition entries for the
AMOUNT field.

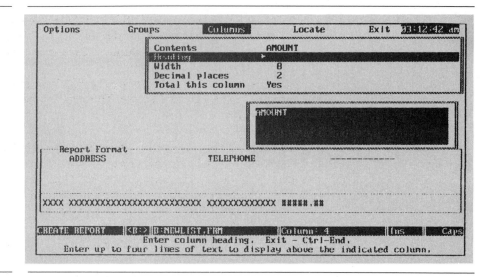

                          ABC COMPANY
                CUSTOMER NAME AND ADDRESS REPORT
                      IN ORDER BY ZIP CODE

NAME	ADDRESS	TELEPHONE	AMOUNT
Reza Ghorbani	4033 N. Wolcott Chicago, Il 61702	(312)245-0324	125.00
Ann Ghorbani	4033 N. Wolcott Chicago, Il 61712	(312)245-0324	250.00
Douglas Acklin	408 E. Monroe Bloomington, Il 61701	(312)663-8976	55.00
Barbara Walters	1981 Crestlawn Arlington, Va 13411	(703)237-3727	75.00
Arthur Adams	115 Ginger Creek Ct. Bloomington, Il 61701	(309)828-7290	35.00
Davis Russell	707 Vale St. Bloomington, Il 61701	(309)662-1759	0.00
Debbie Acklin	408 E. Monroe Bloomington, Il 61701	(309)827-1395	35.00
Harvey Posio	1013 Hillcrest San Diego, Ca 94307	(619)271-9871	1250.00
Ben Pietrowiak	3334 N. Foster Normal, Il 61761	(309)452-9126	20.00
Sandy Acklin	408 E. Monroe Bloomington, Il 61701	(309)829-9901	35.00
Fred Ficek	1215 Tamarack Normal, Il 61761	(309)454-7123	0.00
Juan Decesario	1214 Flores Miami, Fl 12562	(305)719-1363	10.00

*** Total ***

                                              1890.00

Calculations
Embedded within
a Report Template

The REPORT command of dBASE III Plus also enables you to specify calculations to be performed as the written report is generated. These calculations can involve fields of data, numeric constants, or a combination of fields and constants.

To explore this feature of dBASE, load the INVENTRY.DBF file from your disk and activate that file. The structure of the INVENTRY.DBF file can be seen below.

```
Structure for database: B:INVENTRY.dbf
Number of data records:      28
Date of last update   : 11/12/86
Field  Field Name  Type        Width   Dec
    1   INVID       Character     10
    2   NAME        Character     36
    3   ONHAND      Numeric        4
    4   REORDER     Numeric        4
    5   OPTIMUM     Numeric        4
    6   PRICE       Numeric        7      2
** Total *                        66
```

The report to be generated for this application has the title INVENTORY VALUATION REPORT. The following fields and headings are to appear on each line:

Field Name	Field Heading
INVID	ID
NAME	ITEM NAME
ONHAND	CURRENT
	LEVEL
PRICE	ITEM
	PRICE
Calculated field	TOTAL VALUE

Select the Create option of the Assistant menu and indicate to dBASE that you wish to create a new report called INVLIST. Enter the report heading but leave the other entries on the Options screen alone. Enter in the report the field specifications for each field as given above. When you are ready to enter the field specification for the last field, use the following entry: ONHAND * PRICE. Save the report template to disk.

Once you have activated this report template for use and told dBASE to send the output to the printer, your report should look like this:

```
Page No.       1
04/15/87
                    INVENTORY VALUATION REPORT
ID             ITEM NAME                    CURRENT      ITEM     EXTENSION
                                            LEVEL        PRICE

3625a1         crt lamp                        13       149.00      1937.00
4545a1         ready files set                 30        39.50      1185.00
8093a1         serial microbuffer              45       379.00     17055.00
6137a1         IBM nylon cartridge ribbon      47         5.95       279.65
6582 a1        computer vacuum                 85       139.00     11815.00
3970-8a1       multi-purpose back shelf        25       110.00      2750.00
4400a1         workstations                     9       699.00      6291.00
```

4430a1	workstations	5	650.00	3250.00
4440	triangle extension	15	185.00	2775.00
4442	rectangle extension	100	175.00	17500.00
4444	copyholder	55	99.00	5445.00
4446	wristrest	35	39.00	1365.00
4838	footrest	120	35.00	4200.00
4858a1	manager's chair	8	549.00	4392.00
4857	associate's chair	12	359.00	4308.00
4856	clerical chair	33	299.00	9867.00
4765	associate's chair	55	340.00	18700.00
4447a1	copyholder	88	120.00	10560.00
4270	42" customizer	30	190.00	5700.00
4271	72" customizer	22	250.00	5500.00
4272a1	42" side extension	50	115.00	5750.00
4273	72" side extension	45	135.00	6075.00
4279	back extension foot	9	40.00	360.00
4276	flat shelf	85	68.00	5780.00
4276	suspension bar	53	39.00	2067.00

*** Total ***

		1074	5208.45	154906.65

When the report is generated, the contents of the ONHAND field are multiplied by the contents of the PRICE field, and the result is placed in the last column (the column with the PRICE*AMOUNT entry).

Special Headings

When you are using the Report feature of dBASE to make queries to your data file, you may want to place a label on the report so that you can identify its contents later. Unless such a method is used, you may not be able to determine what your selection criteria were for the records in the report.

If you want to label a report with the dBASE III Plus package, you must use the HEADING option of the REPORT command. The text comprising the heading must be enclosed between quotes. For instance, the following example generates a report using the THANKYOU.FRM report template, inserts the heading "First Group of Thank-You Letters," and sends the report to the printer.

```
REPORT FORM THANKYOU HEADING 'First Group of
Thank-You Letters' TO PRINT
```

Generating Mailing Labels

The dBASE III Plus REPORT command has the ability to generate mailing labels directly from name and address information contained in a file via the LABEL command. The LABEL command enables you to define the physical attributes of your labels and then, once the labels are mounted, print the information on them.

To create a label template for the CUSTOMER.DBF file requires that you take the Create option of the Assistant menu and then select the Label option from that submenu. Enter the template name as ZIPLABEL (see Figure 22.9). The Labels menu contains three options: Options, Contents, and Exit.

The Options entry enables you to specify the size of the labels and the number of labels that appear on each row. The default size label (3½ × 15/16 inches, one across) allows you to print up to five lines of text on a label and

Figure 22.9

Options screen of Label for
the ZIPCUST labels.

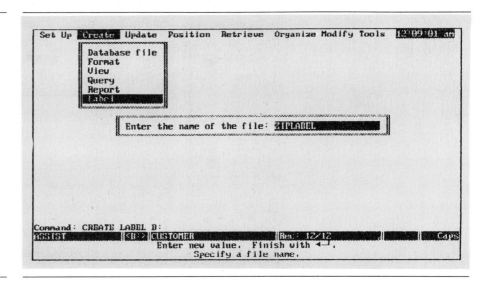

contains one blank line to enable you to get to the next label. Six lines, therefore, must be accounted for on each default size label. The following size labels
are supported by the LABEL feature of dBASE III Plus.

Size of Label	Number Across
3 1/2 × 15/16	1–3
4 × 1 7/16	1
3/2/10 × 11/12	3 (Cheshire)

The Options entries have a number of defaults that change according to
which label type is highlighted. Each default has a number of values that
can be manually changed by highlighting that option and pressing the
ENTER key:

1. The Label Width option determines the maximum number of
   characters (1 to 120) that can be printed on a single line of a label.

2. The Label height option determines the number of lines (1 to 16)
   than can appear on each label.

3. The Left margin option works the same as on the REPORT command.

4. The Lines between labels option indicates the vertical distance between rows of labels and can accept the values 0 to 16.

5. The Spaces between labels option indicates the horizontal
   distance in spaces and allows the values 0 to 120.

6. The Labels across page option indicates the number of labels
   printed on the same line across the page and allows the values 1 to 15.

Once the physical characteristics of the labels have been defined, press
the right-arrow key to activate the Contents entry of the Labels menu to
define the print contents for the labels. If you need help remembering your
field names, simply press the F10 key, highlight the desired field, and press
the ENTER key to copy that field name into this label line (see Figure 22.10).

The comma entry in the preceding field provides an alternate method of
combining and trimming fields when no punctuation is desired immediately
after a field.

Figure 22.10
The Help facility (key F10)
when entering field names.

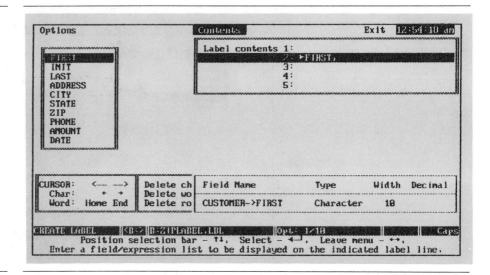

Finish entering the other label files. For line 2, enter the field ADDRESS, and for line 3 enter TRIM(CITY)+', '+STATE+' '+ZIP (see Figure 22.11). Exit the LABEL command and save the file.

To print the labels requires the following steps: take the Retrieve option of the Assistant menu and select Labels from that submenu; indicate that the .LBL file is on the default drive (in this example drive B); select the correct label file, ZIPLABEL.LBL; and execute the command so that the output is sent to the printer (don't worry if you do not have labels mounted).

Your printed output should now appear like the following partial listing:

```
Juan Decesario
1214 Flores
Miami, Fl 12562

Barbara Walters
1981 Crestlawn
Arlington, Va 13411

Sandy Acklin
408 E. Monroe
Bloomington, Il 61701
```

Modifying a dBASE III Plus File

Suppose that you decided that the existing CUSTOMER file does not provide enough information about sales by geographic region; you would like to add a one-byte region field (in character data) to each record to hold that information, and you want to place it after the ZIP field. The MODIFY STRUCTURE **command** is used for this purpose. When you are using the MODIFY STRUC-TURE command, CTRL + N enables you to insert a field at the cursor position, and CTRL + T enables you to delete a field at the cursor position.

To add a REGION field between the ZIP and PHONE fields in the CUS-TOMER file, the following steps are executed from the Assistant menu, once the CUSTOMER file is invoked and the Modify Data Base options are selected:

1. Position the cursor at the PHONE field.
2. Enter the CTRL + N command.

Figure 22.11
The entry for concatenating the city, state, and zip information.

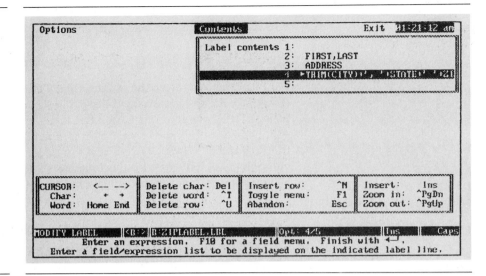

3. Enter the REGION C and 1 field width information in the appropriate entries.
4. Enter the CTRL + W to tell dBASE that the modifications are done.
5. Press ENTER to confirm that everything has been properly changed.

A message is now displayed that indicates that the records have been added to the file.

Listing the file shows that the region field consists of blanks for each record. If you add a *numeric* field to a record, that field will contain zeros rather than blanks. You can now use the EDIT or BROWSE command to add the appropriate REGION field information for each record.

Creating Files with Existing Files

There are a number of ways to create files using dBASE III Plus. Aside from the CREATE command, structures from existing files can be used to create files.

File Backup

One of the preceding sections described how to create a **backup copy** of an existing file. For example, you could copy CUSTOMER from drive A to drive B by using the following statements from the dot prompt:

```
. use a:customer
. copy to b:customer
```

Copy Structure

If you want to pick and choose from various fields that are currently on a record, you can use the COPY STRUCTURE command, which copies only the information from the header record to the receiving file. The field structures are copied, but data are not. You can then modify the new structure by adding and/or deleting field(s). For example, you could issue the following commands in copying structures from the CUSTOMER file:

```
. use customer
. copy structure to temp
. use temp
. modify structure
```

Another characteristic of the COPY STRUCTURE command is that if the temporary file already exists, the existing records are deleted. Using the COPY STRUCTURE command is easier and takes less time than issuing a DELETE ALL command followed by a PACK command. For example, you may have a transaction file TRAN whose records are deleted at the end of each day. Provided that you have previously copied its structure to a file called TEMPTRAN, all you have to do is enter the following commands:

```
. use temptran
. copy structure to tran
```

The TRAN file is now empty.

Copy Field

The COPY FIELD **command** can be used to copy selected fields and their contents to another file. This method can be used when you want to create intermediate files that contain only a portion of the data in a much larger file. It enables you to take a portion of a file contained on hard disk and transfer it to a diskette.

Suppose you want to create a name and address file containing only the FIRST, LAST, ADDRESS, CITY, STATE, and ZIP fields from the CUSTOMER file. The following steps would be required:

```
. use customer
. copy field first,last,address,city,state,zip to newcust
      12 records copied
. use newcust
. list
  1  Reza      Ghorbani    4033 N. Wolcott          Chicago       Il 60712
  2  Ann       Ghorbani    4033 No. Wolcott         Chicago       Il 60712
  3  Douglas   Acklin      408 E. Monroe            Bloomington   Il 61701
  4  Barbara   Walters     1981 Crestlawn           Arlington     Va 13411
  5  Arthur    Adams       115 Ginger Creek Ct.     Bloomington   Il 61701
  6  Russell   Davis       707 Vale St.             Bloomington   Il 61701
  7  Debbie    Acklin      408 E. Monroe            Bloomington   Il 61701
  8  Harvey    Posio       1013 Hillcrest           San Diego     Ca 94307
  9  Ben       Pietrowiak  3334 N. Foster           Normal        Il 61761
 10  Sandy     Acklin      408 E. Monroe            Bloomington   Il 61701
 11  Fred      Ficek       1215 Tamarack            Normal        Il 61761
 12  Juan      Decesario   1214 Flores              Miami         Fl 12562
```

As you can see, only the information from the desired fields is copied to the receiving file.

Creating ASCII Files for Other Packages

Information contained in a dBASE file can easily be passed to applications packages that accept (or are capable of translating) standard ASCII files. An

ASCII file contains a field of data followed by a comma. If there are embedded commas in a field, that field must be enclosed in double quotes. The data must be converted from the storage format used by dBASE III Plus to a standard ASCII format that is recognizable by your software package. These data can then be used for such applications as generating personalized letters. The COPY command is used in concert with the DELIMITED **parameter** in this type of application.

It is important that there be no embedded commas in a field of data. You must, therefore, be careful when creating application files to keep the city and state information in separate data base fields or not to embed a comma between the city and state during data entry. Any field that does contain a comma will be interpreted as two fields. If it is necessary to have commas embedded in a field, that field must also have double quotes (") around it to force your application software to evaluate the data as one field. This is automatically handled by dBASE III Plus. Simple commands that can be used to create a file for merge operations are as follows:

```
. use newcust
. copy to names.dat delimited with "
  12 records copied
```

A copy of the NAMES.DAT file just created is displayed below. Notice that each field is separated by a comma. The NAMES.DAT file is now a standard ASCII file rather than a data base file; any program that is capable of accessing such a file can now process these data.

From DOS, you can now enter the following statement to view the NAMES.DAT file:

```
TYPE NAMES.DAT
"Reza","Ghorbani","4033 N. Wolcott","Chicago","Il","60712"
"Ann","Ghorbani","4033 N. Wolcott","Chicago","Il","60712"
"Douglas","Acklin","408 E. Monroe","Bloomington","Il","61701"
"Barbara","Walters","1981 Crestlawn","Arlington","Va","13411"
"Arthur","Adams","115 Ginger Creek Ct.","Bloomington","Il","61701"
"Russell","Davis","707 Vale St.","Bloomington","Il","61701"
"Debbie","Acklin","408 E. Monroe","Bloomington","Il","61701"
"Harvey","Posio","1013 Hillcrest","San Diego","Ca","94307"
"Ben","Pietrowiak","3334 Foster","Normal","Il","61761"
"Sandy","Acklin","408 E. Monroe","Bloomington","Il","61701"
"Fred","Ficek","1215 Tamarack","Normal","Il","61761"
"Juan","Decesario","1214 Flores","Miami","Fl","12562"
```

Chapter Review

The dBASE package has a number of advanced report features. One of these is the subtotal feature, which can be used only on ordered files (files that have previously been sorted or indexed). A report in which subtotals are generated for groups of records is called a control break or level break.

Although it might appear that dBASE allows you to print only one line per record, concatenation and field separation techniques can be used to generate multiple print lines per record. Joining fields so that they wrap within the same area and thereby create multiple lines within a column requires the concatenation command (+) and the end of line indicator (;). The field must be the proper width when you define it.

An existing report template (stored in a .FRM file) can be changed to incorporate the above items by means of the MODIFY REPORT command.

Mailing labels as well as arithmetic within a report template can also be specified to dBASE.

The dBASE software makes it possible to build files a number of different ways using data from existing files. Backup data files can easily be created using the COPY command. The COPY FIELDS command is used to build a new file with the data from only a few fields of the existing file. An empty file with a matching structure can be created using the COPY STRUCTURE command.

The MODIFY STRUCTURE command uses a straightforward method and automatically performs the steps for adding or deleting fields and then copying the records from the old file to the new, changed file.

Text files can easily be created using the DELIMITED parameter of the COPY command. These files can then be used as input to applications programs.

Key Terms and Concepts

arithmetic in a report template
backup copy
COPY FIELD command
COPY STRUCTURE command
DELIMITED parameter
LABELS command

level break (control break)
MODIFY STRUCTURE command
subtotals
TO PRINT parameter
TRIM function

Chapter Quiz

Multiple Choice

1. Which of the following statements is true for forcing multiple lines to appear within a data column?
    a. The semicolon (;) must be placed where each line is to end within a column.
    b. Both the + and the ; may be required.
    c. Only the colon is needed to indicate the end of a line.
    d. Full-screen editing places each heading on a separate line.

2. Which of the following characters is used to concatenate fields?
    a. &
    b. :
    c. ;
    d. +
    e. None of the above

3. Subtotals can be used only with which of the following files?
    a. Indexed files
    b. Sorted files
    c. Sequential files
    d. None of the above

4. Which of the following is not a version of the COPY statement?
    a. Copy Structure to temp
    b. Copy Field first,last to temp
    c. Copy to temp
    d. Copy to temp delimited with ,
    e. All of the above are valid examples of the COPY statement.

5. Using the MODIFY STRUCTURE command will result in which of the following?
   a. Erasing all records in the file
   b. Enabling you to add new fields
   c. Enabling you to delete unwanted fields
   d. Forcing you to make a copy of the file beforehand
   e. All of the above

True/False

6. The TRIM command is used to delete blanks on the left-hand side of a field.

7. Up to a maximum of two lines can be printed per specified field using the Report feature of dBASE.

8. Subtotals can result in a page break.

9. The LABEL command enables you to print up to three labels across.

10. Arithmetic statements in a report template can contain only field names.

Answers

1. a&b 2. d 3. a&b 4. e 5. b&c 6. f 7. f 8. t 9. t 10. f

Exercises

1. Define or describe each of the following:
   a. level break   c. Delimited with
   b. Trim( )   d. Copy Structure

2. A _____ is generated when the contents of a field change from one record to the next.

3. The _____ option of the REPORT command sends output directly to the printer.

4. Subtotals can be generated only on _____ data fields.

5. The _____ command instruction is issued to make mailing label templates.

6. The command sequence _____ inserts a blank line at the cursor location when using the dBASE MODIFY STRUCTURE command.

7. The command sequence _____ deletes the field at the cursor location when using the dBASE MODIFY STRUCTURE command.

8. The command sequence _____ aborts the modify process and returns you to the Assistant menu.

9. The character _____ is used to break a column entry into two lines.

10. The character _____ is used to join two fields for printing.

11. The _____ function is used to delete any lower-order blanks (blanks that appear in the rightmost portion of a field).

12. The _____ STRUCTURE command deletes all dBASE records in a file.

13. The simple _____ command is used to create a backup of a data file.

14. The _____ option of the COPY command enables you to create a file in which each field is separated by a specified character.

15. dBASE can pass specially formatted files to general application programs such as _____.

Computer Exercises

The following exercises require the PAYMAST file, created previously.

1. Use the technique covered in this chapter for adding fields to a record. Add the following fields to the PAYMAST file. Give each field an appropriate length.

   Address
   City
   State
   Zip

2. Use the BROWSE or EDIT command to fill in data for each record.

3. Using the DOS COPY command, make a copy of the .FRM report template that you have already created. Call the copy NEWPYREP.FRM (New Pay Report).

4. Using the NEWPYREP.FRM, create a multiple-line report like that shown in this chapter. Design the report layout yourself.

5. Use the COPY FIELD command to create a data base file with the name and address information for each employee.

6. Create an ASCII text file with the information from Task 5.

7. Using the file created in Task 6, generate mailing labels for all employees via the LABEL command.

Chapter 23

Advanced Features of dBASE III Plus

After completing this chapter, you should be able to:

Discuss the ability of dBASE to build special data entry screens

One problem that many people have with data base applications is that the paper form (source document) that is used to originally capture (collect) the data does not bear any resemblance to the screen displayed by dBASE after the data is entered via the APPEND command. The APPEND screen shows only the field name and a highlighted area for entering data. The field name is often a cryptic notation of the information that is to be placed in each field and may give a novice few indications of exactly what should be placed in each field.

dBASE III Plus provides a solution to this type of problem by enabling you to create a data entry form that is similar to the original document that contains the data. The dBASE **screen painter** quickly generates forms (see Figure 23.1) that look like printed paper forms and are easy to use.

Once the form is created, you can use it for entering new data via the APPEND command or for displaying data via the LIST or DISPLAY commands. This entry-form feature of dBASE enables you to dictate which fields of a data base are to be included in a form, to change the descriptive data displayed on the screen, and to control what types of data are to be entered for each field in the form. There are two basic parts to the form screen: the descriptive data (labels and titles) and the field-related information, which indicates the field length and the type of data that is allowed in each field (see Figure 23.2).

Creating a Data Entry Form

Creating an entry form requires that the Assistant feature of dBASE be active. Once the Assistant is active, use the Tools option to set the default drive. Once that is done, select the Create option of the Assistant menu and then select the Format option. Indicate to dBASE that the entry form is to be saved to the default disk, and when dBASE displays the prompt Enter the name of the file: respond with CUSTFORM.

dBASE now displays the screen painter menu (see Figure 23.3) which contains the following options: (1) Set Up, which enables you to select the data base for which the entry form is to be built and to specify which fields from this file are to be contained in the form; (2) Modify, which enables you to change the form by adding or changing fields or even modifying the structure of the invoked file; (3) Options, which enables you to create a text file image of the form and to draw lines and boxes; and (4) Exit, with which you can save the screen to disk or abandon it.

Use the Set Up option from the screen painter menu to select the file to be used by this entry form. Since the pointer is already on the Select Database File, simply press the ENTER key. A list of files is now displayed on your screen. Select the CUSTOMER.DBF file, use the up and down arrow keys to highlight that file and press the ENTER key. Highlight the Load Fields option of the Set Up menu. A list of the fields in the Customer file is displayed. To select a field to be included in the form, you must highlight that field and press the ENTER key. Once a field has been selected, an arrow appears to the left of the field name. Since all fields are to be used, mark them all (see Figure 24.4). After all fields have been marked, press an UP or DOWN ARROW key to activate the screen painter.

Designing the Form

Once the screen painter has been invoked and the fields selected, information about the fields appears in the left-hand portion of the screen (see Figure 23.5). This information includes the field name and a highlighted bar indicating the field length. Inside each bar are characters indicating the type of information that can be stored in each field (An X represents character fields, and a 9

Figure 23.1
Data entry form created for the CUSTOMER.DBF data base file.

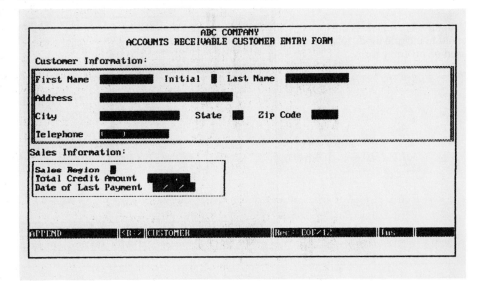

Figure 23.2
Entry form showing the descriptive and field information for the CUSTOMER.DBF file, created with the screen painter of dBASE.

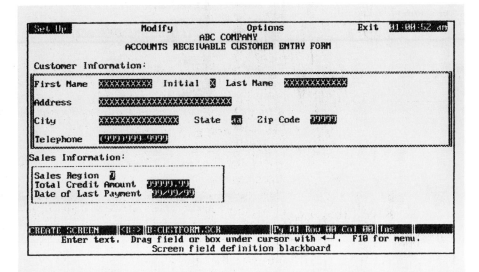

Figure 23.3
The screen painter menu used by dBASE for building data entry forms.

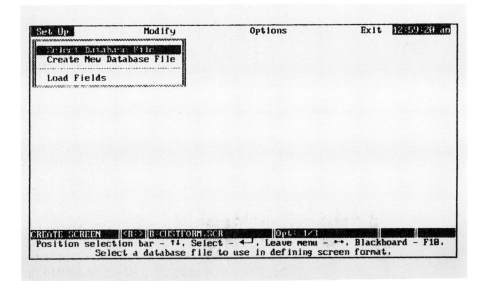

Figure 23.4
Using the Load Fields command to include fields to be used on an entry form.

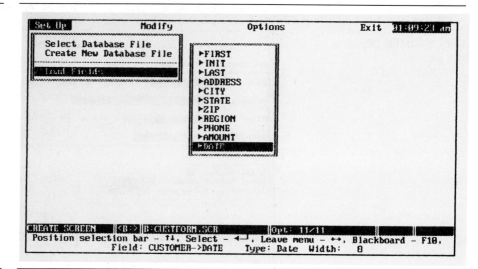

Figure 23.5
List of selected fields on the screen painter blackboard.

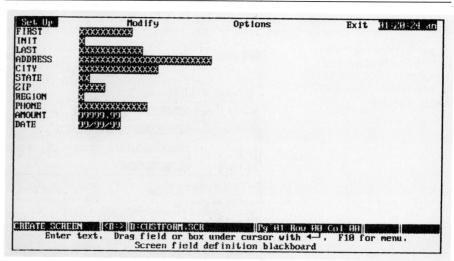

represents numeric fields). This screen is now referred to as the **blackboard**. You use this blackboard to tell dBASE exactly how your form should appear on the screen.

Using the blackboard to create the CUSTFORM **data entry screen** (see Figure 23.1 and 23.2) is accomplished via a number of editing commands that are available to you while you are in blackboard mode. These include the following:

Command	Function Performed
INS or Ctrl + V	Toggles the blackboard between insert and overwrite mode.
Ctrl + N	Inserts a blank line above the current cursor position.
Ctrl + C or PgUp	Scrolls the screen up 18 lines.
Ctrl + R or PgDn	Scrolls the screen down 18 lines.
Arrow key	Moves the cursor one position in the indicated direction.

`Ctrl + A or Home`	Moves the cursor to the beginning of the current word or to the beginning of the previous word.
`Ctrl + B or Ctrl` + right arrow	Moves the cursor to the end of the line.
`Ctrl + F or End`	Moves the cursor to the first character of the next word.
`Ctrl + M or Enter`	Moves the cursor to the beginning of the next line or, if Ins mode is on, inserts a blank line. When the cursor is positioned in a field, you can drag (move) that field. When the cursor is positioned on the outline of a box, you can change the size of the box.
`Ctrl + Z or Ctrl` + left arrow	Moves the cursor to the beginning of the line.
`Ctrl + G or Del`	Deletes the character at the cursor location or decreases the width of the field on the form.
Backspace	Deletes the character to the left of the current cursor location.
`Ctrl + T`	Deletes all characters beginning at the current cursor location to the end of the word.
`Ctrl + Y`	Deletes the line at the cursor.
`Ctrl + U`	Deletes the field or box at the cursor location.

The bottom three lines of the blackboard also provide information:

1. The status bar indicates the current cursor location and whether or not you are in insert or overwrite mode. If an Ins appears in the box to the right of the cursor location status, the blackboard is in insert mode. Any text you enter is added to the line at the cursor location and moves current text to the right. The blackboard activates with overwrite mode in effect. NOTE: Make certain that you do not accidentally have the cursor positioned in a highlighted field; entering insert mode in this situation adds or deletes positions in the field itself, rather than in the text around the field.

2. The navigation line contains additional hints about what actions to take.

3. The message line contains the current status or displays error messages.

You probably noticed the reference to **dragging** fields. A field is dragged from one position on the blackboard to another in the following manner: (1) The cursor is placed in the field highlight, (2) the ENTER key is pressed once, (3) the cursor is moved to the position on the blackboard to which you want to move the field, and (4) the ENTER key is pressed. The field highlight then moves from its original location to the indicated position on the blackboard.

You are now ready to build your `CUSTFORM` entry screen by carrying out the following steps.

Enter descriptive information at the top of the screen:

1. If your cursor is not at Pg 01 Row 00 Col 00, move it there.

2. Place the blackboard in insert mode by pressing the Ins key. You should now see Ins to the right of the cursor location in the status bar.

3. Press the ENTER key five times to insert five blank lines at the top of the blackboard.

4. Position your cursor to column 32 of row 0 and type ABC COMPANY.

5. Position your cursor to column 18 of row 1 and type ACCOUNTS RECEIVABLE CUSTOMER ENTRY FORM.

6. Position the cursor to column 1 of row 3 and type Customer In-formation:.

Rearrange the customer name and address fields for easy data entry, as follows:

1. Position the cursor at row 5 column 0 and press the spacebar once. This embeds a space before the word FIRST.

2. Press the Ins key to place the blackboard in overwrite mode.

3. Position the cursor at the I of FIRST and type irst Name.

4. Drag the INITIAL field to a new location: Position the cursor at the highlighted field for INITIAL (row 6 column 12), press the ENTER key, position the cursor at row 5 column 34, and press the ENTER key again. The highlighted initial field should now be at the new location.

5. Perform the same steps for the highlighted LAST field and position it at row 5 column 48.

6. Move the cursor to row 5 column 37 and type the label Last Name.

7. Move the cursor to row 5 column 25 and type the label Initial.

8. Position the cursor at row 6 and delete that row with a Ctrl + Y command.

9. Use the Home key to position the cursor at the beginning of the word LAST and enter the command Ctrl + T to delete the word.

10. Place the blackboard in insert mode and move the cursor to row 7 column 0 and insert a space in front of the word ADDRESS.

11. Put the blackboard in overwrite mode and change the upper-case characters DDRESS to ddress.

Rearrange the city, state, and zip fields for easy data entry:

1. Position the cursor anywhere in row 8 and insert a blank line by using the Ctrl + N command.

2. Place the blackboard in insert mode and then position the cursor to the C of CITY and press the spacebar to insert a blank.

3. Place the blackboard in overwrite mode, position the cursor at the I of CITY and type the characters ity.

4. Drag the highlighted STATE field to row 9 column 39.

5. Drag the highlighted ZIP field to row 9 column 54.

6. Position the cursor at row 9 column 32 and type State.

7. Position the cursor at row 9 column 44 and type Zip Code.

8. Position the cursor at row 10 and insert a row using the Ctrl + N command.

Figure 23.6
The CUSTFORM entry
screen with the fields and
accompanying text.

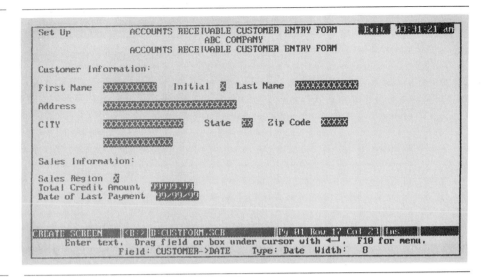

9. Position the cursor at the S of STATE and issue the Ctrl + T command to delete that word.

10. Drag the highlighted phone field to row 11 column 13.

11. Position the cursor at Row 11 Column 1 and type Telephone.

Clean up the area in the middle of the screen:

1. Position the cursor at row 12, press the Home key, and issue the Ctrl + T command to delete the word ZIP.

2. Insert two lines by issuing the Ctrl + N command twice.

3. Position the cursor at row 13 column 1 and type Sales Information:.

Prepare the remaining fields:

1. Position the cursor at row 16 and issue the Ctrl + Y command to delete that row.

2. Place the blackboard in insert mode, position the cursor at row 15 column 0, enter a space, issue the Ctrl + T command to delete the word REGION, and type Sales Region followed by two spaces.

3. Position the cursor at row 16 column 0, enter a space, issue the Ctrl + T command to delete the word AMOUNT, and type TOTAL Credit Amount followed by two spaces.

4. Position the cursor at row 17 column 0, enter a space, issue the Ctrl + T command to delete the word DATE, and type Date of Last Payment followed by two spaces.

The process of arranging the fields and typing the identifying text to label the fields is now complete (see Figure 23.6).

Even though you have changed the labels on the fields, dBASE is still able to store the information on the entry form to the correct field in the data base file.

You may include a field on your entry form that you did not really mean to include. To get rid of such a field, position the cursor to that highlighted

Figure 23.7
The Modify menu of the
paint screen facility.

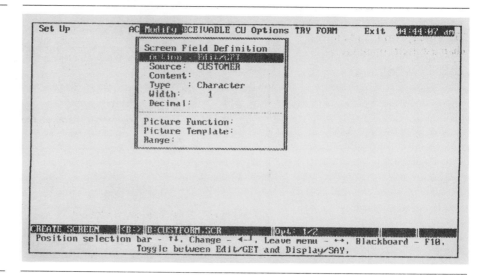

field and issue the Ctrl + U command. dBASE now displays the prompt Do you wish to also delete field from database? [Y/N]. Enter a Y to have dBASE delete the field from the entry form and from the data base.

If you forget to load a field, simply place the cursor in an unused area of the screen (for example, on a blank line) and invoke the print screen menu by pressing the F10 key. After you select the Set Up option, you can issue the LOAD FIELDS command, point to the desired field and press the ENTER key, and then press the F10 key again to return to the blackboard. The marked field is now at the indicated position in your entry form.

Having arranged the fields and entered the identifying labels, your task of developing a data entry screen is not necessarily over. You may, for instance, want to change the size of a field, limit the type of characters that can be entered in a field, change the way the field is to be used (is it available to a user for changes or simply displayed?), or add a new field to the form. The position of the cursor is important since it determines which field is to be modified.

Once you press the F10 key, the **Modify menu** is displayed on your screen (see Figure 23.7). A number of entries in this menu provide flexibility in how data are to be handled on the form. Remember, the cursor has to be positioned on the desired field before the F10 command is issued. A discussion of each entry follows.

Action. The Action option describes how the data in a field are to be handled by dBASE. If the data display is Edit/Get, the field is available to a user for entries or changes. If the data display is Display/SAY, the data in this field can be seen by a user but cannot be changed.

If you want to change the Action entry, use the up and down arrow keys to highlight the entry and press the Enter key. The entry has now switched. For example, an Edit/GET entry has changed to Display/SAY); after you press the F10 key and return to the entry form, the Edit/GET field is no longer highlighted. Be careful when you use this command, because field labels can be lost when you switch the action.

Picture Function. The **Picture Function** entry enables you to specify any special conversion of data before the data appear on the screen. When you select this option, a table of acceptable values appears to the right of the

Figure 23.8
The Modify menu and the character function table.

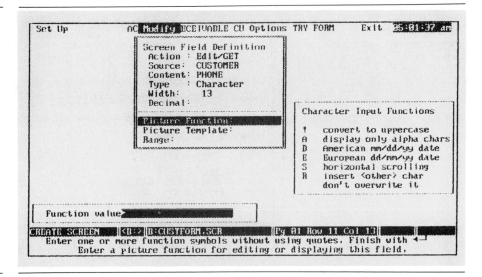

Figure 23.9
The Picture Template help menu of the Modify command.

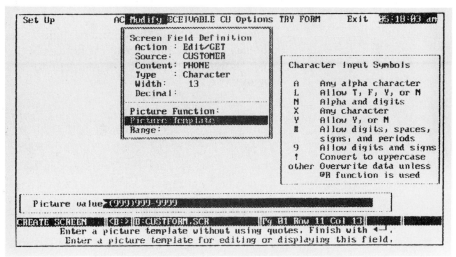

Modify menu (see Figure 23.8), and dBASE waits until you enter your choice at the bottom of the screen.

Even though nothing appears in the field highlight on the entry screen, when you use the form for adding information to the data base file, any data conversion occurs before the information is stored to the file. For example, if you enter the !, all data are converted to upper-case characters before they are sent to the record.

Picture Template. The **Picture Template** enables you to specify exactly the kind of data that is to be allowed in a field on a character-by-character basis. Once this option is selected, a help menu appears on the screen (see Figure 23.9).

The Picture Template contains the same number of characters as the Width entry on the Modify menu. For example, if the PHONE field is currently selected, and you want to limit entries to parentheses, digits, and dashes, enter the following template:

(999)999-9999

This template accounts for all thirteen of the PHONE positions and appears on your data entry screen during an APPEND operation as (   )   -   . If

Figure 23.10
The CUSTFORM entry form
after picture templates have
been added.

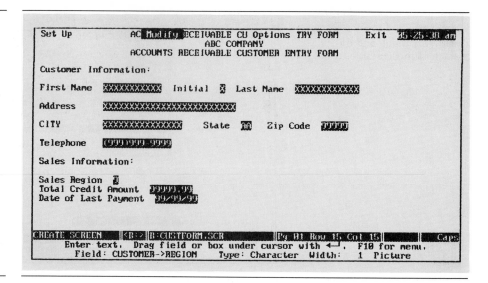

any characters other than numeric digits are entered, the computer beeps and
displays an error message at the bottom of the screen.

Enter the above Picture Template for the phone field as well as the ones
below:

Field	Picture Template
PHONE	(999)999-9999
ZIP	99999
STATE	AA
REGION	9

Why isn't the name and address information limited to alphabetic (A)
characters? Because with alphabetic data the characters are limited to A
through Z and spaces. Many people have special characters in their names,
which could not, therefore, be stored properly in the field. Address data is
always a combination of numbers and characters.

Range. The **Range** option is limited to use on fields that have been defined
as numeric in the data base file template; it enables you to specify a lower and
upper numeric limit to entries. If a value outside the established range is
entered, the computer beeps, displays an error message, and then waits for
you to make the correction.

Once you have made the appropriate changes for each of the fields (see
Figure 23.10), you are ready for drawing the various boxes displayed in Figure 23.1.

Adding Graphics

All that remains to do is to add the graphics to the entry screen on the blackboard. Boxes can be added to emphasize a single field or group of fields and
can either be **double-line** or **single-line** boxes. The entry screen on the blackboard requires two boxes: a double-line box to surround the customer identification data and a single-line box to surround the sales information. It should
be noted that unless you have run the GRAPHICS.COM DOS command or
have a special graphics utility activated on your computer, a Print Screen
command will display some garbage when it prints a screen containing dBASE
graphics.

Figure 23.11
The Options menu from the screen painter menu.

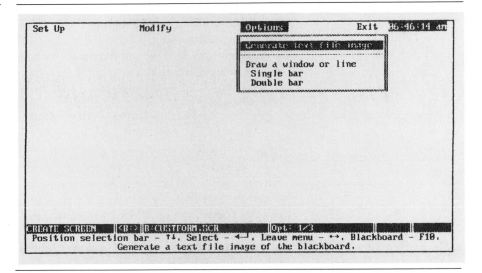

Drawing lines on the screen requires issuing the F10 command to get to the Paint Screen menu and then selecting the Options item. Once the Options item is selected (see Figure 23.11), you can highlight the desired line type: single or double bar. You are now returned to the blackboard and must tell dBASE where to place the line. To draw a box requires you to tell dBASE where two diagonally opposite corners are on the blackboard. Drawing a double-line box around the customer identification data requires the following steps:

1. Issue the F10 command to display the Modify Menu.
2. Press the right arrow to select the Options item from the screen painter.
3. Highlight the `Double Bar` option and press the ENTER key.
4. Position the cursor at Row 4 Column 0 and press the ENTER key. This tells dBASE where the upper left-hand corner of the box is located.
5. Position the cursor at row 12 column 0, press the left arrow key, press the down arrow to get the cursor to row 12, position the cursor at column 71, and press the ENTER key. This marks the lower right-hand corner of the box.

Drawing a single-line box around the sales information fields requires the following steps:

1. Issue the F10 command to display the Modify Menu.
2. Press the right arrow to select the Options item from the screen painter.
3. Highlight the `Single bar` option and press the ENTER key.
4. Position the cursor at row 14 column 0 and press the ENTER key to mark the upper left-hand corner of the box.
5. Position the cursor at row 17 column 37 and press the ENTER key to mark the lower right-hand corner of the box.
6. Whoops! The box is too small. To expand the box, press the ENTER key, press the down-arrow key once, and press the ENTER key again. The box is now expanded by one line.

When the box you draw doesn't include enough rows or columns, simply place the cursor on the side you want to expand, press the ENTER key, issue the appropriate number of arrow key commands, and press ENTER again. The box should now be expanded. If it still is not large enough, go through the commands again.

From time to time you may want to erase a line or box from the screen. This is accomplished by placing the cursor anywhere on one of the lines and issuing the Ctrl + U command. Once this command is issued, the line or box is erased.

Saving the Entry Form

Before you save your form to disk, you might first want to select the Generate text file image option of the Options entry on the Screen Painter menu. This creates a text file with a .TXT extension that describes in detail the screen just generated. Once you have the entry form arranged exactly as you want it (or if you have simply run out of time and want to finish it later), you are ready to save it to disk. This is accomplished by entering the F10 command, selecting the Exit option, highlighting the SAVE command, and pressing the ENTER key.

Using the Entry Form

Now that you have created the entry form, you can test it to see if it actually works. Once the entry form is saved, you are returned to the Assistant menu. To test the CUSTFORM entry screen, select the Set Up option of the Assistant menu. From that submenu take the Database File option and activate the CUSTOMER.DBF file, then indicate that the file is indexed and specify the ZIP.NDX as the master index, and then activate the other indexes (press the left arrow to indicate that you are finished). You must now select the Format for Screen option and indicate that the entry form is on drive B and is called CUSTFORM.FMT. You now select the Update option from the Assistant menu and issue the APPEND command.

A screen similar to that in Figure 23.12 now appears, on which you can enter information for a new record. The entry form operates exactly as the APPEND command does. That is, if the first field contains blanks, dBASE assumes that you have finished with this APPEND session and saves the file to disk. Enter the following data for the individual below:

Name:	John W. Forsythe
Address:	1617 W. Barton
Location:	Chicago, Il. 61701
Phone:	(312)545-0923
Region:	3
Amount:	150

Once you have saved the data entry screen, you can use it any time that you want to append or edit records in the CUSTOMER.DBF data base file.

Files Created for a Data Entry Form

For the example in this chapter, dBASE created three files: CUSTFORM.SCR, CUSTFORM.FMT, and CUSTFORM.TXT. The **.SCR file** contains the blackboard information and is needed any time that you want to use the MODIFY command to change the data entry form. It cannot be accessed with a word processing package. The **.FMT file** contains all of the dBASE program code that is used to generate the data entry form for an EDIT or APPEND command and can be accessed with a word processor. The CUSTFORM.TXT **file**

Figure 23.12
Completed data entry screen using the APPEND command for the Forsythe record.

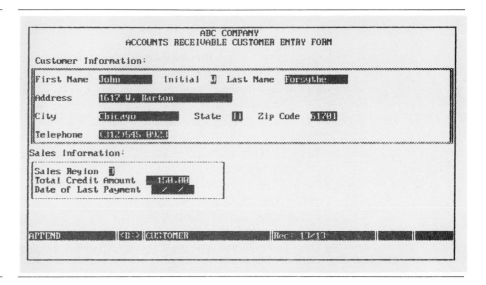

contains documentation about the fields and the screen to be generated and can also be accessed with a word processor.

WARNING! Never make any changes to a .SCR or .FMT file. Both files are needed for a MODIFY command. If the .SCR file is deleted, you will have to start from scratch and recreate the data entry screen using the screen painter of dBASE. If you make any changes to the .FMT file, they are lost any time the MODIFY command is used to change this data entry screen using the View option.

The CUSTFORM.TXT File

The CUSTFORM.TXT file can be accessed using the programming mode of any word processor. Your file looks like the following:

```
Field definitions for Screen: B:CUSTFORM.scr


Page   Row   Col   Data Base    Field                  Type      Width   Dec
  1     5    23    CUSTOMER     INIT                   Character           1
  1     5    49    CUSTOMER     LAST                   Character          12
  1     7    13    CUSTOMER     ADDRESS                Character          25
  1     9    13    CUSTOMER     CITY                   Character          15
  1     9    39    CUSTOMER     STATE                  Character           2
PICTURE AA
  1     9    54    CUSTOMER     ZIP                    Character           5
PICTURE 99999
  1    15    15    CUSTOMER     REGION                 Character           1
PICTURE 9
  1    11    13    CUSTOMER     PHONE                  Character          13
PICTURE (999)999-9999
  1    16    22    CUSTOMER     AMOUNT                 Numeric             8
   2
  1    17    23    CUSTOMER     DATE                   Date                8
  1     5    13    CUSTOMER     FIRST                  Character          10
  1     5    35    CUSTOMER     INIT                   Character           1
```

```
Content of page :   1


                              ABC COMPANY
                 ACCOUNTS RECEIVABLE CUSTOMER ENTRY FORM

Customer Information:

First Name  XXXXXXXXXX  Initial  X  Last Name  XXXXXXXXXXX

Address      XXXXXXXXXXXXXXXXXXXXXXXXX

CITY         XXXXXXXXXXXXXX     State  XX   Zip Code   XXXXX

Telephone    XXXXXXXXXXXX

Sales Information:

Sales Region  X
Total Credit Amount  XXXXXXXX
Date of Last Payment  XXXXXXXX
```

The first part of the report lists the cursor location (page, line, and column) of this entry. It also lists the file from which each entry was taken, the field name, the data type, and the field width. The second part of the report shows the text entries that will be used to create the data entry screen. Note that all of the field widths are represented by Xs regardless of the type of data that was specified for a field. Since this is a text file, none of the graphics data for boxes is shown.

The CUSTFORM.FMT File

```
@  0, 31   SAY "ABC COMPANY"
@  1, 18   SAY "ACCOUNTS RECEIVABLE CUSTOMER ENTRY FORM"
@  3,  1   SAY "Customer Information:"
@  5,  1   SAY "First Name"
@  5, 13   GET CUSTOMER->FIRST
@  5, 23   GET CUSTOMER->INIT
@  5, 26   SAY "Initial"
@  5, 35   GET CUSTOMER->INIT
@  5, 38   SAY "Last Name"
@  5, 49   GET CUSTOMER->LAST
@  7,  1   SAY "Address"
@  7, 13   GET CUSTOMER->ADDRESS
@  9,  1   SAY "CITY"
@  9, 13   GET CUSTOMER->CITY
@  9, 32   SAY "State"
@  9, 39   GET CUSTOMER->STATE PICTURE "AA"
@  9, 44   SAY "Zip Code"
@  9, 54   GET CUSTOMER->ZIP PICTURE "99999"
@ 11,  1   SAY "Telephone"
@ 11, 13   GET CUSTOMER->PHONE PICTURE "(999)999-9999"
@ 13,  1   SAY "Sales Information:"
@ 15,  1   SAY "Sales Region"
@ 15, 15   GET CUSTOMER->REGION PICTURE "9"
```

```
@ 16,  1   SAY "Total Credit Amount"
@ 16, 22   GET CUSTOMER->AMOUNT
@ 17,  1   SAY "Date of Last Payment"
@ 17, 23   GET CUSTOMER->DATE
@  4,  0   TO 12, 71      DOUBLE
@ 14,  0   TO 18, 37
```

The CUSTFORM.FMT file contains the dBASE code necessary for generating the data entry screen. This set of dBASE program statements is executed any time a View command is executed and the CUSTFORM.FMT file is specified as the file to use in creating the data entry screen. The following discussion covers exactly what happens when this code is executed by dBASE.

Notice that each line starts with the character @. The @ symbol tells dBASE to display what follows on the active output device, in this case, the screen. Following the @ symbol are two numbers: The first refers to the row on the output device, and the second refers to the column in the output device. Next you will see either a GET or a SAY command. A SAY command merely displays text (found between double quote marks) to the screen. A GET command tells dBASE where the information entered is to be placed and how that data should appear.

Notice that each of the above fields of data has the prefix CUSTOMER->. This indicates that this field is to be placed in the CUSTOMER file. The entry that follows is the name of the field in the CUSTOMER file to which the information is to be saved. Finally, the PICTURE clause (if any) that appears is the picture template that you entered using the MODIFY command of the screen painter. Fields that do not have a PICTURE clause were not changed using the Picture Template option of the Modify menu.

Invoking a View File from the Dot Prompt

You may not always want to use the Assistant to activate a data entry form. To input data using an existing data entry form, you must enter the following statements from the dot prompt:

```
. use customer
. set format to custform
```

The only difference in creating a data entry screen from the dot prompt is that you have to enter the following command. Everything else stays the same.

```
. create screen custform
```

Chapter Review

dBASE III provides you with the ability to generate self-documenting screens that resemble a paper document. These screens can then be used for inputting or changing data using the APPEND and EDIT commands.

Before an input screen can be created, a data base file must be specified. The screen will directly tie any information to this activated file. Once the file has been selected, fields that will actively participate in the inputting or changing of data must be identified and marked using the Set Up option of the screen painter menu.

Once the fields have been selected, you are placed in the blackboard of the screen painter. The selected field names appear as text, while the fields themselves appear as highlighted areas in the upper left-hand corner of the screen. The blackboard now enables you to change the field names to anything you want. No matter what you label a field, dBASE automatically links the highlighted entry with the appropriate field in the data base.

You can also move the highlighted fields from one area of the blackboard to another via a process called dragging. A drag operation starts by positioning the cursor in the highlighted area of a field, pressing the ENTER key, positioning the cursor to the new field location on the screen, and again pressing the ENTER key. The field now moves to the current cursor location.

Once fields have been positioned, you can dictate how data are to be entered within a field by using the Picture Template of the Modify menu. The Modify menu is reached by pressing the F10 key. The field at the current cursor location can now be more appropriately defined. To return to the blackboard, you must again press the F10 key.

The Options entry of the screen painter menu allows you to save the screen entries to a .TXT file. It also allows you to draw lines and boxes on your screen by moving the cursor to the beginning corner, pressing the EN-TER key, moving the cursor to the ending (diagonally opposite) corner, and pressing the ENTER key again. The line or box is then drawn automatically. If a mistake has been made, the line or box can be deleted by issuing the `Ctrl + U` command with the cursor on any line.

Once a screen is created, you should never change or delete the .FMT file or the .SCR file. The .TXT file contains a text description of the data entry screen.

Key Terms and Concepts

.FMT file	dragging
.SCR file	`Edit/GET`
.TXT file	L data type
! data type	Modify menu
# data type	Options menu
9 data type	Picture Function
A data type	Picture Template
blackboard	Range
data entry screen	screen painter
`Display/SAY`	single line
double line	X data type

Chapter Quiz

Multiple Choice

1. Which of the following statements is true with respect to screen forms?
   a. They are more self-documenting than edit screens.
   b. They allow little control over the data entered.
   c. They do not allow automatic integration of a data screen field with a data base field.
   d. None of the above statements is true.

2. The fields to be included on a data form are specified using which option of the screen painter menu?
   a. Set Up
   b. Modify
   c. Select
   d. Options

3. The process of moving a field is referred to as
   a. Moving
   b. Transferring
   c. Copying
   d. Dragging

4. Which of the following picture characters allows you to enter only a letter of the alphabet?
   a. #
   b. !
   c. L
   d. A

5. Which of the Modify options allows you to specify how data are sent to the data base file?
   a. Picture template
   b. Range
   c. Picture function
   d. Content

True/False

6. Only the .SCR and .FMT files can be changed once a data entry screen is generated.

7. Once a line is drawn it cannot be extended or changed without deleting and starting over.

8. Once fields have been selected for a data entry form and you are at the blackboard, other fields from the same file can also be selected.

9. When you delete a field using the Ctrl + U command, you are also given the option of deleting the same field in the data base file.

10. When it creates a .FMT file, dBASE actually writes a program and stores that set of program instructions in the file.

Answers

1. a 2. a 3. d 4. d 5. c 6. f 7. f 8. t 9. t 10. t

Exercises

1. The _____ feature of the blackboard enables you to locate like fields together.

2. The current cursor location is shown in the _____ .

3. The _____ key allows you to toggle between insert and overwrite mode.

4. The command _____ is used to insert a blank line at the current cursor location.

5. The _____ used to delete a word of text at the cursor location.

6. The _____ command (key) is used to leave the blackboard and return to the Paint Screen menu.

7. The _____ command deletes the line at the cursor location.

8. You can always tell where a field of data is on the screen, because it is _____ .

9. The _____ command is used to delete the field or line or box at the current cursor location.

10. Text can be pushed to the right by pressing the _____ key.

11. If the blackboard is in _____ mode, a field can be expanded by depressing the spacebar.

12. The _____ option of the Paint Screen menu is used to change the characteristics of a field.

13. The _____ option of the Modify menu determines how data are stored to a data base file field.

14. The _____ provides control over the kind of characters that can be entered in a field on a data entry screen.

15. The range option enables you to specify minimum and maximum values for _____ fields.

16. The picture character _____ enables you to enter any character in a field.

17. The file with a ._____ extension contains graphics data and cannot be accessed via a word processor.

18. The graphics feature can be used to draw either a _____ or a _____ on a data entry screen.

19. When you specify a picture template for a field, this results in a _____ statement in the .FMT file for this screen.

20. If a data field can only be displayed on the screen and no changes can be made, it is an Action type of _____ .

Computer Exercises

1. Design and create a data entry screen for your PAYROLL file.

2. Using the APPEND option of the Assistant menu add two records to the file.

Chapter
24

Other dBASE III Plus
Advanced Features

After completing this chapter, you should be able to:

Discuss how to create complex queries of a data base

Discuss the multiple file feature of dBASE

Discuss the UPDATE *command of dBASE*

Discuss the dBASE word processor

Discuss elementary dBASE command files

This chapter introduces you to the following dBASE III Plus topics: complex queries, query files, multiple file feature, the UPDATE command, the dBASE word processor, and elementary dBASE command files.

Complex Queries and Query Files

The examples of queries in the text have so far been straightforward and easy to understand, because each query has involved only one field and one condition. Many times, however, you will want to involve two or more fields in a query. Complex queries can require many keystrokes every time the query is executed. The QUERY command from the dBASE Assistant menu enables you to store these keystrokes in a Query file and execute the query simply by invoking the file.

Complex Queries

A simple query contains a dBASE display command, one field to be examined, a relational operator, and some value. For example, a simple query could be the following command:

```
LIST FOR CITY = 'Normal'
```

As you can see, only those records containing the value Normal in the CITY field will be displayed. The **relational operator** is the equal sign (=). Other relational operators that can appear in a query are the following:

<	Less than
>	Greater than
=	Equal to
< > or #	Not equal
< =	Less than or equal
> =	Greater than or equal
$	Substring comparison (for example, if the fields NAME1 and NAME2 contain character data, NAME1$NAME2 returns a logical True if NAME1 is either identical to NAME2 or contained within NAME2)

These relational operators are sufficient when you have a simple query to perform. However, when more than one field must be checked for specific data before records are displayed, two or more selection criteria must be linked. This linkage is accomplished with **logical operators**, which include (note that periods are required before and after):

.NOT.	The opposite of this expression must occur for this action to take place.
.AND.	The .AND. condition requires that both conditions must be true before any action will be taken.
.OR.	The .OR. condition requires that only one of the conditions be true for an action to be taken.
( )	Parentheses can be used for grouping relations together. If nested parentheses are used, dBASE evaluates an expression by starting with the inner-most set and working outward.

Assume that you want to list any records from Chicago or San Diego that contain an amount owed greater than $100. This query would require the following dBASE statement:

Figure 24.1
The blank Set Filter menu.

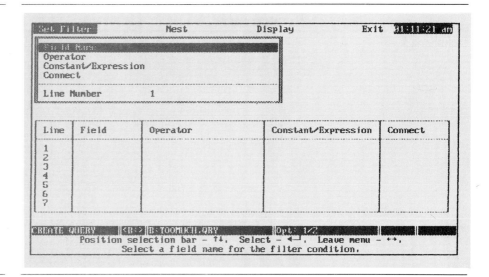

```
  ◆   LIST WHILE CITY = 'Chicago' .AND. AMOUNT > 100 .OR.
            CITY = 'San Diego' .AND. AMOUNT > 100
```

As you can probably guess, since the statement was too large to fit on one line, it was broken for readability. From the dot prompt, such a command would have to be typed on one line.

If you want to create this command from the Assistant menu, the following steps are required after the CUSTOMER file has been invoked:

1. Select the Retrieve option from the Assistant menu.
2. Select the List option of the Retrieve submenu.
3. Select the Build a Scope condition.
4. Select the CITY name field.
5. Select the = from the next submenu.
6. Enter the text Chicago.
7. Select the .AND. operator.
8. Select the field AMOUNT.
9. Select the relational operator >.
10. Enter the value 100.
11. Select the .OR. operator.
12. Repeat steps 1 through 10 for San Diego.

As you can see, this query from the Assistant requires 22 different steps. dBASE stores all of the statements into a Query file, which you can invoke when you so desire.

Building a Query File

Building a **Query file** from dBASE for the preceding example requires that you have invoked the Assistant, specified the default drive, and made the CUS-TOMER file active. From the Assistant menu, select the Create option and then select the Query option from the Create submenu. Now indicate that the Query file to be created is to be stored to the default drive (B in this example). Enter TOOMUCH as the name of the Query file. The Filter menu (see Figure 24.1) appears on your monitor with the following options:

Figure 24.2
Field menu on the Set Filter
screen.

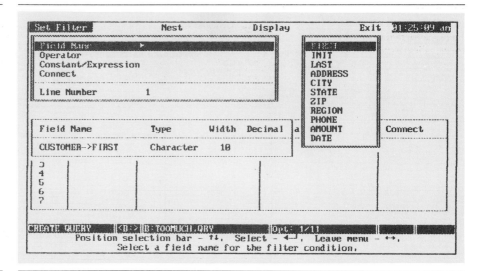

Figure 24.3
The relational operators
displayed on the Set Filter
screen.

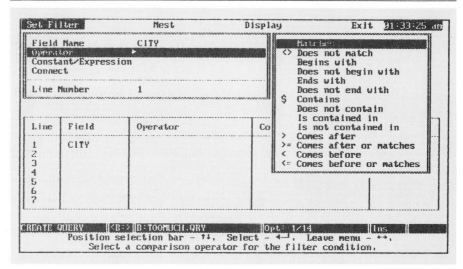

Set Filter	Enables you to enter the condition(s).
Nest	Enables you to enter parentheses to define the order of multiple conditions.
Display	Displays records that match the query instructions.
Exit	Saves the Query instructions to the filename specified with a .QRY file extension.

You must now highlight the Field Name entry and press the ENTER key to display a menu of fields from the CUSTOMER file (see Figure 24.2). Highlight the CITY field, press the ENTER key, and when the Operator entry is highlighted, press the ENTER key again. A menu of relational operators (see Figure 24.3) then appears, from which you must select = (dBASE now displays MATCHES in the operator box of your screen). Now highlight the Constant/Expression entry, press the ENTER key, enter the text 'Chicago' (be sure to include the single quotes), and press the ENTER key again. Once the Connect entry is highlighted, press the ENTER key to display the menu of logical operators (see Figure 24.4); then select the .AND. operator.

You are now ready to enter the second part of this set of selection criteria (AMOUNT > 100) on line 2. Select the Amount field, specify the > operator,

Figure 24.4
Menu of logical operators on the Set Filter screen.

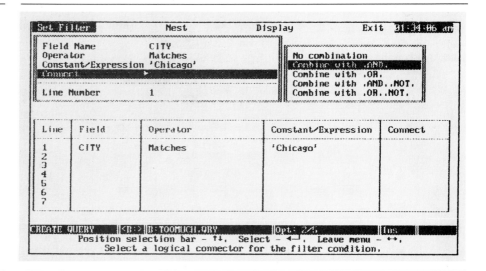

Figure 24.5
The completed Set Filter screen.

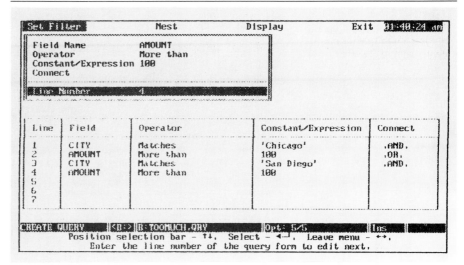

enter 100 for the constant expression, and specify the .OR. as the Connect operator.

Now perform the same steps for the remaining portion of the selection criteria (CITY = 'San Diego' .AND. AMOUNT > 100). Once you have finished, your Set Filter screen should appear like that in Figure 24.5.

You can now test the logic of your selection criteria by pressing the right arrow to highlight the Display option of the Filter menu. The first eight fields of selected records are displayed at the top of the monitor (see Figure 24.6). You can see other selected records by pressing the PGUP and PGDN keys. Once you have determined that the appropriate records have been selected, save the file with the Save option of the Filter menu. The file TOOMUCH.QRY has now been saved to disk.

Once the Query file has been created, you can use it to update or print just those records specified. To accomplish this requires that you select the appropriate data base and Query files from the Set Up menu (in this case, select the CUSTOMER data base and the TOOMUCH query file). Now select either the Update or Retrieve entries. In this example, select the Retrieve menu option, highlight the Report option, and direct dBASE to execute the command. A report with only the records selected by the Query command is generated (see Figure 24.7).

Figure 24.6
Records specified in the
selection criteria can be
displayed on the screen by
using the Display command
of the Filter menu.

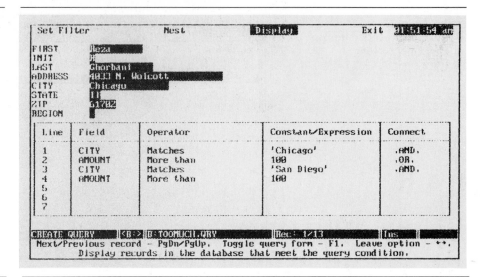

Figure 24.6
Records specified in the
selection criteria can be
displayed on the screen by
using the Display command
of the Filter menu.

Figure 24.7
The report generated via the
TOOMUCH.QRY using the
NAMEADDR.FRM.

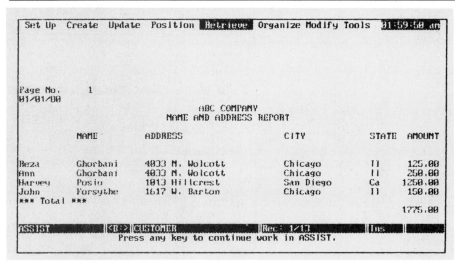

The Query Feature at the Dot Prompt

Using the Query option from the dot prompt for the above example requires
the following commands:

Building a Query file:

```
.  create query toomuch
```

Activate the query file and print a report:

```
.  use customer
.  set filter to file toomuch
.  report form nameaddr
```

To deactivate the Query file so that all records will print using the
NAMEADDR.FRM report template requires the following <u>SET FILTER TO</u>
command:

```
.  set filter to
```

Relating and Linking Files

Assume that you have an inventory application that has a master file containing every inventory item and its inventory stock information. You also have an inventory transaction file that keeps track of the number of items and the dates of transactions. Your objective is to get dBASE to link these two files together so that reports or queries containing information from both files can be contained, for example, in one report. This is easily accomplished by using the View feature of dBASE III Plus. You can create a **View file** to display and edit records from more than one file on the same screen or report.

The first data base file used in this application is the INVENTRY.DBF master file. The structure for this file is shown below:

```
Structure for database: B:Inventry.dbf
Number of data records:       25
Date of last update   : 01/01/89
Field   Field Name  Type        Width   Dec
    1   INVID       Character      10
    2   NAME        Character      36
    3   ONHAND      Numeric         4
    4   REORDER     Numeric         4
    5   OPTIMUM     Numeric         4
    6   PRICE       Numeric         7     2
** Total **                        66
```

The contents of this file are as follows:

Record#	INVID	NAME	ONHAND	REORDER	OPTIMUM	PRICE
1	3625a1	crt lamp	13	50	100	149.00
2	4545a1	ready files set	30	15	45	39.50
3	8093a1	serial microbuffer	45	30	100	379.00
4	6137a1	IBM nylon cartridge ribbon	47	35	55	5.95
5	6582a1	computer vacuum	85	75	120	139.00
6	3970-8a1	multi-purpose back shelf	25	30	50	110.00
7	4400a1	workstations	9	12	20	699.00
8	4430a1	workstations	5	8	15	650.00
9	4440	triangle extension	15	18	20	185.00
10	4442	rectangle extension	100	120	150	175.00
11	4444	copyholder	55	50	80	99.00
12	4446	wristrest	35	45	50	39.00
13	4838	footrest	120	130	150	35.00
14	4858a1	manager's chair	8	10	12	549.00
15	4857	associate's chair	12	15	18	359.00
16	4856	clerical chair	33	40	54	299.00
17	4765	associate's chair	55	60	75	340.00
18	4447a1	copyholder	88	92	99	120.00
19	4270	42" customizer	30	40	45	190.00
20	4271	72" customizer	22	30	35	250.00
21	4272a1	42" side extension	50	35	60	115.00
22	4273	72" side extension	45	10	30	135.00
23	4279	back extension foot	9	10	12	40.00
24	4276	flat shelf	85	90	100	68.00
25	4278a1	suspension bar	53	65	85	39.00

The structure for the inventory transaction file can be seen below:

```
Structure for database: B:Invtrans.dbf
Number of data records:      14
Date of last update   : 01/01/89
Field   Field Name  Type         Width   Dec
    1   INVID       Character       10
    2   UNITS       Numeric          2
    3   MDATE       Character        8
** Total **                         21
```

The contents of the INVTRANS file can be seen below:

```
Record#    INVID        UNITS   MDATE
      1    3625a1          9    12/13/87
      2    8093a1         45    12/13/87
      3    6582 a1        85    12/13/87
      4    4400a1          9    12/13/87
      5    4444           55    12/13/87
      6    4838           12    12/13/87
      7    4857           35    12/13/87
      8    4765           55    12/13/87
      9    4270           88    12/13/87
     10    4272a1         50    12/13/87
     11    4279            9    12/13/87
     12    4276           85    12/13/87
     13    4278a1         45    12/13/87
     14    4545a1         20    12/13/87
     15    6137a1         10    12/13/87
     16    3970-8a1        5    12/13/87
     17    4430a1          5    12/13/87
     18    4440            2    12/13/87
     19    4442            7    12/13/87
     20    4858a1          5    12/13/87
     21    4856           28    12/13/87
     22    4447a1         18    12/13/87
     23    4271            2`   12/13/87
     24    4273            1    12/13/87
```

Notice that all of the files contain an INVID field name (this is the **common field** that enables us to link the master and transaction files). Also notice that the two files do not have the data arranged in order by the INVID field. dBASE requires that any files that you want to relate contain one common field name and be in the same order (this can be achieved via an index). Create an index on the INVID field for the master file called MASTRIND and one called TRANSIND for the transaction file.

This process of relating or linking two files together is accomplished via the dBASE VIEW command. This command can be accessed under the Create option of the Assistant menu. Select the View command and indicate that you want any **View files** to be placed on the default disk. Call the View file to be created INVENTRY and press the ENTER key. dBASE now displays the View menu. Highlight the INVENTRY.DBF (see Figure 24.8) file and then highlight the MASTIND.NDX index file (up to seven indexes can be specified at one time). Press the right-arrow key to return to the Set Up menu.

Figure 24.8

Specifying the INVEN-TRY.DBF file and its corresponding MASTIND.NDX file for use by the View command.

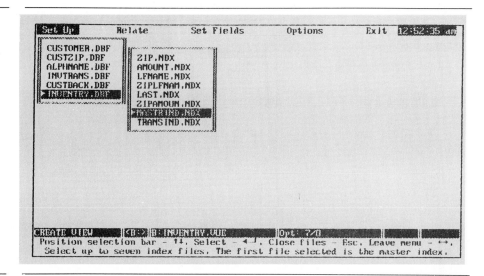

Figure 24.9

Setting up the relation chain between two files.

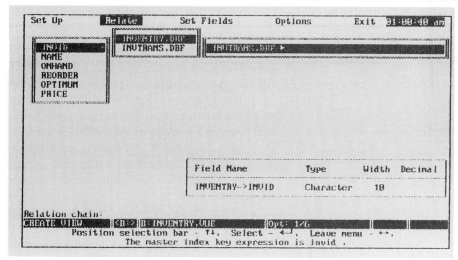

You must now perform the same tasks for the transaction file; mark the INVTRANS.DBF file and its corresponding TRANSIND.NDX index file.

The next task is to indicate to dBASE what common field is to be used to link the two files. Highlight the INVENTRY.DBF file from the View list (there are only two files for this example) and press the ENTER key. You are now prompted for the name of the field to be used; press the F10 key to obtain a field list if you are in doubt as to which field to use (see Figure 24.9). Press the right arrow to get back to the View menu.

You have just linked the INVENTRY and INVTRANS files via the INVID field contained in both files. The relation chain INVENTRY.DBF -> INVTRAN.DBF specifies that the INVENTRY file is the main (or controlling) file because it was selected first. This means that the INVTRANS record order will match the INVENTRY file record order.

More than two files can be related if they were specified in the Set Up option of the View menu.

You must now select which fields are to be used in the View file from the INVENTRY and INVTRANS files via the Set Fields option of the View menu. Select the INVENTRY.DBF file and a **Field menu** appears that includes all fields selected. Deselect (by highlighting and pressing the ENTER

Figure 24.10
Deselecting fields to be included in the View file.

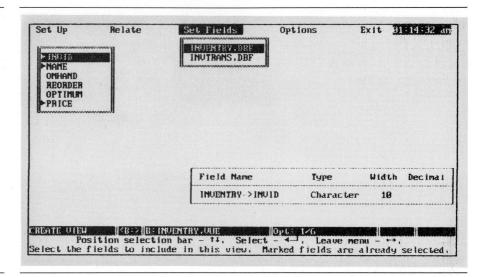

key) the ONHAND, REORDER, and OPTIMUM fields (see Figure 24.10).
Press the right arrow and select the INVTRANS.DBF file. After pressing the
ENTER key, deselect the INVID and MDATE fields.

The Options selection of the View menu allows you to display these
related data on an entry form via the Format option. The Filter option enables
you to enter a search criteria condition such as UNITS > 100.

Save this View file by pressing the right arrow to highlight the Exit option
of the View menu, and then issue the SAVE command. The file called IN-
VENTRY.VUE, which contains the above data relations, has now been created
on disk.

To use the View file just created requires that you select it from the Set
Up option of the Assistant menu. You can use it to display or update the
component data base files or to print by using a report or label template.

If you executed the EDIT command from the Update option of the
Assistant menu, you would see the four fields specified on your edit screen
(see Figure 24.11).

IMPORTANT NOTE! Do not use the EDIT command to change the contents
of any common fields of data. Rather, you must invoke that file independently
via a Use command and then issue an EDIT command. You cannot use an
APPEND command either, since such a command would work only on the
activated fields of the selected files.

A LIST command executed from the Retrieve option of the Assistant
menu would result in the following output on the screen:

Record#	INVID	NAME	PRICE	UNITS
1	3625a1	crt lamp	149.00	9
6	3970-8a1	multi-purpose back shelf	110.00	5
19	4270	42" customizer	190.00	88
20	4271	72" customizer	250.00	2
21	4272a1	42" side extension	115.00	50
22	4273	72" side extension	135.00	1
24	4276	flat shelf	68.00	85
25	4278a1	suspension bar	39.00	45
23	4279	back extension foot	40.00	9

Figure 24.11
An EDIT command performed using the INVEN-TRY.VUE View file.

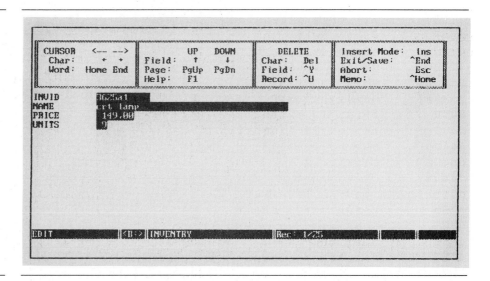

7	4400a1	workstations	699.00	9
8	4430a1	workstations	650.00	5
9	4440	triangle extension	185.00	2
10	4442	rectangle extension	175.00	7
11	4444	copyholder	99.00	55
12	4446	wristrest	39.00	
18	4447a1	copyholder	120.00	18
2	4545a1	ready files set	39.50	20
17	4765	associate's chair	340.00	55
13	4838	footrest	35.00	12
16	4856	clerical chair	299.00	28
15	4857	associate's chair	359.00	35
14	4858a1	manager's chair	549.00	5
4	6137a1	IBM nylon cartridge ribbon	5.95	10
5	6582 a1	computer vacuum	139.00	85
3	8093a1	serial microbuffer	379.00	45

A report template can now be generated that uses the various fields from two files once the View command is executing. For example, in the following INVSALES report the units field is from the INVTRANS file and the other fields are from the INVENTRY master file. The extension field is also calculated in the report and does not result in any changes to the INVTRANS file.

Page No.   1
01/01/88

                              Inventory Sales Report

Item	Description	Price	Units Sold	Extension
3625a1	crt lamp	149.00	9	1341.00
3970-8a1	multi-purpose back shelf	110.00	5	550.00
4270	42" customizer	190.00	88	16720.00
4271	72" customizer	250.00	2	500.00
4272a1	42" side extension	115.00	50	5750.00

4273	72" side extension	135.00	1	135.00
4276	flat shelf	68.00	85	5780.00
4278a1	suspension bar	39.00	45	1755.00
4279	back extension foot	40.00	9	360.00
4400a1	workstations	699.00	9	6291.00
4430a1	workstations	650.00	5	3250.00
4440	triangle extension	185.00	2	370.00
4442	rectangle extension	175.00	7	1225.00
4444	copyholder	99.00	55	5445.00
4446	wristrest	39.00	0	0.00
4447a1	copyholder	120.00	18	2160.00
4545a1	ready files set	39.50	20	790.00
4765	associate's chair	340.00	55	18700.00
4838	footrest	35.00	12	420.00
4856	clerical chair	299.00	28	8372.00
4857	associate's chair	359.00	35	12565.00
4858a1	manager's chair	549.00	5	2745.00
6137a1	IBM nylon cartridge ribbon	5.95	10	59.50
6582 a1	computer vacuum	139.00	85	11815.00
8093a1	serial microbuffer	379.00	45	17055.00
*** Total ***				
		5208.45	685	14153.50

Linking Files from the Dot Prompt

You do not have to go through the Assistant menu to link files. The following commands issued at the dot prompt can also be used:

```
.  select 1
.  use inventry index mastrind
.  select 2
.  use invtrans index transind
.  set relation to invid into inventry
.  list invid, inventry->name, units
```

When you are using multiple files, dBASE requires you to specify them by using a file alias. The SELECT command is an example of using an alias of 1. An alias can be either a numeric digit or a letter, and you can refer to a file by using either alias. For example, the file INVENTRY can be referenced as 1 or A, and the INVTRANS file can be referenced as 2 or B.

The last file opened (in this case INVTRANS) is the one that dBASE has direct access to. If you want to refer to a previous file (in another file buffer), you must reference the filename first and then the field name; hence the entry INVENTRY->NAME means the field NAME from the file INVENTRY. Since the fields INVID and UNITS are both in the INVTRANS file, no file has to be specified before the field name.

Using the Update Command for Multiple Files

The dBASE package has a facility that enables you to take data from one designated file (transaction) and use them to update fields in another file (master). The file to be updated must be the active file. dBASE accomplishes the changes by matching the records in the two data base files on a single key field. Here is the syntax for the UPDATE command:

UPDATE ON {key} FROM {alias} REPLACE WITH {expression} RANDOM

Both files, the master as well as the transaction file, must have been previously referenced with a USE command.

The *key* portion of the command specifies the key field you use to accomplish the update. Both data base files must have the same key field name for the Update command to work. If both files do not have the same key field name, only the first record will be updated.

Both files must be either sorted or indexed on the key field unless the RANDOM option is selected. RANDOM requires that the file to be updated must be indexed on the key field. The transaction file can be in any order when the RANDOM parameter is used.

For the Alias option, dBASE automatically assigns another abbreviated name (alias) to files as they are referenced in a USE command. The first file's alias is *a* or *1*, the second file's alias is *b* or *2*, and so forth. The typical alias to be used in the FROM area for an update involving two files is *b*.

The *expression* involves any formulas or constants necessary for the UPDATE command to work. If fields from the various files are required for updating, the filename or Alias, followed by the field name, must be given. For example, suppose that the ONHAND field of the INVENTRY file is to be updated using the information contained in the UNITS field of the INVPURCH file. The first ten records of the file are listed below:

Record#	INVID	NAME	ONHAND	REORDER	OPTIMUM	PRICE
1	3625a1	crt lamp	13	50	100	149.00
2	4545a1	ready files set	30	15	45	39.50
3	8093a1	serial microbuffer	45	30	100	379.00
4	6137a1	IBM nylon cartridge ribbon	47	35	55	5.95
5	6582a1	computer vacuum	85	75	120	139.00
6	3970-8a1	multi-purpose back shelf	25	30	50	110.00
7	4400a1	workstations	9	12	20	699.00
8	4430a1	workstations	5	8	15	650.00
9	4440	triangle extension	15	18	20	185.00
10	4442	rectangle extension	100	120	150	175.00

The following list shows the first ten records of the purchase transaction file:

Record#	INVID	UNITS	MDATE
1	3625a1	9	12/13/87
2	8093a1	45	12/13/87
3	6582 a1	85	12/13/87
4	4400a1	9	12/13/87
5	4444	55	12/13/87
6	4838	12	12/13/87
7	4857	35	12/13/87
8	4765	55	12/13/87
9	4270	88	12/13/87
10	4272a1	50	12/13/87

The following commands tell dBASE that the transaction file 2 is INVPURCH and that the master file 1 is INVENTRY. The UPDATE command tells dBASE that the key field is INVID and that information is to be taken from the INVPURCH file and used to update the ONHAND field of the INVENTRY file. This is accomplished by taking the contents of the UNITS field from the INVPURCH file and adding it to the contents of the ONHAND field of the INVENTRY file. (The semicolon indicates the command is continued to the next line.)

```
. select 2
. use invpurch index purchind
. select 1
. use inventry index mastrind
. update on invid from invpurch replace onhand with onhand;
  +invtrans->+units random
```

The first ten updated records of the updated INVENTRY file are as follows:

Record#	INVID	NAME	ONHAND	REORDER	OPTIMUM	PRICE
1	3625a1	crt lamp	22	50	100	149.00
2	4545a1	ready files set	50	15	45	39.50
3	8093a1	serial microbuffer	90	30	100	379.00
4	6137a1	IBM nylon cartridge ribbon	57	35	55	5.95
5	6582a1	computer vacuum	170	75	120	139.00
6	3970-8a1	multi-purpose back shelf	30	30	50	110.00
7	4400a1	workstations	18	12	20	699.00
8	4430a1	workstations	10	8	15	650.00
9	4440	triangle extension	17	18	20	185.00
10	4442	rectangle extension	107	120	150	175.00

Command Files

Command files enable you to store in a disk file your frequently used data base commands or series of commands that are entered at the dot prompt, so that they can be easily repeated by people who have little knowledge of dBASE. This ability of dBASE to create command files is a feature that sets it apart from many other data base management packages. The purpose of this module is to introduce command files, memory variables, and some special features that can be used with the Report command.

By now you are acquainted with dBASE *immediate mode* commands that are entered at the dot prompt. Immediate mode commands are executed as soon as you press the ENTER key. These commands and many others can be placed in files and executed at any time. You can develop complete programmed systems using this feature of dBASE. The one thing to remember, however, is that dBASE requires any command file to have a .PRG file extension.

Command files can be created by using the **Modify Command** (filename) feature of dBASE, or, alternatively, by using the nondocument or programming mode of a word processing package such as WordPerfect or WordStar. Each of these methods has advantages and disadvantages.

The Modify Command alternative of creating a command file makes use of the built-in text editor of dBASE. The Modify Command (filename) automatically places a .PRG file extension on the file being created. It has a cursor/command menu at the top of the screen that shows commonly used commands. Since many of these commands are almost intuitive, you do not have to learn many others if you are acquainted with that package.

The maximum file size that the MODIFY COMMAND command can handle is 5,000 bytes unless an external word processor is specified in the dBASE III Plus CONFIG.SYS file. A warning message is issued if an attempt is made to exceed this limit, and the text in the file may not be reliable after it is saved.

Figure 24.12
The dBASE editor screen
available via the MODIFY
COMMAND command.

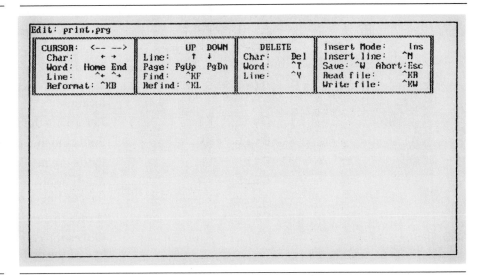

When you type a line that is longer than 66 characters, the editor automatically wraps some of it onto the next line. If a line contains a long command, you can divide it into several parts by entering a semicolon (;) at the end of a line of text and then continue the command on the next line.

The preferred method of creating large command files is by using the programming or nondocument mode of a word processing package. Do not use document mode or a word processing package that embeds special control codes within the body of the document. These special control codes cause dBASE to generate a syntax error when it evaluates a command, since it expects to find only a standard ASCII text file.

The examples in this chapter make use of the dBASE editor accessed via the MODIFY COMMAND <filename>. The <filename> portion of the above command is any filename of not more than eight characters. If no file extension is specified, dBASE automatically places a .PRG extension on the file. When the command is entered, dBASE first looks to the default drive for a .PRG file with the name specified; if one does not exist, it creates one with the name you entered. Once the editor is invoked, a blank screen with a command menu at the top is displayed on your monitor (see Figure 24.12).

The line at the top of the screen contains the message EDIT: and the name of the file being edited. The next area in the box is the command menu. The area under the command menu is available for entering dBASE instructions.

The following commands are available to you once you have invoked the dBASE editor via the MODIFY COMMAND.

Command	Action
Arrow key	Moves the cursor one position in the indicated direction.
Backspace	Deletes the character to the left of the cursor.
F1	Toggles the cursor menu on and off.
Ctrl + A or Home	Moves the cursor to the beginning of the current or previous word.
Ctrl + B or Ctrl + right arrow	Moves the cursor to the end of the line.
Ctrl + C or PgDn	Scrolls the screen up 18 lines.

Ctrl + D	Same as a right-arrow command.
Ctrl + E	Same as an up-arrow command.
Ctrl + F or End	Moves the cursor to the beginning of the next word.
Ctrl + G or Del	Deletes the character at the current cursor location.
Ctrl + KB	Reformats the paragraph.
Ctrl + KF	Finds the first occurrence of a specified string.
Ctrl + KL	Finds the next occurrence of a specified string.
Ctrl + KR	Reads another file into the file being edited at the current cursor location.
Ctrl + KW	Writes the entire file to another file.
Ctrl + M or Enter	Moves the cursor to the beginning of the next line. If the editor is in insert mode (an Ins at the top of the screen), it inserts a blank line.
Ctrl + N	Inserts a blank line after the cursor.
Ctrl + Q or Esc	Exits without saving the changes to disk.
Ctrl + R or PgUp	Scrolls the screen down 18 lines.
Ctrl + S	Same as a left-arrow command.
Ctrl + T	Deletes all characters from the current cursor position to the beginning of the next word.
Ctrl + V or Ins	Toggles between insert and overwrite mode. Insert mode stays on until it is toggled off or until you exit from dBASE III Plus.
Ctrl + KW or Ctrl + End	Exit and save the file to disk.
Ctrl + X	Same as the down-arrow command.
Ctrl + Y	Deletes the current line.
Ctrl + Z or Ctrl + right arrow	Moves the cursor to the beginning of the line.

Assume that you want to replace the commands used to update the INVENTRY file with information contained in the INVPURCH file and then print a report using the INVLIST.FRM template, which shows the current inventory level and the value of inventory. The commands in Figure 24.13 are needed to perform this process.

Once the file has been saved to disk, this set of dBASE commands can be executed simply by telling dBASE to execute the PRINT.PRG file via the DO command. The format of the DO command is as follows:

DO <filename>

When the DO PRINT command is issued, dBASE goes to the PRINT.PRG file and executes the stored instructions one at a time starting at the beginning of the file. When the last command has been executed, dBASE returns to the dot prompt (.).

Figure 24.13
The commands contained in the PRINT.PRG file for updating the INVENTRY file and then generating a report.

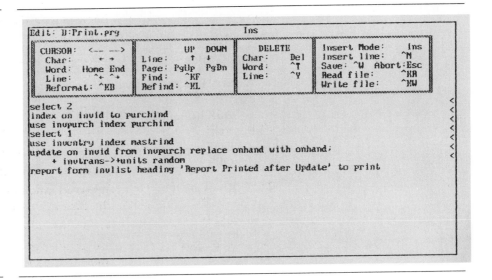

Chapter Review

The dBASE III Plus software package provides you with the ability to create complex queries at the dot prompt or build them using the Assistant menu. Since many key strokes are required, frequently used queries should be saved to a .QRY file.

Once the Query file has been built, it can be invoked via the SET UP command of the Assistant menu or via the SET FILTER TO command at the dot (.) prompt. The Query file can now be used in conjunction with the DISPLAY and PRINT commands to list only the desired records.

dBASE also provides the ability to link or relate files contained in an application via common fields. Once the file relation has been established, fields from different files can be edited, displayed, or printed. It is not advisable, however, to edit the common field that was used to set up the relation. Neither should you use the Update command of the Assistant menu or the APPEND command to change records.

The UPDATE command can also be used from the dot (.) prompt to tell dBASE to take the information from a field of one file and update the contents of a field in another file. Again, both files must have a common field linking them.

For frequent tasks, dBASE provides the ability to store sets of instructions in a file and execute them via a Do command. The file containing the dBASE instructions must have a .PRG file extension, which is automatically included when the built-in editor is used to create such a command file. This built-in editor is accessed via the MODIFY COMMAND filename command.

Key Terms and Concepts

common field
field menu
logical operators
MODIFY COMMAND
Query file

relational operators
SET FILTER TO
SET RELATION TO
UPDATE command
View file

Chapter Quiz

Multiple Choice

1. A query file created by dBASE contains which of the following file extensions?
   a. .ASK
   b. .VUE
   c. .FMT
   d. .QRY

2. Which of the following commands is definitely *not* recommended for use by a VIEW file?
   a. EDIT
   b. REPORT
   c. APPEND
   d. LIST

3. Which of the following commands allow you to link files together?
   a. QRY
   b. VIEW
   c. SET RELATION TO
   d. EDIT

4. Which of the following commands allow you to link files together from the dot (.) prompt?
   a. UPDATE
   b. MODIFY COMMAND
   c. SET QUERY
   d. SELECT

5. The internal editor of dBASE does not have which of the following limitations?
   a. A maximum file size of 5,000 bytes
   b. A default line length of 66 characters
   c. A default insert mode
   d. A command menu at the top of the screen

True/False

6. Unless told otherwise, the dBASE editor places a .PRG file extension on any file it creates.

7. A command file can be executed only via a DO command.

8. There may be more than one editor command available to accomplish the same task.

9. The dot prompt command to invoke a View file is SET VIEW TO.

10. Only two files can be linked using the View feature of dBASE III Plus.

Answers

1. d 2. c 3. b&c 4. a 5. c 6. t 7. t 8. t 9. f 10. f

Exercises

1. A complex query typically makes use of one or more relational operators as well as one or more _____ operators.

2. The _____ are used for grouping relations.

3. The _____ at the dot (.) prompt is used to invoke a Query file.

4. The logical operators are _____, _____, and _____.

5. Before data in files can be linked, both files must have a _____ field.

6. You should never use a(n) _____ command on linked files.

7. An output command that can be used on linked files is the _____ command.

8. The _____ at the dot (.) prompt can be used to relate files.

9. From the Assistant menu, information about linked files is placed in a file with a _____ file extension.

10. The dBASE _____ command can be used to change the content of a field of one file based on the content of a field in another file.

11. The dBASE editor is invoked via the command _____ _____.

12. The maximum file size for a file created by the dBASE editor is _____ bytes.

13. A _____ is used to indicate to dBASE that a command is continued on the next line.

14. A file created by the dBASE editor, unless otherwise indicated, contains a _____ file extension.

15. The _____ editor command is used to save a file to disk.

16. A dBASE command file is invoked via the dBASE _____ command.

17. The editor command used to delete the line at the cursor location is _____.

18. The _____ editor command is used to switch from overwrite to insert mode.

19. The _____ editor command is used to delete a word.

20. The _____ editor command is used to reform a paragraph.

Appendix A

Instructions for Using Educational Versions of Software

Introduction

The diskettes provided by Wadsworth Publishing Company that accompany the textbook *Four Software Tools*, Alternate Edition contain the educational versions of WordPerfect 4.2, VP-Planner, and dBASE III Plus. **The educational versions differ from the business versions in the following ways:**

WordPerfect 4.2 The characters *WP occasionally appear in a document when it is printed using the Training Version of WordPerfect. Files size is unlimited. Otherwise, the training version of WordPerfect contains all of the features of the business edition. Note that the Speller and Thesaurus contain only the words necessary for examining the README.WP file that appears on the disk with the training version of WordPerfect.

VP-Planner The spreadsheet contains all of the spreadsheet capabilities except the multidimensional data base ability. The student version allows 64 columns and 256 rows.

dBASE III Plus The word **(demo)** appears before the dot prompt. The student version of dBASE III Plus limits a file to 31 records.

IMPORTANT! When you want to leave WordPerfect, always use the proper Exit method. Remove the WordPerfect program disk only when the DOS prompt (A>, B>, C>, or D>) appears on the screen. If you remove the program disk while the computer is running, you can destroy the disk.

If you turn off the computer without properly exiting WordPerfect, unallocated clusters (sectors) are placed on the disk. If you consistently exit WordPerfect improperly, your diskette will eventually fill with these unallocated sectors, and you will receive a disk full error.

Starting
WordPerfect 4.2

If your WordPerfect 4.2 diskette contains DOS, perform the following:

1. Insert the diskette containing WordPerfect 4.2 in disk drive A of the computer (with the label up) and close the door.

2. Either turn the computer on, or, if already on, press the Del key while simultaneously holding down the Ctrl and Alt keys. The "boot" process will now load the operating system into memory.

3. If you want to "date stamp" your files, enter the date and time when you are prompted to do so.

4. In a moment, you should see the system prompt A> on your screen. This indicates that disk drive A is the so-called *default disk*. Change the default drive to B by entering B: and pressing the ENTER key.

5. Type A:WP and press the ENTER key.

6. WordPerfect 4.2 will now be loaded into memory (RAM) and be ready to use. All data files will be stored on the disk in drive B.

7. When you are finished with WordPerfect 4.2 and wish to exit to DOS, issue the Exit command (F7). The B> prompt will then appear.

If your WordPerfect 4.2 diskette does not contain DOS, perform the following:

1. Insert a system diskette—a diskette containing the IBM Personal Computer Disk Operating System (PC-DOS) 2.0 or higher, or a com-

patible version of MS-DOS—into disk drive A of the computer and close the disk drive door.

2. Turn the computer on. The computer "boot" process will now load the operating system into the computer memory.

3. If you want to "date stamp" your files, enter the date and time when prompted.

4. The system prompt A>, indicating that disk drive A is the default disk, should now appear on your screen. Change the default drive to B by entering B: and press the ENTER key.

5. Remove the system disk from drive A and place the diskette containing WordPerfect 4.2 in its place.

6. Type the letters A:WP and press the ENTER key.

7. WordPerfect 4.2 is now loaded into memory (RAM) and starts to execute.

8. WordPerfect 4.2 is now ready to use. WordPerfect 4.2 automatically saves all files to the diskette in drive B.

9. When you are finished with WordPerfect 4.2 and want to exit to DOS, issue the Exit command (F7). DOS will display the following prompt:

```
Insert disk with COMMAND.COM in drive A and strike
any key when ready
```

Insert any disk that contains the operating system in drive A, close the door, and strike a key; the A> prompt will then appear.

Steps for Using VP-Planner

Note 1: Your VP-Planner student disk is copy protected. This means that you cannot make a copy of the VP.COM file, execute the DISKCOPY command to make a copy of the diskette, or copy VP-Planner to a hard disk.

Note 2: If you cannot see graphs on the screen with the View command, you must change the hardware video default setting by using the following sequence of commands once VP-Planner is running: / Worksheet Global Default Hardware Video. You can now select the appropriate video display for your computer and execute the Update command to make the change permanent. Return to Ready mode by executing the Update command. To properly display graphs using the Hercules graphics option, you must first execute the HGC.COM file before starting VP-Planner.

Note 3: VP-Planner, unless it has been told otherwise, looks for worksheet files on drive A. To change the default location to drive B enter the following commands: / Worksheet Global Default Directory. Enter B: / and press the ENTER key. To make this change permanent execute the Update command; then execute the Quit command to return to Ready mode.

1. Insert a system diskette—a diskette containing the IBM Personal Computer Disk Operating System (PC-DOS) 2.0 or higher, or a compatible version of MS-DOS—into disk drive A and close the disk drive door.

2. Turn the computer on. The computer "boot" process will now load the operating system into the computer memory.

3. If you want to "date stamp" your files, enter the date and time when prompted.

4. The system prompt A>, indicating that disk drive A is the default disk, should now appear on your screen.

5. Remove the system disk from drive A and place the diskette containing VP-Planner in its place.

6. Type the command VP and press the ENTER key.

7. The VP-Planner Menu now appears on the screen. Press the ENTER key to start the spreadsheet.

8. VP-Planner is now loaded into memory (RAM) and starts to execute.

9. VP-Planner is now ready to use. VP-Planner automatically saves all worksheet files to the diskette in drive B.

10. When you are finished with VP-Planner and want to exit to DOS, issue the / Quit Exit commands. DOS will display the following prompt:

```
Insert disk with COMMAND.COM in drive A and strike
any key when ready
```

Insert any disk that contains the operating system in drive A, close the door, and strike a key; the A> prompt will then appear.

11. *Alternate Method to Finish.* If you want to end the session and you have saved your worksheet to disk, remove your diskette(s) from the drive(s) and turn off the machine.

Steps for Using dBASE III Plus

1. Insert a system diskette—a diskette containing the IBM Personal Computer Disk Operating System (PC-DOS) 2.0 or higher, or a compatible version of MS-DOS—into disk drive A of the computer and close the disk drive door.

2. Turn the computer on. The computer "boot" process will now load the operating system into the computer memory.

3. If you want to "date stamp" your files, enter the date and time when prompted.

4. The system prompt A>, indicating that disk drive A is the default disk, should now appear on your screen.

5. Remove the system disk from drive A and place the sampler 1 diskette containing dBASE III Plus in its place. If your sampler disk 1 has DOS, omit step 5.

6. Type the command DBASE and press the ENTER key.

7. The first part of dBASE III Plus is now loaded into memory (RAM) and you are prompted to insert sampler disk 2 in drive B and press the ENTER key.

8. dBASE III Plus is now ready to use.

9. When you are finished with dBASE III Plus and want to exit to DOS, issue the QUIT command. If you do not enter the QUIT command, data in files may be lost. After this has been accomplished, DOS will display the following prompt:

```
Insert disk with COMMAND.COM in drive A and strike any key when ready
```

Insert any disk that contains the operating system in drive A, close the door, and strike a key; the A> prompt will then appear.

One of the more important concerns for users of 1-2-3 and its clones is the issue of compatibility. The 1-2-3 package itself is not compatible from Release 1A to Release 2. Although the latest version, Release 2.01, has addressed some of these concerns, the problem is compounded when an individual also wishes to use VP-Planner.

This issue is solved simply by avoiding advanced features in either 1-2-3 Release 2(.01) or VP-Planner that are not supported in 1-2-3 Release 1A. This means that any worksheet that can be used for 1-2-3 Release 1A can also be read by VP-Planner or by Release 2(.01) of 1-2-3. If you avoid some of the "bells and whistles" used in Release 2(.01), you can use the Translate facility to convert a .WK1 worksheet to a Release 1A (.WKS) format. Such a worksheet, of course, can also be read by VP-Planner.

Features of VP-Planner to Avoid

Range column width of zero

Autokey macros

The 1-Custom and 2-Custom format options

The 4(M/D/Y), 5(D/M/Y), 6(Y M D), and T(HH:MM:SS 24-hour time) format options

Multiple windows

Page numbers and row and column numbers from the Other Menu of the Print Menu

The $ (substring search), < (less than), and > (greater than) for data management queries

You should also avoid using the following functions:

```
@TIME    @POLY    @ROOT
@STDS    @VARS    @DSTDS
@DVARS
```

Features of Release 2(.01) to Avoid

International date formats using the / Worksheet Global Format Date Time command

Use of the Hide command

Hard coded page breaks

Exploded/colored pie charts

Data regression

Data parse

Avoid use of the following macro commands:

```
{BEEP}        {FILESIZE}     {LET}
{BLANK}       {FOR}          {LOOK}
{BRANCH}      {FORBREAK}     {MENUBRANCH}
{BREAKON}     {GET}          {MENUCALL}
{BREAKOFF}    {GETLABEL}     {OPEN}
{CLOSE}       {GETNUMBER}    {ONERROR}
{CONTENTS}    {GETPOS}       {PANELON}
{DEFINE}      {IF}           {PANELOFF}
{DISPATCH}    {INDICATE}     {PUT}
```

```
{QUIT}           {RESTART}        {WINDOWSOFF}
{READ}           {RETURN}         {WRITE}
{READLN}         {SETPOS}         {WRITELN}
{RECALC}         {WAIT}
{RECALCCOL}      {WINDOWSON}
```

Avoid use of the following functions as well as all string functions:

```
@ISNUMBER(x)
@ISSTRING(x)
@@(cell address)
@CELL(att,rnge)
@CELLPOINTER(att)
@COL(rnge)
@COL(rnge)
@INDEX(rnge,row,col)
@ROWS(rnge)
@DATEVALUE(date str)
@HOUR(time number)
@NOW
@SECOND(time number)
@TIME(hr,min,sec)
@CTERM(int,fv,pv)
@DDB(cost,salvage,life,period)
@RATE(fv,pv,term)
@SLN(cost,salvage,life)
@SYD(cost,salvage,life,period)
@TERM(pmt,int,fv)
```

Appendix
B

WordPerfect Command
Summary

Advance Line   Shift + F1

Advance Up/Down   Shift + F1

Alignment Character   Shift + F8

Append Block (Block on)   Ctrl + F4

Auto Hyphenation   Shift + F8, 5

Auto Rewrite   Ctrl + F3

Binding Width   Shift + F7, 3

Block   Alt + F4

Block, Cut/Copy (Block on)   Ctrl + F4

Block Protect (Block on)   Alt + F8

Bold   F6

Cancel   F1

Cancel Hyphenation   F1

Cancel Print Jobs   Shift + F7, 4

Case Conversion (Block on)   Shift + F7, 4

Center   Shift + F6

Center Page Top to Bottom   Alt + F8

Change Directory   F8. Enter

Change Print Options   Shift + F7

Colors   Ctrl + F3

Column, Cut/Copy (Block on)   Ctrl + F4

Columns, Text   Alt + F7

Column Display   Alt + F7

Concordance   Alt + F5, 6,5

Conditional End of Page   Alt + F8

Copy   F5, Enter

Create Directory   F5, =

Ctrl/Alt Key Mapping   Ctrl + F3

Date   Shift + F5

Delete   Del

Delete (List Files)   F5, Enter

Delete Directory (List Files)   F5, Enter

Delete to End of Line (EOL)   Ctrl + End

Delete to End of Page (EOP)   Ctrl + PgDn

Delete to Left Word Boundary   Home, Backspace

Delete to Right Word Boundary   Home, Del

Delete Word   Ctrl + Backspace

Display All Print Jobs   Shift + F7, 4

Display Printers and Fonts   Shift + F7, 4

Document Comments   Ctrl + F5

Document Conversion   Ctrl + F5

Document Summary   Ctrl + F5

DOS Text File   Ctrl + F5

Endnote   Ctrl + F7

Exit   F7

Flush Right   Alt + F6

Font   Ctrl + F8

Footnote   Ctrl + F7

Full Text (Print)   Shift + F7

Generate   Alt + F5, 6

Go (Resume Printing)   Alt + F5, 6

Go to DOS   Ctrl + F1

Hard Page   Ctrl + Enter

Hard Return   Enter

Hard Space   Home, Space Bar

Headers or Footers   Alt + F8

Help   F3

Home   Home

Hyphen   -

Hyphenation On/Off   Shift + F8, 5

H-Zone   Shift + F8, 5

Indent (right)   F4

Indent (left and right)   Shift + F4

Index   Alt + F5

Insert Printer Command   Ctrl + F8

Justification On/Off   Ctrl + F8

Line Draw   Ctrl + F3

Line Format   Shift + F8

Line Numbering   Ctrl + F8

Lines per Inch   Ctrl + F8

List Files   F5, Enter

List (Block on)   Alt + F5

Locked Documents   Ctrl + F5

Look   F5, Enter

Macro   Alt + F10

Macro Def   Ctrl + F10

Margin Release   Shift + Tab

Margins   Shift + F8

Mark Text   Alt + F5

Math   Alt + F7

Merge   Ctrl + F9

Merge Codes   Alt + F9

Merge E   Shift + F9

Merge R   F9

Minus Sign   Home, −

Move   Ctrl + F4

Name Search   F5, Enter

New Number (Footnote)   Ctrl + F7

New Page Number   Alt + F8

Number of Copies   Shift + F7, 3

Outline   Alt + F5

Overstrike   Shift + F1

Page Format   Alt + F8

Page Length   Alt + F8

Page Number Column Positions   Alt + F8

Page Number Position   Alt + F8

Page (Print)   Shift + F7

Paragraph Number   Alt + F5

Pitch   Ctrl + F8

Preview a Document   Shift + F7

Print   Shift + F7

Print (List Files)   F5, Enter

Print a Document   Shift + F7, 4

Print Block (Block on)   Shift + F7

Print Format   Ctrl + F8

Printer Control   Shift + F7

Printer Number   Shift + F7, 3

Proportional Spacing   Ctrl + F8, 1

Rectangle, Cut/Copy (Block on)   Ctrl + F4

Redline   Alt + F5

Remove   Alt + F5, 6

Rename   F5, Enter

Replace   Alt + F2

Replace, Extended   Home, Alt + F2

Retrieve   Shift + F10

Retrieve (List Files)   F5, Enter

Retrieve Column (Move)   Ctrl + F4

Retrieve Rectangle (Move)   Ctrl + F4

Retrieve Text (Move)   Ctrl + F4

Reveal Codes   Alt + F3

Rewrite   Ctrl + F3, Ctrl + F3

Rush Print Job   Shift + F7, 4

Save   F10

Screen   Ctrl + F3

Search Forward   F2

Search Forward Extended   Home, F2

Search Backward   Shift + F2

Search Backward Extended   Home, Shift + F2

Select Print Options   Shift + F7, 4

Select Printers   Shift + F7, 4

Sheet Feeder Bin Number   Ctrl + F8

Shell   Ctrl + F1

Short Form Marking   Alt + F5

Soft Hyphen   Ctrl + -

Sort   Ctrl + F9

Sorting Sequences   Ctrl + F9

Spacing   Shift + F8

Spell   Ctrl + F2

Split Screen   Ctrl + F3, 1

Stop Printing   Ctrl + F7, 4

Strikeout (Block on)   Alt + F5

Super/Subscript   Shift + F1

Suppress Page Format   Alt + F8

Switch   Shift + F3

Tab   Tab

Tab Align   Ctrl + F6

Tab Ruler   Ctrl + F3, 1

Table of Authorities (Block on)   Alt + F5

Table of Contents (Block on)   Alt + F5

Tab Set   Shift + F8

Text In (List Files)   F5. Enter

Text In/Out   Ctrl + F5

Text Lines   Alt + F8, 4

Thesaurus   Alt + F1

Time   Shift + F5, 2

Top Margin   Alt + F8

Typeover   Ins

Type Thru   Shift + F7

Undelete   F1

Underline   F8

Underline Style   Ctrl + F8

Widow/Orphan   Alt + F8

Window   Ctrl + F3

Word Count   Ctrl + F2

Word Search   F5, Enter

Cursor Control

Go To Ctrl + Home (enter page number)
Word Left Ctrl + Left Arrow
Word Right Ctrl + Right Arrow
Screen Left Home, Right Arrow
Screen Right Home, Left Arrow
Screen Down +
Screen Up −
Page Down PgDn
Page Up PgUp
Beginning of Text Home, Home, Up Arrow
End of Text Home, Home, Down Arrow
Beginning of Line (Text) Home, Home, Left Arrow
Beginning of Line (Codes) Home, Home, Home, Left Arrow
End of Line End of Home, Home, Right Arrow

Appendix C

dBASE III Plus Command Summary

Lower case   User-supplied information

Upper case   Explicit portions of dBASE III Plus commands

[. . .]   Optional portions of dBASE III Plus commands

<. . .>   User-supplied portions of dBASE III Plus commands

<cstring>   Character strings

<ex>   Valid item or group of items and/or operators

<exp list>   List of expressions separated by commas

<field>   Record field name

<field list>   List of record field names separated by commas

<file>   Name of a file to access or create

<index file>   Name of an index file to create or access

<key>   Portion(s) of a file used to create an index file

<n>   Number that dBASE III Plus is to regard as a literal value

<numeric exp>   An ⟨exp⟩ whose content is defined as numeric

<scope>   Command option that specifies a range of records that dBASE III Plus must treat in executing a command; has three possible values: ALL records in the file; NEXT *n* records in the file; and RECORD *n* (default value varies from command to command)

<skeleton>   Allows batch manipulation of files of the same type and/or having matching cstrings in filename

Operators

Logical Operators (in Order of Precedence)

( )   Parentheses for grouping

.NOT.   Logical not

.AND.   Logical and

.OR.   Logical or

$ Substring operator

Arithmetic Operators

( )   Parentheses for grouping

/   Division

*   Multiplication

+   Addition

−   Subtraction

Relational Operators

<   Less than

>   Greater than

=   Equal to

<>   Not equal to

<=   Less than or equal to

>=   Greater than or equal to

String Operator

+ String concatenation

Functions

* Delete indicator identifies record marked for deletion

$(exp,start,length) Substring extracts the specified part of **(exp)** from the given starting position for the given length

DATE( ) Invokes name of the system variable containing the system date

EOF End-of-file function evaluates as a logical true/false whether the last record of the file in use has been processed

STR(exp,length,decimals) String function converts the specified portion of **(exp)** into a character string

TRIM(exp) Trim function removes trailing blanks from a specified string variable

Selected dBASE
Commands

APPEND[BLANK] Adds record(s) or blank formatted record(s) to the data base file in use

APPEND FROM ⟨file⟩ Appends data from a data base

ASSIST Activates the Assistant menu

AVERAGE ⟨explist⟩ [WHILE ⟨condition⟩] [FOR ⟨condition⟩] Calculates the arithmetic average for numeric fields

BROWSE [FIELDS ⟨field list] Provides full-screen editing for changing a file

CLEAR Erases the screen

CLEAR ALL Closes all data base files, index files, format files, and relations; releases all memory variables and selects work area one

CONTINUE Continues a LOCATE command

COPY TO <file> STRUCTURE [FIELD <list>] Copies the structure of the file in use into the designated file

COPY TO <file> [FIELD <list>] Copies the file or fields from the file in use to the designated data base file

CREATE [<file>] Starts the creation process for a data base file

CREATE LABEL <.lbl file name> Activates the LABEL menu and enables you to create a label form file

CREATE QUERY <.qry file name> Activates the QUERY menu and enables you to create a filter condition and store it to a .qry file

CREATE REPORT <.frm file name> Activates the REPORT menu and enables you to create a report template and store it to a .frm file

CREATE SCREEN <.scr file name> Activates the SCREEN menu and enables you to create a custom screen format and store it to a .scr file

DELETE [<scope>] [FOR<exp>] Marks record(s) for deletion

DELETE FILE <file> Deletes the specified file

DIR [<drive>] [<path>] Shows the files on the specified drive or path

DISPLAY [<scope>][<field list>][FOR<exp>][OFF]   Displays selected records from the data base file in use

DISPLAY MEMORY   Displays current memory variables

DISPLAY STATUS   Displays current information about active data bases, index files, alternate files, and system parameters

DISPLAY STRUCTURE   Displays the structure of the file in use

EDIT [n]   Starts selective editing of the file in use

EJECT   Sends a form feed to the printer

ERASE <file name>   Deletes the specified file from the directory

FIND <character string>   Positions the record pointer to the first record with an index key that matches the specified character string, which does not have to be delimited

GO or GOTO <n> or TOP, or <BOTTOM>   Positions the pointer at a specific record or place in the file in use

INDEX ON <key> TO <file>   Creates an index file for the file in use

LABEL FORM <.lbl file name> [WHILE <condition>] [FOR <condition.] [TO PRINT]   Prints labels using the indicated label form file

LIST [<scope>][<field list>][FOR <exp>][OFF]   Lists records from the file in use

LIST FILES [ON<disk drive>][LIKE<skeleton>]   Lists files from disk

LIST STRUCTURE   Displays the structure of the file in use

LOCATE [<scope>][FOR<exp>]   Finds the first record that satisfies the specified condition; the CONTINUE command is then used to locate the next record meeting the condition

MODIFY COMMAND <file>   Calls dBASE III's text editor and brings up the designated file for modification

MODIFY LABEL <file name>   Activates the LABEL menu for changing .lbl file parameters

MODIFY QUERY <file name>   Activates the QUERY menu for changing .qry file parameters

MODIFY REPORT <file name>   Activates the REPORT menu for changing .frm report template parameters

MODIFY SCREEN <file name>   Activates the SCREEN menu for changing .scr file parameters

MODIFY STRUCTURE   Allows structural modification of a data base file

PACK   Eliminates records marked for deletion

QUIT   Terminates dBASE III and returns control to the operating system

RECALL [<scope>][FOR<exp>]   Recovers records previously marked for deletion

REINDEX   Rebuilds existing active index files

RENAME <oldfile> TO <newfile>   Enables you to rename a file

REPLACE [<scope>]<field>WITH<exp>[FOR<exp>]   Replaces the value of the specified field of specified records with stated values

REPORT [FORM <filename>][<scope>][FOR<exp>][TO PRINT]   Generates or accesses an existing .FRM file for output of data in a defined format

SEEK <expression>   Positions the record pointer to the first record with an index key that matches the specified expression

SELECT <work area/alias>   Activates the specified work area for accessing a file

SET   See SET commands

SKIP [+ − n]   Moves the pointer forward or backward within the file

SORT ON <key> TO <file> [ASCENDING] or [DESCENDING]   Creates another data base file, sorted in the order specified by the named key

SORT TO <new file name> ON <field list>[/A][C][/D]   Creates an ordered copy of a data base, arranged according to one or more fields

SUM <field list> [TO<membar list>][<scope>][FOR<exp>]   Computes and displays the sum of numeric fields

USE <file> [INDEX <file list>]   Opens a data base file and (optionally) opens desired index files

ZAP   Removes all records from the active data base file

Selected SET Commands

SET commands enable you to redefine the environment in which you are working with dBASE. The default value of each SET command of ON/OFF type is indicated by the order of presentation: OFF/ON indicates that the default is OFF; ON/OFF indicates that the default is ON.

SET BELL ON/OFF   ON rings the bell when invalid data are entered or a field boundary is passed; OFF turns off the bell

SET CONFIRM OFF/ON   Does not skip to the next field in the full-screen mode

SET DATE TO <MM/DD/YY>   Sets or resets the system date

SET DECIMALS TO <expN>   Sets the minimum number of decimals displayed in the results of certain operations and functions

SET DEFAULT TO <drive>   Commands dBASE III Plus to regard the specified drive as the default drive for all future operations

SET DELETED OFF/ON   ON prevents dBASE III Plus from reading/processing any record marked for deletion following a command that has <scope>; OFF allows dBASE III Plus to read all records

SET FILTER TO [FILE <.qry filename>]   Causes a data base file to appear to contain only records that meet the specified condition

SET INTENSITY ON/OFF   ON enables inverse video or dual intensity to appear during full-screen operations; OFF disables these features

SET MARGIN TO <n>   Sets the left-hand margin of printer to <n>

SET MENU ON/OFF   Turns menus on or off

Full-Screen Cursor
Movement Codes

All Commands

CTRL + X Moves the cursor down to the next field (also CTRL + F)

CTRL + E Moves cursor up to the previous field (also CTRL + A)

CTRL + D Moves cursor ahead one character

CTRL + S Moves cursor back one character

CTRL + G Deletes character under cursor

<Rubout> or DEL Deletes character to left of cursor

CTRL + Y Blanks out current field to right of cursor

CTRL + V Toggles between overwrite and insert modes

CTRL + W Saves changes and returns to command (.) prompt

In Edit Mode

CTRL + U Toggles the record delete mark on and off

CTRL + C Writes current record to disk and advances to next record

CTRL + R Writes current record to disk and backs to previous record

CTRL + Q Ignores changes to current record and returns to command (.) prompt

CTRL + W Writes all changes to disk and returns to command (.) prompt

In Browse Mode

CTRL + B Pans the window right one field

CTRL + Z Pans the window left one field

In Modify Mode

CTRL + T Deletes current line and moves all lower lines up

CTRL + N Inserts new line at cursor position

CTRL + C Scrolls down one-half page

CTRL + W Writes all changes onto disk and returns to command (.) prompt

CTRL + Q Ignores all changes and returns

In Append Mode

ENTER Terminates APPEND when cursor is in first position of first field

CTRL + W Writes record to disk and moves to next record

CTRL + Q Ignores current record and returns to command (.) prompt

Control Key Strokes Operable When dBASE Is Not in Full-Screen Mode

CTRL + P Toggles printer ON and OFF

CTRL + R Repeats last executed command

CTRL + X Clears command line without executing command

CTRL + H Back-space

CTRL + M Emulates a carriage return

CTRL + S Starts/stops CPU operation

Appendix
D

VP-Planner
Command Menus

VP-PLANNER COMMAND STRUCTURE CHART

WORKSHEET RANGE COPY MOVE FILE PRINT GRAPH DATA QUIT

Global Insert Delete Col-Wid Erase Titles Window Status Auto Key

Displays Current VP-Planner Default Setting
Label-Prefix, Col-Wid
Recalculation Procedure and Cell Protection

Row Column

Row Column

Set Reset

1-72

No Yes

Horizontal Vertical Sync Unsync Clear

Both Horizontal Vertical Clear

Format Label-Prefix Col-Width Recalculation Protection Default*

Left Right Center

1-72

Enable Disable

Natural Columnwise Rowwise Automatic Manual Iteration

Fixed Sci Currency ,(comma) General +/- Percent Date Text 1 2

Printer Directory Status Update Custom Ext Dirs Hardware Quit

Interface Auto-LF Left Right Top Bottom Page-Len Wait Setup Quit

1 2 3 4

Yes No

Default 4

Default 76

Default 2

Default 2 Default 66

VP-PLANNER COMMAND STRUCTURE CHART

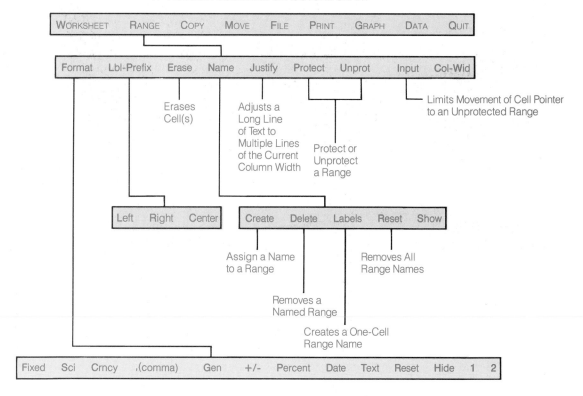

VP-PLANNER COMMAND STRUCTURE CHART

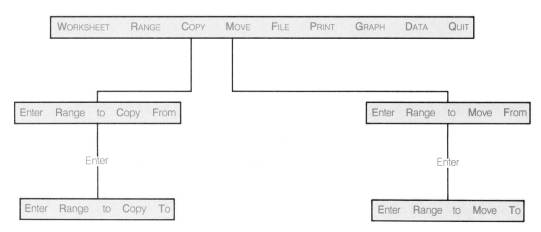

VP-PLANNER COMMAND STRUCTURE CHART

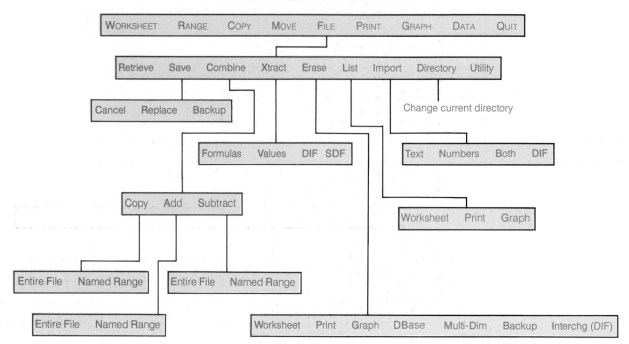

VP-PLANNER COMMAND STRUCTURE CHART

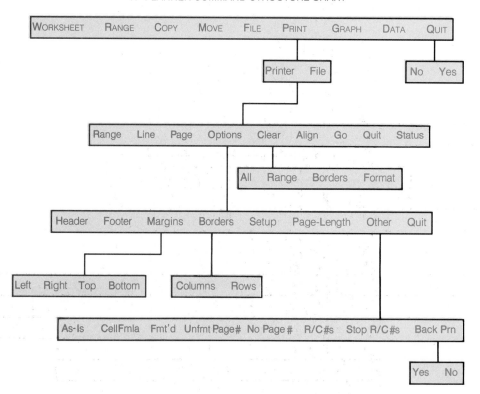

VP-PLANNER COMMAND STRUCTURE CHART

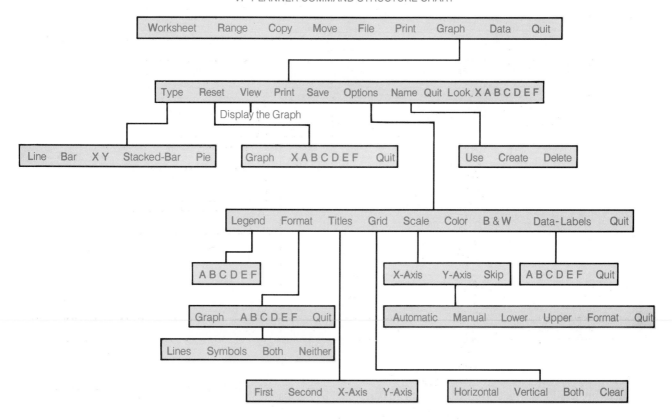

VP-PLANNER COMMAND STRUCTURE CHART

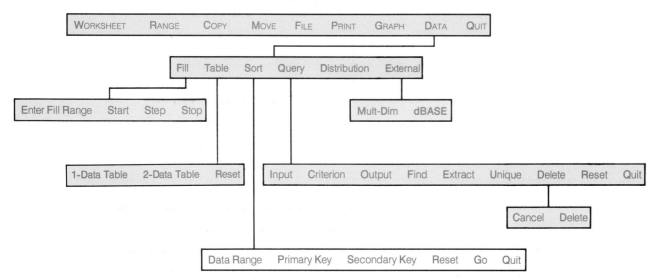

Macro Design Form

1. Name of macro _____

2. Overall task or objective of the macro _____

   _____

3. Range names to be used in the macro:

   Range Name   Purpose

   _____   _____

   _____   _____

   _____   _____

   _____   _____

   _____   _____

4. Steps involved in accomplishing the task to be performed by the macro:

   Keystrokes   Purpose

   _____   _____

   _____   _____

   _____   _____

   _____   _____

   _____   _____

   _____   _____

   _____   _____

   _____   _____

   _____   _____

   _____   _____

   _____   _____

   _____   _____

Macro Design Form

1. Name of macro _____

2. Overall task or objective of the macro _____

   _____

3. Range names to be used in the macro:

   Range Name   Purpose

   _____   _____

   _____   _____

   _____   _____

   _____   _____

   _____   _____

4. Steps involved in accomplishing the task to be performed by the macro:

   Keystrokes   Purpose

   _____   _____

   _____   _____

   _____   _____

   _____   _____

   _____   _____

   _____   _____

   _____   _____

   _____   _____

   _____   _____

   _____   _____

   _____   _____

   _____   _____

Macro Design Form

1. Name of macro _____

2. Overall task or objective of the macro _____

   _____

3. Range names to be used in the macro:

   Range Name   Purpose

   _____   _____

   _____   _____

   _____   _____

   _____   _____

4. Steps involved in accomplishing the task to be performed by the macro:

   Keystrokes   Purpose

   _____   _____

   _____   _____

   _____   _____

   _____   _____

   _____   _____

   _____   _____

   _____   _____

   _____   _____

   _____   _____

   _____   _____

   _____   _____

   _____   _____

Macro Design Form

1. Name of macro _____

2. Overall task or objective of the macro _____
   _____

3. Range names to be used in the macro:

   Range Name   Purpose

   _____   _____

   _____   _____

   _____   _____

   _____   _____

   _____   _____

4. Steps involved in accomplishing the task to be performed by the macro:

   Keystrokes   Purpose

   _____   _____

   _____   _____

   _____   _____

   _____   _____

   _____   _____

   _____   _____

   _____   _____

   _____   _____

   _____   _____

   _____   _____

   _____   _____

   _____   _____

   _____   _____

Macro Design Form

1. Name of macro _____

2. Overall task or objective of the macro _____

   _____

3. Range names to be used in the macro:

   Range Name   Purpose

   _____   _____

   _____   _____

   _____   _____

   _____   _____

   _____   _____

4. Steps involved in accomplishing the task to be performed by the macro:

   Keystrokes   Purpose

   _____   _____

   _____   _____

   _____   _____

   _____   _____

   _____   _____

   _____   _____

   _____   _____

   _____   _____

   _____   _____

   _____   _____

   _____   _____

   _____   _____

Macro Design Form

1. Name of macro _____

2. Overall task or objective of the macro _____

   _____

3. Range names to be used in the macro:

   Range Name   Purpose

   _____   _____

   _____   _____

   _____   _____

   _____   _____

   _____   _____

4. Steps involved in accomplishing the task to be performed by the macro:

   Keystrokes   Purpose

   _____   _____

   _____   _____

   _____   _____

   _____   _____

   _____   _____

   _____   _____

   _____   _____

   _____   _____

   _____   _____

   _____   _____

   _____   _____

   _____   _____

   _____   _____

Appendix
E

A Brief Introduction
to Lotus 1-2-3

Introduction

This supplement supplies information about Release 1A and Release 2 of Lotus 1-2-3 for the VP-Planner version adopters of *Four Software Tools*. The information is arranged in chapter order to correspond to *Four Software Tools*. Any items that are related only to Release 2 of 1-2-3 are noted with asterisks (***).

Chapter 11
Fundamentals
of Spreadsheets

Lotus 1-2-3 is the progeny of Mitch Kapor, a colorful character who taught himself programming. His first spreadsheet success was VisiTrend/Plot, a statistical and graphics package, that he designed and programmed; it was purchased by VisiCorp and was capable of receiving data from VisiCalc.

With the money that he earned from the sale of VisiTrend/Plot, plus some venture capital, Kapor set out to beat VisiCorp at its own game. He realized that the VisiCalc-VisiTrend/Plot hookup was cumbersome, since it required passing data, leaving one program, and then starting the other. He felt that this whole process could be made transparent to the end user.

Kapor and his staff designed 1-2-3 specifically for the IBM PC microcomputer; it was introduced early in 1983. A tremendous publicity campaign (and the superior quality of the software) helped Lotus 1-2-3 become an immediate success in the business community.

Introduction to Lotus 1-2-3

The **Lotus 1-2-3** software package, as the name implies, has three totally *integrated* parts: spreadsheet, data management, and graphing. Because 1-2-3 is integrated you do not have to leave the spreadsheet program, for instance, to get to the graphing or data management programs.

Parts of 1-2-3

Spreadsheet. The extremely powerful **spreadsheet** portion of Lotus manipulates the tabular accounting-like data. You can enter numbers, labels, or formulas into the worksheet. For example you can list twelve numbers in a column and define one cell to hold the sum of those twelve numbers; thereafter, when any one of these numbers is changed, the sum is automatically updated to reflect the change.

Data Management. The **data management feature** of Lotus 1-2-3 allows you to sort, summarize, and extract (make reports) portions of the individual records contained in a file. The major difference between this type of data management and other types is that the entire file is contained in a worksheet.

Graphics. The Graphics feature allows you to take information that you have entered in a worksheet and display it graphically to the screen (assuming you have graphics screen capability) or to the printer. You can display information in the form of a pie chart, bar chart, stacked bar chart, line, or xy. A regular monochrome monitor will not display a graph. Rather, the computer will simply beep.

Starting Lotus 1-2-3

Lotus 1-2-3 is a menu-driven software package, meaning that lists of options (menus) are displayed for you to choose from. Lotus 1-2-3 allows you to make

Figure 1
The Lotus Access System
Menu.

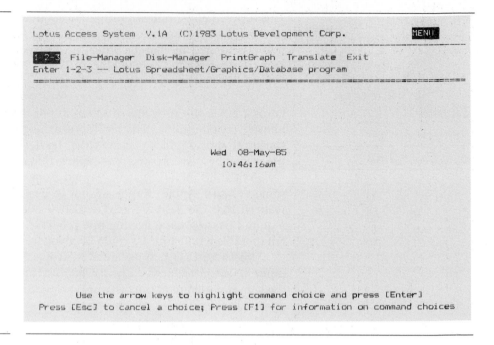

a selection by either entering the first character of the option at the keyboard or positioning the pointer using a right or left arrow key and then depressing ENTER.

Release 1A. Starting Lotus 1-2-3 is a straightforward process. Simply place the Lotus System disk in drive A, and place your data disk in drive B. Turn on the computer (if the computer is already on simply enter LOTUS). The computer will then display the Lotus Access System depicted in Figure 1. At this time enter either a 1 or depress the ENTER key. After some disk processing, a screen will appear indicating that you are in Lotus 1-2-3 and should depress any key to continue. The screen depicted in Figure 2 will now be displayed, and the directory of the disk in drive B will be read by the system.

***Release 2. Starting Lotus 1-2-3 is a straightforward process. After you have booted the system with a system disk (a disk containing DOS), simply place the Lotus System disk in drive A, and place your data disk in drive B, and enter LOTUS. The computer will then display the Lotus Access System depicted in Figure 2a. At this time enter either a 1 or depress the ENTER key. After some disk processing, a screen will appear indicating that you are in Lotus 1-2-3 (refer to Figure 2b) and should depress any key to continue. The screen depicted in Figure 2c will now be displayed, and the directory of the disk in drive B will be read by the system.

Lotus 1-2-3 Screen

At first there may not appear to be much to the worksheet screen. But looks in this case are deceiving. The following pieces are part of the worksheet screen: control panel, mode indicator, border, worksheet, pointer/cursor, error message area, and indicators. Each of these will now be described.

Figure 2a
Lotus Access System Menu
for 1-2-3 Release 2.

```
┌──────────────────────────────────────────────────────────────┐
│ 1-2-3  PrintGraph  Translate  Install  View  Exit              │
│ Enter 1-2-3 -- Lotus Worksheet/Graphics/Database program       │
└──────────────────────────────────────────────────────────────┘

┌──────────────────────────────────────────────────────────────┐
│                      1-2-3 Access System                       │
│                  Lotus Development Corporation                 │
│                        Copyright 1985                          │
│                       All Rights Reserved                      │
│                          Release 2                             │
│                                                                │
│ The Access System lets you choose 1-2-3, PrintGraph, the Translate utility,│
│ the Install program, and A View of 1-2-3 from the menu at the top of this  │
│ screen.  If you're using a diskette system, the Access System may prompt   │
│ you to change disks.  Follow the instructions below to start a program.    │
│                                                                │
│ o  Use [RIGHT] or [LEFT] to move the menu pointer (the highlight bar at    │
│    the top of the screen) to the program you want to use.      │
│                                                                │
│ o  Press [RETURN] to start the program.                        │
│                                                                │
│ You can also start a program by typing the first letter of the menu        │
│ choice.  Press [HELP] for more information.                    │
└──────────────────────────────────────────────────────────────┘
```

Figure 2b
Release 2 copyright screen.

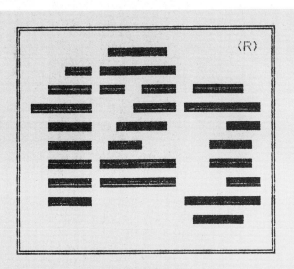

```
                                                        (R)




                    Copyright (C) 1985
              Lotus Development Corporation
                   All Rights Reserved
                    1200916-2725123
                       Release 2
```

Control Panel. The Control Panel is contained on the top three lines of your screen and consists of (first) the status line, (second) the entry line, and (third) the prompt line. The **status line** tells where you are, displaying the cell address, data format (if any), and the cell contents; information is given about

Figure 2c
Lotus 1-2-3 screen.

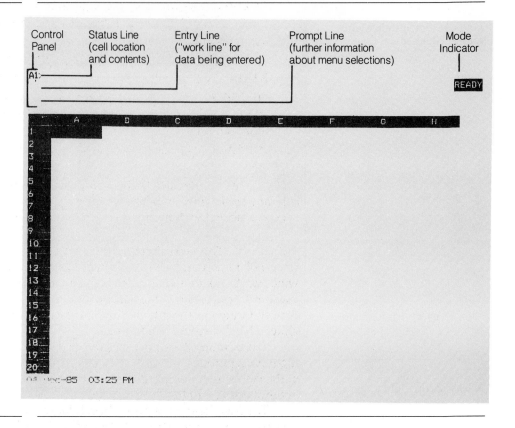

how the data in that particular cell are being processed by Lotus and about whether the cell contains a label, a value, or a formula.

The **entry line** corresponds to a "scratch" area that contains any data you happen to enter. It also contains any "pre-entered" information destined for the cell location given in the status line. This information is not placed in either the cell or the status line until the ENTER key is pressed. The entry line may also contain a menu of options for performing various operations on your worksheet. The Main Menu can be invoked any time by entering the slash (/) command.

The **prompt line** contains further options or an explanation of a specific command when a 1-2-3 menu is displayed.

Mode Indicator. The **mode indicator,** in the upper right-hand corner of the screen, displays status information about what 1-2-3 is doing. Some mode indicators that you will be seeing while you are working in this book will be:

READY—Lotus 1-2-3 is waiting for you to tell it to do something.

VALUE—You are entering a number or formula to be contained in a cell.

LABEL—You are entering text information to be contained in a cell.

EDIT—You are changing the contents of a cell via the edit feature of 1-2-3.

POINT—You are pointing to a cell or to a range of cells.

MENU—You have a menu displayed and are selecting from it.

HELP—You are using the 1-2-3 help facility.

ERROR—Something went wrong, and 1-2-3 is waiting for you to depress the ENTER or ESC key to acknowledge the error.

WAIT—1-2-3 is calculating the spreadsheet or performing a read/write operation and cannot accept more commands.

FIND—1-2-3 is using its data management feature to perform a find operation.

***FILES—Appears any time you select the FILES command from the Main Menu.

***NAMES—Appears any time you work on a named range.

Border. The **border** labels the rows and columns of your worksheet. The columns are labeled with letters of the alphabet (A, B, C, and so on), and the rows are labeled with numbers (1, 2, 3, and so on).

Worksheet. The **worksheet** contains whatever space is available to the user for problem solving. The worksheet has three key parts: cell, pointer, and window. As noted earlier, a cell is the intersection point of a row and column and is referred to by its cell address COLUMN/ROW. For example, B5 refers to the cell located at the intersection of column B and row 5. A cell can contain either a label, a value, or a formula.

The **pointer,** also sometimes referred to as the cursor, is the reverse-video (light background with dark characters) bar. Its width depends on the width of the cell being referenced. The contents of the referenced cell are displayed in the status line of the control panel.

The 1-2-3 Release 1A worksheet is large compared to many other spreadsheet packages. It contains 256 columns (A, B, C, D, . . . , IV) and 2,048 rows for a grand total of 524,288 cells. How large a piece of paper would you need to hold this size spreadsheet? If each cell were 1/4 inch high and 1 inch wide, a piece of paper that could hold all of these rows and columns would have to be 42.6 feet high and 21.3 feet wide. The 1-2-3 worksheet is, indeed, large.

The 1-2-3 Release 2 worksheet is even larger. It contains 256 columns and 8,192 rows. Because this number of rows can never be used with 640K, Lotus has made 1-2-3 capable of addressing up to four additional megabytes of RAM. Using the same criteria as above, this worksheet would also require a piece of paper 21.3 wide, but the height would now be 170.6 feet.

It goes without saying that all these cells cannot be displayed at one time on your small display screen. Instead, only small, rectangular amounts of these 524,288 cells can be displayed at one time. The display will always have 20 rows. The number of columns displayed will be dependent on the column width. This area displayed on the screen is referred to as the **window**.

Error Message Indicator. **Error messages** appear in the lower left-hand corner of the screen, giving a brief explanation of what has gone wrong. They are accompanied by a beep from the computer when a Lotus 1-2-3 rule has been broken. After you have read the message and wish to return control back to the worksheet, simply depress the ESC or ENTER key.

Indicators. The IBM keyboard does not tell you whether the SCROLL LOCK, CAPS LOCK, or NUM LOCK keys are on or off. The Lotus 1-2-3 indicators for each of these provide this information. If one of these keys is on, a message in reverse video will be displayed in the lower right-hand corner of the screen. A fourth indicator is CALC, which will be discussed in a later chapter.

Navigating Around the 1-2-3 Worksheet

Because Lotus 1-2-3 was designed for the IBM PC, it makes full use of all of the keys on the keyboard—an especially important feature when it comes to moving the pointer quickly around the worksheet. Most pointer movement commands are accomplished by using the ten-key pad found on the right-hand side of the keyboard, and Lotus 1-2-3 automatically places these keys in cursor movement mode rather than numeric mode. The movement keys work as follows:

The **down arrow** moves the pointer down one cell position (down one row).

The **up arrow** moves the pointer up one cell position (up one row).

The **right arrow** moves the pointer to the right one cell position (to the right one column).

The **left arrow** moves the pointer to the left one cell position (to the left one column).

The **PG UP** key moves the cursor up 20 lines (one page) in the present column.

The **PG DN** key moves the cursor down 20 lines (one page) in the present column.

The **HOME** key moves the pointer to cell position A1.

The **END** key, when entered prior to an error key, positions the cursor in the same direction as the arrow key at the next nonblank boundary cell. For example, a worksheet will typically have blocks of cells with data, followed by blocks of blank, empty cells that are in turn followed by other cells with data. If the pointer is in a blank/empty region and the END key is depressed, followed by an arrow key, the pointer will be moved to the first nonblank cell. If the same command sequence is entered again, the pointer will be moved to the last nonblank cell in that block. Entering the same command sequence moves the pointer to the next nonblank area. When there are no longer any nonblank cells remaining in one direction of pointer movement, one of 1-2-3's boundaries will have been reached (for example, column IV).

The **Tab** key, located above the CTRL key, moves the cursor to the right one screen (72 characters) at a time. The **Tab** plus the **Shift** key moves the cursor to the left a screen (72 characters) at a time.

***Moving to the right one screen at a time is now referred to as a big right (CTRL + right arrow).

***Moving to the left one screen at a time is now referred to as a big left (CTRL + left arrow).

***Expanded Use of Setup and Print Commands

Chapter 12

More on Ranges,

Copying, Formatting,

Printing,

and Functions

Release 2 provides you with much more flexibility in printing a worksheet than Release 1A. Rather than relying on the 1-2-3 line counter, Release 2 allows you to specify exactly where a page break should occur.

A page break is placed within a document using the / Worksheet Page command. The Page command is an option of the Worksheet Menu. To embed a page break within a worksheet, simply place the pointer at the cell where you wish to have the page break occur, and enter the / Worksheet Page command. 1-2-3 now appears to insert a blank row in your worksheet (don't worry; this is a nonprinting row) and a double colon (::) appears in column A of that row. The double colon indicates to 1-2-3 that this is the last line of a worksheet page. When 1-2-3 encounters this line, it automatically advances the paper to the top of the next page and resets the line counter.

This page break can be erased from your worksheet by either performing a / Range Erase command on the cell with the double colon or by erasing the row in which the double colon appears.

***File Commands

Files that are created by Release 2 do not have the same extension as those created by 1A. Release 1A creates worksheet files with a .WKS extension, whereas Release 2 uses a .WK1 file extension. You are allowed to access both types of files with Release 2. When you save the file, however, the new version places a .WK1 extension on the file. When you access files, 1-2-3 displays any files that have a .WK? extension; that is, any file with an extension of WK is displayed on the prompt line.

Release 2 provides you with the ability to password-protect your worksheet files. **WARNING**: If you have a bad memory, you should not use passwords. Once you save a file with a password, you will always be prompted for it before 1-2-3 will allow you to access the file. If you forget your password, 1-2-3 will deny you access to the worksheet.

The following example shows how to save the worksheet YEAREND with the password FINLCOPY.

/	Invoke the Main Menu.
F	Select the File option.
S	Tell 1-2-3 to save the worksheet file.
YEAREND P	Enter the name of the file, press the space bar, and enter a P. The P indicates to 1-2-3 that a password is to be assigned to this file.
FINLCOPY	Enter the password. (It does not appear on your screen, so be careful to enter it correctly.) The password may contain up to 15 characters.
FINLCOPY	1-2-3 now asks you to verify the password. To do so, you must reenter the original password and press the ENTER key. In this case, the FINLCOPY password is now operational.

To change or cancel a password, you must enter the / File Retrieve command and enter the appropriate file name. 1-2-3 now prompts you for the password. You must enter the appropriate password before you can cancel it or enter a new one. To cancel a password, save the worksheet and press ESC or BACKSPACE when you are prompted for the password. The worksheet will now be saved to disk without a password.

Chapter 13
Maintaining
and Enhancing
Your Worksheets

***Range Transpose

The / Range Transpose command allows you to rearrange the rows and columns within a range in your worksheet. Any alphanumeric or numeric label can be rearranged; however, you are not allowed to arrange any relative address formulas. Trying to do so will result in ERR messages in any cells that have formulas. If formulas are desired, rearrange the labels and then add the formulas.

Assume that you wish to rearrange the following worksheet's rows and columns so that the columns are rows (and vice versa):

```
COMPSALS
Department   Last Year   This Year
Deli             700.00      575.00
Bakery         1,000.00    1,100.00
Liquor         1,200.00    1,400.00
Grocery        2,500.00    2,900.00
Produce          950.00    1,000.00
Meat           1,500.00    1,410.00
```

You would need to enter the following commands:

/	Gets the Main Menu.
R	Selects the Range option.
T	Selects the Transpose option.
B3.D10 ENTER	Enter the Copy From Range (Transpose Range) either by entering the actual cell addresses or by manual pointer movement "painting" the affected area.
B16 ENTER	Tell 1-2-3 where to place the transposed range.

You will now see the following worksheet on your screen.

```
COMPSALS
Department   Last Year   This Year
Deli             700.00      575.00
Bakery         1,000.00    1,100.00
Liquor         1,200.00    1,400.00
Grocery        2,500.00    2,900.00
Produce          950.00    1,000.00
Meat           1,500.00    1,410.00

Department  Deli      Bakery    Liquor    Grocery   Produce   Meat
Last Year   700.00    1,000.00  1,200.00  2,500.00  950.00    1,500.00
This Year   575.00    1,100.00  1,400.00  2,900.00  1,000.00  1,410.00
```

Remember, only text can be moved using the Transpose command. Any formulas will move improperly, causing ERR messages to appear in the affected cells.

Chapter 15

Graphing with 1-2-3

***Exploded Pie Chart

1-2-3 now provides you with the ability to create an exploded pie chart showing one or more slices separated from the rest of the chart. To create this effect, you must set up a separate B data range. The A range contains the values to be plotted. The B range tells 1-2-3 the colors (or patterns, if viewed on a noncolor screen) to be used and which wedges (if any) are to be exploded.

Plotting an exploded pie chart requires you to set up a new B data range in column G with values for the colors of each wedge to be plotted. These are given as single digits 0 through 8. The digits 0 and 8 are used for nonshaded wedges, the digits 1 through 7 for a shade or pattern. Add 100 to the appropri-

Figure 3a
Worksheet for generating the
graph in Figure 3b.

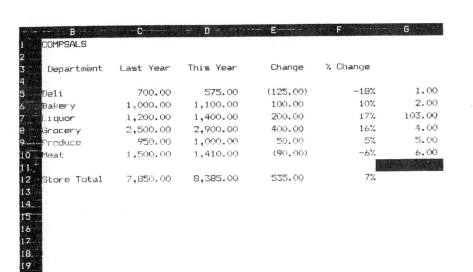

ate shading value of exploded wedges. For example, if the shaded value of a wedge is 4 and you wish to have that wedge appear exploded from the pie, enter 104.

The worksheet displayed in Figure 3a generates the exploded pie chart in Figure 3b. Don't worry if the graph appears a little "squashed"; as you can see from Figure 3c, it will appear fine when printed.

Introduction to Graph Printing

Lotus 1-2-3 does not provide you with facilities for directly printing your graphs from the 1-2-3 spreadsheet program. This is one of the few areas in which Lotus's integration breaks down; but if this feature had been implemented, 1-2-3 would require much more RAM memory than it does now.

To print a graph, you must leave the 1-2-3 spreadsheet software and return to the Lotus Access System Menu, where you take the **PrintGraph** option. If you have been using 1-2-3, you will be instructed to insert the PrintGraph disk in drive A. If you have previously saved your graph files and wish to print them out, you can boot directly from the PrintGraph disk, which also contains a copy of the Lotus Access System.

Make certain that the disk containing the graphs you have saved is inserted in drive B, and get your PrintGraph disk ready. If you have 1-2-3 running on your computer, follow the instructions below. If the computer is off, you can simply insert the PrintGraph disk in drive A: and boot the system with that disk, skipping the instructions below. The steps involved in accessing PrintGraph from 1-2-3 are as follows:

/—Gets the Main Menu.

Q—Selects the Quit option.

Figure 3b
Exploded pie chart viewed
on the screen using a Hercules graphics board.

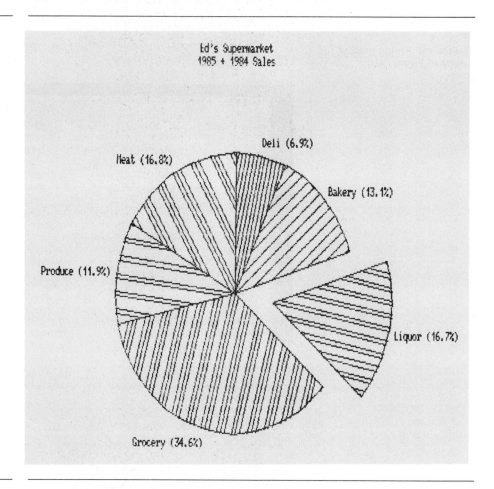

Figure 3c
Printed pie chart using
PrintGraph.

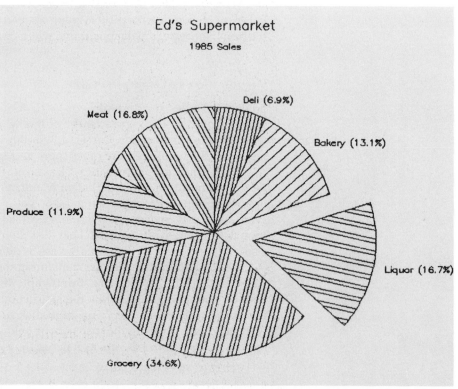

Figure 4
Directions displayed when the PrintGraph option is selected.

```
Insert Lotus PrintGraph disk in drive A and press [Enter]; press [Esc] to quit.
```

Figure 5
The PrintGraph Menu.

```
Copyright 1982, 1983 Lotus Development Corp.  All Rights Reserved.        MENU
----------------------------------------------------------------------------
Select  Options  Go  Configure  Align  Page  Quit
Select pictures
============================================================================
 SELECTED GRAPHS    COLORS            SIZE    FULL        DIRECTORIES

                    Grid:     Black   Left Margin:  .500   Pictures
                    A Range:  Black   Top Margin:   .250   B
                    B Range:  Black   Width:       6.852   Fonts
                    C Range:  Black   Height:      9.445   A:\
                    D Range:  Black   Rotation:   90.000
                    E Range:  Black                        GRAPHICS DEVICE
                    F Range:  Black   MODES
                                                           Epson FX80/4
                    FONTS             Eject: No            Parallel
                                      Pause: No
                    1: ROMAN2                              PAGE SIZE
                    2: SCRIPT2
                                                           Length  11.000
                                                           Width    8.000
```

Y—Affirms leaving 1-2-3, and in a few seconds, elicits a display of the Lotus Access System Menu.

P—Selects the PrintGraph option.

At this point you will be directed to insert the PrintGraph disk in drive A: (see Figure 4). To get the PrintGraph Menu (see Figure 5), you must depress the ESC key.

PrintGraph Menu

The information displayed beneath the PrintGraph Menu details status information about the various options used by the utility, including what the expected paper sizes are, what fonts have been selected, where files are to be found, and what type of printer PrintGraph is currently configured for. When you have properly started the PrintGraph utility, the following menu will be displayed:

```
Select   Options   Go   Configure   Align   Page   Quit
```

When the **Select option** is taken, a display of all graph files contained on the disk in drive B appears on the screen. Across the top file is a wide pointer, which is moved up and down by means of the up and down arrow keys. To tag or mark a file for printing, simply depress the space bar; a **pound sign (#)** will then appear to the left of that graph file entry. (See Figures 6 and 7.)

Up to sixteen graph files can be selected for printing. If more than one file is selected, they are printed in the order in which they appear, from top to bottom. The computer then prints each graph in turn and automatically takes care of advancing the paper for the next graph. When you have selected all

Figure 6
Pointer at the Select option of
PrintGraph.

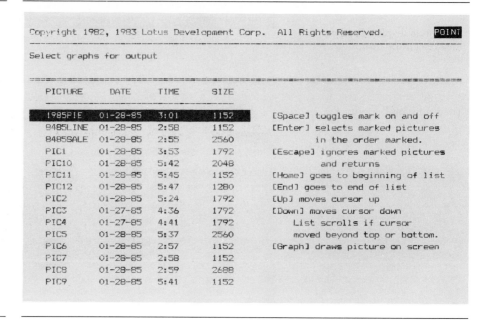

the files you wish to print, simply depress the ENTER key to return to the
PrintGraph Menu. Depressing the ENTER key a second time will "unmark"
the file.

This feature, known as **batch printing,** is very convenient because it
allows you to do something else (like catch up on your reading) while the
graphs you want are being printed.

Options.   The options selection of the PrintGraph Menu allows you to tailor
the printing of any graphs you have selected. The following menu is displayed:

    Color   Font   Size   Pause   Eject   Quit

Color. The **Color option** allows you (if you have a color printer or plotter) to
tell the printer or plotter to do various parts of the graph in different colors.

Font. The **Font option** allows you to select up to two fonts to use in generating
dot matrix output: font 1 is used only for the first line of the graph title; font 2
is used for any other text. Fonts are selected in the same way that files to be
printed are. A pointer is used to highlight the desired option, but in this case
the ENTER key is pressed to choose the font. (See Figure 8.)

Size. The **Size option** allows you to specify whether or not you want full-page
graphs, half-page graphs, or graphs of some other size that you specify (the
default is half).

Pause. The **Pause option** allows you to load single sheets of paper and then
stop the printer between graphs in order to load another sheet (the default
is NO).

Eject. The **Eject option** allows you to determine whether or not the printer
should issue a "go to top of form" message when it has finished printing a
graph (the default is YES).

Figure 7
1985PIE and 8485LINE files marked for printing.

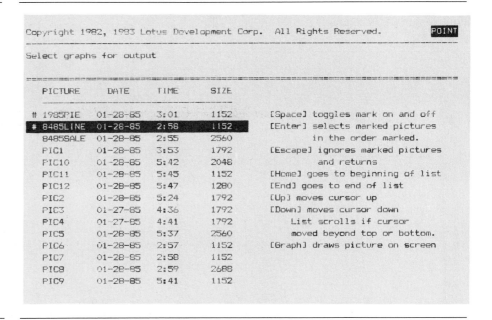

Figure 8
Pointer at the block1 option, after selection of font 1.

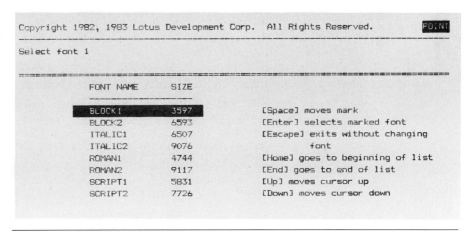

Quit. The **Quit option** returns you to the PrintGraph Menu.

Go. The **Go option** tells PrintGraph to start printing a graph.

Configure. The **Configure option** allows you to change the various printers and defaults for the PrintGraph program. (Consult your 1-2-3 manual for more details.)

Align. The **Align option** operates exactly as the PrintGraph option does in resetting to the top of the page for the printer. It allows you to move the platen so that the print head is at the top of a new sheet of paper—an especially important ability if you are using the roller, instead of the page option, to move the paper.

Page. The **Page option** automatically advances the paper in the printer to the top of the next page without losing track of the top of the page.

Figure 9
Printed-out 1985PIE graph.

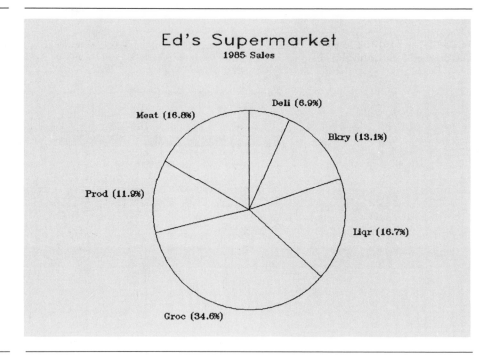

 Step-by-Step PrintGraph Instructions

Following are the steps necessary to print the graph files 1985PIE and 8485LINE that you created earlier. You'll start from the PrintGraph Menu.

1. Move the pointer to the Select option (see Figure 6).
2. Move the pointer (via the up and down arrows) to position at the two desired graph names. Mark them by pressing the space bar so that a # symbol appears to the left of each. Hit ENTER when both have been marked (see Figure 7).
3. Take the Options selection.
4. Take the Font entry of the Options Menu. Select font 1, and choose block 2 by pointing and then hitting the ENTER key (see Figure 8).
5. Take the Font entry of the Options Menu again. Select font 2, and choose Roman2 by pointing and then hitting the ENTER key.
6. You're finished with the options, so take the Quit option.
7. Make sure the printer is at the top of a new page; then select the Align option.
8. You're going to accept all the defaults for printing. The next step is to take the Go option to start printing.

The following actions are now executed by PrintGraph:

1. The font files are loaded.
2. The graph file is loaded, and the picture is generated.
3. The graph file is printed.

You will notice that PrintGraph's printing process is very slow in comparison to regular printing. This is because the printer has shifted to graphics mode, and graphics mode is generally slower than text mode.

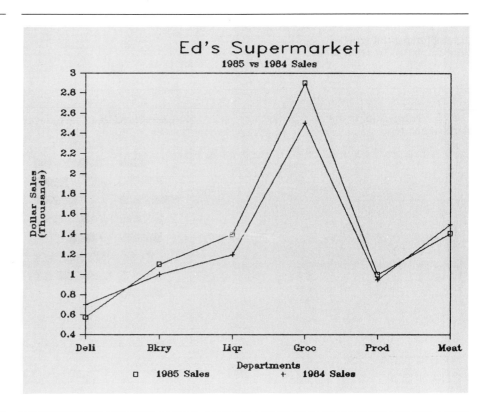

Figure 10
Printed-out 8485LINE
graph.

PrintGraph displays various pieces of status information while it is printing. In the menu area, it identifies the graph file currently printing; and below the current printing file, it displays a list of the files that were selected for printing.

The files selected for printing can be seen in Figures 9 and 10.

***Graph Printing with Release 2

See Figures 11a and 11b.

***PrintGraph Menu

The information displayed beneath the PrintGraph menu details status information about the various options used by the utility, including what paper sizes are expected; what fonts have been selected; where files are to be found; and what type of printer PrintGraph is currently configured for. When you have properly started the PrintGraph utility, the following menu will be displayed:

```
Image-Select  Settings  Go  Align  Page  Exit
```

Image-Select. This option is used to mark graphs for printing and operates exactly the same as the Select option of Release 1A. When you select the Image-Select option, a display of all graph files contained on the disk in drive B appears on the screen. Across the top file is a wide pointer, which is moved

Figure 11a
Prompt for inserting the
PrintGraph disk in drive A.

Figure 11b
The 1-2-3 screen prior to the
PrintGraph Menu.

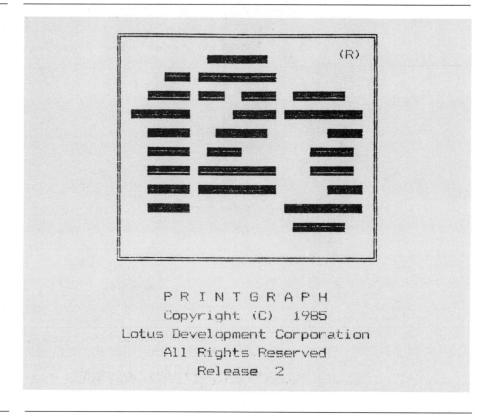

up and down by means of the up and down arrow keys. To tag or mark a file
for printing, simply depress the space bar; a pound sign (#) will then appear
to the left of that graph file entry. (See Figures 13 and 14).

 Up to sixteen graph files can be selected for printing. If more than one
file is selected, they are printed in the order in which they appear, from top to
bottom. The computer then prints each graph in turn and automatically takes
care of advancing the paper for the next graph. When you have selected all
the files you wish to print, simply depress the ENTER key to return to the
PrintGraph Menu. Depressing the ENTER key a second time will "unmark"
the file.

This convenient feature, known as **batch printing,** allows you to do
something else (like catch up on your reading) while your graphs are being
printed.

Settings. This option combines aspects of both the Options and Configure
selections of Release 1A. Upon selecting the Settings option, the following
menu is displayed (see Figure 15):

Image Hardware Action Save Reset Quit

Figure 12
The new PrintGraph Menu.

```
Copyright 1985 Lotus Development Corp.  All Rights Reserved.  Release 2   MENU

Select graphs for printing
Image-Select  Settings  Go  Align  Page  Exit
_____

   GRAPH      IMAGE OPTIONS                    HARDWARE SETUP
   IMAGES     Size            Range Colors     Graphs Directory:
   SELECTED   Top      .395   X                  A:\
              Left     .750   A                Fonts Directory:
              Width   6.500   B                  A:\
              Height  4.691   C                Interface:
              Rotate   .000   D                  Parallel 1
                             E                 Printer Type:
              Font           F
              1  BLOCK1                        Paper Size
              2  BLOCK1                          Width     8.500
                                                 Length   11.000

                                              ACTION OPTIONS
                                                Pause: No   Eject: No
```

Figure 13
Menu of graph (OPIC) files.

```
Copyright 1985 Lotus Development Corp.  All Rights Reserved.  Release 2   POINT

Select graphs for output
_____

   PICTURE    DATE      TIME    SIZE
   ----------------------------------
   8584BAR    12-04-85  15:49   2551       [SPACE] turns mark on and off
   8584LINE   12-04-85  15:49   1031       [RETURN] selects marked pictures
   EXPPIE1    12-04-85  15:46   2599       [ESCAPE] exits, ignoring changes
   EXPPIE2    12-04-85  15:47   2639       [HOME] goes to beginning of list
   TITLES     12-04-85  15:50   2681       [END] goes to end of list
                                           [UP] and [DOWN] move cursor
                                              List will scroll if cursor
                                              moved beyond top or bottom
                                           [GRAPH] displays selected picture
```

Figure 14
Graphs marked for printing.

```
Copyright 1985 Lotus Development Corp.  All Rights Reserved.  Release 2   POINT

Select graphs for output
_____

   PICTURE    DATE      TIME    SIZE
   ----------------------------------
   8584BAR    12-04-85  15:49   2551       [SPACE] turns mark on and off
   8584LINE   12-04-85  15:49   1031       [RETURN] selects marked pictures
 # EXPPIE1    12-04-85  15:46   2599       [ESCAPE] exits, ignoring changes
   EXPPIE2    12-04-85  15:47   2639       [HOME] goes to beginning of list
 # TITLES     12-04-85  15:50   2681       [END] goes to end of list
                                           [UP] and [DOWN] move cursor
                                              List will scroll if cursor
                                              moved beyond top or bottom
                                           [GRAPH] displays selected picture
```

Figure 15
Settings Menu.

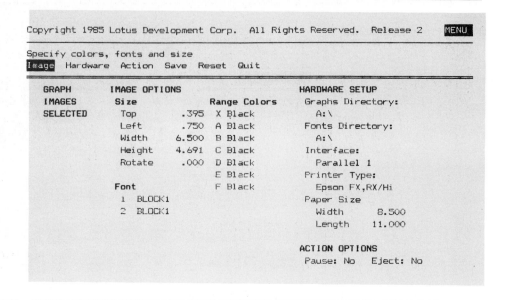

Copyright 1985 Lotus Development Corp. All Rights Reserved. Release 2   MENU

Specify colors, fonts and size
Image Hardware Action Save Reset Quit

```
GRAPH        IMAGE OPTIONS                    HARDWARE SETUP
IMAGES         Size              Range Colors   Graphs Directory:
SELECTED       Top       .395    X Black          A:\
               Left      .750    A Black        Fonts Directory:
               Width    6.500    B Black          A:\
               Height   4.691    C Black        Interface:
               Rotate    .000    D Black          Parallel 1
                                 E Black        Printer Type:
               Font              F Black          Epson FX,RX/Hi
                1  BLOCK1                       Paper Size
                2  BLOCK1                         Width     8.500
                                                  Length   11.000

                                               ACTION OPTIONS
                                                 Pause: No   Eject: No
```

Image. The image option (see Figure 16) displays the following submenu when it is selected:

> Size   Font   Range-Colors   Quit

Size   Allows you to specify the height and width of the graph to be printed.

Font   Allows you to select up to two fonts from eleven possible fonts in generating dot matrix output. Font 1 is used only for the first line of the graph title, font 2 for any other text. Fonts are selected in the same way that files are: Use a pointer to highlight the desired option, and then press the ENTER key to choose the font (see Figure 17).

Range-Colors   Allows you to assign a different color to each data range. This option is selected if you have the ability to generate color graphs.

Quit   Returns you to the Settings Menu.

Hardware. This option allows you to configure 1-2-3 to the type of print that your printer is capable of printing, as well as to tell 1-2-3 where to find the graph files and font files. Most likely these tasks have already been done for readers of this textbook, so this option—as well as the remaining options—will not be covered here.

Quit. Returns you to the PrintGraph Menu.

Go. This option results in the graph being printed.

Align. This option resets the top-of-page. If the graph did not print properly (for example, if there is a blank area in the middle), simply move the paper manually to a perforation and press the ALIGN command. PrintGraph now knows where the top of the page is.

Figure 16
Image Menu.

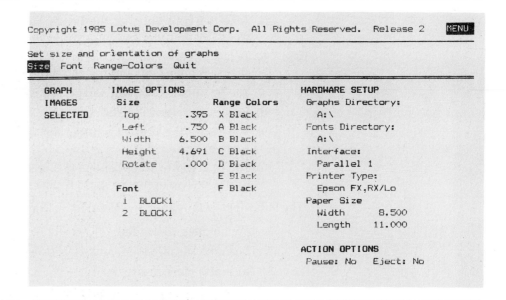

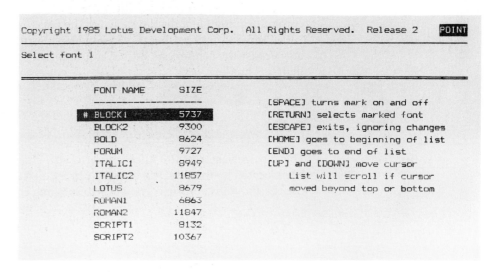

Figure 17
Font marked for use.

Page. This option moves the paper in the printer forward to the top of the next page.

 ***Step-by-Step PrintGraph Instructions**

To print the graph files EXPPIE1 and TITLES that were created earlier, start from the PrintGraph Menu. Then:

1. Move the pointer to the Image-Select option (see Figure 13) and press ENTER.
2. Move the pointer (via the up and down arrows) to position at the two desired graph names. Mark them by pressing the space bar so that a # symbol appears to the left of each. Hit ENTER when both have been marked (see Figure 14).
3. Take the Settings selection.

4. Take the Image option.

5. Take the Font entry of the Image Menu. Select font 1 and choose block2 by pointing and hitting the ENTER key (see Figure 17).

6. Take the Font entry of the Image Menu again. Select font 2, and choose Roman2 by pointing and hitting the ENTER key.

7. You've finished with the Image, so take the Quit option.

8. Quit from Settings Menu.

9. Make sure the printer is at the top of a new page; then select the Align option.

10. You're going to accept all the defaults for printing. The next step is to take the Go option to start printing.

The following options are now executed by PrintGraph:

1. The font files are loaded.

2. The graph file is loaded, and the picture is generated.

3. The graph file is printed.

PrintGraph displays various pieces of status information while it prints. In the menu area it identifies the graph file currently printing, and below the current printing file it displays a list of the files that were selected for printing.

PrintGraph's printing process is very slow in comparison to regular printing because the printer has shifted to graphics mode, which is generally slower than text mode.

Chapter 16

Data Management

Find Command and Editing/Changing Records

The new release of 1-2-3 allows you to edit/change records after they have been located by the FIND command. Once you have located a record, you can use the standard editing commands for making changes to the record.

Appendix F

IBM's PS/2 Computers

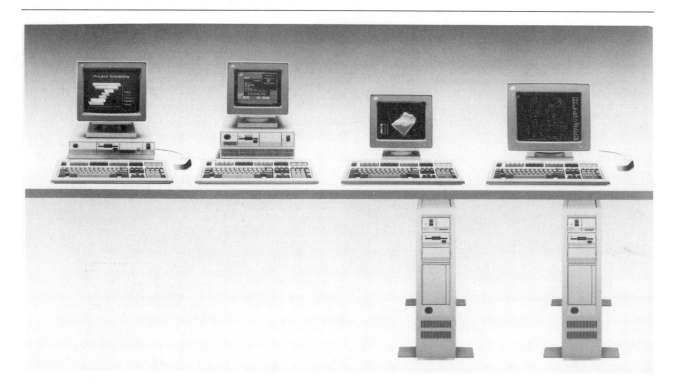

Figure F.1

IBM's Personal System/2 Family. Left to right: Models 30, 50, 60, and 80. (Photograph courtesy of International Business Machines Corporation.)

On April 2, 1987 IBM introduced a new line of computers to take the place of its older PCs (see Figure F.1). These new computers will, according to many industry observers, revolutionize the microcomputer arena. They use a different size disk, have improved video and faster CPU chips, incorporate new manufacturing techniques, and have a faster bus system.

New Features

New Disk Size

The most significant difference between the original PC and the new computer is the size of diskette used for secondary storage. The PC uses the 5¼-inch diskette, but the new series of PC/2 machines use the 3½-inch rigid diskette. Although the physical size is smaller, the smaller, rigid diskette contains twice the storage (720K) of the original diskette. The new rigid disk not only allows you to store more information, but its smaller size makes it much easier to carry.

The one drawback to the new disk is the ability to transfer information from a larger format to the smaller format or vice versa. To achieve this easily requires that you have a 5¼-inch disk drive and DOS 3.x. The 3.x (3.2 or 3.3) DOS is the only release that recognizes the 3½-inch format. If you do not have a recent release of DOS or you have two machines (one with 5¼-inch drives and one with 3½-inch drives), you can solve this problem by purchasing a transfer program from IBM (Data Migration Facility) or another vendor that allows you to mix operating systems and computers.

Such a program requires that you hook a cable between the two computers either via the parallel printer port or via the serial port on the machine. Once the transfer software is running, you can transfer programs or files from one machine to another. As more and more machines with 3½-inch drives appear in the market, this process will no doubt become easier.

New Video

With its new line of computers, IBM also introduced two new video adapters (methods of displaying graphics): the Multicolor Graphics Array (MCGA), which is built into the low-end computer, and the Video Graphics Array (VGA), which is built into the high-end models and can also be purchased as an add-on board for the low-end model. Each of these video adapters is capable of emulating prior graphics modes (CGA and EGA), so most existing software can run without a problem.

In addition, each of these video adapters support 640×480 graphics resolution rather than the old 640×200 resolution. This means that images are more in proportion when they are displayed on the screen; the old modes resulted in rather elongated images. The advantage here is that images can be easily digitized and moved from one system to another without fear of distortion.

Another advantage of the new video is the number of colors that can be displayed. Because of its use of analog technology, IBM can display many more shades of the same color (with digital technology a color is either on or off). This new technology provides for 262,144 different colors or shades of colors. You cannot, however, display all of these colors at one time to your screen, because of memory limitations. Instead, only 256 of these colors can be displayed at one time. This is still a dramatic improvement from the 64 maximum in the old color (CGA) graphics.

The new video adapters from IBM allow a user to generate striking graphics displays. These are especially useful in computer-aided design (CAD) applications, business graphics, or games. Even if a monochrome monitor is used, up to 64 shades of gray can be shown.

New Bus System

With the exception of the low-end machine, the new line of PS/2 machines comes equipped with a new bus system called the Micro Channel bus, which handles all communication within the computer. Unlike the old PC, this new bus system allows more than one message or task to be executed at one time. This feature allows the computer to support multi-tasking. The new bus system also will automatically detect devices/cards that are present and adjust the machine accordingly. This feature frees a user from having to set dip switches telling the computer what types of devices are hooked up.

New Manufacturing Techniques

The new line of computers makes extensive use of new manufacturing technologies that make it much easier to manufacture and repair. The outside of the computer itself is composed of plastic, and the inner components are subassemblies that can be disassembled in a matter of minutes.

The case is high-impact plastic with the inner surfaces painted silver. This silver paint provides the shielding that prevents electronic emissions from exceeding the FCC restrictions placed on microcomputers. The only metal within the case is on the top and sides.

IBM's Personal System/2
Model 30 with IBM Personal
System/2 color display Model
8512 and IBM Proprinter II.
(Photograph courtesy of
International Business
Machines Corporation.)

The inside of the machine is spartan in comparison to the former PC. There are no loose cables connecting components. The computer consists of plug-together subassemblies. Snaps rather than screws hold components together.

The system board contains the regular circuitry along with many components that were originally contained on separate expansion boards on older PCs. These include the serial and parallel ports, the clock, and the video.

The components on the board are all surface mounted. In prior computers, each separate part was installed on a conventional printed circuit board by inserting leads through holes in the circuit board and then soldering each lead into place. Surface-mount technology allows a manufacturer to literally combine several chips into one package and then solder this package to the surface of the board. This process, of course, requires special machinery that can operate within very small tolerances.

New Computers

These new computers actually belong to two different families (based on the type of microcomputer chip used). The low-end computer is the Model 30. The high-end computers are the models 50, 60, and 80.

Model 30

This is the only computer in the PS/2 line that uses the 8086 chip (this is a 16-bit computer that uses an 8-bit bus). The Model 30 (see Figure F.2), also the least expensive of the new computers, is positioned by IBM to take the place of the original PC and PC/XT. It comes equipped with two 720K, 3½-inch drives. A 20-megabyte hard disk is an available option. It also has a RAM limit of 640K, and the MCGA graphics is standard. This machine is the only one in

Figure F.3
IBM's Personal System/2
Model 50 with IBM Personal
System/2 monochrome display Model 8503. (Photograph courtesy of International Business Machines
Corporation.)

the PS/2 line that can use existing expansion boards, since it does not have the IBM Micro Channel. It accepts up to three expansion boards. While this does not seem to be enough in comparison with the eight expansion boards for the PC/XT, many of the features that formerly required an expansion board (parallel port, serial port, video adapter, and clock, for example) are all contained on the system board.

The Model 30 also comes with a new 101-key keyboard and contains a port for a mouse. The keyboard has a six-foot cable, 12 function keys, LED displays, a separate numeric keypad, and separate cursor movement keys. The optional two-button mouse plugs into the computer next to the keyboard.

Models 50 and 60

These two machines replace the old IBM/AT microcomputers. The Model 50 (see Figure F.3) is much smaller (has a smaller footprint) than its predecessor.

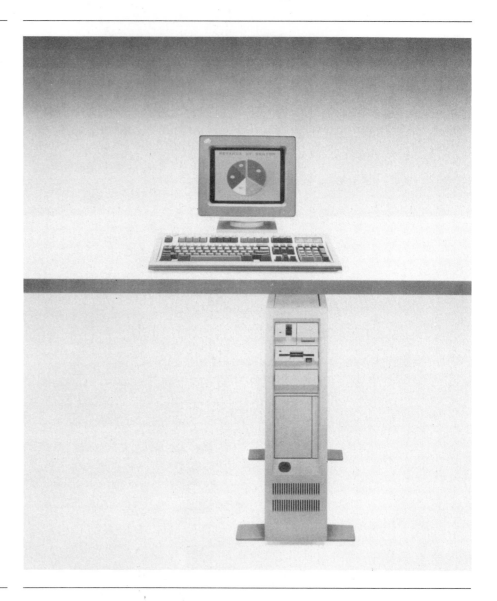

This machine was designed to be used as a single-user workstation. It comes equipped with the Micro Channel, four expansion slots (of which only three are available to the user), VGA graphics, and 1 Mbyte of RAM. One floppy disk drive is standard and another floppy drive or a hard disk can be added.

The Model 60 (see Figure F.4) was designed as a multi-user system. The computer itself was designed to sit on the floor with the keyboard and monitor on a desk. Since this device is for multiple users, it comes equipped with a 44-megabyte hard disk. It also has eight expansion slots and room for more hard disk drives.

Model 80

The Model 80 (see Figure F.5) was also designed to be a multi-user system. It has a much faster CPU chip (80386) than the other machines.

Figure F.5
IBM's Personal System/2
Model 80. (Photograph cour-
tesy of International Business
Machines Corporation.)

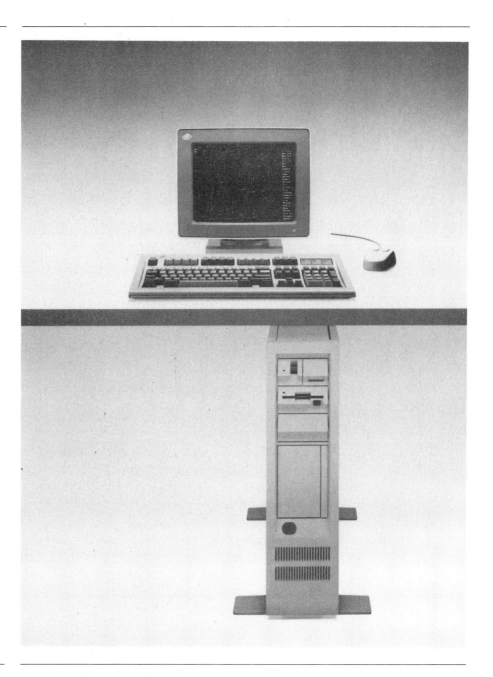

Glossary

Absolute address: Cell location that does not change in the course of copying a formula to other cells. In a cell marked for absolute address, the formula contains dollar signs.

Acronym: Word formed from letters or syllables in a name or phrase. For example, FORTRAN is an acronym for Formula Translator.

Address: (As a noun) number associated with each memory location; (as a verb) to refer to a particular memory location.

Align: Command that tells VP-Planner to expect the top of page at this page position.

Alphanumeric: Contraction of the words *alphabetic* and *numeric*. A set of alphanumeric characters usually includes special characters such as the dollar sign and comma.

Alt: Key label for the Alternate key.

Alternate key: Key used for the following purposes: to create a second set of function keys in some application programs, to enter the ASCII character code directly from the keyboard, and (together with letters) to enter BASIC commands.

APPEND: dBASE command that enables you to add records at the end of an existing file.

Application program: Precoded set of generalized instructions for the computer, written to accomplish a certain goal. Examples of such programs include a general ledger package, a mailing list program, and PacMan.

Arrow keys: Keys (down, up, right, and left) found on the numeric keyboard and typically used to move a pointer or cursor.

ASCII: Acronym for American Standard Code for Information Interchange (pronounced *ass-key*). Often called USASCII, this code is a standard method of representing a character with a number inside the computer. Knowledge of the code is important only if you write programs.

Assembler: Program that converts the mnemonics and symbols of assembly language into the opcodes and operands of machine language.

Assembly language: Language similar in structure to machine language but made up of mnemonics and symbols. Programs written in assembly language are slightly less difficult to write and understand than programs in machine language.

Auto-dial: Feature frequently found in modems that enables you to place a call to a specified number without having to dial it yourself.

AUTOEXEC.BAT: File that is executed by the computer as soon as the boot process is completed. This type of file is used in building a turn-key application that requires very little input from a user before starting.

Automatic recalculation: Feature that enables the worksheet automatically to recalculate itself after any change.

Available memory: Amount of RAM that is available for use by VP-Planner in building a worksheet.

Backspace key: Key used to erase the last character typed. It is labeled with an arrow that points toward the left.

Back-up file: .BAK-extension file that WordPerfect automatically creates as protection against loss of an original file. It can also be an additional copy of an important file created by the user via the DOS **Copy** command.

Banked memory: Usually two sets of 64K memory used to give a computer a total memory of 128K. Only one set of 64K can be active at a time.

BASIC: Acronym for Beginners All-Purpose Symbolic Instruction Code, a common, easy-to-learn computer programming language. The advanced version of BASIC is called BASICA. BASIC was developed by Kemeney and Kurtz at Dartmouth College in 1963 and has proved to be the most popular language for personal computers.

Baud rate: Speed at which modems can transmit characters across telephone lines. A 300-baud modem can transmit about thirty characters per second.

Bell: Sound produced by your computer or line printer, often used by programs to get your attention or to reassure you that computer processing is underway.

Binary: Number system consisting of two digits, 0 and 1, with each digit in a binary number representing a power of two. Most digital computers are binary. A binary signal is easily expressed by the presence or absence of an electrical current or magnetic field.

Bit: Binary digit, the smallest amount of information a computer can hold. A single bit specifies a single value of 0 or 1. Bits can be grouped to form larger values (see Byte and Nibble).

Block: Designated portion of text, consisting of one or more lines, that is to be copied, moved, or deleted.

Boldface text: Darkened text, accomplished by striking or printing the same character three or four times.

Booting: Process of starting the computer. During the boot process a memory check is performed, the various parts of DOS are loaded, and the date and time are requested.

Boot record: Record that resides on sector 1 of track 0 of a file and contains the program responsible for loading the rest of DOS into the microcomputer.

Bootstrap (boot): Procedure used to get a system running from a cold start. The name comes from the machine's attempts to pull itself off the ground by "tugging on its own bootstraps."

Border: Set of labels for the rows and columns of a worksheet. The columns are labeled with letters, and the rows are labeled with numbers.

`BOTTOM`: dBASE command that enables you to position the pointer at the end of the file.

Break: Function for halting the program in progress. Usually the program returns to some higher-level program such as DOS, BASIC, or the main application program; but not all programs have this function. It is invoked by holding the Ctrl key down while pressing Scroll Lock.

`BROWSE`: dBASE command that displays a number of records on the screen at one time, enabling you to edit a file quickly.

B-tree structure: Structural arrangement that provides the ability to develop indexes that establish the relations for a relational data base file.

Bug: Error. A hardware bug is a physical or electrical malfunction or design error; a software bug is an error in programming, either in the logic of the program or in typing.

Bus: Entity that enables the computer to pass information to a peripheral and to receive information from a peripheral.

Byte: Basic unit of measure of a computer's memory. A byte usually has eight bits, and therefore its value can be from 0 to 255. Each character can be represented by one byte in ASCII.

Caps Lock key: Key used to switch the case of letters A through Z on the keyboard. This key does not affect numbers and special characters.

Card: General term for a printed circuit board with electronic components attached. It is also called an interface card, a board, a circuit card assembly, and other similar names.

Cartridge: Removable hard disk storage unit that typically holds 5 or 10 megabytes of storage.

Cell: Intersection point of a row and a column. It is referenced by the cell address `COLUMN/ROW`.

Centering command: Word processing or spreadsheet command that centers text in a document or cell.

Centering hole: Large hole on a diskette that allows the mylar plastic disk inside the diskette envelope to center on the capstan for proper rotation.

Central processing unit (CPU): Device in a computer system that contains the arithmetic unit, the control unit, and the main memory. It is also referred to as the computer.

Centronics: Standard method of passing information through a parallel data port.

Character: Any graphic symbol that has a specific meaning to people. Letters (both upper- and lower-case), numbers, and various symbols (such as punctuation marks) are all characters.

Character field: Field capable of holding any alphanumeric or special character. In dBASE, such a field can hold up to 254 characters.

Character overprint: Function that enables you to create text using diacritical marks such as tildes. It also creates special effects in printing.

Character pitch: Number of characters printed per horizontal inch of space. Twelve pitch (elite) prints twelve characters per inch; ten pitch (pica) prints ten characters per inch.

Chip: Electronic entity containing one or more semiconductors on a wafer of silicon, within which an integrated circuit is formed.

CHKDSK: DOS command that checks the status of a disk and prepares the status report.

Circular reference: Cell's effect depends on both its contents and the contents of other cells.

Clear screen: Procedure that blanks the screen of all characters. It can be accomplished by pressing the Home key while holding down the Ctrl key.

Closed bus system: Type of computer system that comes with plugs, called established ports, that accept device cables from the peripheral.

CLS: DOS command that clears the display monitor.

Cluster: Entity composed of two adjacent sectors. Storage is allocated to a file one cluster at a time.

COBOL: Acronym for Common Business Oriented Language, a high-level language oriented toward organizational data processing procedures.

Code: Method of representing something in terms of something else. The ASCII code represents characters in terms of binary numbers; the BASIC language represents algorithms in terms of program statements. *Code* also may refer to programs, usually in low-level languages.

Cold start: Booting process used to begin operating a computer that has just been turned on.

Color monitor: Display device that is capable of showing red, green, and blue colors.

Column: Vertical line of text.

Column block: Command that specifies a column of data within a document to copy, move, or delete.

Combination key: Key that must be used together with another key to perform a task. Combination keys include the Ctrl, Alt, and Shift keys.

COMMAND.COM: Command processor of DOS, containing built-in functions or subroutines that enable you to copy a file or get a directory listing of a disk.

Command line: Third line of the VP-Planner control panel. It contains the VP-Planner commands that can be issued from the current menu.

Communications packages: Hardware packages that enable you to obtain and/or transmit information over telephone lines.

Compiler: Software that translates a program into machine language. As it performs this translation, it also checks for errors made by the programmer.

Computer: Any device that can receive and store a set of instructions and then act upon those instructions in a predetermined and predictable fashion. The definition implies that both the instructions and the data upon which the instructions act can be changed: a device whose instructions cannot be changed is not a computer.

Concatenation: Process of joining two character strings, usually accomplished through use of the + sign.

Conditional page break: Word processing technique that checks to see if a page break is going to occur in the next *n* lines and, if so, moves the specified text to the top of the next page.

Configured software: Software that has been customized to the specific hardware configuration currently used.

CONTINUE: dBASE command that finds the next record in a Locate command search.

Constant information: Information that remains the same from one document to the next.

Control (CTRL) character: Character in the ASCII character set that usually has no graphic representation but serves to control various functions inside the computer.

Control key: General-purpose key whose uses include invoking breaks, pauses, system resets, clear screens, print echos, and various edit commands. In instructions, the Control key is often represented as a caret (^).

Control panel: Bottom four lines on the VP-Planner worksheet screen, consisting of the status line, the entry line, the command line, and the prompt line.

Coprocessor: Microprocessor chip that is placed in a microcomputer to take the burden of manipulating numbers off the CPU, allowing it to perform other tasks.

COPY: dBASE and DOS command that copies one or more files onto the current disk or onto another disk. In spreadsheets, it enables you to copy the contents of a cell into one or more other cells; in WordPerfect, it enables you to copy a block of text to another location in a document.

CREATE: dBASE command that enables you to build a data base and describe the fields and the data type of each field.

Criterion range: Area of the worksheet on which you specify the records to be included in an operation.

CRT: Acronym for *cathode ray tube*, meaning any television screen or device containing such a screen.

Ctrl: Key label for the Control key.

Cursor (pointer): Display screen's special character (__) used to indicate where the next character will be typed, that is, where you are in a file.

Cursor control key: One of the four arrow keys on the numeric key pad used to move the cursor left, right, up, or down on the screen.

Cursor movement: Operation of moving the cursor over the text.

Cylinder: Entity composed of all like-numbered tracks from all recording surfaces of a disk.

Daisy wheel printer: Letter-quality printer that uses a solid-font printing mechanism (the mechanism is shaped like a flower or a thimble).

Data (datum): Information of any kind.

Data entry: Process of placing text, values, labels, or formulas into a text document, data file, or worksheet.

Data entry window: The 14- or 23-line by 79-column area of the screen in which you can enter or edit text.

Data base: Collection of data related to one specific type of application. *Data base* is often used synonymously with *file*.

Data table: VP-Planner feature that enables you to perform sensitivity analysis on a worksheet easily by asking multiple what-if questions.

DATE: DOS command that enables you to change the system date.

dBASE II: Relational data base package.

dBASE III: Updated version of dBASE II.

Debug: To find hardware or software faults and eliminate them.

Default: Original (or initial) setting of a software package.

Default disk drive: Disk drive that is accessed automatically by the microcomputer when a file-oriented command is executed.

Default pitch: Pitch (usually pica) used to print a document unless some other pitch is specified.

DEL: DOS command used to delete one or more files from disk.

Del: Key label for the Delete key.

DELETE: dBASE command that enables you to mark a record for later deletion.

Delete indicator: Asterisk (*) that appears in a record when it has been marked for deletion.

Delete key: Key used to erase the character to the left of the current cursor position.

Delimiter: Character that indicates to the computer where one part of a command ends and another part begins. Typical delimiters are the space, the period, and the comma.

DIR: DOS command that is used to list the files in the directory.

Directory: Part of a diskette that holds the names of files stored on it. The directory also contains information about file size, file extensions, their location on diskette, and the dates and times files were created or changed.

DISKCOPY: DOS command used to copy a complete disk.

Disk drive: Rectangular box, connected to or situated inside the computer, that reads and writes into diskettes.

Diskette: Square recordlike objects used for storing information from the computer.

Display: (As a noun) any sort of output device for a computer, usually a video screen; (as a verb) to place information on such a screen.

Document file: WordPerfect file that contains embedded codes to tell the monitor how text is to be displayed and to tell the printer how it is to be printed.

DOS: Acronym for Disk Operating System, the program responsible for enabling you to interact with the many parts of a computer system. DOS (pronounced *doss*) is the interface between you and the hardware. To perform system functions, DOS commands are typed on the keyboard, but DOS is actually a collection of programs designed to make it easy to create and manage files, run programs, and use system devices attached to the computer.

Dot matrix printer: Printer that generates characters by firing seven or nine tiny print heads against a ribbon.

Double-density disks: Disks that have approximately twice the storage of a single-density disk. This is achieved by using a higher quality read/write surface on the disk, so that data can be stored in a denser format.

Double-sided disks: Disks on which data can be stored on both surfaces. A double-sided disk has been certified (tested) on both sides.

Double-strike text: Text somewhat darkened by striking or printing each character two times.

Edit: Process by which the format of data is modified for output by inserting dollar signs, blanks, and so on. Used as a verb, to validate and rearrange input data.

Editing a document: Inserting, deleting, and changing existing text in a word processing text file.

Electronic spreadsheets: Programs used to manipulate data that can be expressed in rows and columns.

End key: Key used together with the Ctrl key to erase characters on the screen from the current cursor position to the end of the line.

Enter key: Key used to tell the computer program that you are finished typing. It is principally used when more than one character is required in the typing input.

Erase: DOS command used to delete one or more files from disk.

Error message: Message informing you that you did not type something the program can process or that some other system failure has occurred.

Error message indicator: Brief explanation of what went wrong, appearing in the lower left-hand corner of the worksheet screen.

Esc: Key label for the Escape key.

Escape key: Key used for general purposes, usually to cause some change in computer processing. In DOS and BASIC, it is used to erase a line of input; in application programs, it is often used to transfer to another section of the program.

Execute: To perform the intent of a command or instruction; to run a program or a portion of a program.

Expansion board: Printed circuit board that can be inserted into an open bus expansion slot, expanding the computer configuration to include such items as modems and plotters.

Extension: One- to three-character portion of a file name. Extensions are typically used to indicate families of files, such as backups (.BAK), regular data base files (.DBF), and indexes (.NDX).

External DOS commands: Utility commands that are not part of the COMMAND.COM command processor. They reside on disk as separate files.

Extract: Command used for creating reports from a VP-Planner data base.

Field: Subdivision of a record that holds one piece of data about a transaction.

File: Collection of data or programs that serves a single purpose. A file is stored on a diskette and given a name so that you can recall it.

File allocation table (FAT): Entity that keeps track of which sectors belong to which files and of how much available space remains on the diskette (so that new files can be created and stored in unused areas of the diskette).

Filename: Unique identifier of a file, composed of one to eight characters. If an optional one- to three-character extension is used, there must be a period between the filename and the filename extension.

Filter program: Program that performs some type of data manipulation on a file, such as sorting or breaking it down into displayable chunks.

`FIND`: dBASE command used to locate records in an indexed file, using the index.

Find and replace: Ability of a word processing package to find a character string and replace it with another character string.

Font: Character set for printing. Pica, Elite, Helvetica, Courier, and Orator are among the many common fonts.

Footer: Line of text that appears at the bottom of every page of a document.

FORMAT: DOS command that prepares a disk so that it can be used by the computer. It defines every sector of a diskette, finds and write-protects any tracks having bad sectors, sets up the directory, sets up the File Allocation Table, and puts the boot record program at the beginning of the diskette. *Format* also refers to how data are stored in a worksheet cell, for example, as character or numeric data.

Formula: Series of characters containing cell references and arithmetic operators for numeric data manipulation.

FORTRAN: Acronym for Formula Translator, a programming language designed for writing problem-solving programs that can be stated as arithmetic procedures.

Fragmentation: Characteristic of files whose sectors are not in adjacent locations. A fragmented file can be stored on a disk in a number of different physical locations.

Full-screen editing: Editing format that enables you to move about the entire screen using cursor movement keys. This makes changes to a worksheet, document file, or data file much easier.

Function key: One of ten keys (F1–F10) that allow special functions to be entered with a single user keystroke. Computer programs (DOS, BASIC, and so on) use these keys for different purposes.

Function key line: Bottom line on many application software display screens. It identifies the task performed by each function key.

Functions: Formulas or processes built into a software package. These functions save a user a tremendous amount of effort and tedium.

GOTO: dBASE command used to position the pointer at a specific record in a file.

Global: Spreadsheet command that allows changes entered thereafter to affect the entire worksheet.

Global characters: DOS characters (? and *) that are used to specify a number of files by entering a single command.

Graphics: System used to display graphic items or a collection of such items.

Hard carriage return: Special carriage return recorded in a document when the ENTER key is pressed, usually at the end of a paragraph.

Hard copy: Printed document on paper.

Hard disk: Rigid medium for storing computer information, usually rated in megabytes (millions of bytes) of storage capacity.

Hard page break: Convention of word processing packages to show where one page ends another page begins. WordPerfect uses a line of equal signs.

Hard-sectored: Disks that have already had their tracks divided into sectors.

Hard space: Space inserted by pressing the Home plus the spacebar.

Hardware: Physical parts of a computer.

Header: Line of text that appears at the top of every page of a document.

Hexadecimal: Number system that uses the ten digits 0 through 9 and the six letters A through F to represent values in base 16. Each hexadecimal digit in a hexadecimal number represents a power of 16.

Hidden file: File that exists but does not appear to a user in the file directory. Since it is not visible in the directory, such a file is very difficult to erase mistakenly.

Hierarchical (tree) structure: Structural arrangement in which data elements are linked in multiple levels that graphically resemble an organization chart. Each lower level is owned by an upper level.

High-level language: Language that is more intelligible to humans than it is to machines.

Home: Upper left-hand corner screen position, where the first printable character can be placed. This is also referred to as the initial cursor position.

Home key: Key used to send the cursor to the Home position. If used with the Control key, a clear screen results.

IBMBIO.COM: Hidden file in DOS that manages each character that is typed, displayed, printed, received, or sent through any communications adapter.

IBMDOS.COM: Hidden DOS file that handles any information to be passed to disk.

Index: dBASE feature used to order information logically within a file without physically reordering the records themselves. Indexes may be single- or multiple-field.

Indicators: Signals that appear in the lower right-hand corner of the worksheet screen, telling the user which toggle keys are currently activated.

Initialization: Process during the boot routine when the computer activates the various peripherals hooked to the computer.

Ink-jet printer: Printer that sprays ink in droplets onto paper to form characters. It is much quieter than a dot matrix or letter-quality printer.

Input line: Second line in the control panel, corresponding to a scratch area. The entry line contains any information you are currently entering for the cell location contained in the status line.

INS: Key label for the Insert key.

Insert key: Key used to tell the computer program that you want to insert characters to the left of the cursor. The insert mode continues until you press the key again or until you press another special key (cursor arrows, Del, End), indicating that you want to go on to a different editing operation.

Instruction: Smallest portion of a program that a computer can execute.

Integrated circuit: Small (less than the size of a fingernail and about as thin) wafer of glassy material (usually silicon) into which an electronic circuit has been etched. A single IC can contain from 10 to 10,000 electronic components.

Integration: Process that combines a number of applications under one software umbrella. For instance, VP-Planner combines spreadsheets, graphing, and data base applications.

Interface: Adapter or circuit board containing the electrical components that connect a peripheral with the computer's bus system.

Internal DOS command: Command that is part of the COMMAND.COM command processor.

Interpreter: Program, usually written in machine language, that understands and executes a higher-level language one statement at a time.

Inverse: Command to the computer that tells it to display the characters on the screen as dark characters on a light background instead of the normal display of light on dark.

Justification: Alignment of word processing text flush with the right (and left) margins. This produces straight margins on both the left-hand and right-hand sides of a document.

K: Abbreviation for the Greek prefix *kilo-*, meaning *thousand*. In computer-related usage, K usually represents the quantity 2^{10}, or 1,024.

Key: Data item (field) that identifies a record.

Keyboard: System hardware used to input characters, commands, and functions to the computer. The keyboard consists of 83 keys and is organized into three sections: the function keys, the typewriter keyboard, and the numeric key pad.

Label: Alphanumeric information used to identify a portion of a row or column.

Language: Code that both the programmer and the computer understand. The programmer uses the language to express what is to be done, and the computer understands the language and performs the desired actions.

Language processor: Software that translates a high-level language such as COBOL or BASIC into machine-understandable code.

Laser printer: Printer that uses laser-based technology to form characters on paper via electronic charges and then place toner on the charges to display the characters. The toner is fixed in place by a heat process.

LCD monitor: Liquid crystal display frequently used on notebook-size portable computers.

Legend: VP-Planner graph feature used to label sets of data so that a graph can be easily understood.

Letter-quality printer: Printer that generates output of a quality comparable to that produced on a typewriter.

Line editor: Low-level word processing package that allows you to work on only one line of text at a time.

Line spacing: Number of filled and blank lines that are established with each generated line. Double spacing produces one blank line after each generated line.

LIST: dBASE command used to display records from a data file contained on disk.

List structure: Structural arrangement containing records that are linked together by pointers.

Local area networks (LAN): Networks used to connect a number of micro-computers to share data or expensive peripheral devices.

LOCATE: dBASE command used to find data in a sequential file.

Lock key: Key used to cause subsequent key operations to be interpreted in a specific manner by the computer. Lock keys are toggle keys; they include Caps, Num, and Scroll.

Logged device: Disk specified to be searched automatically for any needed files.

Logical field: Field capable of holding the values of .T. (true) or .F. (false) or Y (yes) or N (no). Logical fields are always one-byte fields.

Lower case: Small letters (a–z).

Low-level language: Language that is more intelligible to machines than to humans.

Machine language: Lowest-level language. Machine language is usually binary; instructions in machine language are single-byte opcodes, sometimes followed by various operands.

Macro: Entity that contains keystroke commands stored for later execution.

Mag typewriter: Predecessor of the computer, developed by IBM in the 1960s.

Main logic board: Large printed circuit board at the bottom of the computer.

Manual recalculation: Functional mode in which a worksheet can only recalculate itself when the F9 key is pressed.

Margin: Unused border around a page of a document.

Megabyte (meg): One million characters of storage, a quantity usually used as a measure of available storage on a hard disk.

Memory location: Smallest subdivision of the memory map to which the computer can refer. Each memory location has a unique address and a certain value.

Menu: List of commands available to anyone using a software package.

Microcomputer: Computer based on a microprocessor (8-bit or 16-bit) that can execute a single user's program.

Microcomputer system: Combined computer, disk drives, monitor, and input and output devices for data processing.

Microprocessor: Integrated circuit that understands and executes machine-language programs.

Microsoft: Company that originally developed PC DOS for IBM (an operating system known, with some minor differences, as MS DOS).

Mixed cell address: Address in which the row or column portion (not both) of the cell address can change to reflect a new cell location.

Mnemonic: Any acronym or other symbol used in place of something more difficult to remember.

Mode indicator: Status information that appears in the upper right-hand corner of the VP-Planner worksheet screen.

Model: Symbolic representation of an entity or process that is difficult to observe.

MODEM: Acronym for modulator-demodulator, a device that converts digital computer signals into analog telephone signals and reverses the procedure at the other end of the line.

Monitor: TV-like device that gives users of microcomputer equipment video feedback about their actions and the computer's actions.

Monochrome monitors: Devices similar to one-color monitors except that their pixels are much closer together, producing clearer characters.

MORE: DOS filter command that displays one screen of data on the monitor at a time.

Motherboard: Another name for the main logic board.

Mouse: Hand-held controller that electronically signals the computer to move the cursor on the display screen. The same movements can be accomplished via the cursor control pad.

MS DOS: Operating system developed by Microsoft. It is the same as PC DOS except that there is no ROM BASIC provision. This operating system is used by most IBM-compatible computers.

Nested function: Function that resides inside another function. The innermost function must be executed before any outer ones.

Network structure: Arrangement permitting the connection of data elements in a multidirectional manner. Each mode may thus have several owners.

Nibble: Slang for half a byte (four bits).

Nondocument mode: Operating mode used to create a file that has no control character sequences to provide instructions to the printer. This mode must be selected when you are creating computer programs or building data files.

Nonvolatile storage: Form of storage that does not lose its content when the system's power is turned off. It may take the form of bubble memory, or it may be powered by batteries.

Numeric data: Consists of the digits 0 through 9.

Numeric entry: Process of entering numbers into the computer. The numeric key pad can be set into numeric entry mode by using the Num Lock key; after this has been done, numbers and number symbols (decimal, minus, plus) can be entered.

Numeric field: Field that can hold only a number or a decimal point. No alphabetic or special characters can be placed in such a field.

Numeric key pad: Section of the keyboard containing numeric entry and editing keys.

Numeric Lock key: Key used to switch the numeric key pad back and forth between numeric entry and editing.

Num Lock: Key label for the Numeric lock key.

Object code: Machine-language code created by the compiler. It is the object code that is actually executed by the computer.

Operating system: Interface between the computer and the user, which provides the user with flexible and manageable control over the resources of the computer.

Operating system prompt: Signal to the user that some type of DOS command or a command to start a program can be entered. The prompt also shows which drive has been specified as the default drive.

Orphan line: Last line of a paragraph when it appears as the top line of a page.

Output: Computer-generated data whose destination is the screen, disk, printer, or some other output device.

Output range: VP-Planner range that holds any report generated in an Extract operation.

`PACK:` dBASE command that physically removes any records marked for deletion.

Page: One screen of information on a video display; quantity of memory locations addressable with one byte.

Page breaks: Marks that show where one page ends and another begins. In WordPerfect, they are represented by a line of dashes across the screen.

Page Down key: Key that is sometimes used to cause text on the screen to move down. Text on the bottom of the screen moves off-screen while text is added at the top.

Page number setting: WordPerfect command used to specify the page number of the first page of a file to be printed. It also resets the page number to a specific value inside a document.

Page Up key: Key that is sometimes used to cause text on the screen to move up. Text on the top of the screen moves off-screen while text is added at the bottom.

Parallel interface: Interface arrangement that transmits all nine bits of a character at one time.

Parameter: Modifying piece of information that constitutes part of a DOS or dBASE command. It might, for example, indicate which files or fields are to be included in an operation.

Pause: Computer function that can be used at any time to temporarily halt the program in use. Pause is invoked by pressing the Num Lock key while holding the Ctrl key down. Pressing any key after a Pause causes the computer to continue from the point of interruption. Pause can also be performed with one hand by pressing the key combination Ctrl + S.

Peripheral: Something attached to the computer that is not part of the computer itself. Most peripherals are input and/or output devices.

Personal computer: Computer equipped with memory, languages, and peripherals, well suited for use in a home, office, or school.

PgUp: Key label for the Page Up key.

PgDn: Key label for the Page Down key.

Piping: System arrangement that allows a number of different programs to share generated input and output, since the output from one program becomes the input to another. Temporary files are created to achieve this.

Pitch: Refers to the number of characters per inch of a type style.

Pixel: Dot that is turned on or off depending on what character is being displayed on the screen.

Platen: Hard rubber roller that moves the paper in the printer.

Plotter: Device that moves a pen on X and Y axes to draw graphs or pictures. For one of the axes, the paper may move instead of the pen.

Pointer: Reverse-video bar, sometimes referred to as the cursor. Its width is dependent on the width of the cell it is referencing.

Precedence: Order in which calculations are executed.

Press any key to continue: Message often displayed by a program when the computer is waiting for you to do something (read text or load a diskette, for example) and does not know when you will be done. Some keys are generally inactive and do not cause the program to continue when depressed; these include the Alt, Shift, Ctrl, Scroll Lock, Num Lock, and Caps Lock keys.

Primary key: In dBASE, the record number; in sorting, the major sort field.

Primary memory: Internal memory used by the computer for a number of different functions. It can contain data, program instructions, or intermediate results of calculations.

PRINT: DOS command used to queue and print disk-based data files.

Print echo: Function performed by pressing the Print Screen (PrtSc) key while holding the Ctrl key down. Once this key is pressed, whatever is displayed on the screen is printed. The simultaneous printing (screen and printer) continues until the key combination is pressed again. Print echo can also be performed using the key combination Ctrl + P.

Printed circuit board: Sheet of fiberglass or epoxy onto which a thin layer of metal has been applied and then etched to form traces. Electronic components are then attached to the board with molten solder, and thereafter they can exchange electronic signals via the etched traces on the board. Small printed circuit boards are often called cards, especially if they are meant to connect with edge connectors.

Printer: Device used to make a permanent copy of any output.

Print screen: Function produced when the Print Screen (PrtSc) key is pressed while the Shift key is held down. Once this key combination is pressed, the current information on your screen is printed.

Print Screen key: Key that, when pressed with the Shift key, results in the screen contents being printed.

Procedures: Written instructions on how to use hardware or software.

Program: Set of instructions that tells the computer how to perform a certain task. DOS, BASIC, and the Instructor are all programs.

Programming language: Special means of providing instructions to the computer to get it to perform a specific task. Examples of programming languages are BASIC, COBOL, PASCAL, and FORTRAN.

PROM: Acronym for Programmable Read-Only Memory. A PROM is a ROM whose contents are alterable by electrical means. Information in PROMs does not disappear when the power is turned off. Some PROMs can be erased by ultraviolet light and then reprogrammed.

Prompt line: Last line in the control panel. When a VP-Planner menu is displayed, it contains a further explanation about a specific command.

Protected cell: VP-Planner cells that cannot be changed by the user. The worksheet has been globally protected by the global protection command.

Protection: In VP-Planner, a way of prohibiting changes on either the entire worksheet or specific cells.

PrtSc: Key label for the Print Screen Key.

Quit: dBASE command that returns you to the operating system.

QWERTY: Standard keyboard arrangement, first used with manual typewriters in the early 1900s.

Random access memory (RAM): Main memory of a computer. The acronym RAM can be used to refer either to the integrated circuits that make up this type of memory or to the memory itself. The computer can store values in distinct locations in RAM and then recall them, or it can alter and restore them.

Range: Rectangular or square area of a worksheet.

Range name: Function used to give a specific name to a range of a worksheet; by using it, you can refer to formulas by meaningful names instead of by cell address only.

Read only memory (ROM): Memory usually used to hold important programs or data that must be available to the computer when power is first turned on. Information in ROM is placed there during the process of manufacture and is unalterable. Information stored in ROM does not disappear when power is turned off.

Read/write access hole: Oval opening on a diskette that allows the read/write heads to record or access information.

Recalculation: Process by which a spreadsheet changes all cell contents that are affected by a change to any other cell in a worksheet.

RECALL: dBASE command used to retrieve or unmark records that have been marked for deletion.

Record: Entity that contains information about a specific business happening or transaction.

Record number: Identification used by dBASE as the primary key for a record; the physical location in the file for a given record.

Redirection: System arrangement that allows the IBM PC to accept input from a device other than the keyboard and to send output to a device other than the display screen.

Reform: WordPerfect feature that automatically readjusts text within existing margins.

Relational structure: Structural arrangement consisting of one or more tables. Data are stored in the form of relations in these tables.

Relative addressing: Automatic changing of cell locations in a copy or move operation to reflect their new locations.

RENAME: DOS command used to rename a disk file.

REPLACE: dBASE command used to change several or all records within a data file quickly.

REPORT: dBASE command used to create or access a parameter file modifying how a specific printed report is to be generated.

Reserved tracks: Tracks of disk storage that contain a bad sector and have been set aside so that data cannot be recorded on them.

Reset: Command that usually results in the return of a piece of software to its original default values.

Root node: Top node of a tree structure.

Row: Horizontal axis on a spreadsheet or document.

Ruler line: Line on the display screen that identifies the location of the right-hand margin, the left-hand margin, and tab stops.

Run: Action of following a sequence of instructions to its completion.

Scaling: Description of how data values will be displayed on a VP-Planner graph.

Scroll: Function that moves all the text on a display (usually upward) to make room for more (usually at the bottom).

Scrolling: Moving the text under the cursor. The relative position of the cursor does not have to change.

Scroll Lock key: Key that is little used in modern programs but is intended for use as a Lock-type key, causing displayed text (rather than the cursor) to move when a cursor control key is pressed.

Secondary key: Defining key used to order information within the primary key.

Sector: One part of a track. For the IBM microcomputer, each track is divided into eight or nine sectors of 512 bytes each. It is the sector that holds the data.

Sensitivity analysis: Procedure used to ask a number of "what if" questions about the effect of various changes to a worksheet.

Serial interface: Interface arrangement that transmits a character one bit at a time.

Set-up string: VP-Planner feature used to vary the pitch of printed information.

SHIFT key: Key used to select the upper-case character on keys that have two characters or to reverse the case of letters A through Z, depending on the status of the CAPS LOCK key.

SKIP: dBASE command used to move the pointer forward or backward within a data file.

Slave disk: Disk that has been formatted but does not contain the operating system. You cannot boot the computer by using such a disk.

Soft carriage return: Carriage return accomplished by the word-wrap feature.

Soft-sectored: Disks that have each track divided into sectors during the format process.

Software: Program that gives the hardware something to do.

SORT: DOS filter command used to sort data files; also the dBASE command used to reorder a data base file physically; also a VP-Planner command used to resequence a portion of a worksheet.

Source code: Set of program instructions written in a high-level language.

Source drive: Drive that contains any files to be copied.

Spreadsheet: Software package that can manipulate rows and columns of data.

Stand alone word processors: Computers that do only word processing.

Standard input device: Device that DOS assumes will be used to enter commands or data. Unless otherwise specified, this device is the keyboard.

Standard output device: Device that DOS assumes will be used to receive any output generated by the computer. Unless specified otherwise, this device is the printer.

Standard pitch: Default pitch, usually pica, for most printers.

Status line: Top line of the control panel, which displays the cell address, the format of the data, and the cell contents.

Storage: Term that applies to either RAM or external disk memory.

Strike-out text: Text produced by placing a dash (–) over each character as it is printed.

Structured walkthrough: Process of having a number of individuals review a program or worksheet and check it for accuracy, logic, and readability.

Subroutine: Segment of a program that can be executed by a single call. Subroutines perform the same sequence of instructions at many different places in a single program.

Subscript: Characters printed half a line beneath the current line.

SUM: dBASE command used to total the contents of a field for all records within a file.

Superscript: Characters printed half a line above the current line.

Synchronized: In VP-Planner, the state of having the contents of one or more windows move in a like fashion.

Syntax: Structure of instructions in a language. If you make a mistake in entering an instruction and garble the syntax, the computer sometimes calls this a SYNTAX ERROR.

SYS: DOS command used to place DOS on a disk.

System disk: Disk that has been formatted and has DOS on it. This type of disk can be used to boot the system.

System reset: System function that restarts your computer just like a power on/off. This is accomplished by pressing the Del key while holding the Ctrl and Alt keys down. Three keys are required to ensure that you know what you are doing and to avoid an accidental system reset.

Tab: Point on a line (also called a tab stop) to which the cursor will position itself whenever the Tab command is issued. Tab stops are usually represented as marks in the ruler line of WordPerfect.

Tab key: Key used to set automatic spacing for typing input. The Tab key has both a forward and a backward capability.

Target drive: Disk to which files will be copied.

Telecommunications: Data communication using communications facilities.

Template: Form that contains the prepackaged worksheet instructions needed to perform some type of application. It can be viewed as a piece of application software on which someone has already performed the planning, design, and implementation of the logic involved.

Temporary file: File that is used temporarily in an application. Such a file will have a randomly assigned file extension such as .$$$ or .%%%. When the file is no longer needed, it is erased.

Testing: Process by which a program or worksheet is examined and tried out to make certain that it generates the proper results.

Text characters: Letters and numbers, usually in English.

Thermal printer: Printer that uses specially treated paper to "burn" in dots to form characters.

TIME: DOS command used to change the time for the system.

Timing hole: Small hole to the right of the centering hole on a diskette.

Titles option: VP-Planner feature used to freeze text on the screen so that it will act as row or column headings.

Toggle key: Key with two states, on and off, that causes subsequent key operations to be processed in a predetermined manner. Toggle keys include the Caps Lock, Num Lock, and Scroll Lock keys.

T̲O̲P̲: dBASE command used to position the pointer at the beginning of a data file.

Track: Concentric circle of storage on a disk's read/write surface on which data are stored.

TYPE: DOS command that displays file contents on the screen.

Typewriter keyboard: One of the three main key groupings of a computer system keyboard. It contains the QWERTY typewriter keyboard, as well as some special keys such as Enter, Backspace, Tab, Esc, and Alt.

Underlined text: Text that has an underscore under every character. Usually underscores are not placed between words.

Unique: VP-Planner data base command used to get only one record for each data type within a data base file.

Upper case: Set of upper characters on two-character keys and capital letters (A–Z). Any upper-case character can be typed by holding the Shift key down while pressing the desired key.

Unsynchronized: In VP-Planner, the state of having the contents of the windows move independently of each other.

U̲S̲E̲: dBASE command that makes a file available for manipulation.

Variable data: Data that change from one document to the next in a mail merge operation.

VER: DOS command that displays the DOS version number being used.

Video: Anything visual, usually information presented on the face of a cathode ray tube.

Virtual word processors: Word processors that enable you to work on a document even when it is longer than the amount of available RAM. Only the needed part of the document is in RAM at any time.

VisiCalc: First spreadsheet introduced for microcomputers.

VOL: DOS command used to display the volume I.D. of a diskette.

Volatile memory: Memory that is erased when the electrical current to the computer is turned off.

Warm start: Booting process used to restart a computer after you have lost control of its language or operating system.

Widow line: First line of a paragraph when it occurs at the bottom of a page.

Wild cards: Characters that enable you to include a number of files or fields in an operation by using only one command.

Window: Displayed portion of a worksheet or document. A window can be split into two or more smaller windows, horizontally or vertically.

Word processing: Automated manipulation of text data via a software package that usually provides the ability to create, edit, store, and print documents easily.

Word wrap: Feature that automatically places a word on the next line when it will not fit on the current line.

Worksheet: Model or representation of reality that is created using a spreadsheet software package. The worksheet is contained inside the spreadsheet border.

Write-protected: Diskettes that have been protected from having information stored on them, from being altered, or from being deleted; this is accomplished by placing a write-protect tab over the small rectangular hole on the side of a diskette.

X axis: Horizontal (left-to-right) axis.

Y axis: Vertical (up-and-down) axis.

Index